MOVEMENT, EXCHANGE AND IDENTITY IN EUROPE IN THE 2ND AND 1ST MILLENNIA BC

MOVEMENT, EXCHANGE AND IDENTITY IN EUROPE IN THE 2ND AND 1ST MILLENNIA BC

BEYOND FRONTIERS

edited by

ANNE LEHOËRFF AND MARC TALON

OXBOW | books

Oxford & Philadelphia

Published in the United Kingdom in 2017 by
OXBOW BOOKS
The Old Music Hall, 106–108 Cowley Road, Oxford OX4 1JE

and in the United States by
OXBOW BOOKS
1950 Lawrence Road, Havertown, PA 19083

© Oxbow Books and the individual authors 2017

Hardback Edition: ISBN 978-1-78570-716-2 (hardback)
Digital Edition: ISBN 978-1-78570-717-9 (epub)

A CIP record for this book is available from the British Library and the Library of Congress

Printed in Malta by Melita Press
Typeset in India by Lapiz Digital Services, Chennai

For a complete list of Oxbow titles, please contact:

UNITED KINGDOM
Oxbow Books
Telephone (01865) 241249, Fax (01865) 794449
Email: oxbow@oxbowbooks.com
www.oxbowbooks.com

UNITED STATES OF AMERICA
Oxbow Books
Telephone (800) 791-9354, Fax (610) 853-9146
Email: queries@casemateacademic.com
www.casemateacademic.com/oxbow

Oxbow Books is part of the Casemate Group

Front cover: © Anne Lehoërff for BOAT 1550 BC.

Contents

Preface

The political vocabulary of Europe in the early part of the 21st century has resonated with themes of boundary and difference, of boundaries between states, concepts of 'them' and 'us', a concern to resist change, to maintain the *status quo*. The concerns of today do not reflect the nature of the long sweep of European history, however. Archaeologists and historians have long known about the ebb and flow of people as they moved across the continent over the millennia, of the ever-changing and porous borders between groups of people, the exchange of goods, ideas and the evolution of identities over time.

More particularly, the integration of professional archaeological research into the planning legislation of many European countries since the *Valetta Convention for the Protection of the Archaeological Heritage of Europe* in 1992 has resulted in an explosion of new knowledge about our European ancestors and the way they lived their lives. It was the recognition of the implications of this new data for the close maritime connections between peoples living in the Transmanche zone of northwestern Europe during the Bronze Age – around 3500 years ago – that led to the creation of the European project 'Boat 1550 BC' project in 2011. The project sought to bring together this new evidence of the strong ancient cultural links between the peoples of the region and present it to a wider audience. It brought together seven partners from three countries: the University of Lille 3/Maison européenne de l'homme et de la société de Lille, the Institut National de Recherches Archéologiques Preventives (INRAP), the Département du Pas-de-Calais and the town of Boulogne-sur-Mer from France, the Canterbury Archaeological Trust and Canterbury Christ Church University from England, and Ghent University from Belgium. It was financially supported by the European Union Interreg IV A '2 Mers Seas Zeeën' programme and the Conseil régional du Nord-Pas-de-Calais.

It was in the context of the 'Boat 1550 BC' project that a major academic conference was planned in collaboration with APRAB (l'Association pour la Promotion des Recherches Archéologiques sur l'Âge du Bronze) that brought together academic and professional archaeologists from all over Europe (and beyond) to discuss the new discoveries and research into the connections between people in the past. Its remit went beyond the study of the Transmanche zone and indeed the Bronze Age, but instead extended right across Europe, reflecting on a period of two millennia, from the middle of the 3rd millenium BC to the middle of the 1st millenium BC. The conference was held on 3–5 October 2012 at the Université du Littoral in the beautiful historic town of Boulogne-sur-Mer, France.

The proceedings of the conference are a co-production of Oxbow Books and APRAB, with the financial support of the Ministère de la Culture et de la communication, INRAP, and the UMR (Unité Mixte de Recherche) 8164 Halma.

The conference organisers would like to thank The Université du Littoral, the Centre de la Mer Nausicaa, and the service archéologique de la Ville de Boulogne for their assistance and the warm welcome extended to this international symposium.

Thanks should also go to the conference steering committee for their work in making the conference a success; Sylvie Boulud, Peter Clark, Alain Henton, Isabelle Kerouanton, Thibault Lachenal, Emmanuelle Leroy-Langelin, Armelle Masse, Claude Mordant, Pierre-Yves Milcent, Théophane Nicolas, Brendan O'Connor and Rebecca Peake.

Peter Clark, Mark Duncan and Jane Elder of the Canterbury Archaeological Trust are also acknowledged for their help in bringing this volume to publication.

Taken together, these varied contributions offer a new and different perspective on the relationships between the peoples of Europe in the distant past, a perspective that we hope will find a wide audience and help inform all about the prehistoric context of our modern world and our appreciation of European identity today.

Lastly, we pause to remember and celebrate the lives of two outstanding scholars of European prehistory who have recently passed away; Richard Darrah, perhaps best known for his ground-breaking work on the Dover Bronze Age boat, and Colin Burgess, whose magisterial command of the European Bronze Age inspired generations of archaeologists. We hope this volume represents a modest tribute to their outstanding contribution to our knowledge of Europe's ancient history.

1

To think of leaving: mobility and identities in Western Europe during the Bronze Age

Anne Lehoërff

'There are three kinds of men: the living, the dead and those who sail the sea'
Quote attributed to: Aristote, Plato or Anacharsis

Keywords: mobility, exchange, frontiers, Bronze Age, identities

Human mobility

The Europe of ancient oral societies, before Classical Antiquity, is sometimes perceived as a closed world, stable – immobile even. This widespread perception, inherited from 19th century historiography and nourished by classical texts such as the *Gallic War* by Julius Caesar, seeks to limit the people of these bygone times to their birth places, when not conjuring up an image of their all too miserable way of life. However, nothing is less true than the idea of static communities over the millennia of Protohistory, from the Neolithic to the end of the Metal Ages (Lehoërff 2009; 2011).

In 1992, the discovery of a Bronze Age boat in the port of Dover (Kent, UK) was a revelation for many, even if, for the archaeological specialists of this period, this type of discovery was only down to a matter of time (Clark 2004a; 2004b).

For decades, archaeologists have studied human mobility through time (Scarre and Healy 1993). During prehistory (the Palaeolithic and Mesolithic periods), populations moved from one place to another following the rhythm of the places they lived, the seasons and the changing climate, seeking out food to eat and essential materials. This mobility, be it over short or long distances, leaves tenuous traces often difficult to interpret, precisely because they are inherent to this way of life. It constitutes nevertheless a scientific challenge for scholars studying these very ancient times, focussing on seasonality, for example, or on the relationship between people and their environment drawing together the threads of influences leading to *Homo sapiens*.

Agricultural mobility

The beginning of Protohistory heralded new relationships between individuals, space and time. In choosing to become farmers, people tied themselves to the land, but this did not mean that society in general was a prisoner. The process of Neolithisation itself is defined by movements of people, of ideas, by the adoption of new subsistence practices (production, storage, consumption) and more generally by the emergence of new types of societies. The creation of an agricultural Europe was 'arythmic' (Guilaine 2015), taking place over the course of millennia, but nevertheless permanent. The rhythm of this revolution, marked by episodes of stasis and then rapid expansion, was largely dependent on the rhythm of human movement and the capacity of communities to develop new ways of life within each new territory, some of which were already populated by nomadic or semi-nomadic groups. In this context, one cannot explain everything by imagining that people had chosen simply to walk (Lehoërff 2016a, 225–61). Sea level was already high because of the melting ice and coastal areas were thus far apart from one another. To cross these spaces without boats was impossible. It follows that the success of Neolithisation was dependant on seafaring. Taking this evidence into account we must recognise that people probably navigated the sea from very early on, from at least the Neolithic if not before (in Europe the first dug out boats date to the Mesolithic), which leads us to two questions: the first concerning the peoples of the past, and the second to the scholars who study them.

The concept of space and the study of frontiers

To travel, to cross borders and to create territories supposes that the individuals who took part in such an adventure understood space on two levels: the real and the symbolic. To dare to travel to known and unknown lands, by land and by sea, braving real and imaginary dangers (especially at sea), one must consider what lies beyond the visible horizon. It is of course difficult to address these questions for oral societies that have now disappeared. Some, however, have the temerity to tackle this fundamental subject. Working from archaeological data, together with ways of thinking about places or animals (such as birds in the sky or on the water), avenues of speculation can be proposed (Clark, Huth, this volume). Of course, this raises questions on the approaches, the methods available to archaeology, a science based on materiality, that allow it to approach the immaterial, the cognitive. When one thinks about ancient oral societies, long disappeared, that make up the greater part of our history, there are no written texts to clarify things for us. It is necessary to understand the meaning of the evidence, to interpret it, to translate it into a set of beliefs, into a language. Archaeologists are not totally bereft of help. Firstly, and most importantly, they have the archaeological record. They study and compare data, debate concepts, compare results, return to excavation, to the original data and thus work in a continually renewed dynamic. They fuel their own hypotheses with the results of others, those studying literate societies or those working in anthropology. They rule nothing out, whilst remaining wary of everything. The exercise can seem difficult. It is. But even if one does not have a mental map of maritime space of the coastal communities of the Channel, one imagines that they had some form of representation, with a system of reference points on land and sea. These clues go to demonstrate a knowledge of the stars (essential for the sailor!) and their cycles (how could it be otherwise in an agricultural society?). The Nebra disc (Germany), the metal chariots and pottery vessels decorated with birds, and the Scandinavian pictograms of boats are just some of the material evidence. So, if one has every reason to think that European Bronze Age societies had a representation of space, then one can also imagine that the question of the length of voyages was not ignored, that of the (more or less) rapid time needed to travel in contrast to the slow tempo of sedentary life in the agricultural world. Past communities gave much thought to the means of travel. Moreover, a

boat like that of Dover, evidence of a craftsmanship of exceptional quality, shows that society (or at least certain individuals) had devoted an important investment to make possible the existence of such a vessel, in order to meet the essential requirements of travel (McGrail 2001; Pomey and Rieth 2005). Such expertise in boatbuilding did not come about overnight, but we know that navigation went hand in hand with the rise in sea levels in Europe and the creation of seas after the last glacial maximum and the beginning of global warming. Navigation is, profoundly, an integral part of recent humanity, of Protohistory (Cunliffe 2001; 2008), with all of its attendant constraints, from boatbuilding to knowledge of the maritime environment and its ever-present dangers. The Dover Boat provides direct proof of this reality at a particular moment in time.

In order to understand the journeys undertaken, the movement of people and territorial identities, the archaeologist relies mostly on material data, albeit indirect. This is how the idea of a Transmanche zone came into being (see below). The houses, pits, ditches and tombs brought to light by excavation were compared and an internal logic became apparent: the structures and techniques demonstrated similar choices, common identities. This one can see in the buildings, in the important rites surrounding the treatment of the dead, and which can also resonate in everyday objects such as pottery or the more exotic, such as metal objects which necessarily require systems of exchange. In addition, the importation of the same foreign materials (such as amber) for the same use (small worked objects deposited in funerary contexts, etc.) underscore certain theories and comparisons (Jennings 2014). These clues, when put together, produce distribution maps, sometimes at different scales (the distribution of everyday pottery is not that of gold objects, which covers a much larger area) and demonstrate actual, real-life borders, not just those imagined by archaeologists today. Over decades of discoveries and research, this type of territorial reconstruction has become possible at precise moments in Protohistory, with continuities and discontinuities varying according to place and time. For the Atlantic zone, if each region demonstrates its originality little by the little, and with more and more clarity, the forms of continuity from the Middle and Late Neolithic to the Bronze Age can be made out (Harding and Fokkens 2013).

The Atlantic Bronze Age and the Transmanche area

Adopting a chronological framework for the period between the 3rd and the beginning of the 1st millennium BC meets two expectations: on one hand, it places the Bronze Age at the heart of ongoing debates consistent with the Dover Boat and its symbolism; on the other, its links this same

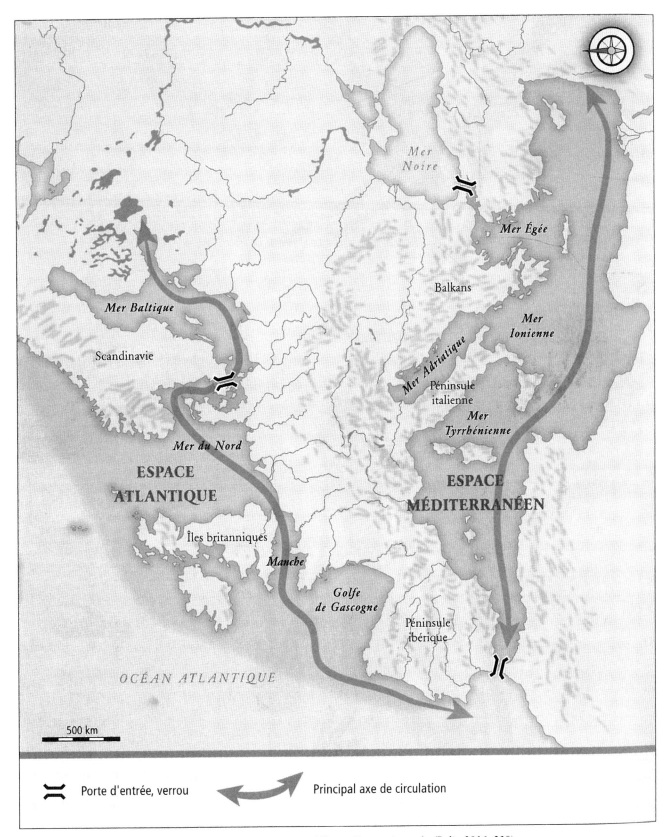

Fig. 1.1. Map of Europe inverted/Carte, Europe inversée (Belin 2016, 230).

Bronze Age to the periods (and realities) which come before and after it, the Neolithic on one side (Late Neolithic and Beaker Culture) and the Early Iron Age on the other. The discovery of a sewn plank boat in the port of Dover in 1992 throws a spotlight on the middle of the 2nd millennium BC, the Middle Bronze Age to use the technical term. This discovery was made during a period of European-wide reassessment of data relating to the Bronze Age. The development of preventive archaeology played its part but is not enough to completely explain the dynamic work during the 1990s and beyond (Chevillot and Coffyn 1990 for the concept of 'Atlantic Bronze Age'; for more recent research, see the bibliographies in this volume). Since this date, excavations have proliferated, the methods of scientific analyses have been enriched, scientific analyses and funerary archaeology has acquired new approaches. The themes of study and research questions have evolved at the same time and particular attention is now centred on environments, territories and the opening up of large areas as well as the growing importance of palaeo-environmental studies to facilitate this perspective. The improved conditions for excavation and the interrogation of data are thus brought together to propose new theoretical models for study. We know that each generation of scholars sits on the shoulders of its predecessors. It is by combining old and new results that the concept of the 'Atlantic Bronze Age' has been identified as a coherent entity for a large area of Western Europe, within which the sea, from the Atlantic to the North Sea, plays a key role.

Today, a new generation of scholars has joined the ranks of their teachers bringing with them a fresh integrative approach to the subject (Matthew, Milcent, this volume). In this vast Atlantic horizon, the boat discovered in Dover, recent excavations in the south of Britain, the coastal areas of Belgium, the north of France to the shores of Normandy, brings one to concentrate one of the foci of spatial analyses of the 'Atlantic Bronze Age' (which is also discussed) on the Transmanche area (Brun, Needham, Marcigny *et al.*, this volume). Put into the perspective of the history of research (De Mulder and Bourgeois, Leclercq and Warmenbol, this volume), the recent data reinforce the idea of a common identity on either side of this narrow stretch of sea that boats, products of exceptional craftsmanship, can cross relatively easily. Furthermore, archaeology invites us to reconsider the idea of a border that has long been put forward as 'natural'. This notion can be applied to the sea (either an obstacle or a routeway), but also to other landscape features which have equally been presented or understood as barriers, such as rivers or mountains (David-Elbiali, Huth, this volume). The study of societies over the *longue durée*, and in particular work on the movement of people, travel and the successive creation of territories and their shifting but never impassable borders, show that geographical determinism comes up against human

free will and it is often the latter that prevails. During the 2nd millennium BC people, goods and ideas circulated over great distances. Links can be identified between the coastal areas of Portugal or Brittany with Ireland and as far north as Scandinavia. The similarities of practices and objects (especially metal objects) are unequivocal. At the scale of the narrow passage between the Channel and the North Sea, the proximity of the two facing coasts is even more marked. Exemplified by the similarities in prestigious objects (made out of gold for example), the common identity of this Transmanche zone can be seen in the choice of dwelling (Leroy-Langelin *et al.*, this volume), funerary practices (Buchez *et al.*, Billand *et al.*, Issenmann *et al.*, this volume) and at certain times, pottery (Buchez *et al.*, Manem, Henton and Buchez, this volume).

The European project 'BOAT 1550 BC' provided an opportunity to assess the results in the context of the history of research during the many conferences of the project (2011–2014) and even after (Lehoërff 2016b). It has also allowed greater public awareness of old and new data brought together in a travelling exhibition in three languages (Lehoërff 2012). One of the themes specifically addressed the movement of people and voyages. The visitors, themselves mainly from the modern-day Transmanche area, were asked to think about the idea that, 3500 years ago, the sea was a route of communication and not a supposedly natural barrier. Pushing aside preconceived ideas and showing how inappropriate they are for our distant ancestors, was a clearly stated and even sought after desire, using the methods and scientific results from archaeology alone. Children were specifically targeted (in the exhibition and with the teaching kit) with a clear aim; to encourage future citizens to think about the question of space, of territories and of people's responsibility in their creation. The project therefore included a strong emphasis on the sharing of knowledge and the links between societies of the past and those of today. Led by scientists, it also included a more specialised presentation, showing hitherto unseen results and syntheses that open up the way to new research, probably less accessible to the general public but rather dedicated to specialised archaeologists. This was the essence of the Boulogne-sur-Mer conference in 2012 (this volume) and the Dover conference in 2013: to make accessible the fruits of this research.

Current work on human mobility

To conclude, the proceedings of this international conference will be published at a time when the question of human mobility has never been more topical. And with mobility comes the question of borders. The archaeologist is not responsible for resolving the issues of the modern world except for one notable exception: when the past physically intersects with the world of today.

More generally, the archaeologist's work is to understand the past, to give voice and words to people who are now silent, to shine a light on their history by way of buried or submerged finds, to bring knowledge to contemporary society and to put into perspective – over the *longue durée* – the phenomena whose traces are archaeological.

Archaeologists would however fail in their mission if they allowed us to believe that societies were in some way 'set down' in one place forever. Communities started to permanently claim territories about 8000 years ago in a Europe whose borders and territorial limits have not stopped moving since that time, at varying rhythms and over different spaces. The notion of irrevocable permanence does not exist within the perspective of the *longue durée*. At best, a period of relative stability can equate to a certain historical reality. In this context, the definition of borders becomes an ongoing territorial and social challenge. There is no evidence in relation to this question. Archaeology stresses that, for millennia at least, from the beginning of the Neolithic at the dawn of Protohistory, territories and borders are human, cultural and political constructions which constitute very strong elements of power. Nothing exists in a 'natural' state, written in the landscape. Natural features can create lines, ways and obstacles but not impassable barriers. Nothing, furthermore, in the reality of the shifting territories on the scale of human history (tens of thousands of years for the most recent 'us', *Homo sapiens*) could justify any form of legitimisation of original territories. In addition, has the (very) recent history of the last centuries, highly concentrated and complicated, succeeded in creating a form of spatial division whose maintenance in a crowded world can be preserved by political and territorial choices and a desire for peace?

Human society moves across the land, the sea or the mountains and creates and recreates its territories in relation to a moment in time and in accordance with its needs and possibilities. Nothing, *a priori*, might let us suppose that around 1500 BC the stretch of water between Britain and the continent was only a place of passage between two very similar and very close coastal worlds. The archaeological record has imposed this reality, contrary to what was expected, especially when considering today's difficulties. Managing a cross-border project which emphasised this very long history has thus been a good scientific lesson. Working together as a group drawn from three countries on the 'BOAT 1550 BC' project (France, Britain and Belgium), which was broadened internationally for the conference on voyaging in Europe between the 3rd and the 1st millennium BC, has also been an important human engagement. At the end of the project, one must draw some lessons about weaving a link between the past and the future. In particular,

we must call for vigilance, so as not to oversimplify complex human realities that cannot be understood either in their crude immediacy nor the red herring of an obsession with 'origins', something which Marc Bloch had good reason to be wary of!

Bibliography

Bloch, M. [1941] (1974) *Apologie pour l'histoire ou le métier d'historien*. Paris, Armand Colin.

Chevillot, C. and Coffyn, A. (eds) (1990) *L'âge du Bronze Atlantique: ses faciès, de l'Ecosse à l'Andalousie et leurs relations avec le bronze continental et la Méditerranée*. Actes du 1er Colloque du Parc Archéologique de Beynac, 10–14 Septembre 1990. Beynac.

Clark, P. (2004a) *The Dover Bronze Age Boat*. London, English Heritage.

Clark, P. (ed.) (2004b) *The Dover Bronze Age Boat in context*. Oxford, Oxbow Books.

Cunliffe, B. (2001) *Facing the Ocean: The Atlantic and its Peoples*. Oxford, Oxford University Press.

Cunliffe, B. (2008) *Europe Between the Oceans. Themes and Variations: 9000 BC–AD 1000*. New Haven-London, Yale University Press.

Guilaine, J. (2015) *La seconde naissance de l'homme. Le Néolithique*. Paris, Odile Jacob.

Harding, A. F. and Fokkens, H. (eds) (2013) *The Oxford Handbook of the European Bronze Age*. Oxford, Oxford University Press.

Jennings, B. (2014) *Travelling Objects: Changing Values*. Oxford, Archaeopress.

Lehoërff, A. (2009) Les paradoxes de la Protohistoire française. *Annales HSS*, Septembre-Octobre 2009, 5, 1107–1134.

Lehoërff, A. (2011) L'Âge du bronze est-il une période historique? In D. Garcia, (ed.), *L'Âge du bronze en Méditerranée. Recherches récentes*, 13–26. Paris, Errance.

Lehoërff, A. (ed.) (2012) *Par-delà l'horizon, Sociétés en Manche et mer du Nord il y a 3500 ans/Beyond Horizon. Societies of the Channel and North Sea 3500 years ago/Voorbij de Horizon. Samenlevingen in Kanaal en Noordzee 3500 jaren geleden*, avec la collaboration de J. Bourgeois, P. Clark, M. Talon. Paris, Somogy, Editions d'art.

Lehoërff, A. (2016a) *Préhistoires d'Europe. De Neandertal à Vercingétorix. –40 000/–52*. Paris, Belin (collection 'Mondes anciens').

Lehoërff, A. (2016b) *L'Âge du bronze en Manche et mer du Nord. Vingt ans d'études, des découvertes archéologiques à la réalisation du projet européen BOAT 1550 BC*, Institut de France, Académie des inscriptions et Belles Lettres, 30 janvier 2015. *CRAI*, février 2016, 187–206.

McGrail, S. (2001) *Boats of the World from the Stone to Medieval Times*. Oxford, Oxford University Press.

Pomey, P. and Rieth, É. (2005) *L'archéologie navale*, Paris, Errance ('Archéologiques').

Scarre, C. and Healy, F. (eds) (1993) *Trade and Exchange in Prehistoric Europe*. Oxford, Oxbow Monograph 33.

«Au miroir des voyages: mobilités et identités en Europe occidentale à l'Âge du bronze»

Anne Lehoërff

« Il y a trois sortes d'hommes, les vivants, les morts, et ceux qui vont sur la mer »
Citation attribuée à : Aristote, Platon ou Anacharsis

Mots-clés: mobilité, échanges, frontières, l'Âge du bronze, identités

Mobilités humaines

L'Europe des sociétés orales très anciennes, antérieures à l'Antiquité, est parfois perçue comme un monde fermé, stable, voire immobile. Cette vision populaire, héritée d'une historiographie bâtie au XIXe siècle et nourrie de textes antiques comme *La guerre des Gaules* de César, cantonne volontiers les individus de ces époques reculées dans leur lieu de naissance quand ce n'est pas également dans des cadres de vie assez miséreux. Pourtant, rien n'est plus faux que cette image de sociétés statiques au long des millénaires de la Protohistoire, du Néolithique à la fin des âges des métaux (Lehoërff 2009; 2011).

En 1992, la découverte fortuite d'un bateau de l'Âge du bronze dans le port de Douvres (Kent, Angleterre) fut une révélation pour certains. Les archéologues spécialistes de cette époque, eux, y étaient préparés (Clark 2004a; 2004b).

Depuis des décennies, les archéologues suivent la mobilité des hommes à travers le temps (Scarre and Healy 1993). Durant la Préhistoire (Paléolithique et Mésolithique), les populations se déplacent au rythme des implantations, des saisons et des changements climatiques, des approvisionnements alimentaires et de matériaux indispensables. Cette mobilité laisse des traces ténues et délicates d'interprétation, précisément car elle est inhérente au mode de vie, sur de courtes ou de longues distances. Elle constitue néanmoins un enjeu scientifique actuel pour les chercheurs travaillant sur ces temps très anciens, préoccupés des saisonnalités par exemple ou des modes de relations entre ces hommes et les milieux, intégrant les filiations d'implantation jusqu'à *Homo sapiens*.

Mobilités paysannes

Les débuts de la Protohistoire ouvrent à de nouveaux rapports entre les individus l'espace et le temps. En choisissant de devenir paysan, l'homme s'attache à la terre, ce qui ne signifie aucunement que la société dans son ensemble en est prisonnière. Le processus lui-même de la néolithisation s'inscrit dans un mouvement des hommes, des idées, d'adoption de nouveaux moyens de subsistance (production, conservation, consommation) et plus globalement de types de sociétés. La création d'une Europe agricole s'est faite de manière arythmique (Guilaine 2015), au cours de plusieurs millénaires, mais de manière définitive. Le rythme de cette révolution, marquée par des temps lents et des accélérations, a été largement tributaire de celui des déplacements des hommes et de leurs capacités à développer de nouveaux modes de vie à l'échelle de chaque territoire, pour certains déjà habités par des populations nomades ou semi-nomades. Dans ce cadre, si les hommes ont pu choisir tout simplement la marche à pied, ce mode de déplacement est insuffisant pour tout expliquer (Lehoërff 2016a, 225–61). Le niveau des mers était alors déjà partiellement remonté en raison de la fonte des glaces et les côtes s'étaient alors éloignées les unes des autres. Franchir ces espaces sans bateau a été impossible. Aboutir la néolithisation sans les voies de mer l'a été tout autant. Devant cette évidence, il faut donc admettre que les hommes ont navigué très tôt en mer, au moins depuis le Néolithique, et peut-être même avant (les pirogues sont connues dès le Mésolithique en Europe), ce qui conduit à deux types d'interrogations : les premières du côté des hommes du passé, les secondes de celui des chercheurs qui les étudient.

Concevoir les espaces et étudier les frontières

Voyager, franchir des frontières, créer des territoires suppose, de la part des individus qui se lancent dans une telle aventure, une représentation des espaces de deux ordres : réelle et symbolique. Il faut avoir envisagé ce qui se trouve au-delà de l'horizon visible, à terre comme en mer et oser se lancer dans des mondes connus ou inconnus, en bravant les dangers imaginaires et réels, surtout en mer. Il est bien sûr très délicat d'aborder ces questions pour des sociétés orales disparues. Certains, pourtant, osent traiter de ce sujet essentiel. À partir des données archéologiques associés aux modes de représentations de lieux ou d'animaux (tels les oiseaux dans le ciel ou sur les eaux), des pistes de réflexion peuvent être proposées (Clark, Huth, dans ce volume). Bien sûr, cela ouvre des questionnements sur les moyens, les méthodes possibles de l'archéologie, science d'une certaine matérialité, pour aborder l'immatériel, le cognitif. Lorsque l'on étudie les sociétés orales anciennes et disparues, qui constituent notre histoire la plus longue, aucun écrit ne vient nous éclairer. Il faut concevoir le sens des formes produites, les interpréter, les traduire d'une certaine manière en des croyances, un langage. Les archéologues ne sont pas totalement démunis pour y parvenir. Bien sûr, tout d'abord, et de manière essentielle, ils ont à leur disposition la documentation archéologique. Ils étudient les données, les comparent, renversent les points de vue, confrontent les résultats, reviennent au terrain, aux données premières et travaillent ainsi dans une dynamique sans cesse renouvelée. Ils nourrissent aussi leurs propres hypothèses des résultats d'autrui. De ceux qui travaillent sur des sociétés de l'écrit ou de ceux qui travaillent en anthropologie. Ils ne s'interdisent rien, en se méfiant de tout. L'exercice peut sembler difficile. Il l'est. Mais, même si l'on ne possède pas la carte mentale des espaces maritimes des sociétés littorales de la Manche, on conçoit qu'elles en aient eu une forme de représentation, avec un système de repères, sur terre et en mer. Des indices concourent pour démontrer une connaissance des astres (repères essentiels du marin!), des cycles (comment pourrait-il en être autrement dans une société agricole ?). Le Disque de Nébra (Allemagne), les chars métalliques et céramiques surmontés d'oiseaux ou les pictogrammes scandinaves de bateaux n'en sont que la trace matérialisée. Si l'on a donc toutes les raisons de penser que les sociétés de l'Âge du bronze européen avaient une représentation

des espaces, on peut également concevoir que la question des durées de voyage n'était pas ignorée, celle du temps (plus ou moins) rapide du déplacement en opposition au temps long de la vie sédentaire de ce monde paysan. De manière directe, la question des moyens a été également, et visiblement, prise en considération par les hommes du passé. Plus encore, un bateau comme celui de Douvres, qui atteste un savoir-faire artisanal d'une qualité exceptionnelle, démontre que la société (ou certaines d'entre elles au moins) a consacré un investissement important à rendre possible l'existence d'une telle embarcation, pour répondre à des nécessités jugées primordiales de voyage (McGrail 2001 ; Pomey et Rieth 2005). Un tel art de la batellerie n'est pas né en un jour, mais on sait que la navigation accompagne la remontée des eaux en Europe et la création des mers après le maximum glaciaire et le début du réchauffement. Naviguer fait, profondément, partie de l'humanité récente, celle de la Protohistoire (Cunliffe 2001 ; 2008), avec toutes les contraintes que cette pratique inclut, de la fabrication des bateaux, à la connaissance des milieux maritimes et de leurs dangers permanents. Le bateau de Douvres constitue, juste, une preuve directe de cette réalité à un moment particulier.

Pour comprendre les voyages, les déplacements, et les identités territoriales, le plus souvent, le travail archéologique s'appuie sur une documentation matérielle, mais indirecte. C'est ainsi que l'idée d'une aire transmanche a vu le jour (voir *infra*). Mises au jour lors de fouilles, les structures de maisons, de fosses et fossés, de sépultures sont comparées et des logiques apparaissent : des formes et des techniques attestent des choix similaires, des identités communes. Ce que l'on peut voir dans les constructions, dans des gestuelles aussi fortes que la prise en charge des défunts, peut également avoir des échos dans des objets du quotidien telles les céramiques, ou plus exceptionnels, en particulier métalliques qui impliquent nécessairement des échanges. En outre, des importations de matériaux exogènes de même type (de l'ambre par exemple), pour des usages identiques (des petits mobiliers travaillés, déposés dans des sépultures, etc.) renforcent certaines thèses, certains rapprochements (Jennings 2014). Des indices, mis en faisceaux, livrent des cartographies de lieux, parfois avec des échelles différentes (la carte des céramiques du quotidien n'est pas celle des objets en or qui couvre une superficie beaucoup plus importante) et mettent en évidence des frontières vécues, réelles, et non seulement imaginé par les archéologues d'aujourd'hui. Au terme de décennies de découvertes et de recherches, ce type de reconstitutions territoriales devient possible pour bien des moments de la Protohistoire, avec des continuités et des discontinuités selon les lieux et les époques. Pour ce qui de l'espace atlantique, si chaque espace régional affirme de plus en plus, et de mieux en mieux, ses originalités, des formes de continuité entre Néolithique moyen et final et Âge du bronze existent (Harding and Fokkens 2013).

Bronze atlantique et espace transmanche

Adopter un cadrage chronologique entre le IIIe millénaire et le début du Ier millénaire répond à deux attentes : d'une part, placer l'Âge du bronze au cœur des débats, en cohérence avec le bateau de Douvres et la symbolique qu'il incarne ; d'autre part, lier ce même Âge du bronze avec les périodes (et les réalités) qui l'encadrent, Néolithique d'un côté (final ici et Campaniforme) et premier Âge du fer de l'autre. La découverte d'un bateau à bords cousus en 1992 dans le port de Douvres a jeté un coup de projecteur sur le milieu du IIe millénaire avant notre ère, le Bronze moyen dans les terminologies spécialisées. Cette découverte s'est faite dans un contexte de renouvellement de la documentation relative à l'Âge du bronze de manière globale en Europe. L'essor de l'archéologie préventive n'y est pas étranger mais il n'est pas suffisant pour expliquer de manière exhaustive le dynamisme des travaux dans ces années 1990 et au-delà (Chevillot et Coffyn 1990, pour le concept de « Bronze atlantique » ; pour les travaux plus récents, voir bibliographies dans ce volume). Depuis cette date, les fouilles se multiplient, les méthodes s'enrichissent de moyens d'analyses, l'archéologie funéraire se dote de nouveaux types d'approches. Les thématiques, les problématiques de recherche évoluent également et une attention particulière est désormais accordée aux milieux, aux territoires, les ouvertures de larges surfaces comme la place grandissante du paléoenvironnement facilitant cette perspective. Les conditions sur le terrain, et dans l'exploitation de la documentation, sont donc alors réunies pour proposer de nouveaux modèles théoriques de réflexion. On le sait, chaque génération de chercheurs est portée sur les épaules de ses prédécesseurs. C'est en faisant la synthèse des anciens et des nouveaux résultats que le concept de « Bronze atlantique » a ainsi été précisé comme entité cohérente pour un large espace occidental européen, au sein duquel la mer, de l'Atlantique à la Mer du nord joue un rôle clef.

Aujourd'hui, une nouvelle génération de chercheurs est venue rejoindre celle de ses maîtres et permet des regards croisés sur le sujet (Matthews, Milcent dans ce volume). Dans ce vaste horizon atlantique, le bateau mis au jour à Douvres, les fouilles récentes dans le sud de l'Angleterre, la Belgique littorale, le Nord de la France jusqu'aux abords de la Normandie, invitent à resserrer une des focales d'analyse spatiale du 'Bronze atlantique' (lui-même discuté) sur l'espace transmanche (Brun, Needham, Marcigny *et al.* dans ce volume). Mises en perspective dans une histoire de la recherche (De Mulder et Bourgeois, Leclercq et Warmenbol dans ce volume), les données récentes renforcent l'idée d'une identité de part et d'autre de ce bras de mer, finalement étroit, que les bateaux, produits d'un savoir-faire exceptionnel, franchissent relativement aisément. Plus encore, la documentation archéologique invite à repenser la notion de frontière que l'on a tant cherché à nous proposer comme « naturelle ». La question se pose bien sûr pour la mer (obstacle ou lieu de passage), mais également pour toutes ces composantes des paysages qui ont été présentées, appréhendées comme des barrières telles les rivières ou les montages (David-Elbiali, Huth dans ce volume). L'étude des sociétés sur la longue durée, et en particulier les travaux sur les déplacements, les voyages, les créations successives des territoires et de leurs frontières mouvantes mais jamais infranchissables, démontrent que le déterminisme géographique se heurte à la volonté des hommes, et que cette dernière semble régulièrement l'emporter. Au IIe millénaire avant notre ère, les hommes, les biens et les idées circulent sur de très grandes distances. On identifie des liens entre la façade maritime du Portugal ou de la Bretagne avec l'Irlande et jusqu'en Scandinavie. Les similitudes de pratiques ou de mobiliers (en particulier métalliques) sont explicites. À l'échelle de cet étroit passage entre Manche et Mer du nord, la proximité entre les deux littoraux qui se font face est plus marquée encore. Perceptible dans des analogies de mobiliers prestigieux (en or par exemple), l'identité commune de cet espace transmanche se mesure dans les choix d'habitation (Leroy-Langelin *et al.*, dans ce volume), les pratiques funéraires (Buchez *et al.*, Billand *et al.*, Issenmann *et al.*, dans ce volume), les données céramiques à certains moments (Buchez *et al.*, Manem, Henton et Buchez dans ce volume).

Le projet européen « BOAT 1550 BC » a été l'occasion de présenter un état des résultats, replacés dans l'histoire de la recherche, dans le cadre de nombreuses conférences dans le temps du projet (2011–2014) et même au-delà (Lehoërff 2016 b). Il a permis également de porter à connaître, pour un public large, des données anciennes et nouvelles de manière croisée dans le cadre d'une exposition internationale, trilingue et itinérante (Lehoërff 2012). Une des thématiques portait précisément sur les déplacements et les voyages. Les visiteurs, pour l'essentiel eux-mêmes habitants de l'espace transmanche actuel, étaient invités à s'interroger sur la mer comme lieu de communication il y a quelque 3 500 ans et non comme barrière supposée naturelle. Le fait de bousculer les idées reçues et de démontrer leur caractère erroné pour nos lointains ancêtres relevait d'une volonté clairement affirmée, voire recherchée, en prenant appui sur les méthodes et les résultats scientifiques de la seule archéologie. Une attention toute particulière avait été accordée au public enfant (dans l'exposition, puis le kit pédagogique), dans une perspective assumée : faire réfléchir les futurs citoyens sur la question des espaces, des territoires et de la responsabilité des hommes dans leur construction. Le projet incluait donc un axe fort tourné vers le partage de la connaissance et les liens entre les sociétés d'hier et celles d'aujourd'hui. Mené par des scientifiques, le projet ne pouvait pas se passer également une réflexion spécialisée, proposant des résultats inédits et des synthèses ouvrant la voie vers de nouveaux travaux, de fond, moins accessibles sans doute au grand public mais dédiés plutôt aux archéologues spécialisés. C'est tout l'enjeu du colloque de Boulogne-sur-Mer de 2012 (ce volume), comme celui de Douvres en 2013 : rendre accessible le fruit de ces travaux.

L'actualité des mobilités humaines

En forme de conclusion, on pourra dire que la question des mobilités humaines n'a jamais semblé autant d'actualité qu'au moment où paraissent les actes de ce colloque international. Et avec les mobilités, la question corolaire des frontières. L'archéologue n'a pas pour mission de résoudre les enjeux du temps contemporain, à une exception près, notable, qui engage alors sa responsabilité : lorsque le passé croise, matériellement, le monde d'aujourd'hui. De manière plus générale, son travail est de comprendre le passé, de redonner la parole aux hommes qui se sont tus, d'éclairer leur histoire au travers des vestiges enfouis ou engloutis, d'apporter de la connaissance aux sociétés actuelles et de mettre en perspective sur la très longue durée des phénomènes dont les traces sont archéologiques.

Ici, toutefois, il faillirait à ses missions s'il laissait croire à ses contemporains que les sociétés sont en quelque sorte « posées » en un lieu pour toujours. Elles ont commencé à s'approprier des territoires de manière pérenne il y a quelque 8000 ans dans une Europe dont les contours territoriaux et les frontières n'ont cessé de bouger depuis cette date, à des rythmes et pour des espaces variables. La notion de définitif n'a pas de sens mis en perspective sur la longue durée. Au mieux, celle de stabilité relative peut recouvrir une certaine réalité historique. Dans ce cadre, la définition des frontières relève de défis territoriaux et sociaux permanents. Aucune évidence ne s'impose sur cette question. L'archéologie souligne que, depuis des millénaires au moins et les débuts du Néolithique à l'aube de la Protohistoire, les territoires et les frontières sont des constructions humaines, culturelles, politiques et qu'ils constituent des enjeux de pouvoir très

forts. Rien n'existe à l'état 'naturel', inscrit dans les paysages. Le milieu environnemental peut former des lignes, des axes, des obstacles, mais pas des barrières infranchissables. Rien, non plus, dans ces réalités territoriales fluctuantes à l'échelle de l'histoire humaine (plusieurs dizaines de millénaires pour le plus récent, le « nous » *sapiens*), ne saurait justifier une forme de légitimation de territoires originels. Au plus, l'histoire (très) récente des derniers siècles, très dense et compliquée, a-t-elle abouti à une forme de répartition spatiale dont le maintien, dans un monde très peuplé, peut espérer être préservé, par des choix politiques, territoriaux et pas une volonté de construction de paix.

La société des hommes traverse les terres, les mers ou les montagnes et compose/recompose ses territoires en fonction des moments, de ses besoins et des possibles. Rien, *a priori*, ne devrait laisser supposer que, vers 1 500 avant notre ère, la mer entre l'Angleterre et le continent n'est qu'un lieu de passage entre deux mondes côtiers très proches et très similaires. L'archéologie a imposé cette réalité, contraire aux possibles attendus, en particulier au regard des difficultés actuelles. Conduire un projet transfrontalier, qui en a souligné la très longue histoire, a donc été une belle leçon de science. Travailler collectivement à l'échelle des trois pays réunis dans le projet « BOAT 1550 BC » (France, Angleterre, Belgique), élargi à l'occasion du colloque sur les voyages en Europe entre le IIIe et le Ier millénaire, a également été un engagement humain important. Au terme de ce travail, on se doit de tirer quelques leçons en tissant le lien entre passé et futur. On se doit en particulier de faire un appel à la vigilance, afin que ne soient pas simplifiées, à outrance, des réalités humaines complexes qui ne sauraient être appréhendées ni uniquement dans leur immédiateté réductrice, ni dans une fausse vision uniforme d'une hantise des origines, dont Marc Bloch avait bien raison de se méfier!

2

On migrations: Sigfried Jan De Laet (1914–1999): his role in Belgian Bronze Age archaeology after the Second World War and the diffusion of cultural characteristics

Guy De Mulder and Jean Bourgeois

Abstract

In the second half of the 20th century Prof. Dr S. J. De Laet was the director of the Seminar for Archaeology at Ghent University. His research interests covered a wide chronological range from the Neolithic to the medieval period. Concerning the first part of the Bronze Age, his research focused on the Hilversum culture, mainly in cooperation with his Dutch colleague, W. Glasbergen. Another of his topics of research were the Urnfield cemeteries, mainly in western Belgium. His archaeological thinking about both subjects was strongly influenced by the idea of migrations.

Keywords: S. J. De Laet, history of archaeology, culture, migrations

Résumé

Dans la deuxième moitié du vingtième siècle, le professeur S. J. De Laet était le directeur du Séminaire d'Archéologie d'Université de Gand. Ses centres de recherche couvraient un large arc chronologique du Néolithique à la période médiévale. Pour la première partie de l'Âge du Bronze, ses recherches étaient centrées sur la culture d'Hilversum, surtout dans une collaboration avec son collègue néerlandais W. Glasbergen. Un de ses autres sujets de recherche portait sur les cimetières, surtout dans l'ouest de Belgique. Ses réflexions archéologiques sur tous ces sujets étaient influencées par les idées sur les migrations.

Mots-clés : S. J. De Laet, l'histoire d'archéologie, culture, migrations

Introduction

The concept of migrations as the major motor for cultural changes is already present in much 19th century archaeological literature. A detailed overview of the evolution of these concepts would be completely out of the focus of this paper and the literature about it is extensive (amongst many others: Kristiansen 2009; Renfrew and Bahn 2012, 463–7; Trigger 2006, 217–34). The role of major archaeologists such as Oscar Montelius (Gräslund 2014) and Vere Gordon Childe in this matter does not need to be stressed (Bintliff 2014). At the very moment when this concept is having a kind of new revival, thanks to studies of Strontium isotopes or DNA, it seemed interesting to follow the history of this idea through one of the major archaeologists for the Bronze and Iron Age in Belgium.

In Belgium, the idea of migrations was much favoured in 20th century archaeology. Alfred de Loë, keeper of the collections at the Royal Museums for Art and History in Brussels, wrote a comprehensive and major opus on the prehistory of Belgium (de Loë 1931). Terms as 'invaders', 'occupation' and 'migrations' are very present in this book.

We quote (de Loë 1931, 146, our translation):

'Hallstatt people or Proto-Celts probably came from the east, along the Danube. The Gallic Celts and Belgian Celts came probably from the north. Whatever, all these invaders are of a type that anthropologists would call *Hallstatt type*. They were tall and strong; they had … blond, almost red hair, blue eyes and a white skin.'

On the contrary, for the beginning of the Bronze Age, interestingly, de Loë stresses the fact that bronze must have been introduced by commerce and that, therefore, there was no new ethnic input (de Loë 1931, 11).

Many other examples of the same kind can be cited: the concept of migration and invasion of superior cultures over minor cultures was generally accepted in Belgium. Sigfried J. De Laet and Marc E. Mariën both began their archaeological careers after the Second World War and played a major role in the success of that diffusion and migration model, in scholarly literature as well as in large audience papers.

Fig. 2.1. De Laet at the excavation of Hofstade in 1947 (© Department of Archaeology, Ghent University).

In this paper, we would like to stress the place and role of S. J. De Laet in Belgian archaeology of the Bronze Age and Iron Age, and analyse where his preference for migration as a factor for cultural change originated.

S. J. De Laet: a brief overview of his career

'Pure luck played an important part in determining my scientific career'. With this quote S. J. De Laet began an overview of his career published in *Antiquity* (De Laet 1985). He was born in Ghent on 15 June 1914 and passed away on 13 May 1999. De Laet started his studies at Ghent University and obtained the degree of '*licentiaat*' in Classical Philology in 1936. In 1937 he became a doctor with a thesis on the Roman senate (De Laet 1937) (Fig. 2.1).

After a short period as a school teacher his academic career started in 1942 as a research fellow of the National Fund for Scientific Research (NFWO) at the Ghent University and 1 year later as assistant of Professor Hubert Van de Weerd.[1] During the first years De Laet published regularly about Roman historical subjects. His first archaeological paper also focused on a Gallo-Roman topic, i.e. the Gallo-Roman artefacts excavated in the 19th century at the Gallo-Roman *vicus* of Asse and preserved in the museum of Aalst, where he had been working as a teacher (De Laet 1942; 1943). During the Second World War he had his first contact with prehistoric archaeology. Kurt Tackenberg (see http://www.ulb.uni-muenster.de/sammlungen/nachlaesse/nachlass-tackenberg.html and http://de.wikipedia.org/wiki/Kurt_Tackenberg) was one of the so-called 'guest-professors' at the university during the German occupation. Tackenberg's papers on the subject of the *Germanenforschung* inspired De Laet to study prehistoric archaeology from a critical point of view (De Laet 1985). This resulted in a first paper on the Bronze and Iron Age in western Europe (De Laet 1944). This first paper was clearly much indebted to the concept of superior civilisations and migrations. We quote (our translation):

'Our country did not form in the prehistoric times neither a political nor a cultural unity. It was always subject to the influence of superior civilisations that flourished in North-western Germany, then South Germany or North-east France and radiated to our country. Major migrations also touched our countries, from the Illyrians, the Celts or the Germans.' (De Laet 1944, 56)

In 1947 he was appointed lecturer (full professor in 1951) at the Institute for Art History and Archaeology still at Ghent University. This led to the creation of the Seminar for Archaeology with its own excavation team within Ghent University, faculty of Arts and Philosophy. From then on De Laet's research focus shifted completely to archaeology. He published on different general and methodological archaeological themes, next to a large series of contributions on subjects of national archaeology, ranging from the Neolithic until the medieval period. His research on the Bronze Age focused on Early Bronze Age/ Middle Bronze Age barrows and Late Bronze Age Urnfield cemeteries (Fig. 2.2).

S. J. De Laet and the Early and Middle Bronze Age barrows in Flanders

From 1946 on, S. J. De Laet had regular contact with the leading Dutch archaeologist Albert Egges van Giffen (1884–1973), professor at the universities of Groningen and Amsterdam (Brongers 2013; De Laet 1973; Knol *et al.* 2005). In this period he participated in some of his excavations in the Netherlands (De Laet 1985). This cooperation influenced the research methods as for example by adopting the 'quadrants method' to excavate barrows.

In 1951 De Laet excavated for the first time a Late Neolithic – Early Bronze Age barrow at the site of Ruien/ Kluisberg (Fig. 2.3) (De Laet and Roosens 1952). Ruien is located on one of the tops of the Flemish Ardennes in western Belgium, an area where already in the 19th century some preserved barrows were excavated at the site of Ronse/Muziekberg (Fourny 1985). This funerary monument at the Kluisberg was already discovered in 1949 during digging by an amateur archaeologist, but a scientific excavation was carried out only two years later, in cooperation with the National Service for Excavations (Service National des Fouilles – Nationale Dienst voor Opgravingen) (Fig. 2.4). In 1953 and 1954 two barrows in the eastern part of Flanders at Mol/Postel were excavated (Fig. 2.5). (De Laet 1954a). The last barrow excavated by De Laet and his team was located at Eksel/De Winner (De Laet 1961a). This brought De Laet to write a new short

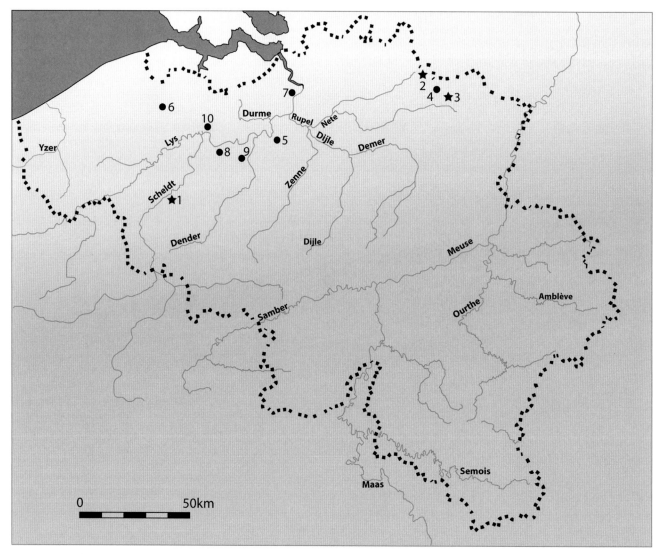

Fig. 2.2. Localisation of the Bronze Age sites excavated by De Laet and mentioned in this paper (Drawing: J. Angenon). 1. Ruien/ Kluisberg; 2. Mol/Postel; 3. Eksel/De Winner; 4. Lommel/Kattenbos; 5. Malderen; 6. Aalter/Oostergem; 7. Temse/Velle; 8. Massemen; 9. Hofstade; 10. Destelbergen.

Fig. 2.3. Visitors at the excavation of the Bronze Age barrow at Ruien/Kluisberg. Right: S. J. De Laet (© Department of Archaeology, Ghent University).

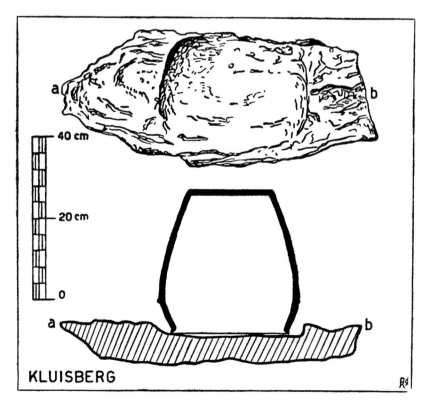

Fig. 2.4. Reconstruction of the inverted urn on a stone base (De Laet 1954b, Fig. 4).

synthesis on the Bronze Age based on recent excavations (De Laet 1954b).

Through his relationship with A. E. van Giffen, S. J. De Laet came also in contact with Willem Glasbergen (1923–1979) who was working, first as a student and later as an assistant of the former. In the early 1950s Willem Glasbergen focused his research on the barrows in North-Brabant (the Netherlands). Glasbergen defended his PhD thesis in 1954 with a study on the barrows of Toterfout-Halve Mijl, the so-called 'Eight Beatitudes' (Glasbergen 1954a; 1954b). Fully in the line of the idea of migration, he introduced the concept of the Hilversum culture which was, according to him, introduced by English immigrants who had moved over the Channel as bronze traders. English influences were visible in the local pottery style from the Middle Bronze Age and also in the funerary traditions (Theunissen 1999; 2009).

S. J. De Laet and W. Glasbergen cooperated to study Bronze Age burial rituals and barrows in the south of the Netherlands and the Belgian Campine region. Both also integrated new scientific approaches such as the use of radiocarbon dating and pollen analysis to reconstruct the landscape, but also as chronological markers. De Laet

and Glasbergen stressed similarities in the funerary ritual along both sides of the border and the presence of English influences in the funerary practices (De Laet and Glasbergen 1957; 1959). This hypothesis was further developed; based on new research results from northern France the arrival of the immigrants was located in the region of Boulogne-sur-Mer. They passed through the western part of Belgium, where a so-called group of English immigrants settled in the Flemish Ardennes, and moved across the Scheldt into the Campine region (De Laet 1961b).

The concept of migration continued to live in his later publications, for the Bronze Age as well as for the Iron Age (De Laet 1982).

The impact of the cooperation with A. E. van Giffen and especially W. Glasbergen is not to be underestimated, although the idea of migrations is already present in De Laet's earliest papers on the Bronze Age. Interestingly, De Laet refers in these early papers, alongside mainly German archaeologists, to Belgian authors such as A. de Loë, although V. Gordon Childe and his study of the Bronze Age in 1930 are mentioned only once. Specifically, the work of E. Sprockhoff (1942) is then considered by him

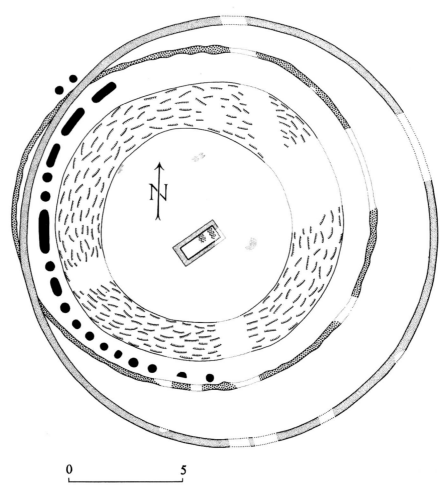

0　　　　　　　5

Fig. 2.5. Plan of barrow II at Mol/Postel (De Laet 1954a, fig. 6).

as a major contribution (De Laet 1944, 59). In his later papers, references to English archaeologists, such as C. F. C. Hawkes or J. D. Cowen make their appearance, along with W. Glasbergen (De Laet 1954b; 1956). Sprockhoff is still cited, but the impact of German studies seems to vanish.

Recent research has changed ideas about the Hilversum culture which is seen nowadays as local farming communities with their own specific material culture and funerary practices which evolved through time by indigenous human processes and by influence from outside (Theunissen 1999; 2009). Since 1980 aerial photography in western Belgium has proven that a testimony of levelled barrows is preserved in (or better under) the landscape. The ditches surrounding the barrows are visible as circular structures from the air. At the present more than 1000 monuments are recorded in the region of geographical name (Cherretté and Bourgeois 2005; De Reu 2012; De Reu *et al.* 2011). These monuments in western Belgium are related to funerary monuments in northern France and southern England. They belong to the Channel–North sea cultural area, characterised by mobility of people, ideas and goods (Bourgeois and Talon 2009; Lehoërff *et al.* 2012).

These observations partly revive the former idea of migrations from De Laet and Glasbergen but in another setting that places the accent more on mobility of material and immaterial goods and values than on people.

Urnfields in the province of East Flanders

Another topic of De Laet's research was the Late Bronze Age and urnfields, mainly in western Belgium. After the Second World War research into urnfields was on the rise again. Publications by German scholars such as Wolfgang Kimmig (1940) and Emil Vogt (1930) and, to a lesser degree, R. Stampfuss (1927) or O. Doppelfeld (1934) in the 1930s and 1940s set the agenda and the focus on Switzerland and Germany. M. E. Mariën makes much reference to German scholars such as W. Kimmig (1948).

Wolfgang Kimmig had written a few stimulating papers about the French Late Bronze Age, which he had been studying in the French museums during the German occupation in the Second World War (Kimmig 1951). In Belgium, the first papers on the Late Bronze Age urnfields were published at the same time (Mariën 1948; see Leclercq and Warmenbol in this volume). The paper by W. Kimmig (1951) on the French Late Bronze Age '*Où en est l'étude de la civilisation des champs d'urnes…*' echoes interestingly a paper published some years earlier by Marc E. Mariën '*Où en est la question des champs d'urnes …*' (Mariën 1948).

New excavations of urnfields were carried out by different institutions in the first decade after the end of the Second World War (De Mulder 2011). S. J. De Laet and Ghent University were amongst them. One of the first urnfields to be excavated by De Laet was the site of Lommel/Kattenbosch in the province of Limburg (De Laet and Mariën 1950). With the exception of an isolated find of an urn grave at Malderen (province of Flemish Brabant) (De Laet 1960) De Laet's later urnfield research concentrated in the province of East Flanders. The first site to be excavated was at Aalter/Oostergem (1952–1954). Later he excavated at Temse/Velle (1955), Massemen (1957–1959) (Fig. 2.6) and Destelbergen (1960–1984) (Fig. 2.7 and 2.9) (de Laet *et al.* 1986; 1958a; 1958b; 1958c; De Mulder and Bauters 1997).

These new excavations combined with the study of ancient archives and preserved urns resulted in some new hypotheses on the urnfields in Flanders. In 1948 M. E. Mariën ascribed the cemetery of Temse/Veldmolenwijk, excavated in the late 19th–early 20th century, to the *Niederrheinische Grabhügelkultur* (Mariën 1948). In 1958 S. J. De Laet and his team proposed a different hypothesis. The urnfields in the province of East Flanders formed a different regional group, called 'the Flemish group' (De Laet *et al.* 1958a). This regional definition was based on the different types of graves that displayed other ways of deposition of cremated remains, a scarcity of the grave goods and different

Fig. 2.6. Original drawing of cremation grave 25 at Massemen (© Department of Archaeology, Ghent University).

pottery styles. The publication of this research led indirectly to the discovery of the urnfield of Destelbergen. An amateur archaeologist contacted De Laet about an old find of urns at a place called Eenbeekeinde during sand digging in 1927–28. A first trial excavation began in 1960 and resulted in the discovery of a well preserved urn grave. This was the start of a long term excavation project that would continue until 1984 (de Laet *et al.* 1986; 1958c). Destelbergen is still the largest excavated urnfield in the province of East Flanders, with 105 cremation burials, a circular structure, six so-called 'longbeds' (*Langgraben*) and six quadrangular funerary structures (Fig. 2.7).

De Laet's papers on the Late Bronze Age in the late 1950s and early 1960s (De Laet and Glasbergen 1959; De Laet 1963) contain many references to migrations and invasions. References to W. Kimmig are almost completely missing. Obviously, De Laet and Mariën, the two major scholars in the Late Bronze Age at that time, published.

In the later 1960s, a student of De Laet, later a collaborator of the Seminar for Archaeology, Marcel Desittere, continued research on the Late Bronze Age. His masters thesis was dedicated to the bronze weapons of the Bronze Age and Early Iron Age in the Low Countries (Desittere 1959). Interestingly, bronze artefacts received little attention from De Laet. Desittere's later doctoral thesis covered the urnfield culture between the Lower Rhine and the North Sea during the Late Bronze Age (Desittere 1968). In contrast with S. J. De Laet, German scholars such as Stampfuss and Kersten are much more present, though W. Kimmig is also missing (Desittere 1968). Both De Laet and Desittere interpreted the urnfield culture, following in this the mainstream of concepts

in European continental archaeology, as a migration from Central European groups which mingled with the local Middle Bronze Age population. The interaction between immigrants and autochthonous elements resulted in the development of four separate regional groups with their own cultural characteristics in funerary ritual and pottery style. These groups were classified as the Flemish group, a North-western group, a Middle Belgian group and the Famenne group (De Laet 1974a; Desittere 1968). M. Desittere, who was also using metal objects in his reflection on what happened in the Late Bronze Age, started over the years to mitigate the idea of immigrants. The title of his paper published at the IVth Atlantic colloquium is clear: '*Autochtones et immigrants…*' (Desittere 1983). He stresses the fact that two elements of the material culture, a local and a non-local element, can be distinguished in the southern part of the Low Countries. We quote (our translation):

'This kind of cultural image cannot be explained by the theory of a "large scale" invasion that would have installed, in one piece, a new material culture in an area without culture. This kind of cultural vacuum is only possible in a region with low population density… Foreign elements are such a strong part of the Late Bronze Age material culture that they can only have been introduced by immigrants… As a conclusion, the material culture of the Late Bronze Age in the southern part of the Low Countries developed under the common influence of autochthonous elements and immigrants, bearers of the Urnfield civilization.' (Desittere 1983, 79).

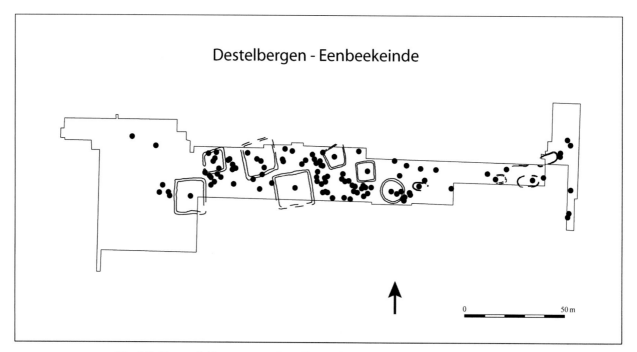

Fig. 2.7. The urnfield cemetery at Destelbergen/Eenbeekeinde (Drawing: J. Angenon).

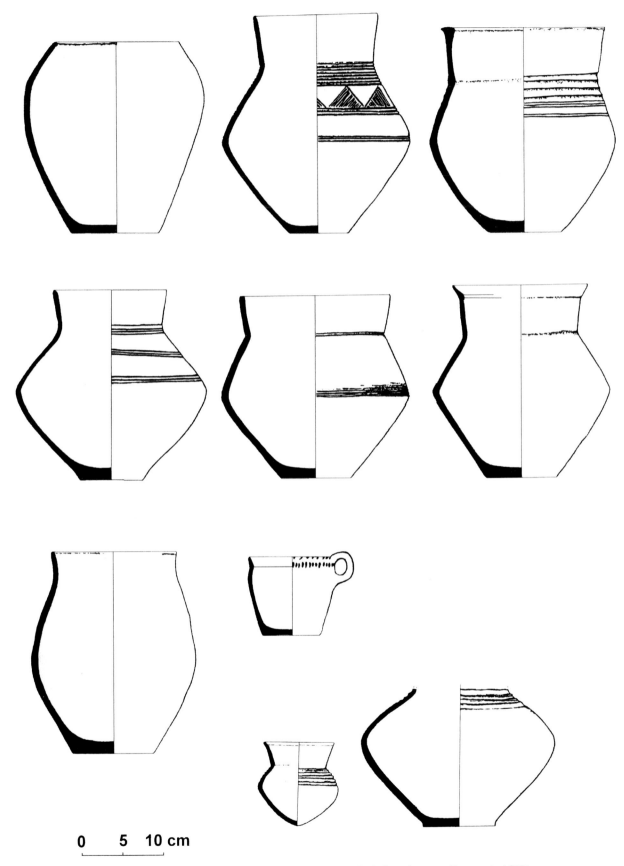

Fig. 2.8. Some RSFO-influenced pottery in the so-called Flemish group (Bourgeois 1989).

As for the former period of the Bronze Age the concepts of migrating groups of people have been reviewed. P. Brun proposed, in the 1980s, a model based on socio-economic dynamics between a Continental cultural and economic area and an Atlantic cultural complex. The idea of the urnfield culture was replaced by the concept of the 'groupe Rhin-Suisse-France orientale (RSFO)' the core region from where the socio-economic changes spread out in a westerly direction (Brun 1988). This model is accepted by the French archaeological community and also functions quite well for the Belgian Late Bronze Age. In the Netherlands, the influence of the RSFO is less visible and is also not much used as a concept in German archaeology.

RSFO cultural influence spreads through Central Belgium (Warmenbol 1988) in the Scheldt valley, but is less dominant. Pottery in RSFO style does not reach the same level of quality as in the southern Meuse valley and is only found in limited numbers in funerary contexts (Fig. 2.8) (De Mulder 2011). Atlantic influences are still visible in the material culture from this area, being it ceramic form or the copying of bronze objects (De Mulder 2013). The definition of the regional urnfield groups is also questioned. The River Scheldt at Antwerp was seen as the border between the Flemish and the North-western group. Recent research has proven that this region east of the River Scheldt was a transitional area between two different regional cultural entities. In this area there is also influence visible of the RSFO group, which is not ascertained in the eastern part of the so-called North-western group (Leclercq 2014; De Mulder 2013).

Urnfield research by De Laet and his department led to the creation of a typology of the different kind of cremation deposits recognised in the cemeteries of East Flanders (Fig. 2.9). This typology is based on the manner of deposition of the cremated remains from the pyre in the burial pit. This typological scheme is still used as a mainstay for identifying cremation burials. It has been enlarged to incorporate some newly ascertained ways of depositing cremated remains in the Scheldt valley. This scheme can also be used for the Late Iron Age. Radiocarbon dates are being used to support the chronological framework of this burial typology (Bourgeois *et al.* 1989; De Mulder 2011).

Conclusion

S. J. De Laet was, together with M. E. Mariën, one of the driving forces in the Bronze Age research in Belgium in the second half of the 20th century. His research was focused on two topics. First the Early and Middle Bronze Age barrows and the Hilversum culture together with his Dutch colleague W. Glasbergen. His second interest was in urnfields, especially in the province of East Flanders and their relation to the Central European urnfield culture.

Note

1   The biographical elements on De Laet's career have been extracted from De Laet (1974b). This document has also been used for several *In memoria* (Van Caenegem 1999; Van Looy 2000).

Bibliography

Bintliff, J. (2014) Vere Gordon Childe. 1892–1957. Revolutions in prehistory. In B. Fagan (ed.), *The Great Archaeologists*, 258–262. London, Thames & Hudson.

Bourgeois, J., Semey, J. and Vanmoerkerke, J. (1989) *Ursel. Rapport provisoire des fouilles 1986–1987. Tombelle de l'âge du bronze et monuments avec nécropole de l'âge du fer.* Scholae Archaeologicae 11. Gent, Rijksuniversiteit Gent.

Bourgeois, J. and Talon, M. (2009) From Picardy to Flanders: Transmanche connections in the Bronze Age. In P. Clark (ed.) *Bronze Age Connections. Cultural Contact in Prehistoric Europe,* 38–59. Oxford, Oxbow Books.

Brongers, J. A. (2013) *Giffen, Albert Egges van (1884–1973).* Biografisch Woordenboek van Nederland. http://resources.huygens.knaw.nl/bwn1880-2000/lemmata/bwn3/giffen

Brun, P. (1988) L'entité Rhin-Suisse-France orientale; nature et évolution. In P. Brun and C. Mordant (eds) *Le Groupe Rhin-Suisse-France Orientale,* 599–620, Mémoires du Musée de préhistoire d'Île-de-France 1. Nemours, Association pour la promotion de la recherche archéologique.

Cherretté, B. and Bourgeois, J. (2005) Circles for the dead. Excavation of a Bronze Age cemetery, discovered by aerial survey (Oedelem-Wulfsberge, West Flanders, Belgium). In J. Bourgeois and M. Meganck (eds) *Aerial Photography and*

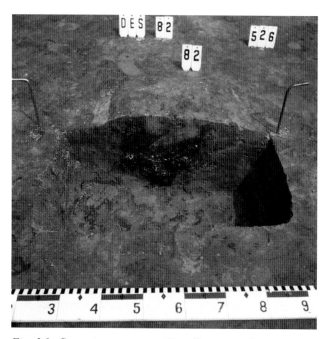

Fig. 2.9. Cremation grave type Destelbergen at the eponymous urnfield (© Department of Archaeology, Ghent University).

Archaeology 2003. A Century of Information. Papers presented during the Conference held at the Ghent University December 10th–12th, 2013, 255–65. Archaeological Reports Ghent University 4. Gent, Academia Press.

De Laet, S. J. (1937) *De samenstelling van den Romeinschen Senaat gedurende de eerste eeuw van het Principaat (28 v. – 68 na Kr.) en de politieke houding van de keizers tegenover deze hoge vergadering.* Gent, Rijksuniversiteit Gent.

De Laet, S. J. (1942) Figurines en terre-cuite de l'époque romaine trouvées à Assche-Kalkhoven. *Antiquité Classique* 11, 41–54.

De Laet, S. J. (1943) De terra sigillata van Assche-Kalkoven. *Revue Belge d'Archéologie et d' Histoire de l'Art* 13, 95–115.

De Laet, S. J. (1944) Enkele recente studies over het Metaaltijdperk in West-Europa. *Handelingen van de Maatschappij voor Geschiedenis en Oudheidkunde te Gent, Nieuwe Reeks* 1, 55–80.

De Laet, S. J. (1954a) Opgraving van twee grafheuvels te Postel (gemeente Mol, provincie Antwerpen). *Handelingen van de Maatschappij voor Geschiedenis en Oudheidkunde te Gent, Nieuwe Reeks* 8, 1–24.

De Laet, S. J. (1954b) De bronstijd en het begin van de ijzertijd in Vlaanderen in het licht van recente opgravingen. *Gentse Bijdragen tot Kunstgeschiedenis* 15, 161–187.

De Laet, S. J. (1956) Etudes récentes et documents nouveaux sur la civilisation de Michelsberg. *Bulletin de la Société Royale Belge d'Anthropologie et de Préhistoire* 67, 73–79.

De Laet, S. J. (1960) Een urnengrafveld te Malderen (Brabant). *Antiquité Classique* 29, 24.

De Laet, S. J. (1961a) De opgraving van een grafheuvel op 'De Winner' te Eksel. *Limburg* 11, 158–165.

De Laet, S. J. (1961b) Quelques précisions nouvelles sur la civilisation de Hilversum en Belgique. *Helinium* 1, 120–6.

De Laet, S. J. (1963) Eléments autochtones dans la civilisation des champs d'urnes en Belgique et aux Pays-Bas. In *A Pedro Bosch-Gimpera En El Septuagésimo Aniversario de Su Nacimiento*, 119–127. México, Instituto Nacional de Antropologia e Historia.

De Laet, S. J. (1973) In memoriam Albert Egges Van Giffen 1884–1973. *Helinium* 13, 4–9.

De Laet, S. J. (1974a) *Prehistorische kulturen in het Zuiden der Lage Landen.* Wetteren, Universa.

De Laet, S. J. (1974b) *Curriculum Vitae en Bibliografie* (unpublished document s.l. private document with copy in Ghent University).

De Laet, S. J. (1982) *La Belgique d'avant les Romains.* Wetteren, Universa.

De Laet, S. J. (1985) Archaeological retrospect 7. *Antiquity* 59, 7–12.

De Laet, S. J. and Glasbergen, W. (1957) Begrafenisritueel in de kempische bronstijd. *Vlaamse Gids*, 3–19.

De Laet, S. J. and Glasbergen, W. (1959) *De voorgeschiedenis der Lage Landen.* Brussel, J. B. Wolters.

De Laet, S. J. and Mariën, M. E. (1950) La nécropole de Lommel-Kattenbosch. *Antiquité Classique* 19, 309–363.

De Laet, S. J. and Roosens, H. (1952) Opgraving van een bronstijdgrafheuvel op de Kluisberg (Gem. Ruien, Prov. Oost-Vlaanderen). *Cultureel Jaarboek der Provincie Oostvlaanderen* 2, 45–59.

De Laet, S. J., Nenquin, J. A. E. and Spitaels, P. (1958a) *Contributions à l'étude de la civilisation des champs d'urnes en Flandre.* Dissertationes Archaeologicae Gandenses IV. Brugge, De Tempel.

De Laet, S. J., Thoen, H. and Bourgeois, J. (1986) *Les fouilles du Séminaire d'Archéologie de la Rijksuniversiteit te Gent à Destelbergen-Eenbeekeinde et l'histoire la plus ancienne de la région de Gent (Gand). I. La période préhistorique*, Dissertationes Archaeologicae Gandenses XXIII. Brugge, De Tempel.

De Laet, S. J., Nenquin, J. A. E., Spitaels, P. and Van Doorselaer, A. (1958b) Het urnengrafveld van Massemen. *Nieuwe Oudheidkundige Opgravingen en Vondsten in Oost-Vaanderen* II, 6–37.

De Laet, S. J., Nenquin, J. A. E., Spitaels, P. and Van Doorselaer, A. (1958c) Het urnenveld van Destelbergen. *Nieuwe Oudheidkundige Opgravingen en Vondsten in Oost-Vaanderen* II, 38–54.

de Loë, A. (1931) *Belgique ancienne. Catalogue descriptif et raisonné. II Les âges du métal.* Bruxelles, Vromant.

De Mulder, G. (2011) *De funeraire rituelen in het Scheldebekken tijdens de late bronstijd en de vroege ijzertijd. De grafvelden in hun maatschappelijke en sociale context.* Unpublished PhD, Department of Archaeology Ghent University.

De Mulder, G. (2013) La céramique du Bronze final dans l'ouest de la Belgique. Entre le monde atlantique et le groupe Rhin-Suisse-France orientale. In E. Warmenbol and W. Leclercq (eds) *Échanges de bons procédés. La céramique du Bronze Final dans le nord-ouest de l'Europe. Actes du Colloque International organisé à l'Université Libre de Bruxelles les 1er et 2 Octobre 2010*, 223–244. Bruxelles, CReA-Patrimoine.

De Mulder, G. and Bauters, L. (1997) Het urnengrafveld van Massemen (O.–Vl.). *Lunula, Archaeologica Protohistorica* 5, 43–44.

De Reu, J. (2012) *Land of the Dead. A Comprehensive Study of the Bronze Age Burial Landscape in Northwestern Belgium.* Unpublished PhD, Department of Archaeology Ghent University.

De Reu, J., Deweirdt, E., Crombé, P., Bats, M., Antrop, M., De Maeyer, P., De Smedt, P., Finke, P. A., Van Meirvenne, M., Verniers, J., Zwertvaegher, A. and Bourgeois, J. (2011) Les tombelles de l'âge du bronze en Flandre sablonneuse (nord-ouest de la Belgique): un status quaestionis. *Archäologisches Korrespondenzblatt* 41, 491–505.

Desittere, M. (1959) *De bronzen aanvalswapens der Lage Landen uit de bronstijd en de vroege ijzertijd.* Unpublished MA paper, Ghent University.

Desittere, M. (1968) *De urnenveldenkultuur in het gebied tussen Neder-Rijn en Noordzee.* Dissertationes Archaeologicae Gandenses XI. Brugge, De Tempel.

Desittere, M. (1983) Autochtones et immigrants en Belgique et dans le sud des Pays-Bas au Bronze Final. In S. J. De Laet (ed.) *Acculturation and Continuity in Atlantic Europe, Mainly during the Neolithic Period and the Bronze Age*, 77–94, Dissertationes Archaeologicae Gandenses XVI. Brugge, De Tempel.

Doppelfeld, O. (1934) Die Hallstattzeit im niederrheinischen Raum. *Prähististorische Zeitschrift.* 25, 3–51.

Fourny, M. (1985) Nouvelle contribution à l'étude de la nécropole de la civilisation de Hilversum/Drakenstein (âge du bronze ancien/moyen). Examen des anciennes collections du musée du Centenaire à Mons. *Vie Archéologique, Bulletin de la Fédération des Archéologues de Wallonie* 5, 41–68.

Glasbergen, W. (1954a) *Barrow Excavations in the Eight Beatitudes. The Bronze Age Cemetery between Toterfout and Halve Mijl, North Brabant, I: The excavations. Palaeohistoria* II (1), Groningen, 1–134.

Glasbergen, W. (1954b) *Barrow Excavations in the Eight Beatitudes. The Bronze Age Cemetery between Toterfout and Halve Mijl, North Brabant, II: The implications. Palaeohistoria* II (2), Groningen, 1–204.

Gräslund, B. (2014) Oscar Montelius. 1843–1921. Developing accurate chronologies. In B. Fagan (ed.) *The Great Archaeologists*, 31–33. London, Thames & Hudson.

Kimmig, W. (1940) *Die Urnenfelderkultur in Baden*, Römisch-germanische Forschungen 14. Berlin, Walter de Gruyter.

Kimmig, W. (1951) Où en est l'étude de la civilisation des Champs-d'Urnes en France, principalement dans l'Est? *Revue Archéologique l'Est* 2, 65–81.

Knol, E., Bardet, A. C. and Prummel, W. (2005) *Professor Van Giffen en het geheim van de wierden*. Groningen, Groniger Museum – Heveskes Uitgevers.

Kristiansen, K. (2009) The discipline of archaeology. In B. Cunliffe, C. Gosden and R. A. Joyce (eds) *The Oxford Handbook of Archaeology*, 3–45. Oxford, Oxford University Press.

Leclercq, W. (2014) Les nécropoles de l'âge du Bronze final entre les bassins de l'Escaut et de la Meuse moyenne: approche chronologique et culturelle de l'occupation. In A. Cahen-Delhaye and G. De Mulder (eds) *Des Espaces aux Esprits. L'organisation de la mort aux Âges des Métaux dans le nordouest de l'Europe*, 15–27, Etudes et Documents, Archéologie. Namur, Institut du Patrimoine Wallon.

Lehoërff, A., Bourgeois, J., Clark, P. and Talon, M. (2012) *Par-delà l'horizon. Sociétés en Manche et mer du Nord, il y a 3500 ans. Catalogue de l'exposition du projet européen Interreg IVa 2 Mers Seas Zeeën 'Boat 1550 BC'*. Paris, Somogy Art Publishers.

Mariën, M. E. (1948) Où en est la question des Champs d'Urnes? *Antiquité Classique* 17, 413–444.

Renfrew, C. and Bahn, P. (2012) *Archaeology. Theories, Methods and Practice*, 6th edition. London, Thames & Hudson.

Sprockhoff, E. (1942) Niedersachsens Bedeutung für die Bronzezeit Westeuropas: zur Verankerung einer neuen Kulturprovinz. *Bericht der Römisch-Germanischen Kommission* 31, 1–138.

Stampfuss, R. (1927) Beiträge zur Nordgruppe der Urnenfelderkultur. *Mannus* 5, 50–100.

Theunissen, E. M. (1999) *Midden-bronstijdsamenlevingen in het zuiden van de Lage Landen. Een evaluatie van het begrip 'Hilversum-cultuur.'* Unpublished PhD, University of Leiden.

Theunissen, L. (2009) British immigrants killed abroad in the seventies: The rise and fall of Dutch culture. In P. Clark (ed.) *Bronze Age Connections: Culture Contact in Prehistoric Europe*, 60–67. Oxford, Oxbow Books.

Trigger, B. G. (2006) *A History of Archaeological Thought*, 2nd edition. Cambridge, Cambridge University Press.

Van Caenegem, R. (1999) In memoriam Professor Siegfried De Laet (1914–1999). *Handelingen der Maatschappij voor Geschiedenis en Oudheidkunde. te Gent, Nieuwe Reeks* LIII, 1.

Van Looy, H. (2000) In memoriam Sigfried De Laet (1914–1999). *Antiquité Classique* 69, 5.

Vogt, E. (1930) *Die spätbronzezeitliche Keramik der Schweiz und ihre Chronologie*. Zurich, Denkschrift der schweizerischen naturforschenden Gesellschaft 66.

Warmenbol, E. (1988) Le groupe Rhin-Suisse-France orientale et les grottes sépulcrales du Bronze final en Haute-Belgique. In P. Brun and C. Mordant (eds) *Le Groupe Rhin-Suisse-France Orientale*, 153–8. Mémoires du Musée de préhistoire d'Île-de-France 1. Nemours, Association pour la promotion de la recherche archéologique

3

Marcel Édouard Mariën (1918–1991) and the metal ages in Belgium. Undoing the Atlantic wall

Walter Leclercq and Eugène Warmenbol

Abstract

Marcel Édouard Mariën (1918–1991) is one of the 'founding fathers' of protohistoric studies in Belgium. His career was mainly devoted to the publication of the archaeological material kept in the Musées royaux d'Art et d'Histoire in Brussels. His study of the material culture of the Bronze and the Iron Age in the Low Countries is still useful, especially as it goes with (his) high-quality drawings. He was one of the first to recognise specificity to the material culture of the Bronze Age of the Scheldt basin, perceiving its close relationship to the material culture of northern France and southern Britain. He did not call it 'Atlantic', though.

Keywords: Bronze Age, Iron Age, Belgium, Mariën, historiography, Atlantic.

Résumé

Marc Édouard Mariën (1918–1991) est un des « pères fondateurs » des études protohistoriques en Belgique. Il consacra l'essentiel de sa carrière à la publication du matériel archéologique conservé aux Musées royaux d'Art et d'Histoire de Bruxelles. Ses études de la culture matérielle de l'Âge du bronze et de l'Âge du fer de Belgique et des Pays-Bas rendent toujours service, d'autant qu'elles sont toujours accompagnées de dessins de sa main de très haute qualité. Il a été un des premiers à reconnaître une spécificité au matériel de l'Âge du bronze du bassin de l'Escaut, tout en soulignant ses relations étroites avec celui trouvé dans le nord de la France ou dans le sud de l'Angleterre. À l'époque, il ne fera pas usage du terme « atlantique », toutefois.

Mots-clés : l'Âge du bronze, l'Âge du fer, Belgique, Mariën, historiographie, Atlantique

Introduction

Nearly 25 years after his death, Marcel Édouard Mariën (Fig. 3.1) has become, for most young archaeologists, no more than a name accompanying some bibliographical references, much too often considered obsolete (Anonymous 1983). This scholar, who curated the rich collection of Belgian archaeological material belonging to the Musées royaux d'Art et d'Histoire in Brussels, deserves to be better known, as he was, with Sigfried De Laet, one of the men who gave substance to the Bronze and Iron Ages in Belgium. He was also an excellent draughtsman and his drawings are still of much use to the present generation. Up to the most recent synthesis, his work remains quoted, because it is not obsolete (Milcent 2012).

Biography

Marcel Édouard Mariën (Lefrancq 1991; 2003; Leclercq 2016) was born in Antwerp on 23 June 1918. He preferred to be called Marc E. Mariën by the end of his career.[1] He did his Classical Humanities in his hometown and graduated in Classical Philology at Ghent University, 12 September 1940

(Archives MRAH, Dossier Mariën). He also got his doctorate there, 26 March 1942, submitting an original dissertation on Roman burial practices: *Het Gallo-Romeinsche graf bij de Treviri en in de Rijnstreek*, directed by Hubert Van de Weerd (1878–1951) (Lambrechts, 1949; De Laet 1951).

A few months later, a position as (attaché) in the 'Belgique ancienne' department at the Musées royaux du Cinquantenaire (later the Musées royaux d'Art et d'Histoire)

Fig. 3.1. M. E. Mariën in the midst of 'Découvertes à la Grotte de Han', an exhibition organised by him in 1964 (photo: Marc Jasinski).

in Brussels opened up, and that supposedly suited him well. He applied, but as Belgium had by then been 2 years under Nazi occupation, practical considerations had to be weighed. While reminding Jean Capart (1877–1947), an Egyptologist who was then head-curator of the Musées, how much his candidacy was 'adequate', he also had to excuse himself for not going to Brussels more often, as providing for food was so difficult and took so much time. In October 1942, he asked for an interview with the new head-curator, Henry Lavachery (1885–1972), to make sure his candidacy was not forgotten. He was by then well 'sponsored' by Hubert Van de Weerd (Fig. 3.2). He was the author of an *Inleiding tot de Gallo-Romeinse archeologie* (published in 1944), very much in the spirit of Mariën's first publications. Our man was successful. By January 1943, Marcel Édouard Mariën was indeed (attaché) of the Musées royaux, at work in the 'Belgique ancienne' department, then headed by Jacques Breuer (1892–1971) (Mertens 1994; Roosens 1971) (Fig. 3.3).

As also appears, through his brilliant paper cataloguing the bell beakers found in Belgium (1948a), that he seems to have been quite keen to follow up on new finds and to check on accidental discoveries. He was constantly on the road in the late 1940s and the 1950s, driving his little Morris Oxford, and building a network of friends and acquaintances among the local actors of Belgian archaeology. Among the sites then (re)discovered are Biez (Brabant wallon), Harchies (Hainaut) and Lommel (Limburg).

How keen he was transpires through a letter, dated 8 March 1953, written to Comte Joseph de Borchgrave d'Altena (1895–1975), the new head-curator of the Musées royaux d'Art et d'Histoire (since 1951). M. E. Mariën asks for an authorisation to accompany Professor S. J. De Laet (1914–1999) and Doctor F. Twiesselmann to Sinsin (Namur), where they were about to look for some 'factual

Fig. 3.2. M. E. Mariën paying hommage to H. Van de Weerd on the cover of an offprint of one of his papers (Mariën 1948a 2d) (author's collection).

Fig. 3.3. Jacques Breuer and M. E. Mariën (in shorts) with the official van of the Service des fouilles near the Gallo-Roman site of Liberchies (Hainaut), 1946 (ex-collection Joseph Mertens).

Fig. 3.4. M. E. Mariën at work with Albert Henin on the Lesse near the Trou de Han, 1960s (photo: Marc Jasinski).

information'. They were most certainly visiting the *Trou del Leuve* at Sinsin (Mariën 1952, fig. 255), a cave with important Bronze Age material.

But a network never reaches everywhere, and M. E. Mariën, for instance, could do nothing but register the complete destruction of an 'urnfield' near the Galgestraat in Sint-Niklaas (Oost-Vlaanderen), amongst other disappointments.

All along his career M. E. Mariën was particularly sensitive to the doing and undoing of private collections, especially when they were to be auctioned. Quite typically, in a letter dated 4 February 1956, he rather bitterly reminds the head-curator he was not allowed to follow up the sale of the gold torques of Frasnes-lez-Buissenal (Hainaut), which were sold to the US National Tennis Championship winner Alistair Bradley Martin (1915–2010), the man behind the Guennol collection, who bought them for $65,000. They have been exhibited in the Metropolitan Museum of Art in New York since the early 1950s (Rubin 1975, 129–40. Lately: Warmenbol 2011; Cahen-Delhaye and Doyen 2014).

The curator of the department, Jacques Breuer, was pensioned in 1957. M. E. Mariën, assistant-curator since 1 October 1950, replaced him, curating a department still called 'Belgique ancienne'. The Service des Fouilles de l'État, founded by Baron Alfred De Loë in 1903, had by then been detached from the Musées royaux to become the Service National des Fouilles (Lefrancq 1985). The archaeological activities considerably enriched the Museum collections and Jacques Breuer had begun the classification of the collections. M. E. Mariën continued his work and suggested a reorganisation of the exhibition rooms. He suggested a chronological sequence, very much in the spirit of the 1950s. The new curator also launched a new collection, the Monographies d'Archéologie Nationale, dedicated to the publication of the major sites he had in his care. The first four volumes of this collection are by his hand. The

first presents the Hallstatt material of Court-Saint-Étienne (Brabant wallon) (Mariën 1958); the second the La Tène material from sites such as Leval-Trahegnies (Hainaut) (Mariën 1961); the third the Hallstatt and early La Tène material of Saint-Vincent (Luxembourg) (Mariën 1964a), yet another necropolis; the fourth the material of (very) different periods found in the 'Trou de l'Ambre' of Eprave (Namur).[2]

He curated two exhibitions at the Musées royaux d'Art et d'Histoire, one in 1964, the other in 1965 (Mariën 1964b; Mariën and Vanhaeke 1965), illustrating the new finds in the cave of Han-sur-Lesse (Namur), mostly from the bottom of the Lesse (Fig. 3.4), which flows right through the cave. He was indeed the first archaeologist to recognise the special nature of this major site, of international importance, though we cannot agree any more with his interpretation of the cave, never used for anything else but a temporary refuge in his mind (see, for instance Mariën 1974. For another view: Warmenbol 2009; 2013).

M. E. Mariën had a special relationship with the area of Rochefort, where he had a small property, and published a few synthetic papers on the archaeology of the area (Mariën 1960; 1961). He also excavated in the cave of Han-sur-Lesse (the *Galerie des Petites Fontaines* between 1963 and 1967 (Fig. 3.5), the *Trou du Salpêtre* in 1964–1965 (Mariën and Borremans 1970) and in the *Trou de l'Ambre* at Eprave (1957–1959 and 1961–1963; Mariën 1970, 21–3), though he was not a 'natural' field worker.

He was a teacher at the Kunsthistorisch Instituut of Antwerp as early as 1945 (teaching 'L'Art antique'), and at the Institut Supérieur d'Histoire de l'Art et d'Archéologie de Bruxelles, under the roof of the Musées royaux d'Art et d'Histoire (teaching 'Préhistoire européenne') from 1964 until 1991. After his accreditation to teach at university

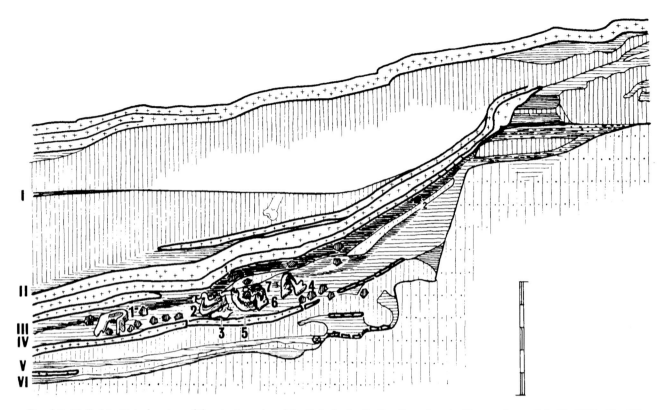

Fig. 3.5. M. E. Mariën's drawing of the stratigraphy of the Galerie des Petites Fontaines in Han-sur-Lesse (Mariën 1970, Fig. 73).

level, (he became 'Agrégé de l'enseignement supérieur' in 1970)[3], he was called upon by the Vrije Universiteit Brussel to teach there (as 'chargé de cours'). He kept this assignment until 1985, 2 years after retiring from the Musées royaux d'Art et d'Histoire, on 1 July 1983 (Lefrancq 1991, 273), and was succeeded by our colleagues and friends Anne Cahen-Delhaye at the Musées and Jean Bourgeois at the University.

Mariën was a member of the 'Conseil permanent' of the Union Internationale des Sciences Pré- et Protohistorique, and a member of a great number of societies in Belgium and abroad, such as the Société royale d'Anthropologie de Bruxelles, and many others. Marcel Édouard Mariën died in Brussels on 24 July 1991 following a long fight against cancer (Lefrancq 1991).

The Bronze Age

Marcel Édouard Mariën's main work was on the Bronze and Iron Age material in custody of the Musées royaux d'Art et d'Histoire, but he also studied the Roman period in the provinces. Early in his career, he studied the Roman sculptures from Belgium, and the (funerary) monuments they were part of (Mariën 1943; 1945). He eventually crowned his study of the Roman period with a magnificent synthesis titled *L'empreinte de Rome* (1980), a lush volume without parallel in Belgium.

His most original contribution, as stated, was on the Bronze and Iron Age material he curated, with a first contribution, in 1945, on a bronze lozenge-shaped sword chape found in Gentbrugge (Oost-Vlaanderen; MRAH B 451), and a first major contribution, in 1950, on a number of hoards characterised by bracelets with everted terminals (Fig. 3.6), including those from Spiennes 'Camp-à-Cayaux' (Hainaut; MRAH B 4235), and actually the only ones from the Brussels museum in his paper, as Mariën was also well informed of the content of other public (and private) collections.

Less than 10 years after his introduction to pre- and protohistory, M. E. Mariën published his first monograph, *Oud-België. Van de eerste landbouwers tot de komst van Caesar* (1952), which was awarded the *Prix Maréchal* by the Académie royale de Belgique, but was not much read outside of Belgium and the Netherlands, as it was never translated from its original Dutch. The book mainly but not only features the collections of the Musées royaux d'Art et d'Histoire, studying the material remains in Belgium and the Southern Netherlands from the earliest Neolithic (then dated 2600–2300 BC ...) to the latest Iron Age. Unlike de Loë's work, the material was put into a European context and perspective, which was quite innovatory then. The four volumes entitled *Belgique ancienne* published by his predecessor Baron Alfred de Loë (1858–1943; see Cahen-Delhaye 1999) between 1928 and 1939, and stretching

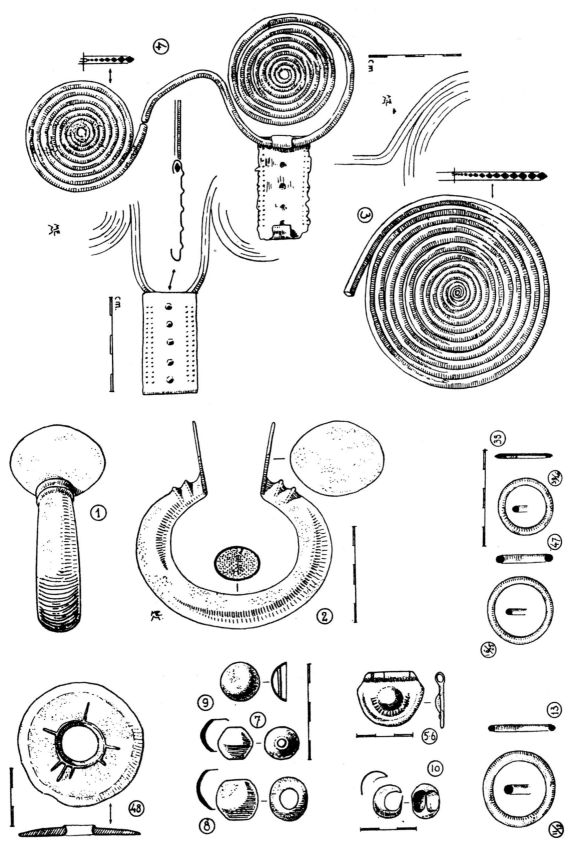

Fig. 3.6. M. E. Mariën's excellent drawings of the bronzes in the Gent 'Port Arthur' hoard, with its characteristic bracelet with everted terminals (Mariën 1950, pls v and vi).

from the Paleolithic to the early medieval period, indeed constitute the only pre-war synthetic studies of Belgian archaeological finds. This was actually 'only' an extensive catalogue of the material to be found in the Musées royaux d'Art et d'Histoire. The scope of Marcel Édouard Mariën's work is so much wider!

A major concept introduced by him, is that of a subdivision of Belgium into, more or less, a northern and a southern part, or, more accurately, a subdivision of the country according to the two major river basins, that of the Scheldt and that of the Meuse (Fig. 3.7). According to him:

'as the Bronze Age evolves towards its final phase, we become more and more aware of the differences in civilization between the Scheldt basin and the Meuse basin. These differences seem not only to reflect a specific commercial orientation of each zone, but also to translate a specific nature of the population, one in the Scheldt area, one in the Meuse area' (Mariën 1951a).[4]

We do not believe he was looking for the origins of the Flemings or the Walloons, and Mariën was surely aware of the fact that archaeology can easily be misused in this context.

He never uses the term 'Atlantic' or 'Alpine' in the 1950s, but it is quite clear that he considers the Scheldt basin as part of what Patrice Brun will call the 'complexe techno-économique atlantique', and the Meuse basin as part of the 'complexe techno-économique nord-alpin' (Brun 1987, 8). This position can still be defended, but only for the Late Bronze Age. His main sources are Christopher Hawkes, on the one hand (see also Mariën 1953a), and Wolfgang Kimmig on the other hand (see also Mariën 1948b; 1951b). They will both contribute to Mariën's *Festschrift* in 1983, showing enduring relationships between these 'founding fathers'. After the coming down of the Atlantic Wall, the Continent ceased to be 'isolated': this is also true of the archaeology of the Continent. An Atlantic 'community' was quickly established through the work of Vere Gordon Childe,

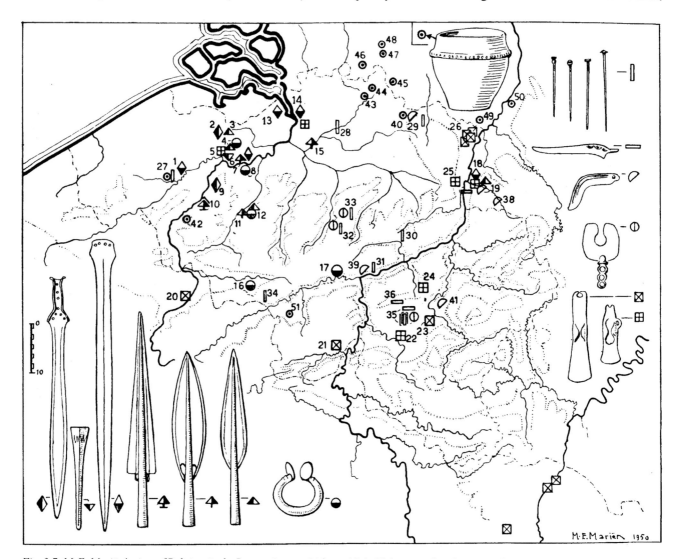

Fig. 3.7. M. E. Mariën's view of Belgium in the Bronze Age: an 'Atlantic' Scheldt basin and a 'Continental' Meuse basin (Mariën 1951a, 46).

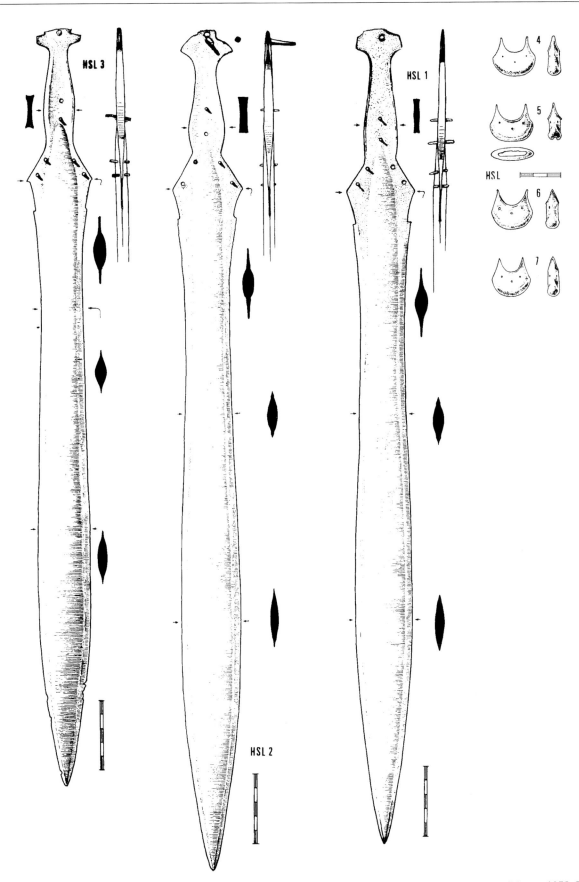

Fig. 3.8. *The Thames-type swords and their chapes from Han-sur-Lesse, as professionally drawn by M. E. Mariën (Mariën 1975, Fig. 1).*

Margaret Dunlop, Christopher Hawkes and Hubert Savory. Sigfried De Laet and Marcel Édouard Mariën, Willem Glasbergen and Harm Waterbolk were on the 'receiving' end (De Laet 1989; Theunissen 1999, 10–33).

Marcel Édouard Mariën eventually uses the term 'Atlantic' close to the end of his life (Mariën 1989, 10). He indeed states in 1989 that the 'sword-bearers', dear to Hubert Savory (1948), were responsible for an 'Atlantic' invasion, spreading Thames-type swords all over the place (Fig. 3.8); soon to be followed by a 'Continental' invasion, replacing the former by Gündlingen type swords. A paper too far? One must not forget that he was certainly not the only one to reason in terms of invasions in those years, but for sure the fashion was on the way out (lately: Warmenbol and Leclercq 2009). We cannot resist quoting Christopher Hawkes (1983, 30), looking at things from the other side of the Channel: 'Of course no conquering invasions *en masse* were ever possible in prehistoric Britain. Not because disliked by certain modern British archaeologists! The cause was the sea, and the restricted means of navigation'. After *BOAT 1550 BC* it is quite clear he, and many others were grossly misguided. The British Isles have also ceased to be 'isolated'. Marcel Édouard Mariën certainly made his contribution towards that.

Mariën's interpretation of the cultural contexts and dynamics of the Bronze and Iron Age (Mariën 1989) has of course not survived processual and post-processual archaeology, but his detailed study of the artefacts (Mariën 1975) cannot but stand despite the many changes archaeology has gone through, as he was an extraordinary erudite scholar.

L'Union fait la force

Marcel Édouard Mariën (Fig. 3.9) was fully aware of the greater importance of certain finds for a better understanding of pre- and protohistory on a larger scale – the European one – and thus was one of the initiators of an European inventory which was first discussed during the *IVe Congrès International des Sciences Pré et Protohistoriques* of August 1950 in Zürich (Mariën 1951c). His aim was to break through actual or intellectual borders. To him, if the relevant material is not included 'in studies of a more general nature, or mentioned in general works looking across national borders, few foreign archaeologists will suppose its existence'.[5] The inventory-project was adopted by the 'Conseil permanent' of the ISPP-Congresses. A provisional international committee was then designated by the 'Conseil permanent' (of which Mariën was a member) during the 1952 meeting in Namur. The first volumes of the *Inventaria Archaeologica* soon followed, with a first volume for Belgium edited by Mariën in 1953. He was one of the first Belgians to play a role in what is called the Union Internationale des Sciences Pré- et Protohistoriques since 1955. Sigfried De Laet was Secretary General of the Executive Committee from 1952 until 1966,

Fig. 3.9. The 'official' M. E. Mariën, or his only picture published previously (Lefrancq 1991, 273; 2003, 26).

Jacques Nenquin from 1980 until 1996 and Jean Bourgeois from 1996 until 2006, the latter becoming President in 2011. *Horum omnium fortissimi sunt Belgae*. But this is another story…

Notes

1   To distinguish himself from the surrealist artist Marcel Mariën, also born in Antwerp?

2   But not last: there is a posthumous volume (Mariën 1994) containing the Roman material from his excavations in Overhespen (Vlaams Brabant) and Thorembais-Saint-Trond (Brabant wallon).

3   Thanks to his work on the *Trou de l'Ambre* at Eprave.

4   'A mesure que l'âge du Bronze chemine vers sa phase finale, nous percevons davantage la différenciation entre la civilisation de la zone scaldéenne et celle de la zone mosane. Cette différence ne semble pas seulement provenir d'une orientation commerciale spécifique de chacune des deux zones, mais semble traduire aussi un caractère particulier chez les peuplades des régions de l'Escaut et celles de la région de la Meuse'.

5   [Si le matériel n'est pas repris dans des] 'études à caractère
    plus général, ou mentionné dans des synthèses répandues au
    delà des frontières nationales, peu d'archéologues étrangers
    en soupçonnent l'existence' (Mariën 1951c, 380).

Bibliography

Anonymous (1983) Beknopte bibliografie van M. E. Mariën. *Bulletin des Musées royaux d'Art et d'Histoire* 54, 109–111.

Brun, P. (1987) *Princes et princesses de la Celtique. Le premier âge du Fer en Europe, 850–450 av. J.-C.* Paris, Editions Errance.

Cahen-Delhaye, A. (1999) De Loë, Alfred. *Nouvelle Biographie Nationale* 5, 106–8.

Cahen-Delhaye, A. and Doyen J.-M. (2014) De l'or pour les dieux celtiques? De Frasnes-lez-Buissenal aux trésors de Thuin. In M. Demelenne and G. Docquier (eds), *Trésor? Trésor! Archéologie au Cœur de l'Europe*, 74–85. Bruxelles, Editions Safran.

De Laet, S. J. (1951) Hubert Van de Weerd (1878–1951). *L'Antiquité Classique* 20, 289–292.

De Laet, S. J. (1989) Sigfried J. De Laet. In G. Daniel and C. Chippindale *The Pastmasters. Eleven Modern Pioneers of Archaeology*, 126–136. London, Thames & Hudson.

Hawkes, C. (1983) Belgium and Britain in the Urnfield and Hallstatt Periods. *Bulletin des Musées royaux d'Art et d'Histoire 54 (= Festschrift M. E. Mariën)*, 25–35.

Kimmig, W. (1983) Das Fürstengrab von Eigenbilzen. Neue Überlegungen zu einem alten Fund. *Bulletin des Musées royaux d'Art et d'Histoire 54 (= Festschrift M. E. Mariën)*, 37–53.

Lambrechts, P. (1949) *Prof. dr. H. van de Weerd, een vooraanstaand figuur der Gentse Universiteit, Gent.* Werken uitgegeven door de Faculteit van de Wijsbegeerte en Letteren, Rijksuniversiteit te Gent, 104.

Leclercq, W. (2016) Mariën, Marcel Edouard. *Nouvelle Biographie nationale*, 236–238.

Lefrancq, J. (1985) Le Service des Fouilles du Musée: les fouilles en Belgique. *Liber Memorialis 1835–1985*, 195–200. Bruxelles, Musées Royaux d'Art et d'Histoire.

Lefrancq, J. (1991) In memoriam Marc Mariën. *Bulletin des Musées royaux d'Art et d'Histoire* 62, 272–3.

Lefrancq, J. (2003) Marc E. Mariën (1918–1991). *Institut supérieur d'Histoire de l'Art et d'Archéologie de Bruxelles, 1903–2003. Centième anniversaire*, 26–27. Bruxelles, Atelier Ledoux Editions.

Mariën, M. E. (1943–1944) Les monuments funéraires de Buzenol. *Bulletin des Musées royaux d'Art et d'Histoire* 15, 2–10, 58–69, 104–114; 16, 28–36, 59–70.

Mariën, M. E. (1945) *La sculpture à l'époque romaine.* Bruxelles, Editions du Cercle d'Art.

Mariën, M. E. (1948a) La civilisation des 'Gobelets' en Belgique. *Bulletin des Musées royaux d'Art et d'Histoire* 20, 16–48.

Mariën, M. E. (1948b) Où en est la question des Champs d'Urnes. *L'Antiquité Classique* XVII/Miscellana Philologica, Historica et Archaeologica in honorem Huberti Van de Weerd/, 413–44, Bruxelles, Fondation Archéologique.

Mariën, M. E. (1950) Les bracelets à grandes oreillettes en Belgique à l'âge du bronze final. *Handelingen der Maatschappij voor Geschiedenis en Oudheidkunde te Gent, Nieuwe Reeks* IV, 41–77.

Mariën, M. E. (1951a) Les axes Escaut et Meuse à l'âge du Bronze. *Bulletin des Musées royaux d'Art et d'Histoire* 23, 45–48.

Mariën, M. E. (1951b) Coup d'œil sur l'étude de l'âge du Bronze en Belgique. *Handelingen der Maatschappij voor Geschiedenis en Oudheidkunde te Gent, Nieuwe Reeks, V*, 215–224.

Mariën, M. E. (1951c) Recueil des ensembles de trouvailles de l'âge des Métaux, comportant des éléments de portée chronologique. *L'Anthropologie 55 (3–4)*, 380–5.

Mariën, M. E. (1952) *Oud-België. Van de eerste landbouwers tot de komst van Caesar.* Antwerpen, De Sikkel.

Mariën, M. E. (1953a) Quelques trouvailles de l'âge du bronze final dans le bassin de la Meuse. In *Congrès International des Sciences Préhistoriques et Protohistoriques. Actes de la IIIe session, Zürich 1950*, 234–8. Bonn/Zürich, Fondation Goethe.

Mariën, M. E. (1953b) *Inventaria Archaeologica. Corpus des ensembles archéologiques. Âges des Métaux. Belgique. I.* Anvers, De Sikkel.

Mariën, M. E. (1958) *Trouvailles des Champs d'Urnes et des tombelles hallstattiennes de Court-Saint-Étienne.* Bruxelles, Monographies d'Archéologie Nationale 1.

Mariën, M. E. (1960–1) Vestiges archéologiques de la région de Lesse-et-Lomme, des origines aux Mérovingiens. *Parcs Nationaux* XV, 127–158; XVI, 55–97.

Mariën, M. E. (1961) *La Période de La Tène en Belgique. Le Groupe de la Haine.* Bruxelles, Monographies d'Archéologie Nationale 2.

Mariën, M. E. (1964a) *La nécropole à tombelles de Saint-Vincent.* Bruxelles, Monographies d'Archéologie Nationale 3.

Mariën, M. E. (1964b) *Découvertes à la Grotte de Han.* Bruxelles Société d'Archéologie de Bruxelles.

Mariën, M. E. (1970) *Le Trou de l'Ambre au Bois de Wérimont, Éprave,* Bruxelles, Monographies d'Archéologie Nationale 4.

Mariën, M. E. (1974) Les habitats du Trou de Han. Éléments chronologiques du Bronze final. *Bulletin des Musées royaux d'Art et d'Histoire* 46, 219–243.

Mariën, M. E. (1975) Épées de bronze 'proto-hallstattiennes' et hallstattiennes découvertes en Belgique. *Helinium* XV, 14–37.

Mariën, M. E. (1980) *L'empreinte de Rome. Belgica Antiqua.* Anvers, Fonds Mercator.

Mariën, M. E. (1989) Aperçu de la période hallstattienne en Belgique. In M. Ulrix-Closset and M. Otte (eds), *La civilisation de Hallstatt, bilan d'une rencontre, Liège 1987.* Liège, Études et Recherches Archéologiques de l'Université de Liège 36.

Mariën, M. E. (1994) *Quatre tombes romaines du IIIe siècle. Thorembais-Saint-Trond et Overhespen.* Bruxelles, Monographies d'Archéologie Nationale 8.

Mariën, M. E. and Borremans, R. (1970) Fouilles 1958–1969. II. Âges des Métaux. Han-sur-Lesse. *Bulletin des Musées royaux d'Art et d'Histoire* 40–2, 309–315.

Mariën, M. E. and Vanhaeke, L. (1965) *Nouvelles découvertes à la grotte de Han.* Bruxelles Bruxelles, Société d'Archéologie de Bruxelles.

Mertens, J. (1994) Breuer, Jacques. *Nouvelle Biographie Nationale* 3, 50–52.

Milcent, P.-Y. (2012) *Le temps des élites en Gaule atlantique. Chronologie des mobiliers et rythmes de constitution des depots métalliques dans le contexte européen (XIIIe–VIIe s. av. J.-C.).* Rennes, Presses Universitaires de Rennes.

Roosens, H. (1971) In memoriam Jacques Breuer, 1892–1971. *Helinium* 11, 209–212.

Rubin, I. E. (1975) (ed.) *The Guennol Collection. I.* New York, The Metropolitan Museum of Art.

Savory, H. (1948) The 'Sword-bearers'. A reinterpretation. *Proceedings of the Prehistoric Society* 14, 155–176.

Theunissen, L. (1999) *Midden-bronstijdsamenlevingen in het zuiden van de Lage Landen. Een evaluatie van het begrip 'Hilversum-cultuur'.* Leiden, Liesbeth Theunissen.

Warmenbol, E. (2009) Natures mortes. Les dépôts subaquatiques de Han-sur-Lesse (Belgique). In S. Bonnardin, C. Hamon, M. Lauwers and B. Quilliec (eds) *Du matériel au spirituel. Réalités archéologiques des 'dépôts' de la Préhistoire à nos jours.* Actes des XXIXe Rencontres internationales d'Archéologie et d'Histoire d'Antibes, 16–18 octobre 2008, 143–54. Antibes, Editions pour la Promotion et la Diffusion des Connaissances Archéologiques.

Warmenbol, E. (2011) Le trésor celtique de Frasnes-lez-Buissenal. In J.-M. Duvosquel and D. Morsa (eds) *La Maison d'Arenberg en Wallonie, à Bruxelles et au G.-D. de Luxembourg depuis le XIVe siècle. Contribution à l'histoire d'une famille princière, 410–12.* Enghien, Fondation d'Arenberg.

Warmenbol, E. (2013) Le deuxième âge du Fer (fin Vᵉ–début Ier s. avant notre ère) dans la grotte de Han (commune de Rochefort, province de Namur, Belgique). *Revue du Nord* 95 (= Hommages à Germaine Leman-Delerive), 91–112.

Warmenbol, E. and Leclercq, W. (2009) Les débuts de l'âge du Fer en Belgique. Chronologie relative, chronologie absolue. In M. Roulière-Lambert, A. Daubigney, P.-Y. Milcent, M. Talon and J. Vital (eds) *De l'âge du Bronze à l'âge du Fer en France et en Europe occidentale (Xe–VIIe siècle av. J.-C.).* La moyenne vallée du Rhône aux âges du Fer. Actes du XXXe colloque international de l'AFEAF, co-organisé avec l'APRAB, Saint-Romain-en-Gal, 26–28 mai 2006, 373–384. Dijon, Société archéologique de l'Est.

4

Transmanche in the Penard/Rosnoën stage.
Wearing the same sleeve or keeping at arm's length?

Stuart Needham

Abstract

This paper assesses the extent and nature of cross-Channel relations for just one phase of the Bronze Age, thereby minimising diachronic factors in the system. The contemporary seabed assemblages of Salcombe and Dover are used to illuminate the problem of low-visibility circulation and its effect on comprehending metalwork 'distributions'. The Channel conundrum – the conflict between roles as conduit or obstacle – is discussed in relation to the special properties of coastal territories, preferential interaction decisions, and the infrastructure of the 'Channel super-highway'. In considering apparent cross-Channel unity, a distinction is made between time-immemorial factors that helped forge a degree of cultural commonality, and specific behavioural traits that, although based on minority evidence, differentiated social practice. It is proposed that future study needs to focus more on regional-scale interactions than broad-scale systems.

Keywords: Bronze Age; Penard/Rosnoën phase; cross-Channel relations; shipwrecks; super-highway; metalwork deposition patterns; low-visibility circulation

Résumé

Cet article révise l'ampleur et la nature des relations transmanches pour une seule phase de la fin de l'Âge du bronze, ce qui réduit les facteurs diachroniques dans le système. Les ensembles contemporains des fonds maritimes de Salcombe et de Douvres sont utilisés pour éclairer le problème de la faible visibilité des circulations et ses effets sur les compréhensibles « distributions » métalliques. L'énigme du Channel – l'opposition entre son rôle de voie de circulation ou d'obstacle – est discuté, en relations avec les caractéristiques propres des territoires côtiers, tout particulièrement les décisions en interaction et l'infrastructure du « Channel super-highway ». Concernant l'unité apparente du Channel, une distinction est faite entre les facteurs chronologiquement immémoriaux, qui contribue à forger une sorte de fond culturel commun, et les et les traits comportements spécifiques qui, bien que basés sur peu de données, différencient les pratiques sociales. Il est proposé que les études futures se resserrent sur une approche régionale plutôt que sur une vision large en système.

Mots-clés : Âge du bronze, Penard/Rosnoën, relations Transmanche, épaves, super-highway, modèles de dépôt de métal

The purpose of this paper is to consider the extent to which the Channel zone (southern England, northern France and part of the Low Countries) is a closely unified cultural zone in one phase of the later Bronze Age. To do so I have chosen to focus on the period of the two shipwreck sites located just off the southern English coastline – Salcombe,

Devon, and Langdon Bay, Kent. The whole of the Langdon assemblage and most of that recovered at Salcombe date to the Penard/Rosnoën stage of metalworking, a phase probably contained within two centuries (1300–1100 BC); indeed, these particular finds can be assigned to the first half of the period (Fig. 4.1; Needham *et al.* 2013, 111–12). The shipwreck sites are pertinent because analysis of their assemblages has raised fundamental questions about our ability to recognise circulation zones of given metalwork types, but at the same time has highlighted some potential distinctions from one side of the Channel to the other. The cultural phenomenon that has come to be known as the 'Channel Bronze Age', a constituent part of the so-called 'Atlantic Bronze Age', is widely understood to be a long-lived entity during which doubtless much changed. It was probably an ever-shifting set of inter-community relationships and alignments, so by focusing on one relatively short-lived phase, we can have more confidence that we are dealing with much the same interaction system whatever particular evidence is being considered. It is also perhaps a bonus that this phase falls somewhere near the middle of the entity's accepted life-span (*c.* 1750–800 BC), since this avoids any peculiarities that might accompany inception and demise.

Recent years have seen the publication of many and sometimes diverse views on the chronology of the Atlantic later Bronze Age (e.g. Gerloff 2007; Burgess and O'Connor 2008; Milcent 2012; Burgess 2012; Matthews, this volume). These involve the sub-division of Penard and parallel material in varied ways and, in one case, a reiteration of the conclusion that its Wallington component is entirely separate and later (Burgess 2012). This is not the place to address the complexities of the evidence relating to this debate, but the best understanding of the spatio-temporal structure of regional material can only come in the first instance from analysis at the specifically regional level. An analytical review of the evidence will appear elsewhere (Needham 2017).

The main empirical divisions in the Penard Assemblage relate to the dominance of weapons, tools or ornaments respectively – these are referred to as 'Aspects' (Fig. 4.1). More refined 'Groups' have only been discerned as yet amongst the weapon-dominant deposits; they involve deduced temporal changes in sword design (Ambleside, Penard) and a socially and to some extent geographically determined focus on long fancy spearheads, especially those with tear-drop blades, instead of swords (Farnley). Associations containing swords are entirely exclusive of those containing tear-drop blade spearheads, and it is this latter, Farnley Group that Burgess thought was entirely later than Penard metalwork (2012). However, the swords that have come to preoccupy those concerned with fine chronologies – understandably so because

of the evidence for more rapid morphological change over time – only occur in seven insular associations. This has two important ramifications. Firstly, any finer chronology implied by the swords can only be applied to a small minority of finds – in other words it has very limited utility when it comes to considering the broader metalwork evidence. Secondly, it is clear that swords never became widely accepted as a type to include in hoard deposits, even in those areas in which they do occur thus; the mainstay of Penard weapon deposition *in hoards* comprised spearheads and rapiers despite the presumed social importance of the newly introduced weapon type, the sword. Appreciating this point diminishes the importance of a supposedly separate Wallington complex defined, *inter alia*, on non-sword weaponry. A final point to make here is that the inclusion of swords in hoards may become even rarer late in Penard metalwork currency, for none of the Limehouse family of swords (a collective term to embrace insular Types Clewer, Limehouse, Mortlake, Taplow and Teddington – Colquhoun and Burgess 1988) occurs in association with any non-sword type and they sit uncomfortably outside any definable Assemblage (Fig. 4.1; Needham 2017).

The two seabed finds that are central to this paper must also sit outside the Penard Assemblage, although for different reasons. Being interpreted as the result of shipwrecks or ships in trouble means that the formation of the deposits is governed by an entirely different process from most/all of the association finds on land. To include them in analysis would potentially skew patterns of conscious selection of material for deposition. A second reason is that both finds include a large component of non-insular metalwork types whose inclusion in analysis would be inappropriate to attempts to understand insular deposition customs. These seabed finds do nevertheless provide rich information on the contemporaneity of a multitude of types, and this information can be fed in to chronological evaluations in the same way as other external correlations are.

The special properties of shipwreck/cargo metalwork assemblages

It is paradoxical that the most difficult physical environment for the survival and recording of metalwork assemblages – the seabed – should be one that has the greatest potential for new insights into their interpretation. That potential, of course, has to be realised by assiduous archaeological surveillance and, thus far, too few underwater sites yielding Bronze Age metalwork have been subjected to systematic survey. Most of the ground covered in this article therefore has to rely heavily on the two large seabed finds of metalwork found off the

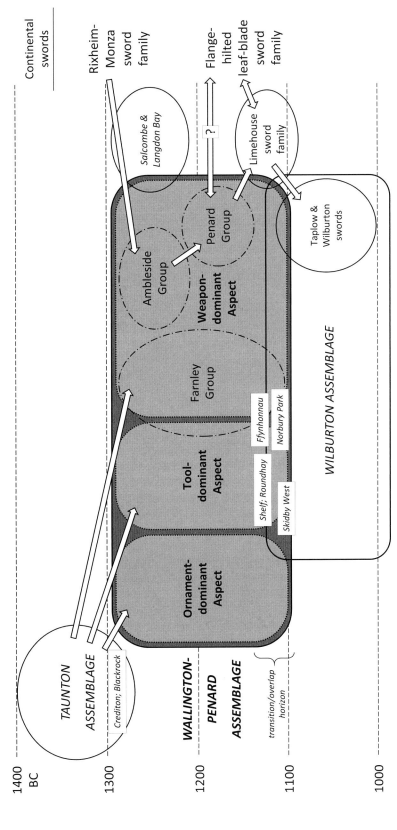

Fig. 4.1. The chronology and immediate relationships of the Wallington-Penard Assemblage and its constituent Aspects and Groups; a few association finds with specific dating evidence are also shown (after Needham 2017).

southern English coast – Salcombe, Devon, and Langdon Bay, Kent – detailed analysis of which has recently been published in the *Claimed by the Sea* volume (henceforth CBTS; Needham *et al.* 2013). That analysis drew the conclusion that these assemblages resulted from the wrecking of boats, or at least the jettisoning of cargoes from boats in trouble. The arguments leading to this conclusion will not be reiterated here, but it was demonstrated that the character-cum-size of the two assemblages cannot be matched in any other known contexts, whether from terrestrial or other watery environments (Needham *et al.* 2013, 150–7).

Although not alone in this respect, shipwrecks, as contexts directly representing material in the process of circulation, are particularly good at throwing into sharp focus questions about metalwork (and other material if it survives) in routine circulation relative to that being habitually deposited. This is not to suggest that shipwreck assemblages are in any way fully representative of the life assemblage. Shipwrecks, or rather their cargoes, are almost by definition specialised – this is one particular mode of distribution of a critical material good, perhaps one amongst many, and there can be no guarantee that the material in question would be fully representative of the source area(s). Selection processes for the purposes of exchange will undoubtedly have affected assemblage composition and the very particular conditions of sea transportation may have done so differently than for transit over land or along rivers. The concept of shipwreck assemblages being 'exchange frozen in time' (Muckelroy 1980, 108) may be valid but should not be taken to imply that they will be any more representative of the full repertoire of material than metalwork from any other kind of context.

The shipwreck is, however, a unique context in capturing material in the actual course of transit. It is hard to imagine comparable archaeological fall-out surviving in terrestrial environments, now that the concept of hoards being deposited for temporary safe-keeping by people who were on the move, such as 'merchants', has been left behind. This in-transit character in combination with their rarity makes shipwrecks an exceptionally informative context type on the matter of life assemblages. Both Salcombe and Langdon Bay have thrown up surprises to support this claim.

The issue of hidden and low-visibility circulation

One conclusion from the analysis of the shipwreck assemblages with potentially wide ramifications is that circulation may be hidden for some types of metalwork. This could be with respect to either the geographic extent or the time-span of the type's circulation. I referred to this phenomenon as *hidden circulation* in the CBTS volume (Needham *et al.* 2013, 144), but in reality this

term reflects the extreme case where *no* examples had previously entered the archaeological record for the given phase and region. More often we are probably, strictly speaking, dealing with *low-visibility circulation*, whereby some of the given type *did* come to be lost or deposited rather than all being recycled, but that recovered examples lacked useful contexts and hence their true date was not apparent.

Low-visibility circulation, in which the poverty of a recovered distribution belies the actual level of systemic circulation, can obviously have a significant impact on understanding the temporal and geographical span of types. But it also has repercussions back on the interpretation of the shipwreck assemblages themselves. This can be shown best with some schematic illustrations of a series of interlinked regions in regular exchange with one another; different scenarios are modelled against a simple distance-decay profile for an individual type of metal object manufactured only at one end of the chain (Fig. 4.2). Scenarios 1 and 2 represent, through different circle sizes, the actual quantities of the type in circulation in the successive regions. In scenario 1 (Fig. 4.2.1) it is also assumed that the material 'caught in transit' is most likely to have come direct from the production zone. It is obvious, however, that this is a simplistic and poor assumption with regards to the *immediate* source of the type even if its manufacture was truly confined to a restricted zone. Lower levels of circulation, for whatever reason, do not mean the object type is unavailable, although there may be constraints on the quantity that could be supplied over a short time period. Objects of the type found well away from zones of production and/or high circulation (these can be termed 'core' zones) could have been from any accessible region in which the type was circulating (Fig. 4.2.2) as happens, for example, in down-the-line exchange. This is therefore certainly not a problem unique to shipwrecks and jettisoned cargoes, but perhaps is more acute in these instances because of their 'caught-in-transit' status and the natural desire to deduce whence the cargo was collected prior to its carriage by boat. Low-visibility circulation exacerbates our interpretative difficulties. Distinct depositional strategies adopted by neighbouring social groups can lead to a given type being represented very variably in proportion to its circulation (Fig. 4.2.3) and this can result in fewer apparently viable source zones for the type.

It should be apparent from the above discussion, that it is no easy matter to draw up a map of the sources of the object types in a given cargo, so conventional 'distribution maps' were avoided in the CBTS volume (their absence was criticised by one reviewer; Brandherm 2014). The interpretative predicament was highlighted in the volume by contrasting two models: at one extreme was the simplistic assumption that the greatest archaeological

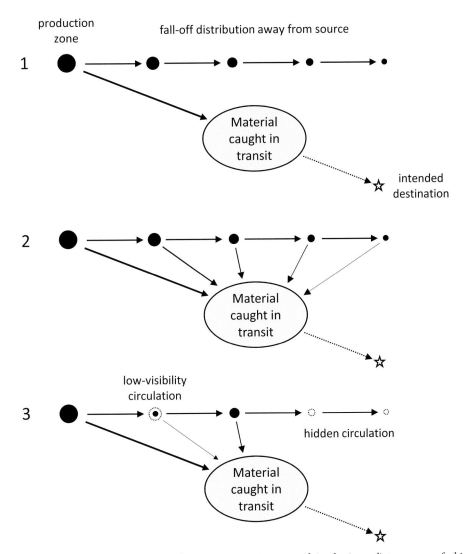

Fig. 4.2. Systemic and archaeological models giving alternative scenarios to explain the immediate source of objects in an in-transit deposit such as a shipwreck; all are modelled against a straightforward distance-decay profile from the production zone of the type in question: 1) Systemic scenario A, material comes direct from production zone; 2) Systemic scenario B, material can derive from any down-the-line zone of the distribution; 3) Archaeological scenario, different regional deposition rates lead to low-visibility circulation, thereby restricting the apparent range of immediate source zones.

density of a type ('core distribution') indicated its source; at the other, the immediate source was allowed potentially to be almost anywhere that the given type is known to have occurred (Fig. 4.3; Needham *et al.* 2013, 161–5). The former model was termed a *tentacled view* because with a large assemblage like that from Langdon Bay it can result in a series of apparent links in different directions. The latter was termed *restrictive* because this model makes it feasible to narrow down on a much more restricted geographical range where type ranges are known to overlap; this might even include arguing that the circulation of some types was truly 'hidden' in the consensus geographical area. Both models have their problems, but it may be a mistake to deduce far-reaching

itineraries for a single voyage, as implied for the Langdon Bay assemblage as seen from a *tentacled* viewpoint, when there are perfectly reasonable alternative explanations involving more *restrictive* views. It is worth exploring some of the problems discussed through examples from both the shipwreck sites and other contexts.

The best case for low-visibility circulation comes undoubtedly from the tanged-and-collared chisels, six of which come from the Langdon Bay assemblage. Were it not for their association on that site, we might still be reluctant to accept their existence at a stage prior to the British Late Bronze Age and equivalent Continental phases. Investigation of the type's occurrence shows that it is virtually absent from hoards until the Ewart/Plainseau

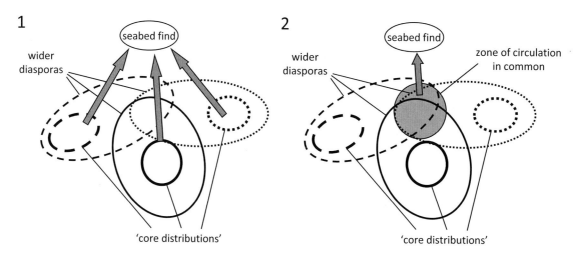

Fig. 4.3. Contrasting models for the sources of object types in shipwrecked cargoes: 1) Tentacled view, sources are assumed to lie in the zones of highest archaeological visibility; 2) Restrictive view, sources are allowed to be almost anywhere that the respective types are known to have occurred, and the most likely immediate source(s) of the cargo is narrowed to a minimum zone of overlap (after Needham et al. 2013, 162, Fig. 5.4)

stage, with just one in Britain (Doncaster) of Penard date and one in France of *Bronze Final II* date (Briard and Onnée 1972, no. 87; Needham *et al.* 2013, 94–5). Low-visibility circulation appears to be the norm on both sides of the Channel for this type.

Another type worth considering in this context is the Langdon Bay loop fastener (object no. 157). Although the known distribution is confined to France (Needham *et al.* 2013, 96–7), we are aware of only four examples in total and their findspots are very widely spread north to south (Eure-et-Loir to Gard). This could well suggest that the type suffers from low-visibility and, if so, its true distribution could easily be wider than is apparent. At present there are no similar fittings in British contexts, although a cautionary point is that the contemporary Penard hoards rarely contain small ornaments and fittings; this ornament-poor pattern is in distinct contrast (in the south at least) to the previous Taunton Assemblage deposits.

As can be seen, identifying low-visibility circulation is fraught with difficulty by the very nature of the evidence – its near-absence. Diagnostic casting moulds may help address this issue, since production in an area would normally be associated with use in the same area. There are various cases in Britain of mould finds lying outside of the 'core distributions' of their respective types – just to give one example, the clay mould assemblage from Dainton, Devon, represents types that are barely known in the south-west peninsula of England (Needham 1980, 211). Similarly, the bronze mould for a Grigny type median-winged axe from France comes from Saint-Aignan, Loir-et-Cher (Millotte *et al.* 1968, no. 81), which lies on the western periphery of the apparent 'core distribution'

of the type. A slightly different situation bearing on the same issue has been provided by a recent mould find from an excavation at Trevalga, Cornwall. The mould would have cast a type of *racloir*, which is poorly represented anywhere and had previously been linked mistakenly to a later type known as hog-backed knives (O'Connor in Jones and Quinnell 2014, 64–5). Individual examples of moulds might sometimes be explained away as curios which were passed beyond the normal range of the type's use or manufacture, but this will become an increasingly difficult argument to sustain if the phenomenon becomes more regular. Moreover, fragmented clay moulds are perhaps less likely than more durable moulds to be valued outside their relevant social context in this way. In time, therefore, moulds might become a major source of evidence to redress the voids and uncertainties left by low-visibility circulation.

Real outliers

If the difficulties outlined above are accepted, then there are no easy ways to wholly circumscribe either the production zones or regular circulation zones of any given type of metalwork. Yet it remains imperative for us to make judgements on such matters in order to take interpretation forward. I shall start at the easier end of the interpretative spectrum – the relatively easy, if very occasional, identification of 'real outliers'. One such case is the Sicilian *strumento con immanicatura a cannone* from the Salcombe B site (Needham and Giardino 2008). This class of bronze implement is diagnostic of Sicily and is not even found on the adjacent Italian mainland, let alone further into the European land-mass. It is

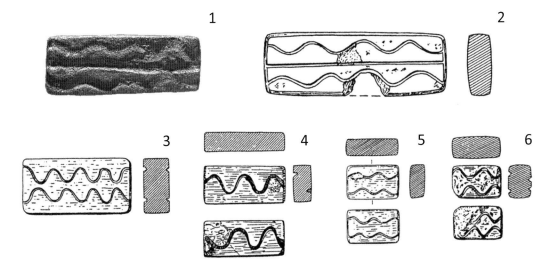

Fig. 4.4. Wavy-line weights; a possible case of low-visibility circulation outside the Urnfield burial zone: 1) one of two rectanguloid weights from Salcombe, Devon; 2) possibly the Sologne region, France; 3) Richemont-Pépinville, Moselle, France; 4) Barbuisse-Courtavant 7, Aube, France; 5) Maintal/Wachenbuchen, Hessen, Germany; 6) Wallerstädten, Hessen, Germany. Scale 1:1 (1, photo: British Museum; 2–6, after Pare 1999)

therefore reasonable to suppose that its zone of regular circulation stopped considerably short of the Channel. This object, above all, highlights the potential of shipwreck assemblages to open new windows on the far reach of occasional pieces. Whether displaced in a single move or in a down-the-line process will rarely be possible to determine for a single example; it requires very specific contexts or patterning in the archaeological data to throw light on this issue.

A second object of Sicilian type, a shaft-hole axe from off the south English coast at Southbourne, Hampshire (Needham *et al.* 2013, 118–19), is of almost comparable status as a 'real outlier'. Although there is a scatter of up to seven finds of shaft-hole axes across France (Coffyn 1985, 157, map 25; Milcent 2006, 324; Needham and Giardino 2008, fig. 4), these are disparate in form and few in number compared to such objects in Italy and Sicily. While one should not wholly rule out the circulation of such objects in parts of the Continent close to the western Mediterranean, it is extremely unlikely that it ever saw wider circulation anywhere near the Channel. The Bohemian type palstave found on Horridge Common, Dartmoor, Devon (Fox and Britton 1969) is also a good example of a 'real outlier'; Dennis Britton summarised the long-distance links that might well explain the westward passage of this central European object, but it remains the case that the type is not found anywhere near to the Channel coasts.

More problematic are types that are not particularly common anywhere and yet isolated examples do seem to lie beyond the known range. Examples of this pattern include the bronze rectanguloid weights from Salcombe.

One of them bears an incredibly distinctive design involving wavy furrows (Needham *et al.* 2013, 89, fig. 3.22) that can be matched exactly in the central European series catalogued by Chris Pare (1999) (Fig. 4.4). Prior to the Salcombe find, the extant distribution stopped in the Champagne-Ardennes region of north-eastern France with a possible example further into the centre (Sologne area?). Although not necessarily as early as these Reinecke D-dated examples, there are other rectanguloid blocks from Britain which are plain (Needham *et al.* 2013, 100). These may urge some caution about assuming that such weights were not already an accepted part of cross-Channel and insular systems during a longer span of the later Bronze Age. There may therefore be grounds for seeing rectanguloid weights as suffering from low-visibility, especially outside of the early Urnfield sphere, where archaeological representation was ensured by their occasional placement in graves.

Channel-delimited types

One question of tremendous relevance to our understanding of cross-Channel relationships is whether some bronze metalwork types were only accepted on one side or the other, especially if the types concerned can be interpreted as having a strong role in the definition of social identities. The issue of low-visibility circulation, however, makes evaluation of one-sidedness ever more problematic. Deciding that a 'distribution' is one-sided is inevitably an interpretation of contextual evidence; it is not something that appears magically out of a raw map of recovery. It is necessary, for example, to consider more explicitly different contexts of occurrence in a region; some of the main contexts can be summarised as: 1) local production zone (usually implying regular local use), 2) regular use of a type produced elsewhere, 3) regular presence as a dominant component of imported 'scrap' metal destined for conversion into local types, or 4) low-scale presence due to movement of people or objects over some distance, or across major cultural boundaries. Contexts (1) and (2) have the *potential* to be highly visible archaeologically, but only insofar as the particular deposition regime of the region allows. Context (3) is inherently unlikely to be very visible, except where material has been interrupted unexpectedly in transit (as in the case of shipwrecks), or when examples have been abstracted from a local metalworkers' stockpile for permanent deposition. Context (4) should, by definition, not be represented very strongly for otherwise it would be constitute context (2) as a kind of regular use. The importance of distinguishing context (4) is that small-scale intrusions of that kind should not necessarily be equated with a broad social acceptance of the type in question. It might relate, for example, to occasional gifts given by distant elites, or to 'real outliers' which had been displaced an exceptional distance from their source areas and then for some reason had escaped the melting pot.

The problem of low-visibility circulation can be alleviated sometimes by comparing the occurrence of functional equivalents within the same object class. This is, in effect, what we are frequently doing by recognising the regionalised distributions of, say, palstaves or socketed axes. Even this methodology, however, is not without its problems since it makes the assumption that there was no concurrent use of two or more styles of the object category in a given region and that overlap in distributions was instead due to interpretative contexts (3) and (4) above. Nevertheless, it is still sometimes helpful to develop a working hypothesis on the basis of fairly tight regionalisation in the symbolic or representational value of the respective styles.

This is the case for the Saint-Ouen type swords (formerly Pépinville A type; Muckelroy 1980, 106; Needham *et al.* 2013, 98), one of which was recovered from Salcombe. Only a handful of examples have been recorded, so we can hardly claim to have a good knowledge of their deposited occurrence, let alone any sound basis for interpreting their original circulation zone. However, in contrast to the low-visibility circulation outlined for the weights above, here there may be grounds for suspecting that this really was a rather regionalised type in northern France. Comparable and equally early heavy-blade swords are found in Britain that are stylistically related, but distinct (and varied) in design (Needham 1982 – dubbed the *Ambleside-Bardouville* series). Although a few more-or-less good parallels occur in northern France

Ambleside-Bardouville swords appear to be a largely insular response to northern French variants (Saint-Ouen and Grigny types) of the complex early sword spectrum of western central Europe. On this line of argument, although the Saint-Ouen sword from Salcombe, and for that matter the probable Grigny type sword from Langdon Bay, demonstrate that these types might be seen along the coasts of Britain (and one could not rule out inland appearances either), they should *not* on current evidence be seen as culturally accepted styles here. As 'British' dots on the map, therefore, the shipwreck occurrences have to be qualified.

Rosnoën swords are much more frequent finds on the Continent and would appear to have had a much wider distribution than the Saint-Ouen type. The full spread of the type was described fully in the CBTS volume (Needham *et al.* 2013, 97–9) and I shall only concern myself here with understanding their occurrence north of the Channel. Setting aside the two major seabed sites, Rosnoën swords have only been found at six sites in Britain (Needham *et al.* 2013, 97–9; Colquhoun et Burgess 1988, nos 4, 5, 7–9; plus the Limpsfield, Surrey, example: Needham 1987, 115, fig. 5.11). The relative abundance of early swords of other types in Britain, especially from the Thames (Colquhoun and Burgess 1988, pls 115, 118 and 119), suggests that if the Rosnoën sword style was accepted locally, it was quickly supplanted by regional sword variants. Another possible interpretation is that the complete Rosnoën swords were occasional intrusions due to gift exchange or the movement of warriors. However, it should be noted that there is a complementarity between the British distributions of Rosnoën and heavy-blade Ambleside swords (Needham 1982, 25, fig. 7), so it is possible that early in the Penard phase there were different regional sword preferences within Britain.

The phenomenon of 'Channel-as-style-boundary' has always appeared to be demonstrated most eloquently by the median-winged axes in the Langdon Bay find, where over 60 examples were recovered. This contrasts with a mere four finds of median-winged axes from British soil or rivers (Needham *et al.* 2013, 91), only one of them being of the relevant phase (Rosnoën/Penard) and type (Grigny). Had the type seen regular circulation in parts of Britain, it is hard to understand why such fine axeheads would have been deliberately kept out of insular hoards and single deposits when palstaves of many varieties were being deposited in abundance; the conclusion has long seemed clear, that this class of axe was not accepted for circulation by insular communities. It is nevertheless not difficult to explain away the sheer weight of median-winged axes at Langdon Bay since the broader patterns of metal composition show that south-eastern Britain was at this time locked into a far-flung skein of metal flow deriving ultimately from deep in mainland Europe (e.g. Rohl and Needham 1998, 96–101, 179–80; Northover 2013). The implication is that median-winged axes, when landed in Britain, were viewed as a source of metal, not as usable axes (Muckelroy 1980, 101). Again, the Langdon Bay dot on the map for median-winged axes must be qualified as probably having a completely different significance from most Continental dots.

A secondary question arises, however, from the fact that the median-winged axes have a statistically deviant metal composition from other major types in the Langdon Bay find (Northover 2013; Needham *et al.* 2013, 164). This deviance suggests that although the type was in regular circulation right up to the Channel coast it may not have been produced in the coastal regions themselves. Butler and Steegstra (1999–2000, 135) regarded the Dutch finds of the type as imports from further south and the same could be true of those from northern French regions. If this is a correct deduction, then the Channel is in this case the limit for social acceptance of this type rather than for the metalworking tradition that manufactured it. In this scenario, median-winged axes produced a little further south were accepted into the circulation pool of the coastal communities, deposited singly and in hoards, and presumably used by them to some extent (Fig. 4.5). However, when the axes became defunct and returned for recycling, they must have been turned into other types more central to the traditions of those coastal communities or their metalworkers. In this process the aggregate compositions tended to shift because of random mixing with other material not all emanating from the

same metal pool. Although there is a genuine Channel-as-style-boundary phenomenon, this is actually seen to be but one change within a more complex geographical system (Fig. 4.5).

A case has also been made for differentiation either side of the Channel at this stage amongst socketed axes/chisels (Needham *et al.* 2013, 93, 161), although the evidence is less conclusive. The poor rate of recovery of early socketed forms from the French side could in part be due to low-visibility, but the few examples known there lack the loops that are normally present on the larger number of British examples. Evidence for loops is present on the Langdon Bay examples where they are well enough preserved (Needham *et al.* 2013, 93, 161) and this is taken as grounds for suggesting that the seabed finds did *not* originate on the southern shore of the Channel, even if socketed axe/chisel circulation there was greater than is apparent from the archaeological record.

Two contemporary types not found amongst the seabed assemblages deserve mention here because they paint a very vivid picture of mutual exclusion – shields and helmets. In both cases the full chronology extends beyond Penard/Rosnoën, but the pattern remains consistent. Shields are only found on the British side of the Channel, helmets only on the Continental side (Uckelmann 2012, Tafn 154–5 and 162–3; Hencken 1971, fig. 1). While the helmets from the Channel zone of France and Belgium are part of a wider Continental helmet phenomenon that crosses major culture-block divisions, detailed typology sets them apart. Only the Schoonaerde example from Belgium (Uckelmann 2012, 190–3) is of the generic 'cap'

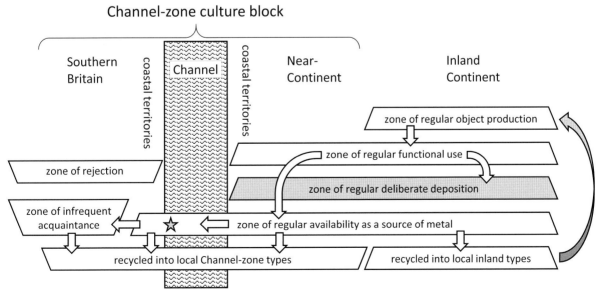

Fig. 4.5. A model for the spatial zones of production, use, rejection, deposition and recycling of Type Grigny median-winged axes in relation to the Channel-zone culture block; the toned bar largely accounts for the metalwork record as found and the star represents the Langdon Bay find.

form which is otherwise found in central and southern Europe. All sixteen helmets from northern France, coming from eight find locations, are of two 'crested' types that can be seen to be regional products (I have included the example from Mantes, Seine-et-Oise, which is better placed here than with cap helmets: Hencken 1971, 126–8). The only close parallels from further into Europe are those from Pockinger Heide, Lower Bavaria, and the River Main at Mainz-Kostheim (Hencken 1971, 65, fig. 38 and 73, fig. 47) and it seems highly probable that these derive from the southern Channel zone tradition either as exports or through the re-location of craftsmen. The objects associated with the fragmentary helmet at Le Thiel, Loir-et-Cher, including a Type Grigny median-winged axe (cf. variant Nauheim; Kibbert 1984, nos 102–15), can be dated to early Urnfield.

A group of pointed rivets from Flag Fen, Cambridgeshire, might possibly be from a helmet (Coombs 2001, 290), but there are other options and metal analysis suggests these rivets are later than the period under consideration here. The key point with regard to shields and helmets is not whether there might have been some overlap in their systemic zones of use, but that these complementary types of prestige armour were chosen for deliberate deposition on a regionally exclusive basis. This betrays a crucial difference in attitude to the most flamboyant of martial deposits on either side of the Channel.

Channel-crossing types

Several types belonging to the Penard/Rosnoën phase, some of them represented in the seabed assemblages, are found in reasonable numbers on both sides of the Channel, although often there is an apparent imbalance from one side to the other. Where there is unequal representation, it is easy to jump to the conclusion that the lesser occurrence is due to importation of metalwork made on the opposite side of the water. We have already looked at the example of Rosnoën swords, but such patterns may have varied backgrounds. Intriguingly, respective numbers of finds of the slightly later Ballintober swords (O'Connor 1980, 809 map 33; Coffyn 1985, 127 carte 13) suggest similar levels of circulation on the two sides of the Channel, although it should be noted that there still may have been regional variants seen, for example, in Coffyn's recognition of a *type évolué*.

Twisted gold-bar torcs, a type represented as fragments at Salcombe (Needham *et al.* 2013, 86; plus subsequent finds), are another of the types in question. They are much more frequent finds in southern Britain than in northern and western France (Eogan 1994, 71, fig. 32), but this could be due to a range of factors relating to access to gold, consequent deposition rates and then the historical vagaries of later disturbance and recovery. It is of note that although the technical intricacy of the multi-strand example from the Guînes hoard, Pas-de-Calais (Armbruster and Louboutin 2004) is without good parallel in France, so too, it cannot be matched in Britain or Ireland; consideration should certainly be given to this masterpiece being due to regional innovation and inspiration. Given a range of other similarities in goldwork types, it may be more appropriate to think in terms of a *shared tradition* on either side of the Channel in which there was a high degree of common ground in techniques and styles, but still autonomous production in both regions.

Local production on the southern side of the Channel has never really been questioned for Rosnoën palstaves because of their presence in Rosnoën associations across north-west France, yet they are not actually common finds either in the hoards or as single finds. Good parallels for these amongst the British *Transitional* series (including those classified in the CBTS volume as Langdon types 1–3) are much more frequent finds north of the water (Needham *et al.* 2013, 92). A similar bias is found for Group IV notched-butt rapiers/dirks (Needham *et al.* 2013, 99) and for triangular basal-looped spearheads (Davies 2012, types 9B and 9C), a class of weapon not recovered from the seabed sites yet. The latter continue the pattern seen for the preceding leaf-shaped basal-looped form (O'Connor 1980, 803 map 27; Davies 2006, pls 74 and 75; Coffyn 1985, 132 carte 17 – for all basal-looped types) and Peter Schauer has actually suggested manufacture on the Continent (Schauer 1973).

Despite uncertainties over the real production and circulation zones of many of the constituent types discussed so far in this paper, these types show a spectrum of spatial patterns in relation to the geography of the Channel-flanking lands which likely do reflect variability in the systemic sphere. However, the uncertainties make it impossible to be dogmatic about the composition and balance of source regions contributing to the recovered cargoes and we may have to satisfy ourselves with more fluid interpretative frameworks in this regard.

A leapfrog connection?

Some British metalwork of the Penard phase could suggest quite different connections going beyond the Channel zone. In the CBTS volume, I argued against the relevance of the conical ferrule and Taunton-Hademarschen axe links to central and northern Europe respectively (Needham *et al.* 2013, 161–2). The reasoning for the latter type may remain valid in that socketed axe/chisels had apparently already become established in southern Britain during the Taunton stage and continued to be developed into local style variants during the Penard. Since the examples in the Langdon Bay find have good parallels amongst the

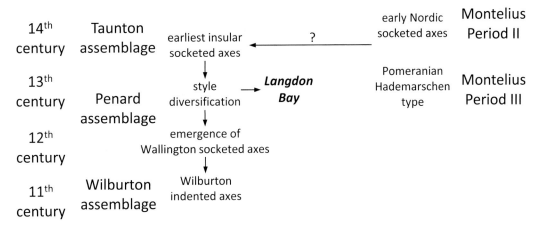

Fig. 4.6. The insular development of socketed axe/chisels in relation to the earliest examples in Britain and their assumed prototypes in northern Europe. It shows that the examples in the Langdon Bay find can be derived direct from those circulating in southern Britain without needing to invoke an origin in Pomerania.

insular corpus, there is thus no need to invoke a distant origin for them at this date of some decades or as much as a century later (Fig. 4.6).

The case for the conical ferrules is more open to reconsideration. It is true that smaller conical fittings appear in Britain in a few Taunton phase contexts (O'Connor 1980, 90–1, plus additional finds) and could have served as a prototype for enlarged spear-butt fittings, but another metalwork link in much the same direction is inescapable – that attested by the Nipperwiese type shields (Needham 1979). The five known north European examples occur fairly close to both the Hademarschen axes of Pomerania and the conical ferrules of the Middle Elbe and Bohemia. Nipperwiese shields stand at the head of metal shield development in northern Europe and Britain, probably having emerged at the very beginning of Penard in terms of the British sequence (Needham 1979; Needham *et al.* 2012). Likewise, conical ferrules must have started early on the evidence of the Ambleside hoard (Needham 1982), perhaps early in the 13th century BC. The potential Taunton horizon connection for socketed axes/chisels, especially if late in the assemblage (a possibility raised by Steve Matthews, pers. comm.), could still have been relatively recent history at this time. Unless intervening absences of the respective types are due to hidden circulation, it would appear that there was some kind of special 'leapfrog' connection here that accounted for the mutual adoption of these very few types. Other links have been suggested in this broadly easterly direction in the past to account for the style of ornaments in British Taunton phase contexts, but this is less convincing given much broader European distributions of interrelated, neckring, bracelet and pin styles, including many in northern France. On the other hand, occasional Nordic palstaves of Montelius Period II, equivalent to Taunton, occur in

Britain (O'Connor 1980, 785 map 9; a newer find comes from a hoard at Malmains Farm, Kent: Keith Parfitt, pers. comm.) and a Nordic dirk handle occurs in the Blackrock hoard, Sussex (Piggott 1949, 108, fig. 1.1), which on the evidence of its Group IV dirk should date close to the Taunton/Penard transition.

Acknowledgement of this more easterly orientation of contacts shows that southern British communities were not totally locked in to cross-Channel relations and that they also took advantage of the wider opportunities provided by the northwestern seaways. The north French connections with the Nordic world suggested by Gabillot (2003) relate to pre-Rosnoën phases and it is not clear any such links exist amongst Rosnoën metalwork.

The culture-block backdrop

The existence of large-scale similarities in mid- to later Bronze Age cultural packages on either side of the Channel needs to be contextualised in relation to both historical processes and other broad-scale cultural complexes, such as that of the Nordic zone, or the Urnfield zone. These are unities which emerge from a group's need to ally itself with one set of political, social and religious paradigms, in the process also distinguishing itself from others. Such processes of alliance in relatively small-scale societies are unlikely to result in a high degree of homogeneity because there is no state mechanism exerting pressure to conform to that degree. The self-identifying group retains its identity through certain distinctive characteristics, whether it be through local variants in the ceramic repertoire or particular styles of costume fitting – to take but two material examples recognisable in archaeological evidence. Although the group will at some point in history have either made a conscious decision to ally with one particular cultural umbrella, or drifted on a convergent path to the same end, this may have been pragmatic to some extent, may have been strongly influenced by (*not* determined by) geographical position, and may have happened with little concept of what was being tied into at more than the local (that is regional) scale. An Urnfield group in the southern Netherlands may have cared little that social groups on the farthest perimeter of that culture block had some recognisably similar beliefs and material goods. The same might be the case in north-west Europe too, although the seaways would have offered more ready passage to distant parts of the culture block (and beyond) and arguably, therefore, better one-to-one acquaintance with them. It is worth recalling here David Fontijn's suggestion that Middle Bronze Age communities in the Netherlands may not have distinguished between palstaves coming from southern Britain or northern France; they were very similar looking objects which basically came from the west by way of the seaways (Fontijn 2009).

A second important point needs to be made about these broadly held commonalities that we see conveniently as culture blocks. The decision or trajectory initially leading to convergence or 'conversion' may have happened over a limited passage of time. Yet once brought about, a tied relationship may have stood for centuries for a variety of reasons such as inertia, the lack of any more attractive propositions, coercion by neighbouring groups (threats of violence or sanctions) and predispositions arising from geographical position. These processes would have helped keep developments within the particular social group more or less in tandem with those in the broader complex, but unless that group can be seen to have subscribed to *all* attributes of a neighbouring group (in which case they come to be absorbed into that neighbouring culture definition), it still remains a recognisable group with its own identity. The sharing of a general signature over the full extent of a given culture block may often be as much a consequence of incidental historical processes as the result of an ongoing heart-felt desire to belong.

Conceptualising these big culture blocks in this way allows us to divert attention more towards individual group identity and the way that intra-block variability maps out. It is clear for example that in Britain, as we track away from the south-eastern coastlands we see certain aspects of change in the nature of the archaeological evidence, whether it be in the ceramic repertoire, in regionally diagnostic metalwork types, burial patterns or patterns of deposition or land-use. There is little doubt that the cultural ensemble in the far north was very removed from that in the far south, but many of the changes take place gradually over a long distance. Across the much shorter distance of the Channel, we have no intervening

'culture' to act as buffer or filter, a factor only partly offset by the greater difficulty and risk in making the crossing. If then we are investigating the possibility of a pattern of gradational changes over geographical space, perhaps we should not expect *genuinely different* social groups on either side of the Channel to be particularly strongly differentiated since they are close to being 'neighbours'. Indeed, taking the transverse along-Channel axis, the same sense of being almost neighbours might be stretched to communities not just directly opposite, but those bordering the coast further *along* the Channel in either direction. The long, parallel-sided stretch of uninhabited water allows much more untrammelled passage over longer distances – this can be lead more readily to 'leapfrogging' in the formation of socio-economic ties (Fig. 4.7.2) and can have the effect of distorting geography. This then has profound implications for the pattern of networks which can develop relative to a typical land-locked situation (Fig. 4.7.1) and future analyses need to test whether such effects can be seen in the archaeological data.

The Channel conundrum

It is commonly recognised that a wide passage of water such as the Channel can be both an obstacle and a conduit at one and the same time. This two-sided coin deserves further examination. The Channel *was* an obstacle of sorts, but the story of the Bronze Age in this part of the Europe is the early 'conquest' of the seas to a degree that they came to be embodied in the everyday life, or at least in the annual cycles of the flanking territories. Crossing the sea was just something that had to be done to achieve contact in certain directions, different only from crossing a mountain range or a large marshy plain, or travelling along a long river in that different preparations, permissions and equipment were needed. Sea-crossing had been added to the range of mechanisms routinely available for inter-regional interaction and was there to be put into service as required. The sea was only an obstacle insofar as it may limit the scale and regularity of physical interaction between 'neighbours' in a way that is not the case for land-based interactions between neighbours and near-neighbours. Those limitations can be partially overridden by the technology available in conjunction with social imperatives. Once seafaring is mastered and long-distance voyaging is seen to be desirable, the balance tips towards the Channel being a conduit. It is not just the short crossings that facilitate connections; it is the long-axis passage, because, unlike on land, this is untrammelled passage. As already noted, this wholly changes the shape of interaction patterns (Fig. 4.7.2) and can 'distort' proximity patterns more than is normally the case for terrestrial landscapes (David-Elbiali this volume).

We should no longer be surprised at the many similarities between societies on the two sides of the Channel. It is precisely *because* sea travel had become embedded in the cultural psyche early on that it was possible for a 'culture block' to straddle this stretch of sea. For populations through much of the Bronze Age this was a time-immemorial reality resulting from circumstances that evolved many generations earlier in vaguely remembered

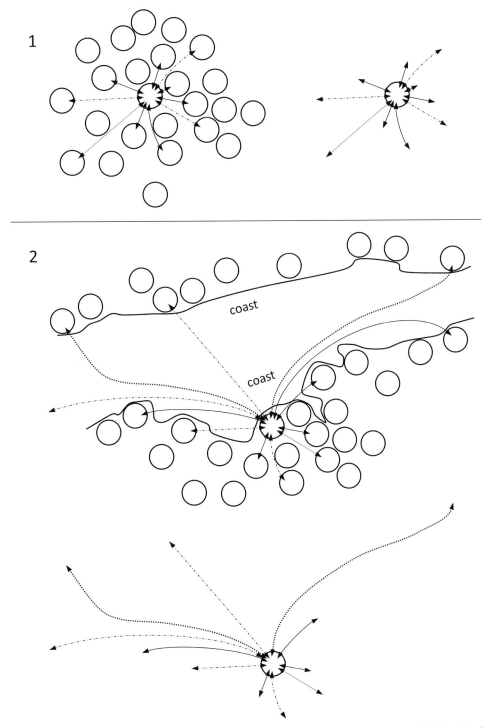

Fig. 4.7. Hypothetical models to show the possibility of typical differences in the interaction networks of: 1) land-locked, and 2) coastal territories. Each circle represents a social group occupying a territory and it is assumed that the strength of links will vary according to a range of factors, not just distance between two; the patterns divorced from background noise emphasise the potential attenuation and asymmetry of coastal relative to land-locked networks.

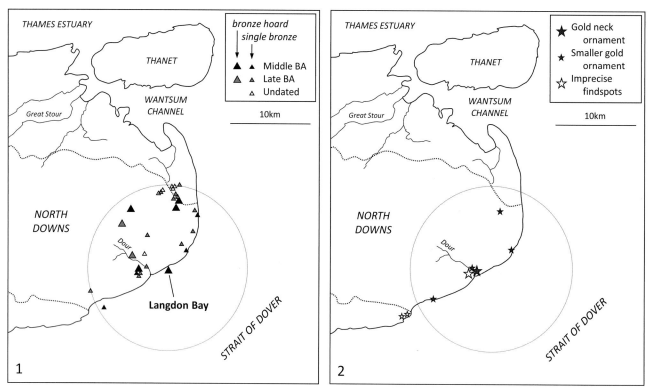

Fig. 4.8. Middle and Late Bronze Age metalwork from the immediate hinterland of Langdon Bay: 1) bronze metalwork finds; 2) gold metalwork finds. The circle has a radius of 10 km.

ancestral time. For people of any subsequent stage, this was just the way their world was and they found it convenient, expedient or least disruptive (by and large) to maintain that pre-existing network of affinities with its resulting material correlates.

The relative ease with which connections can be made once the sea has been encompassed may seem to erode all sense of obstruction, but this misses two points. Firstly, the mere fact that any given group typically has a greater choice of socio-economic allies than they would as a land-locked group could easily lead to them distancing themselves from relatively near groups more readily than land-locked societies could afford to, all other factors being equal. Distancing could be done with relative impunity for groups on opposing shores simply because there *was* the buffer of the Channel. Obviously, if relationships were strongly antagonistic this might lead to the launching of seaborne war-bands – in such circumstances the state of impunity may be suspended briefly or sporadically.

The second point is that the sea presents an almost unparalleled fixed boundary; in times of strife coastal territories are much less prone to be under pressure in this direction relative to land boundaries. The coast may consequently be seen to be a stable, time-honoured entity for a coastal territory, and even if a coastal strip

were seized either from the sea itself or from a coastal neighbour, it is not the boundary fixed by the coast that changes, merely instead its occupation. Although inland topographic features such as significant ridges and rivers are also stable in human experience and can exert a strong influence, territorial boundaries need not be so deterministically tied to them. The relative boundary stability of the coast is likely to have been understood, subconsciously at least. To this 'special property' of the coast one should add another, that of it being the 'gateway' to the already mentioned untrammelled access to many valued contacts. It is easy to see, especially when account is also taken of the rich and distinctive food resources and its non-diurnal rhythm (e.g. O'Sullivan 2003), how the coast itself could come to be viewed as a special and unique place in the local social landscape, a place to be cherished and respected for all that it offered the coastal community.

Relevant to respect for the coast is a feature of metalwork distributions that emerged from study of the Langdon Bay hinterland in east Kent (Needham *et al.* 2013, 50–5). A difference was found between the archaeological distributions of bronzework and goldwork of the later Bronze Age (Fig. 4.8). While bronze finds occur quite widely across the landscape, the contemporary goldwork was mainly deposited

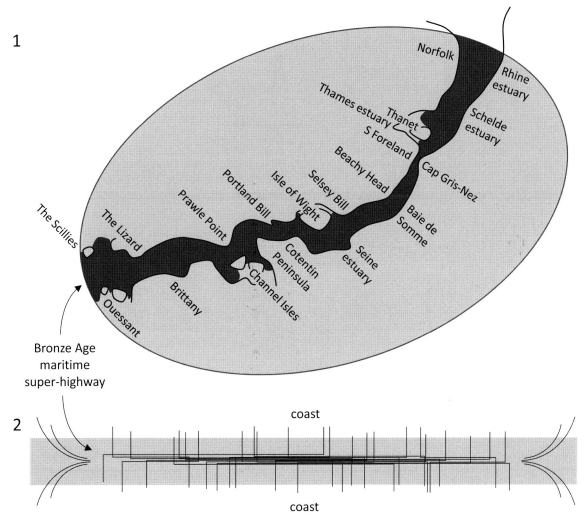

Fig. 4.9. The Channel as a Bronze Age maritime super-highway. 1) closing up the Channel to show geographical proximities in terms of lack of intervening communities; 2) the collective 'wiring' of coastal communities based on many overlapping, yet unique, favoured interconnections.

in coastal locations. This pattern may extend further around the Kentish coast, but is nevertheless specific to this small part of Britain. Elsewhere, other aspects of behaviour potentially indicative of respect for the *terre/mare* interface will need to be sought. While the Kent-coast focus for gold deposition appears to be boundary behaviour of a kind, it may have been directed towards relations with a particular part of the supernatural realm, rather than with other living communities – the focus of the above discussion.

In terms of the evidence we have for the later Bronze Age, the Channel clearly *does* become a super-highway facilitating connections (Fig. 4.9). But enhanced flux does not automatically bring coherence or convergence. As with any super-highway, different travellers have different interests and expectations leading them to favour some ports

of call and shun others. High interconnectedness along and across the Channel does not preclude its two coasts being treated as boundaries; in reality, each of these was actually the conjunction of a multitude of separate boundaries defined by individual social groups.

Given, then, our current understanding of interactions around the Channel zone during the Bronze Age, it is hardly surprising that by the advanced stage seen in the Penard/Rosnoën phase there were extensive similarities in material culture, and probably also in beliefs. The 'Channel-crossing' metalwork types discussed above are testimony to this, as are the similarities in ceramic assemblages etc. Against this backdrop, rather more significance should be attached to evidence for real differences in the acceptability of certain metalwork types from one side of the Channel to the other. The Channel-bounded distributions discussed (and argued not to be caused by low archaeological visibility) involve different classes of object – weaponry and defensive armour in the Penard/Rosnoën phase and, in the previous Taunton/ Baux-Sainte-Croix phase, certain fancy ornament types (such as quoit-headed pins and Sussex loops) – classes which are likely to have been very important to the definition of identity and affiliation. This is also potentially true of the median-winged axe whose functional capabilities presumably did not differ significantly from those of palstaves. It is intriguing that Channel-zone communities south of the Channel were relatively receptive to the type, whereas their close neighbours on the northern side were not; this may have something to do with different exposure to and relationships with the west Urnfield groups (RSFO) that generated this object type.

Other Channel-bounded distributions occur at the object variant level. Variant distinctions may have less to do with the current socio-political needs of the respective elites, more to do with particular regional preferences of style which were maintained through regional production traditions. Nevertheless, they can still bear on community identity and they show that there was not felt to be a need to harmonise cross-regionally in these respects – to express regionality was good, necessary and normal.

In addition to the hard archaeological evidence, it might be speculated that a particular historical circumstance may militate in favour of different attitudes, perceptions and behaviour from one side of the Channel to the other. The sudden curtailment of the Channel-zone block southeastwards, where it meets the (northwestern) Urnfield block, could have led to substantially heightened perceptions of pressure or threat. Societies in southern Britain were relatively insulated from this major ideologically rift on the Continental side. Meanwhile, many groups in northern France and the Low Countries would have been constantly coping with friction at the culture-block interface. Faced with such circumstances, the need of Channel-zone groups on the Continental side for the consolidation of intra-block political alliances may have been greater than those of the reciprocal British groups. Such an asymmetric cross-Channel consolidation process could help explain the apparently greater desirability of British-style metalwork in the Continental side than vice versa. A southern desire for consolidation may not have been confined to importing goods, but could have extended to importing the diagnostic insular styles and techniques, thereby facilitating local production in the same mould ('shared traditions'). Nor should we rule out a need at times for British mercenaries. In essence, Channel-zone communities on the southern side could have been buying support through the northward flow of metal and perhaps other goods. The fact that Britain was an offshore island could even have encouraged the view that it was also a supernaturally protected bastion

of the umbrella culture – somewhat akin to the island of Anglesey with respect to Late Iron Age druidism.

Conclusions

This paper has not tried to offer a holistic interpretation of the Channel Bronze Age. It has focused on one branch of evidence – the metalwork – and one metalworking phase – the Penard/Rosnoën. This evidence is nevertheless useful as a case-study because it minimises the dangers of diachronic complexity and yet the range of objects involved can still address varied aspects of the life-styles, interactions and different concerns of communities. The analysis presented gives sufficient reason for being cautious about how unified societies were on either side of the Channel without detracting from the on-going political opportunism provided by the Channel culture-block.

Much has been said in this paper about the difficulties of understanding systemic occurrences of metalwork from archaeologically recorded 'distributions'. These are real problems for some areas of understanding, but actually, for other areas of interpretation we may be able to side-step these difficulties. One major reason (although not the only one) for the mismatch is undoubtedly down to different social groups having different ways of expressing their concerns in the realm of deliberate deposition (thus leading to archaeological visibility). Such matters surely go to the core of fundamental distinctions in ways of dealing with the world – dependent on 'world views'. So, ironically, the fact that recovered material may not relate closely to that in circulation may be of lesser importance to the question of identifying self-distinguishing groups. On the contrary, it may offer some of the best evidence we could hope to have in order to shed light on them. We have to start regarding the archaeological metalwork record as one of the best proxies we have for differential behaviour; it is likely to speak volumes about different attitudes or beliefs. And sometimes, perhaps normally, it may be that a minority of clear-cut differences between regional assemblages, especially if they can be connected to critical aspects of behaviour, tell us more than do a much greater number of similarities. Much is made of the fact that the most prestigious of metalwork types are those that have the most international distributions, contrasting with tools which can have very regionalised distributions. However, this is not a universal correlation, as the contrast made in this paper between shields and helmets demonstrates.

The issues raised above question whether debating or celebrating the existence of a Channel Bronze Age should be a key concern any longer. It has almost become a redundant question, not least because its definition will probably eternally change according to what material is considered and with every new analysis of it. It would be far more useful to examine the finer relationships within this Channel zone *and* between it and its congener 'Atlantic' cultures. The need now is to focus more on smaller-scale entities and how they fit in to the wider interaction system; and this needs to be done through rigorous analysis for each constituent phase, because it is variations and changes in those workings that will be most important for understanding the real histories of social groups at whatever scale we wish to consider them.

Acknowledgements

I am grateful to the conference organisers for inviting me to speak at Boulogne, to the British Museum for permission to use Figure 4.1, and to Steve Matthews for letting me see his paper for these proceedings in draft. Special thanks go to Brendan O'Connor for his support in analysing the metalwork in the CBTS volume and for various comments on this paper.

Bibliography

Armbruster, B. R. and Louboutin, C. (2004) Parures en or de l'Âge du Bronze de Balinghem et Guînes (Pas-de-Calais): les aspects technologiques. *Antiquités Nationales* 36, 133–146.

Brandherm, D. (2014) *Review of Claimed by the Sea: Salcombe, Langdon Bay, and other Marine Finds of the Bronze Age*. http://www.prehistoricsociety.org/files/reviews/Claimed_by_the_sea_Final_review.pdf

Briard, J. and Onnée, Y. (1972) *Le Dépôt du Bronze Final de Saint-Brieuc-des-Iffs (Île-et-Vilaine)*. Rennes, Université de Rennes, Travaux du Laboratoire Anthropologie Préhistoire-Protohistoire et Quaternaire Armoricains.

Burgess, C. B. (2012) Alignments: revising the Atlantic Late Bronze Age sequence. *Archaeological Journal* 169, 127–158.

Burgess, C. B. and O'Connor, B. (2008) Iberia, the Atlantic Bronze Age and the Mediterranean. In S. Celestino, N. Rafael and X.-L. Armada (eds) *Contacto Cultural entre el Mediterráneo y el Atlántico (Siglos XII–VIII ane), 41–58*. Madrid, C. S. I. C.

Butler, J. J. and Steegstra, H. (1999-2000) Bronze Age metal and amber in the Netherlands (III: I): catalogue of the winged axes. *Palaeohistoria* 41, 127–148.

Coffyn, A. (1985) *Le Bronze Final Atlantique dans la Péninsule Ibérique* Publications du Centre Pierre Paris 11. Paris, Diffusion de Boccard.

Colquhoun, I. and Burgess, C. B. (1988) *The Swords of Britain*. Munich, Prähistorische Bronzefunde IV (5).

Davies, R. (2006) *Basal-looped Spearheads: Typology, Chronology, Context and Use*, British Archaeological Report S 1497. Oxford, Archaeopress.

Davies, R. (2012) *The Early and Middle Bronze Age Spearheads of Britain*, Prähistorische Bronzefunde V, 5. Stuttgart, Franz Steiner

Eogan, G. (1994) *The Accomplished Art: Gold and Gold-working in Britain and Ireland during the Bronze Age*. Oxford, Oxbow Books.

Fox, A. and Britton, D. (1969) A continental palstave from the ancient field system on Horridge Common, Dartmoor. *Proceedings of the Prehistoric Society* 35, 220–8.

Gabillot, M. (2003) *Dépôts et Production Métallique du Bronze Moyen en France Nord-Occidentale*, British Archaeological Report S1174. Oxford, Archaeopress.

Gerloff, S. (2007) Reinecke's ABC and the chronology of the British Bronze Age. In C. Burgess, P. Topping and F. Lynch (eds) *Beyond Stonehenge: Essays in Honour of Colin Burgess*, 117–161. Oxford, Oxbow Books.

Hencken, H. (1971) *The Earliest European Helmets: Bronze Age and Early Iron Age*. Cambridge MA, Peabody Museum of Archaeology and Ethnology.

Jones, A. M. and Quinnell, H. (2014) *Lines of Archaeological Investigation along the North Cornish Coast*, British Archaeological Report 594. Oxford, Archaeopress.

Kibbert, K. (1984) *Die Äxte und Beile im mittleren Westdeutschland II, Prähistorische Bronzefunde* IX (13). Munich, Beck.

Milcent, P.-Y. (2006) Les importations Italiques au nord-ouest du midi Gaulois (milieu du Xe – début du IVe s. av. J.-C.): inventaire et perspectives d'interprétation. In *Gli Etruschi da Genova ad Ampurias: Atti del XXIV Convegno di Studi Etruschi ed Italici*, 319–355. Rome, Istituti Editoriali e Poligrafici Internazionali.

Milcent, P.-Y. (2012) *Le Temps des Élites en Gaule Atlantique: Chronologie des Mobiliers et Rythmes de Constitution des Dépôts Métalliques dans le Contexte Européen*. Rennes, Presses Universitaires de Rennes

Millotte, J.-P., Cordier, G. and Abauzit, P. (1968) Essai de typologie protohistorique: les haches à ailerons médians. *Revue Archéologique de l'Est et du Centre-Est* 19, 7–67.

Muckelroy, K. (1980) Two Bronze Age cargoes in British waters. *Antiquity* 54, 100–9.

Needham, S. P. (1979) Two recent British shield finds and their continental parallels. *Proceedings of the Prehistoric Society* 45, 111–134.

Needham, S. P. (1980) An assemblage of Late Bronze Age metalworking debris from Dainton, Devon. *Proceedings of the Prehistoric Society* 46, 177–216.

Needham, S. P. (1982) *The Ambleside Hoard: a Discovery in the Royal Collections*, British Museum Occasional Paper 39. London, British Museum

Needham, S. P. (1987) The Bronze Age. In J. Bird and D. G. Bird (eds) *The Archaeology of Surrey to 1540*, 97–137. Guildford, Surrey Archaeological Society.

Needham, S. (2017) Assemblage, structure and meaning in bronze metalwork studies; an analysis of the British Penard Assemblage. *Oxford Journal of Archaeology 36, 111–156.*

Needham, S. and Giardino, C. (2008) From Sicily to Salcombe: a Mediterranean Bronze Age object from British coastal waters. *Antiquity* 82, 60–72.

Needham, S. P., Northover, J. P., Uckelmann, M. and Tabor, R. (2012) South Cadbury: the last of the bronze shields? *Archäologisches Korrespondenzblatt* 42, 473–492.

Needham, S., Parham, D. and Frieman, C. J. (eds) (2013) *Claimed by the Sea: Salcombe, Langdon Bay and Other Marine Finds of the Bronze Age*. Council for British Archaeology Research Report 173. York, Council for British Archaeology.

Northover, P. (2013) Metal analysis. In S. Needham, D. Parham and C. J. Frieman (eds) *Claimed by the Sea: Salcombe, Langdon Bay and Other Marine Finds of the Bronze Age, 101–11, Council for British Archaeology Research Report 173*. York, Council for British Archaeology.

O'Connor, B. (1980) *Cross-Channel Relations in the Later Bronze Age*, British Archaeological Report S91. Oxford, British Archaeological Reports.

O'Sullivan, A. (2003) Place, memory and identity among estuarine fishing communities: interpreting the archaeology of early medieval fish weirs. *World Archaeology* 35, 449–468.

Pare, C. F. E. (1999) Weights and weighing in Bronze Age central Europe. In *Eliten in der Bronzezeit: Ergebnisse zweier Kolloquien in Mainz und Athen, 421–514*, Römisch-Germanisches Zentralmuseum, Monographien 43 (2). Mainz, Römisch-Germanisches Zentralmuseum.

Piggott, C. M. (1949) A Late Bronze Age hoard from Blackrock in Sussex and its significance. *Proceedings of the Prehistoric Society* 15, 107–121.

Rohl, B. and Needham, S. P. (1998) *The Circulation of Metal in the British Bronze Age: the Application of Lead Isotope Analysis*, British Museum Occasional Paper 102. London, British Museum.

Schauer, P. (1973) Kontinentaleuropaïsche Bronzelanzenspitzen vom *Typ Enfields. Archäologisches Korrespondenzblatt* 3, 293–8.

Uckelmann, M. (2012) *Die Schilde der Bronzezeit in Nord-, West- und Zentraleuropa*, Prähistorische Bronzefunde III, 4. Stuttgart, Franz Steiner.

5

At World's End: the Channel Bronze Age and the emergence and limits of the Atlantic complex

Steven Matthews

Abstract

The significance of the Channel in the later Bronze Age is best understood in terms of its relationship to the Atlantic Bronze Age complex. Sometime around the beginning of the 14th century the relationship between other parts of the British Isles and southern England changed, re-orientating the interests of the latter toward the near Continent, and in particular northern France. Locally the distinction can be summed up as the transformation from the earlier Channel 'maritories', those communities that serviced the movement of artefacts across the Channel, to a full Channel Bronze Age 'culture', where the communities on both sides shared widely in the same artefacts and social practices. The difference is significant. Rowlands has described the latter grouping of communities as encompassing a Channel 'core zone' and it was this that was integral to the development of the Atlantic complex. We should not confuse the Bronze Age of the Atlantic region, representative only of contemporary societies related by a shared geography, with the Atlantic Bronze Age complex, a social and political phenomenon that shared in similar artefacts and practices, but which did not encompass all the geographic regions of the Atlantic. The latter was facilitated by the geography of the Atlantic region but was by no means shaped nor constrained by it. As we shall see, it is the Channel communities of north France and southeast England, those regions that do not even face the Atlantic that very much came to form the core of this complex. However, just as the extent of the complex has been exaggerated in the past, so too has its homogeneity.

Keywords: Atlantic Bronze Age, Atlantic complex, Channel Bronze Age, Later Bronze Age, Rapiers, Swords, Typology, Chronology

Résumé

La place du Channel est mieux comprise dans ses relations avec le complexe atlantique à la fin de l'Âge du bronze. Quelque part du côté du XIVe siècle avant notre ère, les relations entre les différentes parties du sud de l'Angleterre et des îles britanniques changent, réorientant ses centres d'intérêt vers le continent et tout particulièrement le nord de la France. Localement, la distinction peut être mise en évidence d'une transformation depuis les premières « maritories » du Channel, qui ont servi les déplacements des artefacts par le Channel, jusqu'à une pleine culture de l'Âge du bronze, dans laquelle les communautés des deux côtés partagent les mêmes artefacts et pratiques sociales. La différence est claire. Rowlands a décrit les derniers regroupements de communautés comme une englobante « Core zone » du Channel, et c'est cela qui a été intégré au développement du complexe atlantique. Nous ne devrions pas confondre l'Âge du bronze avec l'Atlantic région, représentative seulement des sociétés contemporaines reliées par une géographie commune et le Complexe du Bronze Atlantique, entendu comme un phénomène social et politique qui regroupe des objets et des pratiques similaires, mais qui ne rassemble pas toutes les régions géographiques du monde atlantique. L'aboutissement du phénomène a été facilité par la géographie de la région atlantique, mais il n'a pas été façonné ou contraint par elle. Comme nous allons voir, ce sont les communautés du Channel du nord de la France et du sud-ouest de l'Angleterre – régions qui ne font pas face à l'Atlantique – auxquelles on doit le cœur de ce complexe. Cependant, son extension a été exagérée par le passé, tout comme son homogénéité.

Mots-clés : Âge du bronze Atlantique, Complexe Atlantique, Âge du bronze transmanche, Âge du bronze final, rapières, épées, typologie, chronologie

Introduction

The significance of the Channel in the later Bronze Age is best understood in terms of its relationship to the Atlantic Bronze Age complex. Sometime around the beginning of the 14th century the relationship between other parts of the British Isles and southern England changed, re-orientating the interests of the latter toward the near Continent, and in particular northern France. Locally the distinction can be summed up as the transformation from the earlier Channel 'maritories' (cf. Needham 2009, 16–18, fig. 2.3), those communities that serviced the movement of artefacts across the Channel, to a full Channel Bronze Age 'culture' (e.g. O'Connor 1980; Burgess 1996, fig. 3), where the communities on both sides shared widely in the same artefacts and social practices. The difference is significant. Rowlands (1980, 37) has described the latter grouping of communities as encompassing a Channel 'core zone' and it was this that was integral to the development of the Atlantic complex. We should not confuse the Bronze Age of the *Atlantic region*, representative only of contemporary societies related by a shared geography, with the *Atlantic Bronze Age complex*, a social and political phenomenon that shared in similar artefacts and practices (e.g. Burgess and O'Connor 2008), but which did not encompass all the geographic regions of the Atlantic. The latter was *facilitated* by the geography of the Atlantic region but was by no means shaped nor constrained by it. As we shall see, it is the Channel communities of north France and south-east England, those regions that do not even face the Atlantic that very much came to form the core of this complex. However, just as the extent of the complex has been exaggerated in the past, so too has its homogeneity.

Atlantic Bronze Age complex

There have been attempts to address the Atlantic complex as a broad, uniform cultural phenomenon. However, the Atlantic complex during the later Bronze Age has long been recognised as a product wholly represented by the occurrence of a limited number of bronzes types, particularly weapons. As Burgess and O'Connor (2004, 191) so succinctly put it:

> In following the development of the Atlantic Bronze Age it must be made clear from the start that as a

concept this is all about metal, and has nothing to do with settlement, burials, religion and ritual, ceramics or any aspect of the Bronze Age of the Atlantic fringes.

This Atlantic complex shared widely in the arts, fashion and commerce, all of which gravitated around regional elites whose status was based on a specific ethos of a weapon-bearer. The entire period was well furnished with ornaments and decorative fittings (O'Connor 1980, 74–92, 119–27, 153–4), with local adaptations and innovations always outnumbering imports from other areas, and the same approach was taken in aspects of defensive armour (Hencken 1971; Uckelmann 2012), and ostentatious feasting vessels and their accoutrements (Burgess and O'Connor 2004; Needham and Bowman 2005; Gerloff 2010). Gold inevitably played its part (e.g. Eogan 1994) but differs in distribution and connections, and may be representative of a further specialist group, class or role. Evidence for esoteric rites survive largely as depositional practices involving metalwork, were entirely Atlantic in character and distinctly weapon orientated (Coombs 1988). Despite this sharing in a rich and varied Atlantic maritime material culture, their occurrence is neither homogenous nor uniform. Instead, the wider unity of the complex is predicated entirely on the occurrence of certain types of weapons, of a uniquely Atlantic style, in repeated association together (e.g. Savory 1958, 28; Coombs 1988). These arms clearly show signs of use (York 2002; Quilliec 2007; Matthews 2011a, forthcoming) but were not simply about primitive displays of aggressive force but rather displays of social and political symbolism.

The height of the Atlantic complex is traditionally synonymous with Late Bronze Age 3/Bronze Final III and the Vénat group (e.g. Briard 1965, 228–39; Brun 1991 – traditionally known as the Carp's Tongue group). However, there have occurred a number of recent studies that have fundamentally reshaped both its chronology and geographical extent. The first of these was confirmation of the long suspected view that the majority of so-called Carp's Tongue swords in the Iberian Peninsula, as well as some in France, were not, in fact, of the same type as those of the Vénat group but representative of an earlier proto-Vénat series (Savory 1949, 152–3, fig. 4; Coffyn 1985, 205; Burgess 1991, 38–9). These have been termed

Type Huelva (Brandherm 2007, 56–88) after the large assemblage of such weapons recovered from the Ría de Huelva, Huelva, prov. Huelva (Almagro Basch 1958). These Huelva swords were found to align better with the preceding Late Bronze Age 2/Bronze Final II or Wilburton/Saint-Brieuc-des-Iffs phase (Burgess 1991, 36), severely curtailing the distribution of the Vénat group and shifting the greatest extent of the Atlantic complex back to the mid-12th to mid-10th centuries BC.

The second development was the realisation that the eponymous British and French deposits of this phase, from Wilburton Fen, Cambridgeshire (Evans 1884), and Saint-Brieuc-des-Iffs, Ille-et-Vilaine (Briard and Onnée 1972), were not contemporary (Gerloff 2007, 145–6; Matthews 2011a, 28, tab. 1; Burgess 2012b; Milcent 2012, 103–7). The two groups that these deposits represent were never entirely synchronous to begin with, with British researchers aligning the Wilburton phase with Reinecke's Ha B1, whilst French colleagues aligned the Saint-Brieuc-des-Iffs phase with Ha A2 and Ha B1. In Britain, Ha A2 was instead the later facies of the Penard phase (Penard 2), which as a whole was considered contemporary with the preceding French Rosnoën phase (cf. Burgess 1979, fig. 15. B).

On the basis of a number of AMS dates obtained from organic materials found in association with bronzes representative of these British phases, Needham *et al.* (1997) pushed back their absolute date ranges, resulting in the respective French and British phases finally being aligned. Unfortunately, when the Penard phase was back dated, the assemblage associated with its later Penard 2 aspect, comprising an almost exclusively southern English assemblage, was subsumed within the duration of this 'new' Penard phase, alongside its earlier (Penard 1) types (Rohl and Needham 1998, 98–101, figs 34–35 – the existence of late types within the phase was intimated). This has long seemed untenable, and Gerloff (2007, 145–146) established that this southern English assemblage, particularly its Atlantic types, should be realigned with Ha A2, contemporary with the deposit at Saint-Brieuc-des-Iffs, whilst the Wilburton deposit was representative of the subsequent phase, relative to Ha B1.

The French predilection for U-shouldered swords, seen in the deposit at Saint-Brieuc-des-Iffs, over the V-shouldered swords common at Wilburton, was originally interpreted as a product of regional taste (Burgess 1968a, 9–14). Now these different sword choices can be seen to be chronologically successive, with the U-shouldered swords of this southern English assemblage matching those of Saint-Brieuc-des-Iffs, as well straight- and shallow V-mouthed chapes, as opposed to the various U-mouthed Wilburton chapes, an absence of socketed axes, and with the exception of those with lunate opening, none of the complex spearheads found at Wilburton. Apart from the small deposit at Mickleham, Norbury

Park, ct. Surrey (Needham 2003; Williams 2008), which contained a shallow V-mouthed chape and two 'Late' type palstaves, there is no eponymous deposit to name this southern English assemblage after. Milcent (2012, 103, pl. 77) named it after the deposit from Nettleham, Lincolnshire (Davey 1973, fig. 29) but the hollow-cast pegged spearhead and indented Type Sturry socketed axes date to the subsequent Wilburton-Isleham phase. As well as Mickleham, the deposit at Ffynhonnau, Breconshire, Wales (Savory 1958, 28–28, fig. 3) is also contemporary with this southern English assemblage but this is more representative of late Penard developments outside of southern England, as is the Wallington group (Burgess 1968b). This southern English assemblage has also been identified by Burgess (2012b, 136–8, ill. 2), who termed it the 'Limehouse' phase, after the characteristic leaf-shaped sword type of this phase (Colquhoun and Burgess 1988, 33–6, nos 95–114) and seems most appropriate. These developments, and the realignment of respective British and French phases, inevitably require changes across all respective Atlantic chronologies (Fig. 5.1).

This division of Late Bronze Age 2/Bronze Final II into an earlier Limehouse/Saint-Brieuc-des-Iffs phase and a later Wilburton/Brécy phase, means that many of the earlier discussions of the contents of this period (e.g. Savory 1958, 28; 1965, 182–7; Coombs 1988) are now too general to be used in identifying developmental trends within the Atlantic weapons complex. This is less of a problem in Britain and the Iberian Peninsula, where the weapon developments of this period have been illustrated and described in typological detail (Colquhoun and Burgess 1988; Brandherm 2007), and such divisions can be achieved reasonably easily. For France, however, such a division is more problematic to identify. Regional studies of these weapons have appeared (e.g. Briard 1965; Mohen 1977; O'Connor 1980; Gaucher 1981; Blanchet 1984) but no comprehensive typology or illustrated catalogue has been produced, creating a particular hindrance to the study of the important cross-Channel relations that so clearly underpinned the development of the Atlantic complex. Lacking these, it is impossible, for example, to know which sword series, that of Saint-Brieuc-des-Iffs or Brécy phase, are represented in the distribution maps published by Coffyn (1985, carte 16) and Brun and Mordant (1988, type 33). However, fully illustrated typologies and distributions for the main Atlantic weapon series of the French later Bronze Age (*c.* 1400–960 BC) have now been compiled by the author (Matthews forthcoming). These allow for a detailed understanding of the development of the Atlantic complex and its weapons during this period, and provide for the first time a broader appreciation of the relationship between the Channel and Atlantic regions during the later Bronze Age according to this new chronological scheme.

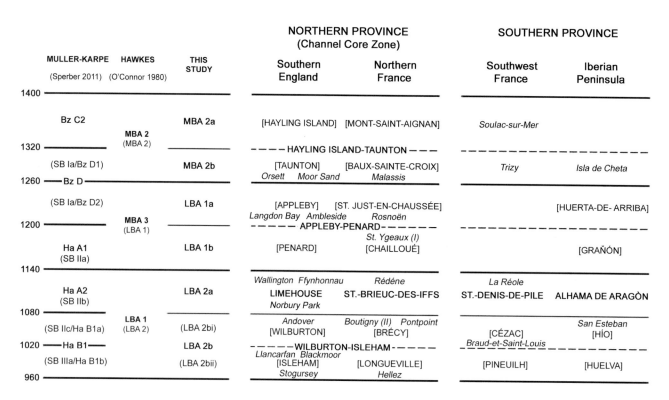

Fig. 5.1. Chronology of the Atlantic complex of Western Europe during the later Bronze Age. Key: phases are in bold text, horizons (subdivisions of phases) are in normal text, and important deposits are in italics (after Matthews forthcoming).

The emergence of the Atlantic complex, north and south

The Atlantic complex has been argued by Burgess and O'Connor (2008, 42) not to have emerged until the beginning of the Appleby-Penard phase. However, much of the extent of the distribution of the main Atlantic bronze types, and by implication the underpinning relationships that facilitated their distribution or stylistic similarity that constitute the later complex, were clearly already established during the preceding Hayling Island-Taunton phase. This is most obvious in respect of the Atlantic rapiers of this phase and in particular their distribution (Fig. 5.2). The majority of these are concentrated in the Channel core zone of northern France and southern England. Beyond, their numbers are far fewer but their distribution significant.

Of these, Group III rapiers of Type Wandsworth-Rouen (Burgess and Gerloff 1981, 50–5; Matthews 2010, 82) are the most numerous and widely distributed. Although mainly concentrated in southern England and north France, they still have a wide distribution across France, including the Loire Valley and in the southwest. During the later Taunton horizon, early Group IV 'archaic' rapiers (Burgess and Gerloff 1981, 63–74; Matthews 2010, 83) developed, their flattened blade section demonstrated to be representative of a change in combat techniques (Matthews forthcoming). Whilst not as widely distributed in England, being largely restricted to the south-east, rapiers of Type Battersea-Sèvres (with Group II affinities) and Type Battersea-Oissel (with Group III affinities) have the same distribution in France as the other weapons of this phase. Whilst Group III rapiers appear not to have reached the Iberian Peninsula, archaic Group IV rapiers did, as seen in the Spanish deposit at Isle de Cheta, Puentecesures, Pontevedra (Brandherm 2007, nos 2, 3), as well as unprovenanced examples held by the Museo Arqueológico Nacional, Madrid (Brandherm 2007, no. 4) and the Museu de Etnografia e História do Douro Litoral, Porto (Brandherm 2007, no. 5). These have traditionally been identified as Type Appleby rapiers (Brandherm 2007, 17; Burgess and O'Connor 2008, 43) and consequently assigned to the subsequent phase. However, the shape of the butt plate and the positioning of the rivet holes clearly mark them as of the archaic Group IV tradition. This earlier date is supported by the pegged, ogival spearhead from Isle de Cheta (Brandherm 2007, lam. 54.A, no. 3) which is identical to one from the Taunton horizon deposit at Orsett, ct. Essex (Burgess and Gerloff 1981, pl. 128.A, no. 5), which contained Group III and Group IV archaic rapiers.

The distribution of these Hayling Island-Taunton phase rapiers and their associated weapon deposits can already be seen to have established the extent and regional relationships that underpinned the Atlantic complex in later phases. Importantly, the distribution and concentration of certain

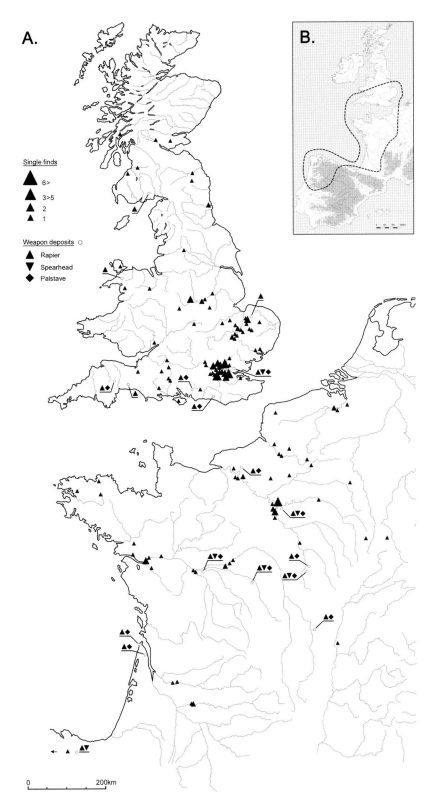

Fig. 5.2. A. Distribution of Atlantic rapiers during the Taunton phase. Includes only those rapier types shared between southern England and France: Group III early rapiers (Types Chatham and Surbiton: Burgess and Gerloff 1981, 47–9), Group III Wandsworth rapiers (Types Wandsworth and variants Cambridge, Newcastle, Chatteris, Aston Ingham and Amboise: Burgess and Gerloff 1981, 50–5) and Group IV Archaic rapiers (Types Brentford and Battersea: Burgess and Gerloff 1981, 65–9). (After Matthews 2010; forthcoming). B. Extent of Atlantic complex.

types also demonstrates that the complex was initiated by developments from within the Channel core zone. Comprising southern England, north and northwest France, these Channel regions have understandably been described as the centres of innovation for the Atlantic complex (Burgess 2012b, 146). Whilst this is certainly true in the earlier stages of the complex, during the Hayling Island-Taunton phase and the early part of the Appleby-Penard phase (the Appleby horizon), subsequent phases are typified by greater variation in weapon types north and south of the Loire.

At the transition from the Penard horizon (Ha A1) to the Limehouse phase (Ha A2), a number of regional sword forms developed not only in the Channel core zone but also in south-west France and the Iberian Peninsula (Fig. 5.3). The earliest of these were Type Vilar Maior (Brandherm 2007, 39–43), followed by Type Fontanguillère (Matthews

forthcoming), as found together from the Garonne at La Réole, Gironde (Coffyn 1985, figs 35.3, 5) and in the Spanish deposit at Grañón, La Rioja (Fernández and Echevarría 2009). Unlike the Channel core zone, south-west Europe was largely sheltered from direct Central European influence resulting in innovations that drew instead upon established Western European traditions. Of particular significance were parallel- and kite-shaped blades, the latter being those with largely straight blade edges that expand outward to their widest point relatively close to the point, as seen on swords of Type Fontanguillère and Type Évora (Brandherm 2007, nos 25, 27–9). From these Fontanguillère swords also developed the earliest Type Mortlake swords of variant Saint-Denis-de-Pile (Matthews forthcoming), with hilt fragments of both found in the southwest French deposit of the same name from dept Gironde (Coffyn 1985, fig. 34, 12–13). These have often been misidentified as

Northern province (Channel core zone)   /   Southern province (southwest France and northwest Iberia)

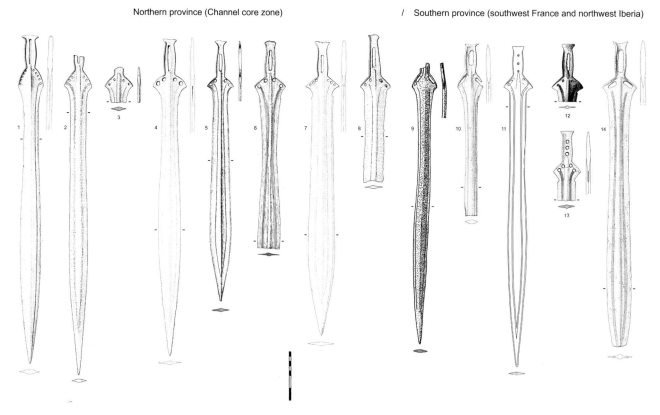

Fig. 5.3. Atlantic swords of the Penard horizon (Ha A1) and Limehouse phase (Ha A2). 1) Barrow, Suffolk; 2) Seine at Corbeil-Essonnes, Essonne; 3) Kerguerou in Rédené, Finistère; 4) River Thames at Battersea, Greater London; 5) Trieux, Cotes d'Armor; 6) Aisne at Pasly, Aisne; 7) River Thames at Brentford, Greater London; 8) Seine at Essonne, Essonne ; 9) Lot at Peyroulie, Sainte-Livrade-surLot, Lot-et-Garonne ; 10) 'prov. Leon'; 11) Dordogne at Condat, Libourne, Gironde; 12) Saint-Denis-de-Pile, Gironde; 13) Saint-Denis-de-Pile, Gironde; 14) Évora, Alto Alentejo. Types: Northern province (Channel core zone). Type Clewer: 1–2; Type Limehouse: 3 (var. Rédené), 4 (var. Yvelines), 5 (var. Trieux); Type Mortlake: 6 (var. Saint-Denis-de-Pile), 7–8 (var. Brière). Southern province (southwest France and northwest Iberia). Type Vilar Maior: 9–10; Type Fontanguillère: 11–12 ; Type Mortlake: 13 (var. Saint-Denis-de-Pile); Type Évora: 14 (nos 1, 4, 17 after Colquhoun and Burgess 1988, nos 93. 102. 128; 2, 8 after Mohen 1977: nos 445. 440; 3 after Briard 1965, Fig. 57, B; 5 after Briard 1977, 60; 6 after Blanchet 1973, no. 7; 9 after Beyneix et al. 1994, Fig. 3,2; 10, 14 after Brandherm 2007, no. 19. 27; 11 after Matthews forthcoming; 12 after Coffyn 1985, Fig. 34,12; 13 after Gaucher and Mohen 1973, Fig. 3, B).

later swords of Type Saint-Nazaire. In a rare occurrence of south to north influence, this early variant of Type Mortlake spread to the Channel core zone. From these developed the northern series of swords with kite-shaped blades such as Type Limehouse, variant Trieux (Matthews forthcoming), and Type Mortlake, variant Brière (Colquhoun and Burgess 1988, 37–8) and Type Teddington (Colquhoun and Burgess 1988, 39). It is the view of this author that it is these swords with parallel- and kite-shaped blades that should be considered the true Atlantic swords of the Limehouse/ Saint-Brieuc-des-Iffs phase, not the Urnfield-influenced swords with leaf-shaped blades.

The most common of these leaf-shaped swords was Type Limehouse, of which there were a number of variants. In southwest France, however, we find only variant Mugdrum (Colquhoun and Burgess 1988, 35–6). Interestingly, these swords are the most widely distributed variant in Britain and the least common in southern England and northern France. At Barrow, Suffolk, a Mugdrum sword was found associated with a sword of Type Clewer (Colquhoun and Burgess 1988, nos 180, 202), the northern equivalent of Type Vilar Maior, suggesting a similarly early date for these Mugdrum swords. Instead, variants Rédené and Yvelines (Matthews forthcoming) are the most common Type Limehouse swords in the Channel core zone but are absent from southwest France. Limehouse swords are equally rare in the Iberian Peninsula with just one example each of variant Rédené and Yvelines (Brandherm 2007, nos 24 and 22 respectively), as well as local copies (nos 23, 32).

Southwest France and the Iberian Peninsula also shared in a number of exclusive types during the subsequent Wilburton-Isleham phase, such as Type Cordeiro (Brandherm 2007, 50–4), which are again absent from the Channel core zone. Here similar sword forms are widely distributed on both sides of the Channel but rare beyond the Loire and are entirely unknown in the Iberian Peninsula.

Connections beyond the Atlantic complex

We have already mentioned that the extent of the Atlantic complex should not be confused with the geography of Atlantic Europe. The complex was restricted in its northern aspect to the Channel regions of England and France – the Channel core zone – and to the south by Atlantic France and the northwest of the Iberian Peninsula. Beyond these northern and southern provinces lay different traditions. Nonetheless, connections abound across the frontiers of the complex within Western Europe and the western Mediterranean.

In the south of the Iberian Peninsula developed a further sword form, Type Huelva (Brandherm 2007, 56–88; Brandherm and Burgess 2008). These have been identified as of Atlantic type but are, in fact, entirely absent from the Atlantic weapon deposits of the Wilburton and Brécy

groups. A number of blade fragments from the deposits at Waldershare, Kent (Dover Museum, Dover, unpublished), and Isleham, Cambridgeshire (Colquhoun and Burgess 1988, pl. 154, 16.21), have been interpreted as coming from these Huelva swords (cf. Brandherm and Burgess 2008, 139). However, there are no end of contemporary French swords of Wilburton/Brécy type that also have similar blade sections (e.g. Guillaumet et al. 1999, fig. 20.2). Moreover, Isleham is not strictly an Atlantic weapon deposit but rather a scrap deposit, containing late types related to the Atlantic Wilburton group and types from the contemporary (non-Atlantic complex) Whittingham-Tarves group, which were more common to northern England and Scotland. There are only two certain Huelva swords in Britain, from Llanddety, Brecon, Powys (Colquhoun and Burgess 1988, no. 674), and in the deposit at Llancarfan, Glamorgan (Gwilt 2005/6). Further fragments suspected of being from Huelva swords also appear in the deposits at Yattenden, Berkshire (Burgess et al. 1972, fig. 18.58), and Stogursey, Somerset (McNeil 1973, fig. 5.66). Whilst these may also be from French Wilburton swords, like Isleham neither is an Atlantic or Wilburton group deposit. Instead, their similarity to Llancarfan and their more westerly distribution in Britain might mean true Huelva sword fragments. This western bias is further emphasised by the occurrence of an unprovenanced Huelva sword from Ireland (Eogan 1965, no. 562). Related Atlantic weapon deposits from France similarly lack certain evidence of Huelva swords, only equivocal blade fragments. The only exception is the deposit from Longueville, Calvados (Verney unpublished; Milcent 2012, pl. 51), which contained two hilt fragments of Huelva swords. However, with its contents dominated by axes Longueville is not a weapon deposit either but is instead similar in character to that of Stogursey and Llancarfan, with which it is also contemporary. The distinction between these deposits is important, as it demonstrates that there were alternative traditions operating outside of the complex within Western Europe.

The absence of Type Huelva swords from the Atlantic weapon deposits raises the question as to what degree they were ever part of this complex. Whether they developed in France or the Iberian Peninsula is still unclear (cf. Brandherm and Burgess 2008, 142; Burgess and O'Connor 2008, 54), though we favour a southern Iberian origin, developing as a consequence of interaction with the western Mediterranean, and spreading northwards. The distribution of early Atlantic swords in the Iberian Peninsula during the Penard horizon and subsequent Limehouse phase is largely concentrated to the north and west (Brandherm 2007, lam. 45–6). Swords of Type Cordeiro, contemporary with the earliest Wilburton group swords of Types Wilburton, Witney and Richmond (Matthews forthcoming; largely equivalent to variants A, C and D in the scheme of Colquhoun and Burgess 1988), also have a similar distribution in the peninsula (Brandherm 2007, lam. 46). That this is an Atlantic type is supported by the occurrence of a Cordeiro sword in a small but not atypical Atlantic weapon deposit at San Esteban, Ribas del Sil, Orense, Spain (Brandherm 2007, no. 39, lam. 54, B), which included a hollow bladed pegged spearhead common to the Wilburton group. Huelva swords, however, are concentrated almost entirely in the south (lam. 47).

One possible explanation for the absence of Type Huelva swords from these Atlantic weapon deposits is their being later, contemporary with the early part of the Ewart Park phase (Burgess 2012a, 240–1; Milcent 2012, 123–31). However, when Huelva swords were first identified they were aligned with Ha B1 and the Wilburton horizon (e.g. Burgess 1991, 36, 38; Burgess and O'Connor 2004, 192), and there remains good reason to maintain this date. For example, whilst the Huelva assemblage was likely deposited late in the phase, contemporary with the Isleham horizon, it contains types common to the preceding Wilburton horizon, such as Type Cordeiro swords (Brandherm 2007, no. 37). In Iberia this is contemporary with the northern Spanish deposit from Hío, Cangas de Morrazo, Pontevedra (Coffyn 1985, pls lx–lxi), which contained bronze types common to the Atlantic weapon deposits of the Wilburton/Brécy groups, as well as a Huelva sword of variant Marmolejo. Whilst an internal chronology has been difficult to establish for the different Huelva variants (Brandherm and Moskal-del Hoyo 2010, 434–6), swords of variant Marmolejo do share a number of morphological traits with those of Type Cordeiro. Despite the chronological changes in the alignment of the Saint-Brieuc-des-Iffs and Wilburton groups described above, there is no reason not to align Huelva swords and the Hío phase with Ha B1 and the Wilburton/Brécy groups (cf. Burgess 2012b, 148).

Originally, these Type Huelva swords were conceived of as the southern equivalent of the Atlantic swords of Type Saint-Nazaire (Burgess 1991, 38–9; Burgess and O'Connor 2004, 192) which, with the exception of their narrow-shouldered Moncontour variant, are largely confined to the Channel core zone. This relationship has been subsequently modified with the identification of Huelva swords in France and Britain (Burgess and O'Connor 2008, 52). However, a relationship between Huelva and Saint-Nazaire swords is not without merit, particularly as the latter also have a rather ambiguous relationship to the Atlantic complex and its weapon deposits. Burgess and O'Connor (2008, 47) have noted the absence of the latter swords from French deposits of this phase, which was explained as a consequence of the majority being deposited earlier in the phase. Many of these deposits now belong to the preceding Limehouse/Saint-Brieuc-des-Iffs phase, as described above. However, Saint-Nazaire swords remain absent even from those deposits of the Brécy group. In Britain, the situation is much the same: there are no certain Saint-Nazaire

swords found in any Wilburton group deposit! The blade fragments from the deposits at Waldershare and Bentley I, Hampshire (Lawson 1999, 102–3, fig. 11, 7), assumed to be from Saint-Nazaire swords, could equally belong to any number of decorated Limehouse or Wilburton group types with similar decoration. At Wicken Fen, Cambridgeshire, a hilt fragment (Colquhoun and Burgess 1988, no. 251) was found associated with fragments of ferrule and chape, as well as several blade fragments but all are too fragmentary to tell if they are Wilburton or Whittingham-Tarves types, whilst the complete spearhead could belong to either. Only at Isleham have unequivocal Saint-Nazaire swords (Colquhoun and Burgess 1988, nos 253, 254) been found alongside Wilburton types. But as already noted Isleham is neither a typical Atlantic nor Wilburton group deposit. This latter point is significant as Saint-Nazaire swords are known instead from several deposits where Ewart Park swords, characteristic of the contemporary Whittingham-Tarves group, are found, such as the deposits at Blackmoor, Hampshire (Colquhoun 1979, fig. 4.5, 94) and High Easter, Essex (Cuddeford and Sealey 2000, fig. 6, no. 36). There is only a single French association, from the Seine at Paris (Gaucher 1981, fig. 20), which was associated with a Huelva sword. Like the latter then, Saint-Nazaire swords stand somewhat apart from the Atlantic complex of this phase, contemporary with the later Isleham horizon.

In Britain the Atlantic complex appears not to have extended much beyond southern England, where other traditions lay. Here weapon deposits are also found (Fig. 5.4), containing swords and spearheads, and their accoutrements but their Atlantic swords having been replaced by those of early Ewart Park type (Burgess 1974, 211; Coombs 1975, 54, fig. 6). In the north, these weapon deposits represent the Whittingham-Tarves group, and its southern aspect by deposits such as Blackmoor. Understanding the relationship of the latter to the Wilburton group has always proved somewhat problematic, given their similar contents but containing instead Ewart Park swords. It has long been suspected that these swords developed first in northern Britain (cf. Brown 1982, 29; Colquhoun and Burgess 1988, 68; Needham 1990, 265–6), contemporary with the Wilburton group. As a consequence, the southern deposits such as Blackmoor are largely late in the Wilburton-Isleham phase, its swords hybrid between the two traditions. The contents of the Blackmoor deposit can no longer, therefore, be considered the earliest representatives of the Ewart Park type, nor Wilburton their ultimate ancestor. This fusion of traditions can also be seen in the contemporary clay sword moulds deposited on the site at Springfield Lyons, Essex (Needham and Bridgford 2013, 57–9). The entire Ewart Park series now needs to be looked at afresh and their development considered perhaps in terms of derivation from swords distributed to the north and west during the Limehouse phase.

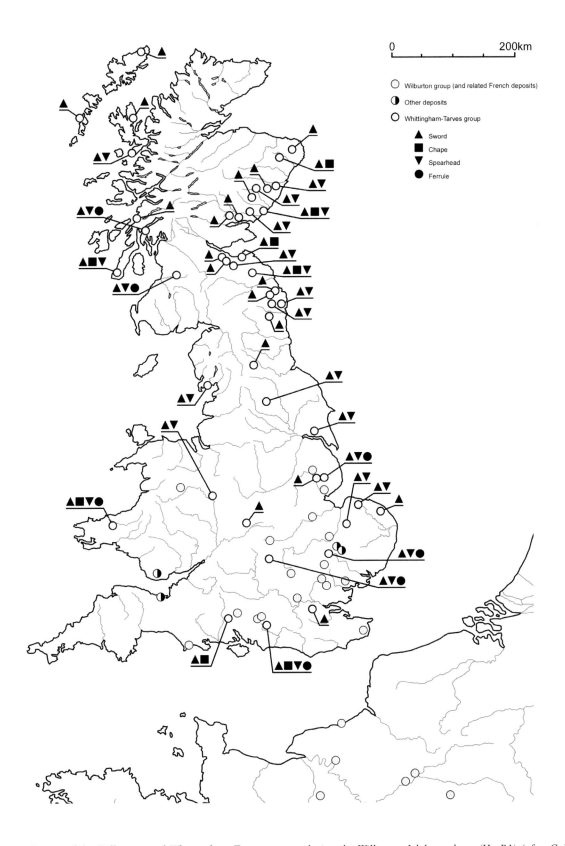

Fig. 5.4. Distribution of the Wilburton and Whittingham-Tarves groups during the Wilburton-Isleham phase (Ha B1) (after Colquhoun and Burgess 1988; Coombs 1988; Matthews forthcoming).

There are four such Atlantic swords of this Limehouse phase in Ireland (Eogan 1965, nos 24, 27, 28, 31), where their role was filled instead by a developed form of Type Ballintober with extended tang and primitive ricasso notches (Matthews 2011a, 89–90). The late date for these is demonstrated by its occurrence in the deposit at Kerguerou in Rédené, Finistère (Briard 1965, fig. 57.B), alongside a Type Limehouse sword. The remaining Class 2 Irish swords (Eogan 1965, 28–32) are instead earlier Appleby-Penard swords. During the subsequent Wilburton-Isleham phase, there are similarly few Atlantic swords, with just four of the 20 Class 3 swords being of Wilburton types (Eogan 1965, nos 48, 50, 60, 61), the rest being instead early Ewart Park forms. Similarly, few of the bronze types that go to make up the southern English Limehouse or Wilburton-Isleham

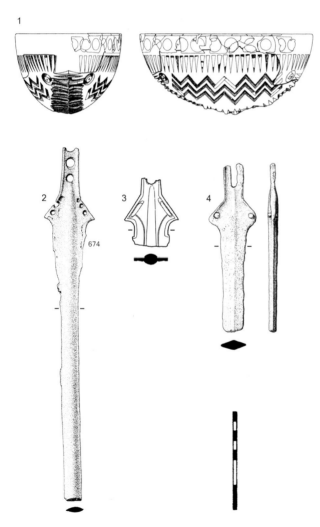

Fig. 5.5. Atlantic connections in Wales during the Wilburton-Isleham phase (Ha B1). 1. Caergwrle, Flintshire; 2. Llanddety, Brecon, Powys; 3. Llancarfan, Vale of Glamorgan; 4, St Mary Hill, Glamorganshire (no. 1 after Savory 1980, Fig. 10; 2 after Colquhoun and Burgess 1988, no. 674; 3 after Matthews forthcoming; 4 after Green 1985, Fig. 2).

phases are to be found in Ireland. There is no evidence of Limehouse phase types in Wales, which might suggest that the Irish swords came from northwest France, given the Rédené connection. The subsequent phase is rather better represented (Fig. 5.5), though the Wilburton group in Wales largely comprises the deposit at Guilsfield, ct. Powys (Savory 1965), as well as single sword of Type Twickenham from St Mary Hill, ct. Glamorganshire (Green 1985, 285, fig. 2). Otherwise the connections of the western seaways, distinct from those of the Channel core zone, are again prevalent, such as in the only certain British examples of Type Huelva swords at Llancarfan and Llanddety, and the remarkable bowl from Caergwrle, ct. Flintshire (Savory 1980, 69–70, fig. 10), which has been suggested to be a boat-model of southern Iberian or western Mediterranean derivation (Hawkes 1969, 191, fig. 2). Beyond the Channel core zone, peripheral connections with Belgium and the Netherlands are also to be found. Following on from the small number of Hayling Island-Taunton and Appleby-Penard phase rapiers (e.g. Warmenbol 1986), a few French Atlantic swords of the Limehouse and Wilburton-Isleham phases also reached the Low Countries (e.g. Desittere 1976, fig. 5, 1–2; Warmenbol 2009, figs 1–2). This Atlantic influence was also found as far afield as Sardinia in the western Mediterranean, where a number of swords with kite-shaped blades have been found (Burgess and O'Connor 2004, 195). The occurrence of these Atlantic weapons (Fig. 5.6) is evidence for important connections during this period but in none of these lands can we truly talk of an Atlantic complex.

Conclusion: Atlantic maritories

On the basis of the distribution of sword types during late Ha A1 to Ha B1, the Atlantic complex can be divided into two distinct but related provinces. The northern Atlantic province is represented by the Channel core zone, consisting of southeast England and north and northwest France. South of the Loire lay the southern Atlantic province, consisting of southwest France and the northwest of the Iberian Peninsula. During the formative stages of the complex in the Hayling Island-Taunton phase, the weapon types found distributed across these provinces are identical. This was likely as a consequence of their being exports from the Channel core zone. With the transition to the Appleby horizon, a significant degree of regionalism was beginning to emerge in weapon types within the Channel core zone, resulting in each having a much more restricted distribution. As a consequence, the Iberian Peninsula and south-west France drew more directly on those traditions found more commonly on the French side of the Channel, such as early Type Rosnoën rapiers, than those found in southern England, such as Type Appleby rapiers. Despite this regionalism within the Channel core zone, the weapons found to the south should still be considered imports. During the Penard horizon this southern province developed a precocious tradition in regional sword types, represented first by Type Vilar Maior, and at the transition to the subsequent Limehouse phase by swords of Type Fontanguillère and Type Évora. None of these types were distributed north of the Loire. In the Channel core zone, we find instead swords of Type Clewer during the Penard horizon and during the subsequent phase the eponymous swords of Type Limehouse and its variants. The latter occur in considerable number in the north but are actually quite rare south of the Loire, where they are replaced by these Type Fontanguillère and Type Évora swords. Swords of Type Mortlake are one of the few Limehouse phase weapons with a wide distribution, with variant Saint-Denis-de-Pile possibly developing earliest in the south and spreading northwards where it influenced the development of the northern Mortlake swords of variant Brière, Type Teddington and Type Limehouse, variant Trieux.

Despite the central role the Channel core zone played in initiating the Atlantic weapons complex, in a rare reversal of influence, south-west sword traditions had a considerable impact on the north. Compared to south-west France and Iberia, leaf-shape blades had predominated on late Penard and early Limehouse swords in the Channel core zone. The re-introduction of parallel-sided and kite-shape blades during the late Limehouse phase was of considerable significance, as can be seen in the greater variety of blade shapes seen on swords of Wilburton form during the subsequent phase. Nonetheless, these Wilburton swords remain largely exclusive to the Channel core zone. Instead, the south-west and Iberia have swords of Type Cordeiro, and finally Type Huelva, which were to so influence French traditions during the subsequent phase.

The earliest grip-tang swords were ultimately based upon imported early Urnfield sword traditions. However, such swords are rare in south-west France and the Iberian

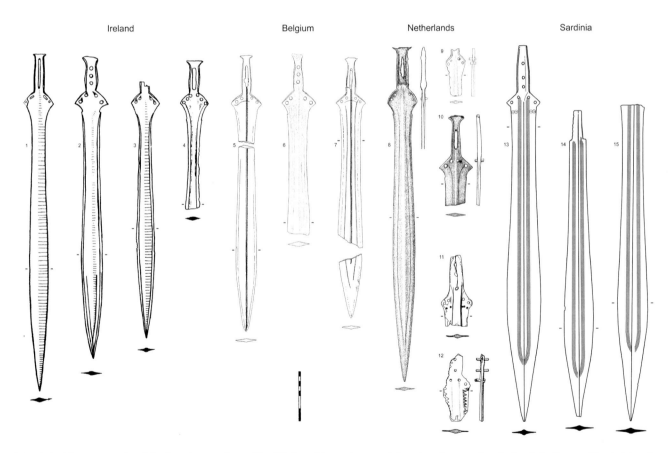

Fig. 5.6. Atlantic swords of the Limehouse phase (Ha A2) found in regions peripheral to the complex. Ireland: 1. Toome, Co. Antrim; 2. Athy, Co. Kildare; 3. Barrowford, Co. Kildare; 4. 'Ireland'. Belgium: 5. Zele, East Flanders; 6. Mechelen, Antwerp; 7. Schoonaarde, East Flanders; Netherlands: 8. 'Noord-Brabant'; 9. Neer, Limburg; 10. Near Cuijk, Noord-Brabant. Sardinia: 11. Bolotana, Nuoro; 12. Su Tempiesu, Orune, Nuoro; 13-5. Siniscola, Nuoro. Types: Type Limehouse: 1–5, 8. 9; Type Mortlake: 6 (var. Saint-Denis-de-Pile), 7, 10 (var. Brière); Type Siniscola: 11–15 (nos 1–4 after Eogan 1965, nos 24. 27. 28. 31; 5, 7 after Warmenbol 2009, figs 1–2; 6 after Desittere 1976, Fig. 5, 1; 8–10, courtesy Groningen Institute of Archaeology; 13–15, S. Matthews; 11–2 after Lo Schiavo 1991, Fig. 4, 3–4).

Peninsula (Brun and Mordant 1988, types 27, 28, 30; Brandherm 2007, lam. 45). Whilst this might suggest that the tradition in this area was instead derived second-hand from the Channel core zone, these southern Atlantic traditions appear equally early as their northern counterparts. Moreover, the typological difference of these southern types also rules out importation from the north. The distribution of regional types and their contemporaneous occurrence suggests instead the development of an inter-regional industry in Atlantic weapon types. The ultimate purpose of their production – beyond their crude function as weapons – was likely as elite status markers for familial alliance, helping to bind together ultimately distinct communities (Rowlands 1980, 37–38), as represented by the regional palstave traditions of the Atlantic and Channel regions (e.g. Savory 1949, 134; O'Connor 1980, 95–8, 132–4).

Whilst the Early Bronze Age maritory of the Channel region developed into a fuller Channel Bronze Age community from the Hayling Island-Taunton phase onward (cf. Needham 2006, 81; 2009, 33), there was clearly not a synchronous development throughout the territory that eventually came to constitute the Atlantic complex. Later Bronze Age relations within the Channel core zone are too stable and complex for them to still be described in terms of a maritory (Needham 2009, 15–20). The connections between the northwest of the Iberian Peninsula and south-west France might be considered similarly meaningful. However, the very specific set of elite-driven craft relationships that constituted the Atlantic complex, concerned as they were almost entirely with weapons and their accoutrements, during the later Bronze Age were clearly of the same form as those of the Channel region during the Early Bronze Age, underwritten by some form of elite community of Atlantic sea peoples.

Acknowledgements
This paper is in part based on my doctoral research, which was generously funded by an Ubbo Emmius scholarship from the University of Groningen and supported by the Groningen Institute of Archaeology. Studies of this scale are only ever achievable through the support of colleagues, and in this respect I have been most fortunate, and my thanks must go to Muriel Mélin, Muriel Fily, Dirk Brandherm, Richard Davis, Marion Uckelmann, John Smythe and Claudia Czert. I am most grateful to Anne Lehoërff for inviting me to speak at the conference in Boulogne-sur-Mer. Pierre-Yves Milcent was kind enough to provide a copy of his significant new book on the French Bronze Age and Colin Burgess generously shared his thoughts on Late Bronze Age chronology. Particular thanks must go to Stuart Needham and Sylvie Boulud-Gazo for thoroughly reviewing the paper and suggesting corrections. I alone, however, must take responsibility for the above.

Bibliography

Almagro Basch, M. (1958) Depósito de la Ría de Huelva. *Inventaria Archaeologica España* 1–4, E. 1.

Beyneix, A., Garnier, J.-F. and Pons, J. (1994) Les épées du Bronze moyen et final draguées dans le cours inférieur du Lot (Lot-Garonne). *Bulletin de la Société préhistorique française* 91 (3), 191–5.

Blanchet, J.-C. (1973) Objets de l'âge du Bronze dans des collections privées à Compiègne (Oise). *Revue Archéologique de l'Oise* 3, 45–57.

Blanchet, J.-C. (1984) *Les premiers métallurgistes en Picardie et dans le Nord de la France*. Mémoires de la Société préhistorique française, t.17. Paris, Société préhistorique française.

Brandherm, D. (2007) *Las Espadas del Bronze Final en la Península Ibérica y Baleares*, Prähistorische Bronzefunde IV, 16. Stuttgart, Franz Steiner

Brandherm, D. and Burgess, C. (2008) Carp's-tongue problems. In F. Verse, B. Knoche, J. Graefe, M. Hohlbein, K. Schierhold, S. Siemann, M. Uckelmann and G. Woltermann (eds), *Durch die Zeiten ... Festschrift für Albrecht Jockenhövel zum 65. Geburtstag*, 133–68. Internationale Archäologie, Studia honoraria 28. Rahden/Westfahlen, Marie Leidorf.

Brandherm, D. and Moskal-del Hoyo, M. (2010) Las espadas en lengua de carpa: aspectos morfológicos, metalúrgicos y culturales. *Trabajos de Prehistoria* 67, 431–456.

Briard, J. (1965) *Les dépôts bretons et l'Âge du Bronze atlantique*. Rennes, Travaux du laboratoire 'Anthropologie – Préhistoire – Protohistoire – Quaternaire Armoricains', Université de Rennes.

Briard, J. (1977) Épées de l'Âge du Bronze draguées dans le Trieux (Côtes-du-Nord). *Dossiers du Centre Régional Archéologique d'Alet, Saint-Malo* 5, 59–64. 15

Briard, J. and Onnée, Y. (1972) *Le dépôt du Bronze final de Saint-Brieuc-des-Iffs (I et V)*. Rennes, Travaux du laboratoire 'Anthropologie – Préhistoire – Protohistoire – Quaternaire Armoricains', Université de Rennes.

Brown, M. A. (1982) Swords and sequence in the British Bronze Age. *Archaeologia* 107, 1–42.

Brun, P. (1991) Le Bronze atlantique et ses subdivisions culturelles: essai de définition. In C. Chevillot and A. Coffyn (eds) *L'âge du Bronze atlantique: ses faciès, de l'Écosse à l'Andalousie et leurs relations avec le Bronze continental et la Méditerranée. Actes du 1er Colloque du Parc Archéologique de Beynac*, 11–24. Beynac-et-Cazenac, Association des Musées du Sarladais.

Brun, P. and Mordant, C. (eds) (1988) *Le groupe Rhin-Suisse-France orientale et la notion de civilisation des Champs d'Urnes: Actes du Colloque de Nemours 1986*, Mémoires du Musée de préhistoire d'Île-de- France 1. Nemours, Association pour la promotion de la recherche archéologique

Burgess, C. (1968a) The Later Bronze Age in the British Isles and north-western France. *Archaeological Journal* 125, 1–45.

Burgess, C. (1968b) *Bronze Age Metalwork in Northern England, c. 1000 to 700 BC*. Newcastle, Oriel Press.

Burgess, C. (1974) The Bronze Age. In C. Renfrew (ed) *British Prehistory: A New Outline*, 165–232, 291–329. London, Duckworth,

Burgess, C. (1979) A find from Boyton, Suffolk, and the end of the Bronze Age in Britain and Ireland. In C. Burgess and D. Coombs (eds) *Bronze Age Hoards: Some Finds Old and*

New, 269–83, British Archaeological Report 67. Oxford, British Archaeological Reports

Burgess, C. (1991) The East and the west: Mediterranean influence in the Atlantic world in the later Bronze Age, *c* 1500–700 BC. In C. Chevillot and A. Coffyn (eds) *L'âge du Bronze atlantique: ses faciès, de l'Écosse à l'Andalousie et leurs relations avec le Bronze continental et la Méditerranée*. Actes du 1er Colloque du Parc Archéologique de Beynac, 25–45. Beynac-et-Cazenac, Association des Musées du Sarladais.

Burgess, C. (1996) 'Urns', culture du Wessex et la transition Bronze ancien – Bronze moyen en Grande Bretagne. In C. Mordant and O. Gaiffe (eds) *Cultures et sociétés du Bronze Ancien en Europe*. Actes du 117ième Congrès National des Sociétés Savantes, Clermont-Ferrand, 1992, 605–621. Paris, Éditions du C. T. H. S.

Burgess, C. (2012a) South Welsh socketed axes and other carp's tongue conundrums. In W. J. Britnell and B. Silvester (eds) *Reflections on the Past. Essays in Honour of Frances Lynch*, 237–253. Welshpool, Cambrian Archaeological Association.

Burgess, C. (2012b) Alignments: Revising the Atlantic Late Bronze Age sequence. *Archaeological Journal* 169, 127–158.

Burgess, C. and Gerloff, S. (1981) *The Dirks and Rapiers of Great Britain and Ireland, Prähistorische Bronzefunde* IV, 7. Munich, Beck. 16

Burgess, C. and O'Connor, B. (2004) Bronze Age rotary spits: finds old and new, some false, some true. In H. Roche, E. Grogan, J. Bradley, J. Coles and B. Raftery (eds) *From Megaliths to Metals: Essays in Honour of George Eogan*, 184–199. Oxford, Oxbow Books.

Burgess, C. and O'Connor, B. (2008) Iberia, the Atlantic Bronze Age and the Mediterranean. In S. Celestino, N. Rafel and X.-L. Armada (eds) *Contacto Cultural Entre el Mediterráneo y el Atlántico (Siglos XII–VIII ane), 41–58*. Madrid, C. S. I. C.

Burgess, C., Coombs D. and Davis D. G. (1972) The Broadward Complex and barbed spearheads. In F. Lynch and C. Burgess (eds) *Prehistoric Man in Wales and the West*, 211–283. Bath, Adams and Dart.

Coffyn, A. (1985) *Le Bronze final atlantique dans la péninsule Ibérique*. Paris, Publications du Centre Pierre.

Colquhoun, I. A. (1979) The Late Bronze Age hoard from Blackmoor, Hampshire. In C. Burgess and D. Coombs (eds) *Bronze Age Hoards: Some Finds Old and New, 99–115*. British Archaeological Report 67. Oxford, British Archaeological Reports.

Colquhoun, I. and Burgess, C. (1988) *The Swords of Britain*, Prähistorische Bronzefunde IV, 5. Munich, Beck

Coombs, D. (1975) Bronze Age weapon hoards in Britain. *Archaeologia Atlantica* 1, 49–81.

Coombs, D. (1988) The Wilburton Complex and Bronze Final II in Atlantic Europe. In P. Brun and C. Mordant (eds) *Le groupe Rhin-Suisse-France orientale et la notion de civilisation des Champs d'Urnes: Actes du Colloque de Nemours 1986, 575–81*. Mémoires du Musée de préhistoire d'Île-de-France 1. Nemours, Association pour la promotion de la recherche archéologique

Cuddeford, M. J. and Sealey, P. R. (2000) A late Bronze Age hoard from High Easter. *Essex Archaeology and History* 31, 1–17.

Davey, P. J. (1973) Bronze Age metalwork from Lincolnshire, *Archaeologia* 104, 51–127.

Desittere, M. (1976) Autochtones et immigrants en Belgique et dans le Sud des Pays-Bas au Bronze final. In S. J. De Laet (ed) *Acculturation and Continuity in Atlantic Europe, mainly during the Neolithic period and the Bronze Age: Papers presented at the IV Atlantic Colloquium, Ghent*, 77–94. Brugge, De Tempel.

Eogan, G. (1965) *Catalogue of Irish Bronze Swords*. Dublin, National Museum of Ireland.

Eogan, G. (1994) *The Accomplished Art: Gold and Gold-working in Britain and Ireland during the Bronze Age (c. 2300–650 BC)*, Monograph 42. Oxford, Oxford University Committee for Archaeology.

Evans, J. (1884) On a hoard of bronze objects found in Wilburton Fen, near Ely. *Archaeologia* 48, 106–114.

Fernández, C. A. and Echevarría, J. J. (2009) El Depósito de armas del Bronce Final de 'Los Cascajos', Grañón, (La Rioja). *Gladius* 29, 7–38.

Gaucher, G. (1981) *Sites et cultures de l'Âge du Bronze dans le Bassin Parisien*. Paris, C. N. R. S.

Gaucher, G. and Mohen, J.-P. (1972) *Typologie des objets de l'âge du Bronze en France. Fascicule I: épées*. Paris, Société préhistorique française.

Gerloff, S. (2007) Reinecke's ABC and the chronology of the British Bronze Age. In C. Burgess, P. Topping and F. Lynch (eds) *Beyond Stonehenge: Essays on the Bronze Age in Honour of Colin Burgess, 117–61*. Oxford, Oxbow Books.

Gerloff, S. (2010) *Atlantic Cauldrons and Buckets of the Late Bronze Age and Early Iron Ages in Western Europe*. Prähistorische Bronzefunde II, 18. Stuttgart, Franz Steiner.

Green, H. S. (1985) Four Bronze Age sword-finds from Wales. *Bulletin of the Board of Celtic Studies* 32, 3, 283–7.

Guillaumet, J.-P., Blanchet, J.-C., Bouet-Langlois, B., Boulud, S., Roussot-Larroque, J. and Verney, A. (1999) La collection Henri Lamarre (1904–1982). *Antiquités Nationales* 31, 45–115.

Gwilt, A. (2005/06) Llancarfan, Vale of Glamorgan: Late Bronze Age hoard. *Treasure Annual Report 2005/6*, 221.

Harrison, R. J. (2004). *Symbols and Warriors: Images of the European Bronze Age*. Bristol, Western Academic Press.

Hawkes, C. F. C. (1969) Las relaciones Atlanticas del mundo Tartesico. In M. De Motes(ed.) *Tartessos y sus Problemas: V Symposium International de Prehistoria Peninsular*, 185–197. Barcelona, Instituto de Arqueologia.

Hencken, H. (1971) *The Earliest European Helmets. Bulletin of the American School of Prehistoric Research 28*. Cambridge MA, Peabody Museum.

Lawson, A. J. (1999) The Bronze Age hoards of Hampshire. In A. F. Harding (ed.) *Experiment and Design: Archaeological Studies in Honour of John Coles*, 94–107. Oxford, Oxbow Books.

Lo Schiavo, F. (1991) La Sardaigne et ses relations avec le Bronze Final atlantique. In C. Chevillot and A. Coffyn (eds) *L'âge du Bronze atlantique: ses faciès, de l'Écosse à l'Andalousie et leurs relations avec le Bronze continental et la Méditerranée. Actes du 1er Colloque du Parc Archéologique de Beynac*. 213–226. Beynac-et-Cazenac, Association des Musées du Sarladais.

Matthews, S. (2010) Notes on a typological scheme for Atlantic Rapiers in France. *Bulletin de l'Association pour la Promotion des Recherches sur l'Âge du Bronze* 7, 82–85.

Matthews, S. (2011a) Chelsea and Ballintober swords: Typology, chronology and use. In M. Uckelmann and M. Mödlinger (eds)

Bronze Age Warfare: Manufacture and Use of Weaponry, 85–106, British Archaeological Report S2255. Oxford, Archaeopress.

Matthews, S. (2011b) Wrapping bronzes: Pottery encased metalwork in southern England and northern France during the Late Bronze Age. *Bulletin de l'Association pour la Promotion des Recherches sur l'Âge du Bronze.* 8, 67–69.

Matthews, S. forthcoming. *Weapons of the West: The Techniques and Technology of Bronze Age Warcraft in Northwest Europe, c. 1400–950 BC.* PhD thesis, University of Groningen, Groningen.

McNeil, R. (1973) A report on the Bronze Age hoard from Wick Park, Stogursey, Somerset. *Proceedings of the Somerset Archaeological and Natural History Society* 117, 47–64.

Milcent, P.-Y. (2012) *Le temps des élites en Gaule atlantique.* Rennes, Presses Universitaire de Rennes.

Mohen, J.-P. (1977) *L'âge du Bronze dans la région de Paris: Catalogue synthétique des collections conservées au Musée des Antiquités Nationales.* Paris, Musée des Antiquités Nationales.

Needham, S. (1990) The Penard-Wilburton succession: new metalwork finds from Croxton (Norfolk) and Thirsk (Yorkshire). *Antiquaries Journal* 70 (2), 253–270.

Needham, S. (2003) Mickleham, Surrey: Late Bronze Age base-metal hoard. In A. Gannon, L. Voden-Decker and R. Bland (eds) *Treasure Annual Report 2003, 21–2,* 198. London, D. C. M. S.

Needham, S. (2006) Chapter 8: Networks of contact, exchange and meaning; the beginnings of the Channel Bronze Age. In S. Needham, K. Parfitt and G. Varndell (eds) *The Ringlemere Cup: Precious Cups and the Beginning of the Channel Bronze Age, 75–81, Research Publication 163.* London, British Museum.

Needham, S. (2009) Encompassing the sea: 'Maritories' and Bronze Age maritime interactions. In P. Clark (ed.) *Bronze Age Connections: Cultural Contact in Prehistoric Europe, 12–37.* Oxford, Oxbow Books.

Needham, S. and Bowman, S. (2005) Flesh-hooks, technological complexity and the Atlantic Bronze Age feasting complex. *European Journal of Archaeology* 8, 2, 93–136.

Needham, S., Bronk Ramsey, C., Coombs, D., Cartwright, C. and Pettitt, P. (1997) An independent chronology for British Bronze Age metalwork: the results of the Oxford radiocarbon accelerator programme. *Archaeological Journal* 154, 55–107.

O'Connor, B. (1980) *Cross-Channel Relations in the Later Bronze Age: Relations between Britain, North- Eastern France, and the Low Countries during the Later Bronze Age and the Early Iron Age, with Particular Reference to the Metalwork,* British Archaeological Reports S91. Oxford, British Archaeological Reports.

Qulliec, B. (2007) *L'épée atlantique: échanges et prestige au Bronze final.* Paris, Mémoire de la Société Préhistorique Française n°XLII.

Rohl, B. and Needham, S. (1998) *The Circulation of Metal in the British Bronze Age: the Application of Lead Isotope Analysis,* Occasional Paper 102. London, British Museum.

Rowlands, M. (1980) Kinship, alliance and exchange in the European Bronze Age. In J. Barrett and R. Bradley (eds) *Settlement and Society in the British Later Bronze Age, 15–55.* British Archaeological Report 83. Oxford, British Archaeological Reports.

Savory, H. N. (1949) The Atlantic Bronze Age in south-west Europe. *Proceedings of the Prehistoric Society* 15, 128–155.

Savory, H. N. (1958) The Late Bronze Age in Wales. *Archaeologia Cambrensis* 107, 3–63.

Savory, H. (1965) The Guilsfield hoard. *Bulletin of the Board of Celtic Studies* 21, 2.

Savory, H. (1980) *Guide Catalogue of the Bronze Age Collections.* Cardiff, National Museum of Wales.

Sperber, L. (2011) Bronzene Schutzwaffen in Gräbern der Urnenfelderkultur: Beinschienen- und helm (?) fragmente aus dem Gräberfeld Volders in Nordtirol. *Bayerische Vorgeschichtsblätter* 76, 5–45.

Uckelmann, M. (2012) *Die Schilde der Bronzezeit in Nord-, West- und Zentraleuropa.* Prähistorische Bronzefunde IV, 16. Stuttgart, Franz Steiner.

Warmenbol, E. (1986) British rapiers with trapezoidal butt found in Belgium. *Proceedings of the Prehistoric Society* 52, 153–8.

Warmenbol, E. (2009) À propos des épées atlantiques trouvées en Belgique (Étape 2 du Bronze Final). *Lunula* XVII, 23–26.

Williams, D. (2008) A Late Bronze Age hoard from Norbury Park, Mickleham. *Surrey Archaeological Collections* 94, 293–301.

York, J. (2002) The life cycle of Bronze Age metalwork from the Thames. *Oxford Journal of Archaeology* 21, 1 77–92.

6

Rythmes et contours de la géographie culturelle sur le littoral de la Manche entre le IIIe et le début du Ier millénaire[1]

Cyril Marcigny, Jean Bourgeois et Marc Talon

Abstract

In northern France, from Brittany to Flanders, as well as in England or in Belgian Flanders, information about the landscape and territories in the Bronze Age has much improved in the last 20 years. This is mainly due to the development of preventive or rescue archaeology and to the use of new tools for spatial analysis. Very quickly, convergences between France and the neighbouring countries appeared, especially with southeast England and Belgian Flanders. This enabled us to open up our view and to define a vast, but changing, technocultural group called Manche-Mer du Nord (MMN). The history of this group and its changing borders are revealed by analysis of the material culture, from artefacts (ceramics, lithics, metal objects) to domestic and funeral contexts, even through the choices made for using and organising rural space (agricultural system and structures). Beginning from a cultural geography, as defined by Pierre Vidal de la Blache and later Marc Bloch, and adding the integration of other parameters, such as the social and ideological structure of a culture, it is possible to define homogeneous territories. This Manche-Mer du Nord territory built on and developed from the remnants of the great Early Bronze Age cultures, such as the Wessex culture, the Armorican or the Hilversum culture, all cultures that seem to vanish in the 17th–16th centuries BC. In the 11th and 10th centuries, this territory seems to be undermined, especially in its agricultural system, most probably due to pressure from groups coming from the north-alpine complex.

Keywords: Cultural geography, Bronze Age, cross-Channel contact, material culture.

Résumé

Dans le Nord de la France, de la Bretagne aux Flandres françaises, la connaissance des territoires de l'Âge du bronze a été grandement modifiée ces vingt dernières années avec le développement de l'archéologie préventive et l'utilisation de nouveaux outils de modélisation spatiale. Très rapidement des points de convergences avec les pays limitrophes, en particulier le sud de l'Angleterre et les Flandres belges, ont permis d'élargir notre focale et de définir un vaste groupe techno-culturel aux contours mouvants dénommé Manche-Mer-du-Nord (MMN).

L'histoire de ce groupe et de ces limites peut être cernée à travers l'analyse de la culture matérielle dans son acceptation la plus large, des mobiliers – céramiques, lithiques, métalliques – aux contextes domestiques et funéraires, en passant par les choix opérés par ces sociétés en matière d'utilisation de l'espace rural (choix en matière d'agrosystème et de structure agraire). Le passage de cette géographie culturelle, chère à Paul Vidal de la Blache puis Marc Bloch, à l'intégration d'autres facteurs comme les composantes sociales et idéologiques de la culture permet aujourd'hui véritablement de parler d'un territoire homogène.

Celui-ci s'épanouirait sur les cendres des grandes cultures du Bronze ancien comme la culture du Wessex ou celle des tumulus armoricains qui semblent péricliter au cours des XXVIIe–XXVIe siècles avant notre ère. Au cours du Bronze moyen et du début du Bronze final, ce territoire est florissant et a une production agricole et métallurgique très dynamique qui participe au renforcement de la cohésion sociale. Ce n'est qu'au cours des XIe–Xe siècles que le territoire est ébranlé dans ces fondements, en particulier dans son système de production agricole, sûrement sous la poussée des groupes issus du complexe nord-alpin.

Mots-clés: Géographie culturelle, Âge du bronze, contact transmanche, culture matérielle.

Introduction

Le développement des recherches archéologiques au XXe siècle et des interprétations historiques qui en découlent, entachées de présupposés sur le dynamisme d'un monde continental (centre européen) élément moteur de l'Âge du bronze face à un monde atlantique (sur les bords de la Manche, de la mer du Nord ou de l'Atlantique) qui participerait moins aux innovations culturelles, sociétales et politique du IIe millénaire, a durablement grevé notre analyse de la protohistoire ancienne des rivages de la Manche et de la mer du Nord. Ce point de vue, très largement tributaire de théories élaborées dans les années 40 et 50, a durant près d'un demi-siècle, freiné la lecture et l'analyse de la géographie culturelle et des mouvements socio-économiques qui ont sous-tendu l'histoire de cette vaste région dont nous ne verrons ici que la partie septentrionale: dans l'ouest et le nord de la France (région Bretagne, Normandie, Picardie et Nord-Pas-de-Calais), dans le sud de la Grande-Bretagne et en Belgique (Fig. 6.1).

Le renouvellement de la documentation archéologique, depuis la fin du XXe et le début du XXIe siècle, pour une large part lié au développement de l'archéologie préventive (Carozza *et al.* 2009 ; Carozza et Marcigny 2007), offre une opportunité sans précédent de tenter une lecture de la configuration géopolitique des régions bordant le littoral de la Manche et de la mer du Nord entre la fin du IIIe millénaire et le début de l'Âge du fer. À partir de ces nouveaux matériaux de recherche et en les examinant sous les angles des processus de transmission des idées ou des savoirs, de construction des identités et de l'établissement de normes culturelles, il est possible de proposer une lecture dynamique des différents groupes qui ont occupé ce secteur.

Créer un outil d'analyse commun

En préalable à ce travail, il a été nécessaire d'établir un langage chronologique et archéologique commun entre les différents chercheurs regroupés autour de cette restitution historique. Il a donc été décidé de créer dans un premier temps un canevas chronologique faisant fi des découpages chronoculturels internes à chaque région au profit d'un séquençage, certes moins fin, en cinq séquences de 300 à 350 ans (soit de 12 à 14 générations). Ce séquençage, qui

peut paraître au premier abord bien réducteur, repose sur une précédente périodisation proposée dans l'ouest de la France à partir de l'étude croisée de différentes variables, indicateurs archéologiques et environnementaux (Marcigny 2009 a) dont l'ancrage chronologique repose sur une chronométrie fine (modélisation des dates radiocarbones, statistique bayésienne).

Ce cadre a été élargi aux régions plus septentrionales, du nord de la France et de la Belgique, et a fait l'objet de modifications en fonction des données disponibles dans les autres secteurs de notre espace d'étude. L'ensemble n'est ici proposé qu'à titre d'hypothèse (Fig. 6.2), mais il reflète bien le rythme des occupations dans chacune des régions étudiées. Ce cadre à l'avantage par ailleurs d'être bien calé sur la chronologie anglaise et néerlandaise qui à notre sens reflète mieux la réalité du tempo historique des régions du littoral de la Manche et de la mer du Nord. A un autre niveau de lecture, ce découpage s'adapte très bien aux modifications climatiques de l'Âge du bronze (Fig. 6.3), telles qu'elles sont enregistrées à partir des variations de la teneur de l'atmosphère en radiocarbone résiduel (Stuiver *et al.* 1998). Elles sont considérées comme un enregistrement des fluctuations de l'activité solaire (Hoyt et Schatten 1997 ; Bond *et al.* 2001) et donc, comme un bon indicateur empirique des variations du climat (Magny 1993), sachant que pour l'heure le détail des variations climatiques du nord-ouest de l'Europe reste sujet à discussion en l'absence d'un travail paléoenvironnemental multiscalaire sur cette question. Il n'est bien entendu pas dans notre propos ici de s'engouffrer dans une analyse déterministe où le climat jouerait un rôle essentiel dans les conjonctures socio-économiques de la protohistoire, mais plutôt d'utiliser cette information, au même titre que d'autres, dans un contexte d'étude multi-proxy où les indicateurs culturels, économiques, sociologiques etc. forment autant de courbes d'introspection participant à un modèle de lecture de la géopolitique de l'Âge du bronze.

Autre pierre d'achoppement, les indicateurs utilisés dans la modélisation proposée ici ont dû faire la part des choses en trois niveaux de valeurs, là encore extrêmement variable d'une zone à l'autre. Il a donc été nécessaire de bien identifier et distinguer ce qui contribue à une lecture des phénomènes politiques, économiques et sociaux à l'échelle

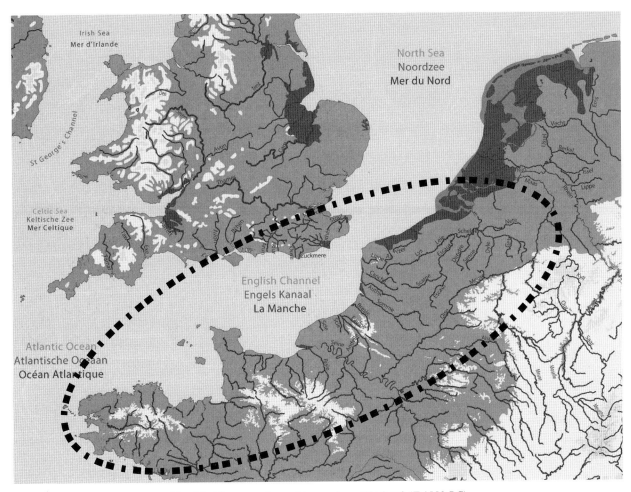

Fig. 6.1. L'espace géographique retenu (DAO BOAT 1550 BC).

suprarégionale, régionale ou interrégionale et locale. Dans l'approche proposée dans cet article, seule les faits de rang suprarégional ou interrégional ont été retenus.

Dans l'ensemble, même si ce travail, sur la chronologie ou les phénomènes socio-économiques vus à large échelle géographique, n'est pas encore mené à son terme, il pourrait constituer un véritable programme de recherche international que nous espérons développer dans les prochaines années. Les premières analyses permettent aujourd'hui, malgré les problèmes inhérents à la documentation archéologique variable d'une région à l'autre, de proposer une première ébauche de géographie culturelle aboutissant à une première lecture historique, entaché d'incertitudes il est vrai, mais particulièrement stimulante.

Séquence 1 : entre 2400 et 2100 avant notre ère

La première séquence est placée entre la fin du Néolithique et le début de l'Âge du bronze, de 2400 à 2100 avant notre ère. Elle correspond à la phase d'épanouissement des différentes cultures porteuses de gobelets campaniformes,

dont les articulations chronologique et régionale restent à préciser malgré les nombreuses recherches menées sur le sujet. Dans le cadre de notre travail, nous avons principalement utilisé un indicateur de lecture de la géographie culturelle. Ce comparateur porte sur les pratiques funéraires dont les caractéristiques, pour cette période, sont bien mieux identifiées et reconnues que celles caractérisant l'habitat et la culture matérielle (Vander Linden 2006).

Notre zone d'étude se partage très grossièrement en deux groupes correspondant très probablement à au moins deux entités distinctes d'obédience campaniforme (Fig. 6.4). A l'ouest, de la Bretagne aux marges du Bassin parisien, la réutilisation des sépultures collectives mégalithiques pour l'inhumation semble être la norme (ou en tous cas une tendance plus forte ; Salanova 2007). Il n'est pas rare ainsi de retrouver un ou deux à trois individus enterrés au sein d'une couche sépulcrale bien plus ancienne, datée du Néolithique final. Il s'agit toutefois systématiquement d'un individu seul accompagné d'éléments du viatique classique – gobelet, boutons à perforation en V, poignard etc., la vocation collective des lieux n'étant que fortuite à notre sens.

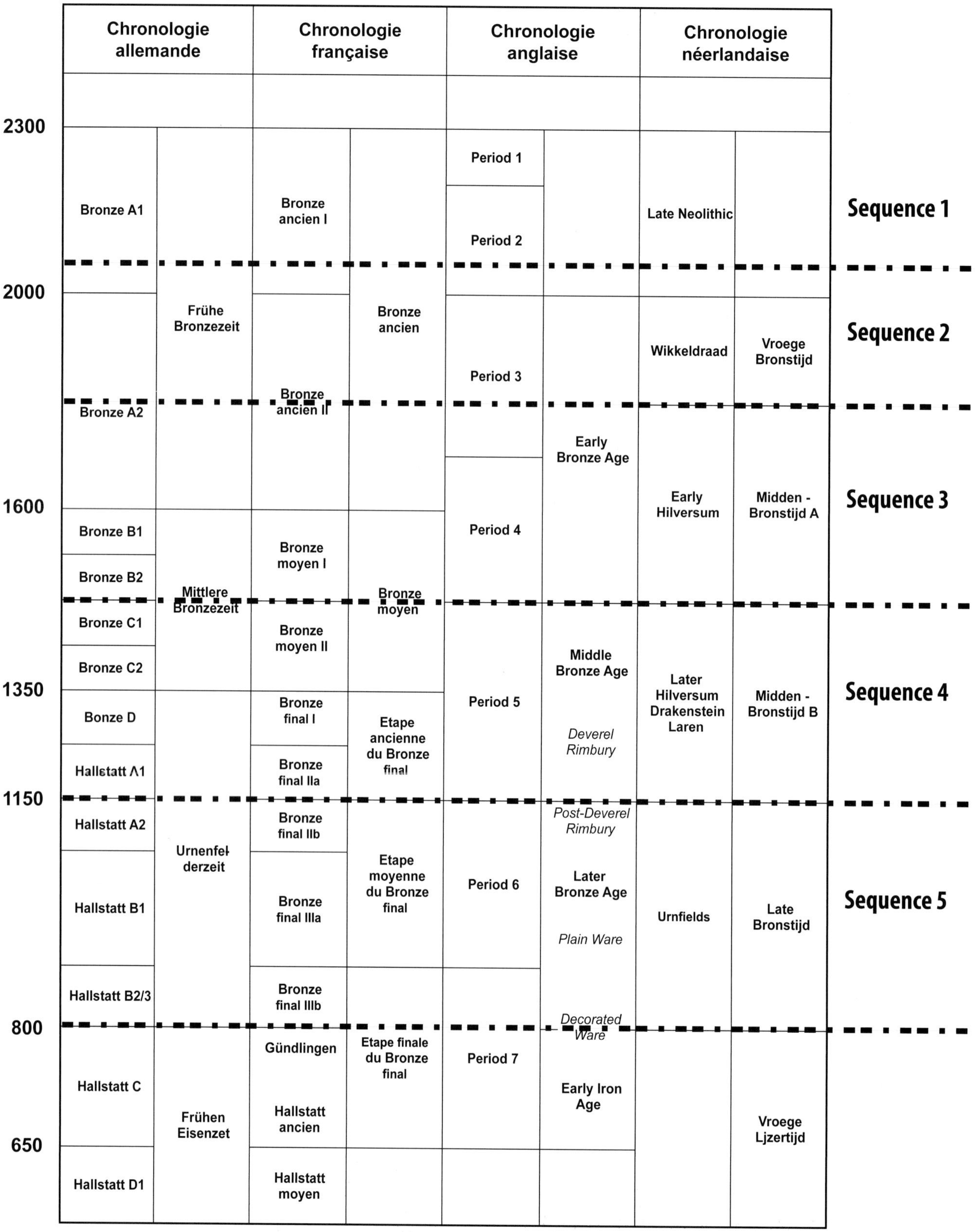

	Chronologie allemande		Chronologie française		Chronologie anglaise		Chronologie néerlandaise		
2300									
	Bronze A1		Bronze ancien I		Period 1	Late Neolithic			Sequence 1
					Period 2				
2000	Frühe Bronzezeit		Bronze ancien						Sequence 2
					Period 3	Wikkeldraad	Vroege Bronstijd		
	Bronze A2		Bronze ancien II						
					Early Bronze Age				
1600	Bronze B1		Bronze moyen I		Period 4	Early Hilversum	Midden - Bronstijd A		Sequence 3
	Bronze B2	Mittlere Bronzezeit		Bronze moyen					
	Bronze C1		Bronze moyen II			Middle Bronze Age	Later Hilversum Drakenstein Laren	Midden - Bronstijd B	Sequence 4
	Bronze C2								
1350	Bonze D		Bronze final I	Etape ancienne du Bronze final	Period 5	*Deverel Rimbury*			
	Hallstatt A1		Bronze final IIa						
1150	Hallstatt A2	Urnenfelderzeit	Bronze final IIb	Etape moyenne du Bronze final	Period 6	*Post-Deverel Rimbury*	Urnfields	Late Bronstijd	Sequence 5
	Hallstatt B1		Bronze final IIIa			Later Bronze Age			
						Plain Ware			
	Hallstatt B2/3		Bronze final IIIb			*Decorated Ware*			
800	Hallstatt C		Gündlingen	Etape finale du Bronze final	Period 7	Early Iron Age			
		Frühen Eisenzet	Hallstatt ancien					Vroege Ljzertijd	
650									
	Hallstatt D1		Hallstatt moyen						

Fig. 6.2. *Confrontation des différentes chronologies utilisées dans l'espace géographique retenu et définition des cinq séquences utilisées (DAO J. Bourgeois, C. Marcigny et M. Talon).*

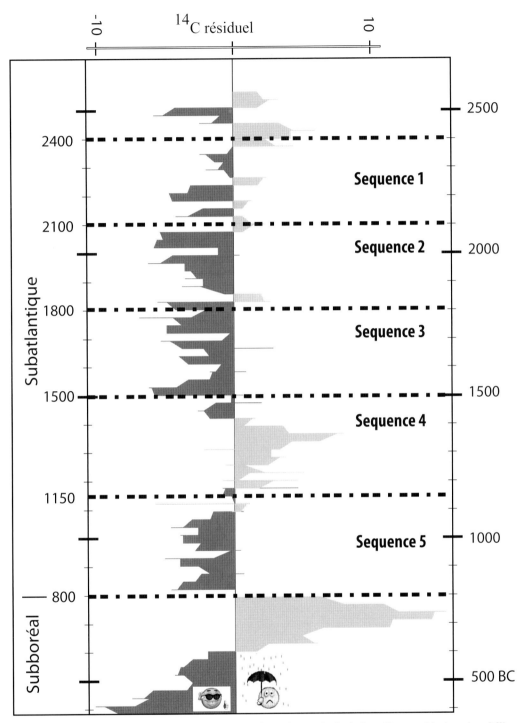

Fig. 6.3. Corrélations entre le climat (variations du taux de radiocarbone résiduel dans l'atmosphère) et les différentes séquences chronologiques (d'après Stuiver et al 1998; DAO M. Magny modifié C. Marcigny).

C'est plus la volonté d'utiliser un monument mégalithique et de donner à l'inhumé un sépulcre empreint d'une certaine monumentalité qui prime, la distance chronologique entre l'utilisation princeps du monument et sa réutilisation (souvent d'ailleurs séparée par un laps de temps de deux à trois siècles ; Salanova *et al.* 2014) peut alors être interprétée de deux manières: une pratique uniquement opportuniste visant à acquérir un monument remarquable (prestige de l'individu et potentiel géosymbole à vocation territoriale) ou un désir manifeste de s'inscrire dans la continuité et le lignage d'aïeux même si cette filiation reste factice.

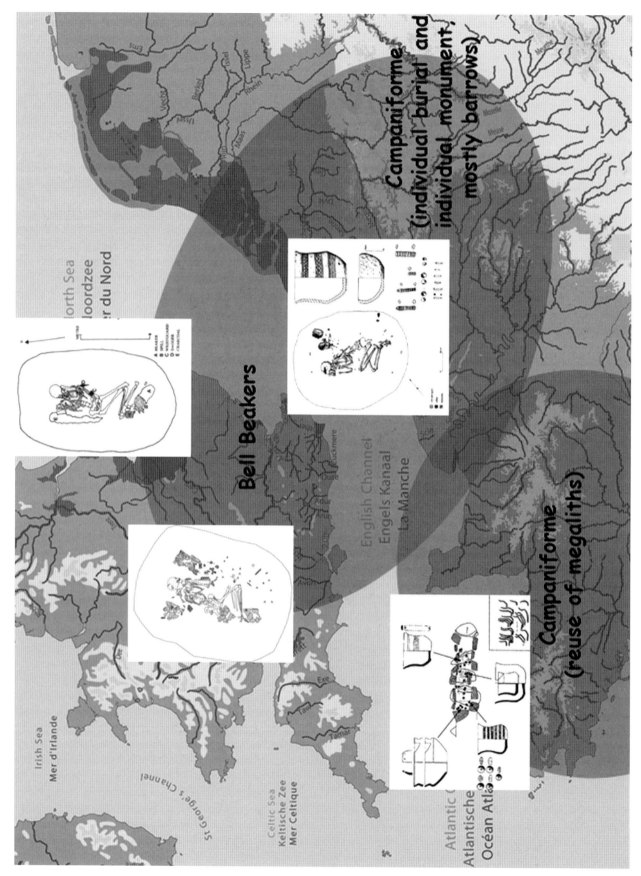

Fig. 6.4. Géographie culturelle de la séquence 1, entre 2400 et 2100 avant J.-C. (DAO J. Bourgeois, C. Marcigny et M. Talon).

Au nord, du sud de la Grande Bretagne et des marges du Bassin-parisien aux Flandres, la sépulture individuelle est aussi la norme, mais c'est la tombe creusée en pleine terre qui forme la tendance la plus forte des pratiques sépulcrales. On y retrouve le même langage symbolique dans le mobilier qui accompagne les tombes avec le même type de viatique qu'à l'ouest même si d'une part, dans le détail, il existe de nombreuses variations dans les types de vases, de parures, de poignards et d'autre part, les pointes de flèche sont plus nombreuses dans les sépultures du groupe oriental. Là aussi, la mise en avant de l'individu constitue une donnée forte qui est renforcée sur certains sites par la constitution de monuments consacrés à ces sépultures, sous la forme de tumulus circulaires délimités par des fossés, ou sous la forme d'espaces limités par des palissades. Ces monuments peuvent dans certains cas polariser de véritables ensembles funéraires (Vander Linden 2006 ; Salanova et Tchérémissinoff 2011) constitués de quelques tombes implantées au fil des générations dans les masses des tertres, le comblement des fossés ou à proximité immédiate, formant ainsi des sépulcres dont la vocation lignagère peut être évoquée même si dans la grande majorité des cas les données formelles manquent.

Cette première séquence, formative pour ce qui est la géographie culturelle de l'Âge du bronze, pose encore de nombreux problèmes de caractérisation. La lecture sociale et économique des faits historiques qui ont sous-tendu ces trois siècles échappe pour une grosse part à l'analyse et il est difficile d'aller très en avant dans les interprétations. C'est toutefois durant cette phase que se met en place un nouvel élan dynamique qui modifie profondément la géographie culturelle héritée des dernières siècles du Néolithique et qui insuffle une transformation des constructions identitaires à une large échelle de chaque côté des rives de la Manche et de la mer du Nord. La place du métal et sa plus large diffusion (tant au niveau des objets que des savoirs techniques), à la fin du IIIe millénaire, a invariablement provoqué ces modifications dont il reste à préciser avec exactitude les modalités.

Séquence 2 : entre 2100 et 1800 avant notre ère

A la charnière entre les IIIe et IIe millénaires, de 2100 à 1800 avant notre ère, la polarité culturelle identifiée précédemment existe toujours mais il semble qu'il y ait un basculement de la géographie proposée lors de la séquence 1, formant trois entités très contrastées (Fig. 6.5). Là encore les données sont très disparates d'une région à l'autre et les indicateurs mis à contribution sont dans le détail sujet à caution.

Du nord du Bassin parisien aux Flandres, les données sont encore très lacunaires, mais elles montrent de nombreux points communs. On retrouve, du sud au nord, les groupes des urnes à décor plastique et à cordons « arciformes »,

proches du « Hilversum ancien » et du « *Wikkeldraad* » (Bourgeois et Talon 2009). A l'ouest, proche de ce groupe et très probablement en interaction, une bonne part de la Grande-Bretagne et de l'Ecosse est caractérisée par le groupe des « *Collared Urn* » que l'on connaît aussi un peu plus vers le sud-ouest à une date un peu plus récente. Ces deux groupes, aux liens probables, facilités par le passage entre le nord de la France et la pointe sud-ouest de l'Angleterre, présentent de fortes similitudes dans les modes funéraires (pratiques et constructions funéraires) et les types d'habitat (même s'ils restent rares en France et en Angleterre).

Dans l'ouest de la France et le sud de l'Angleterre, les données sont bien plus importantes. Ces deux zones géographiques se caractérisent entre autre par la présence de volumineux tertres funéraires (culture du Wessex ou des tumulus armoricains ; Briard 1984 ; Burgess 1980), réservés à des hauts personnages accompagnés d'un important matériel funéraire. Ces pratiques funéraires, qui renvoient à d'autres phénomènes sociaux de même nature (tombes monumentales, viatiques ostentatoires, matériaux exotiques, …) et qui se développent à la même époque dans d'autres régions d'Europe (Unetiče, El Argar etc.), sont les stigmates de l'existence d'une plus forte complexification sociale reposant sur l'avènement d'une élite dont les codes funéraires – poignards, pointes de flèches, gobelets en matériaux précieux ou exotiques, brassards d'archer, etc. – sont directement inspirés du package campaniforme dont seule la valeur ajoutée des matériaux est amplifiée. Le développement de cette hiérarchisation sociale, dont le pouvoir politique s'appuie sur le contrôle des ressources en cuivre et en étain, s'accompagne d'une plus grande structuration de l'espace rural très visible dans l'analyse de l'habitat, les réseaux viaires ou la création d'une véritable planimétrie agraire. Cette dernière n'est pas sans conséquence historique puisqu'elle témoigne d'un acte fondateur, d'appropriation du territoire, qui doit s'accompagner de changements importants, quant à la notion de propriété foncière et de gestion de l'espace (Brun et Marcigny 2012).

Si notre zone nord-occidentale semble exclue de ces bouleversements sociaux, la présence dans ces régions de monuments funéraires aux dimensions importantes (généralement placés sur le littoral de la Manche ou le Cambrésis, Desfossés dir. 2000) et la découverte récurrente de dépôts d'objets métalliques (en particulier sur la façade littorale) sont peut-être les indices de changements politiques durant cette phase dont les pratiques funéraires au sein de la tombe ne présenteraient pas les mêmes caractéristiques ostentatoires.

Cette seconde séquence, fondée sur les bases de notre première séquence même si elle présente une géométrie différente, paraît être une époque de consolidation culturelle. Les élites de l'ouest de la France et du sud de

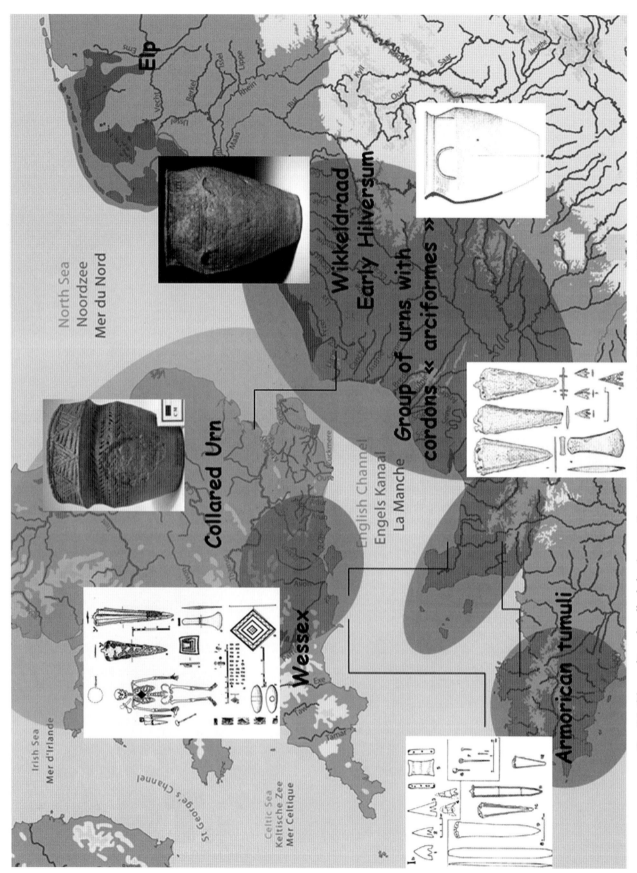

Fig. 6.5. Géographie culturelle de la séquence 2, entre 2100 et 1800 avant J.-C. (DAO J. Bourgeois, C. Marcigny et M. Talon).

la Grande-Bretagne opèrent une mainmise sur le territoire favorisant ainsi une plus forte homogénéisation culturelle. Au nord-est, les informations sont plus complexes à analyser, mais à notre sens là-aussi un pouvoir fort semble s'imposer. Ces élites, bien plus discrètes que celle de l'ouest même si elles se font inhumer dans des monuments aux dimensions imposantes (comme à Fréthun « Les Rietz », par exemple, Bostyn *et al.* 1992), fondent leur puissance sur les transferts économiques (et culturels) entre les zones occidentales et orientales, entre ce qui va devenir au fil du temps les domaines atlantique et continental. La présence de dépôts terrestres conséquents, dont les objets thésaurisés témoignent de liens avec les régions orientales (dépôt de Saint-Valéry-sur-Somme, Picardie, avec des lingots du type *Spangenbarren et Rippenbarren* ; Blanchet et Mille 2008) ou plus septentrionales (dépôts de haches du type anglais d'Escalles – Nord Pas-de-Calais – découvert récemment et en cours d'étude ; Fig. 6.6), sont là pour témoigner de l'importance économique de cette zone (Needham 2009).

Séquence 3 : entre 1800 et 1500 avant notre ère

Au cours de la séquence 3, on assiste à un effondrement apparent des élites mises en place au cours de la séquence 2 (en tout cas, elles ne sont plus visibles à partir des contextes funéraires) et à une recomposition culturelle. On distingue quatre entités.

A l'extrême ouest, un groupe apparenté au groupe du Centre-Ouest semble faire pression sur la partie occidentale de la Bretagne, s'implantant à l'emplacement de la zone des tumulus armoricains (Fig. 6.7). Ce groupe, dont on suit la diffusion géographique jusqu'en dans le centre-ouest de la France (à l'emplacement du groupe des Duffaits qui se développera à partir du XVe siècle avant notre ère), forme une vaste zone couvrant la façade atlantique.

Vers le nord, deux zones disposées en vis-à-vis de chaque côté de la Manche présentent des similitudes, mais aussi des différences qui ne permettent pas pour l'instant de les rattacher strictement au même horizon culturel. En Grande-Bretagne c'est le groupe à *Cordoned Urns* qui prend le relais des *Collared Urns* et du groupe de Wessex. En France

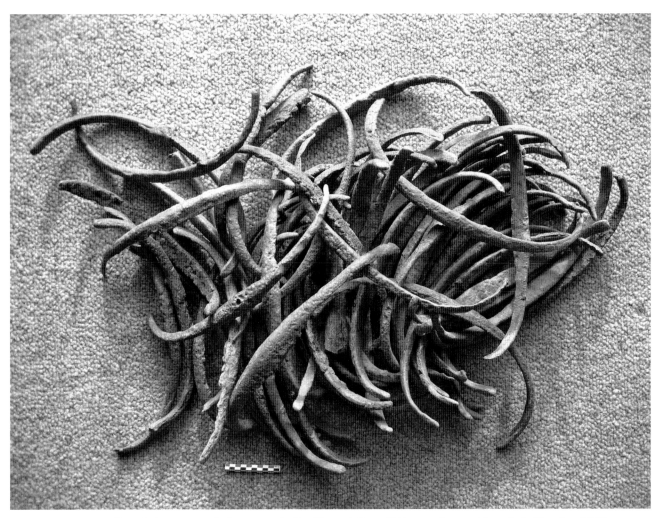

Fig. 6.6. Le dépôt de lingots en métal cuivreux du Cap Hornu à Saint-Valéry-sur-Somme (photo J. C. Blanchet, MCC)

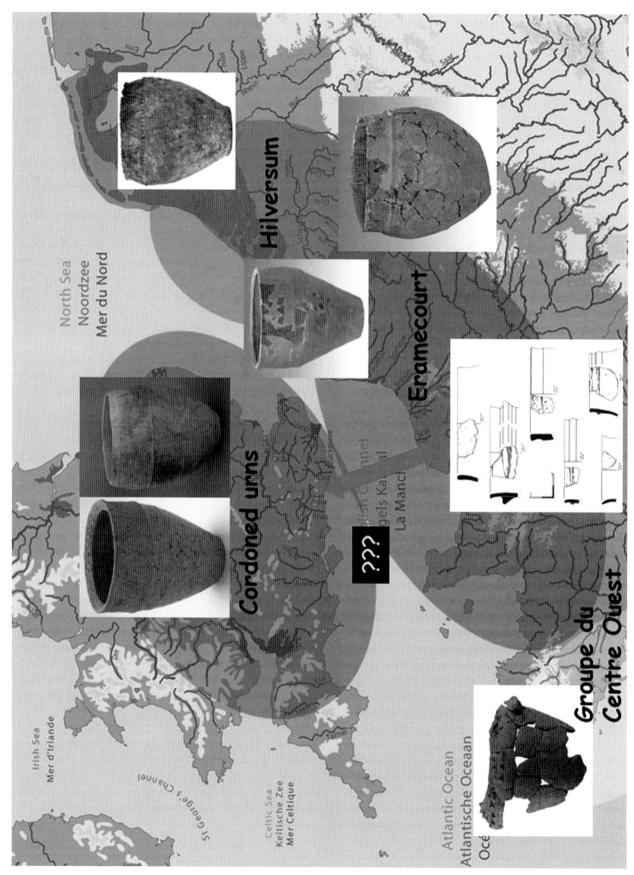

Fig. 6.7. Géographie culturelle de la séquence 3, entre 1800 et 1500 avant J.-C. (DAO J. Bourgeois, C. Marcigny et M. Talon).

et au Benelux, on retrouve du sud au nord les groupes d'Eramecourt et de Hilversum (Bourgeois et Talon 2009). Là aussi, il existe de profondes différences entre ces deux groupes même s'ils présentent de fortes affinités sur le plan de la culture matérielle et des rites funéraires. Les formes de l'habitat, par exemple, sont différentes, alors qu'il existe des comparaisons entre certaines constructions contemporaines (comme l'existence de système de clôture délimitant les fermes, Marcigny et Ghesquière 2008) des *Cordoned Urns* et d'Eramecourt. L'ensemble formé par ces trois groupes semble donc avoir des accointances tout en développant certaines caractéristiques autonomes, interdisant de fait d'en faire une construction culturelle homogène.

Dans l'ensemble de ces régions, on assiste à un même processus sociétal qui accompagne le déclin puis la disparition des élites de la séquence 2. Toutefois, l'existence d'une construction politique et sociale reposant sur un système hiérarchisé, voire très hiérarchisé, ne peut être totalement rejetée de l'analyse. Il semble que les signes ostentatoires de cette hiérarchie soient pour partie effacés. L'accroissement des sépultures sous tumulus (aux dépôts généralement peu abondants et le plus souvent absents) renvoie au contraire l'image d'un tassement généralisé de la pyramide sociale. Dans le domaine de l'habitat, les choses sont moins évidentes à décrypter, mais dans cette région, la multiplication de sites avec les mêmes statuts semble témoigner du même mouvement. Lorsque les études de territoires sont suffisamment poussées, il est possible d'avoir une analyse fine de ce basculement entre les séquences 2 et 3. Ainsi, dans le sud de la Grande-Bretagne et en Normandie, on assiste entre les XVIIe et XVIe siècles au passage progressif de « fermes pionnières » (à statut social élevé dans certains cas) associées à la mise en place de parcellaires, à un réseau de fermes qui se partagent le même espace sans distinction formelle de statut et sur une période de fréquentation s'étalant sur plusieurs générations (plus grande fixité des territoires ; Marcigny 2012). Ce système d'utilisation collectif d'un « terroir », au cours de la séquence 3, n'est pas sans évoquer les interprétations économico-sociales proposées par A. Fleming dans le Dartmoor (Fleming 2008). On a l'impression, dans ces régions, que les constructions de l'espace agraire, mises en place sous l'égide d'un pouvoir fort, se sont durant cette phase affranchie de ces systèmes politiques pour être mises à disposition d'un groupe plus large, à une époque où le climat, particulièrement favorable, a dû favoriser l'expansion des établissements agricoles.

Dans une perspective historique plus large, on aurait là le même processus que celui qui s'est mis en place dans la société féodale française, puis au début de l'époque moderne. Avec initialement une société rurale fondée sur de fortes inégalités sociales où la terre était contrôlée par une classe, minorité de la communauté. Sachant que peu à peu, ce modèle, selon un processus long et complexe, a

cédé la place à un autre où les classes de cultivateurs se sont réappropriées la terre et son exploitation formant une société de petite propriété paysanne (comme probablement durant notre séquence 3).

Séquence 4 : entre 1500 et 1150 avant notre ère

Ce mouvement se poursuit au cours de la séquence 4 entre 1500 et 1150 avant notre ère, à une époque où la géométrie de la géographie culturelle se modifie. Durant cette phase, les liens tissés au cours de la période précédente vont se densifier comme en témoigne par exemple la découverte du bateau de Douvres datée du début du XVIe siècle (Clark 2009 ; la majorité des bateaux reconnus jusqu'à présent datent toutefois de la période précédente avec la série de North Ferriby), formant peu à peu une entité dont les composantes présentent de très fortes corrélations. Ce complexe, qui rassemble plusieurs groupes comme le Deverel-Rimbury, le Hilversum tardif ou le Drakenstein, voire même le Trevisker, est dénommé en France le Manche Mer-du-Nord (MMN) (Marcigny *et al.* 2007 ; Fig. 6.8).

Le MMN n'est pas une culture au sens strict du terme, mais plutôt un vaste ensemble aux paramètres culturels fluctuant d'une région à l'autre. Cet ensemble prend sa genèse dans les liens économiques construits lors des phases précédentes qui, au cours du Bronze moyen, ont probablement abouti à la constitution d'un modèle unique de développement économique qui a effacé pour partie la diversité culturelle de ces régions. Ce phénomène de globalisation et de fragilisation des identités culturelles renvoie bien entendu à des préoccupations actuelles beaucoup plus larges, mais il a pu constituer, à une moindre échelle et pour des époques plus reculées, une dynamique qui a touché pour partie les cultures des rives de la Manche et de la mer du Nord. Certains constituants de la culture matérielle se trouvent fortement impactés par ce phénomène de « mondialisation » à l'échelle des rives de la Manche et de la mer du Nord. Les formes céramiques, par exemple, présentent de nombreux points de comparaison, le développement des constructions de plan circulaire participent du même mouvement, tout comme certains objets artisanaux à l'instar des pesons pour le tissage. Le mobilier métallique, entre autre, se trouve par contre en dehors de ce processus d'homogénéisation avec au contraire l'apparition d'écoles métallurgiques régionales en capacité de surproduction. Ces objets et surtout ce matériau, une des ressources essentielles de l'économie de l'Âge du bronze, gardent ainsi des spécificités à petite échelle (signatures à vocation identitaire clairement exprimée) permettant à ce type de fabrication artisanale de pleinement participer au jeu des échanges qui se mettent en place à l'intérieur de l'espace MMN.

Ces mouvements socio-économiques accompagnent une péjoration climatique qui a dû impacter pour partie les ressources vivrières. Les modalités de l'occupation de

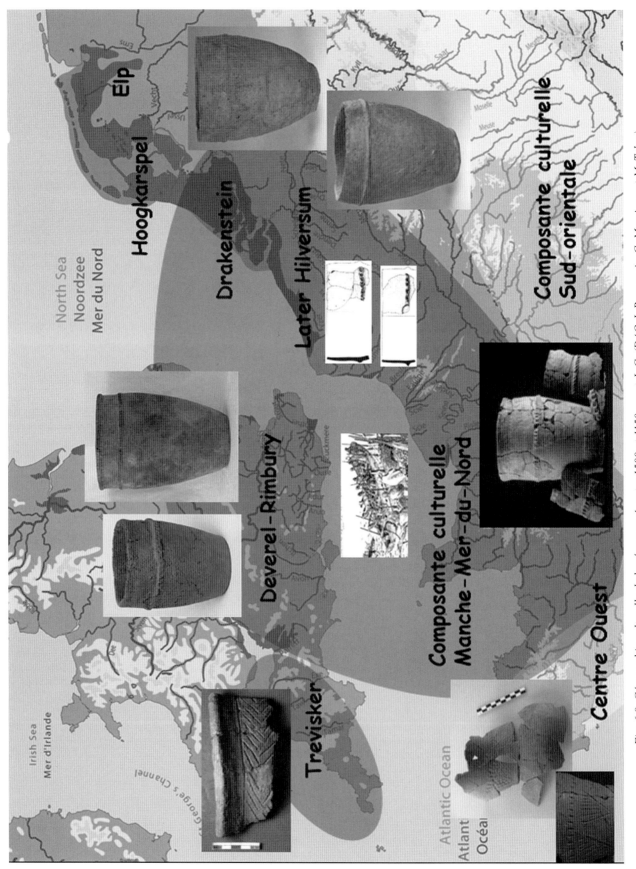

Fig. 6.8. Géographie culturelle de la séquence 4, entre 1500 et 1150 avant J.-C. (DAO J. Bourgeois, C. Marcigny et M. Talon).

l'espace agraire changent alors durant cette phase. Dans certains secteurs, les systèmes parcellaires sont encore occupés, mais ils ne font plus l'objet de travaux de réfections et ils sont, dans la plupart des cas, peu à peu abandonnés au cours des XIIe et XIe siècle avant notre ère (Marcigny 2012). Les fermes changent aussi de configuration et il est de plus en plus fréquent d'avoir affaire à des occupations de courtes durées (sur une ou deux générations) se déplaçant au sein d'un même terroir, revenant parfois, de manière cyclique, au même lieu (donnant des sites très complexes où les structures d'habitat se recoupent). La fixité des terroirs et des territoires qui caractérisait les occupations des séquences 2 et 3 ne semble plus de mise au profit d'une utilisation moins pérenne des espaces.

C'est à cette période qu'apparaissent les premiers cimetières familiaux avec de modestes fosses à résidus de combustion (Le Goff et Billand 2012) comprenant quelques poignées d'ossements incinérés mélangés à des cendres et charbons de bois, sans autre matériel ou alors une simple urne, voire un *hair-ring*, petit anneau doré constitué d'un alliage cuivreux recouvert d'une feuille d'or que l'on retrouve essentiellement dans les îles britanniques et le territoire MMN sur le continent (Billand et Talon 2007). Dans certains cas, les sépultures semblent s'organiser autour de tumulus qui ont pu servir de point de repère dans le paysage, mais dans d'autres cas, il n'y a pas de monument. Ces tombes ne se recoupant pas, elles devaient bénéficier d'une stèle ou d'un marqueur de surface.

Autour du complexe MMN, d'autres composantes culturelles se constituent. A l'ouest, sur le Finistère breton, ce sont les cultures appartenant au Centre-Ouest. Plus au sud de notre zone, ce sont les cultures sud-orientales qui présentent d'ailleurs de fortes affinités avec celles du Centre-Ouest (Gomez de Soto 1995).

Séquence 5: entre 1150 et 800 avant notre ère

Le complexe MMN perdure durant la séquence 5 (entre 1150 et 800 avant notre ère) sur les mêmes bases économiques que précédemment et avec les mêmes effets sur la culture matérielle, comme la céramique de type *plain ware* que l'on retrouve de chaque côté de la Manche (Brun 1998 ; Marcigny et Talon 2009), ou la perduration des constructions de plan circulaire. L'aire de ce groupe semble toutefois se réduire au fil du temps et se rétracter sur les rives de la Manche peut-être sous la « pression » de la composante culturelle nord-alpine de plus en plus prégnante (Fig. 6.9). Cette dernière prend le relais de la composante culturelle sud-orientale et affiche des caractéristiques identitaires très fortes (en particulier pour ce qui est du vaisselier céramique) que l'on retrouve jusque dans le groupe MMN en particulier sur des sites à statut probablement élevé comme les *ring-fort*, les sites de hauteur ou les villages (Manem *et al.* 2013).

Ces nouvelles catégories de site que l'on ne connaissait pas auparavant apparaissent au cours des XIIe et XIe siècles avant notre ère, à une époque où l'espace rural fait l'objet de profondes modifications : abandon des parcellaires, abandon des systèmes de clôture pour les fermes, délocalisation des sites au profit de nouveaux espaces géographiques, etc. Ces changements qui affectent le Bronze final vont s'accentuer au cours des Xe et IXe siècle avec le développement de l'habitat groupé (sous forme de hameau ou de village, auquel on préfèrera le terme typologique d'« *agro-town* ») et des systèmes de protection sur les sites à la fonction défensive affirmée ou même sur des territoires complets (*dikes*) (Marcigny et Talon 2009). Ce phénomène de concentration et de protection initie un mouvement qui continuera au-delà de l'Âge du bronze au début de l'Âge du fer.

Cette volonté de se protéger et de se regrouper est à mettre en parallèle avec le développement de l'armement défensif (casques, boucliers, cnémides) et offensif, en particulier l'épée qui connaît une évolution morphologique régulière et une production importante au cours de cette période. Ces témoignages dans la culture matérielle sont pour nous la traduction d'évènements géopolitiques majeurs répondant probablement à un sentiment d'insécurité peut-être pour partie lié à des tensions avec le complexe nord-alpin. Il reste bien entendu à définir ces tensions et il faut bien dire que dans ce cadre, l'information archéologique est bien souvent peu diserte, les rites funéraires restant sobres et de même nature que pendant la séquence précédente avec l'utilisation de cimetières familiaux pauvres en mobilier.

Pour la fin de la séquence et le début de l'Âge du fer, un évènement semble se surimposer avec l'avènement de la péjoration climatique, qui signe le passage Subboréal/ Subatlantique. Cette modification du climat a eu des incidences sur le comportement des sociétés. De profonds changements s'opèrent alors en ce début de Ier millénaire : changement de pratiques agraires, habitats désertés alors que d'autres sont créés, etc. Ce changement dans les pratiques agricoles et les formes de l'habitat est probablement à mettre en relation avec une crise agraire sans précédent qui a dû briser l'élan économique des âges du Bronze moyen et final. De cette crise, peu d'éléments sont perceptibles pour l'archéologue, si ce n'est peut-être l'utilisation de nouvelles semences. En France, par exemple, l'orge à grains nus est peu à peu remplacée par l'orge à grains vêtus à partir du début de l'Âge du fer (Marcigny et Ghesquière 2008). En Angleterre, le déclin de l'orge nue coïncide avec la mention du seigle.

Perspectives

Ce premier essai de lecture géopolitique des rives de la Manche et du sud de la Mer-du-Nord met en place les premières pierres d'un travail qu'il serait nécessaire

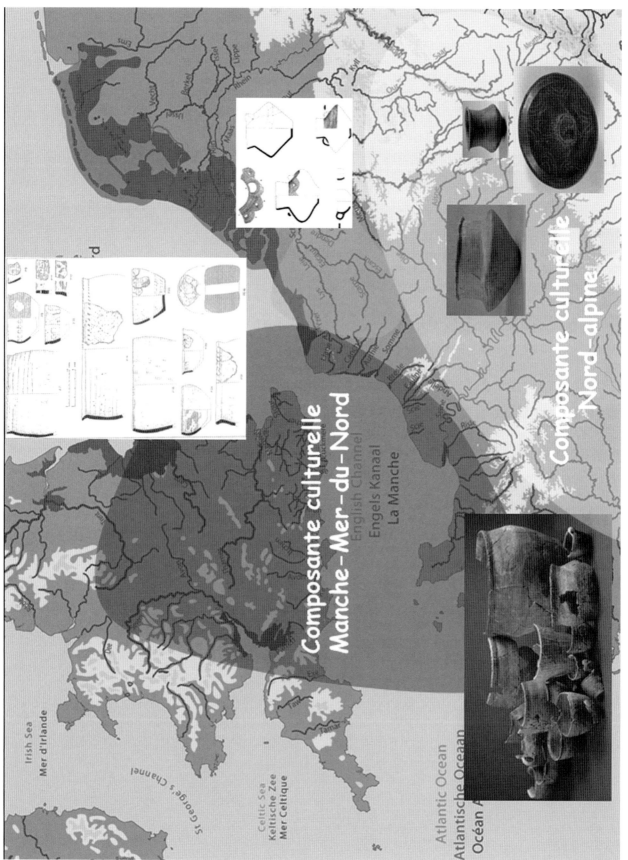

Fig. 6.9. Géographie culturelle de la séquence 5, entre 1150 et 800 avant J.-C. (DAO J. Bourgeois, C. Marcigny et M. Talon).

d'affiner et de développer de manière à confirmer ou infirmer certaines des hypothèses émises ici. L'analyse multi-proxy et interdisciplinaire ne peut être que la clef pour aboutir à des interprétations au plus près des réalités historiques et environnementales des 1500 ans couverts par l'Âge du bronze. La définition d'indicateurs utilisables à une échelle suprarégionale, la constitution de courbes d'analyse commune et la confrontation de données macro-archéologiques forment à notre sens l'armature d'un programme de recherche international qu'il reste à mettre en place sur ces espaces géographiques.

Note

1   Cet article reprend pour une grosse partie un papier similaire proposé dans le cadre du colloque « Cultural Mobility » d'Aarhus complété à l'occasion du colloque de Boulogne-sur-Mer.

Bibliographie

Billand, G. et Talon, M. (2007) Apport du Bronze Age Studies Group au vieillissement des 'hair-rings' dans le Nord de la France. Dans C. Burgess, P. Topping and F. Lynch (eds) *Beyond Stonehenge, Essays on the Bronze Age in Honour of Colin Burgess*, 342–351. Oxford, Oxbow Books.

Blanchet, J.-C. et Mille, B. (2008) Découverte exceptionnelle d'un dépôt de lingots de l'Âge du Bronze ancien à Saint-Valéry-sur-Somme. Dans *L'isthme européen Rhin-Saône Rhône dans la Protohistoire ; approches nouvelles en hommage à Jacques-Pierre Millotte, 177–82.* Besançon Presse universitaires de Franche-Comté.

Bond, G., Kromer, B., Beer, J., Muscheler, R., Evans, M.-N., Showers, W., Hoffmann, S., Lotti-Bond, R., Hajdas, I. et Bonani, G. (2001) Persistent solar influence on North Atlantic climate during the Holocene, *Science* 294, 2130–6.

Bostyn, F., Blancquaert, G. et Lanchon, Y. (1992) Un enclos triple du Bronze ancien à Fréthun (Pas-de-Calais). *Bulletin de la Société Préhistorique Française* 89, 393–412.

Bourgeois, J. et Talon, M. (2009) From Picardy to Flanders: Transmanche connections in the Bronze Age. Dans P. Clark (ed.) *Bronze Age Connections: Cultural Contact en Prehistoric Europe*, 38–59. Oxford, Oxbow Books.

Briard, J. (1984) Wessex et Armorique, une révision. In *Les relations entre le continent et les îles Britanniques à l'Age du Bronze*, Actes du Colloque de Lille, 77–87. Paris, Société Préhistorique Française et Revue Archéologique de Picardie.

Brun, P. et Marcigny, C. (2012) Une connaissance de l'âge du bronze transfigurée par l'archéologie préventive. Dans *Nouveaux champs de la recherche archéologique, 132–9. Archéopages hors-série 10 ans.*

Burgess, C. (1980) *The Age of Stonehenge*. London, Dent.

Carozza, L. et Marcigny, C. (2007) *L'âge du Bronze en France*, colloques Archéologies de la France. Paris, éditions La découverte.

Carozza, L., Marcigny, C. et Talon, M. (2009) Ordres et désordres dans l'économie des sociétés durant l'âge du Bronze en France. Dans M. Bartelheim et H. Stäuble (eds) *The Economic Fondations of the European Bronze Age, Die wirtschaftlichen Grundlagen der Bronzezeit Europas*, 23–64, Rahden/Westf : VML 2009.

Clark, P. (2009) *Bronze Age Connections: Cultural Contact in Prehistoric Europe*. Oxford, Oxbow Books.

Desfossés, Y. (dir) (2000) *Archéologie préventive en vallée de Canche, les sites protohistoriques fouillés dans le cadre de la réalisation de l'autoroute A16*. Berck-sur-Mer, Nord-Ouest Archéologie 11.

Fleming, A. (2008) *The Dartmoor Reaves: Investigating Prehistoric Land Divisions*. Oxford, Windgather Press.

Gomez de Soto, J. (1995) *L'âge du Bronze en France, 5 : Le Bronze moyen en Occident. La Culture des Duffaits et la Civilisation des Tumulus*. Paris, Picard.

Hoyt, D.-V. et Schatten, M. (1997) *The Role of the Sun in Climate Change*. Oxford, Oxford University Press.

Le Goff, I. et Billand, G. (2012) De la détection des structures fugaces à la reconnaissance d'un système funéraire: les fosses à résidus de combustion de l'âge du Bronze, *Archéopages* hors-série, 138–146.

Magny, M. (1993) Solar influences on Holocene climatic changes illustrated by correlations between past lake-level fluctuations and the atmospheric 14C record, *Quaternary Research* 40, 1–9.

Manem, S., Marcigny, C. et Talon, M. (2013) Vivre, produire et transmettre autour de la Manche. Regards sur les comportements des hommes entre Deverel Rimbury et post Deverel-Rimbury en Normandie et dans le sud de l'Angleterre. Dans W. Leclercq et E. Warmenbol (éd.) *Echanges de bons procédés. La céramique du Bronze final dans le nord-ouest de l'Europe, 245–65, Études d'archéologie 6.* Bruxelles, Éditions du CReA–Patrimoine.

Marcigny, C. (2012a) Au bord de la mer. Rythmes et natures des occupations protohistoriques en Normandie (IIIe millénaire–fin de l'âge du Fer). Dans M. Honegger et C. Mordant (eds) *Au bord de l'eau, Archéologie des zones littorales du Néolithique à la Protohistoire*, 135e Congrès CTHS (Neuchâtel, Suisse, 2010), 345–364. Neuchâtel, Cahier d'Archéologie Romande.

Marcigny, C. (2012b) Les paysages ruraux de l'âge du Bronze, structures agraires et organisations sociales dans l'Ouest de la France. Dans V. Carpentier et C. Marcigny (eds) *Des Hommes aux Champs, Pour une archéologie des espaces ruraux du Néolithique au Moyen Age*, Actes de la table ronde de Caen (Octobre 2008), 71–80. Rennes, Presses Universitaires de Rennes.

Marcigny, C. et Ghesquière, E. (2008) Espace rural et systèmes agraires dans l'ouest de la France à l'âge du Bronze: quelques exemples normands. In J. Guilaine (ed.) *Villes, villages, campagnes de l'Âge du Bronze*, séminaires du Collège de France, 256–278. Paris, Editions Errance.

Marcigny, C. et Talon, M. (2009) Sur les rives de la Manche. Qu'en est-il du passage de l'âge du Bronze à l'âge du Fer ? In *De l'âge du Bronze à l'âge du Fer (X–VIIème siècle av. J.-C.)* Actes du colloque international APRAB-AFEAF de St Romain-en Gal 2005, 385–403. Dijon, Revue Archéologique de l'Est.

Marcigny, C., Ghesquière E. et Kinnes, I. (2007) Bronze Age cross-Channel relations. The Lower-Normandy (France) example: Ceramic chronology and first reflections. Dans C. Burgess, P. Topping and F. Lynch (eds) *Beyond Stonehenge, Essays on the Bronze Age in Honour of Colin Burgess*, 255–267. Oxford, Oxbow Books.

Needham, S. (2009) Encompassing the sea: 'Maritories' and Bronze Age maritime interactions. In P. Clark (ed.) *Bronze Age Connections, Cultural Contact in Prehistoric Europe*, 12–37. Oxford, Oxbow books.

Salanova, L. (2007) Les sépultures campaniformes: lecture sociale. Dans J. Guilaine (dir.), Le Chalcolithique et la construction des inégalités, t. I: Le continent européen, Séminaires du Collège de France, 213–28. Paris, Éditions Errance.

Salanova, L. et Tchérémissinoff, Y. (dir.) (2011) *Les sépultures individuelles campaniformes en France*. XLIe supplément à *Gallia Préhistoire* Paris, CNRS éditions.

Stuiver, M., Reimer, P. J., Bard, E., Beck, J.-W., Burr, G.-S., Hughen, K.-A., Kromer, B., McCormac, G., Van der Plicht, J. et Spurk, M. (1998) Incal98 radiocarbon age calibration, 24,000–0 cal BP, *Radiocarbon* 40, 1041–1083.

Vander Linden, M. (2006) *Le phénomène campaniforme dans l'Europe du 3ème millénaire avant notre ère: Synthèse et nouvelles perspectives*, British Archaeological Report S1470. Oxford, Archaeopress

7

The Atlantic Early Iron Age in Gaul

Pierre-Yves Milcent

Abstract

The concept of the Atlantic Early Iron Age in Gaul is a recent one and is thus not necessarily self-evident. It was presented for the first time in 2005 during a round table in Italy focusing on Celtic prehistory (Milcent 2006) in order to explicitly define its scope and update our understanding of the concept. In order to gain a better grasp of the pertinence of the term, it is important to recall how the Early Iron Age of the northwestern regions of Gaul was identified, then dispel any tenacious biases inherited from former strata of research, particularly for the Champagne region. In addition, we will see that this article slightly overruns the traditionally allotted chronological framework for the first Iron Age, as materials and sites from the whole of the 5th century BC are also taken into consideration.

Keywords: Early Iron Age; Atlantic networks; Medio-Atlantic societies; Champagne; La Tène genesis.

Résumé

«Le concept de premier Âge du fer atlantique en Gaule est récent et ne va donc pas de soi. Il a été présenté une première fois en 2005 durant une table ronde en Italie consacrée à la «Préhistoire des Celtes» (Milcent 2006). Je souhaite ici en détailler l'explicitation, la portée, et actualiser son appréhension. Pour mieux saisir la pertinence du concept, il est important de rappeler de quelle manière on a pu, ou non, identifier par le passé le premier Âge du fer des régions nord-occidentales de la Gaule. Il est nécessaire aussi de dissiper les préjugés tenaces hérités des premiers temps de la recherche, en particulier pour la Champagne rattachée à tort au monde hallstattien. Cet article débordera légèrement du cadre chronologique traditionnellement attribué au premier Âge du fer en prenant en considération l'ensemble du Ve siècle avant notre ère. Il s'agira notamment de mettre en évidence certains des traits principaux des cultures matérielles du premier Âge du fer atlantique».

Mots-clés: premier Âge du fer, réseaux atlantiques, sociétés médio-atlantiques, Champagne, genèse des cultures matérielles de La Tène

An Early Iron Age without a name: historiographical overview

In the most northern and western regions of Gaul in the geographical sense of the term (Fig. 7.1), the notion of the Early Iron Age remained vague for a long time. Its existence was at times denied, and at best often limited to a transitional stage between the Late Bronze Age and the Early La Tène period (Déchelette 1913 [1927], 40, 43 and 76; Giot *et al.* 1979). This period was at times the focus of Bronze Age specialists, serving as a conclusion to their research (Briard 1965; Blanchet 1984), and at times analysed by specialists of the Late Iron Age, as a prelude to their work (Hatt and Roualet 1976; 1977; Demoule 1999). Therefore, apart from some exceptions (Mariën 1958), the Early Iron Age of these northwestern regions was not treated as a fully-fledged period with its own characteristics.

The thesis that these zones were distant peripheries, turned towards the Atlantic and more or less lagging behind the supposed central regions, prevailed for a long time and has still not totally disappeared. It stipulated that these lands were barely affected by the development of iron metallurgy, or only at a late period corresponding to the Late Hallstatt, or even the Early La Tène of continental regions, giving rise to the idea of a prolongation of the Late Bronze Age in these regions, which was more or less equivalent to the Early Hallstatt and sometimes even to the Middle Hallstatt of continental cultures (Giot 1950, 338; Brun 1987, 53–4). Even today in scientific publications, it is not rare to come across Armorican socketed pseudo-axes incorrectly attributed to an 'extended Late Bronze Age', or, for the more massive specimens, to the Atlantic Late Bronze Age 3. Even when they are not functional, they are presumed to represent the persistence of mainly bronze tool production until the 6th century BC, and the ignorance of iron smelting and iron forging.

As for the emergence of a full Iron Age, it was deemed to result mainly from external stimuli, driven by the migrations of Proto-Celtic Hallstattian populations, according to early works (Déchelette 1913 [1927], 168; Mariën 1958), or by contributions and influences from both the continental domain and the Mediterranean, according to more recent approaches (Giot *et al*. 1979; Hatt and Roualet 1977; Brun 1987). Note that the emergence of typical La Tène culture features in these regions is generally considered to follow a comparable centrifugal schema, with a late Celtisation resulting from a more or less cumulative acculturation process, depending on the authors.

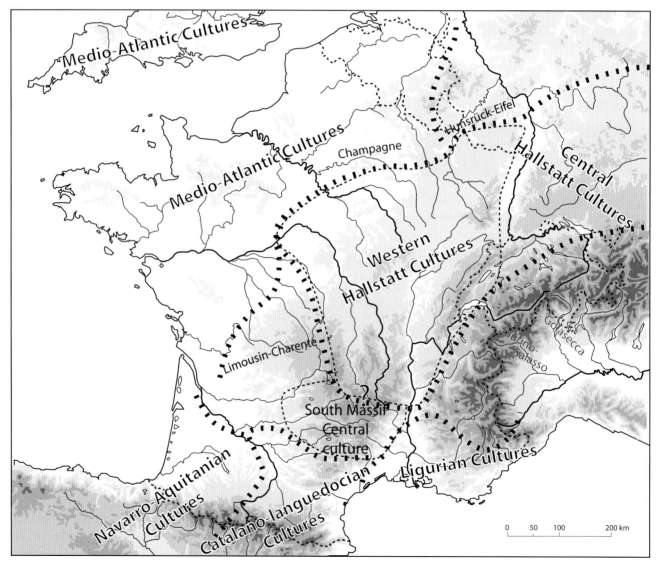

Fig. 7.1. Cultural entities in Gaul in the Early Iron Age.

These diffusionist, or at times even migrationist paradigms are based on 'centre-periphery'-type models and evoke images of northwestern regions submerged by migrations, or lagging behind, in a process of acculturation. Towards the end of the 1980s, they were abandoned, although no detailed models replaced them, or they were revised, without being entirely rejected, by the world-economy concept assigning a role of passive procurement to these territories on behalf of allegedly more dynamic and advanced regions in Central Europe and the Mediterranean.

Thus, the same concept always prevails when a model is formulated; that is to say innovation and civilisation are located in the Mediterranean, the active reception of these stimuli is based in Central Europe and beyond that, inertia and passivity are associated with the west and north of Europe. This idea is extremely ancient as it is more or less the same as that presented by Greek historians, and Herodotus in particular.

Nonetheless, it would be very unfair to formulate this severe review without recalling that the materials and archaeological sites from the Early Iron Age in northwestern regions remained very poorly identified for a long time, mainly on account of more modest-looking or more difficult remains to identify than elsewhere. Unlike the Hallstattian or Mediterranean regions of Gaul, pottery in these zones bears little decoration and displays rather simple profile shapes, settlements are never clustered together to form large agglomerations, and those that have been excavated have yielded few objects. In the same way, tombs can be rare or only exceptionally preserve spectacular objects, even for the most privileged graves. In such conditions, it is a difficult challenge to identify a northwestern Early Iron Age and we cannot criticise our predecessors for not having clearly identified this chrono-cultural facies.

However, over the past 20 years discoveries have multiplied, mostly from rescue archaeology, and at last we have evidence of settlements. In the same way, grave mapping is beginning to take shape, after remaining extremely scant for a long period of time. Nevertheless, the identification of a northwestern Early Iron Age in its own right, and not one modelled on that of regions further south or east, is still difficult to establish. For a long time, this period had no specific name. As proof of this, we only need to refer to the widespread use of the German nomenclature passed on from the work of P. Reinecke. In this way, over the past 20 years, remains found in the northwest of France are said to date from the 'Hallstatt C' or the 'Hallstatt D'. This chronological nomenclature and associated periodisation cannot, however, be adopted, or even adapted: firstly because from a methodological point of view, it is preferable not to associate a cultural dimension with chronological nomenclature (cf. for example the chronology of the Urnfields by W. Kimmig, laden with questionable historical implications), as explained by

J. Collis (1986) among others, and secondly and especially because this chrono-cultural construction was developed and defined on the basis of funerary goods from Central Europe, and particularly from southern Germany. Connections with materials from the northwest of France or Belgium are thus rarely substantiated, apart from for several very particular and rare metallic objects, whereas nothing leads us to reasonably consider that the evolution of societies near the Atlantic Ocean and the Channel could have occurred in step with their Central European counterparts. Apart from the fact that this transposition of the 'Reinecke' chronology appears to be totally methodologically arbitrary and incongruous, it implicitly recalls that the Early Iron Age of the northwestern regions of Gaul is not considered to be autonomous, with its own chronological dynamics. In other words, this reveals that the old diffusionist stereotypes that we thought we had discarded 30 years ago, relegating this western zone to the back-benches of Europe at the beginning of the Iron Age, remain very present today and still colonise minds and vocabulary.

Deconstructing preconceived notions

Before envisaging the existence of a specific Early Iron Age in northwestern Gaul, it appears essential to recall the main preconceived notions altering its perception, in order to demonstrate that they are unfounded. Our aim is not to establish an inventory of these notions, but simply to deconstruct the main concepts.

Until the 6th century BC, an exclusive bronze metallurgy and hoard practices inherited from the Late Bronze Age?

Like in most of the other regions of temperate Europe, the metallurgy of copper alloys during the Early Iron Age remains in fact poorly known in northwestern Gaul. Quantitatively, Armorican socketed pseudo-axes provide most of the information. These productions follow on from functional Late Bronze Age socketed axes and mainly date from the 7th–6th centuries BC (Gomez de Soto *et al.* 2009; Milcent 2012, 161–7; Milcent in press). In actual fact, they have little in common with their 'precursors' from the end of the Bronze Age: apart from some rare older models, they were cast using an alloy rich in lead; they are small in size, often miniatures; their socket is deep and hardly leaves room for the cutting edge; they are not functional tools and therefore do not present any traces of sharpening. Apart from rare exceptions, they are assembled as roughouts, but with traces of circulation, in over 300 very monotonous hoards exclusively made up of these objects. They thus have no connection whatsoever with the real Late Bronze Age socketed axes, which are morphologically varied and often found used and broken, along with other heteroclite objects, in jumbled hoards predating the 8th century BC. The production and depositing of the Armorican pseudo-axes thus corresponds to a very original phenomenon, specific to the Armorican Early Iron Age. This phenomenon can probably be explained by the pre-monetary use of these pseudo-axes and by their definitive abandonment as part of ritualised practices (Milcent in press). We cannot thus use them to argue for the continuity of an industry and hoard practices from the Atlantic Late Bronze Age. On the contrary, these sets of pseudo-axes provide evidence of a profound mutation of the position accorded to copper alloy products in the socio-economic sphere during the Early Iron Age.

A late emergence of iron metallurgy under Hallstattian, or even Mediterranean influence?

From the end of the Late Bronze Age, small iron objects found throughout the zone of Atlantic network circulation, from Extremadura to Scotland (Vilaça 2013; Milcent 2012, 141; Needham 2007, 49–52), provide evidence of knowledge of a new metal, albeit limited, as in temperate Europe. It is difficult to identify the place of fabrication of these elements, which do not constitute proof of the mastery of iron metallurgy as they could be imported or made from imported refined iron bars. However, it is important to recall the existence of forge waste (scalings) associated with a settlement apparently dating from the 10th century BC in the south of England (Hartshill Quarry in Berkshire; Collard et al. 2006) and iron work slag from the 9th century BC at Bonnée in the Centre region of France, on the fringes of the Bronze Atlantic zone (Joly *et al.* 2011). Above all, it is imperative to reiterate the fact that evidence of iron metallurgy during the Late Bronze Age in the continental domain is no more frequent or more impressive (Gomez de Soto and Kerouanton 2009).

More significantly, from the beginning of the Early Iron Age, during the 8th century BC, we find several large-sized Atlantic iron productions: Holme-Pierrepoint type swords, looped socketed axes, to cite but a few examples (Milcent 2012, 143; pl. 65, no. 7 and 9; pl. 72, no. 17). These exceptional objects were undoubtedly reserved for the elite and demonstrate for the first time a real mastery of forge techniques. They do not appear to be less frequent than their very rare equivalents from the east of France or Languedoc. In western Languedoc, in contact with Phoenician, Greek or Etruscan tradesmen and artisans, the 'Launacian' industry, fossilised in non-funerary hoards, shows that essential instruments, such as axes and spearheads, were still produced in bronze until the beginning of the 6th century BC. In these conditions, it is not legitimate to envisage any significant lag in iron metallurgy in the northwest of Gaul compared to more eastern or more southerly regions. In addition, for a period corresponding to the 7th century, a site such as Choisy-au-Bac (Oise) yielded two major forges

(Blanchet 1984, 423–5, fig. 245). During the Boulogne colloquium, the discovery of forge residues dating from the beginning of the Iron Age at Saultain (Nord) was reported by N. Buchez and A. Henton.

Traces of primary iron production are now very well established for the Early Iron Age in the region of Le Mans (Sarthe), in Upper Brittany, as well as in the Evreux region in Upper Normandy (at least 11 sites). Paradoxically, these oldest bloomeries, for once-off use and of trapped slag type, are much better known and more frequent in the northwest than in the east of France (Cabboi *et al.* 2007, 58), even though this mainly denotes differential research. The discoveries of these past 15 years did not come as much of a surprise as hoards of more or less refined bi-pyramidal iron bar masses have been known for a long time in some of these northwestern regions, particularly in Brittany (where 130 bars have been recorded, corresponding to about 800 kg of metal). As most of these bars present a specific morphology which is not found elsewhere, apart from occasional finds in the south of England (elongated bars, variant BLS5 of Marion Berranger's classification; Berranger 2014, 69, 90; fig. 32), there is no reason to assume that these objects were produced outside northwestern Gaul.

A world under continental pressure or influence?

The theory that the Late Bronze Age in Atlantic regions was under pressure from the Continent, as shown in particular by Rhine-Swiss-eastern France (RSFO) influences, then Hallstattian influences, is widespread. In this way, vast regions in the north and west of France were considered to have integrated into the orbit of the Continental domain, as a result of migrations, or more recently in a more moderated vision, on account of cultural transgression and acculturation. After 800 BC in particular, the Atlantic cultural area would have shrunk rapidly on the Continent, to such an extent that it would be difficult to envisage that it was not a peripheral facies of the Hallstattian world, or under Hallstattian influence, apart perhaps from the Armorican Massif and the Channel coastline. According to this paradigm, most of the material culture of these northwestern regions would be importations or the influence of Central Europe. We will not revisit the very complex and rather balanced exchange dynamics operating during the Late Bronze Age between the Atlantic and the continental domains (Milcent 2012) as we would not have enough space to assess this question, which is, moreover, not the central issue of this paper. For the ensuing period, it is clear that these links are much less simple and asymmetric than previously thought, and that the cultural area preferentially opened towards the Channel and the Atlantic, does not appear to be specially confined to a fringe of Gaul. Several cases will be cited as examples here, such as hand weapons, domestic and funerary architecture. A special mention should be reserved for the Champagne region, which was responsible for some of the intellectual barriers inhibiting the identification of an Atlantic Early Iron Age.

In relation to weapons, we will not examine in any detail an argument presented for the past 15 years, *i.e.* that grip-tongue swords with pistiliform blades from the beginning of the Iron Age, incorrectly referred to as 'Hallstattian', are originally North Atlantic products, and that they were adopted from the 8th century BC onwards by the majority of the continental elite, with adaptations. What is new, is that the examination of other emblematic objects from the early continental Hallstatt, also reveals Atlantic heritage or strong Atlantic influences. This is true of razors, certain horse harnessing and wagon elements, vessels and situlae in bronze sheets (Milcent 2009; 2012, 149–53; 2015). These are thus forms of an 'Atlantic way of life' that spread a little everywhere throughout middle Europe during the 8th century BC.

A rather similar process is at work at the end of the Early Iron Age, with tanged hilt Medio-Atlantic daggers, often called 'Jogassians'. These arms and their metallic sheaths appear simultaneously for the first time on either side of the eastern Channel, particularly in Champagne and in the lower Thames Basin, and are then adopted and distributed from the second half of the 5th century onwards, throughout what was in the process of becoming the Latenian domain (Milcent 2009). The parallel diffusion from west to east, of filiform fibulae with short springs and a pellet or disc-shaped foot (Dehn and Stöllner 1996; Milcent 2006, 96, fig. 10) implies that other material culture traits of Atlantic ancestry or dispatched through the Atlantic domain, also accompanied these weapons in one way or another.

The case of architecture is more original as it is not called upon to account for the cultural dynamics of the Early Iron Age. As far as the domestic buildings are concerned, we know that the circular plan examples discovered in north-west Gaul are taken to be Atlantic, or to be more precise, closely linked with the British Isles, as comparable 'houses' from an architectural and technical viewpoint were identified across the Channel. In the British Isles, these circular buildings are by far the predominant architectural form, but are not exclusively used for the construction of houses. Links on either side of the Channel appear to be all the more likely in light of the fact that continental circular 'houses' are rare and are concentrated in the regions bordering the Channel, at least during the Early and Middle Bronze Age (Fig. 7.2). Unlike traditional perspectives would have us believe, these circular houses do not become rarer during the Late Bronze Age and do not disappear from the continent during the Early Iron Age. On the contrary, the sites on which we find them appear to be more frequent than at the beginning of the sequence, and above all, clearly advance inland during the Early Iron Age, particularly towards the

south of Champagne (Fig. 7.2). The observed dynamics are thus opposed to usual assumptions. Unfortunately, due to dating problems, it is not yet possible to accurately date these buildings in the Early Iron Age and to provide details on the dynamics of this extension into Gaul. However, it is important to underline that circular buildings are still well recorded in northwestern Gaul during the Late Iron Age (Dechezleprêtre and Ginoux 2005).

If we now consider funerary architecture, a similar process may be observable, but on a totally different scale. Generally, in middle Europe, the emergence of funerary enclosures made up of a more or less square ditch, often lined with a palisade, containing a group of family burials, is associated with the advent of La Tène cultures, during the 5th century BC. The model of these funerary structures with strong ritual and cosmological connotations was attributed to regions considered to correspond to the birth of material La Tène cultures, particularly Bohemia, Hunsrück Eifel and Champagne. Although trenched quadrilateral funerary enclosures are known there from the 5th century BC onwards, they were not exclusive to these regions, as shown by the example of contemporaneous necropolises in Brittany (Villard *et al.* 2013) or in eastern Languedoc (Séjalon and Dedet 2003), to cite only a few distant examples. But, above all, recent discoveries confirm that prototypes exist from the end of the 7th century BC, on the Continental Channel coastline, from Lower Normandy to Pas-de-Calais (Fig. 7.3, nos 4–5). Similar, yet older funerary enclosures are sporadically recorded in Flanders and the north of France, during the Atlantic Late Bronze Age 2 and the Atlantic Early Iron Age 1 (Fig. 7.3, nos 1–3). Like certain canonical Latenian examples, square enclosures from the full Atlantic Early Iron Age can be associated with a palisade and delimit burial pit graves that appear to correspond to family groups, like in Basly in Calvados (Fig. 7.3, no. 5). This transition from circular funerary enclosures to quadrangular enclosures must represent a major change in mentalities and it is interesting to attempt to identify the leading regions of this transformation.

Champagne: on the fringes of the Atlantic area

These cases show that it is no longer possible to consider today that the northwestern societies of Gaul were accountable to or under the influence of Hallstattian regions during the Early Iron Age. But we must refrain from adopting the opposite model to that criticized here, by inversing the poles in a caricatured way. In view of their extension, the regions linked by the networks referred to as Atlantic were never a centre in relation to others, no more than the Hallstattian world. All of this argues in favour of abandoning 'centre-periphery' type models for the European Early Iron Age. The question now is to comprehend the links between the

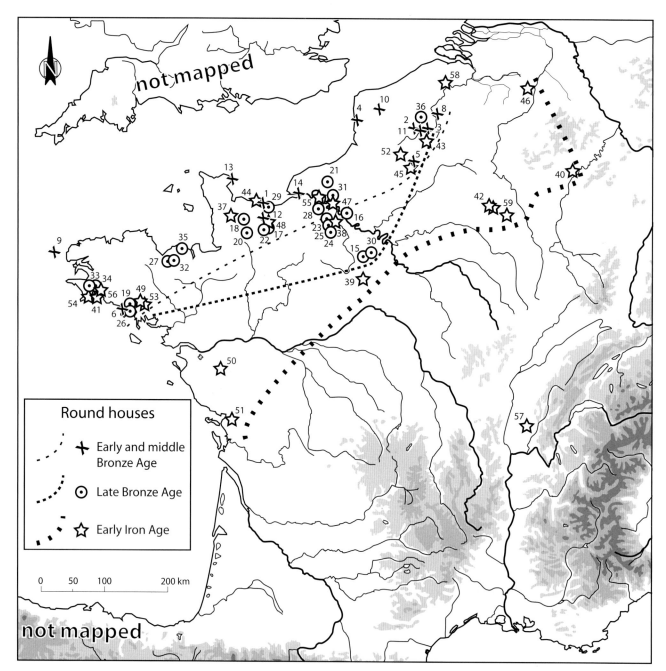

Fig. 7.2. Distribution of round houses dating to the Bronze Age or Early Iron Age. Early and Middle Bronze Age: Bernière-sur-Mer (1); Brebières (2); Erre (3); Etaples-sur-Mer (4); Eterpigny-Barleux (5); Guidel (6); Lauwin-Planque (7); Lesdain (8); Ouessant (9); Rebecques (10); Roeux (11); Saint-Martin-de-Fontenay (12); Saint-Vaast-la-Hougue (13); Saint-Vigor-d'Ymonville (14). Late Bronze Age: Auneau (15); Bouafles (16); Cagny (17); Cahagnes (18); Caudan (19); Condé-sur-Noireau (20); Etaimpuis (21); Fontenay-le-Marmion (22); Gravigny (23); Grossoeuvre (24); Guichainville (25); Guidel (26); Lamballe (27); Malleville-sur-le-Bec (28); Mathieu (29); Mignières (30); Mont-Saint-Aignan (31); Plédéliac (32); Pluguffan (33); Quimper (34); Saint-Jacut-de-la-Mer (35); Seclin (36). Early and transitional Later Iron Age: Agneaux (37); Alizay (38); Allaines-Mervilliers (39); Beaufort (40); Bénodet (41); Bezannes (42); Bourlon (43); Courseulles-sur-Mer (44); Ennemain (45); Grote-Spouwen (46); Honguemare-Guénouville (47); Ifs (48); Inzizac-Lochrist (49); La Gaubretière (50); Longèves (51); Méaulte (52); Pluvigner (53); Pont l'Abbé (54); Poses (55); Quimper (56); Saint-Just (57); Sint-Martens-Latem (58); Suippes (59).

societies of this period in a more complex, dynamic and multilateral way. This is in particular why the term 'Medio-Atlantic' and not 'Central-Atlantic' Early Iron Age was

coined to describe regions in the northwest of Gaul and the south of Great Britain, in an intermediary situation in the area of networks preferentially constructed in westernmost

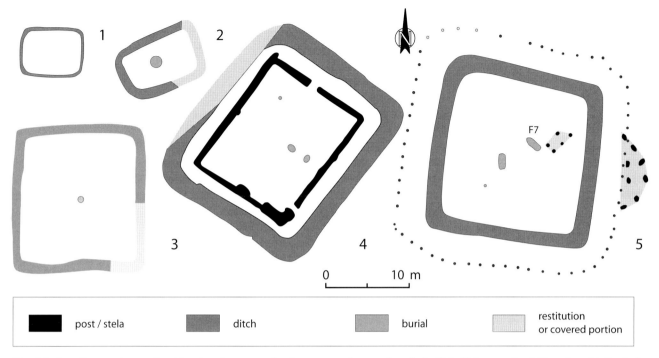

Fig. 7.3. *Late Bronze Age medio-Atlantic sub-rectangular funerary enclosures (nos 1–2: 11th–10th centuries BC) to the mid–Early Iron Age (no. 3: 8th–first half of the 7th century BC; nos 4–5: 2nd half of the 7th–early 6th century BC). No. 1: Tagnon, Ardennes (after Le Goff and Guillot 1992); no. 2: Thourotte, Oise (after Blanchet and Talon 2005); no. 3: Destelbergen, Flandres occidentales (after De Laet et al. 1986, Fig. 29) ; no. 4: Eterville, Calvados (after Jahier 2005) ; no. 5: Basly, Calvados (after San Juan and Le Goff 2003).*

Europe. This does not imply that the Atlantic networks would be in competition with the others to the point that clear limits could be observed around their peripheries, and still less that monothetic groups existed, that is, where all the main traits would be purely Atlantic. Instead, we observe the occurrence of complex interconnections and many examples of cultural transitions with no clear-cut limits, apart from some exceptions, which creates difficulties when we attempt to visually and cartographically depict these phenomena. Champagne provides a good example of this cultural mixing. This region warrants special consideration as for a long time it was the focus of attention and still serves as a reference for the cultural characterisation of the most northern and western regions of Gaul. Champagne has many points in common with these latter regions, is considered as Hallstattian, and would be a key element arguing for the inexistence of original and Atlantic cultural entities during the Early Iron Age. It is thus crucial to correctly identify and analyse the main cultural features of Champagne.

The very particular historiographical status of this region is explained by the abundant funerary discoveries dating from the end of the Early Iron Age and particularly from the beginning of the Late Iron Age, as well as the early exploration of settlements from these periods. The Champagne geological substratum is mainly made up of chalky plateaus, which explains why sites are easier to detect than elsewhere, and why they appear to be more frequent or rich. Due to fact that abundant sites were excavated as early as the 19th century, Champagne was often considered as one of the main centres of the cradle of Latenian societies, supposed to occupy a wide crescent extending beyond the classical Hallstattian domain, from Champagne to Hunsrück Eifel to Bohemia. However, this was not based on any detailed or decisive argument. The earliest Iron Age graves from the Champagne region were attributed to the end of the Hallstatt Early Iron Age on account of several discoveries of fibulae of Hallstattian morphology and technology. But also because, due to circular reasoning, the Early Latenian Champagne tombs were affiliated to an ancestral Hallstatt material culture (Hatt and Roualet 1977, 11). For all these reasons, the material culture from the end of the Early Iron Age in Champagne and the outlying areas, described as Jogassian (from the eponymous necropolis at Chouilly 'Les Jogasses') following the terminology of P. M. Favret, or Aisne-Marne stage 1 according to that of J.-P. Demoule, is still considered by most protohistorians as one of the westernmost manifestations of a strictly Hallstattian cultural facies. This is why the recurring perceived affinities between the northwesternmost regions of Gaul and Jogassian culture are sometimes deemed to be surprising, and generally interpreted in terms of profound diffusions of Hallstattian influences towards the northwest.

In reality, the link between Jogassian culture and the Hallstatt complex should not be taken for granted and disproportionate weight has been given to the Hallstattian fibulae from Champagne as regards the identity of the region in terms of material culture. What really remains of this allegedly Hallstatt material culture if we exclude these fibulae from the debate, a lot of which (in particular the drum fibulae) are in actual fact importations from more southerly neighbouring and truly Hallstattian regions? What is left if we leave out the elements of personal adornment that appear to point to the presence of foreigners or adhesion to an 'international' elite fashion, such as basket-shaped pendants, glass beads, bronze tubular torcs or 'armlet' type bracelets? When these are discounted, nothing specifically Hallstattian remains in Jogassian necropolises and settlements. The weapons, especially the aforementioned Jogassian daggers, but also the spear heads, the bows and arrows for which we sometimes find the quiver (Hatt and Roualet 1976, pl. ii), have no exact equivalent in the Hallstattian domain, strictly speaking. Annular adornments other than those mentioned above are specific to Champagne, or else very simple and ubiquitous. As for Champagne pottery productions, they are mainly characterized by angular carinated profiles which later become widespread during the 5th century BC and are more similar to those from regions situated further west or further north (Fig. 7.4). But, above all, funerary practices, which are, with pottery, one of the best criteria of cultural identification, display few associations with the Hallstattian world. Jogassian graves are practically exclusively inhumation burials, and are not installed in tumuli used as family cemeteries supprimer virgule, like in the Hallstattian world from Ha D1-2 and Ha D3. Individual inhumations are laid out in a sub-rectangular pit, which can be deep, and is not overlain by a tumulus of sufficient dimensions to have left any trace, apart from a few exceptions. They often form small groups of aligned or parallel pits, prefiguring the organisation of certain Latenian necropolises, but have no equivalent in the West Hallstattian world. In addition, they often contain a food deposit, probably corresponding to the remains of a funerary meal, made up of one or several pottery vessels and animal bones. These food deposits never appear in Hallstattian tombs in the eastern centre and the east of France. Only the presence of drinking vessels has been recorded in several of these latter tombs.

On a different level, the absence of elitist graves corresponding to the Hallstattian model of the tomb with a four-wheeled wagon beneath a large tumulus, or to the west Hallstattian model of a cremation deposited in a bronze urn under a tumulus (cf. map of these tombs: Verger 1995, fig. 1 and 47; Milcent 2003, fig. 234), is a sign that the Champagne elite never adhered to the very specific funerary ideologies of the east and the eastern centre of Gaul. As observed before, exceptions have been discovered only in the south of Champagne, in the region of Troyes-Lavau, in a sector bordering the Hallstattian world in the strict sense of the term (Verger 1995, 363; Milcent 2014, ill. 4.11).

More generally, our knowledge of settlements, the territorial and socio-economic organisation of Champagne at the end of the Early Iron Age and the very beginning of the following period, does not point to any particular affinities with Hallstattian Gaul. There are no similar proto-urban agglomerations, like that of Bourges and no princely residences, such as Vix (Milcent 2014). Settlement appears to be relatively dispersed and at most, we can identify large hamlets or small villages with loose organisation, alongside very structured farms (Villes 2000).

In the same way, it is significant that in spite of the fact that thousands of tombs have been excavated in Champagne, early Mediterranean imports are only anecdotally represented and belong to very banal products (elements of at times unrefined coral, perhaps glass beads).[1] They thus have nothing to do with the hundreds of very diversified Mediterranean imports present in west Hallstattian regions, which are sometimes issued from prestigious productions (Guggisberg 2004). This implies that Champagne remained rather hermetic, like most of northwestern Gaul, to the major ideological and material exchange currents that structured the tight relations established between the Hallstattian and Mediterranean domains at this time.

For all these reasons, Champagne should now be removed from the Hallstattian world, strictly speaking, in the same way as Hunsrück-Eifel. Widening the Hallstattian world to Champagne was an interpretative illusion, inherited from the confusion of the first half of the 20th century, which muddles the issue and the understanding of cultural dynamics at the end of the Early Iron Age. We cannot deny that Champagne remains original in certain respects and that it presents affinities with adjacent Hallstattian regions, which is logical given its geographical location in contact with the eastern centre of Gaul and the polythetic aspect of the material cultures, but it is increasingly apparent that it shares a majority of cultural traits with more northern and western regions. It is notably on this basis that it seems possible to identify an Early Iron Age in the northwestern arc of Gaul, i.e., from Gironde to Meuse, with different cultural and socio-economic traits to those of continental regions. We now propose to describe this Atlantic Early Iron Age and to consider its geographic influence and also the links that it appears to maintain with the Atlantic Late Bronze Age, identified during the 1940s.

Assessing the Atlantic Early Iron Age in Gaul

As its name suggests, the concept of the Atlantic Early Iron Age is based on two main dimensions, one of which is chronological, the other geographic and cultural. In concrete terms, this implies that we can identify this period by differentiating it from the preceding Late Bronze Age and the ensuing Late Iron Age. It also suggests that the archaeological materials from this period present a

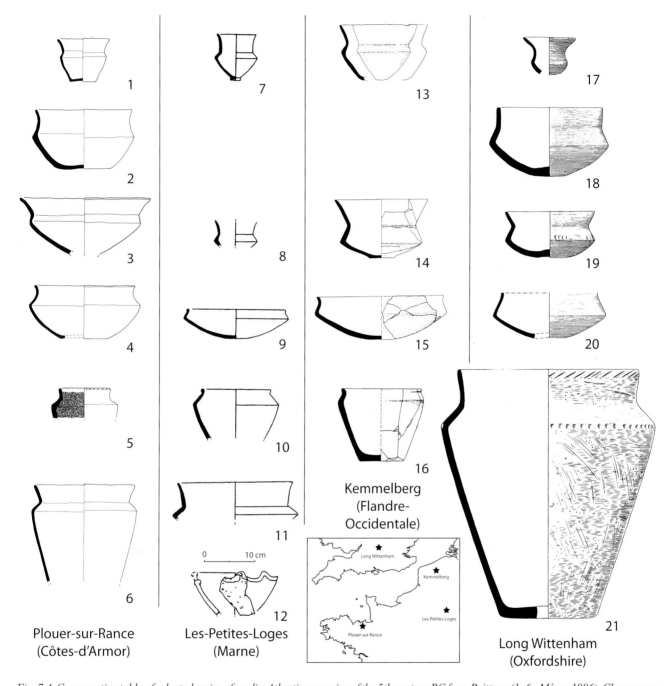

Fig. 7.4. Comparative table of selected series of medio-Atlantic ceramics of the 5th century BC from Brittany (1–6 ; Ménez 1996), Champagne (7–12 ; Saurel 2007), Belgian Flanders (13–6 ; Van Doorselaer et al. 1987) and southern England (17–21 ; Harding 1972). At same scale.

sufficient number of specific features to distinguish them from continental or southern cultures. In order for these traits to be considered specific, they must be preferentially distributed throughout regions close to the Atlantic and the seas (the Channel and the southwest of the North Sea) and rivers (Loire, Seine ...), sometimes prolonging this ocean a long way from its shorelines.

Assuming that the Atlantic Early Iron Age represents a kind of continuum with the Atlantic Late Bronze Age,

this would also imply that it would not be confined to the northwestern regions of Gaul. As in the past, there would be shared material culture traits with other European regions bordering the northern Atlantic and its eastern ramifications, particularly Great Britain. Forms of exchange and links with these other regions should also be perceptible. From our perspective, it is not a case of identifying a homogeneous super or supra-cultural complex extending over the westernmost European territory, beyond Atlantic

Gaul. The concept of the Atlantic Early Iron Age, like that of the Atlantic Late Bronze Age, corresponds rather to the identification of the importance of a network of contacts preferentially linking, for diverse regions (geographic, historical, socio-economic…), different cultures through different aspects, to the point of revealing convergences between these cultures, perhaps in the same way that certain Mediterranean regions shared cultural traits designated as Orientalising, during the same period.

As for the chronological dimension, it is not necessary to revisit the individualisation of a true Early Iron Age as this is more or less generally accepted. Today, the remaining challenge is its internal periodisation and absolute chronological order. Proposals to this end only really

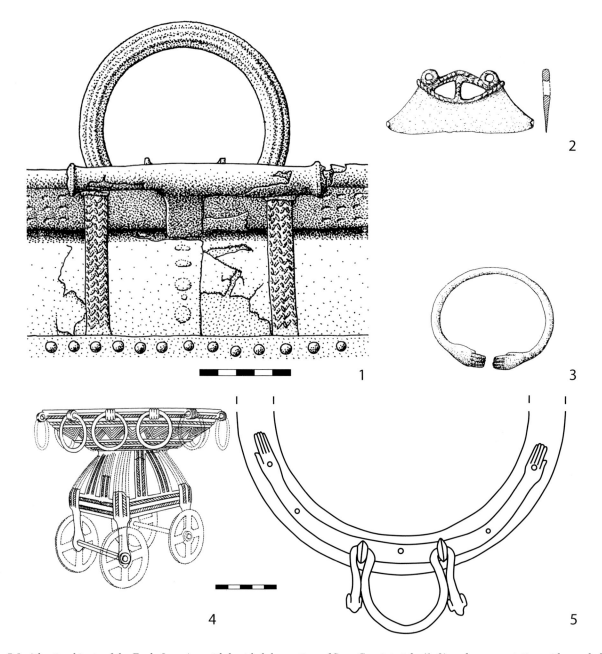

Fig. 7.5. Atlantic objects of the Early Iron Age with braided decoration of Syro-Cypriot style (1–2) and ornamentation with prophylactic hands of Near Eastern inspiration (3). For comparison, objects of Punic inspiration discovered in the Iberian Peninsula (4–5). 1: attachment loop of a cauldron from Llyn Fawr (Wales) of the Early Iron Age (Gerloff 2010, pl. 73); 2: razor from Saint-Leu-d'Esserent (Oise) of the Early Iron Age (Blanchet et al 1978); 3: bracelet from Saint-Pierre-sur-Dives (Calvados) of the Early Iron Age (Verney 1993 Fig. 8 no. 11); 4: miniature chariot from the Baiões hoard (Beira Alta) dated to the Late Bronze Age (Silva 1986); 5: Western Phoenician basin attachment from Cañada de Ruiz Sánchez in Carmona (Sevilla), of the 7th century BC (after Jimenez Avila 2002, pl. xvi). 1–3: scale 1:2; 4–5: scale 1:3.

concern the first stage of the Atlantic Early Iron Age (Milcent 2012, 142–67), and occasionally what appears to be an intermediary stage (Milcent in press). Most of the relative chronology work in this domain has yet to be carried out, and we hope that the dendrodates will lead one day to the establishment of an independent absolute chronology, i.e., that is not dependent on comparisons with the typo-chronologies and absolute dates obtained for the other cultures of the European Early Iron Age.

As for material culture affinities, the very marked recorded differences observed from one region to another in Atlantic Gaul in terms of the intensity and quality of excavations and publications are of considerable weight. One only has to compare Champagne with a vast region such as Pays-de-la-Loire for which practically no archaeological data have been published. Nonetheless, some indicators and information mark out the way: for the Atlantic Early Iron Age 1 (800–625 BC), individual inhumation below a tumulus is a virtually unknown funerary practice in northwestern Gaul, whereas it is predominant at the same time in the western Hallstattian domain. Generally speaking, tombs are rare, which points to the generalised use of funerary practices leaving few or no material traces, like for the Atlantic Late Bronze Age. The exception to this is what Eugène Warmenbol called the Mosan group, a culture with strong Atlantic affinities, with a rather original and mixed aspect, with tombs under tumuli, at times with a long pistiliform sword in bronze or iron. In spite of the adoption of the tumulus, the Mosan

group practices in elitist tombs remain different to those found in west Hallstatt cultures as cremation is exclusive, sometimes concerns several deceased at a time and is generally accompanied by a 'defunctionalisation' of the sword in that it is broken and burnt (Warmenbol 1993). In several of these cremations, a reduced drinking service was found (three recipients at the most: Reinhard 1993), but this does not enable us to establish close links with elitist cremation tombs with swords from the central and eastern Hallstattian domains, as the latter contain sets of tableware, for both eating and drinking.

On another scale, reference should be made to the links that seem to bind the north of Gaul to the British Isles, judging by the distribution of the earliest variants of the pistiliform swords from the Gündlingen group (Milcent 2004, fig. 57–58; 2009, fig. 11). We also observe the persistence of tenuous contacts with the southwest of the Iberian Peninsula, in the form of locally produced objects during the 7th century BC, but bearing for the first time decoration inspired by Syrian-Cypriot toreutics and Phoenician religious symbolism (hand-amulet depicting the heavenly goddess Tanit; Fig. 7.5, nos 1–3). Prototypes of these decorations are depicted on objects brought from the southwest of Spain and Portugal at the end of the Late Bronze Age by Phoenicians, then imitated on site (Fig. 7.5, nos 4–5). This implies that the long distance Atlantic contacts towards the southwest were not broken, even if they no longer attained the same intensity as during the Atlantic Late Bronze Age 2 and 3 early (1140–900 BC);

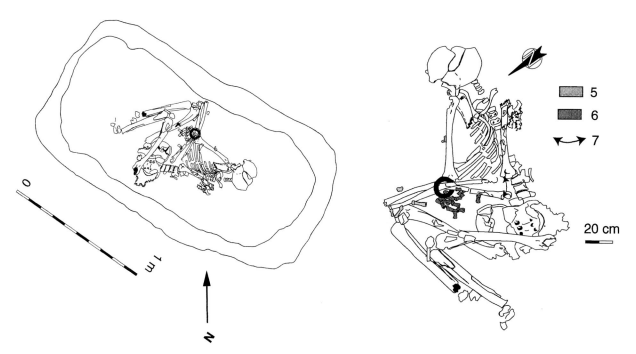

Fig. 7.6. Example of an inhumation placed on its side, with lower limbs flexed, in a large rectangular pit: Basly (Calvados, Normandy) tomb F7 (beginning 6th century BC) (after San Juan and Le Goff 2003). The grave was set in a square enclosure (cf Fig. 7.3 n°5).

during the Atlantic Early Iron Age 2 (625–525 BC), we note the exceptional development of the fabrication of pseudo-axes with sockets and massive hoards of these objects, but this phenomenon is hardly any different to the Armorican Massif, although it sporadically affects regions as far away as Picardy, Beauce and Touraine.

We will not describe in detail the original phenomenon observed from Brittany to Champagne to Pas-de-Calais, with what appears to be the abrupt development of inhumation burials in a deep rectangular pit, and not directly on the ground below a tumulus. Buried individuals are placed in a lateral position, generally on their right side, with the legs bent, and the head towards the south or southeast (Fig. 7.6).

This phenomenon is also reflected in other regions in the extreme west of Europe, perhaps in England and peculiarly in the southwest of Portugal where burials in a lateral bent position (mostly on the right side) were recently discovered in rectangular pits, at times delimited by a quadrangular earthwork enclosure (Arruda *et al.* in press). But, if we return to Atlantic Gaul, it is true that a significant deficit of burials remains observable for this stage in most regions, pointing to the widespread use of funerary practices leaving no archaeological trace. On a very wide scale, the diffusion of small or large cup mark decorations on pottery extends overs a vast Atlantic area. These decorations persist during the following stage (Milcent 2006, map fig. 6); at the end of the Early Iron Age and the beginning of the following period (525–425 BC), the most remarkable phenomenon is the generalisation of the production of hand-made pottery with angular profiles, while these forms remain practically unknown in the Hallstattian domain.

The multiplication of settlement excavations in the west of France reveals that very comparable productions extend

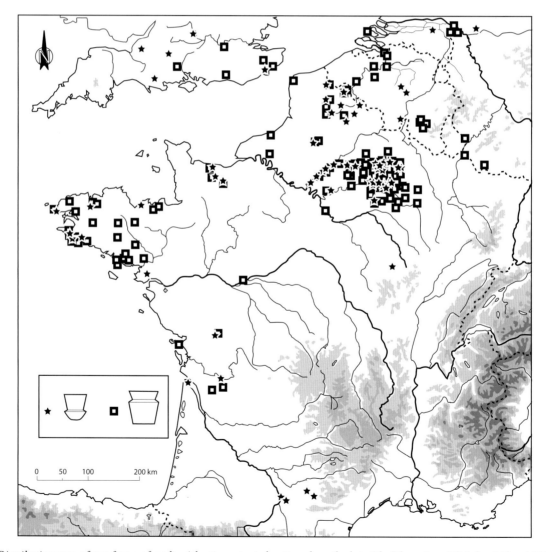

Fig. 7.7. Distribution map of two forms of medio-Atlantic carinated pottery from the late 6th–5th century BC (after Milcent 2006, Fig. 4).

from Flanders to Vendée, right through Normandy and Brittany (Fig. 7.7), whereas until recently these productions appeared to be limited to Champagne and the neighbouring regions. Prototypes of these forms (low carinated goblets and high carinated pots) were known from the beginning of the 6th century BC in western Languedoc (see for example the C family vases from the Castrais necropolis classification: Giraud *et al.* 2003, vol. 1, fig. 40–41).

During the 5th century BC, several regional groups from the south of England participate in the regional production area of these angular carinated vases, but in lesser proportions. The distribution map for what we can call truly Medio-Atlantic pottery largely overlaps with that of a new clothing fashion, materialized by the diffusion of filiform fibulae with a raised foot and ending in a widened appendage during the course of the 5th century BC (Fig. 7.8). We observe that these fibulae with short springs are

the first to be undeniably produced on site as they have practically no equivalent in west Hallstattian regions where the fibula with an drum foot and crossbow spring are largely dominant (Milcent 2004, 245, fig. 106). On the other hand, they are clearly affiliated to the Gulf of Lion type Iberian-Languedoc productions with prototypes going back until at least the beginning of the 6th century BC. Once again, they demonstrate that the contacts established with regions in the southwest of Europe were not necessarily less significant than those established with the Hallstattian world.

Lastly, the use of funerary practices with archaeologically materialized tombs appears to intensify. Whereas burials are predominant in the north of Atlantic Gaul and appear to develop in the south of England,[2] conversely cremation appears to prevail in the west, particularly in the Armorican Massif. This latter aspect may not be unrelated to the extension of cremation in southern Gaul throughout the

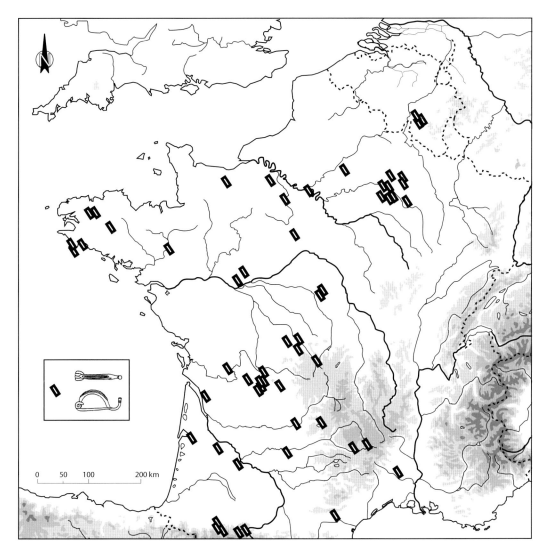

Fig. 7.8. Distribution map of brooches with upright foot and spring of La Tène style of the 5th century BC (after Milcent 2006, Fig. 10). Southern England and Western Germany are not mapped.

Early Iron Age (Dedet 2004), by means of specific practices denoting an adaptation to distinct cultural contexts. As for the contacts established beyond the Channel, it is interesting to note that burials with non-dismantled two-wheeled chariots from the 5th century BC are now known in Yorkshire and the southeast of Scotland (Boyle 2004; Carter *et al.* 2010), which could provide evidence of affinities with Champagne. On the Continent and in the northwest, these 5th century chariot tombs are not confined to Champagne, as they are also known in the Belgian Ardennes, the south of Holland, in Brittany and Charente-Périgord. The first well-dated burials in lateral position with bent lower limbs

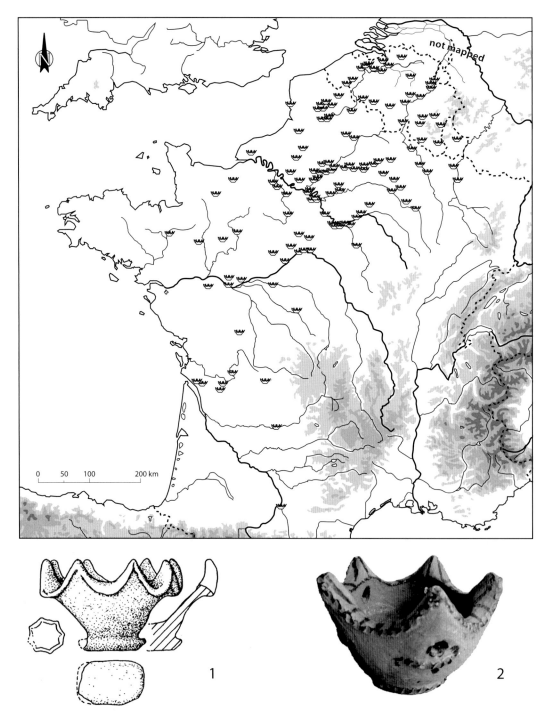

Fig. 7.9. Distribution of 'cups' with scalloped edges and a drawing of an example from Epraves in Belgium (1). For comparison, a Kanoun (cooking brazier) from the Maghreb (2).

in Yorkshire are also attributed to this period. As we have already seen, this funerary ritual is well documented several decades earlier in the north of Gaul and we can question whether certain Yorkshire tombs without objects might not be older but rather contemporaneous with their continental counterparts.

In a more diachronic perspective, let us mention the very particular form of vessel, the large bowl with festooned edges, known from the beginning of the Iron Age in northern Gaul, and which spreads to the whole west of Gaul, apart from Armorica, at the beginning of the Late Iron Age (Fig. 7.9). This distribution almost completely disregards the Hallstattian world. It undoubtedly signifies a form of cultural community if we admit that this utensil was used for a specific culinary practice: these festooned recipients may not be lamps, but brazier pots for embers used to cook food slowly in a pot placed above them, in the same way as the present-day *kanouns* in the Maghreb (Fig. 7.9, nos 1–2).

As far as settlement is concerned, let us recall that 'circular' houses are now known everywhere throughout Atlantic Gaul, although they are not very frequent. It is important to underline that these buildings with very British affinities appear several times in an enclosed settlement

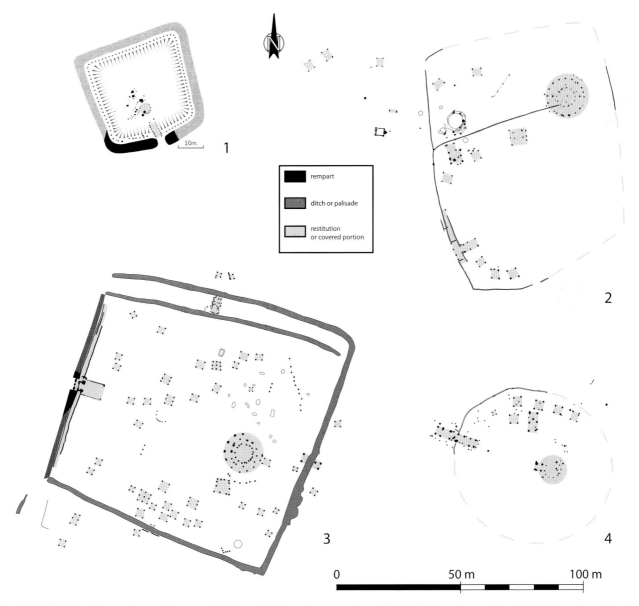

Fig. 7.10. *The Late Bronze Age enclosure at Highstead in Kent for comparison (Clark 2012), and examples of ditched and/or palisaded farmsteads of the Early Iron Age, with round house in Atlantic Gaul. 2: Bezannes (Marne) 'La Bergerie' (after Desbrosse et al 2012, modified); 3: Courseulles-sur-Mer (Calvados) 'La Fosse Touzé' (after Jahier 2011, modified); 4: Méaulte (Somme) 'ZAC du pays des Coquelicots' (after Buchez 2012, modified).*

context, with an elitist vocation or appearance, throughout the Early Iron Age (Fig. 7.10, nos 2–4). Although they are not common, this typically Atlantic architectural model appears to be socially valued and seems to be used at times as a strong identity marker.

In the same way, and in spite of the fact that we could be tempted to establish connections with the '*Herrenhöfe*' from the Bavarian Early Iron Age, it is increasingly clear that large centres of agro-pastoral domains with ditched or quadrilateral palisaded enclosures emerge at an early stage in the Atlantic

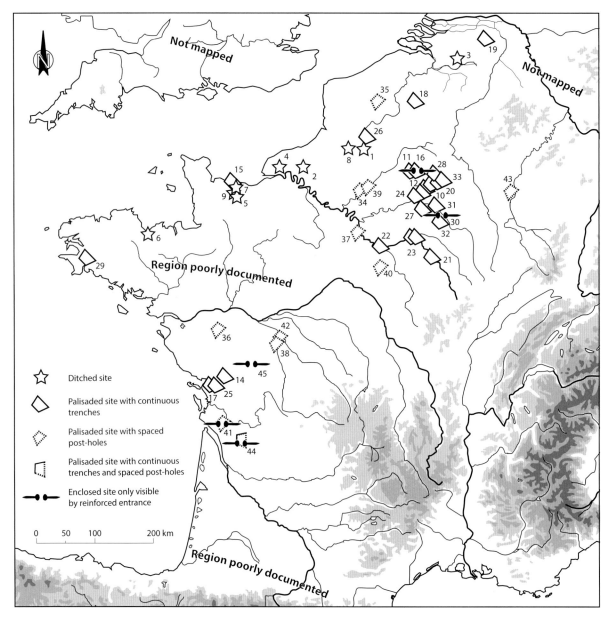

Fig. 7.11. Distribution of enclosed agricultural sites and farmsteads dating from the end of the Bronze Age to the middle Early Iron Age (10th–mid-6th centuries BC) in Atlantic Gaul. The scarcity of palisaded sites to the west of the Paris Basin is explained by bias rather than cultural or historical reality. Ditched sites: Amiens (1); Beautot (2); Beerse (3); Epretot (4) ; Fontenay-le-Marmion (5); Lamballe (6); Mathieu (7); Pont-de-Metz (8); Saint-Martin-de-Fontenay (9). Sites with palisades based on continuous trenches : Bazancourt (10); Beaurieux (11); Bezannes (12); Coulon (14); Courseullessur-Mer (15); Cuiry-lès-Chaudardes (16); Dompierre-sur-Mer (17); Ghislenghien (18); Gemert Bakel (19); Isles-sur-Suippe (20); La Chapelle-Saint-Luc (21); La Grande-Paroisse (22); La Saulsotte (23); Les Mesneux (24); Longèves (25); Méaulte (26); Oger (27); Pomacle (28); Quimper (29); Saint-Germain-la-Ville (30); Saint-Gibrien (31); Saint-Martin-sur-le-Pré (32); Warmeriville (33). Sites with palisades based on spaced post-holes : Boran-sur-Oise (34); Brebières (35); Cholet (36); Cesson (37); Ingrandes-sur-Vienne (38); Ponpoint (39); Préfontaines (40); Préguillac (41); Pussigny (42); Woippy (43). Sites with mixed palisade types (based on trenches and spaced post-holes: Barbezieux (44). Sites with enclosure visible only by reinforced entrance : Barbezieux (44); Chasseneuil-du-Poitou (45); Cuiry-lès-Chaudardes (16); Préguillac (41); Saint-Germain-la-Ville (30).

arc of Gaul. They appear from the end of the Late Bronze Age or the very beginning of the Early Iron Age, which is to say clearly before their west Hallstattian counterparts and at the same time as their Bavarian counterparts. Furthermore, they are part of an earlier tradition that appeared during the Atlantic Middle Bronze Age and is well evidenced during the Late Bronze Age in the south-east of England, then sporadically in the north of France (palisaded circular enclosures of Brebières, Saint-Martin-sur-le-Pré in Marne and Ghislenghien in Hainaut). Mapping of the earliest sites, before the end of the 6th century BC shows a clear concentration in the north and the west of Gaul, in spite of the disparities due to the unequal development of rescue archaeology (Fig. 7.11). During the 5th century BC, these enclosed establishments remain much more frequent in Atlantic Gaul than in continental Gaul, probably pointing once again to a rather distinctive trait of Atlantic settlement.

Ultimately, and paradoxically, the evidence for characterising an Atlantic cultural entity appears to be more diversified during the Early Iron Age than during the Late Bronze Age, for which the identification of Atlantic cultures is mainly based on bronze productions and metallic hoards. This Atlantic Gaul during the Early Iron Age is also made up of a mosaic of cultures and maintains rather clear links with the southeast of England. All of these regions, from Yorkshire to Charente, are in a pivotal Medio-Atlantic area, within a network of more extensive links. However, in the absence of more substantial archaeological evidence, the contours of these networks have yet to be defined, particularly towards the south.

Conclusion

The notion of the Atlantic Early Iron Age is valid as it provides an explanatory framework for the analysis of remains contrasting with the material remains discovered in Hallstattian and southern Gaul, mainly on account of their early chronology or original characteristics. The discovery of large palisaded agro-pastoral domains in the western centre region, the multiplication of the discoveries of those enclosed by a ditch in Brittany and Normandy, their rarity in the eastern centre region and in the east, consolidate a predictive model outlined several years ago (Milcent 2006, 97–8).

In a traditional perspective centred on the Mediterranean and the Hallstattian world, Atlantic Gaul could be perceived as peripheral during the Early Iron Age, but this was certainly not the case judging for example by its important contribution to the genesis of Latenian material cultures. It could also appear to be conservative in certain respects. Effectively, the rupture with the Late Bronze Age appears to be less clear than in the Continental domain: non-funerary metallic hoard practices are still well represented, at least during the 7th–6th centuries BC. In the same way, unlike in the western and central Hallstattian world, we do not

observe a process of increasing socio-economic complexity that would lead to more developed centralisation: princely tombs remain exceptional and are dispersed throughout areas with strong cultural mixing; there is no evidence of proto-urban agglomerations and no traces of trade with the Mediterranean, even though Mediterranean imports come in sporadically. In other words, in terms of socio-economic organization, the Medio-Atlantic societies of the Early Iron Age appear to be less complex and less hierarchical than elsewhere. But they also appear to be more stable and less prone to fluctuations than their eastern or southern counterparts. And they were perhaps more solidly organised than elsewhere. All this explains that the transition from the Early to the Late Iron Age also seems to be more gradual in the Medio-Atlantic domain than elsewhere.

To extend this reflection, the concept of the Early Iron Age resonates singularly well with the ethnical situation described in Gaul just before the Roman invasions (Milcent 2012, 23). According to Caesar, the celtic speaking populations of the most northern and north-western regions of Gaul were respectively designated as Belgian and Armorican (Julius Caesar, *B. G.*, I, 1; V, 53 and VII, 75), while certain earlier authors (Posidonius?), reiterated by Strabo (*Géogr.*, IV, 1–4), describe all the populations located near the Atlantic and the Channel, between Gironde and the mouths of the Rhine as Belgian.

These associations raise questions as to the existence of an Atlantic Late Iron Age on one hand, which cannot be ruled out, and the hypothesis of a form of long-term ethnic identity stability on the other.

To conclude, the Atlantic Early Iron Age is also fundamental as it is a way of no longer focusing, like in the past, on the Mediterranean or the Hallstattian world, and thus of adopting a new approach to the European Early Iron Age. It is an indispensable intellectual lever for assessing the history of this period in a different, more dynamic and multipolar way. It is, in particular, an essential concept for bringing to light the multiplicity and the 'international' aspect of the networks that gave rise to the emergence of the material La Tène cultures. In this paper, there is no question of replacing centre-periphery models that have served their time by 'Atlantico-centric' models. From this point of view, the position adopted here is different to recent work by B. Cunliffe (2010), arguing for an Atlantic origin for the Celts, as these new hypotheses only inverse existing perspectives without really changing the more problematic foundations.

Notes

1   It would be appropriate to reexamine the detailed study of the elements found in Champagne assimilated to red Mediterranean coral. Indeed, recent research shows that substitutes, bone in particular, could have been used instead of real Mediterranean coral.

2   Here, we refer to the oldest known pit burials in Yorkshire and Cornwall (Harlyn Bay), with associated metallic objects going back to the 6th–5th century BC, although our British colleagues often advocate short chronologies out of step with the Continent.

Bibliography

Arruda, A., Barbosa, R., Gomes, F. B. and Sousa, A. (in press) *A necropolis da Vinha das Caliças 4. Sidereum* III. Madrid, El Rio Guadiana en Epoca Tartésica.

Berranger, M. (2014) *Le fer, entre matière première et moyen d'échange, en France, du VIIe au Ier siècle avant J.-C. Approches interdisciplinaires.* Dijon, Editions Universitaires de Dijon.

Blanchet, J.-C. (1984) *Les premiers métallurgistes en Picardie et dans le nord de la France.* Paris, Mémoires de la Société préhistorique française 17.

Blanchet, J.-C. and Talon, M. (2005) L'âge du Bronze dans la moyenne vallée de l'Oise: apports récents. In J. Bourgeois et M. Talon (eds) *L'âge du Bronze du nord de la France dans son contexte européen*, 125e congrès de CTHS, Lille 2000, 227–268. Paris, CTHS-APRAB.

Boyle, A. (2004) The Ferrybridge chariot burial. *Current Archaeology* 191, 481–5.

Briard, J. (1965) *Les dépôts bretons et l'Âge du bronze atlantique.* Rennes, Thèse de Sciences naturelles.

Brun, P. (1987) *Princes et princesses de la Celtique. Le premier âge du Fer en Europe 850–450 av. J.-C.* Paris, Errance.

Buchez, N. (2012) La ferme de Méaulte (Somme). In A. Lehoërff (ed.) *Par-delà l'horizon. Sociétés en manche et mer du Nord il y a 3500 ans*, 121–2. Paris, Somogy Editions d'Art.

Cabboi, S., Dunikowski, C., Leroy, M. and Merluzzo, P. (2007) Les systèmes de production sidérurgique chez les Celtes du Nord de la France. In P.-Y. Milcent (ed.) *L'économie du fer protohistorique: de la production à la consommation du métal.* Actes du XXVIIIe colloque international de l'AFEAF, Toulouse 20–23 mai 2004, 35–62. Bordeaux, *Aquitania*, supplément 14/2.

Carter, S., Hunter, F. and Smith A. (2010) A 5th Century BC Iron Age Chariot Burial from Newbridge, Edinburgh. *Proceedings of the Prehistoric Society* 76, 31–74.

Clark, P. (2012) Highstead: un fort de l'âge du Bronze? In A. Lehoërff (ed.) *Par-delà l'horizon. Sociétés en manche et mer du Nord il y a 3500 ans.* 125. Paris, Somogy Editions d'Art.

Collard, M., T. Darvill, M. Watts M. (2006) Ironworking in the Bronze Age? Evidence from a 10th century BC Settlement at Hartshill Copse, Upper Buckelbury, West Berkshire. *Proceedings of the Prehistoric* Society, 72, p.367–422

Collis, J. (1986) Adieu Hallstatt ! Adieu La Tène ! In A. Duval and J. Gomez (eds) Actes du VIIIe colloque sur les Âges du Fer en France non méditerranéenne, Angoulême, 18–19–20 mai 1984, 327–30. Bordeaux, *Aquitania*, supplément 1.

Cunliffe, B. (2010) Celticization from the west: The contribution of archaeology. In B. Cunliffe and J. T. Koch (eds) *Celtic from the West. Alternative Perspectives from Archaeology, Genetics, Language and Literature.* 13–38. Oxford, Oxbow Books.

Déchelette, J. (1913) [1927] *Manuel d'archéologie préhistorique, celtique et gallo-romaine. III, Premier âge du fer ou époque de Hallstatt.* Paris, Picard.

Dechezleprêtre, T. and Ginoux, N. (2005) Les constructions circulaires de la moitié nord de la France: état de la question. In O. Buchsenschutz and Cl. Mordant (eds) *Architectures protohistoriques en Europe occidentale du Néolithique final à l'âge du Fer.* Actes du 127e congrès des Sociétés historiques et scientifiques, Nancy 2002, 77–87. Paris, Editions du Comité des Travaux historiques et scientifiques.

Dedet, B. (2004) Variabilité des pratiques funéraires protohistoriques dans le sud de la France: défunts incinérés, défunts non brûlés. *Gallia* 61, 193–222.

Dehn, W. and Stöllner, T. (1996) Fußpaukenfibel und Drahtfibel (Marzabottofibel) – ein Beitrag zum kulturhistorischen Verständnis des 5. Jh. in Mitteleuropa. In T. Stöllner (ed.) *Europa celtica. Untersuchungen zur Hallstatt- und Latènekultur*, 1–54. Espelkamp, Marie Leidorf.

De Laet, J., Thoen, S. and Bourgeois J. (1986) *Les fouilles du séminaire d'archéologie de la Rijksuniversiteit te Gent à Destelbergen-Eenbeekeinde (1960–1984) et l'histoire la plus ancienne de la région de Gent (Gand) I La période préhistorique.* Dissertationes Archaeologicae Gandenses XXIII. Brugge, De Tempel.

Demoule, J.-P. (1999) *Chronologie et société dans les nécropoles celtiques de la culture Aisne-Marne du VIème au IIIème siècle avant notre ère.* Revue archéologique de Picardie spécial 15, Amiens, The Revue Archéologique de Picardie.

Desbrosse, V., Riquier, V. avec la collaboration de Bocquillon, H., Brun, O. and Kasprzyk, M. (2012) Les établissements ruraux palissadés hallstattiens en Champagne. In M. Schönfelder and S. Sievers (eds) *L'âge du Fer entre la Champagne et la vallée du Rhin/Die Eisenzeit zwischen Champagne und Rheintal*, Actes du XXXIVe colloque international de l'A. F. E. A. F., Aschaffenburg 2010, 3–27, Tagungen Band 14. Mainz, Römisch-Germanisches Zentralmuseum.

Gerloff, S. (2010) *Atlantic Cauldrons and Buckets of the Late Bronze and Early Iron Ages in Western Europe. Prähistorisches Bronzefunde* II, 18, Stuttgart Frank Steiner.

Giot, P.-R. (1950) Remarques préliminaires sur la chronologie de la fin de l'Âge du Bronze et sur celle de l'Âge du Fer en Bretagne. *Bulletin de la Société préhistorique française* t. 47, 336–340.

Giot, P.-R., Briard, J. and Pape, L. (1979) *Protohistoire de la Bretagne.* Rennes, Ouest-France Université.

Giraud, J.-P., Pons, F., Janin, T. (ed.), avec la collaboration de Carozza, J.-M., Duday, H., Forest, V., Gardeisen, A., Lagarrigue, A. and Roger, J. (2003) *Nécropoles protohistoriques de la région de Castres (Tarn). Le Causse, Gourjade, Le Martinet.* Documents d'Archéologie Française 94. Paris, Éditions de la Maison des sciences de l'Homme.

Gomez de Soto, J. and Kerouanton, I. (2009) Les premiers objets en fer en France, à l'âge du Bronze. In M.-J. Roulière-Lambert, A. Daubigney, P.-Y. Milcent, M. Talon and J. Vital (dir.) *De l'âge du Bronze à l'âge du Fer en France et en Europe occidentale (Xe–VIIe s. av. J.-C.). La moyenne vallée du Rhône aux âges du Fer.* Actes du XXXe colloque international de l'AFEAF, co-organisé avec l'APRAB (Saint-Romain-en-Gal, 26–28 mai 2006), 501–6. Dijon, supplément 27 à la Revue archéologique de l'Est.

Gomez de Soto, J., Bourhis, J.-R., Ghesquiere, E., Marcigny, C., Ménez, Y., Rivallain, J. and Verron, G. (2009) Pour en finir avec le Bronze final ? Les haches à douille de type armoricain en France. In M.-J. Roulière-Lambert, A. Daubigney, P.-Y. Milcent, M. Talon and J. Vital (eds) *De l'âge du Bronze à l'âge du Fer en France et en Europe occidentale (Xe–VIIe s. av. J.-C.). La moyenne vallée du Rhône aux âges du Fer*. Actes du XXXᵉ colloque international de l'AFEAF, co-organisé avec l'APRAB (Saint-Romain-en-Gal, 26–28 mai 2006), 507–12. Dijon, supplément 27 à la Revue archéologique de l'Est.

Guggisberg, M. A. (2004) (ed.) *Die Hydria von Grächwil. Zur Funktion und Rezeption mediterraner Importe in Mitteleuropa im 6. und 5. Jahrhundert v. Chr.*, Actes du colloque de Bern. Berne, Schriften des Bernischen Historischen Museums.

Harding, D. W. (1972) *The Iron Age in the Upper Thames Basin*. Oxford, Clarendon Press.

Haselgrove, C. (2007) Rethinking earlier Iron Age settlement in the eastern Paris Basin. In C. Haselgrove and R. Pope (eds) *The Earlier Iron Age in Britain and the Near Continent*, 400–428. Oxford, Oxbow Books.

Hatt, J.-J. and Roualet, P. (1976) Le cimetière des Jogasses en Champagne et les origines de la civilisation de La Tène. Dijon, *Revue archéologique de l'Est* t. 27, 421–448.

Hatt, J.-J. and Roualet, P. (1977) La chronologie de la Tène en Champagne. Dijon. *Revue archéologique de l'Est* t. 28, 7–36.

Jahier, I. (2005) Eterville. Le Clos des Lilas. *Bilan scientifique 2004, 39–41.* Caen, S. R. A. BasseNormandie.

Jahier, I. (2011) *L'enceinte des premier et second âge du Fer de La Fosse Touzé (Courseulles-sur-Mer, Calvados). Entre résidence aristocratique et place de collecte monumentale.* Documents d'Archéologie Française 104. Paris, Editions de la Maison des Sciences de l'Homme.

Jiménez-Ávila, J. (2002) *La Toréutica Orientalizante en la Península Ibérica*. Bibliotheca Archaeologica Hispana 16, Studia hispano-phoenicia. Madrid, Real Academia de la Historia.

Joly, S., Mercey, Fl., Filippini, A., Abenzoar, V., Liard, M. et Poupon F. avec la collaboration de Béziat D. et Coustures M.-P. (2011) Un nouvel habitat du Bronze final IIIb dans le Val d'Orléans: Bonnée, « Les Terres à l'Est du Bourg » (Centre, Loiret), *Revue archéologique du Centre de la France, [En ligne] t. 50.*

Le Goff, I. and Guillot, H. (1992) Étude des ossements incinérés de la nécropole de l'Âge du bronze de Tagnon 'La Fricassée'. *Amphora* 73, 35–44.

Mariën, M.-E. (1958) *Trouvailles du Champ d'Urnes et des tombelles hallstattiennes de Court-Saint-Etienne*. Monographies d'Archéologie Nationale, 1. Bruxelles, Musées royaux d'Art et d'Histoire.

Ménez, Y. (1996) *Une ferme de l'Armorique gauloise. La Boisanne à Plouër-sur-Rance (Côtes-d'Armor)*. Documents d'Archéologie Française 58. Paris, Editions de la Maison des Sciences de l'Homme.

Milcent, P.-Y. (2003) Le contexte historique. In C. Rolley (ed.) *La tombe princière de Vix*, 327–366. Paris, Picard.

Milcent, P.-Y. (2004) *Le premier âge du Fer en France centrale*. Paris, Mémoire de la Société préhistorique française t. XXXIV.

Milcent, P.-Y. (2006) Premier âge du Fer médio-atlantique et genèse multipolaire des cultures matérielles laténiennes. In D. Vitali (ed.) *Celtes et Gaulois, l'archéologie face à l'Histoire, 2: la préhistoire des Celtes*, Actes de la table ronde de Bologne-Monterenzio, 28–29 mai 2005, 81–105. Glux-en-Glenne, Bibracte 12/2.

Milcent, P.-Y. (2009) A l'Est rien de nouveau. Chronologie des armes de poing du premier âge du Fer médio-atlantique et genèse des standards matériels élitaires hallstattiens et laténiens. In A. Lehoërff (ed.) *Construire le temps. Histoire et méthodes des chronologies et calendriers des derniers millénaires avant notre ère en Europe occidentale*. Actes du XXXe colloque international HALMA-IPEL, Lille 7–9 décembre 2006, 231–250. Glux-en-Glenne, Bibracte 16.

Milcent, P.-Y. (2012) *Le temps des élites en Gaule atlantique. Chronologie des mobiliers et rythmes de constitution des dépôts métalliques dans le contexte européen (XIIIe–VIIe s. av. J.-C.)*. Rennes, Presses Universitaires de Rennes, Archéologie & culture.

Milcent, P.-Y. (2014) Hallstattian urban Experience before the Celtic *Oppida* in central and eastern Gaul. Two case studies: Bourges and Vix. In M. Fernández-Götz, H. Wendling and K. Winger (eds) *Paths to Complexity – Centralisation and Urbanisation in Iron Age Europe*, 35–51. Oxford, Oxbow Books.

Milcent, P.-Y. (2015) Bronze objects for Atlantic Elites in France (13th–8th century BC). In F. Hunter and I. Ralston (eds) *Scotland in Later Prehistoric Europe*, Actes de la conférence internationale d'Edimbourg, 19–21 septembre 2008, 19–46. Edinburgh, Society of Antiquaries of Scotland.

Milcent, P.-Y. (in press) Echanges prémonétaires et immobilisation fluctuante de richesses métalliques en Gaule atlantique (XIIIe-Ve s. av. J.-C.). Dynamiques et décryptage des pratiques de dépôts métalliques non funéraires. In B. Toune and E. Warmenbol (eds), *Choice Pieces. The Destruction and Manipulation of Goods in the Later Bronze Age: From Reuse to Sacrifice*. Actes du colloque de Rome 2012, Academia Belgica Rome, Academia Belgica.

Needham, S. (2007) 800 BC, The great divide. In C. Haselgrove and R. Pope (eds) *The Earlier Iron Age in Britain and the Near Continent*, 39–63. Oxford, Oxbow Books.

Pape, J. (2000) Die attische Keramik der Heuneburg und der keramische Südimport in der Zone nördlich der Alpen während der Hallstattzeit. In W. Kimmig (ed.) *Importe und mediterrane Einflüsse auf der Heuneburg*. Heuneburgstudien, XI, 71–175. Mainz am Rhein, P. von Zabern.

Reinhard, W. (1993) Gedanken zum Westhallstattkreis am Beispiel der Ha C – zeitlichen Schwertgräber. *Blesa* 1. 359–387. Metz, Éditions Serpenoise.

San Juan, G. and Le Goff, I. (2003) La nécropole du VIᵉ siècle avant J.-C. de 'La Campagne' à Basly (Calvados). In B. Mandy and A. De Saulce (eds) *Les marges de l'Armorique à l'âge du Fer. Archéologie et histoire: culture matérielle et sources écrites, Actes du XXIIIe colloque de l'A. F. E. A. F.*, Nantes 1999, 59–102. Rennes, Revue archéologique de l'Ouest, supplement 10.

Saurel, M. (2007) Les IVᵉ et IIIᵉ siècles avant notre ère en Champagne-Ardenne: apport de l'étude de la vaisselle des habitats. In Chr. Mennessier-Jouannet, A. Adam and P.-Y. Milcent (eds) *La Gaule dans son contexte européen aux IVe et IIIe s. av. n. è.* Actes du XXVIIe colloque international de l'AFEAF, Clermont-Ferrand, 29 mai–1er juin 2003, 7–33. Lattes, Monographies d'Archéologie Méditerranéenne.

Séjalon, P. and Dedet, B. (2003) Les trois enclos funéraires de Mas de Vignole VII à Nîmes, Gard (Ve s. av. J.-C.). *Documents d'Archéologie méridionale 26, 43–61.*

Van Doorselaer, A., Putman, R., Van der Gucht, K. and Janssens, Fr. (1999) *De Kemmelberg een Keltische bergvesting*. Kortrijk, Westvlaamse Archaeologica Monografieën III.

Verger, S. (1995) De Vix à Weiskirchen. La transformation des rites funéraires aristocratiques en Gaule du nord et de l'est au Ve siècle avant J.-C. *Mélanges de l'École française de Rome Antiquité* 107, 1, 335–458.

Verney, A. (1993) Les nécropoles de l'âge du Fer en Basse-Normandie; bilan de trois siècles de découvertes. In D. Cliquet, M. Rémy-Watté, M. Vaginay and V. Guichard (eds) *Les Celtes en Normandie. Les rites funéraires en Gaule (IIIe–Ier siècle avant J.-C.)*, 95–113, Rennes, Revue archéologique de l'Ouest, Supplément 6.

Vilaça, R. (2013) L'arrivée des premiers fer dans l'Occident atlantique. In L. Callegarin and A. Gorgues (eds) *Les transferts de technologie au premier millénaire av. J.-C. dans le sud-ouest de l'Europe, 39–64*. Mélanges de la Casa de Velázquez, Madrid, Casa de Velázquez.

Villard-Le Tiec, A., Ménez, Y. and Lohro T. (2013) Habitats et nécropoles de l'âge du Fer en Centre-Bretagne. In S. Krausz, A. Colin, K. Gruel, I. Ralston and T. Dechezleprêtre (eds) *L'âge du Fer en Europe. Mélanges offerts à Olivier Buchsenschutz*, 261–279. Bordeaux, Ausonius.

Villes, A. (2000) Entre principautés et chefferies, citadelles et fermes, le Hallstatt final en Champagne: données nouvelles. In A. Villes and A. Bataille-Melkon (eds) *Fastes des Celtes entre Champagne et Bourgogne aux VIIe–IIIe siècles avant notre ère*. Actes du 19e Colloque de l'A. F. E. A. F., Troyes 1995, 11–92. Chalon-en-Champagne, Mémoires de la Société archéologique champenoise 15.

Warmenbol, E. (1993) Les nécropoles à tombelles de Gedinne et Louette-Saint-Pierre (Namur) et le groupe 'mosan' des nécropoles à épées hallstattiennes. In F. Boura, J. Metzler and A. Miron (eds) *Interactions culturelles et économiques aux Âges du Fer en Lorraine, Sarre et Luxembourg*. Actes du XIe colloque de l'A. F. E. A. F., Sarreguemines 1987, 83–114. Metz Archaeologia Mosellana.

Following the Whale's road: perceptions of the sea in prehistory

Peter Clark

Abstract

The inundation of the Northwest European landmass by the melting ice sheets in the earlier part of the Holocene created a new world for the indigenous hunter-gatherers, an interdigitation of land and sea that characterises the region today. This paper explores the perception of the sea by prehistoric communities in both the short and long term; at the same time the destroyer of ancestral homelands and the provider of new opportunities. The marine environment of course requires technological aids – boats – to negotiate its waters and the development of such technologies was an important adaptive response. In addition, navigating the sea, particularly when navigating 'over the horizon' required good navigation skills. How did prehistoric mariners find their way across the seas, and what was their cognitive understanding of the world in which they moved? Modern concepts of space and navigation are inappropriate for prehistory, and this paper explores alternative cognitive perceptions of the sea, drawing on the notions of 'smooth' and 'striated' space put forward by Gilles Deleuze and Felix Guattari to suggest a more satisfying appreciation of prehistoric perceptions of the sea.

Keywords: Prehistoric navigation; cognitive archaeology; Deleuze and Guattari; maritime environment; Holocene inundation

Résumé

L'inondation de la terre européenne du NW, par la fonte des glaces au début de l'Holocène, a créé un nouveau monde pour les chasseurs-cueilleurs autochtones, un entrecroisement de terre et de mer qui caractérise la région aujourd'hui. Cet article explore la perception de la mer par les sociétés préhistoriques, à court terme et sur la longue durée ; tout à la fois destructrice des terres ancestrales et fournisseuse de nouvelles opportunités. L'environnement marin nécessite bien sûr une assistance technologique – les bateaux – pour parcourir ses eaux et le développement de ces technologies a été une réponse adaptative importante. En outre, la navigation en mer, en particulier lors de la navigation « au-delà de l'horizon » nécessite de bonnes compétences nautiques. Comment les marins préhistoriques trouvaient-ils leur chemin en mer, et quelle était leur compréhension cognitive du monde dans lequel ils se sont déplacés ? Les concepts modernes de navigation et d'espace sont inappropriés pour la préhistoire, et cet article explore les perceptions cognitives alternatives, en faisant appel au concept d'espaces « lisse » et « strié » mis en avant par Gilles Deleuze et Felix Guattari pour suggérer une appréciation plus juste des perceptions préhistoriques de la mer.

Mots-clés : navigation préhistorique, archéologie cognitive, Deleuze et Guattari, environnement maritime, inondation holocène

Tranquillas etiam naufragus horret aquas...[1]

Questions regarding the movement of peoples and social identity are critical in understanding the prehistory of the Transmanche Zone. Indeed, these issues remain hugely important in the modern world, where notions of frontier, belonging and otherness are mainstays of our daily news. The Transmanche is quintessentially a maritime domain; the sea is an intimate part of the region's identity, romantically described by the Anglo-Saxon kenning word *hran-rád* or *hrônrâde* (Toller 1898, 556; Kemble 1843, 48, line 1641) – the 'Whale's Road' of this paper's title. Here we take the opportunity to reflect on the nature of the sea itself – the *mysterium tremendum et fascinus* – and how it might have been perceived in prehistory. This must of necessity be an exercise in speculation, but may provide a more nuanced appreciation of the context of early maritime contacts.

Today we are accustomed to the sea being shown as an undifferentiated blue monotone on our modern maps, a 'space between places', a separation and barrier between the comforting security of *terra firma*. The sea is nevertheless an essential part of the identity of western Europe; the eastern edge of the Atlantic Ocean, the North Sea, La Manche, the Irish, Baltic and Wadden Seas all make up a cognitive landscape (*sensu* Farina 2009, 103–41) with which we are all familiar. The sea both divides us and brings us together; it is at the same time a constant companion and an alien environment.

Early records express some ambivalence to the sea; it is an agent of both destruction and creation, a provider and a threat, the realm of history and of mystery (Johnstone 1988, 85; Driessen 2004, 42–5; *cf.* Fischer and Hasse 2001, 83–6). Notwithstanding this, recent history has seen the sea charted and circumscribed, its boundaries traced out and its enormity brought under control by the shackles of latitude and longitude. Modern concepts of navigating these waters represent a cognitive exercise of moving through a known space, proceeding from point to point in a mental map of Cartesian co-ordinates. It is only in relatively recent times that this conceptual model has become commonplace, that the sea has been transformed into what the French philosophers Gilles Deleuze and Félix Guattari describe as 'striated space' (1988, 528–2). It is not the only way of understanding and perceiving the sea, and it seems likely that prehistoric communities had a different relation to and a different perception of the waters of the world.

First impressions

If we are to look to the north and west of Europe, away from the Mediterranean world, then the sea is a relative newcomer. At the end of the last Ice Age, around 10,000 cal BC, the open sea lay to the north and west of a large coherent landmass, christened 'Doggerland' by Bryony Coles in her seminal 1998 paper (Fig. 8.1). It was into this landscape that Mesolithic man returned after the ice had gone and following its colonisation by flora and fauna, a setting of rivers, hills, forests and lakes. Recent excavations have shown that Mesolithic peoples were living in the far north of what is now Scandinavia at an early date, close by the retreating ice sheet (e.g. Lagesidribakti in Norway (9450 cal BC; Blankholm 2008) and Aareavaara in Sweden (8750 cal BC; Möller *et al.* 2012)), whilst finds dredged up from the bottom of the North Sea suggest that the whole area of Doggerland was occupied relatively quickly after the glaciers retreated (e.g. Clark 1932, 115; Louwe Kooijmans 1985; Bjerck 1995; Clark and Godwin 1956; Long *et al.* 1986; Fig. 8.2). People were to live throughout the region for thousands of years, generation after generation, moving through this land on foot or along the rivers and across the lakes in log boats (Beuker and Niekus 1997; Bonnin 2000; Burov 1996), exploiting the animals and plants of the region for food, shelter, clothing and tools. The geography of this lost land has only recently begun to be mapped, tracing the lines of river valleys, great marshes and lakes (Gaffney *et al.* 2007; 2009; Fitch *et al.* 2005; Bicket 2011). We might imagine that the people living in this place might think of it as 'home'; that the rivers, hills, lakes and forests had names, that these natural places were imbued with significance, with stories and myths, connections with memories of ancestors stretching back in time (Bradley 2000; 2002). But as the melting glaciers revealed this land, so ultimately were they to destroy much of it.

Rising sea levels encroached on the low-lying lands throughout the earlier part of the Holocene; the great plain of Doggerland was inundated to create what is now the North Sea, whilst the coast line advanced eastwards along the Channel river, eventually to link with the North Sea to create the island of Britain sometime around 5800–5400 BC (Fig. 8.3; Cunliffe 2012, 56), whilst large areas of land were also submerged in the Baltic (Tikkanen and Oksanen 2002, 15–16; Emeis *et al.* 2002) and the area of the Irish Sea (Devoy 1990). In the area of the North Sea, over 100,000 km² were lost to flooding (Gaffney *et al.* 2009, 138), and by 5890 cal BC the waters around Boulogne-sur-Mer and the Transmanche zone were fully marine (Lambeck 1995). The speed of this inundation of course varied through time and in different places; along the German coast the waters rose around 1.25 cm a year, say 31.25 cm in a single generation (Behre 2007, 85), but in the area of the Dover Strait and along the Dutch and Belgian coast it was just 0.7 cm per year (Beets and van der Spek 2000, 7). At times there were sudden dramatic floods, when the landscape was transformed – lost – almost overnight (Coles 1998, 67–9). Most spectacular must have been the great Tsunami caused by the Storegga

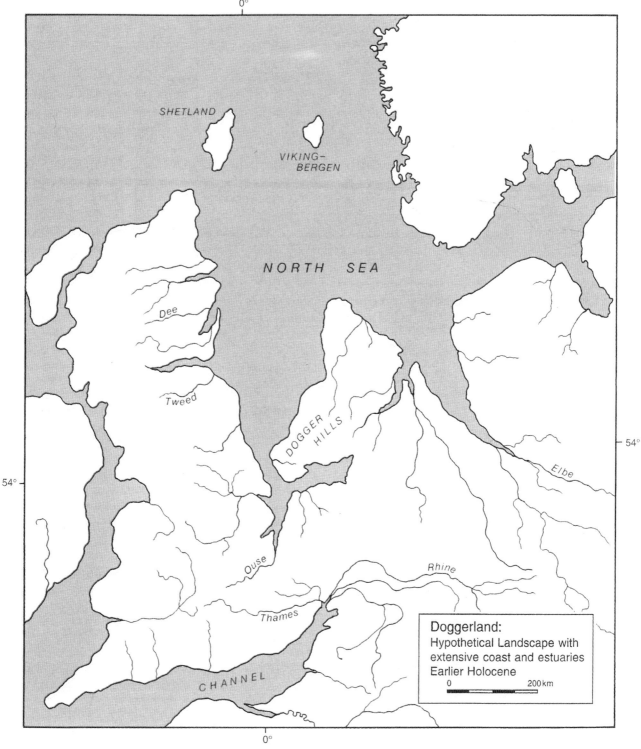

Fig. 8.1. Doggerland in the Earlier Holocene (after Coles 1998).

Slide off the west coast of Norway in around 6200–5950 cal BC (Weninger *et al.* 2008; Bondevik *et al.* 1997; 2003; Haflidason *et al.* 2005; Smith *et al.* 2004). Around 2400–3200 km³ of material slid onto the floor of the North Atlantic, generating a huge wave that reached the coast of Greenland to the west and the Transmanche zone to the south, where the runup may have been as much as 3 m (for comparison, the average runup heights for the 2004 Indian Ocean Tsunami along the southeast Indian Coast were around 3.6 m; Yeh *et al.*, 2005, table 1). Huge

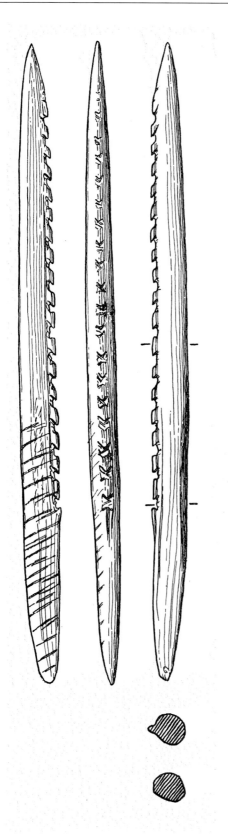

Fig. 8.2. The 218 mm long barbed point of red deer antler dredged from the sea floor between the Leman and Ower banks off the eastern coast of Britain (after Clark and Godwin 1956).

areas of Doggerland must have been inundated in this catastrophic event, with a significant loss of life amongst the Mesolithic populations living here, not just from the violent impact of the wave itself, but from consequences such as the destruction of the biosphere and the loss of food and other resources such as ruined shellfish beds, damaged fishing facilities, etc. One can only imagine the psychological effect of the loss of land had on contemporary people. We might imagine refugees fleeing their drowned homelands, families and social groups separated and isolated by the rising water, but retaining knowledge of their relatives and kinsfolk across the water. Of course, the world of rising sea level was the world to which people were accustomed, something that they lived in, experienced and were part of (De Roest 2013). The loss of parts of the landscape, perhaps closely associated with memories and stories of ancestors in the past would be accommodated, transmogrified in folk memory in a dynamic relationship with a changing world (Leary 2009, 232–5). However, dramatic and catastrophic events such as the Storegga Tsunami must have had an immediate and devastating affect that made a powerful impact on the survivor's perception of the sea as a destructive force, no matter how they were accommodated in myth over the long term or what economic advantages accrued through the extended coastline and increasing diversity of inland resources (Coles 1998, 76).

Thus the broad plains of Doggerland and elsewhere became transformed into a patchwork of sea and land. From a terrestrial perspective, the encroaching seas were in part a negative aspect to the lives of Mesolithic people living there, eroding the landscapes of the past and sometimes causing death and distress. As yet our data will not allow us to understand precisely how the stabilising forces embedded within society interacted with such long-term and occasionally catastrophic destabilising forces – the extent to which the Mesolithic way of life of the inhabitants of Doggerland was 'resilient', accommodating such change and maintaining its essential structures, or underwent significant transformation as the world around them was itself transformed (Redman 2005, 72; Thompson and Turck 2009). In any event, as generations came and went, people must have accommodated this changing environment into their own world view, and the potential opportunities of the marine environment and the increasing access to the resources of the coastal zone became apparent and began to be exploited.

At some point in this story, people began to travel across the sea itself. As we have seen, the rivers and lakes of Doggerland were mostly probably already navigated by simple logboats of pine judging by examples found in the Netherlands (e.g. Pesse (8237–7616 cal BC; Beuker and Niekus 1997) and northern France (e.g. two from Nandy (Fig. 8.4; 7245–6710 cal BC and 7040–6620 cal BC;

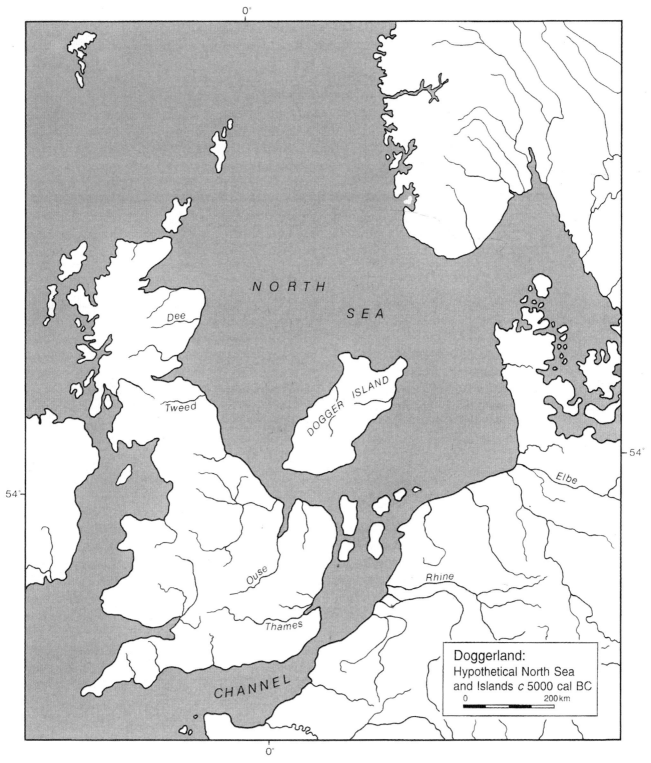

Fig. 8.3. Doggerland in around 500 cal BC (after Coles 1998).

Bonnin 2000) and one from Noyen-sur-Seine (Fig. 8.5; 7136–6601 cal BC; Marinval-Vigne *et al.* 1989; Mordant and Mordant 1989; 1992, 61; Mordant *et al.* 2010)), but the advent of full marine conditions in the new seas of western Europe meant that the earliest navigators had a more difficult – and dangerous – environment to contend with. Of course, this was not a precipitous event, but a gradual adaptation as environmental conditions changed,

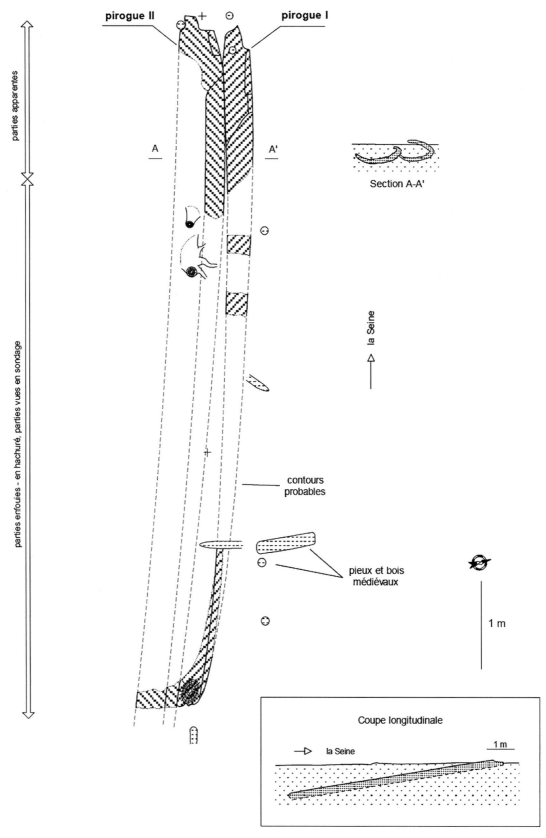

Fig. 8.4. Plan of the two Mesolithic dugouts found near Nandy/Le-Coudray-Montceaux, France (after Bonnin 2000).

but over the *longue durée* this was a significant change. Moreover, the sea is a realm where the relationship between people and their environment is necessarily mediated through technology – the boat. The sea is quintessentially an alien place for man, demanding not just the physical hardware to survive and negotiate the water itself, but deep knowledge of more intangible realities; winds, currents and tides, the changing weather and the ability to find one's way. A new relationship had to be forged with this new maritime landscape, a new perception of the sea beyond its effects on the terrestrial landscapes of the past.

From first steps to over the horizon

Our understanding of the technology of early prehistoric water transport, particularly that of the maritime domain, is based on very little actual data. Despite the discovery of sometimes rather spectacular Mesolithic and Neolithic

Fig. 8.5. The Mesolithic dugout found at Noyen-sur-Seine, France (after Mordant et al 2010, fig. 3A).

monoxylous vessels, these may best be understood as having operated in a riverine or wetland environment. These logboats are generally fairly simple technologically, hollowed tree trunks shaped at the ends and on their exterior. A few, dating to the later Neolithic, have lines of holes cut through their sides along the upper edge (as at Øgårde 3 (*c.* 3190 BC) and Verup I, St Åmose (*c.* 2770 BC) in Denmark (Troel-Smith 1946, 17, fig. 2; Christensen 1990, fig. 11). Some have understood these holes to be evidence for increasing freeboard by attaching washstrakes to the sides of the boat, or for increasing beam by joining two logboats together (like the undated example found in the River Weser near Minden, Germany; Ellmers 1996, 23). Other ways of increasing stability (and thus the possibility of using such craft in marine conditions) might be by fitting outriggers (as is known from ethnographic examples in (for example) India (Edye 1834, 5, pl. 2) and Oceania (Haddon and Hornell 1936–8)) or by expansion, forcing the sides of the logboat apart after heat treatment (McGrail 1987, 66–70). However, despite such speculation, there is no evidence as yet to suggest that any prehistoric logboat was modified by expansion (Arnold 1996, 157–8). Based on archaeological evidence currently available therefore, it seems unlikely that such logboats were used at sea (McGrail 2001, 173).

Another possibility is that skin boats were used for maritime transport. This is an attractive suggestion; such boats were certainly theoretically possible to construct with contemporary technology from the Mesolithic onwards (if not before). Ethnographic parallels suggest that such boats can be eminently seaworthy and capable of carrying significant cargoes (e.g. Clark 2004, 306; Petersen 1986). However, there is very little evidence for such vessels until at least the later Iron Age in western Europe; the unprovenanced fragment of antler from Husum in Schleswig-Holstein in Germany, claimed to be part of the frame of a hide boat (Ellmers 1984) can be interpreted in several other ways (but note the putative hide 'canoe' found at Miennakker in the Netherlands; Nobles 2013). The use of hide boats for maritime navigation in the earlier prehistoric period must, therefore, remain speculative for the moment.

Notwithstanding the difficulty of unequivocally identifying the types of sea-going vessels used in the Mesolithic and Neolithic, certainly there is ample evidence that sea voyages of some length were being undertaken from at least the Mesolithic onwards. In the south of Britain at Bouldnor Cliff off the north-west coast of the Isle of Wight, sedaDNA analysis of a submerged Mesolithic palaeosol has demonstrated the presence of Einkorn wheat (*Triticum monococcum*) dated to around 6000 cal BC (Smith *et al.* 2015a; 2015b, table S1) suggests that long distance social networks existed at this time between the Mesolithic peoples of Britain and the Neolithic communities of southern Europe, necessitating the existence of sea-going vessels at this early time. Similarly, the stone tools of bloodstone (a visually distinctive cryptocrystalline silica outcropping only on the Isle of Rhum in western Scotland; Figs 8.6 and 8.7), are found widely distributed along the coast from the Mesolithic onwards (Wickham-Jones 1990). Clearly the only way this material could have been moved from its island source was by boat. Other evidence for Mesolithic seafaring comes from Ireland, where the remains of domesticated cattle have been found at Dalkey Island and Sutton (Co. Dublin), Kilgreany Cave (Co. Waterford) and Ferriter's Cove (Co. Kerry) dated to the middle of the 5th millennium BC (Woodman *et al.* 1999); presumably these remains – either live animals or carcasses – had been acquired from continental farming communities and imported by boat.

In northern waters, a flint core tool of Mesolithic date was found in Fair Isle some 25 miles/40 km north of the British mainland (Mithen 2000, 15; Saville 2000, 94), whilst analysis of an oyster midden at West Voe in the Shetland Isles 25 miles/40 km further north has shown the presence of humans in the early part of the 5th millennium BC (Melton and Nicholson 2004)

The first signs of a Neolithic way of life (represented by the *Linearbandkeramik* culture) appeared in northwestern Europe in around 5500 cal BC (Whittle 1996a, 157), some time after the islands of Britain and Ireland had come into existence, but only reached them by *c* 4000 cal BC (Whittle *et al.* 2011). The introduction of this new

Fig. 8.6. Bloodstone Hill on the Isle of Rhum, Scotland (courtesy of Caroline Wickham-Jones).

Fig. 8.7. Mesolithic worked stone objects made of Bloodstone (courtesy of Caroline Wickham-Jones).

lifestyle, including the importation of domestic cattle and other livestock, naturally had to come by sea, suggesting the existence of sturdy and potentially quite large vessels (Case 1969). The Neolithic transformation of society throughout these islands seems to have been relatively rapid (Kinnes 2004, 139) and soon affected all parts of the archipelago; Neolithic finds have recently been found on the remote island of St Kilda, 40 miles/64 km off the west coast of the Western Isles of Scotland (Fleming 2005). The nature of the Mesolithic–Neolithic transition in the islands off the western European seaboard remains a topic of fierce debate (e.g. Guilane and van Berg 2006; Garrow and Sturt 2011; Louwe Kooijmans 1993; Vanmontfort 2008; Whittle 1996b; Sheridan 2010), and the extent to which long sea journeys were routinely undertaken and the necessity for close contact between offshore farmers and their continental cousins during the Neolithic is a matter of conjecture. By the 2nd millennium BC long-distance maritime exchange is well attested archaeologically (e.g.

Butler 1963; Clark 2009), and it is during this period that we have the first evidence for complex sea-going sewn-plank vessels (Fig. 8.8; Van de Noort 2006; Green 2004). Such boats are clearly representative of a mature shipbuilding technology that must have its origins in the 3rd millennium BC, if not before. Whilst continuing research and experimental archaeology is giving us a better understanding of the potential seafaring capabilities of such vessels (Clark 2014; Parfitt 2014; Clark and Lehoërff 2014), their purpose and range of operation remains speculative. Were our prehistoric mariners limited by nautical technology and their cognitive understanding of navigational principles so that they were restricted to travel in sight of land, making journeys to offshore lands by the shortest possible route, or were they able navigators, confident to make long voyages beyond the horizon out of sight of *terra firma*?

Theoretically, most of the islands in the north-east Atlantic zone can be reached by boat without losing sight

Fig. 8.8. A half-scale replica of the Dover Bronze Age boat (1575–1520 cal BC) at sea off the English coast (Canterbury Archaeological Trust).

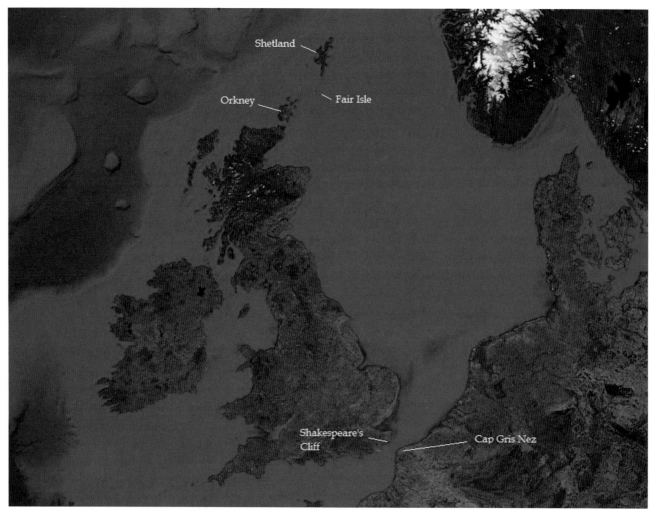

Fig. 8.9. The North Sea (source: NASA World Wind).

of land. The visible horizon when at sea may be calculated by the formula 'the square root of the height one's eye in feet multiplied by 1.17 = distance to the horizon in nautical miles'. Thus, when seated in a boat with one's eye (say) about 3 ft/0.76 m above the water, the horizon would only be around 2 nautical miles away, ignoring the effects of wave and weather. However, the presence of high ground changes this picture dramatically; for example, high cliffs such as Shakespeare's Cliff and Cap Gris Nez would have been visible much further away (Fig. 8.9); the former (just to the west of Dover) rises sheer from the sea to a height of 107 m (*c.* 350 ft) and is thus visible some 22 nautical miles away (24 if seated in a boat). Cap Gris Nez, lying between Boulogne-sur-Mer and Calais is the closest point of France to England, just 20 miles/32 km distant, and rises 45 m (*c.* 148 ft), visible some 16 nautical miles away (18 in a boat).

Thus even the far flung islands of the northern British archipelago could be reached by pilotage (the use of fixed

(terrestrial) reference points to guide one's vessel to a destination); Ward Hill on Fair Isle stands some 217 m (712 ft) high and is thus visible over 30 miles/48 km away, in sight of North Ronaldsay in northern Orkney. Travelling further north, using Ward Hill as a 'back marker', sailors would only have to travel a few miles before Sumburgh Head, the southern tip of Shetland became visible which at 100 m (328 ft) can be seen over 20 nautical miles away. The islands of Faroe and Iceland further to the north and west would necessarily entail voyages out of sight of land (Fig. 8.10), and it is perhaps significant that (to this author's knowledge), there is as yet no evidence that people settled in the Faroe Islands before the middle of the 1st millennium AD (Hannon *et al.* 2001) or Iceland before AD 870–930 (Smith 1995). Further north, however, people crossed the seas to settle the coastal areas of Greenland sometime in the 3rd millennium BC (the *Saqqaq* culture; Larsen and Meldgaard 1958; Appelt and Pind 1996; Grønnow 1990;

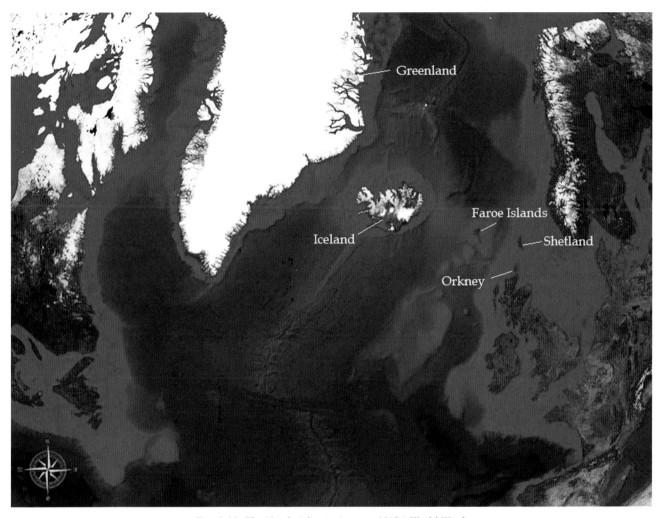

Fig. 8.10. The North Atlantic (source: NASA World Wind).

Møbjerg 1997; Schledermann 1990). These people came from the west; recent DNA analysis suggests that these people originated in the Bering Sea area around 4000 km (2500 miles) away, and that they were not directly related to Native Americans nor the later Neo-Eskimos that replaced them (Gilbert *et al.* 2008). Thus nearly all the lands of the northern and eastern Atlantic zone could in theory be reached by pilotage, without sailing out of sight of land.

Of course, simple pilotage cannot be the complete story of how our ancient mariners found their way across the seas. Notwithstanding our simplistic calculations regarding the visibility of the horizon (which of course require a flat calm and a cloudless sunny day), anyone who has been in a small boat on the open sea knows well that the complexities of tide, current, wind and weather rarely allow a simple direct passage from A to B. Often the land is obscured, and even when significant landmarks are visible, intimate knowledge of local sea conditions

is essential for making a sea journey in relative safety; even today local pilots are critical in negotiating the safe entry of ports and estuaries around the world. Here we are concerned with deliberate voyaging, of journeys undertaken intentionally, and not the possibility of accidental 'drift voyages' recently discussed by Richard Callaghan (2015), nor of initial 'pioneering' voyages that paved the way for later deliberate voyaging. The presumption is that prehistoric seafarers had a clear idea of where they wanted to go, and presumably how they were to return. But how did prehistoric mariners find their way across the seas, and what was their understanding of the world in which they moved?

We may assume that our prehistoric seafarers had an intimate knowledge of the three main elements of the environment in which they moved; the land, at once providing fixed points of reference and the contradictory characteristics of safe haven and perilous shore; the sky, with its manifold meteorological fluctuations changing from season to season and above the ever-moving celestial bodies; and the sea itself, with all its vagaries of tide and current, whirlpools and surface waves. These three elements, of course, interact to create complex and changing conditions that needed to be understood empirically within a *Weltanschauung* very different to our own.

This knowledge was presumably initially acquired through experience, and the detailed information required to make specific voyage from one place to another formalised in the form of sailing instructions, handed down by word of mouth from generation to generation, and memorised word for word by every novice mariner. This was not a static body of knowledge; over time new routes would have been established, comprehension of the natural world enhanced, changes in the physical and cognitive environment accommodated, a 'sealore' developing and evolving as maritime travel continued.

We can only speculate on the nature of this knowledge and how it was transmitted. We might not imagine the use of charts or maps that appear to have been familiar to Roman navigators (Taylor 1956, 55–7), though we might suggest that the concept of 'sailing directions' or 'sailing instructions' would be appropriate in non-literate societies relying on oral traditions. Sailing instructions were committed to writing at an early date. In the Mediterranean world, such information was gathered into 'pilot-books' such as the *Periplous* of Scylax of Caryanda (probably dating to the mid-4th century BC; Counillon 2004; Shipley 2011) or the *Stadiasmus of the Great Sea*, (perhaps from the early 3rd century AD; Bauer and Helm 1955, 43–69). In northern Europe, sailing instructions first appear around the middle of the 1st millennium AD. In the introduction to his translation of the *Historiarum Adversus Paganus* (written by the Spanish priest and historian Paulus Orosius in the 5th century AD; Bately and Englert 2007), the anonymous author records the sailing instructions of two men; the Englishman Wulfstan, who described how to travel from Haithabu to Truso (near Elbing on the Vistula), and a Norwegian, Ohthere, who described a journey from his home in Helgeland (in the far north of Norway) to Skirinssal, a market in Oslofjord, and thence to Haithabu, in addition to a journey from Helgeland round the North Cape to the White Sea. These accounts were documented in around AD 889–899, and are the first evidence we have of what must have been an oral tradition that existed for centuries, if not millennia. Such instructions give details of directions and duration of journey, significant landmarks, directions of winds, species of animals and birds to look out for (instructions for sailing from Norway to Greenland preserved in the Icelandic *Landnámabók* describe the presence of birds and whales, a fixed point in the open sea where the cold polar currents meet the warmer Irminger current about 60–70 miles/ 97–113 km south of Iceland; Schnall 1996, 124). Other natural phenomena recorded in these sailing instructions include the colour of the sea, direction, height and form of waves, characteristic driftwood and clouds; what we might infer from this is that there was no 'open sailing' as such; there were specific instructions on how to go from one place to another.

Another invaluable aid for our prehistoric mariners would have been the sounding lead, a heavy cone with a hollow at the bottom to hold a sticky filler (usually beeswax or tallow) that could be lowered on a cord to take soil samples of the sea bottom (Schnall 1996, 124). We have never found a prehistoric example in northwest Europe, though they must surely have been used (though made of stone rather than lead). We have examples from the 2nd century BC and 1st century AD from the Mediterranean (Fig. 8.11; Oleson 2008), and their use is recorded by Herodotus (*Histories*, Book II, 6). They are certainly referred to without remark in Old English (a *sund-rap* or *sundline*) and in Low German (a *lot*). Knowledge of the nature of the sea bottom could be of great value for finding where you are at sea; in AD 1147 an Anglo-German fleet was lost off the coast of Brittany in thick fog, but found its position accurately by reference to water colour and the sounding lead alone (Schnall 1996, 124).

One of course thinks of celestial bodies when considering navigation, and undoubtedly the sun would be an important guide to direction, whilst the length of shadow at certain times of day can give clues to latitude on long journeys, but this was probably not a highly developed technique in prehistory. Certainly the Pole Star was known about (the Vikings called it the *leiðarstjarna* or *lád-steorra*, the 'way-star'; Taylor 1956, 80), though in earlier prehistory the star Kochab was nearer the pole than Polaris.

The behaviour of animals could also be of help, such as roosting birds (e.g. Fulmars) heading toward land at dusk; an apocryphal tale preserved in the *Landnámabók* tells of the Viking sailor Floki Vilgerðarson who carried three ravens; when he released the first two, they flew around his boat and then returned; the third however, set off towards the horizon. Floki sailed in that direction and eventually found Iceland (Taylor 1956, 72).

There are also various devices purported to be very early navigational aids such as the so-called 'bearing dial' dug up at Unartoq in Greenland in the late 1940s (Fig. 8.12; Sølver 1953; 1954; Seaver 2000; Keller and Christensen 2002) and the various references to 'Sun stones' (*solarsteinn*) in Old Icelandic manuscripts and church inventories, but their interpretation as such is not generally accepted (Schnall 1996, 125–6).

In addition to the natural landmarks of cliffs, river mouths and other distinctive features as an aid to fixing one's position at sea and facilitating pilotage, it seems likely that man-made objects were also used as navigational aids, such as the great burial mounds of the Bronze Age, often situated on coastal settings easily visible from the sea. The later mound built over the tomb of Beowulf was specifically set on the coast so it could be seen far away at sea:

'Geworhton ð   Wedra leode
hleo on hoe,   se wæs heah ond brad,
wægliðendum   wide gesyne...'

('Then the Geat people began to construct
a mound on a headland, high and imposing,
a marker that sailors could see from afar...')

The sea, therefore, was not perceived as the uniform, undifferentiated blank of modern maps, but as a place redolent of signs, forces and places – 'seamarks' – that could be read by the experienced eye to help negotiate this alien environment, a seascape potentially as rich as any landscape. This is not to say that these were charted out, mensurated or spatially systematised in a 'mental map' analogous to the navigational charts of today. The sea is a fluid, dynamic environment, constantly changing so that these 'places' at sea can only be understood within the context of a multitude of interacting phenomena. The spatial precision we take for granted in modern concepts of navigation may not be appropriate when considering early perceptive models of way-finding. Rather than being understood in terms of a static two-dimensional model of the world – the predominant paradigm for understanding spatial and geographical relationships today – places were connected by vectors, trajectories of direction and time.

In the Mediterranean from the early 14th century cardinal and intercardinal directions were given the name of a prevailing wind, so that an entire directional system was based on an ephemeral and shifting natural phenomenon. Thus the direction 'north' was *tramontane*, (from) across the mountains, 'east' was *levanter*, (from) the sunrise, 'northeast' was *greco*, (from) Greece, 'southwest' was *libeccio*, (from) Libya and so on (Frake 1994, 123). The geographical orientation of the these names suggests the system developed in the waters around southern Italy or Sicily, perhaps following the Arabic occupation of the latter in the 9th century AD (Amari 1854; 1858). This nomenclature for spatial direction was used all over the Mediterranean and beyond – the use of the terms was not dependent on the physicality of the winds blowing, nor of the relativity of position to the original direction of the wind. Thus, in the 14th–15th centuries, Italian galleys crossing the English Channel would follow the instruction *porlan e las agujas de varda quarta de leuante al greigo* ('from Portland to the Needles, one heads a quarter from

levante (east) to *greco* (northeast)'; Kretschmer 1909 cited in Frake 1994, 123). The point here is that early mariners managed to make fine directional distinctions and navigate long distances without precision instruments or indeed the cognitive geography that accommodated precise mathematical mapping that became increasingly common from the middle of the 2nd millennium AD onwards. The 'mental map' of early mariners may have been more fluid and less precise than we imagine, and we should be mindful of the 'error of misplaced concreteness that so often distorts our views of the mental schemes of other peoples' (Frake 1994, 125).

The striation of space

We might comfortably assume that these practicalities of finding one's way at sea recorded in early historic times represent a long standing and ancient tradition. Whilst, of course, this must remain speculation, it does not seem unreasonable to extrapolate from early historical methods of 'non-instrumental navigation' back into prehistory (McGrail 1987, 276–84). The much-quoted *Mu'allim* of the Arabian Sea (said to have been written in Sanskrit in AD 434) may well be as applicable to early prehistoric mariners as it was to early historic seafarers;

'He knows the course of the stars and can always orient himself; he knows the value of signs, both regular, accidental and abnormal, of good and bad weather; he distinguishes the regions of the ocean by the fish, the colour of the water, the nature of the bottom, the birds, the mountains, and other indications' (Taylor 1971, 85).

However, this does not approach the cognitive aspects of navigation; how did people understand the world they moved in?

Today, it is normal to understand the world as a totality, even the parts of that totality that are not known – the 'blanks on the map'. Concepts of movement are understood in terms of moving from one place to another within this totality, an understanding of movement within a fixed, immutable space of relative position. This concept of a total space, constrained, controlled by parameters of measurement (longitude, latitude) has been the basis of modern (instrumental or mathematical) navigation for many centuries (Needham 1971, 555), whereby the process of navigation is to move from one point to another in a cognitive universe of known space (notwithstanding those factors that might complicate such movement; tide, wind, current, cloud and so forth).

This conception of the nature of the world in which navigation takes place is essentially the viewpoint described by Deleuze and Guattari as 'striated' space; 'a place where

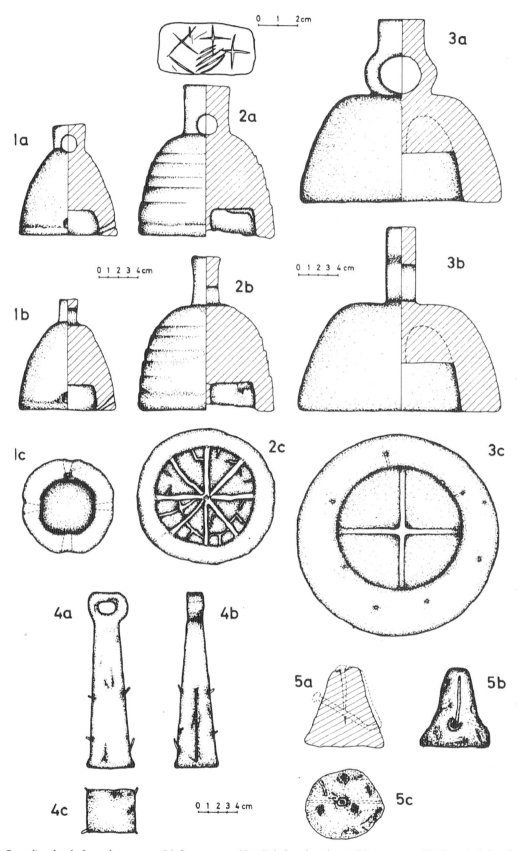

Fig. 8.11. Sounding leads from the western Mediterranean: Nos 1–2 dated to the mid-1st century AD; Nos 4–5 dated to the first half of the middle of the 2nd century BC (after Fiori and Joncheray 1973).

lines and trajectories tend to be subordinated to points: one goes from one point to another' (1988, 528).

It is no coincidence that the latter history of navigation has been characterised as 'mathematical navigation' (McGrail 1987, 275), operating in a cognitive geography 'canopied by the sky as measure and by the measurable visual qualities deriving from it' (Deleuze and Guattari 1988, 529). The notion of striated space is perhaps best understood by comparing it with its sister concept, 'smooth' space. Unlike striated space, smooth space is characterised by the idea that points are subordinate to trajectory; 'the line is therefore a vector, a direction and not a dimension of metric determination' (Deleuze and Guattari 1988, 528). Smooth space is 'occupied by intensities, wind and noise, and sonorous and tactile qualities, as in the desert, steppe or ice' (Deleuze and Guattari 1988, 528–9; cf. Leete 1997);

Fig. 8.12. The 70 mm wooden fragment found in Uunartoq Fjord, Greenland in 1948 (Nationalmuseet, Copenhagen).

'striated space is ordered and regulated by fixed schemata whereas smooth space allows, or requires, irregularities. It is heterogeneous and resists reproduction and universalising' (Phelan 2007, 12).

This dual conception of the nature of space has applications and utility in a multiplicity of disciplines from both synchronic and diachronic perspectives (cf. Lysen and Pisters 2012). To take one example, in the field of musical theory, Pierre Boulez has suggested a dichotomy in the nature of musical space time; in musical striated space time one counts in order to occupy, a space controlled by the stave and the time signature, whereas musical smooth space time is occupied without counting, that of continuous variation, continuous development of form (Boulez 1971, 83–87). Deleuze and Guattari themselves offer a good analogy for the differences between smooth and striated space by comparing the ancient games of Go and Chess. In Chess, with its heterogeneous pieces of different abilities, the underlying principle is of arranging a closed space for oneself, of going from one point to another, of occupying the maximum number of squares (within a finite, 'total' space) with the fewest number of pieces. Go, by contrast, with its undifferentiated and unmoving pieces, is a question of arranging oneself in an open (theoretically infinite) space, of maintaining the possibility of springing up at any point: 'the movement becomes perpetual, without aim or duration, without departure or arrival' (1988, 531–2).

Within this cognitive model, Deleuze and Guattari recognised the sea as a 'very special problem' and in this acknowledged mankind's diachronic trajectory of spatial perception through history which is of particular interest to us here (1988, 528–32). From such a perspective, can we postulate, therefore, that prehistoric mariners understood movement across the seas of the western European seaboard in terms of a mental map of 'smooth' space rather than that of 'striated' space? This is, of course, unknowable, though the possibility is an attractive one. The transition to a fully 'mathematical' method of navigation and the striation of sea and land was in fact a slow process in northern waters, extending well into the historic period. The compass was not introduced until the 13th–14th century and even then was little used by northern sailors (unlike those of the Mediterranean). As late as the 15th century an Italian cartographer annotated his map of the northern seas with the phrase 'in this sea they navigate with neither chart nor compass' (Vogel 1911, 27) and in the 16th century a German seafarer commented:

'Many seamen who sail from Prussia to England and Portugal commonly not only ignore latitude reckoning, but also they heed neither chart nor proper compass … *sie tragen die kunst alle im kopfe*, "they carry their art all in their head"' (Vogel 1911, cited in Frake 1994).

It seems therefore that northern navigators felt no compelling need to adopt the full range of mathematical navigation aids available to them and which themselves were symptomatic of the cognitive striation of maritime space.

If we think of the early historical 'sailing instructions' (like those preserved in the report of Ohthere in the 9th century AD), they might best be understood in terms of 'smooth' space; rather than moving from point to point in a Cartesian mental map of the world, they involve trajectories, timings, relationships to wind, land and current:

> 'Then the land there turned east, or the sea into the land, he did not know which of the two, but he knew that he waited there for a wind from the west and slightly north and then sailed east along the coast as far as he could sail in four days. Then he had to wait there for a wind from the north…' (Bately 2007a, 44; note that the use of cardinal points ('north', 'south', etc.) appear first in the Anglo-Saxon version of this text; the earlier Latin text uses terms such as 'left' and 'right' (Bately 2007b, 22)).

Of course, there is no simple opposition between concepts of smooth and striated space; pilotage, where the presence of land and the knowledge (and perhaps sight) of the point of departure and of destination would imbue a sense of striation – of measurable structure – to people undertaking such journeys. Away from sight of land – 'over the horizon' – a different cognitive understanding of the sea might be appropriate, that of a space negotiated by a deep understanding of the forces and environment present in open water. The transformation of the sea into a striated space was to take a long time, with the eventual imposition of latitude and longitude in the middle of the 2nd millennium AD creating an understanding of the sea as a 'space of sites rather than a region of places' (Casey 1988, 308). 'For the sea is a smooth space *par excellence*, and yet was the first to encounter the demands of increasingly strict striation' (Deleuze and Guattari 1988, 529). An appreciation of such different modes of thought regarding the perception of the sea in prehistory may perhaps enrich a more nuanced understanding in our search for more satisfying explanations of the early history of the Transmanche Zone.

Conclusions: an intimate relationship

We have touched on the early mental attitudes that may have characterised the long-term inundation of Doggerland and the development of the sea and landscapes over the last 8000 years or so that are familiar to us today. We have

speculated on the mechanisms of travelling safely across the alien environment of the sea, reverse engineering from the 'non-instrumental' methods of way-finding set out in early historical records, and we have considered alternative possibilities of the cognitive geographies underpinning seafaring in prehistory. Ultimately, we should not forget that early mariners were dependent on a deep and sophisticated practical knowledge of the sea, of the weather, of the myriad forces and signs that allowed them to make safe passage. This understanding and knowledge of the marine environment was essential to negotiate this 'smooth space', and we must understand that long voyages, particularly 'over the horizon' were redolent with symbolic and magical significance (Helms 1988; Van de Noort 2006). The sea was as much a 'place' as the land, not just a 'space between places', with its own 'seamarks', history and tradition (cf. Bradley 2000; Perring 2000). It is within this context that we might perhaps better understand the technological adaptions of prehistoric ships, social connections and maritime exchange networks.

Note

1 'The man who has experienced shipwreck shudders even at a calm sea'; Ovid, *Letters from Pontus*.

Bibliography

Amari, M. (1854) *Storia dei Musulmani di Sicilia: Volume Primo*, Firenze, Felice Le Monnier.

Amari, M. (1858) *Storia dei Musulmani di Sicilia: Volume Secondo*, Firenze, Felice Le Monnier.

Appelt, M. and Pind, J. (1996) Nunnguaq – a Saqqaq site from the Godthâbsfiord. In B. Grønnow (ed.) *The Paleo-Eskimo Cultures of Greenland – New Perspectives in Greenlandic Archaeology*. Copenhagen, Danish Polar Centre.

Arnold, B. (1995) *Pirogues monoxyles d'Europe centrale: construction, typologie, évolution, tome 1*, Archéologie neuchâteloise 20. Neuchâtel, Musée cantonal d'archéologie.

Bately, J. (2007) Ohthere and Wulfstan in the Old English Osorius. In J. Bately and A. Englert (eds) *Ohthere's Voyages: A late 9th-century account of voyages along the coasts of Norway and Denmark and its cultural context*, Maritime Culture of the North 1, 18–39. Roskilde, Viking Ship Museum.

Bately, J. (ed.) (2007) Text and translation: the three parts of the known world and the geography of Europe north of the Danube according to Orosius' *Historiae* and its Old English version. In J. Bately and A. Englert (eds) *Ohthere's Voyages: A Late 9th-century Account of Voyages along the Coasts of Norway and Denmark and its Cultural Context*, 40–50, Maritime Culture of the North 1. Roskilde, Viking Ship Museum.

Bately, J. and Englert, A. (2007) *Ohthere's Voyages: A Late 9th-century Account of Voyages along the Coasts of Norway and Denmark and its Cultural Context*. Roskilde, Viking Ship Museum.

Bauer, A. and Helm, R. (eds) (1955) *Hippolytus Werke 4, Die Chronik*, Die Griechischen Christlichen Schriftsteller 46 (36). Berlin, Akademie-Verlag.

Beets, D. and van der Spek, A. (2000) The Holocene evolution of the barrier and the back-barrier basins of Belgium and the Netherlands as a function of late Weichselian morphology, relative sea-level rise and sediment supply. *Netherlands Journal of Geosciences* 79 (1), 3–16.

Behre, K.-E. (2007) A New Holocene Sea Level Curve for the Southern North Sea. *Boreas* 36, 82–102.

Beuker, J. and Niekus, M. (1997) De kano van Pesse: De bijl erin. *Nieuwe Drentse Almanak* 114, 122–126.

Bicket, A. (2011) *Submerged Prehistory: Research in Context*, Marine Aggregate Levy Sustainable Fund (MALSF) Science Monograph Series 5, MEPF 10/P150. Salisbury, Wessex Archaeology.

Bjerck, H. (1995) The North Sea continent and the pioneer settlement of Norway. In A. Fischer (ed.) *Man and Sea in the Mesolithic*, 131–144. Oxbow Monograph 53. Oxford, Oxbow Books.

Blankholm, H. (2008) *Målsnes 1: An Early Post-Glacial Site in Northern Norway*. Oxford, Oxbow Books.

Bondevik, S., Svendsen, J., Johnsen, G., Mangerud, J. and Kaland, P. (1997) The Storegga tsunami along the Norwegian coast, its age and runup. *Boreas* 26, 29–53.

Bonnin, P. (2000) Découverte de deux pirogues monoxyles Mésolithiques entre Corbeil-Essonnes (Essonnes) et Melun (Seine-et-Marne). In *Les derniers chasseurs-cueilleurs d'Europe occidentale*, Actes du colloque international de Besançon, octobre 1998, Annales Littéraires 699, Série 'Environment, sociétés et archéologie 1, 305–311. Besançon, Presses Universitaires Franc-Comtoises.

Boulez, P. (1971) *Boulez on Music Today*, (translated by S Bradshaw and R Bennett), Cambridge, Massachusetts: Harvard University Press.

Bradley, R. (2000) *An Archaeology of Natural Places*. London, Routledge.

Bradley, R. (2002) *The Past in Prehistoric Societies*. London, Routledge.

Burov, G. (1996) On Mesolithic means of water transportation in north-eastern Europe. *Mesolithic Miscellany* 17 (1), 5–15.

Butler, J. (1963) Bronze Age connections across the North Sea: a study in prehistoric trade and industrial relations between the British Isles, the Netherlands, north Germany and Scandinavia, *c* 1700–700 BC. *Palaeohistoria* 9, 1–286.

Callaghan, R. (2015) Drift voyages across the mid-Atlantic. *Antiquity* 89 (345), 724–731

Case, H. (1969) Neolithic Explanations. *Antiquity* 43 (171), 176–186.

Casey, E. (1988) *The Fate of Place: A Philosophical History*. Berkeley, University of Californa Press.

Christensen, C. (1990) Stone Age dugout boats in Denmark. In D. Robinson (ed.) *Experimentation and Reconstruction in Environmental Archaeology*, 119–142. Oxford, Oxbow Books.

Clark, J. (1932) *The Mesolithic Age in Britain*. Cambridge, Cambridge University Press.

Clark, J. and Godawin, H. (1956) A Maglemosian site at Brandesburton, Holderness, Yorkshire. *Proceedings of the Prehistoric Society* 22, 6–22.

Clark, P. (2014) The Ole Crumlin-Pedersen puts to sea! *PAST* 76, 4.

Clark, P. (2004) Discussion. In P. Clark (ed.) *The Dover Bronze Age Boat*, 305–322. Swindon, English Heritage.

Clark, P. (ed.) (2009) *Bronze Age Connections: Cultural contact in Prehistoric Europe*. Oxford, Oxbow Books.

Clark, P. and Lehoërff, A. (2014) Naviguer en Manche il y a 3 500 ans. *Dossiers d'Archéologie* 364, 20–21.

Coles, B. (1998) Doggerland; a speculative survey. *Proceedings of the Prehistoric Society* 64, 45–82.

Counillon, P. (2004) *Pseudo-Skylax, Le Périple du Pont-Euxin: texte, traduction, commentaire philogique et historique*, Scripta Antiqua 8. Bordeaux, Ausonius.

De Roest, K. (2013) How to cope with a drowning landscape? A research history into changing representations of Doggerland in relation to climate change. In D. Raemaekers (ed.) *A Kaleidoscope of Maritime Perspectives: Essays on the archaeology, art history and landscape history of the maritime world view*, 7–15. Groningen, Barkhuis.

Deleuze, G. and Guattari, F. (1988) *A Thousand Plateaus: Capitalism and Schizophrenia* (translated by B. Massumi). London, Athlone Press.

Devoy, R. (1990) Sea Level changes and Ireland: past impacts and future prospects. *Technology Ireland* 22 (5), 24–30.

Driessen, H. (2004) A Janus-Faced sea: Contrasting perceptions and experiences of the Mediterranean. *Maritime Studies* 3 (1), 41–50.

Edye, J. (1834) Native vessels of India and Ceylon, *Journal of the Royal Asiatic Society* 1, 4–14.

Ellmers, D. (1984) Earliest evidence for skinboats in late Palaeolithic Europe. In S. McGrail (ed.) *Aspects of Maritime Archaeology and Ethnography*, 41–55. London, National Maritime Museum.

Ellmers, D. (1996) The beginnings of boatbuilding in Central Europe. In R. Gardiner and A.-E. Christensen (eds) *The Earliest Ships: The Evolution of Boats into Ships*, 11–23. Conway's History of the Ship, London, Conway Maritime Press.

Emeis, K.-C., Endler, R., Struck, U. and Kohly, A. (2002) The post-glacial evolution of the Baltic Sea. In G. Wefer, W. Berger, K.-E. Behre and E. Jansen (eds) *Climate Development and History of the North Atlantic Realm*, 205–221. Berlin, Springer.

Farina, A. (2009) *Ecology, Cognition and Landscape: Linking Natural and Social Systems*, Landscape Series 11. Dordrecht, Springer Netherlands.

Fiori, P. and Joncheray, J.-P. (1973) Mobiliers métallique (outils, armes, pièces de gréement) provenant de fouilles sous marines, *Cahiers d'Archéologie subaquatique* 2, 73–94.

Fischer, L. and Hasse, J. (2001) Historical and current perceptions of the landscapes in the Wadden Sea region. In M. Vollmer, M. Guldberg, M. Maluck, D. Marrewijk and G. Schlicksbier (eds) *Landscape and Cultural Heritage in the Wadden Sea Region - Project Report*, Wadden Sea Ecosystem. 12. Wilhelmshaven, Common Wadden Sea Secretariat, Trilateral Monitoring and Assessment Group, 72–79.

Fitch, S., Thomson, K. and Gaffney, V. (2005) Late Pleistocene and Holocene depositional systems and the palaeogeography of the Dogger Bank, North Sea, *Quaternary Research* 64, 185–196.

Fleming, A. (2005) St Kilda: the prehistory of a distant archipelago, *Past* 49, 13–15.

Frake, C. (1994) Dials: a study in the physical representation of cognitive systems. In C. Renfrew and E. Zubrow (eds) *The Ancient Mind: Elements of Cognitive Archaeology*. 119–132. Cambridge, Cambridge University Press.

Gaffney, V., Fitch, S. and Smith, D. (2009) *Europe's Lost World: The Rediscovery of Doggerland*, Council for British Archaeology Research Report 160. York, Council for British Archaeology.

Gaffney, V., Thomson, K. and Finch, S. (2007) *Mapping Doggerland: The Mesolithic Landscapes of the Southern North Sea*. Oxford, Archaeopress.

Garrow, D. and Sturt, F. (2011) Grey waters bright with Neolithic argonauts? Maritime connections and the Mesolithic-Neolithic transition within the 'western seaways' of Britain, *c* 5000–3500 BC. *Antiquity* 85 (327), 59–72.

Gilbert, M., Kivisild, T., Grønnow, B., Andersen, P., Metspalu, E., Reidla, M., Tamm, E., Axelsson, E., Götherström, A., Campos, P., Rasmussen, M., Metspalu, M., Higham, T., Schwenninger, J.-L., Nathan, R., De Hoog, C.-J., Koch, A., Møller, L., Andreasen, C., Meldgaard, M., Villems, R., Bendixen, C. and Willerslev, E. (2008) Paleo-Eskimo mtDNA Genome reveals matrilineal discontinuity in Greenland. *Science* 320 (5884), 1787–9.

Green, C. (2004) Evidence of a marine environment associated with the Dover boat. In P. Clark (ed.) *The Dover Boat in Context: Society and Water Transport in Prehistoric Europe*, 13–16. Oxford, Oxbow Books.

Grønnow, B. (1990) Prehistory in permafrost: Investigations at the Saqqaq Site, Qeqertasussuk, Disco Bay, West Greenland. *Journal of Danish Archaeology* 27, 24–39.

Guilane, J. and van Berg, P.-L. (eds) (2006) *La Néolithisation/The Neolithisation Process*. British Archaeological Report S1520/ Acts of the XIVth UISPP Congress, University of Liège, Belgium, 2–8 September 2001, Symposium 9.2. Oxford, Archaeopress.

Haddon, A. and Hornell, J. (1936–38) *Canoes of Oceania*. 3 vols. Honolulu, Bernice Pauahi Bishop Museum.

Haflidason, H., Lien, R., Sejrup, H., Forsberg, C. and Bryn, P. (2005) The dating and morphometry of the Storegga Slide. *Marine and Petroleum Geology* 22, 123–136.

Hannon, G., Wastegård, S., Bradshaw, E. and Bradshaw, R. (2001) Human impact and landscape degradation on the Faroe Islands. *Proceedings of the Royal Irish Academy* 101B (1–2) (Biology and Environment), 129–139.

Helms, M. (1988) *Ulysses' Sail: An Ethnographic Odyssey of Power, Knowledge, and Geographical Distance*. Princeton, Princeton University Press.

Johnstone, P. (1988) *The Sea-craft of Prehistory*. 2nd edition. London, Routledge and Kegan Paul.

Keller, C. and Christensen, A. (2002) The Uunartoq 'bearing dial' - not an instrument for ocean navigation? In S. Lewis-Simpson (ed.) *Vinland Revisited: The Norse World at the Turn of the 1st Millennium, Selected Papers from the Viking Millennium International Symposium, 15–24 September 2000, Newfoundland and Labrador*, 429–441. St John's, NL, Historical Sites Association of Newfoundland and Labrador.

Kemble, J. (1843) *The Poetry of the Codex Vercellensis, with an English Translation*. London, Ælfric Society.

Kinnes, I. (2004) Context not circumstance: a distant view of Scottish monuments in Europe. In I. Shepherd and G. Barclay (eds) *Scotland in Ancient Europe*, 139–142. Edinburgh, Society of Antiquaries of Scotland.

Kretschmer, K. (1909) *Die italienischen Portolane des Mittelalters*. Berlin, Instituts für Meereskunde.

Lambeck, K. (1995) Late Devensian and Holocene shorelines of the British Isles and North Sea from models of glacio-hydro-isostatic rebound. *Journal of the Geological Society* 152, 437–448.

Larsen, H. and Meldgaard, J. (1958) Paleo-Eskimo cultures in Disko Bugt, West Greenland. *Meddelelser om Grønland* 161 (2), 1–75.

Leary, J. (2009) Perceptions of and responses to the Holocene flooding of the North Sea lowlands. *Oxford Journal of Archaeology* 28 (3), 227–237.

Leete, A. (1997), Regarding the way-finding habits of the Siberian peoples, considering the Khants as an example Translated by E. Uustalu), *Folklore* 3, http://haldjas.folklore.ee/folklore/vol3/soros4.htm

Long, D., Wickham-Jones, C. and Ruckley, N. (1986) A flint artefact from the northern North Sea. In D. Roe (ed.) *Studies in the Upper Palaeolithic of Britain and Northwest Europe*. 55–62. British Archaeological Report S296. Oxford, British Archaeological Reports.

Louwe Kooijmans, L. (1985) *Sporen in Het Land: De Nederlandse Delta in de Prehistorie*. Amsterdam, Meulenhoff.

Louwe Kooijmans, L. (1993) The Mesolithic/Neolithic transition in the Lower Rhine Basin. In P. Bogucki (ed.) *Case Studies in European Prehistory*. 95–145. Boca Raton, CRC Press.

Lysen, F. and Pisters, P. (2012) Introduction: The smooth and the striated. *Deleuze Studies* 6 (1), 1–5.

Malinowski, B. (1922) *Argonauts of the Western Pacific*. London, Routledge.

Marinval-Vigne, M.-C., Mordant, D., Auboire, G., Augereau, A., Bailon, S., Dauphin, C., Delibrias, G., Krier, V., Leclerc, A.-S., Leroyer, C., Marinval, P., Mordant, C., Rodriguez, P., Vilette, P. and Vigne, J.-D. (1989) Noyen-sur-Seine, site stratifié en milieu fluvitile: Une étude multidisciplinaire intégrée. *Bulletin de la société préhistorique française* 86 (10/12), 370–9.

McGrail, S. (1987) *Ancient Boats in NW Europe: the archaeology of water transport to AD 1500*. London, Longman.

McGrail, S. (2001) *Boats of the World*. Oxford, Oxford University Press.

Melton, N. and Nicholson, R. (2004) The Mesolithic in the Northern Isles: the preliminary evaluation of an oyster midden at West Voe, Sumburgh, Shetland, UK. *Antiquity* 78 (299), http://antiquity.ac.uk/ProjGall/nicholson/index.html

Mithen, S. (2000) The Scottish Mesolithic: Problems, prospects and the rationale of the Southern Hebrides Mesolithic Project. In S. Mithen (ed.) *Hunter-gatherer Landscape Archaeology: the Southern Hebrides Mesolithic Project 1988–98*, 9–37. Cambridge, McDonald Institute for Archaeological Research.

Møbjerg, T. (1997) New Aspects of the Saqqaq Culture in West Greenland. In R. Gilberg and H. Gulløv (eds) *Fifty Years of Arctic Research: Anthropological Studies From Greenland to Siberia*. 227–236, National Museum of Denmark Ethnographical Series 18. Copenhagen, National Museum of Denmark.

Möller, P., Östland, O., Barnekow, L., Sandgren, P. Palmbo, F. and Willerslev, E. (2012) Living at the margin of the retreating

Fennoscandian Ice Sheet: The early Mesolithic sites at Aareavaara, northernmost Sweden. *Holocene* 23 (1), 104–116.

Mordant, C. and Mordant, D. (1989) Noyen-sur-Seine, site mésolithique en milieu humide fluviatile. In *L'homme at l'eau au temps de la Préhistoire*, Actes du 112e congrès national des sociétés savantes, 31–52. Paris, Comité des travaux historiques et scientifiques.

Mordant, D. and Mordant, C. (1992) Noyen-sur-Seine: A Mesolithic waterside settlement. In B. Coles (ed.) *The Wetland Revolution in Prehistory*, 55–64. Exeter, Prehistoric Society and WARP (Wetland Archaeology Research Project).

Mordant, D., Valentin, B. and Vigne, J.-D. (2010) Noyen-sur-Seine, vingt-cinq ans après. In B. Valentin, B. Souffi, T. Ducrocq, J.-P. Fagnart, F. Séara and C. Verjux (eds) *Palethnographie du Mésolithique: Recherches sur les habitats de plein air entre Loire et Neckar*, 37–49, Actes de la table ronde internationale de Paris, 26 et 27 novembre 2010, Séances de la Société préhistorique française 2 (1). Paris, Société préhistorique française.

Needham, J. (1971) *Science and Civilization in China, Volume 4: Physics and Physical Technology, Part 3: Civil Engineering and Nautics* (with the collaboration of W Ling and L Gwei-Djen). Cambridge, Cambridge University Press.

Nobles, G. (2013) The canoe. In J. Kleijne, O. Brinkkemper, R. Lauwerier, B. Smit and E. Thunissen (eds) *A Matter of Life and Death at Mienakker (the Netherlands): Late Neolithic Behavioural Variability in a Dynamic Landscape*, 241–7, Nederlandse Archeologische Rapporten 45. Amersfoort, Cultural Heritage Agency of the Netherlands.

Oleson, J. (2008) Testing the waters: The role of sounding weights in ancient Mediterranean navigation. *Memoirs of the American Academy in Rome. Supplementary Volume 6, The Maritime World of Ancient Rome*, 119–176.

Parfitt, K. (2014) A land archaeologist goes to sea. *Current Archaeology* 24 (11), 287, 44–5.

Perring, E. (2000) *Da Fishing Hands O'Fair Isle*. Fair Isle, George Waterston Memorial Centre.

Petersen, H. (1986) *Skinboats of Greenland*, Ships and Boats of the North 1. Roskilde, National Museum of Denmark, Greenland Provincial Museum and the Viking Ship Museum in Roskilde.

Phelan, J. (2007) *Seascapes: Tides of Thought and being in Western Perceptions of the Sea*, Goldsmiths Anthropology Research Paper 14. London, Goldsmiths College, University of London.

Redman, C. (2005) Resilience theory in archaeology. *American Anthropologist* 107 (1), 70–77.

Saville, A. (2000) Orkney and Scotland before the Neolithic period. In A. Ritchie (ed.) *Neolithic Orkney in its European Context*, 91–100. Cambridge, McDonald Institute for Archaeological Research.

Schledermann, P. (1990) *Crossroads to Greenland: 3000 Years of Prehistory in the Eastern High Arctic*, Komatic Series 2. Calgary, Arctic Institute of North America of the University of Calgary.

Schnall, U. (1996) Early shiphandling and navigation in northern Europe. In R. Gardiner and C. Christensen (eds) *The Earliest Ships: The Evolution of Boats into Ships*. 120–8. Conway's History of the Ship. London, Conway Maritime Press.

Seaver, K. (2000) Unanswered questions. In W. Fitzhugh and E. Ward (eds) *Vikings: The North Atlantic Saga*. 270–9. Washington DC, Smithsonian Institution Press.

Sheridan, A. (2010) The Neolithisation of Britain and Ireland: the big picture. In B. Finlayson and G. Warren (eds) *Landscapes in Transition*, 89–105. Oxford, Oxbow Books.

Shipley, G. (2011) *Pseudo-Sylax's Periplous. The Circumnavigation of the Inhabited World: Text, Translation and Commentary*. Exeter, Bristol Phoenix Press.

Smith, D., Shi, S., Cullingford, R., Dawson, A., Dawson, S., Firth, C., Foster, I., Fretwell, P., Haggart, B., Holloway, L., Long, D. (2004) The Holocene Storegga Slide tsunami in the United Kingdom. *Quaternary Science Reviews* 23, 2291–2321.

Smith, O., Momber, G., Bates, R., Garwood, P., Fitch, S., Pallen, M., Gaffney, V. and Allaby, R. (2015a) Sedimentary DNA from a submerged site reveals wheat in the British Isles 8000 years ago. *Science* 347 (6225), 998–1001.

Smith, O., Momber, G., Bates, R., Garwood, P., Fitch, S., Pallen, M., Gaffney, V. and Allaby, R. (2015b) Supplementary materials for sedimentary DNA from a submerged site reveals wheat in the British Isles 8000 years ago. *Science* 347 (998), DOI: 10.1126/science.1261278

Sølver, C. (1953) The discovery of an ancient bearing dial. *Journal of the Institute of Navigation* 6, 294–6.

Sølver, C. (1954) *Vestervejen: Om Vikingernes Sejlads*, Copenhagen, Weilbach.

Taylor, E. (1956) *The Haven-finding Art: A History of Navigation from Odysseus to Captain Cook*. London, Sydney and Toronto, Hollis and Carter for the Institute of Navigation.

Thompson, V. and Turck, J. (2009) Adaptive cycles of coastal hunter-gatherers. *American Antiquity* 74 (2), 255–278.

Tikkanen, M. and Oksanen, J. (2002) Late Weichselian and Holocene shore displacement history of the Baltic Sea in Finland. *Fennia* 180 (1–2), 9–20.

Toller, T. (ed.) (1898) *An Anglo-Saxon Dictionary Based on the Manuscript Collections of the late Joseph Bosworth, D. D., F. R. S.* Oxford, Oxford University Press.

Troels-Smith, J. (1946) Stammebaade fra Aamosen. *Fra Nationalmuseets Arbejdsmark* 1946, 15–23.

Van de Noort, R. (2006) Argonauts of the North Sea – a social maritime archaeology for the 2nd millennium BC. *Proceedings of the Prehistoric Society* 72, 267–287.

Vanmontfort, B. (2008) A southern view on north–south interaction during the Mesolithic-Neolithic transition in the Lower Rhine Area. In H. Fokkens, B. Coles, A. Van Gijn, J. Kleijne, H. Ponjee and C. Slappendel (eds) *Between Foraging and Farming: An Extended Broad Spectrum of Papers Presented to Leendert Louwe Kooijmans*, 85–97. *Analecta Praehistorica Leidensia* 40. Leiden, Leiden University.

Vogel, W. (1911) Die Einführung des Kompasses in die nordwesteuropaïsche Nautik. *Hansische Geschichtsblätter* 17 (38), 1–32.

Weninger, B., Schulting, R., Bradtmöller, M., Clare L., Collard, M., Edinborough, K., Hilpert, J., Jöris, O., Niekus, M., Rohling, E., and Wagner, B. (2008) The catastrophic final flooding of Doggerland by the Storegga Slide tsunami. *Documenta Praehistorica* 35, 1–24.

Whittle, A. (1996a) Prolegomena to the study of the Mesolithic–Neolithic transition in Britain and Ireland. In D. Cahen and M. Otte (eds) *Rubané et Cardial: Actes du Colloque de Liège, Novembre 1988*, 209–227. Liège, Université de Liège.

Whittle, A. (1996b) *Europe in the Neolithic: The Creation of New Worlds*. Cambridge, Cambridge University Press.

Whittle, A., Healy, F. and Bayliss, A. (2011) *Gathering Time: Dating the Early Neolithic Enclosures of Southern Britain and Ireland*. Oxford, Oxbow Books.

Wickham-Jones, C. (1990) *Rhum: Mesolithic and Later Sites at Kinloch. Excavations 1984–86*. Society of Antiquaries of Scotland Monograph 7. Edinburgh, Society of Antiquaries of Scotland.

Woodman, P., Anderson, E. and Finlay, N. (1999) *Excavations at Ferriter's Cove, 1983–95: Last Foragers, First Farmers in the Dingle Peninsula*. Dublin, Wordwell.

Yeh, H., Peterson, C., Chadha, R., Latha, D. and Katada, T. (2005) *Preliminary Report on the 2004 Great Indian Ocean Tsunami: Tsunami Survey along the South-East Indian Coast*. Oakland CA, Earthquake Engineering Research Institute.

9

Circular funerary monuments at the beginning of the Bronze Age in the north of France: architecture and duration of use

Nathalie Buchez, Yann Lorin, Emmanuelle Leroy-Langelin, Armelle Masse, Angélique Sergent and Sébastien Toron with the collaboration of Jérôme Brenot, Kai Fechner, Élodie Lecher, Emmanuelle Martial and Yann Petite

Abstract

Bronze Age circular funerary monuments with periphery features are found in the north and west of Europe. After a reminder of these features classed by type, several different approaches that are used in order to reconstruct the elevations are described. The analysis of ditch fills and pedological contexts provides important information as to the restoration of these places. Furthermore, the archaeological finds provide chronological and cultural data that can reveal practices relating to the funerary sphere or ditch use.

Keywords: round-barrows, pedological analysis, architecture, objects.

Résumé

Les monuments funéraires à aménagement périphérique sont présents dans le nord et l'ouest de l'Europe. Après un rappel typologique de ces vestiges, plusieurs approches sont présentées afin de mieux appréhender leurs élévations. En effet, l'analyse sédimentaire des comblements, et/ou du substrat environnant, apporte des informations essentielles à la restitution des lieux. Ensuite, la question du matériel lié à ces monuments est abordée. Outre son intérêt chrono-culturel, il peut révéler certaines pratiques en lien avec la gestuelle funéraire ou l'utilisation des fossés.

Mots-clés : monuments funéraires, analyse pédologique, architecture, mobilier.

The mapping and excavation of Bronze Age funerary circular monuments as part of development-led archaeology raises two main angles of research into this vast topic: their construction and duration of use.

This paper presents considerations on the databases recorded for the Nord, Pas-de-Calais and Somme departments, flanking the sea coast. By means of a descriptive overview of these data, we evaluate the different methods and analyses required for a better assessment of these monuments.

The systematic application of varied methods of analyses (radiometric dating, pedological, geomorphological) combined with the in-depth study of archaeological structures, fills and associated objects leads to an enhanced approach for understanding the evolution of practices and cultural facies at the beginning of the Bronze Age.

Circular monuments, round-barrows, Ringwalheuvels or tombelles: the context of new regional data

Funerary monuments with peripheral structures are present in the north and west of Europe, in the coastal areas of southeast England, Holland and in Belgian Flanders and the northwest of France. The architecture and funerary practices of these monuments have been defined based on the Early Bronze Age facies in different regions (Wessex, Hilversum, Eramecourt or the group called 'Urnes à décor plastique').

From the 1950s onwards, similarities between the funerary traditions of these groups from the northwest of Europe were broached, in particular through diffusionist and 'invasionist' theories of Bronze Age population movements in the west of Europe (Glasbergen 1954). This model, now largely undermined, has nonetheless led to the identification of the first contacts between local facies and neighbouring regions, such as the eponymous Eramecourt group in France with echoes in the Belgian Ardennes and in the British Isles, as shown by the work of C. Burgess on Trans-Channel relationships (Blanchet 1976; Fourny 1985; Burgess 1987).

These interactions between different cultural groups are now well documented and have been the focus of several regional and international overviews. They provide clearer definitions and a more comprehensive terminology, particularly in relation to funerary practices at the beginning of the Bronze Age, as part of the 'Channel-North Sea' identity called 'Manche-Mer du Nord (MNN)' (Bourgeois and Talon 2005; Toron 2006; De Reu *et al.* 2012).

Descriptive overview

Over a thousand monuments have been identified in the north of France, mainly in the Somme, using aerial photographs. To date, 56 sites have been surveyed or excavated, leading to the identification of a little more than 100 circular ditches, some of which were not recorded by aerial photographs (Fig. 9.1). The typology of the peripheral ditch of these monuments varies little. Almost 90% of the monuments present a single continuous ditch with a diameter oscillating between 4 m and 86 m. However, most of them are in the 10–25 m range, and dimensions at either extreme of the spectrum are rare. During extensive clearing carried out over the past few years, it is increasingly frequent to discover small circles of less than 10 m that cannot be systematically attributed to the Late Bronze Age, as was widely believed for a long time, and as shown by recent discoveries at Avelin (Nord: Germain *et al.* 2010), la Marlière at Courcelles-lès-Lens

(Pas-de-Calais: Blondeau 2015) or Lauwin-Planque (Nord: Leroy-Langelin and Sergent 2015). The ditch of the typical single-ditched monument is on average 2 m wide, although width varies proportionately in relation to the diameter of the enclosure. Average depth is 1 m. Several rare cases of interruptions have been recorded, forming an entrance, as at les Arguillières at Fréthun (Pas-de-Calais: Maréchal 2000) or in the Saint-Nicolas Basin at Ham and Bois Vieil at Vignacourt in the Somme (Feray and Herbert 1998; Baray 1998). Many monuments display several sequences of ditch development with several stages of digging: this is clearly the case in one of the Motel monuments at Fresnes-lès-Montauban, where two arced oblong pits were reworked into a circular ditch (Pas-de-Calais: Desfossés and Masson 1990). But the chronology of the sequences – conservation directly linked to the funerary function of the monument or later use of the site – is not always well known. Several monuments present double or even triple concentric ditches in exceptional cases, or with an annex, like at Au-dessus du Grand Rideau at Saint-Vaast-en-Chaussée in the Somme (Baray 1998), at Rietz at Fréthun (Bostyn *et al.* 2000) and at Frénésie at Conchil-le-Temple in Nord-Pas-de-Calais (Piningre 1990). These multiple monuments represent a characteristic tradition in the northwest of Europe. Again, the chronology of these ditches is not always clear in our regions and thus requires special attention. It could indicate a single construction from the outset or the persistence of an old structure, reused and extended throughout time. These rare cases of concentric enclosures are still poorly understood and necessitate systematic dating and more in-depth sampling in order to assess the principles underlying their construction.

These monuments are characterised by the paucity of objects within the internal circle as well as in the peripheral ditches, and often, the only means of dating is to multiply radiometric analyses (Masse and Toron 2008). Fifty-four dates have been obtained for 16 regional sites on samples taken from the different stages of infilling or burials associated with the monuments. The chronological timespan corresponding to the construction and use of the monuments covers the whole of the Bronze Age, and even the end of the Neolithic and the beginning of the Iron Age, from 2200 to 750 let : cal BC (calibrated) (Fig. 9.2). However, the cumulated dates show a clear increase in site occupation between 1750 and 1350 cal BC. This main phase presents an upsurge in funerary practices as well as monuments. Therefore, greater numbers of circular monuments were erected during the Early and Middle Bronze Age, as is also shown in the bordering territories of England and Belgium (De Reu *et al.* 2012, 272–3). This occupation chronology has now been confirmed at several regional sites. Burials in a flexed side position and cremation are both practised at the same period; however there are no known examples of both practices in contemporaneous deposits within the same

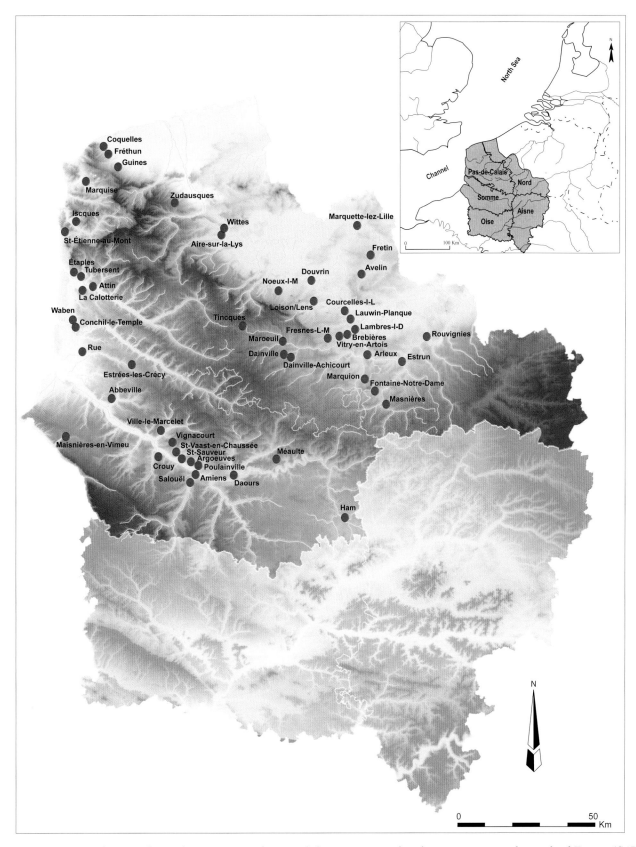

Fig. 9.1. Mapping of sites with circular monuments discovered during rescue archaeology operations in the north of France (CAD: S. Toron, ÉVEHA).

funerary structure (Fig. 9.3). In addition, we differentiate another mode of deposit around 1500 cal BC, where cremated remains are covered by an urn and placed at the centre of the monument, in a shallow pit, which is at times structured, like for example at Chemin des morts at Rue (Somme *et al*. 2000). Simple pit cremation deposits, in the form of small concentrations of bones and charcoal are a

recurrent tradition, as at Lauwin-Planque (Leroy-Langelin and Sergent 2015).

The presence of wooden structures associated with monument architecture has been poorly documented until now in our study area (Maniez 2010). However, these installations have been identified in a zone extending from the Netherlands to Belgian Flanders (Bourgeois and Cherreté

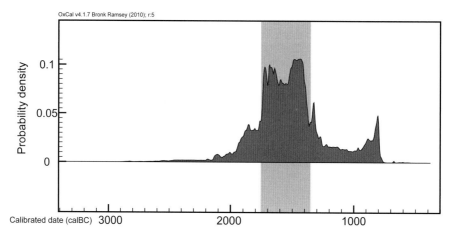

Fig. 9.2. Cumulative summary of the 54 dates obtained on 16 sites with circular monuments in the studied regions (CAD: S. Toron, ÉVEHA).

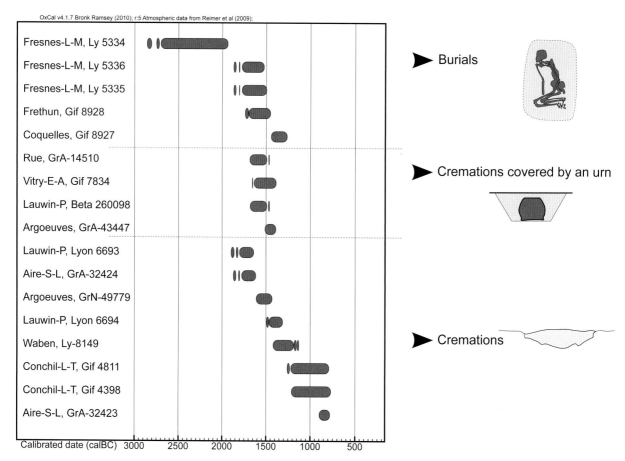

Fig. 9.3. Details of the calibrated dates by burial type in circular monument contexts (CAD: S. Toron, ÉVEHA).

2005; Bourgeois 2013). This could be a specific MMN trait, although we cannot provide confirmation of this owing to the poor state of monument conservation in our region. The detailed analysis of ditch fill could perhaps clarify this issue.

The absence of any above-ground structure is a result of the poor conservation of monuments: most of them must have had a mound in the same way as the better preserved tumuli with peripheral ditches across the Channel. In our regions, only several indirect indications point to the existence of mounds, often due to later reoccupations: a diverted path, implantation of a medieval cemetery adopting the same shape as the mound, etc. Areas with forest cover, such as the Crécy-en-Ponthieu forest in the Somme, provide evidence of conserved tumuli with peripheral ditches (Agache 1978, 110).

This absence of earth mounds, and the scarcity of any visible signs of above-ground architecture, necessitate new approaches in order to provide useful data for the reconstruction of monument architecture, through the analysis of pedological contexts.

In a chalky context: infilling analysis in order to study monument architecture

For monuments built on chalk formations, excavation data comes from the study of the ditch fills. Nonetheless, in very

Fig. 9.4. Plan view of a chalk level in the ditch infilling at Dainville 'Le Champ Bel Air' (photo: A. Masse, CDA CG62).

rare cases, the presence of a specific sedimentary formation at the interface of the substratum and the soil can point to the remnants of an elevation linked to the enclosure, as at the site of Gérico at Dainville Achicourt, Pas-de-Calais (Jacques and Prilaux 2006), or Moulin d'Argoeuves, in the Somme (Buchez 2014).

As this information is only derived from the ditch fill, an in-depth interdisciplinary approach is still required for their analysis.

However, although endeavouring to understand infilling dynamics – run-off phases, stabilisation, renewed digging and final infill – is nothing new, and although several sites have been studied in detail, such as Motel at Fresnes-les-Montauban, in Pas-de-Calais (Desfossés and Masson 1990), in practice, these ditches – remains of monuments – are often only assessed during archaeological evaluation. Consequently, for many of them, only few sections are available and are too often considered to be representative. Proposals relating to the morphology or the history of the monument are thus poorly substantiated, in the absence of:

1) verifying the regularity of the observed phenomena in sections;
2) identifying the recorded anomalies in a more substantial and regular way in the ditch fill;
3) testing field observations by pedological analyses.

For the time being, we thus only have case studies for assessing monument morphology and for identifying any associated activities (*cf. infra see before*).

Ditch profiles can be well marked, with a flat base and rectilinear sides. The hypothesis of wooden walls protecting the ditch cut ditches is still tenuous, as evidence is sparse. We can cite the case of Argoeuves where fine humiferous layers are attested at the base of the fill. Granulometric analyses and thin-section observations suggest that these layers are similar to the formation mode of the palaeo-horizon ('black soil') identified at the site, but nonetheless present several differences (K. Fechner in Buchez 2014). They do not appear to result from the accumulation of the ancient soil at the base of the structure after the collapse of the ditch of the ditch cut, but rather from the *in situ* decomposition of organic matter (leaves, wood, a floor?).

The most frequently noted information is the dissymmetry of the fill, related to the presence of materials at the edge of the ditch, probably the earth mound.

At Champ Bel Air at Dainville (Masse *et al.* 2013; Masse 2014) or rue de Lennes at Douvrin (Henton 2011) in Pas-de-Calais, as at Argoeuves (Buchez 2014), a chalk gravel level concentrated on the outer side of the ditch indicates an external deposit, which may be a bank formed by the chalk taken from digging out the ditch. At Argoeuves, as at Dainville, specific fragmentation of chalk elements – gravel – has been noted, which may result from the exposure of these materials to frost.

The regularity of this deposit is confirmed by the fact that it is visible on the surface during clearing; it is particularly clear at the site of Dainville (Fig. 9.4). In places at Argoeuves and at Dainville, a layer of humus emphasises this chalk backfill. It may mark the early stages of infilling and derive from the humiferous surface of the bank. Interpretation is different at other points in the Argoeuves ditch, suggesting the combined input of externally-derived gravels and of humiferous levels from the interior, that is to say a possible internal elevation. The morphology of the latter – mound or cordon – cannot be determined here.

Loessial contexts: influence of architecture on decarbonation

Work on loess observation began in 2008, with the geomorphologist O. Collette, at the ZAC site at Lauwin-Planque (Leroy-Langelin and Collette 2011), where the influence of ditch digging on the substratum was identified. In northwestern Europe, carbonated loess underwent alteration, probably from the Tardiglacial period onwards (Van Vliet-Lanoé *et al.* 1992), when climatic conditions were propitious. A brunified horizon, also called 'structural horizon' then formed (Fig. 9.5). When the soil becomes very brunified, slight leaching begins, then becomes stronger, creating several horizons of decarbonated silt in the pedological section (Jamagne and Bégon 1984).

Alteration and migration were observed to be stronger due to the effects of digging, when ditches have remained open for some time. On the other hand, earth inputs (mounds or banks) are not always visible on the alteration horizon, but can be represented by a slowing in decarbonation.

These conclusions were published in 2011 (Leroy-Langelin and Collette 2011) and provide a starting point for methodological reasoning. Discussions between researchers have resulted in testing the relevance of the method and the proposal of improvements or new perspectives. Recent discoveries, stemming from the combined intervention of archaeologists and geomorphologists, enhance the observation of loess and occurrences associated with the presence of a monument.

Today, the influence of any anthropogenic activity on the decarbonation level is now accepted. Current challenges now focus on two main points: 1) the pertinence of reconstructing elevations; 2) the methods to implement in order to improve hypotheses of reconstruction.

The first point attempts to understand the impact of elevations on the decarbonation level. In other words, can the fluctuations observed in the uppermost layers be related to anthropogenic activity or to natural variations? And how can they be explained by observations in the field? On account of the innovative nature of this approach, results must be increasingly questioned and placed in a wider context, in practical terms by extending investigations beyond the limits of the monuments, as well as in temporal terms by questioning the conditions of implementation.

The second point aims to provide as accurate a rendition as possible of these variations.

A complete review of the methodology, taking into account all related questions, enables us to draw up new study prospects and to propose, as empirically as possible, the most effective methods and techniques to use in order to address, in particular, the restrictions of rescue archaeology.

Several diagnostic methods have been applied and are listed in a table including a corpus with shared criteria considerations (Table 9.1). This inventory is an intermediary stage in the ongoing centralization of data. It enables us to assess which questions these approaches generate. A detailed comparative analysis is required to gauge the importance of certain factors (depth, slope, exposure to weather conditions?) and the influence of specific contexts (variations linked to the sedimentary record). A series of experiments have been implemented in order to try to address these questions (Fig. 9.6), as shown by the evolution in the way the question was treated in the region of Aire-sur-la-Lys (Lorin and al. 2016). This review identifies the correlation between the pedological signal and palaeo-landforms.

The chosen fieldwork methods are adapted to variations in the diameter of the remains and the depth of the levels to be attained. The most commonly adopted practice consists of a series of trenches (radiating or cross-shaped) and appears to be the best compromise when results present the same variations around the monument. It results in recording the upper limit of the carbonated level on the axes. We can consider that the overlapping of a transect with a standard curve presenting the same protrusions in the same places is proof of human action.

Section analysis remains subjective in so far as different anomalies can appear. Former topography, zones where run-off varies in intensity and vegetation density are all potentially conducive elements to bioturbation and have an impact on soil alteration. Moreover, we can question the influence of the phenomenon when the thickness of decarbonated silts is significant, in which case the decarbonation front is at some distance from the archaeological remains.

These different questions led to the observation of the type of decarbonation outside monuments. Tests were undertaken by opening one or several test trenches, referred

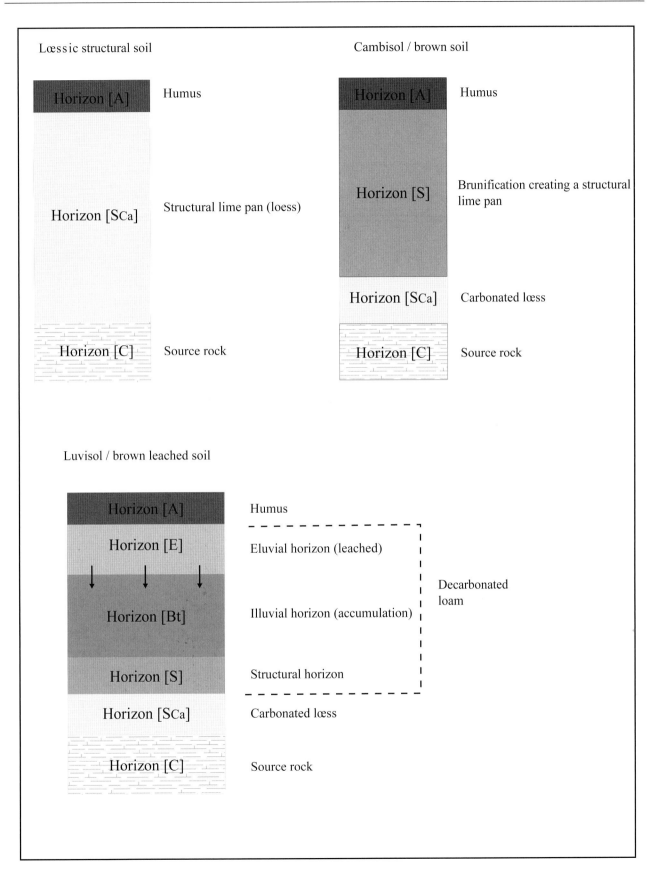

Fig. 9.5. Alteration schemas for loessial soils in our region (Y. Petite, CAD-DAP).

Table 9.1 Observation modes of occurrences linked to decarbonation: list of regional sites and types of operations

Site's names	Ditch			Decarbonatation				observations	Graphic finish
	Type	Diam.	average depth	Depth	Transect	ext. reference	sedimentary record		
Aire sur la Lys - N	simple	49	1.45	1.6	partial radiating	no			sections
Aire sur la Lys - P1	double	50–72	1,4 et 0,45	2	cross-shaped	yes	yes		sections
Aire sur la Lys - P2	simple	51	1.4	2	cross-shaped	yes	yes		sections
Arleux	simple	11	0.7	1.2	cross-shaped	no	yes		sections
Courcelles les lens 1	simple	28	1.6	1.2	radiating	yes	no		sections
Lambres-Lez-Douai	simple	11	0.6	0.7	cross-shaped	no	no		sections
Lauwin-Planque 1	simple	30	1.1	1.1	cross-shaped	no	no		sections
Lauwin-Planque 2	simple	21	1.3	1.1	cross-shaped	no	no		sections
Lauwin-Planque 3	simple	19	1.2	1.1	cross-shaped	no	no	badger burrow	sections
Lauwin-Planque 4	simple	31	1.5	1	cross-shaped	no	no		sections
Lauwin-Planque 5	simple	34	1.7	1.3	cross-shaped	no	no		sections
Lauwin-Planque 6	simple	24	1.2	0.6	cross-shaped	no	no		sections
Lauwin-Planque 7	simple	15	0.5	0.4	partial radiating	no	no		sections
Lauwin-Planque 8	simple	32	1	0.4	partial radiating	no	no		sections
Lauwin-Planque 10	simple	17	1.5	1.3	cross-shaped	yes	no		3 D
Maroeuil	simple	46	1.2	1	cross-shaped	no	yes	badger burrow	sections and plans
Wittes	double	43–58	1.45	1.7	radiating	no	yes		sections

Depth is indicated in meters with topsoil thickness

to as reference trenches, near the archaeological ditch in a zone devoid of archaeological features. These natural variations led to a better evaluation of the topographic context of the site at the time of monument building. This work is based on a comparison between the variations observed under the monuments and those situated outside any known archaeological structure. At the site of Courcelles-lès-Lens (Blondeau 2015), the study of the decarbonation level was based on the statistical analysis of its altimetric variations. By following the amplitude of natural landform variations, it was possible to only take into consideration variations superior to those recorded and thus to propose a more reliable reconstruction of the landform associated with the enclosure. At this stage of the study, this approach is still applied in a very empirical way and needs to be developed further.

When the sequence of decarbonated horizons is complete, the lower limit of the illuvial horizon lying on a brunified horizon provides more ample information. In order to complete the sections in the carbonated level, it is possible to observe this illuvial horizon and the rest of the pedological profile with the help of a geomorphologist. This horizon undergoes fewer disturbances due to plant cover and run-off, giving rise to better interpretations of embankments and their anthropogenic or natural characteristics. During the diagnostic of the chemin de Brunémont at Arleux (Nord), the observation of these levels resulted in the architectural reconstruction of the monument with a mound and an external bank (Julien 2011).

With a view to improving the method, the geomorphologist Y. Petite, removed the top soil from the totality of the last monument at the ZAC at Lauwin-Planque in 2010 after completely excavating the surrounding area (Leroy-Langelin and Sergent 2015). The decarbonated silts were removed from the central zone of the circle (with a 17 m diameter) as well as from the periphery in order to attain the carbonated loess. Along with altimetric recording, this led to the 3D reconstruction of the top of this level, revealing the presence of an internal bank and very probably of an external bank. The multiplication of altimetric measurements reduces the risk of inconsistencies and provides a good overall vision of elevations (Fig. 9.7).

An alternative method was proposed at the site of Maroeuil (Pas-de-Calais: Lorin 2017) by excavating a further 50 cm down, which revealed the presence of badger burrows. Their plan is in keeping with what is commonly described for the burrows of this species, that is, a tunnelled entrance at the edge of the bank and setts further down (Germain-Vallée *et al.* 2007; Langohr 2000; Vanmoerkerke 1990). The presence of these burrows represents an argument in favour of an elevation. The second clearing suggests that the probable mound was located off-centre in the internal area. This operative mode requires considerable logistics (as this double excavation

imputes heavily on mechanical means) and does not seem feasible beyond a certain diameter or when the carbonated level is very deep.

In spite of the difficulties involved, this research is promising and by multiplying different experiences, we should achieve reliable reconstructions.

The objects: evidence of the use duration of monuments

Publications and reports often note sherds and vase portions, chipped flint and burnt or unburnt flint, forming concentrations in the ditch fill, that are at times associated with what is considered to be a hearth, as at Frénésie, at Conchil-le-Temple (Pas-de-Calais: Piningre 1990), or corresponding to the remains of a combustion structure in association with the funerary function.

Due to the way ditches are processed, features are rarely exhaustively recorded and are not always associated with a detailed analysis of infilling events. It is thus often difficult to differentiate between objects pertaining to general refuse contained in backfill indicating former site occupation, or the proximity of a contemporaneous or more recent settlement. It is not always possible to quantify how long the monument was maintained or how long it functioned as a funerary site. Were sites really taken over at relatively recent periods? The question subsists for example, for the Early Iron Age and the Early La Tène in the case of the Pigeonnier monuments with double enclosures at Daours and Au-dessus du Grand Rideau at Saint-Vaast-en-Chaussée, in the Somme (Buchez 2011), or Zac in the hamlet of Saint-Martin at Aire-sur-la-Lys (Lorin 2016, David and Lorin 2016), from the Late Bronze Age/Early Iron Age transition. Again, hypotheses can be formulated from several case studies (as at Argoeuves and Lauwin-Planque, chosen from recent excavations), pending their possible validation based on recurrent observations.

Both of the Argoeuves enclosures were mainly excavated manually, by metric portions, leading to the assessment of different phenomena and in particular, the identification and the piece-by-piece demontage of several lithic concentrations. In both ditches, these concentrations preceded the dismantling of the chalk bank around the monument (*cf. supra - just see below*), and correspond to knapping waste from what appears to be *in situ* flake production, given the remains lying in flat position, the high number of refits, the proximity of the associated elements within the concentration and the representation of all the products and by-products of the operational chain, including chips (E. Martial in Buchez 2014).

For one of the concentrations, we have a date obtained from a deer antler found nearby (GrA-44229: 3100±35 BP, 1441–1270 cal BC 2 sigma). Several years to several centuries may have elapsed between the time of the

Aire-sur-la-Lys

(enclosure 1 - area I)
(enclosure 1 - area M)   2005 : no test
(enclosure 1 - area J)
(Langgraben 1 - area F)

Wittes

                                2011 : radiating trenches
(concentric enclosures
Cornet Road)

Aire-sur-la-Lys

(concentric enclosures   2012 : varied tests
 - area P)
                               area P :
                               int. et ext. transects (1),
(enclosure 2 - area P)   reference curve with several
                               test holes (2)

                               area N :
(enclosure 1 - area N)   tests holes and
                               partial scrapping (3)

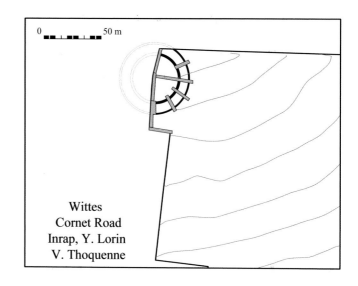

Wittes
Cornet Road
Inrap, Y. Lorin
V. Thoquenne

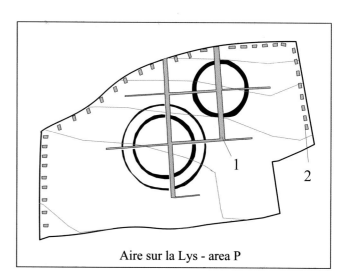

Aire sur la Lys - area P

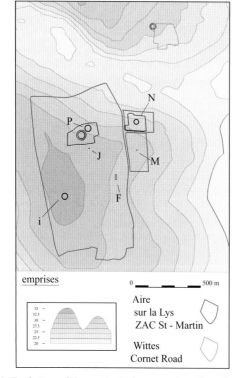

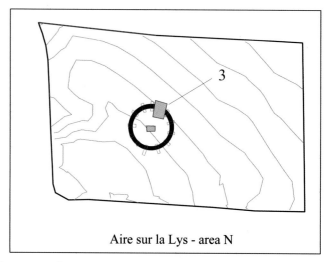

Aire sur la Lys - area N

Fig. 9.6. Evolution of the methods for assessing 'decarbonation' processes during operations around Aire-sur-la-Lys and tests aiming to evaluate contextual data (Y. Lorin, INRAP)

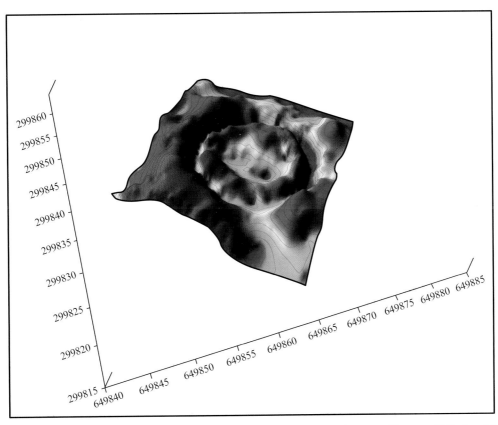

Fig. 9.7. 3D modelling of the upper limit of the carbonated level at the site of Lauwin-Planque. (Y. Petite, CAD-DAP).

cremation indicated by the funerary deposit and flint knapping activity, occurring at a time when the ditch was partially filled in but elevations were still completely or mostly in position. However, the tools are too rare (1.4% in one of the monuments and 3.9%, in the other) to understand the purpose of flint knapping operations: do they relate to the monuments' maintenance or do they result from the opportunistic exploitation of available materials?[1]; did they end up in the ditch as having fallen into it as a result of gravity, having been used at a nearby settlement site? It has been presumed that domestic occupation dating from the end of the Middle Bronze Age to the beginning of the Late Bronze Age was located nearby. Although the all assemblage from both enclosures were found in the same stratigraphic position, they present very clear technical and morphometric differences, in addition to the use of a raw material of better quality in one case. This variability may reflect distinct skill levels between artisans, different functional objectives and/or a chronological discrepancy in monument use, features that seem to point to recurrent activity linked to monument conservation. The Early Bronze Age triple monument at Rietz at Fréthun (Pas-de-Calais) yielded an important lithic assemblage also comprising debitage and a small proportion of tools (3.6% of the corpus; Martial 1995). Excavations at Mont

à cailloux at Abbeville and ZAC du chemin des Prés at Étaples, yielded a considerable quantity of objects (lithic and fauna), which raise questions as to the funerary vocation of the sites.

However, the lithic baked from the sedimentary level sealing the Argoeuves ditches do not present the same characteristics. They comprise disparate elements, directly associated in one case with an almost complete ceramic vessel (broken with sherds discovered lying flat), and correspond to totally different deposition/abandonment conditions. Whole or shattered nodules, which do not appear to have arrived there by gravity, given their position, form a relatively thick layer in this level, with comparatively dense and continuous distribution in the different enclosures (Fig. 9.8). In addition, the same layer contains a small quantity of fired clay and several sparse macro-tool elements in heat-altered sandstone. This bed of flint blocks with sherds can be considered as a more or less floor or path (like at Loisy-sur-Marne, Marne: Fechner 2010), associated with waste from a nearby occupation. It may come from the deterioration of the reworking of an elevation including residual remains – a Beaker occupation has been identified at the site – and funerary structures (whole ceramic vessel), as these hypotheses are not mutually exclusive.

Fig. 9.8. Bed of flint blocks (structure?) in the terminal ditch infilling of one of the Argoeuves monuments Le Moulin d'Argoeuves (photo: N. Buchez, INRAP).

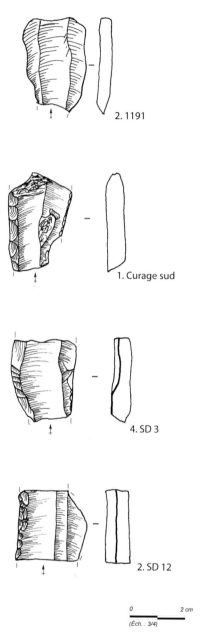

Fig. 9.9. Fragments of burnt blades issued from the ZAC funerary enclosures at Lauwin-Planque (drawings: É. Lecher, CAD-DAP).

The objects found at the site of Lauwin-Planque (Nord) raise another question. Several flint elements were discovered in pits with central cremation deposits or charred pits in the ditch fills, including blade fragments, flakes from polished axes, flake tools, etc. Several artefacts are burnt and the recurrence of some of them is interesting. Indeed, five retouched and non-retouched blade fragments, four of which are burnt, have been recorded. In addition, the observed modules are identical; blades have a trapezoidal section, rectilinear and parallel edges, and are sometimes retouched on both edges (Fig. 9.9). The observation of fractures indicates breaking before heating. Does this represent an intentional deposit of flint artefacts? Were the objects intentionally broken or incidentally re-used? Is this part of funerary practice and is it characteristic of this period? Is there a link with fractured artefacts in bronze deposits? If this type of observation becomes more widespread, it should provide some answers to these questions.

These two case studies of objects demonstrate the need to excavate ditch fills as meticulously as possible, as hasty operations can result in the loss of valuable information for the reconstruction of the global history of circular funerary monuments, which existed and were used for several generations.

Conclusion

The main aim of this regional summary was to present several approaches that address the questions raised by funerary monuments with peripheral structures and to identify recurrences as well as any specific chronological or micro-regional features.

The first findings of this overview can be extended to the areas bordering and beyond our zone of study. It has already been shown that the occurrence of circles at the beginning of the Bronze Age extends further south and west, in particular towards the Plain of Caen and the Oise and Aisne valleys.

Excavations carried out over these past years have called into question a certain number of traditionally accepted ideas, such as:

*   the recent dates of circles with small dimensions. This may be recurrent in the Paris Basin or eastern regions, but it is not the case in the northwest of Europe;
*   the image of the 'typical monument' formed by a ditch and a central mound requires revision, as it is probably

more similar to the architectural assemblages recorded across the Channel and in the Netherlands.

Although today, these remains appear to be well known to archaeologists, this study shows that many areas still require clarification. The diversity of the architecture and objects associated with these monuments shows the importance of continuing their excavation.

Note

1   Hypothesis valid for one of the monuments, but not in the other where the raw material selected is of superior quality.

Bibliography

Agache, R. (1978) *La Somme pré-romaine et romaine d'après les prospections à basse altitude*. Amiens, Mémoires de la Société des Antiquaires de Picardie.

Baray, L. ed. (1998) *Les cimetières protohistoriques de l'autoroute A16 Nord*. Unpublished report, Inrap, SRA Lille.

Billand, G. and Talon, M. (2000) Archéologie en Picardie. Nécropoles de l'âge du Bronze: Rue (Somme) et Thourotte (Oise). Amiens, DRAC-AFAN.

Blanchet, J.-C. (1976) Les tumulus des Combles d'Éramecourt dans leur contexte du Bronze ancien et moyen en France du Nord-Ouest. *Cahiers Archéologiques de Picardie* 3, 39–55.

Blondeau, R. (2015) Courcelles-lès-Lens (62), Éco-quartier de La Marlière, tranche 6. Unpublished report, Eveha, SRA Lille.

Bostyn, F., Blancquaert, G. and Lanchon, Y. (2000) Un enclos triple du Bronze ancien à Fréthun (Pas-de-Calais). supprim, *Habitats et nécropoles à l'âge du Bronze sur le transmanche et le T. G. V. Nord* 89, 10–12, 109–128 Paris, Société Préhistorique Française.

Bourgeois, J. and Talon, M. (ed.) (2005) *L'âge du Bronze du nord de la France dans son contexte européen*, Actes du 125e congrès national des sociétés historiques et scientifiques à Lille 2000. Paris, CTHS.

Bourgeois, J. and Cherretté, B. (2005) L'âge du Bronze et le Premier Âge du Fer dans les Flandres occidentale et orientale (Belgique): un état de la question. In J. Bourgeois and M. Talon (ed.) *L'âge du Bronze du nord de la France dans son contexte européen*, 43–81, Actes du 125e congrès national des sociétés historiques et scientifiques à Lille 2000. Paris, CTHS

Bourgeois, Q. (2013) *Monuments on the Horizon: the Formation of the Barrow Landscape Throughout the 3rd and 2nd Millennium BC*. Unpublished thesis, Leiden University.

Buchez, N. (2011) La protohistoire ancienne. Recherche et fouille des sites de l'âge du Bronze à La Tène ancienne sur les grands tracés linéaires en Picardie occidentale : questions méthodologiques et résultats scientifiques. In N. Buchez, D. Bayard et P. Depaepe (eds) *Quinze ans d'archéologie préventive sur les grands tracés linéaires en Picardie, première partie, 121–99*. Revue Archéologique de Picardie, 3/4.

Buchez, N. (ed.) (2014) *Argoeuves-Saint-Sauveur, Somme Le Moulin d'Argoeuves. Evolution de l'occupation sur le rebord de plateau du Néolithique final à La Tène D*. Unpublished report, Inrap INRAP Nord-Picardie, Amiens.

Burgess, C. (1987) Le rapport entre la France et la Grande-Bretagne pendant l'âge du Bronze: Problèmes de poterie et d'habitats. In J.-C. Blanchet (ed.) *Les relations entre le continent et les Îles britanniques à l'âge du Bronze, 307–18*, Actes du 22e Congrès préhistorique de France Lille 1984. Amiens, Supplément à la Revue Archéologique de Picardie.

Desfossés, Y. and Masson, B. (1990) La nécropole du Bronze ancien des Fresnes-lès-Montauban. In F. Bostyn (ed.), *Catalogue de l'exposition 'Les enclos funéraires de l'Âge du Bronze dans le Nord/Pas de Calais, Décembre 1990–Mars 1991, Lille-Arras-Boulogne-Douai., 17–37*, Villeneuve d'Ascq, Numéro Spécial des Cahiers de Préhistoire du Nord 8.

De Reu, J., Hammond, J., Toron, S. and Bourgeois, J. (2012) Spatial and chronological continuities of Bronze Age cemeteries of north-western Europe. In D. Bérenger, J. Bourgeois, M. Talon and S. Wirth (eds) *Paysages funéraires de l'âge du Bronze, 265–82*, Actes du colloque international sur l'âge du Bronze de Herne 2008. Darmstadt, Bodenaltertümer Westfalens.

Fechner, K. (2010) *Rapport pédologique de terrain du secteur protohistorique de la fouille de Loisy-sur-Marne*. Unpublished report, INRAP Grand-Est Sud, Châlons-sur-Marne.

Feray, P. and Herbert, P. (1998) *Ham 'Bassin St-Nicolas'*. Unpublished report, Inrap INRAP Nord-Picardie, Villeneuve d'Asq.

Fourny, M. (1985) Le 'Muzieleberg' à Renaix. Nouvelle contribution à l'étude de la nécropole de la civilisation Hilversum/Drakenstein (âge du Bronze ancien/moyen). *Vie archéologique* 19, 41–68.

Germain, M., Deckers, M. and Vanbalinghem, C. (2010) *Avelin, Route départementale 549 (Nord), site 552–10*. Unpublished report, Communauté d'agglomération du Douaisis – Direction de l'archéologie préventive INRAP Nord-Picardie, Villeneuve d'Asq.

Germain-Vallée, C., Giraud, P. and Durand, R. (2007) L'enclos funéraire de l'âge du Bronze de Saint-Martin-de-Fontenay (Calvados, Basse-Normandie). *Bulletin de la Société préhistorique française* 104 (3), 565–581.

Glasbergen, W. (1954a) Barrow excavations in the Eight Beatitudes. The Bronze Age cemetery between Toterfout and Halve Mijl, North Brabant. I. The excavations. *Palaeohistoria* 2, 1–134.

Glasbergen, W. (1954b) Barrow excavations in the Eight Beatitudes. The Bronze Age cemetery between Toterfout and Halve Mijl, North Brabant. II. The implications. *Palaeohistoria* 3, 1–204.

Henton, A. (2011) *Douvrin (62), Rue de Lennes. Découverte d'un enclos circulaire de l'âge du Bronze*. Rapport final d'opération. Unpublished report, INRAP Nord-Picardie, Villeneuve d'Asq.

Jacques, A. and Prilaux, G. (2006) *ZAC Dainville Achicourt (62) lieu dit 'Gérico'. Le site gaulois de Dainville-Achicourt au lieu-dit 'Gérico'. Un exemple sur l'évolution d'un établissement celtique de l'arrière-pays atrébate*. Unpublished report, Inrap INRAP Nord-Picardie, Achicourt.

Jamagne, M. and Bégon, J.-C. (1984) Les sols lessivés de la zone tempérée. Apport de la pédologie française. In *Livre jubilaire du Cinquantenaire de l'AFES, 55–76*. Orléans, Association française pour l'étude des sols.

Julien, M. (2011) *Arleux (59), chemin de Brunémont*. Unpublished report, Communauté d'agglomération du Douaisis – Direction de l'archéologie préventive Douai.

Langohr, R. (2000) Creusement, érosion et comblement des fossés; l'approche des sciences de la terre. In Les *enclos celtiques, Actes de la table ronde de Ribemont-sur-Ancre (Somme)*, 57–65. Amiens, *Revue archéologique de Picardie* 1–2.

Leroy-Langelin, E. and Collette, O. (2011) La fouille des enclos circulaires de l'âge du Bronze: une nouvelle approche?: contribution géopédologique à l'étude des monuments arasés sur substrat limoneux de Lauwin-Planque (Nord). *Bulletin de la Société préhistorique française*, 108 (1), 127–138.

Leroy-Langelin, E. and Sergent, A. (2015), ZAC Lauwin-Planque, l'âge du Bronze, Section II, vol. 3a, unpublished report. Douai. Communauté d'agglomération du Douaisis – Direction de l'archéologie préventive.

Lorin, Y. (2017), Maroeuil 'Rue Curie'. Des occupations du Néolithique au Bronze final, unpublished report. INRAP Nord-Picardie, Achicourt. Inrap.

Lorin, Y. (2016), Aire-sur-la-Lys 'ZAC Saint-Martin', phase 2, unpublished report. Amiens, Inrap. INRAP Nord-Picardie, Achicourt.

Maniez, J. (2010) MARQUISE (62), 'Mont de Cappe', Avenue Ferber, unpublished report, Dainville, Centre départemental d'archéologie du Pas-de-Calais.

Maréchal, D. (2000) Frethun 'Les Argillères'/ RD 304, unpublished report. Amiens, INRAP Nord-Picardie.

Martial, E. (1995) *L'industrie lithique à l'âge du Bronze dans le Nord-Pas-de-Calais: les exemples de Roeux et de Fréthun.* Villeneuve-d'Asq. Cahiers de Préhistoire du Nord 15.

Masse, A. and Toron, S. (2008) Construire le Temps, de l'âge du Bronze à l'âge du fer, entre Seine et Meuse. In A. Lehoërff (ed.) *Construire le temps. Histoire et méthodes des chronologies et calendriers des derniers millénaires avant notre ère en Europe occidentale, 179–87.* Actes du XXXe colloque international de Halma-Ipel, UMR 8164 (CNRS, Lille 3, MCC), 7–9 décembre 2006, Lille. Glux-en-Glenne, Collection Bibracte 16.

Masse, A. dir., Merkenbreack, V., Wilket, L., Chombart, J., Delobel, D. and Lachaud, C. (2013) Dainville 'Le Champ Bel Air', unpublished report. Dainville, Centre départemental d'archéologie du Pas-de-Calais.

Masse, A. (2014) *Vie quotidienne et pratiques funéraires de l'âge du Bronze à Dainville 'Le Champ Bel Air' (Pas-de-Calais).* Dijon, Université de Bourgogne, Bulletin de l'Association pour la Promotion des Recherches sur l'âge du Bronze 12.

Piningre, J.-F. (1990) La Nécropole de l'Age du Bronze du Conchil-le-Temple (Pas-de-Calais). *Les Cahiers de Préhistoire du Nord* 8, 79–89

Toron, S. (2006) De la Picardie aux Flandres belges: une approche comparative des enclos circulaires de l'âge du Bronze ancien et moyen. *Lunula Archaeologia protohistorica XIV (Mariemont)*, 71–76.

Vanmoerkerke, J. (1990) *Les structures funéraires du Bronze Ancien et Moyen. In F. Bostyn (ed.), Catalogue de l'exposition 'Les enclos funéraires de l'Âge du Bronze dans le Nord/Pas de Calais', Décembre 1990–Mars 1991, Lille-Arras-Boulogne-Douai, 11–5.* Villeneuve d'Ascq, Numéro Spécial des Cahiers de Préhistoire du Nord 8.

Van Vliet-Lanoë, B. Fagnat, J.-P., Langohr, R., Munaut, A. (1992) Importance de la succession des phases écologiques anciennes et actuelles dans la différenciation des sols lessivés de la couverture lœssique d'Europe occidentale ; argumentation stratigraphique et archéologique. *Science du Sol 30–2*, 75–93. Orléans, Association française pour l'Etude des Sols.

10

Evolution of rites and funerary systems during the Early and Middle Bronze Age in the north-west of France

Ghislaine Billand, Isabelle Le Goff and Marc Talon

Abstract

This paper provides an analysis of funerary practices, carried out over a long period of about a millennium, from the beginning of Middle Bronze Age to the end of the initial stage of the Late Bronze Age. Based on 42 sites phased notably by way of 35 radiocarbon dates (many unpublished), it contributes to broaden our knowledge of the Manche - Mer du Nord complex, one of the regional facies of the Atlantic cultural sphere. The aim is also to enable comparisons between the different cultural entities through the contribution of recent excavations and to highlight the significant features of funerary arrangements.

The analysis is based on five components: the phenomenon of the clustering of the dead in the cemeteries, the architectural form of the burials, the use of ring ditch monuments, the relationship between primary or secondary burial and cremation, and the different ways of burying burned bones and pyre fuel remains. By questioning the specific funerary features of the Manche – Mer du Nord complex, the study shows how they coordinate, interact and succeed one another to form a complex and evolving system. Some features could be attributable to other cultural spheres or correspond to an underlying trend perceptible on a wider geographical scale.

Keywords: Bronze Age chronology, funerary system, cremation, inhumation, funerary space, Manche – Mer du Nord complex.

Résumé

L'article propose une analyse des pratiques funéraires, menée sur un temps long d'environ un millénaire, entre le début du Bronze moyen et la fin de l'étape initiale du Bronze final. S'appuyant sur 42 sites phasés notamment grâce à 35 datations radiocarbones souvent inédites, il contribue à étendre les connaissances sur l'entité Manche - Mer-du-Nord, l'un des faciès régionaux du domaine culturel atlantique. L'objectif est également de favoriser les comparaisons entre les différentes entités culturelles en diffusant l'apport des fouilles récentes et en mettant en évidence les traits significatifs des dispositifs funéraires observés.

L'analyse se base sur cinq composantes : le phénomène du regroupement des morts en nécropole, la forme architecturale des sépultures, l'usage des monuments circulaires fossoyés, la relation entre les pratiques de l'inhumation primaire ou secondaire et de la crémation, les différents modes d'ensevelissement des os brûlés et des restes de combustible du bûcher.

En posant la question des traits funéraires spécifiques à l'entité MMN, l'analyse conduit à montrer comment ils se coordonnent, interagissent ou se succèdent pour former un système complexe et évolutif. Certains seraient attribuables à d'autres sphères culturelles ou correspondraient à une tendance de fond perceptible à une très large échelle géographique.

Mots clés : Chronologie de l'Âge du Bronze, système funéraire, crémation, inhumation, espace funéraire, entité Manche/Mer-du-Nord.

Introduction

Since recent interest in funerary practices, and particularly in cremation (diffusion: PhD by Le-Goff (1998); articles published in the Lille colloquium in 2005), and the Villeneuve d'Ascq round table on 'the treatment of cremation remains at the end of the Bronze Age in northern France' in 2006, the development of analysis methods, the excavation of new sites and the contribution of new dates have considerably widened our knowledge of the evolution and the understanding of rites and funerary systems and their role in defining the Channel/North Sea cultural entity.

In particular these advances raise new questions concerning the different forms of graves (burial and cremation) and the relation between incineration/burial, through the chronological attribution of a number of incineration graves (Appendices 1 and 2), made possible by the radiocarbon dating method of burnt bones using bio-apatite from bone matter (Lanting and Brindley 2005).

It is thus possible to develop identification of the funerary systems used during the Early and Middle Bronze Age by examining the coexistence of different types of corpse treatment – cremation and primary inhumation – and different ways of burying the dead. Throughout the Bronze Age, inhumation is a relatively minor tradition, but is nonetheless important for assessing how funerary systems were interconnected.

In this paper, we propose to examine specific traits of cultural systems at a given moment in the north-west of France (Fig. 10.1), and to discuss their adjustment over a long time period, from the beginning of the Early Bronze Age until the end of the first phase of the Late Bronze Age stage, which represents about 1000 years. The aim of the construction of this approach is to facilitate and extend comparisons of funerary practices between regions from the Atlantic cultural domain and regional facies, including the Channel/North Sea entity, and North Alpine and Nordic regions.

The evolution of funerary practices at the end of the 3rd millennium and individual Bell Beaker graves

Before the Early Bronze Age

In order to assess the evolution of funerary practices during the Bronze Age, and the transition from burial to incineration, it is appropriate to examine existing practices at the end of the final Neolithic, when individual burials prevailed.

The second half of the 3rd millennium is marked by the progressive discontinuation of group burial practices in the north-west of France (Nord/Pas-de-Calais and Picardie), and the widespread reoccurrence of individual burials, coinciding with the appearance of the Bell Beaker culture.

Up until now, the study of several identified Bell Beaker tombs had shown that they were discovered in isolated situations and chronological attribution was based on the single vessel or vessel fragment they contained. Only rarely were skeletons dated (Blanchet 1984).

However, with new studies and radiocarbon measurements (cf. inventory in Salanova 2011), a new Bell Beaker periodisation has been proposed for north-central France (Salanova *et al.* 2011).

The first observation to be made is that the number of graves is very small, with only six occurrences over this vast territory spanning a period of five centuries. In comparison, on the other side of the Channel, about 100 tombs have been identified in Kent over a surface area of 3736 km², which represents less than 15% of the Nord/Pas-de-Calais and Picardy regions combined (25,823 km²). Whereas rescue excavations linked to development work in Kent considerably enriched the corpus, in France, the same research dynamics did not modify the situation, which remains more or less identical to that described by J. C. Blanchet 30 years ago (1984).

Treatment of the inhumed body: underground architecture – monument

In the absence of any mention of incinerated bones, these graves contained buried bodies for which the earliest descriptions indicate a crouched position, when the position of the dead is commented on, with females generally lying on their right side and men and children on their left side. The funerary structures containing these tombs, when they are described, correspond to pits lined with wooden structures, as shown by the recent discovery of Ciry-Salsogne (Hachem *et al.* 2011); some of which are covered with a stone lid (slabs, polisher …). Unlike in Holland or Normandy where remains from ring-ditches point to the possible existence of monuments, structures of this kind have rarely been identified in the north-west of France, except in the Boulonnais region at *la Tombe Fourdaine* at Equihen (Blanchet 1984).

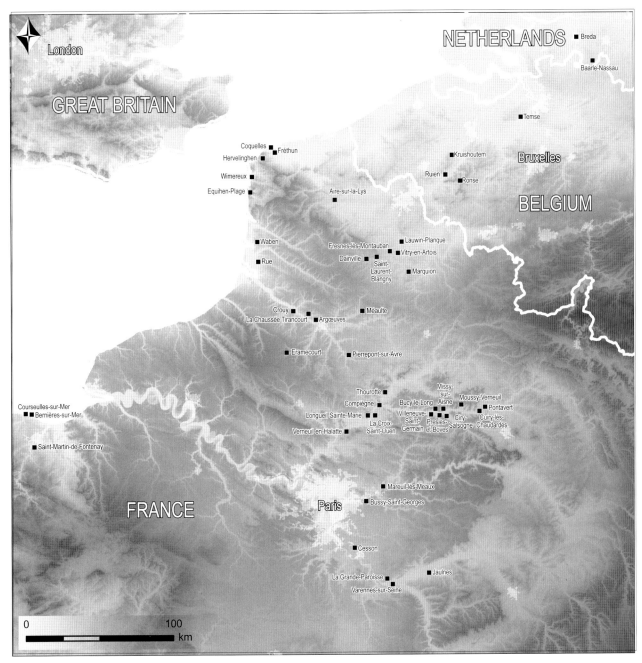

Fig. 10.1. Map of the sites mentioned in the text.

Treatment by cremation: objects

Let us point out that, for the time being, no Bell Beaker cremation grave has been discovered in this territory, whereas a dozen cases have been recorded in Holland (Drenth and Lohof 2005), and such a rite is mentioned in Belgium at Kruishoutem *Wijkjuis* and at Temse *Krekel* (Oost-Vlaanderen). The two latter examples are characterised by an overturned Bell Beaker goblet deposit 'alongside incinerations deposited in pits with burial formats'

(Warmembol 1996). It is also important to note the presence of a wooden funerary chamber in Lorraine, on the site of Hatrize (Meurthe-and-Moselle), with multiple deposits where the buried remains of an adult and a child lie alongside incinerated bones placed in a rectangular container in perishable materials (0.30 × 0.20 m) (Lefebvre *et al.* 2011). The accompanying grave goods, made up of three goblets and a barbed and tanged arrowhead, allow us to attribute this multiple grave to the recent/final Bell Beaker phases.

The Early Bronze Age I (Bronze A1)

Transition from collective inhumations to individual inhumation

Funerary complexes other than Bell Beaker graves remain unknown for the Bronze A1 period. However, several elements demonstrate the use, or reuse, of collective graves showing continuity in funerary practices from the end of the Neolithic (Chambon 2003). This is the case in particular in level III of the collective grave at La Chaussée Tirancourt (Somme: Masset 1995). In the Paris Basin during this period, small wooden vaults were built for several individuals, perhaps illustrating the progressive transition from collective to individual graves. The recently radiocarbon dated Cuiry-les-Chaudardes grave *le Champ Tortu* (Aisne; Bailloud 1982), containing eight buried bodies (including an adolescent), with no objects, demonstrates this in Picardy.

Early evidence of individual tumulus burials

Records are rare and are largely based on early research and even on the first explorations of tumuli which were still standing in the Boulonnais sector (Pas de Calais) during the 19th century and were subject to numerous excavations (Blanchet 1984).

In this way, four skeletons and a copper dagger with a dotted decoration were discovered in tumulus 11 at Hervelinghen. In 1897 at Wimereux, 19 stone vaults were found in the *Ballon* tumulus (diameter of 7 m for a height of 1.50 m), containing buried remains in crouched position, lying on the right side, with no objects apart from several flints and an amber button with a V-shaped perforation (Blanchet 1984).

These early discoveries thus yielded individual burial graves, generally without objects, which appear to be characteristic of Early Bronze Age graves. For the moment, this region contains no rich tombs comparable to those found in Brittany, Wessex, or in contact with the Nordic Bronze Age. On account of the absence of objects it is difficult to date the graves and we are thus deprived of elements conducive to the identification of the social structure.

These excavations of tumuli in the Boulonnais region provide evidence of this type of architecture at the end of the 3rd millennium and at the beginning of the 2nd millennium. However, the simplified description of these structures does not indicate whether or not there is a peripheral ditch. The 19 *Ballon* tumulus vaults laid out in an ellipse at Wimereux have no counterparts in the region, but this concentration of tombs can be compared to the potentially contemporaneous tombs at Bernières-sur-Mer, on the Lower Normandy coast (Noël 2011).

Pit burials related or burials unrelated to monuments

Like for the Bell Beaker culture, discoveries related to rescue archaeology are relatively infrequent, and radiocarbon dated finds are rare.

At Longueil-Sainte-Marie *Les Gros Grès IV* (Oise: Joseph and Pinard 1996; Blanchet and Talon 2005), burial st. 4 (3535±40 BP, 1959–1749 cal BC) of a young adult, buried on its right side (legs folded, lying E–W, with the head towards the east) in a pit placed above the outer slope of a double enclosure (diameter 22 m), is attributed to the Bronze Age A1. This attribution makes this one of the oldest monuments in the region. The meticulous excavation of this structure by F. Joseph demonstrates the phasing of the monument: the building of a first tumulus surrounded by a ditch with an interruption in the east (diameter 7 m), then widening resulting from the digging of a second ditch, the installation of an outer bank and a wooden platform above the large ditch, in the axis of the break in the internal ditch. The residual material, discovered mainly in the final infill of the ditches, is made up of fragmented sherds, flint, stones, pieces of fired clay, a fragment of bronze and an amber bead. A second grave (st. 337), installed in the space between the ditches, can be added to the grave discovered outside the phase 2 enclosure of the monument (st. 4). This grave contained the remains of a young child, but no further material, and was badly damaged by ploughing.

This monument is part of a larger funerary and worship site which contains a second monument (diameter 20 m), about 100 m to the northeast, made up of a circle of 36 regularly spaced postholes, with an interruption in the east serving as an entrance. There are no graves inside or in the immediate vicinity of this monument.

In sum, considering the limited records available for the beginning of the Early Bronze Age, during the 2nd millennium, burial prevails; tombs are individual and contain no objects, apart from rare Bell Beaker graves. The construction of mounds in some sectors seems to be confirmed, in particular on the Boulonnais coastline, as does the use of stone vaults. When conservation conditions are favourable, the existence of wooden vaults is observed. However, tombs are most often in simple isolated pits, which further complicates their detection.

The Early Bronze Age II (Bronze A2)

The second part of the Early Bronze Age, the Bronze Age A2, is better documented and demonstrates of the considerable contribution of rescue archaeology operations carried out in the sandpits in the Aisne (Brun and Pommepuy 1987; Le Goff and Guichard 2005) and Oise valleys (Blanchet and Talon 2005), and on the Trans-Channel and TGV Nord development projects (Collectif 2000).

Appearance of cemeteries and continuity of burial

Graves are mainly individual and no sign of multiple graves or the continued use of collective graves is known at present. Monuments with a circular ditch develop during this period, and are visible in the cultivated lands of north-western France, where erosion has erased mounds and surface installations, and probably many of the graves (particularly secondary) that they must have contained. In addition to this deterioration, the loessial nature of plateau soils is not conducive to the preservation of buried skeletons, in contrast to bones mineralised by fire. Cremation tombs thus tend to be over-represented.

Thousands of enclosures have been identified by aerial photography in the north-west of France and in the neighbouring regions, on both sides of the Channel (De Reu *et al.* 2012). Although they are mostly isolated (Audouze and Blanchet 1981; Toron 2006), the earliest tombs with the first concentrations of monuments interpreted as cemeteries nonetheless appear during this period. This is the case for the funerary complexes of Fresnes-lès-Montauban (Pas-de-Calais: Desfossés and Masson 2000), Lauwin-Planque (Nord: Leroy-Langelin and Sergent 2015) and Bucy-le-Long (Aisne: Brun and Pommepuy 1987), which contain 5–11 monuments. According to the available dates, these cemeteries are used over a long period of time, and in some cases we observe the joint presence of inhumation and cremation graves in the same monument. Buried bodies attributed to the end of the Early Bronze Age by radiocarbon are mostly in laid on the right side with folded legs.

Other forms of burial tombs: flat isolated tombs

As well as the graves generally identified beside monuments – which facilitates their identification – there are isolated, simple pit tombs, often without objects, where the body is dated by radiocarbon.

The discovery made in an aggregates quarry at La Croix-St-Ouen 'le Prieuré' (Oise) (Billand 1992; Pinard 1992) illustrates this point. Two graves 6 m apart each contained a badly preserved primary burial (oriented SE–NE, head towards SE), in a pit the bottom of which was partially lined with coarse gravel. In spite of the poor state of preservation of the body buried in pit 53 (nonetheless identified as an adult), it appears that the bodies were in a similar position: laid on the right side with the legs folded. In tomb st. 52, the remains of a cremated corpse were spread over a buried adult corpse (50–69 years old). Given the ages obtained from dating the occupants of this tomb (3455±35 BP, 1880–1680 cal BC for the buried corpse and 3355±30 BP, 1740–1530 cal BC for the cremated body), these events are attributed to the Early Bronze Age and are not rigorously contemporaneous.

A funerary system with no grave good deposits

Unlike the individual Bell Beaker graves containing at least one goblet as an offering, these burial or cremation tombs contain no objects, apart from the urn used as a container, or as a covering for the incinerated deposits. As for food offerings, the presence of plant macro-remains and food preparations among combustion residues remains to be verified, but no evidence of quarters of meat or animals on the pyre has been found.

However, it is important to point out the presence of several ornamental elements related to personal objects – and not offerings – at Fresnes-lès-Montauban for the woman buried in monument 5 of the cemetery. These objects consist of two perforated dog canines and a vertebral fish disc placed at the right humerus, and a bronze wire earring with three spirals, found near the right auditory canal (Desfossés and Masson 2000).

According to these data, the material investment during the course of funerary proceedings does not seem to be represented by grave good deposits. In the same way, if objects in durable materials were used during ceremonies, they do not appear to have been buried with the dead.

With the first incineration tombs: how was fire used in funerary proceedings?

The first tombs with cremation burials seem to appear at the end of this period in the north-west of France.

Fire is known to have been used in certain recent Neolithic collective graves to burn down the funerary monument or carbonise the corpse, but the crematory practice used during the Early Bronze Age results in the calcination of the bones, the dismemberment of the skeleton and its reduction into fragments. In this way, the bones of the deceased adult buried in the Somme at Pierrepont-sur-Avre *Rue de Boussicourt* (Petit and Billand 2006) are at the calcination stage (white bones), apart from the forehead, which must have been protected from the flames some of the time (Fig. 10.2).

What phases of funerals with cremation are recorded?

The archaeological evidence mainly records the late funeral phase, which concerns the conservation of the burnt remains of the deceased and the pyre remains. On the other hand, for the time being, cremation structures, and the conditions in which they were installed in the funerary area, remain virtually unknown, apart from the example of the funerary pyre from the end of the Early Bronze Age at Pontavert *La Pêcherie* (Aisne). The position of the pyre in the large monument at Pontavert suggests that cremation and burial of the dead could have taken place in the internal area of monuments.

Forms of cremated burials

Although the Early Bronze Age corpus is limited, three important phenomena for the understanding of funerary systems can be detected.

The first relates to the case of a grave with a buried body associated with 460 g of bone from a second cremated individual (Billand 1992; Pinard 1992). This association is one of the first examples of a link between both funerary

Fig. 10.2. Pierrepont-sur-Avre, st. 10. Cephalic skeleton of the deceased is calcined except for part of the frontal bone, at the end of the carbonisation stage. This sector was probably less exposed to flames (photo: I. Le Goff).

systems, although they are frequently connected from this stage of the Bronze Age onwards.

In addition, the corpus of sites provides the earliest evidence of cremation practices in Picardy, and even at this early stage, burial forms present variants. At Pierrepont-sur-Avre, the observed grave presents characteristics of a 'bone-dumping type deposit', in an oval-shaped hollow (1.35 × 1 m), with no added objects. In more detail, the structure (unfortunately vandalised before the excavation) contained at least 760 g of bone, probably issued from successive deposits. First of all, a mixture of small bone splinters, charcoal, ashes and sediment appears to have been

deposited. Then, less fragmented bone portions (4–5 cm long at the most) with no charcoal residues were grouped together in the upper part of the infill.

There is little evidence of honouring the dead; only the grouping of bones extracted from the ashes provides evidence of this. In fact, honouring the dead is more perceptible in the upper part of the tomb in the organisation of the funerary area (central position of the tomb) and the construction of an imposing monument.

This specific way of including pyre remains in the grave or funerary area characterises a practice still in use during the Late Bronze Age. Thus, during the course of the Early Bronze

Age, not only is the custom of burning the body developed, but already a specific funerary system incorporating the remains of the funeral pyre is established. What meaning can be attributed to this action? According to ethnoarchaeological sources, the aims of cremation, which are multiple depending on the culture, give rise to one or several entities, which are then used as the basis of ceremonies after cremation. The creation of a new entity is sometimes materially symbolised by very simple gestures: the separation of bones and combustion residues, the transfer of a selection of burnt remains towards the tomb or by manipulation (Le Goff 2013).

The third trait of this corpus is the diversity of sepulchral forms linked to cremation. In this way, the graves from Lauwin-Planque (Nord, Leroy-Langelin and Sergent 2015) illustrate other operational sequences leading to the burial of an often considerable bone volume in the tomb, this time without charcoal among the fragments. Bones are placed in an urn in a functional container position, representing the only object used in the grave.

Thus, from the first signs of cremating the dead, funerary practices involved several forms of graves. They all display simple architecture (oval pits) and the absence of objects, and they are centred on the inhumation of the entities produced during the funeral. But tombs present divergences regarding the type of buried entity:

- only the bones of the dead, deposited in considerable quantity, with limited fragmentation (460–760 g),
- sometimes accompanied by a fuel residue deposit (charcoal, ashes) with practically no bones (or severely reduced bones),
- just bones, often in considerable quantity, contained in an urn.

These different conceptions of burial do not seem to be hermetic: at Marquion *Plate-forme multimodale – sector 27* (Pas-de-Calais), an urn covered with a small slab contained bones mixed with ashes (Lefèvre 2016).

Relationship between cremation and burial

What can we learn from the beginning of the coexistence of two funerary systems in the studied regions; one based on primary burial, the other on cremation? We will focus here on the observation of certain shared funerary practices.

First of all, the posture of the corpse appears to be the same, whether it is buried or cremated. At the site of Pontavert *la Pêcherie* (Ertlé 1966), the child appears to have been cremated with bent limbs. Elsewhere, in the Middle Bronze Age necropolis of Bussy-Saint-Georges *le Champ fleuri* (Seine and Marne: Le Goff and Guillot 2005), bone remains still in position in the funeral pyres lead to the same conclusion.

As for the dimensions of the tomb: whether they are burnt or buried, the bodies are buried in similar oval-shaped pits with dimensions of more than 1.30 m; with the largest reaching 1.85 m (Table 10.1). During the Middle Bronze Age, the size of cremated graves decreases to such an extent that some of them correspond to the dimensions of the cinerary urn. This tendency is taken to be a progressive adaptation of funerary practices to the introduction of cremation: first the dead are burnt, then the size of the tomb is adapted to the reduced volume of the cremated body. Other dynamics could also be at work, related to the form of cinerary deposits. During the Early Bronze Age, combustion residues were buried alongside bones, whereas later, this stage of the funeral was simplified: a single deposit, often combining bone and charcoal was sufficient for consecrating the grave.

Lastly, in the case of the double *Prieuré* tomb at La Croix-Saint-Ouen (Oise), the use of the same tomb, with a chronological interval between the two deposits, not only points towards the sharing of the same grave, but also the sharing of certain funerary stages and possible commemorations. We note the sobriety surrounding both bodies. The burial of the incinerated corpse involves the same funerary gestures known for that time period: considerable mass of bone, deposit with no perceptible container, bones scattered in the pit fill. The funerary procedure for the buried corpse also follows the currently known standards for the Early Bronze Age. Moreover, the whole body is conserved during the course of the funeral: on account of the primary burial and also of the use of a restraining arrangement, wrapping the body and separating it from the earth.

Middle Bronze Age I (Bronze B 1 and B2)

An increase in the number of sites

For the Middle Bronze Age period, we observe an increase in the number of funerary sites, cremation becomes dominant, with during the first part – the B1 Bronze Age –tombs linked to monuments (Table 10.1), which appear to be isolated like at Dainville *Gérico* (Pas-de-Calais), Vitry-en-Artois (Pas-de-Calais), or Villeneuve-St-Germain (Aisne). But when we explore more extensive surfaces, other enclosures appear, sometimes several tens of metres away, like at Fréthun (Pas-de-Calais), Rue (Somme) or Argoeuves (Somme). In other cases, the initially identified monument turns out to belong to a much more consequential necropolis, like at Fresnes-lès-Montauban, Lauwin-Planque or Coquelles (Pas-de-Calais).

The development of the practice of the overturned urn

The other specific aspect of this first part of the Middle Bronze Age is the concentration of inverted urns placed over incinerations, mainly discovered in the internal area of monuments (Table 10.2). These urns are generally classified in the category of the group of urns with decoration (GDU) defined by J. C. Blanchet. They are linked to the Eramecourt

Table 10.1. Dimensions of cremation tombs and their contents during the Early Bronze Age.

Sites	Dimensions of the tomb (m)	Contents	Chronological attribution
Tombs			
Bucy-le-Long *le Grand Marais* monument 3	Oval pit 1.85 × 1.40	Double deposit: – cist on overturned urn – heap of earth with charcoal	Early Bronze Age A1
Bucy-le-Long *le Grand Marais* monument 1	Oval pit 1.50 × 1	Double deposit (?) – two sheets of bone fragments on the surface on either side – of a cluster of bones in a semi–rounded shape (in a container ?)	Possible attribution to Middle Bronze Age
Pierrepont-sur-Avre *Rue de Boussicourt*	Oval pit 1.35 × 1	Double deposit (?) – group of bones – cluster of ashes with few bones	Early Bronze Age A2
La Croix St Ouen *le Prieuré*	1.50 × 0.90	Double deposit – a crouched body – a spread of burnt bones	Early Bronze Age A2
Pyre			
Pontavert *la Pêcherie*	Rectangular pit with rounded angles 1.05 ×0.61	– child's body cremated *in situ* with personal objects	Possible attribution to final phase of Early Bronze Age

group, which traditionally covers the Early and Middle Bronze Age, also defined by the same author (Blanchet 1984). Thanks to burnt bone dates, we observe that the practice of covering the bone deposits with an urn, and the discovery of GDU-type ceramics, does not occur beyond the Bronze Age C.

The possibility of dating cremated remains from early excavations when they have been conserved – which is rarely the case – recently gave rise to the chronological assessment of the cremation discovered beneath an overturned urn at Crouy (Somme: Bréart and Fagnart 1982). The date (3290±30 BP, 1640–1490 cal BC) obtained for this atypical discovery, which also yielded a small lignite bead in a pit located near the grave, makes it five centuries younger than previously thought.

Focus on an operational sequence: the overturned urn

This funerary form has been known since the Eramecourt excavation, and was noticed in the first place on account of the strange upside down position of the ceramic vessels on their neck. In other respects, it is similar to the funerary systems in our study zone. A certain importance is given to the fuel of the pyre, discovered in the tombs of Vitry-en-Artois (carbonised 45 cm branch) and Bucy-le-Long *le*

Grand Marais (st. C3 – pile of oak charcoal under the urn in monument 3).

Furthermore, the importance of the volume of bone (more than a kilo at Bucy-le-Long), or the exceptional dimensions of the bone portions (Fresnes-lès-Montauban), have drawned attention. With more recent discoveries, like those from Rue (Somme: Billand 1998), Moussy-Verneuil (Aisne: Robert 2013) and Argoeuves (Somme: Buchez *et al.* 2014), the impression of less fragmented bone is substantiated. The portions of long bone diaphyses regularly reach 10 cm at Rue and 5 cm at Moussy-Verneuil. These complementary discoveries also confirm the relatively important volume of bone buried in this type of tomb: respectively 819 g (adult subject), 1 kg and 301 g (5–10-year-old child). The recurring substantial weight does not merely characterise the north-west of France, or simple tombs with an overturned urn. Comparable or ever greater values have been recorded for tombs with bone deposits in an urn. Several examples from Ile-de-France, Normandy, or Oise show that extreme values range between 397 g and 1191 g (Tables 10.3 and 10.4); with a maximum value of 2149 g at the site of Verneuil-en-Halatte *la Petite Remise* (Oise: Gaudefroy and Le Goff 2004).

These latter excavations also provide details of the positioning of the bones under the urn and consequently, of the use of recipients.

Table 10.2. Table of Early-Middle Bronze Age inverted urns discovered in Holland, Belgium and France.

Site	Region	Country	Reference	Date BP	Observations
Baarle-Nassau	N Brabant	Holland	Glasbergen 1954		old excavations
Breda	N Brabant	Holland	Koot and Berkvens 2004		
Kruishoutem *Wijkhuis*	E Flanders	Belgium	De Laet and Rodge 1972	4035±190	Beaker vessel
Temse *Krekel*	E Flanders	Belgium	Van Roeyen 1989		Beaker vessel
Ronse *Muziekberg*	E Flanders	Belgium	Fourny 1985		old excavations
Ruien *Kluisberg, Mont de l'Enclus*	E Flanders	Belgium	De Laet 1961		old excavations
Lauwin-Planque *les Dix-neuf* monument 7 (Nord)	Nord-Pas-de-Calais	France	Langelin and Sergent (forthcoming)	3290±40	
Fresnes-les-Montauban *le Motel* monument 1 (Pas-de-Calais)	Nord-Pas-de-Calais	France	Desfossés and Masson 2000		
Vitry-en-Artois *les Colombiers* (Pas-de-Calais)	Nord-Pas-de-Calais	France	Azagury and Demolon 1990	3220±60	
Argoeuves *le Moulin d'Argoeuvres* monument A (Somme)	Picardy	France	Buchez 2014	3170±35	
Crouy *les Quatre* (Somme)	Picardy	France	Breart and Fagnart 1982	3290±30	
Eramecourt *les Combles* 4-3 (Somme)	Picardy	France	Blanchet 1976		old excavations
Rue *le Chemin des Morts* (Somme)	Picardy	France	Billand and Talon 2000	3295±40	
Moussy-Verneuil *au Glanart* (Aisne)	Picardy	France	Robert 2013		archaeological diagnosis
Bucy-le-Long *le Grand Marais* C3 (Aisne)	Picardy	France	Brun and Pommepuy 1987	3710±200	
Missy-sur-Aisne *le Culot* (Aisne)	Picardy	France	Brun and Pommepuy 1987		
Pontavert *le Marteau* (Aisne)	Picardy	France	Brun and Pommepuy 1987		

For Pontavert *Le Marteau* (Aisne: Boureux 1974), the reconstruction by excavators represents a group of bones concentrated in the opening of the upside down vessel. For Fresnes-lés-Montauban, an urn two-thirds full of a voluminous pile of bones is described. The considerable bone mass in these vessels and the absence of spread-out bone suggests that the contents remained in the container when it was overturned. The use of a system for blocking the opening and preventing the bones from falling out thus appears technically necessary although no hypothesis has been observed by direct traces on these sites. Elsewhere, at Bucy-le-Long and Eramecourt, the urn is turned upside down on a small slab, then covered with stones laid out like for a cist burial. The shape and dimensions of the slab are adjusted to the urn, implying that this was a means of closing the vessel before it was inverted.

This hypothesis was advanced for the Middle Bronze Age graves of Bussy-St-Georges or Cesson (Seine-et-Marne, Legriel *et al.* 2011), where the position of the stones shows that it is customary to deposit them in the opening of the urns, placed in the tomb in a functional position. This practice is also found in Oise and Pas-de-Calais at the end of the Middle Bronze Age at Verneuil-en-Halatte, Compiègne *Carrefour d'Aumont* (Oise: Blanchet 1984) and Marquion 'sector 27' (Pas-de-Calais: Baudry *et al.* 2013).

At Argoeuves, the configuration is different; the urn is upside down in a pit adapted to its dimensions, the base of which is lined with flint nodules (Fig. 10.3). The smaller volume of the child's bones does not fill the space of the urn. Consequently, we could expect the overturned urn to spread its contents on the flint nodules, but this is not the

Table 10.3. Several cases of bone deposits in urns attributable to the Middle Bronze Age, outside the study zone. Note the considerable buried volumes = large quantity of bone?

Site with bone deposit in an urn	Quantity of bone
La Grande Paroisse *Pincevent* (Seine-et-Marne). 1 urn (Grévin *et al.* 1990)	1191 g adult
Cesson *la Plaine du Moulin à Vent* (Seine-et-Marne). Example from urn 113 -12 (Le Goff and Jarmad in Le Griel 2004)	712 g adult
Varennes-sur-Seine *le Marais du Pont* (Seine-et-Marne). 3 urns (Le Goff in Séguier 1996)	748 g adult
	889 g adult
	870 g adolescent & young
	child (2–4 years old)
St-Martin-de-Fontenay *la Grande Chasse* (Calvados). 1 urn (Durant in Germain-Vallée 2007)	919 g
Courseulles-sur-Mer (the département is Calvados) *la Fosse Touzé*. 1 dated urn out of 3. End Middle Bronze Age–beginning of the Late Bronze Age (Jahier with collaboration of I. Le Goff in Jahier 2011)	397 g adult

Table 10.4. Verneuil-en-Halatte la Petite Remise (Oise): possible coexistence of several forms of Middle Bronze Age tombs at the same site.

Form of tombs	Radiocarbon date cal BC	Quantity of buried bone
Tomb with bone cluster in perishable circular container (st. 18) – type 8a	1540–1370. Middle Bronze Age C2	374 g adult
Tomb with bone cluster in urn (st. 20), with piles of residues at bottom of tomb – type 7c	1450–1230. Middle Bronze Age C2	2149 g adult
Tom with poured bone deposit mixed with combustion residues (st. 10) – type 4	1500–1370. Middle Bronze Age C2	328 g adult

case. A more elaborate operational sequence, with the use of a container in perishable matter, combined with a system for closing the ceramic urn, would explain the fact that this heap of bones was maintained in position.

At Rue, the urn seems to have been installed above the bones which were partly covered with pebbles. The urn then seems to have been inserted and to crown the pile of pebbles.

With these new configurations observed in archaeological situations, it is now difficult not to include perishable elements in the operational sequence.

In Great Britain, in Windsor (Berkshire), the excavation of a tomb with an inverted vessel, dated to the end of the Early Bronze Age, points to the use of a 'double' container: a first container in organic matter covering 1153 g of burnt bones from a young person, all placed in a ceramic vessel, closed by fabric or leather. The author envisages the installation of the urn in an upside down position in the tomb (McKinley 2012; 2016).

Another approach entails integrating the blocking of the urn in the sequence of technical gestures. This time, the arguments stem from a functional and symbolic analysis of the ceramic contaners in use at the time. According to the suggestions of H. Fokkens, in the Netherlands, the cord-made decoration, particularly at the neck of the vessel, evokes a way of attaching a leather or another flexible element with a cord enclosing the neck (Fokkens 2005, 24 and 30). The reasons behind this gesture are still unknown, but this type of decoration was in use for a long period of time (Early and Middle Bronze Age) and extended over a large region, including our study zone. What link can be made between these hypotheses and the funerary contexts where these containers were used as cinerary urns? What was the point in turning them upside down in the tomb? It is difficult to develop these themes further, but it is important to emphasise that urns in graves are used more to cover than to contain. And before being deposited there, what were they used for? We may consider that they participate first in regrouping and transporting bones, but perhaps also another liquid (?) element, that was spilled into the tomb when the urn was overturned.

After examining the structure of several pits containing an overturned urn, we note the recurrence of one aspect: the necks of the urns lie on a specific structure and do not come into contact with the substratum. Whether it is at Rue, in a coastal context on a former bar of marine alluviums (sand and pebbles), or at Argoeuves and Eramecourt (Blanchet 1984) on the chalky plateau of the Somme, or again at Bucy-le-Long (Brun and Pommepuy 1987) in the Aisne Valley, the substratum did not only appear to be unsatisfactory for containing the bones, but everything was set up so that the bones of the deceased – even though they were protected in an urn – did not come into contact with it. At Rue, this was manifested by a pocket of pebbles made in the surrounding sand. At Argoeuves, a carefully installed nest of flint nodules lines the base of the pit. The Eramecourt and Bucy-le-Long urns, placed in cists, lie on a small stone slab. Whether the substratum is sandy or chalky, it appeared to be essential to protect the bones from contact with the surrounding sediment. In a way, this amounts to being buried without touching the ground … The overturned urns, combined with

Fig. 10.3. Argoeuves (Somme). Installation of tomb 18 with the internal and external diameters of the urn and the maximum extension of the bone cluster. It takes crushing phenomena into consideration (photo: G. Billand: photo of the urn from Buchez 2014; CAD Le Goff). The offset bone cluster lies against the wall of the urn without spreading into the free space under the inverted recipient.

the specific arrangement of the base of the sepulchral pits, contribute to perfectly 'sealing' the bone remains from the rest of the grave infill, thereby symbolically preserving the entirety of the fragmented but grouped body.

Middle Bronze Age II (Bronze C1 and C2)

From the second part of the Middle Bronze Age, other forms of necropolis without monuments are observed, made up of groups of small pits containing graves with cremation deposits with no objects, as at Verneuil-en-Halatte (Oise: Gaudefroy and Le Goff 2004) and Méaulte (Somme: Billand and Le Goff 2011).

The practice of primary burial in the monument

The burial graves brought to light are pits located in the central area, in the ditch or near the monument (Henton 2014). Discoveries made on terraces in the Aisne Valley, which is conducive to bone preservation, illustrate the different forms of burials (Brun and Pommepuy 1987; Debord 1987). In these pits, the bodies are deposited on their side with the legs folded. They are of both sexes and different ages and display varied orientation. The graves can either be in a central position, or appear as graves in a secondary position, with a tomb

with incineration occupying the centre. But they can also be positioned in the same way as the incineration tombs in the central area. This appears to be the case during the Early Bronze Age at the necropolis of Fresnes-lès-Montauban (Pas-de-Calais: Desfossés and Masson 2000).

The practice of cremation: what use is made of fire?

As for the preceding period, cremation is carried out until bone calcination for the child (Argoeuve**s**), and for adult individuals (Crouy Rue and Fresnes-lès-Montauban). Sometimes, a sector of the body is less burnt (grey bone), for example at the pelvis (Fresnes-lès-Montauban, Barbet in Desfossés and Masson 2000). Although it would be hasty to define a tendency, bone calcination appears to be the aim of exposing the corpse to fire as the less burnt sectors are always limited and at least reach the stage of advanced carbonisation. Moreover, several recorded cases affect the torso, which is known to present technical combustion difficulties.

Modification in ways of depositing the burnt remains of the deceased

Although the use of an overturned container is generally attributed to the beginning of the Middle Bronze Age, several burial forms from the preceding period subsist: simple pits with a deposit of bones, either spread out or contained in an urn. The custom of burying bones in a container diversifies, with use of circular recipients in perishable materials.

Besides bones, the other major component of graves is combustion residues, placed in the space of the tomb or buried nearby. Objects are always used as containers for bones, probably also when they are tipped into the tomb, but are never used as accompanying objects in the grave, and are only exceptionally placed on the pyre.

This diversity encompasses different phenomena. In Picardy and in Nord-Pas-de-Calais, the funerary use of a recipient placed upright in the tomb is recorded (Marquion, Lauwin-Planque, Verneuil-en-Halatte and Compiègne 'Carrefour d'Aumont' (Lefèvre 2016; Leroy-Langelin and Sergent 2015; Gaudefroy and Le Goff 2004; Blanchet 1984), and this practice is also widely known outside the studied zone.

As for tombs with a pile of bones in a perishable container with a circular shape and standard dimensions, there is at least one example from the Middle Bronze Age C1 in Oise, at Verneuil-en-Halatte 'La Petite Remise' (Fig. 10.4). Other later perishable containers were identified in tombs from the middle stage of the Late Bronze Age, discovered especially in the Aisne Valley (Presles-et-Boves *le Bois Planté* and Ciry-Salsogne *la Cour Maçonneuse* (Le Guen and Pinard 2007; Le Guen 2012).

An overview of the extension of this form of grave still remains to be drawn up, but it appears to be better known outside the present study zone during the Middle Bronze

Fig. 10.4. Cluster in a container in perishable matter from Verneuil-en-Halatte la Petite Remise (Oise).

Age, that is, along the Marne Valley (Bussy-St-Georges 'le Champ Fleuri', Mareuil-les-Meaux 'les Vignolles' (Cottiaux and Lawrence-Dubovac 2008) and along the Seine Valley (Cesson 'La plaine du Moulin à Vent': Legriel *et al.* 2011), or further south again, at the Seine-Yonne confluence (Jaulnes 'le Bas des Hauts Champs': Peake and Delattre 2010). Furthermore, at Verneuil-en-Halatte, this kind of cinerary deposit is found alongside tombs with loose bone deposits mixed with combustion remains (see Table 10.4, above).

As for tombs with dispersed deposits, most of them contain bones, ashes and charcoal. The traces of this type of grave become more widespread during this stage of the Middle Bronze Age in the whole zone studied (Table 10.5). In the Somme, they are observed under one of the Eramecourt tumuli *les Combles* (Blanchet 1984), in one of the Argoeuves monuments (st. 151, Buchez 2014), and in the Méaulte cemetery. In Pas-de-Calais, this type of tomb had been identified at Aire-sur-La Lys (Lorin 2016) and in the centre of a monument at Dainville-Achicourt *Gérico* (st 344) (Jacques and Prilaux 2006).

Through this corpus of sites, we know that these traditions are anchored in the north-west of France from the Middle Bronze Age onwards and that they become the practically exclusive burial form.

Already, at this stage, they present characteristic traits: the discharge of the bones directly into the tomb, the restricted dimensions of the pits, important variations in the quantity of buried bones. Pyre residues are always present and pyre deposits are no longer distinct from bone deposits; they are intricately linked. And, as was the case during the Early Bronze Age, grave good deposits are still excluded from the funeral burial phase.

We can cite several examples of the reconstruction of the sequence.

At Méaulte (site 1, st. 25), discharge occurs onto the base of the pit, where bones and pieces of charcoal are spread out.

Grave 344 at Dainville is even more typical of this sepulchral form (Billand and le Goff in Jacques and Prilaux 2006). It appears as a rather large oval hollow (1 m x 0.50 m), filled with black silt with charcoal containing 465 g of cremated bone fragments. The first six centimetres of the charcoal infilling comprise rare, dispersed bone splinters, whereas the next five centimetres include a more important quantity of larger bone fragments (up to 6 cm long). The bones spread out in a narrow band extending across the medial zone of the pit (Figs 10.5 and 10.6). During experiments, this configuration is obtained by spreading bones discharged from a recipient. Consequently, this tomb would result from at least two series of technical actions related to two components of the pyre. The first would involve spreading selected bones and the other discharging combustion remains with very few remaining bones.

At Argoeuves (st. 151), intention only focuses on combustion residues, which fill a large pit of about 1.20 m. Bones are only included as 'background noise' with just 6 g of sparse splinters, and the operation from which they derive (the cremation of a body) is thus not very perceptible. However, even though the information that these bones bear is dissolved in the bulk of fuel residues, they nonetheless link the structure to a series of cremation-linked operations. The considerable volume of ashes, the rarity of bones and the dimensions of the pit point to functions other than grave functions: funeral pyre or pit with an ash deposit?

These discoveries strengthen a typological tool initially developed from a corpus from the Middle Aisne Valley (Le Goff and Guichard 2005). It was based on a commonly used typology established in the 1950s from ancient tombs (Van Doorselear 2001), and adapted to the cultural context in north-western France during the Bronze Age. It takes account of the diversity of the modes of spreading bones and pyre remains. The typological activity was also carried out in a region covering Escaut Basin (Bourgeois 1991; De Mulder 2014, 32 and 33). The results of these simultaneous typological approaches ultimately merge together, backing up the pertinence of the locally identified types. And they especially show the recurrence of the funerary practices observed at different points in the expansive zone of the MMN entity. The types presented here take account of the archaeological situations encountered in the study zone (Fig. 10.7). They are organised into three main categories highlighting bone treatment (1 spread out, 2 contained, 3 absent), then their association with combustion residues.

What of funerary architecture, and in particular the dimensions of the tombs? How did they evolve with the development of the cremation of the deceased and the reduction of the corpse to several grams of bone? The size of the six oval or circular structures considered for the Bronze Age B and C1 remains relatively large (0.75–1.20 m), although the dimensions are much smaller than the several known Early Bronze Age cases (Fig. 10.6). The diameter of others, on the other hand, is no larger than 0.35 m, prefiguring a recurrent characteristic of Late Bronze Age funerary traits. For the several known later structures (between the Bronze Age C2 and D), the tendency appears to be identical.

What quantity of bone was present in the structures? We observe first of all a wide range of quantities: varying between 6 g and a little under 500 g of bone (Fig. 10.8). If we refer to the evaluations of the mass of bone produced for a burnt adult skeleton in modern cremation conditions, these quantities of bone correspond to a small portion of the combustion of an adult or sub-adult body (McKinley 1993). The expected theoretical value is 1604 g (extreme values: 1001–2422.5 g excluding fragments less than 2 mm). Biological factors (small stature of the deceased, osteoporosis …) do not explain the low bone volumes found in the Middle Bronze Age tombs (average weight: 166 g), or the difference between the extreme values (6–500 g/standard deviation: 164). On the other hand, it

is possible to establish a causal link between the volume of bone and the burial mode (Fig. 10.9). The deposits discharged by spreading (type 4) result from a series of actions which generally draw attention to the presence of the bones of the deceased (24–465 g). This is not the case for type 10 (6–10 g). In these structures, the presence of bones as 'background noise' may be unintentional.

The initial phase of the Late Bronze Age (Bronze D–Hallstatt A1) between 1350 and 1150 BC

Very few dated tombs document the initial phase of the Late Bronze Age, or the D Bronze Age–A1 Hallstatt (1350–1150 BC). There are five cases of cremation tombs (Table 10.1), which confirm the important position that this rite holds in the north-west of France during the whole of the Late Bronze Age, when it becomes common. Apart from the Méaulte tomb, which is part of a cemetery with no monument, the other four are linked to a monument, either in a central position, like for the two tombs of Thourotte (St 2 and St 1010; Oise: Blondiau *et al.* 1999), or implanted in a

Table 10.5. Middle Bronze Age sites presenting tombs with discharged deposit of bones mixed with pyre combustion residues.

Site	Type of deposit & proposed function	Sub-type	Bone weight /Maximum fragment size	MNI	Size of pits (m)	MBA stage
Méaulte site1, st. 8	Tomb with discharged deposit of bone with charcoal and ashes	Type 2 or 3: small batches of sparse bone in combustion residues. 'Handful'	118 g/3 cm	1 adult or sub-adult	Diam *c.* 0.35	B
Dainville, st 344	Tomb with discharged deposit of bone with charcoal and ashes	Type 4: bone spread during the charcoal infill	465 g/6 cm	1 adult	1 x 0.50	B
Verneuil-en-Halatte, st. 10	Tomb with discharged deposit of bone with charcoal and ashes	Type 4: bone discharged during the infill	328 g/6 cm	1 adult & 1 young child	0.75 long	C1
Argoeuves monument B, st. 151	Pit with charcoal/ash deposit or remains of a pyre?	Type 10: several sparse bone splinters 'background noise'	6 g	Possible human origin but not confirmed	*c.* 1.20x0.90	B
Méaulte site1, st. 25	Tomb with discharged bone deposit with pieces of charcoal	Type 4: at base of pit	202 g/7 cm	1 immature	Diam *c.* 0.30	C1
Méaulte site1, st. 9	Tomb with discharged deposit of bone with charcoal	Type 4: at base of pit	24 g	1 adult/sub-adult	Diam *c.* 0.30	C2–D
Méaulte site1, st. 2	Pit with charcoal deposit	Type 10: several sparse bone splinters 'background noise'	10 g	Possible human origin	Diam *c* 0.35	C2–D
Méaulte site1, st. 12	Tomb with discharged deposit of bone with charcoal and ashes	Type 4: at base of pit	180 g	1 adult/sub-adult	Diam *c.* 0.65	C2–D

Fig. 10.5. Dainville 'Gérico' (Pas-de-Calais). Tomb with a poured deposit of bone mixed with combustion residues (type 4). In this level of the pit infill, there is a bone spread presumed to has been poured from a recipient (photo: G. Billand).

Fig. 10.6. Experimentation. Aspect of a bone spill obtained by the pouring from a recepient (photo: I. Le Goff).

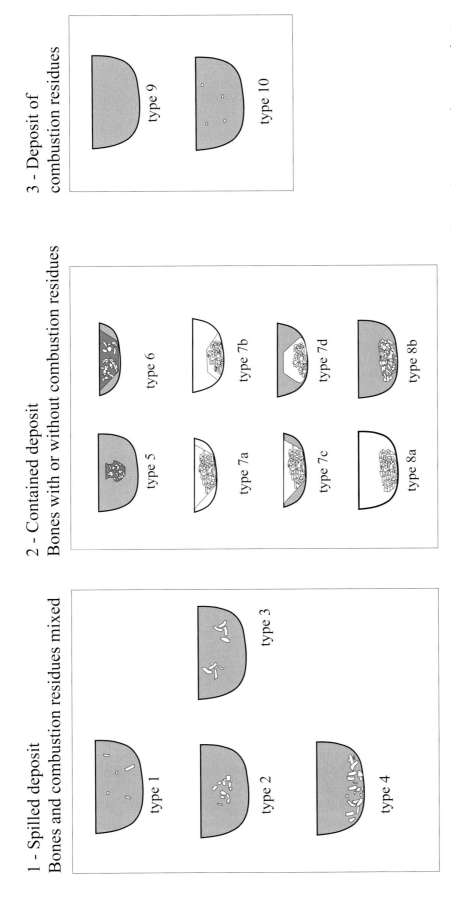

Fig. 10.7. Different types of cremation graves. 1. Structure with a deposit of spilled bone mixed with pyre remains: type 1: several bone splinters scattered among combustion residues, with no regrouping; types 2 and 3: small groups of bone ('handful') dispersed in the infilling of the structure; type 4: group of bones spread out in the structure (at the base, throughout the infill); Type 10: pit with combustion residues and tiny quantities of bone as 'background noise'. 2. Tombs with a contained cinerary deposit: tomb with a bone deposit in an urn with the remains of the pyre: type 5: bones and residues in an urn, placed in the pit infill filled with combustion residues; type 6 a: bones and residues in an urn, placed at the base of the pit filled with combustion residues: tomb with bone deposit in an urn: type 7a: bones in the urn in functional position, without combustion residues (in the urn or in the tomb); type 7b: bones under the upside down urn, with no combustion residues (in the urn or in the tomb); type 7c: bones in the urn in functional position, with charcoal/ashes in the tomb; type 7d : bones under the upside down urn, with charcoal/ashes in the tomb: tomb with contained bone deposit: type 8a: bones in a container in perishable matter; with no combustion residues (in the container or in the tomb); type 8b: bones in a container in perishable matter, with combustion residues in the tomb infill. 3. Structure with combustion residues without bone: type 9: pits with combustion residues with no detected bones.

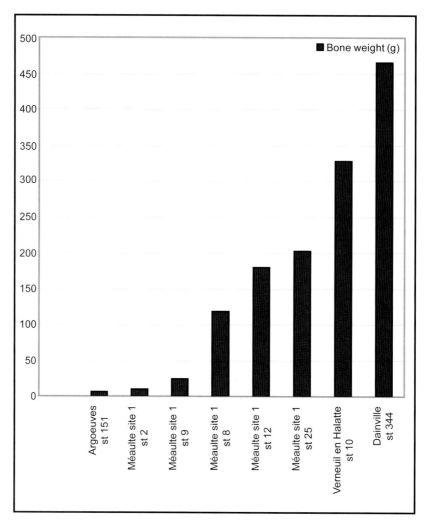

Fig. 10.8. Middle Bronze Age: quantity of bones buried per deposit.

hollow or at the edge of the ditch of a monument, as at Waben (Pas-de-Calais: Feray *et al.* 2000), or at La Croix-St-Ouen *Le Parc Scientifique*, (Oise: Blanchet and Talon 2005). It is important to point out that three of these four sites are classified as 'family' cemeteries.

These sites only include a concentration of small pits with combustion residues with a diameter of less than 75 cm. However, at Verneuil-en-Halatte, we observe a tomb with a cinerary urn (st. 20), dated to the transition between the end of the Middle Bronze Age and the beginning of the Late Bronze Age. It contains a considerable mass of bone; a funerary trait, which appears, on the basis of the use of a ceramic recipient, to be characteristic of the Middle Bronze Age. The bone mass buried in Late Bronze Age tombs is generally smaller. For the sites of the corpus presented in Table 10.6, this mass does not exceed the 500–750 g category. Furthermore, weight varies considerably, ranging from several grams to 750 g of bone. The weight of the bone in the tombs dated between the end of the Middle Bronze Age and

the beginning of the Late Bronze Age (1–423 g) fits into this range. For the whole of the Late Bronze Age, these weights are concentrated in the 30–250 g class. The 250–500 g and 500–750 g classes are present in most necropolises, but concern few individuals at a time. All the tombs are plain, with no added objects, like for the preceding stage.

The initial phase of the Late Bronze Age is thus marked by continuity and the development of 'familial' cemeteries, which appear as small concentrations of pits with combustion residues. Their configuration is either:

- with no associated monument and possibly from the end of the Middle Bronze Age, like at Méaulte and Verneuil-en-Halatte,
- associated with a monument, where they develop in association with an initial monument dated from the beginning of the Late Bronze Age (Thourotte) or belonging to the end of the Middle Bronze Age (La Croix-Saint-Ouen).

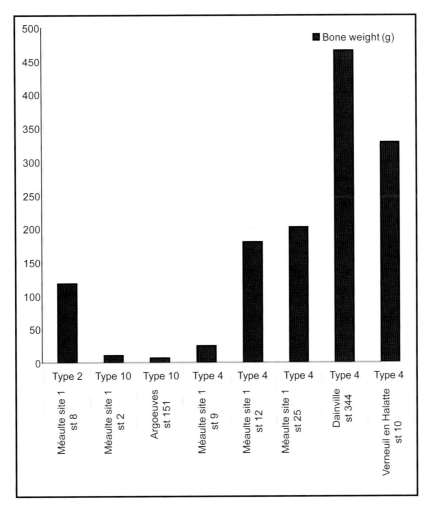

Fig. 10.9. Middle Bronze Age. Link between the volume of bone and type of deposit.

Summary

This first overview sheds light on the contribution of excavations and studies of so-called isolated cemeteries and graves, which significantly enhance the known corpus of sites. It helps to organise the different forms of graves throughout time and updates our understanding of the evolution of rites and practices, which vary over time, but are partly common to the Channel-North Sea entity. But it also reveals the difficulties involved in identifying funerary rituals with few remains of the deceased and in studying sites with no objects.

The aim of this summary is to present a first overview of our understanding of the successive systems and funerary practices during the Early and Middle Bronze Age, based on new contributions from fieldwork, anthropological studies and unpublished radiocarbon dates.

Raising the question of specific Channel–North Sea funerary traits led us to assess traits attributable to other cultural spheres or aspects that go beyond the expression of a single cultural entity (cremation for example), and which correspond to a tendency perceptible over a very wide geographic scale.

At the beginning of the Early Bronze Age, burial prevails, tombs are individual, without objects, apart from rare Bell Beaker graves. The use of mounds is recorded in some sectors, particularly on the Boulonnais coast, as well as stone or wooden vaults. However, most of the tombs are simple isolated pits where the buried corpse is generally placed on its side with folded legs, similar to the Bell Beaker and the Early and Middle Bronze Age.

From the second part of the Early Bronze Age onwards, monuments with ring-ditches and the first concentrations interpreted as cemeteries develop. The earliest cremation tombs in the north-west of France date from this period. These funerary sites are used over a long period of time spanning the Early and Middle Bronze Age. We sometimes observe the presence of burial and cremation graves in the same monument, in a central or another position. Objects

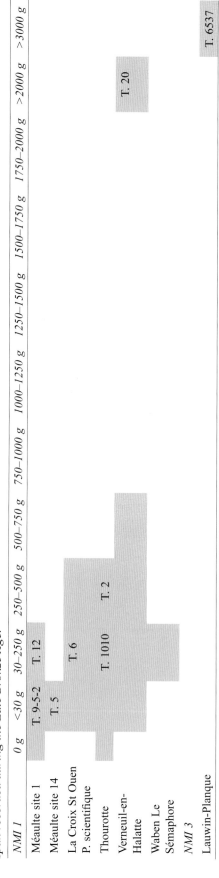

Table 10.6. Quantity of bones buried in the Bronze C/D and Bronze D tombs (adult grave, of adult morphology or immature specimen) compared to the weight span recorded during the Late Bronze Age.

NMI 1	0 g	<30 g	30–250 g	250–500 g	500–750 g	750–1000 g	1000–1250 g	1250–1500 g	1500–1750 g	1750–2000 g	>2000 g	>3000 g
Méaulte site 1		T. 9-5-2	T. 12									
Méaulte site 14		T. 5										
La Croix St Ouen P. scientifique			T. 6									
Thourotte			T. 1010									
Verneuil-en-Halatte				T. 2								
Waben Le Sémaphore											T. 20	
NMI 3												
Lauwin-Planque												T. 6537

Ponderal mass analysis attested on some Late Bronze age sites

T.9   Bronze C/D and Bronze D tombs

are absent, apart from the urn used as a container or to cover the incinerated deposit.

Burnt or buried, the deceased are placed in similar oval-shaped pits, with comparable dimensions. During the course of the Middle Bronze Age, the size of cremation graves decreases to such an extent that it is at times adjusted to the dimensions of the cinerary urn. This trend is considered to be a progressive adjustment of funerary practices to the introduction of cremation. Funerary customs do not include object deposits.

During the Middle Bronze Age, we observe an increase in the number of funerary sites, with incineration becoming predominant during the Bronze Age B. This first part of the Middle Bronze Age is marked by the frequency of deposits in overturned urns on cremations, generally place in the internal area of monuments. This ritual is practiced on both sides of the Channel. Whether they are used as a covering or as a container, these urns are GDU type urns with decoration; however they do not seem to have been used after the Bronze Age C.

The use of an overturned container marks the beginning of the Middle Bronze Age, but several forms of graves from the previous period persist: simple pits with a bone deposit emptied from or contained in an urn, or even in a circular container in perishable matter. The quantity of bones contained in the urn is often considerable. Besides the bones, the other main grave component corresponds to combustion residues which can be placed within the tomb or buried nearby. Inhumation is practiced sporadically. Although the corpus of sites is small, they seem to correspond to secondary graves.

From the second half of the Middle Bronze Age, tombs with dispersed deposits, combining bone, ashes and pieces of charcoal become more frequent and this practice turns into the almost exclusive sepulchral form. It is characterised by: the limited dimensions of pits, the spreading of bones directly in the tomb, pyre residues mixed with bones, important variations in the quantity of buried bone (often small) … and still no grave good deposits.

At the beginning of the Late Bronze Age, in the continuity of the Middle Bronze Age II (which corresponds to the Deverel-Rimbury phase in the English chronology), we observe the development of small cemeteries. These cemeteries, referred to as 'familial' appear at the end of the Bronze Age and have been identified in the south-east of England. They are one of the characteristics of the Channel–North Sea entity.

Bibliography

Audouze, F. et Blanchet, J. C. (1983) Les cercles de l'âge du Bronze en Picardie et ses abords. Un premier bilan. In *Enclos funéraires et structures d'habitat en Europe du Nord-Ouest, 7–29, Table ronde du CNRS Rennes 1981, Travaux du laboratoire « Anthropologie – Préhistoire – Protohistoire – Quaternaire Armoricains ».* Rennes, CNRS.

Azagury, I. and Demolon, P. (1990) Vitry-en-Artois, Les Colombiers. *Cahiers de Préhistoire du Nord* 8, 54–58.

Bailloud, G. (1982) Une sépulture collective Seine-Oise-Marne à Cuiry-les-Chaudardes, Le Champ Tortu (Aisne). In *Vallée de l'Aisne, cinq années de fouilles protohistoriques*, 171–174. Amiens, Revue Archéologique de Picardie numéro spécial 5.

Baudry, A.-C., Buchez, N., Gaillard, D., Lamotte, D., Lefèvre, P., Prilaux, G. and Talon M. (2013) Premiers résultats pour l'âge du Bronze et le premier âge du Fer sur le Canal Seine-Nord Europe. *Bulletin de l'Association pour le Promotion des Recherches sur l'Âge du Bronze* 10, 82–88.

Billand, G. (1992) La Croix Saint Ouen « Le Prieuré » Bilan des fouilles de 1992. In *Programme de surveillance et d'étude archéologique des sablières de la moyenne vallée de l'Oise – Rapport d'activités 1992*, 109–120. Amiens, Service régional de l'archéologie de Picardie.

Billand, G. (1998) *Rue « Le Chemin des Morts » Rapport de sondages 1ère tranche de la carrière Boinet.* Amiens, AFAN, SRA Picardie.

Billand, G. and Le Goff, I. (2011) *Méaulte, Bray-sur-Somme, Fricourt, (Somme) Plate forme aéro-industrielle de Haute Picardie, Méaulte « Le Champ Saint-Pierre » Rapport final d'opération* 3. Amiens, Inrap Nord-Picardie.

Billand, G. and Talon, M. (2007) Apport du Bronze Age Studies Group au vieillissement des 'hair-rings' dans le Nord de la France. In C. Burgess, P. Topping and R. Lynch (eds) *Beyond Stonehenge, Essays on the Bronze Age in Honour of Colin Burgess*, 342–351. Oxford, Oxbow Books.

Blanchet, J.-C. (1984) Les premiers métallurgistes en Picardie et dans le nord de la France, Mémoire de la Société Préhistorique Française 17. Paris, Société Préhistorique Française.

Blanchet, J.-C. and Talon, M. (2005) L'âge du Bronze dans la moyenne vallée de l'Oise apports récents. In J. Bourgeois and M. Talon (eds) *L'Age du Bronze du nord de la France dans son contexte européen*, 232–73, Actes du 125e congrès national des sociétés historiques et scientifiques à Lille 2000. Paris, CTHS.

Blondiau, L., Billand, G. and Le Goff, I. (1999) *Thourotte « ZAC du Gros Grelot » Rapport d'évaluation.* Amiens, AFAN SRA Picardie.

Bostyn, F., Blancquaert, G., Lanchon, Y. and Auboire, G. (1992a) Un enclos triple du Bronze ancien à Fréthun (Pas-de-Calais). *Bulletin de la Société Préhistorique Française* 89 (10–12), 393–412.

Bostyn, F., Blancquaert, G. and Lanchon, Y. (1992b) Les enclos funéraires de l'âge du Bronze de Coquelles RN1 (Pas-de-Calais). *Bulletin de la société préhistorique française* 89 (10–12), 412–428.

Boureux, M. (1974) Rapport de fouilles de sauvetage à Pontavert « Le Marteau ». In *Les fouilles protohistoriques dans la vallée de l'Aisne*, rapport 3, 68–74. Paris, Université de Paris I.

Bourgeois, J. (1991) *Enclos et nécropole du second âge du Fer à Kemzeke (Stekene, Flandre orientale). Rapport provisoire des fouilles 1988*, Scholae Archaeologicae 12. Gent, 1988. Gent, Scholae Archaeologicae 12.

Bourgeois, J. and Talon, M. (ed.) (2005) *L'âge du bronze du nord de la France dans son contexte européen, Actes du 125e congrès national des sociétés historiques et scientifiques à Lille 2000.* Paris, CTHS.

Bourgeois, J. and Talon, M. (2009) From Picardy to Flanders: Transmanche connections in the Bronze Age. In P. Clark (ed.) *Bronze Age Connections: Cultural Contact in Prehistoric Europe*, 38–60. Oxford, Oxbow Books.

Bréart, B. and Fagnart, J.-P. (1982) La sépulture à incinération de Crouy (Somme). Contribution à l'étude des structures funéraires du groupe d'Eramecourt. *Revue Archéologique de Picardie* 2, 7–10.

Brun, P. and Pommepuy, Cl. (1987) La nécropole protohistorique du méandre de Bucy-le-Long/Missy-sur- Aisne. In *Les relations entre le continent et les îles britanniques à l'âge du Bronze, 57–76, actes du colloque de Lille, septembre 1984, dans le cadre du 22e Congrès préhistoire de France*. Paris. Société Préhistorique Française

Buchez, N. and Talon, M. (2005) L'âge du Bronze dans le bassin de la Somme, bilan et périodisation du mobilier céramique. In J. Bourgeois and M. Talon (eds) *L'Age du Bronze du nord de la France dans son contexte européen, 159–88, actes du 125e congrès national des sociétés historiques et scientifiques à Lille 2000*. Paris, CTHS.

Buchez, N., Billand, G., Descheyer, N., Fechner, K., Le Goff, I., Loicq, S., Martial, E. and Pinard, E. (2014) Argoeuvres Saint-Sauveur (Somme) « Le Moulin d'Argoeuvres » Evolution de l'occupation sur le rebord de plateau du Néolithique final à La Tène D, Rapport final d'opération. Amiens, INRAP, SRA Picardie.

Chambon, P. (2003) *Morts dans les sépultures collectives néolithiques en France: Des cadavres aux restes ultimes*. Supplément à *Gallia Préhistoire* 35. Paris, CNRS Editions.

Collectif (2000) *Habitats et nécropoles à l'âge du Bronze sur le Transmanche et le TGV Nord*, Travaux I. Paris, Société Préhistorique Française.

Cottiaux, R. and Lawrence-Dubovac, P. (2008) Un ensemble funéraire de l'âge du Bronze moyen à Mareuil- les-Meaux « Les Vignolles » (Seine-et-Marne). *Revue Archéologique d'Ile de France* 1, 113–124.

David, A. and Lorin, Y. (2016) Aire-sur-la-Lys « ZAC Saint-Martin », phase 2, Rapport Final d'Opération. Achicourt, Inrap Nord-Picardie.

De Laet, S. (1961) Quelques précisions nouvelles sur la civilisation de Hilversum en Belgique. *Helinium* 1, 120–6.

De Laet, S. and Rogge, M. (1972) Une tombelle à incinération de la civilisation aux gobelets campaniformes trouvée à Kruishoutem (Flandre orientale). *Helinium* 12, 209–224.

De Mulder, G. (2014) Les rites funéraires dans le nord du bassin de l'Escaut à l'âge du Bronze final et au premier âge du Fer. In A. Cahen-Delhaye and G. De Mulder (eds) *Des espaces aux esprits. L'organisation de la mort aux âges des Métaux dans le nord-ouest de l'Europe, 29–52, actes du colloque de la C. A. M. et de la S. B. E. C., Moulins de Beez à Namur, 24–25 février 2012. Namur, Etudes et documents Archéologie 32*. Namur.

De Reu, J., Hammond, J., Toron, S. and Bourgeois, J. (2012) Spatial and chronological continuities of Bronze Age cemeteries of North-western Europe. In D. Bérenger, J. Bourgeois, M. Talon and S. Wirth (eds) *Paysages funéraires de l'Age du Bronze, Gräberlandschaften der Bronzezeit, 265–82, actes du Colloque international sur l'Age du Bronze, APRAB et LWL-Archäologie für Westfalen, Herne, 2008 t. 51*. Darmstadt, BAW.

Debord, J. (1987) Fouille d'un enclos funéraire de l'âge du Bronze à Villeneuve-Saint-Germain (Aisne), *Revue Archéologique de Picardie* 3–4, 37–50.

Desfossés, Y. (2000) *Archéologie préventive en vallée de Canche – Les sites protohistoriques fouillés dans le cadre de la réalisation de l'autoroute A 16*. Nord-Ouest Archéologie 11. Berck-sur-mer CRADC.

Drenth, E. and Lohof, E. (2005) Mounds for the dead – funerary and burial ritual in Beaker period, Early and Middle Bronze Age. In L. P. Louwe Kooijmans, P. W. Van den Broeke, H. Fokkens and A. L. Van Gijn (eds) *The Prehistory of the Netherlands I*, 411–454. Amsterdam, Amsterdam University Press.

Ertlé, R. (1966) Etude archéologique de la vallée de l'Aisne : le complexe protohistorique de Pontavert – Berry-au-Bac. I – Les incinérations entourées de fosses circulaires. In *Actes du Ve colloque international d'études gauloises, celtiques et protoceltiques, Amiens, 1965*, 97–120. Rennes, OGAM traditions celtiques.

Favier, D., Jacques, A. and Prilaux, G. (2004) ZAC Actiparc (62), Saint-Laurent-Blangy. Les occupations humaines au lieu-dit « Les Soixante ». De la ferme aristocratique gauloise au complexe militaire romain. Document Final de Synthèse. Arras, Inrap Nord-Picardie, SAM d'Arras.

Feray, P., Lantoine, J. and Lefevre, P. (2000) L'enclos funéraire de Waben « Le Sémaphore ». In *Archéologie préventive en vallée de Canche – Les sites protohistoriques fouillés dans le cadre de la réalisation de l'autoroute A16, 195–214, Nord-Ouest Archéologie 11*. Berck-sur-mer, CRADC.

Fokkens, H. (2005) Le début de l'âge du Bronze aux Pays-Bas et l'horizon Hilversum ancien. In J. Bourgeois and M. Talon (ed.) *L'âge du Bronze du nord de la France dans son contexte européen, 11–33, actes du 125e congrès national des sociétés historiques et scientifiques à Lille 2000*. Paris, CTHS.

Fourny, M. (1985) Le « Muzieleberg » à Renaix. Nouvelle contribution à l'étude de la nécropole de la civilisation Hilversum/Drakenstein, (âge du Bronze ancien/moyen). Examen des anciennes collections du Musée du centenaire à Mons. *Vie archéologique* 19, 41–68.

Gaillard, D. and Jacques, A. (2000) Rocade Ouest d'Arras (Pas-de-Calais). DFS de sauvetage urgent de 1995 à 1998. Arras, AFAN, Service Archéologique Municipal d'Arras et SRA du Nord-Pas-de- Calais.

Gaudefroy, S. and Le Goff, I. (2004) La nécropole du début du Bronze final de Verneuil-en-Halatte (Oise). *Revue archéologique de Picardie* 1/2, 19–32.

Germain-Vallée, C., Giraud, P. and Durand, R. (2007) L'enclos funéraire de l'âge du Bronze de Saint-Martin- de-Fontenay (Calvados, Basse-Normandie). *Bulletin de la Société préhistorique française* 104 (3), 565–581.

Glasbergen, W. (1954a) Barrow excavations in the Eight Beatitudes. The Bronze Age cemetery between Toterfout and Halve Mijl, North Brabant. The excavations, *Palaeohistoria* 2 1–134.

Glasbergen, W. (1954b) Barrow excavations in the Eight Beatitudes. The Bronze Age cemetery between Toterfout and Halve Mijl, North Brabant. The implications. *Palaeohistoria* 3, 1–204.

Gouge, P. and Peake, R. (2005) Aux marges du Bronze atlantique, sites et chronologies de la région du confluent Seine-Yonne. In J. Bourgeois and M. Talon (ed.) *L'Age du Bronze du nord de la France dans son contexte européen*, 333–59, actes du 125e congrès national des sociétés historiques et scientifiques à Lille 2000. Paris, CTHS.

Grévin, G., Baud, C. A. and Susini, A. (1990) Etude anthropologique et paléopathologique d'un adulte inhumé puis incinérés provenant du site de Pincevent (Seine-et-Marne). In E. Crubézy, H. Duday, P. Sellier and A.-M. Tillier (eds) *Anthropologie et archéologie: dialogue sur les ensembles funéraires*, 77–88. Paris, Bulletin et mémoires de la Société Anthropologique de Paris 2 (3–4).

Hachem, L., Allard, P., Convertini, F, Robert, B., Salanova, L., Sidera, I. and Thevenet, C. withthe collaboration of Guichard, Y. and Peltier, V. (2011) La sépulture campaniforme de Ciry-Salsogne 'La Bouche à Vesles' (Aisne). In L. Salanova and Y. Tchérémissinoff (eds) *Les sépultures individuelles campaniformes en France*, 21–35, XLIème supplément à *Gallia Préhistoire*. Paris, CNRS Editions.

Henton, A. (2014) Fouille d'un enclos circulaire à Douvrin (Pas-de-Calais, France) La problématique des sépultures annexes à inhumation de l'âge du Bronze en Nord-Picardie. *Lunula Archeologia protohistorica* XXII, 45–51.

Jacques, A. and Prilaux, G. (2006) ZAC Dainville Achicourt (62) lieu dit « Gérico ». Le site gaulois de Dainville-Achicourt au lieu-dit « Gérico ». Un exemple de l'évolution d'un établissement celtique de l'arrière-pays atrébate. Document final de synthèse. Arras, INRAP Nord Picardie,Service Archéologique Municipal d'Arras.

Joseph, F. and Pinard, E. (1996) Les occupations de l'âge du Bronze sur le site de Longueil-Sainte-Marie 'Les Gros Grès IV'. *Programme de surveillance et d'étude archéologique des sablières de la moyenne vallée de l'Oise: rapport d'activité 1995*, 130–169. Amiens, Service régional de l'archéologie de Picardie.

Koot, C. W. and Berkvens, R. (2004) *Bredase akkers eeuwenoud. 4000 jaar bewoningsgeschiedenis op de rand van zand en klei (ErfgoedStudies Breda 1)*. Breda, Gemeeente Breda/Rijksdienst voor het Oudheidkundig Bodemonderzoek. Rapportage Archeologische Monumentenzorg 102.

Lanting, J. and Brindley, A. (2005) La datation des ossements incinérés. In J. Bourgeois and M. Talon (eds) *L'âge du Bronze du nord de la France dans son contexte européen*, 35–41, actes du 125e congrès national des sociétés historiques et scientifiques à Lille 2000. Paris, CTHS.

Lefebvre, A., Franck, J. and Veber, C. (2011) Les sépultures individuelles campaniformes en Lorrain : l'exemple de Pouilly (Moselle) et d'Hatrize (Meurthe-et-Moselle). In L. Salanova and Y. Tchérémissinoff (eds) *Les sépultures individuelles campaniformes en France*, 97–113, XLIème supplément à *Gallia Préhistoire*. Paris, CNRS Editions.

Le Goff, I. (1998) *De l'os incinéré aux gestes funéraires. Essai de palethnologie à partir des vestiges de la crémation*. Unpublished Thesis in prehistory, ethnology and anthropology, université de Paris I.

Le Goff, I. (2013) Brûler le défunt pour traverser le temps des funérailles. In G. Perreira (ed.) Une archéologie des temps funéraires? Hommage à Jean Leclerc. *Les Nouvelles de l'archéologie* 132, 41–47.

Le Goff, I. and Guichard, Y. (2005) Le dépôt cinéraire comme indicateur chronologique; le cas des nécropoles de l'âge du Bronze de la vallée de l'Aisne. In J. Bourgeois and M. Talon (eds) *L'âge du Bronze du nord de la France dans son contexte européen*, 209–26, actes du 125e congrès national des sociétés historiques et scientifiques à Lille 2000. Paris, CTHS.

Le Goff, I. and Guillot, H. (2005) Contribution à la reconnaissance des gestes funéraires : mise en évidence des modalités de collecte des os humains incinérés. In C. Mordant and G. Delpierre (eds) *Les pratiques funéraires à l'âge du Bronze en France*, 155–167. Paris, CTHS, Société archéologique de Sens.

Le Guen, P. (2012) Ciry-Salsogne « La Cour Maçonneuse » carrière Desmarest : nécropole de l'âge du Bronze final. Rapport d'opération de fouille. Amiens, Inrap Nord-Picardie.

Le Guen, P. and Pinard, E. (2007) La nécropole à incinération de Presles-et-Boves « les Bois Plantés » (Aisne): approche des pratiques funéraires du Bronze final dans la vallée de l'Aisne. In L. Baray, P. Brun and A. Testart (eds) *Pratiques funéraires et sociétés, 101–14*, actes du colloque de Sens 2003. Dijon, Editions Universitaires de Dijon.

Lefèvre, Ph. (2016) Marquion, secteur 27, Rapport d'opération de la Fouille no. 32, plate-forme multimodale de Sauchy-Lestrée-Marquion (62). Croix-Moligneaux, Inrap Projet canal Seine-Nord-Europe.

Legriel, J., Granchon, P. and de Kepper, A.-G. (2011) La nécropole à incinérations de l'âge du Bronze moyen de Cesson 'La Plaine du Moulin à Vent' (Seine-et-Marne): derniers résultats. *Bulletin de l'Association pour la Promotion des Recherches sur l'Âge du Bronze* 8, 5–8.

Lehoërff, A. in collaboration with Bourgeois, J., Clark, P. and Talon M. (ed.) (2012) *Beyond the Horizon, Societies of the Channel and North Sea 3,500 years ago*, catalogue de l'exposition (Château-Musée de Boulogne-sur-Mer, 30 juin 2012–5 novembre 2012 – Erfgoedcentrum de Ename, 16 décembre 2012–30 mai 2013 – Musée de Douvres, 1er juillet–30 décembre 2013). Paris, coédition BOAT 1550 BC/Somogy éditions d'art.

Leroy-Langelin, E. and Sergent, A. (eds) (2015) Lauwin-Planque « ZAC Lauwin-Planque » (Nord): L'âge du Bronze. Vol. III. Rapport final d'opération de fouille, Communauté d'Agglomération du Douaisis-Direction de l'Archéologie Préventive. Douai, S. R. A. Nord-Pas-de-Calais, Douai. section 2. Saint-Martin", phase 2, Rapport final d'opération de fouille. Achicourt, INRAP Nord-Picardie.

Marcigny, C., Ghesquière, E. and Kinnes, I. (2007) Bronze Age cross-channel relations. The Lower-Normandy (France) example: ceramic chronology and first reflections. In C. Burgess, P. Topping and R. Lynch (eds) *Beyond Stonehenge, Essays on the Bronze Age in Honour of Colin Burgess*, 255–267. Oxford, Oxbow Books.

Masse, A. (2014) Vie quotidienne et pratiques funéraires de l'âge du Bronze à Dainville « Le Champ Bel Air » (Pas-de-Calais). *Bulletin de l'Association pour la Promotion des Recherches sur l'Âge du Bronze* 12, 82–88.

Masset, C. (1995) Sur la stratigraphie de la Chaussée Tirancourt (Somme). In *Actes du 19ème Colloque interrégional Néolithique Amiens 1992*, 135–9. Amiens, Revue Archéologique de Picardie spécial 9.

McKinley, J. I. (1993) Bone fragment size and weights of bone from modern British cremations and its implications for the interpretation of archaeological cremations. *International Journal of Osteoarchaeology* 3, 283–7.

McKinley, J. I. (2012) Caley's Department Store, Windsor (65031). Unpublished cremated bone report. Salisbury, Wessex Archaeology.

McKinley, J. I. (2016) Cremated bone, pyre technology and cremation ritual. In N. Cooke, Prehistoric and Romano-British activity and medieval settlement on the site of the former Caley's Department Store, 19–23 High St, Windsor, Berkshire. *Berkshire Archaeological Journal* 82, 33–62.

Noël, J.-Y. (2011) Les sépultures individuelles de Bernières-sur-Mer (Calvados) : une nécropole du début des âges des métaux ? In L. Salanova and Y. Tchérémissinoff (eds) *Les sépultures individuelles campaniformes en France, 47–55*, XLIème supplément à *Gallia Préhistoire*. Paris, CNRS Editions.

Peake, R. and Delattre, V. (2010) Monumentalité de la Mort : la nécropole diachronique de Jaulnes « Le Bas des Hauts Champs », *Bulletin de l'Association pour la Promotion des Recherches sur l'Âge du Bronze* 7, 19–22.

Petit, E. and Billand, G. (2006) Pierrepont-sur-Avre « Rue de Boussicourt » Rapport de diagnostic. Amiens, INRAP, SRA Picardie.

Pinard, E. (1992) Approche anthropologique de cinq sépultures découvertes en 1992 à Longueil-Sainte- Marie « Les Gros Grès III » et La Croix-Saint-Ouen « Le Prieuré » (Oise). Réflexions sur les découvertes anciennes de ce type. In *Programme de surveillance et d'étude archéologique des sablières de la moyenne vallée de l'Oise : rapport d'activité 1992*, 223–239. Amiens, Service régional de l'archéologie de Picardie.

Piningre, J.-P. (1990) La Nécropole de l'Âge du bronze de Conchil-le-Temple (Pas-de-Calais). In *Les Enclos funéraires de l'Âge du bronze dans le Nord/Pas-de-Calais. Catalogue d'exposition, 79–89*, Les Cahiers de Préhistoire du Nord 8 (2). Villeneuve d'Ascq, Cahiers de Préhistoire du Nord 8.

Robert, B. (2013) Moussy-Verneuil (Aisne), au Glanard, le Prée, les Neufs Boeufsn Chemin de la Pâturelle, Carrière Holcim 2. Rapport de diagnostic. Amiens, Inrap Nord-Picardie.

Salanova, L. (2011) Chronologie et facteurs d'évolution des sépultures individuelles campaniformes dans le Nord de la France. In L. Salanova and Y. Tchérémissinoff (eds) *Les sépultures individuelles campaniformes en France, 125–42*, XLIème supplément à *Gallia Préhistoire*. Paris, Éditions CNRS.

Salanova, L., Renard, C. and Mille, B. (2011) Réexamen de la sépulture campaniforme d'Arenberg. In L. Salanova and Y. Tchérémissinoff (eds) *Les sépultures individuelles campaniformes en France, 21–35*, XLIème supplément à *Gallia Préhistoire*. Paris, CNRS Editions.

Salanova, L., Brunet, P., Cottiaux, R., Hamon, T., Langry-François, F., Martineau, R., Polloni, A., Renard, C. et Sohn, M. (2011) Du néolithique récent à l'âge du Bronze dans le centre nord de la France: les étapes de l'évolution chronoculturelle. In F. Bostyn, E. Martial and I. Praud (eds) *Le Néolithique du Nord de la France dans son contexte européen : habitat et économie aux 4e et 3e millénaires avant notre ère, 77–101*, actes du 29ème colloque interrégional sur le néolithique, Villeneuve-d'Asq, 2–3 octobre 2009. Amiens, *Revue archéologique de Picardie* spécial 28.

Toron, S. (2006) De la Picardie aux Flandres belges : une approche comparative des enclos circulaires de l'âge du bronze ancien et moyen. *Lunula Archaeologia protohistorica XIV (Mariemont)*, 71–76.

Van Doorselaer, A. (2001) Les tombes à incinération à l'époque gallo-romaine en Gaule septentrionale : introduction générale. Actes du colloque « Les nécropoles à incinérations en Gaule Belgique. Synthèses régionales et méthodologie. » J. F. Geoffroy et H. Barbé (dir.), tenu les 13 et 14 décembre 1996. *Revue du Nord* 8 hors série (coll. Art et archéologie), 9–14

Van Roeyen, J.-P. (1989) De vroegste menselijke aanwezigheid in Temse en in het Waasland: de Steentijd. In H. Thoen (ed.) *Temse en de Schelde*, 28–43. Brussel, Van Ijstijd tot Romeinen

Warmembol, E. (1996) Les débuts de l'âge du Bronze en Belgique In C. Mordant and O. Gaiffe (eds) *Cultures et sociétés au Bronze ancien en Europe, 637–657*. Paris, CTHS.

Annex 10.1 Table of the dates of radiocarbon dated graves in Nord-Pas-de-Calais and Picardy, from the Early Bronze Age to the beginning of the Late Bronze Age.

Site	District	Feature	Description	Pit (m)	Weight (g)	Lab. no.	Radiocarbon age (BP)	Calibrated date range (BC) 2 sigma	Attribution	Reference
Bucy-le-Long, Le Grand Marais	Aisne	cremation monument 3	central cremation under overturned urn placed in cist; monument Ø 17 m	1.85×1.40			3710±200	2640–1690	Bronze A1	Brun & Pommepuy 1987
Fresnes-les-Montauban, Le Motel	Pas de Calais	burial monument 5	burial in pit of 20-yr-old woman wearing a few modest ornments; monument Ø 25 m	1.10×0.80		Ly-5334	3865±145	2828–1958	Bronze A1	Desfossés & Masson 2000
Longueil-Sainte-Marie, Les Gros Grès IV	Oise	burial st 4	burial in pit of young adult outside a double ring-ditch monument; Ø 22 m	2×1.18		Ly-4703[1]	3535±40	1959–1749	Bronze A1	Joseph & Pinard 1996
La Croix-St-Ouen, Le Prieuré	Oise	burial st 52	burial in pit of adult (50–69-yr-old) without monument	1.63×0.84		Ly-4701[1]	3455±35	1880–1680	Bronze A2	Billand 1992
Lauwin-Planque	Nord	central cremation	central cremation in monument; Ø 31 m	1.80×1.00	550	Ly-6693[1]	3415±35	1866–1628	Bronze A2	Leroy-Langelin & Sergent forthcoming
Aire-sur-la-Lys, ZAC Hameau St Martin	Pas de Calais	central cremation 272	central cremation in monument; Ø 45 m	0.56×0.51	977	GrA-32424[1]	3410±35	1871–1623	Bronze A2	Lorin forthcoming
Fresnes-les-Montauban, Le Motel	Pas de Calais	burial monument 1	burial in pit of 30-yr-old woman in monument; Ø 19 m	1.30×0.90		Ly-5336	3380±50	1858–1541	Bronze A2	Desfossés & Masson 2000
Fresnes-les-Montauban, Le Motel	Pas de Calais	burial monument 3	burial in pit of 16-yr-old young man; monument Ø 25 m	2×1.30		Ly-5335	3355±60	1848–1526	Bronze A2	Desfossés & Masson 2000
La Croix-St-Ouen, Le Prieuré	Oise	cremation in st 52	cremated bones spread over buried adult corpse	1.63×0.84	460	GrA-37955[1]	3355±30	1740–1530	Bronze A2	Pinard 1992
Marquion, Plate forme multimodale, secteur 27	Pas de Calais	cremation 9	few cremated bone frags mixed with fuel residue contained in small urn close to monument	urn covered with slab (Ø 0.12)	45	RICH-20388[1]	3349±35	1739–1531	Bronze A2	Lefèvre forthcoming
Pierrepont-sur-Avre, Chemin de Boussicourt	Somme	central cremation	deposit of cremated bones in oval pit in monument; Ø 27 m	1×1.35	760	GrA-43445	3340±35	1940–1640	Bronze A2	Billand & Legoff,
Saint-Laurent-Blangy, Les Soixante	Pas de Calais	burial st 1482	badly preserved burial of child in ditch of monument; Ø 8,50 m			GrA-59617[1]	3325±35	1690– 1513	Bronze A2	Favier, Jacques & Prilaux 2004

(Continued)

Annex 10.1. Table of the dates of radiocarbon dated graves in Nord-Pas-de-Calais and Picardy, from the Early Bronze Age to the beginning of the Late Bronze Age. (Continued)

Site	District	Feature	Description	Pit (m)	Weight (g)	Lab. no.	Radiocarbon age (BP)	Calibrated date range (BC) 2 sigma	Attribution	Reference
Fréthun, Les Rietz	Pas de Calais	burial st 23	burial of old woman in triple ring-ditch monument; Ø 60 m	2.60×1.70		Gif-8928	3310±60	1736–1466	Bronze B	Bostyn & alii 2000
Rue, Le Chemin des Morts	Somme	cremation 1	cremated bones covered with overturned urn in monument; Ø 33 m	0.95×0.65	819	GrA-14510[1]	3295±40	1683–1462	Bronze B	Billand 1998
Méaulte, Plate-forme aéro-industrielle, site 1	Somme	cremation 8	deposit of adult cremated bones mixed with pyre residues in pit, no monument	Ø 0.37	118	GrA-35263[1]	3290±40	1690–1490	Bronze B	Billand & Le Goff 2011
Lauwin-Planque, Les Dix-Neuf	Nord	cremation 6096	cremated bones covered with overturned urn in monument; Ø 15 m	2.20×1.80	110	Ly-309 (OXA)[1]	3290±40	1682–1464	Bronze B	Leroy-Langelin & Sergent forthcoming
Crouy, Les Quatre	Somme	cremation	cremated bones covered with overturned urn in monument; oval shape 18×14 m	1×0.80		GrA-41825[1]	3290±30	1640–1490	Bronze B	Bréart & Fagnart, 1982
Dainville, Gérico	Pas de Calais	cremation st 344	deposit of adult cremated bones scattered with pyre residues in pit; monument Ø 14 m	0.50×0.30	465g	GrA-59094[1]	3250±35	1515–1447	Bronze B	Jacques & Prilaux 2006
Argoeuves, Le Moulin d'Argoeuves	Somme	st 151 monument B	v. few cremated bone frags in pit/remains of pyre ?; monument Ø 18 m	1.20×0.90	6g	GrN-49779[1]	3240±40	1612–1433	Bronze B	Buchez 2014
Marquion, Plate forme multimodale, secteur 27	Pas de Calais	cremation 2	deposit of few cremated bone frags in pit located off-centre in monument	0.60×0.40	112g	RICH-20384	3238±37	1610–1430	Bronze B	Lefèvre à paraître
Vitry-en-Artois, Les Colombiers	Pas de Calais	cremation	cremated bones covered with overturned urn in monument; Ø 10 m	1.40×1.00		Gif-7258	3220±60	1623–1346	Bronze B	Azagury & Demolon, 1987
Marquion, Plate forme multimodale, secteur 2	Pas de Calais	cremation 6	few cremated bone frags in pit located just outside ring-ditch monument	Ø 0.40	3	RICH-20387	3219±28	1540–1420	Bronze B	Lefèvre forthcoming

(Continued)

Annex 10.1. Table of the dates of radiocarbon dated graves in Nord-Pas-de-Calais and Picardy, from the Early Bronze Age to the beginning of the Late Bronze Age. (Continued)

Site	District	Feature	Description	Pit (m)	Weight (g)	Lab. no.	Radiocarbon age (BP)	Calibrated date range (BC) 2 sigma	Attribution	Reference
Villeneuve-St-Germain, Les Grandes Grèves	Aisne	burial 431	burial of 15–17-year-old woman; monument Ø 13 m	1.47×1.20		Ly-3809	3200±100	1865–1390	Bronze B	Debord 1987
Marquion, Plate forme multimodale, secteur 2	Pas de Calais	cremation 5	deposit of few cremated bone frags in pit located close to ring-ditch monument	Ø 0.40	27	RICH-20386	3193±33	1530–1410	Bronze C	Lefèvre forthcoming
Verneuil-en-Halatte, Parc Alata	Oise	cremation 18	cremated bones of woman over 30–35 ys old placed in perishable container	± Ø 0.30	417	GrA-19556	3180±45	1540–1370	Bronze C	Gaudefroy & Le Goff 2004
Argoeuves, Le Moulin d'Argoeuves	Somme	cremation monument A	cremated bones covered with overturned urn in monument; Ø 18 m	Ø 0.40	301	GrA-43447[1]	3170±35	1512–1391	Bronze C	Buchez 2014
Villeneuve-St-Germain, Les Grandes Grèves	Aisne	burial 437	burial of 18–29-yr-old man in monument; Ø 13 m	?×0.80		Ly-3810	3160±100	1685–1130	Bronze C	Debord 1987
Méaulte, Plate-forme aéro-industrielle, site 1	Somme	cremation 25	scattered cremated bone frags of young child deposited in pit with pieces of charcoal	Ø 0.35	202	GrA-34781[1]	3145±35	1500–1370	Bronze C	Billand & Le Goff 2011
Verneuil-en-Halatte, Parc Alata	Oise	cremation 10	scattered cremated bone frags of young child & young adult deposited in pit with pyre residues	± Ø 0.75	328	GrA 37957	3140±30	1500–1370	Bronze C	Gaudefroy & Le Goff 2004
Dainville, Le Champ Bel air	Pas de Calais	cremation 62	deposit in pit with selective sorting of pyre residues; monument Ø 25 m	0.98×0.64	191	Beta-329806	3140±40	1500–1370	Bronze C	Masse 2014
Marquion, Plateforme multimodale, secteur 3/4	Pas de Calais	cremation 162	cremated bone frags in pit located in filling of ring-ditch	± Ø 0.20	5	Beta-379878	3140±30	1455–1385	Bronze C	Lefèvre à paraître
Marquion, Plateforme multimodale, secteur 2	Pas de Calais	cremation 4	few cremated bone frags in pit located just outside ring-ditch monument	Ø 0.40	41	RICH-20385	3137±34	1500–1360	Bronze C	Lefèvre forthcoming

(Continued)

Annex 10.1. Table of the dates of radiocarbon dated graves in Nord-Pas-de-Calais and Picardy, from the Early Bronze Age to the beginning of the Late Bronze Age. (Continued)

Site	District	Feature	Description	Pit (m)	Weight (g)	Lab. no.	Radiocarbon age (BP)	Calibrated date range (BC) 2 sigma	Attribution	Reference
Verneuil-en-Halatte, Parc Alata	Oise	cremation 20	cremated bones of a man placed in an upright urn	± Ø 0.55	2136	GrA-19557	3095±45	1460–1250	Bronze C/D	Gaudefroy & Le Goff 2004
Coquelles, RN1	Pas de Calais	burial monument 10	burial of woman over 25 yrs old in ditch of monument; Ø 16 m			Gif-8927	3095±40	1453–1273	Bronze C/D	Bostyn & alii 2000
Méaulte, Plate-forme aéro-industrielle, site 1	Somme	cremation 9	deposit of adult cremated bones mixed with pyre residues in pit, no monument	Ø 0.27	24	GrA-34780[1]	3090±35	1440–1260	Bronze C/D	Billand & Le Goff 2011
Lauwin-Planque, Les Dix-Neuf	Nord	st 6537	deposit of 2 adults & 2 children (0–3 & 6–15 yrs) in pit without monument. Vessel placed next to cremated bones	1.20×1	3405	GrA-39120[1]	3080±30	1421–1268	Bronze C/D	Leroy-Langelin & Sergent forthcoming
Dainville, Les Biefs	Pas de Calais	central cremation	v. poorly preserved deposit of cremated bones in monument; Ø 19 m			GrA-14976[1]	3065±45	1427–1134	Bronze C/D	Gaillard & Jacques, 2000
Méaulte, Plate-forme aéro-industrielle, site 1	Somme	cremation 2	few cremated bones mixed with pyre residues in pit, no monument	Ø 0.33	10	GrA-34779[1]	3065±35	1420–1250	Bronze C/D	Billand & Le Goff 2011
Méaulte, Plate-forme aéro-industrielle, site 1	Somme	cremation 12	deposit of adult cremated bones mixed with pyre residues in pit, no monument	Ø 0.60	180	GrA-34784[1]	3060±35	1420–1250	Bronze C/D	Billand & Le Goff 2011
Waben, Le Sémaphore	Pas de Calais	cremation in ditch	cremated bones placed over burnt flints in pit located in ring-ditch of monument; Ø 16 m	0.30×0.20	55	Ly-8149	3040±50	1396–1127	Bronze D	Feray & alii, 2000
La Croix-St-Ouen, Parc Scientifique	Oise	cremation 6	cremated bones in pit located on inner edge of ditch; monument Ø 20 m			GrA-14511	3035±45	1407–1130	Bronze D	Blanchet & Talon 2005
Méaulte, Plate-forme aéro-industrielle, site 14	Somme	cremation 5	deposit of cremated bones mixed with pyre residues in pit, no monument	Ø 0.35	40	GrA-34807[1]	3030±35	1410–1190	Bronze D	Billand & Le Goff 2011

1 = unpublished

La nécropole de Soliers 'PA.EOLE' (14) : nouvelles données en faveur d'un complexe medio-atlantique

*Régis Issenmann, Capucine Tranchant,
Alexis Corrochano et Émilie Dubreucq*

Résumé

La découverte d'une nécropole de la transition premier / second Âge du fer à Soliers (Calvados), a permis d'étudier un petit ensemble de quatre tombes ceintes par un enclos léger, le long d'une voie de circulation. L'une des sépultures et quelques caractéristiques morphologiques de cette nécropole détonent dans le paysage funéraire contemporain dans la plaine de Caen. Les observations effectuées enrichissent le questionnement relatif à la genèse et l'évolution du domaine médio-atlantique.

Mots clés : nécropole, La Tène ancienne, plaine de Caen, architecture funéraire, domaine médio-atlantique

Abstract

The discovery of a cemetery dating from the transition between the Early and Late Iron Age at Soliers (Calvados) has given us the opportunity to study a small group of four tombs located within an enclosure along a right of way. One of the burials and several of the morphological characteristics of the cemetery denote from the contemporary funerary landscape of the Caen plain. The observations enrich the debate relative to the birth and evolution of the mid-Atlantic domain.

Keywords: cemetery, early La Tène, Caen plain, funerary architecture, medio-atlantic domain

Dans le cadre du projet d'aménagement d'un parc d'activités mené par la société SHEMA sur la commune de Soliers (Calvados), au lieu-dit *Le Bon Sauveur*, une équipe du bureau d'études Éveha est intervenue fin 2010 sur une surface de 1000 m², afin de procéder à la fouille d'une nécropole fréquentée à l'orée du second Âge du fer (Fig. 11.1) (Issenmann *et al.* 2011). Installée le long d'un chemin, cette dernière est dotée d'un enclos fossoyé quadrangulaire partiel, qui enceint un espace funéraire de 105 m² environ, au sein duquel ont été creusées quatre sépultures (Fig. 11.2). Bien que modeste, cet ensemble a livré des éléments permettant d'enrichir la réflexion portée sur les relations entre le domaine atlantique et les régions plus orientales.

Cadres d'étude

Le village de Soliers est localisé dans la Plaine de Caen, en rive droite de l'Orne, qui serpente à environ 7 km à l'ouest. La Plaine de Caen englobe un corridor de 60 km de long, orienté selon un axe nord-sud, et marqué par un paysage d'*openfield* et de terres particulièrement fertiles. Elle est enfermée entre le massif armoricain à l'ouest et les reliefs du pays d'Auge à l'est, et s'ouvre au nord vers la

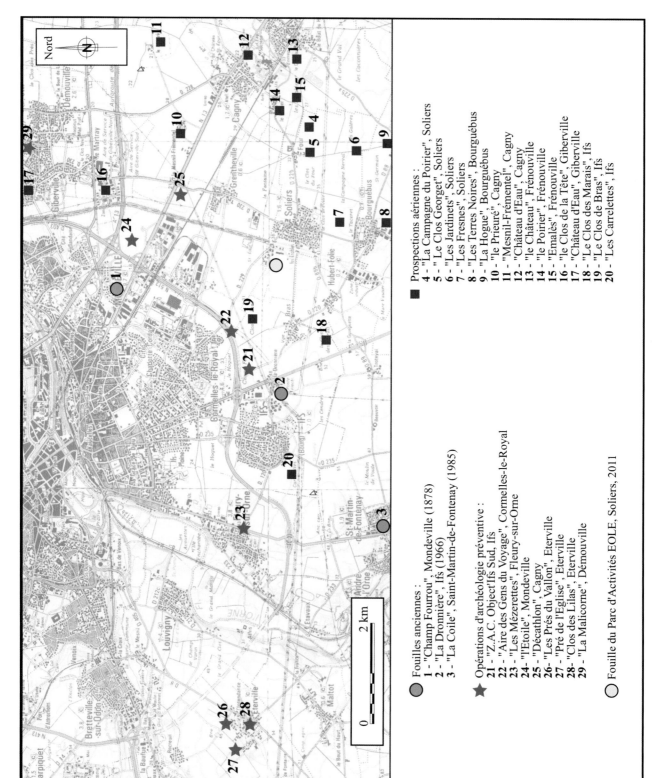

Fig. 11.1. Carte du contexte archéologique funéraire de la transition premier / second Âge du fer autour de Soliers (14) (DAO : R. Issenmann, Éveha).

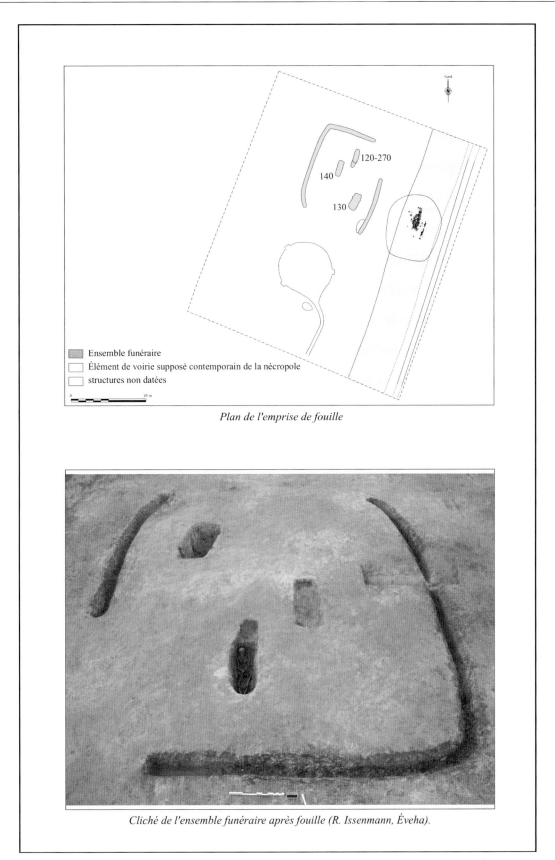

Plan de l'emprise de fouille

Cliché de l'ensemble funéraire après fouille (R. Issenmann, Éveha).

Fig. 11.2. Plan relevé et cliché photographique de l'emprise de fouille (DAO : D. Gazagne, Éveha).

Manche. L'inclinaison de l'intérieur des terres vers la mer est relativement faible sur toute la longueur de la plaine, l'altitude de l'emprise fouillée oscillant autour de 29.50 m NGF. Les argiles rouges holocènes qui recouvrent un substrat calcaire jurassique ont une épaisseur variable qui ne dépasse guère 0.60 m. Elle n'est pas supérieure 0.50 m sur l'emprise de la nécropole et est elle-même dégradée par l'activité agricole, sur une puissance de 0.30 m environ.

D'un point de vue historique, même si elle est aujourd'hui privilégiée, l'archéologie de l'Âge du fer fut particulièrement peu dynamique jusque dans les années 1980. De fait, seules quelques découvertes, remontant pour la plupart à la fin du XIXe siècle, avaient été effectuées avant le lancement de campagnes de prospections aériennes en 1986, 1987 et 1990, ces dernières ayant permis la mise en évidence d'indices de sites interprétés comme des nécropoles protohistoriques.

Durant ces quinze dernières années, le développement périurbain caennais, accompagné du suivi régulier de l'archéologie préventive, a été à l'origine de vastes investigations archéologiques, parfois dépassant la dizaine d'hectares, qui ont révélé une occupation quasi continue du Néolithique au Moyen Âge (Fichet de Clairefontaine et Marcigny 2014). L'extensivité des décapages a permis la reconnaissance, à l'échelle d'un territoire, d'un parcellaire protohistorique cohérent, au sein duquel s'insèrent un large réseau de voirie, un habitat varié, des terres vouées à l'activité agro-pastorale et des ensembles funéraires disséminés. Au sein de ce contexte archéologique riche, le début du second Âge du fer est aujourd'hui plutôt bien représenté (Fig. 11.1).

Ainsi, de grands ensembles funéraires ont été mis au jour ; notons, pour les plus proches de Soliers, les sites d'Ifs *Object'Ifs Sud* (Besnard-Vauterin 2009), de Cormelles-le-Royal *L'Aire des gens du voyage* (Lepaumier 2007), de Fleury-sur-Orne *Les Mézerettes* (Lepaumier 2009), de Mondeville *L'Étoile* (Besnard-Vauterin et Guillon 2010) et de Cagny *Décathlon* (Giraud 2008).

De manière générale, la majorité des ensembles funéraires de la fin du premier et du second Âge du fer découverts en Basse-Normandie sont de taille restreinte, localisés à proximité d'habitats enclos ou le long de voies de circulation. Cette situation paraît toutefois spécifique au Calvados, dans la Plaine de Caen et le Pays d'Auge. Les nécropoles de grande envergure et déconnectées de l'habitat, attestées dans toute la Gaule Belgique jusqu'à la vallée de la Seine font, en l'état actuel de la recherche, totalement défaut en Basse-Normandie. L'exemple ici concerné ne fait pas exception à cette tendance.

L'espace funéraire

L'espace funéraire se compose en effet d'un enclos fossoyé et de quatre sépultures, situés dans la partie nord de l'emprise de fouille (Fig. 11.2). S'ajoute une incinération découverte lors du diagnostic, située à une vingtaine de mètres au sud-est de l'enclos. Intégralement prélevée et fouillée à cette occasion, aucune datation précise n'a pu être apportée. Elle est caractérisée par un vase en céramique qui porte des caractères ubiquistes de l'Âge du bronze au second Âge du fer, et qui était calé par des pierres plates dans une fosse circulaire et contenait les restes d'au moins un individu adulte (Flotté 2010). La pratique de l'inhumation est généralisée à la fin du premier Âge du fer, mais non exclusive : la cohabitation inhumation / incinération est en effet identifiée sur quelques nécropoles régionales, comme à Basly *La Campagne* (San Juan et Le Goff 2003). Si aucune n'a été repérée lors de la fouille, il reste envisageable que d'autres sépultures à incinération aient été présentes hors emprise.

L'enclos funéraire

Ni quadrangulaire ni circulaire, le plan de l'enclos s'apparente plutôt à un « U », qui constitue une forme inédite dans la région. Il présente deux interruptions, l'une sur la totalité du côté sud, l'autre au nord-est, face à la voie. Les deux tronçons sont réguliers, larges d'environ 0.50 à 0.60 m, profonds d'environ 0.30 à 0.40 m sous décapage, et leur profil est en V. Les interruptions ne présentent aucun aménagement excavé. Ils ont livré un mobilier céramique en faible quantité et totalement indigent. Bien qu'il diffère de ceux reconnus pour cette période, cet enclos participe à illustrer l'évolution générale des structures funéraires au cours de l'Âge du fer et à documenter la relative standardisation des monuments à la transition entre le premier et le second Âge du fer, en enclos angulaires (Milcent 2006).

Des sépultures simples

Dans l'espace interne, ont été mises au jour quatre sépultures à inhumation, orientées selon un axe préférentiel (sud-sud-ouest / nord-nord-est) qui correspond globalement à celui de la voie adjacente (Fig. 11.2). La faible densité des tombes n'a permis de déceler aucune organisation spatiale particulière. En raison de l'état médiocre de conservation et de représentation osseuse des défunts, l'étude anthropologique s'est limitée à caractériser l'âge et le sexe des défunts, à l'aide des méthodes classiques utilisées en archéo-anthropologie : étude de l'éruption dentaire (Ubelaker 1978), mesure des os longs (Stloukal et Hanakova 1978) et observation de la fusion des épiphyses (Brothwell 1965 ; Birkner 1980) pour les immatures, diagnose sexuelle sur l'os coxal et diagnose sexuelle probabiliste (Bruzek 2002 ; Murail *et al.* 2005) et enfin observation de la surface sacro-pelvienne iliaque (Schmitt 2005) pour les individus adultes. Une observation générale de l'état sanitaire a été réalisée sans être approfondie.

Table 11.1. Tableau récapitulatif de la morphologie des sépultures.

No de structure	Plan	Profil	Dimensions (m)		
			Longueur	largeur	profondeur
120	oblong	en cuvette irrégulière	2	0.7	0.5
130	rectangulaire	en « U » à fond plat	2.2	1.2	0.97
140	rectangulaire	en « U » à fond plat	2.1	1	0.28
270	oblong	en « U » à fond plat	?	0.7	0.24

La sépulture 140 a été découverte et intégralement fouillée lors du diagnostic (Table 11.1 ; Fig. 11.3). Les ossements sont en mauvais état de conservation, rendant impossible toute documentation sur l'individu ou sur le mode de dépôt. Toutefois, ont été recueillis un anneau en bronze et un anneau en fer de 1.5 cm de diamètre, ayant pu servir de système d'attache d'un vêtement ou de petites amulettes ou pendentifs appartenant au défunt.

La sépulture 120 est composée d'une fosse de forme oblongue, à angles arrondis, sans architecture apparente (Table 11.1 ; Fig. 11.3). Un adulte vraisemblablement masculin y a été inhumé allongé sur le dos, la tête vers le sud, sans mobilier. Cette tombe est recoupée dans sa moitié sud par la sépulture 270, creusée postérieurement dans le comblement supérieur de la tombe 120, donc sans perturber le premier individu. L'individu inhumé dans la tombe 270 est un immature de sexe indéterminé (dont l'âge est estimé autour de dix ans), allongé sur le dos, la tête vers le sud. Les ossements sont mal conservés et la représentation anatomique mauvaise. Aucun mobilier n'a été recueilli. Ces deux inhumations présentent des caractéristiques taphonomiques classiques (fosse simple à colmatage, avec enveloppe souple et pieds resserrés). Elles sont toutefois stratigraphiquement liées, ce qui, dans un espace funéraire où la densité des structures est faible, pourrait être le signe d'un geste particulier, comme le rapprochement volontaire de deux individus d'un même lignage par exemple.

Ces trois sépultures correspondent à des tombes simples, plates, sans dépôt mobilier, et s'intègrent de façon cohérente dans le paysage funéraire de la Plaine de Caen. En revanche la dernière sépulture (st. 130) se distingue par de nombreux aspects de celles sises alentours.

Une sépulture aménagée (st. 130)

Tout d'abord, ses dimensions se démarquent de façon significative : longue de 2.20 m et large de 1 à 1.20 m en surface de décapage, elle est creusée sur une profondeur de 0.97 m où ses mesures sont légèrement moins importantes (longueur : 2 m – largeur : 0.78 m) (Fig. 11.4). De forme sub-rectangulaire, ses parois sont quasi-verticales et son fond plat. Par ailleurs, elle a livré les traces d'un aménagement

architectural sur quatre poteaux plantés au fond de la fosse (deux sur chaque longueur). Les parois verticales ont été également surcreusées sur toute la profondeur afin d'y caler les poteaux. Ces observations permettent d'affirmer que la tombe était munie d'une superstructure signalisant la sépulture en surface, et éventuellement surmontée d'un tertre. Ce type de traces a déjà été observé sur des nécropoles dès le début de l'Âge du fer, les vestiges étant couramment interprétés comme des trous de poteau ayant servi à ancrer un monument de type coffrage ou abri. C'est le cas pour trois tombes situées dans le Bassin parisien, comme celle du Hallstatt ancien de Champlay *Les Carpes* (Yonne), documentée par A. Merlange, qui en propose même une restitution (Merlange 1979) (Fig. 11.5 : 1). Plus récemment découverte, à Jaulnes *Le Bas des Hauts Champs* (Seine-et-Marne), la tombe d'un homme accompagnée d'une épée longue en fer, attribuée au Hallstatt C, présente les traces d'un aménagement similaire (Peake et Delattre 2010) (Fig. 11.5 : 2). Enfin, à Rosières-près-Troyes *Zone Industrielle* (10), une sépulture datée de la transition entre le Hallstatt D3 et La Tène a été mise au jour en 2006 au centre d'un enclos circulaire de 25 m de diamètre (Grisard *et al.* 2012). Un premier individu masculin y était inhumé, vraisemblablement dans un contenant en bois massif de type coffrage reposant sur quatre poteaux reliés par un système d'entretoises. La présence d'un tertre est fortement suspectée, rendant la tombe localisable, puisqu'un deuxième individu a été inhumé dans la même sépulture plus tardivement (Fig. 11.5 : 3). Au sein du domaine Aisne-Marne, quelques fosses sépulcrales dotées de tels aménagements sont répertoriées ; ceux-ci sont essentiellement rencontrés au sein de tombes ayant accueilli un char, comme à Sémide (Ardennes) (Lambot et Verger 1995), donc en lien avec un défunt au statut social privilégié (Baray 2003), même si une superstructure en bois n'est pas forcément considérée comme un marqueur social particulier (Demoule 1999). Certaines tombes de la nécropole Aisne-Marne de Pernant (Aisne) comportaient en effet des trous de poteau qui pourraient n'avoir servi qu'à signaler la tombe en surface, « … surtout si l'on songe au rôle des poteaux de bois sur lesquels était exécutée, à des phases plus récentes, une partie de la sculpture religieuse celtique – les « trunci » dont parlent Lucain et Valerius Flaccus » (Demoule 1999, 183).

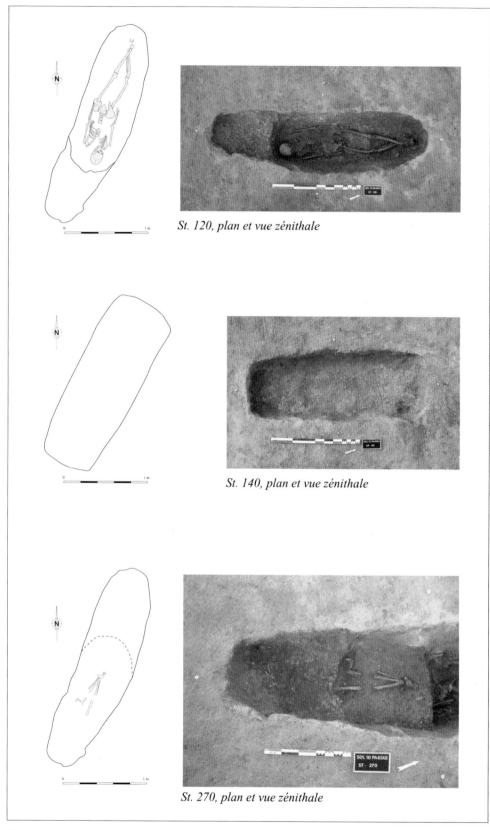

St. 120, plan et vue zénithale

St. 140, plan et vue zénithale

St. 270, plan et vue zénithale

Fig. 11.3. Relevé et cliché photographique des trois tombes simples de la nécropole (DAO : C. Tranchant, Éveha).

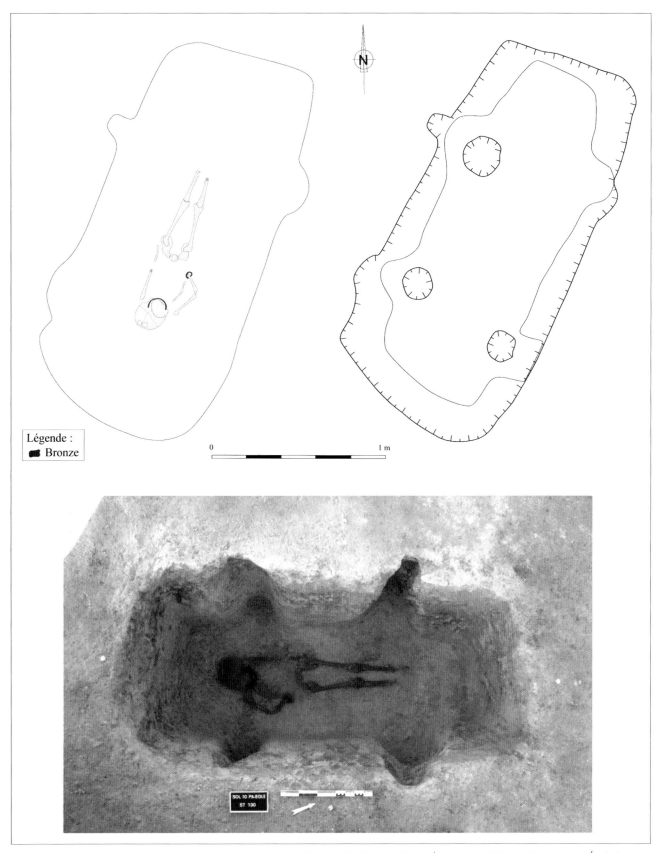

Légende :
🔲 Bronze

0   1 m

Fig. 11.4. Relevé et cliché photographique de la tombe 130 (DAO : C. Tranchant, Éveha et cliché : A. Corrochano, Éveha).

Était inhumé, dans cette sépulture 130, un immature en décubitus avec la tête au sud. Les ossements étaient assez mal conservés et la représentation anatomique mauvaise. Son sexe n'a pu être déterminé, et son âge est estimé dans la tranche 10–14 ans. Il est inhumé dans une enveloppe souple ou un vêtement, et doté d'éléments de parure en position de port.

Ces derniers se composent d'un torque (Fig. 11.6 : 1) et d'un bracelet en alliages cuivreux (Fig. 11.6 : 2).

Le torque est muni d'un jonc simple lisse, de section circulaire. Son système de fermeture se caractérise par l'ajout d'un rivet ou d'une goupille pour fixer les deux extrémités perforées et terminées en biseau. Ce genre de dispositif apparaît sur certains torques de l'étape moyenne du premier Âge du fer (Ha D1-2 récent), notamment en France centrale (Milcent 2004). Il est également présent sur quelques pièces découvertes anciennement dans la région, tel à Soumont-Saint-Quentin (Calvados) et Nonant-le-Pin (Orne) (Vernay 1993, fig. 10, 1 ; fig. 11, 4). Les contextes de ces éléments ne sont pas sûrs, les assemblages trouvés en particulier à Nonant appartiennent au premier et au début du second Âge du fer (*ibid.*). En Bourgogne, un torque de ce type provient également de la sépulture 57, tumulus de Clair-Bois à Bressey-sur-Tille (Côte d'Or) (Chaume 2001, pl. 134) ; il est attribué au tout début de LTA par la stratigraphie (Chaume 2001).

Le bracelet est muni d'un jonc réalisé à partir d'un ruban de tôle, décoré de cercles oculés estampés qui s'organisent selon une alternance 1/2/1/2... En outre, son système de fermeture repose sur la présence d'une extrémité crochetée et d'une perforation circulaire destinée à accueillir la première. La morphologie très spécifique de ce bracelet n'a pas été évidente à corréler. Muni d'un système de fermeture quasi-analogue, il rappelle quelques pièces découvertes en Suisse et en Alsace, dans des ensembles datés du Ha D1 (Schaeffer 1930, fig. 10). Il peut toutefois être rapproché d'une pièce découverte également dans le tumulus de *Clair-Bois* à Bressey-sur-Tille (Chaume 2001, pl. 143, no. 1). Dans cet ensemble daté de LTA2, le bracelet, quasi identique dans sa forme, se distingue par l'application d'un décor différent « en dent de loup » (Chaume 2001). L'ornementation de l'exemplaire de Soliers semble en effet relativement originale. Elle rappelle le motif estampé, dit *occhi di dado* composé de cinq cercles occulés que l'on retrouve sur certaines fibules durant la période hallsttattienne (Ha D2) puis sur les torques de LTA (Charpy et Roualet 1991). Plusieurs pièces découvertes à Chouilly-Les Jogasses dans la Marne disposent de ce genre de décor (Hatt et Roualet 1976, no. 832–928), généralement interprété comme provenant du versant sud des Alpes (Adam 1996, 37). Néanmoins, certains bracelets découverts notamment à Mondeville (Calvados) semblent disposer également du motif simple du cercle occulé, qui

dans ce cas est encadré d'incisions transversales et placé juste sur les extrémités de ces bracelets ouverts (Vernay 1993, fig. 7, 4-5). Quelques bracelets provenant de la nécropole de Bucy-le-Long (Aisne) disposent aussi de ce motif associé à des chevrons ou des lignes. Dans ce dernier cas, il s'agit de pièces massives plutôt attribuées à LT A2 (Desenne *et al.* 2009, fig. 230). Découverte plus récemment, dans la nécropole de Blainville-sur-Orne (Calvados), une tombe datée du Ha D1-D2 récent semble avoir livré un bracelet en tôle, orné lui aussi d'ocelles et d'un décor au trémolo (Lepaumier 2011). Complété du bracelet de Bressey-sur-Tille (*cf. infra*), il s'agit des deux seules pièces, véritablement comparables à l'exemplaire découvert à Soliers.

Que ce soit pour le torque ou le bracelet, les comparaisons trouvées posent donc problème d'un point de vue chronologique car elles convergent vers deux possibilités qu'il s'avère difficile de trancher : une datation au Ha D1-D2 récent ou au début de LTA1. Par ailleurs, les datations du radiocarbone effectuées sur les ossements ne permettent pas d'affiner l'attribution chronologique (voir Annexe 11.1).

La sépulture 130 se distingue donc par ses dimensions, sa profondeur et son architecture très différentes des autres tombes ; de même, le mobilier d'accompagnement évoque fortement les productions caractéristiques de la Champagne et de la Bourgogne du nord. La présence simultanée de ces éléments 'dissonants' dans un contexte médio-atlantique pose à nouveau la question des relations à longue distance et circulations d'individus.

L'élément de voirie

Le diagnostic puis la fouille ont permis de mettre en évidence une voie orientée nord-sud et son fossé bordier à l'est (Fig. 11.2). La voie, d'une largeur de 5.20 m en moyenne, prend l'aspect d'un chemin creux, rechargé de blocs calcaires aux endroits instables, permettant une bande de roulement assez large pour faire passer deux attelages circulant en sens inverse. Des ornières ont d'ailleurs été mises au jour sur certaines portions. Le chemin et le fossé qui le borde n'ont pas livré de mobilier, mais leur cohérence spatiale avec l'enclos funéraire laisse penser à une contemporanéité des deux ensembles ; le cas échéant, l'interruption nord-orientale de l'enclos pourrait ainsi constituer un accès à la nécropole par le biais de la voie.

La nécropole de Soliers et la question du complexe médio-atlantique

La fouille de l'emprise prescrite à Soliers a donc permis la découverte d'un ensemble funéraire protohistorique modeste, intégré à un parcellaire vraisemblablement étendu, et dont la fréquentation semble remonter à la fin du premier Âge du fer ou à la transition avec le second. Si elle s'intègre de façon satisfaisante dans le paysage funéraire de la Plaine de Caen, l'un des apports les plus intéressants de la nécropole est qu'elle présente certaines similitudes avec des ensembles des régions plus orientales. En effet, outre le caractère angulaire – et non circulaire – de l'enclos, la tombe 130 est dotée d'une architecture en matériau périssable, phénomène rencontré plus régulièrement à l'est du Bassin Parisien, similitudes perçues aussi dans la typologie du torque et du bracelet, dont les comparaisons principales sont issues de Champagne et de Bourgogne du nord, ce que réaffirme cet assemblage (torque et bracelet porté à la main droite), qui constitue la majorité des cas découverts dans le Bassin Parisien en tout cas à LTA1 (Baray 2003, tab. lii, 287).

Si des liens avec les populations de l'est du Bassin Parisien ont été reconnus dans le cadre de découvertes récentes (San Juan et Le Goff 2003 ; Lepaumier et Delrieu 2004), l'interprétation de ce phénomène peut être menée selon deux hypothèses, l'une diffusionniste, et l'autre endogène.

L'hypothèse diffusionniste, en place depuis les années la fin du XIXe siècle, considère que les traits caractéristiques les plus anciens de la « culture matérielle de La Tène » sont originaires des régions situées entre la Champagne et la Bohême, matérialisant ainsi un berceau à partir duquel les modèles laténiens se seraient diffusés dans toute l'Europe celtique, par des migrations guerrières notamment (Kruta 2000). Selon ce scénario, la Basse-Normandie et les régions du nord-ouest de la Gaule, entre autres, auraient été celtisées de façon tardive, autour du IVe siècle avant notre ère. À partir de là, il serait aisé de reconnaitre dans la tombe 130, voire dans l'aspect de l'enclos funéraire, les influences exercées par le domaine Aisne-Marne (Demoule 1999 ; Baray 2003) jusque dans la Plaine de Caen.

Si l'attribution chronologique de l'ensemble funéraire solarien n'est pas assurée (liée au milieu du VIe siècle ou au début Ve siècle avant notre ère), cela tendrait de toute façon à vieillir l'appartenance à la sphère laténienne de cette partie de la Gaule. La question de la contemporanéité, voire de l'origine de l'apparition des caractéristiques laténiennes entre les deux régions se pose alors à nouveau.

Jusqu'à ces dernières années, les travaux abordant ces problématiques se sont surtout attelés à mettre en évidence les similitudes culturelles existant entre la culture Aisne-Marne et le domaine nord-alpin, sans envisager réellement les disparités, et surtout sans s'intéresser à ce qui était observé dans le nord-ouest de la Gaule et les îles Britanniques. L'essor des données dans ces dernières régions, dues à l'intensification de l'activité archéologique, permet aujourd'hui de pallier ces écueils et d'envisager l'histoire autrement.

L' hypothèse d' un domaine médio-atlantique ...

Définie pour la première fois en 2006 par Pierre-Yves Milcent lors de la table ronde de Bologne-Monterenzio (Italie), cette entité culturelle englobe les îles Britanniques, « une large portion de la Gaule septentrionale et occidentale, culture Aisne-Marne comprise », et est donc distribuée en résumé à l'ouest d'une ligne reliant la basse Garonne et les bouches du Rhin (Milcent 2006, 95). Sa définition est basée essentiellement sur l'observation de la répartition de types communs (notamment la diffusion des coupes à bord festonné et des vases carénés à col tronconique) dont certains préfigurent les attributs laténiens, au niveau des fibules et sur d'autres traits : rareté des échanges avec le monde méditerranéen, faible hiérarchisation de l'habitat (absence d'agglomération proto-urbaine) ou de certaines pratiques funéraires (enclos funéraires quadrangulaires). Concernant ce dernier point, l'accent est mis sur la prééminence des petits groupements familiaux ou claniques, faiblement hiérarchisés et n'étant associés à un tumulus que très exceptionnellement. Le plus important est que ces caractères n'apparaissent pas à la transition premier/second Âge du fer, mais semblent au contraire constituer l'héritage culturel d'un « premier Âge du fer médio-atlantique », donc plutôt le résultat d'une évolution lente endogène amorcée dès l'Âge du bronze.

... vecteur des traits laténiens

S'ajoutant aux travaux récents ayant également reconnu des liens avec les populations de l'est du Bassin parisien (San Juan et Le Goff 2003 ; Lepaumier et Delrieu 2004), les découvertes effectuées à Soliers apportent des arguments à l'idée que le domaine Aisne-Marne ne peut plus être considéré comme exclusivement tourné vers le domaine nord-alpin, mais plutôt inclus dans un vaste complexe culturel plus nord-occidental, sans que cela ne s'oppose bien entendu à des échanges avec le domaine nord-alpin. L'hypothèse décrivant la lente laténisation ou celtisation de la plaine de Caen à partir d'un pôle aisne-marnien reste, en cela, délicate à retenir.

Mais plus encore, concernant le domaine funéraire, il apparaît que certains caractères laténiens sont attestés plus précocement dans les régions nord-occidentales. C'est le cas pour la généralisation des petites nécropoles familiales à enclos quadrilatéraux et inhumations individuelles, exemptes de monument de type tumulus (Milcent 2006, 98). Ce phénomène est attesté en Basse-Normandie et dans le nord de la France dès le VIIe siècle, à Éterville « Le Clos des Lilas » (Jahier 2009) ou à Basly « La Campagne » (San juan et Le Goff 2003) ou encore à Etaples. Les aménagements ancrés traduisant la présence d'un coffrage, d'un édicule ou d'une stèle apparaissent également à cette

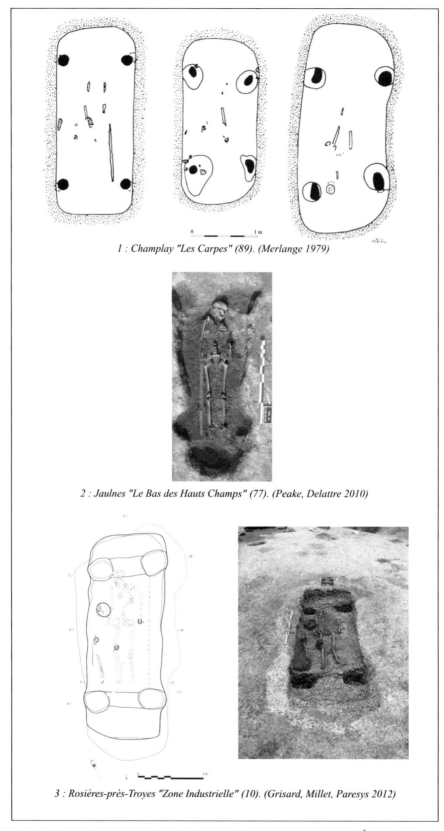

1 : Champlay "Les Carpes" (89). (Merlange 1979)

2 : Jaulnes "Le Bas des Hauts Champs" (77). (Peake, Delattre 2010)

3 : Rosières-près-Troyes "Zone Industrielle" (10). (Grisard, Millet, Paresys 2012)

Fig. 11.5. Exemples comparatifs de tombes à architecture sur poteaux de l'Âge du fer (DAO et clichés : C. Tranchant, Éveha).

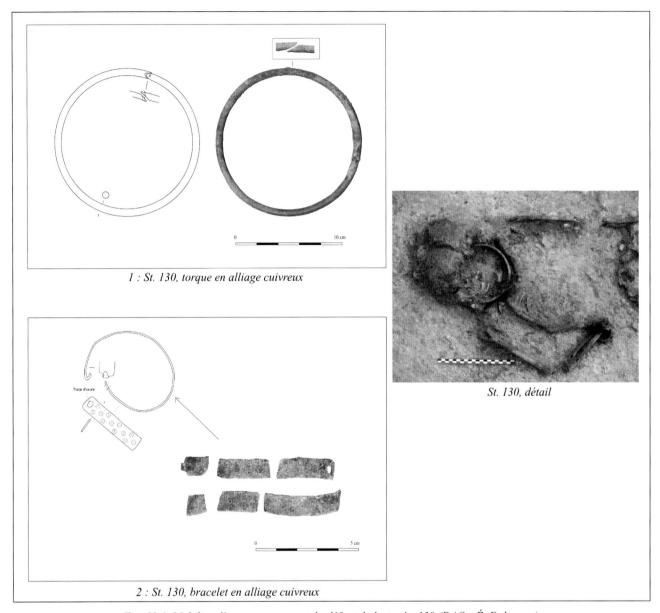

1 : St. 130, torque en alliage cuivreux

St. 130, détail

2 : St. 130, bracelet en alliage cuivreux

Fig. 11.6. Mobilier d'accompagnement du défunt de la tombe 130 (DAO : É. Dubreucq).

époque. De telles pratiques funéraires sont le témoin d'une évolution endogène et vont s'étendre dans le reste du domaine médio-atlantique à la fin du premier Âge du fer, et notamment dans les nécropoles aisne-marniennes (Milcent 2006, 99).

À la lumière de ces observations, la nécropole de Soliers, si modeste soit-elle, offre des arguments en faveur de l'existence d'un domaine culturel médio-atlantique, auquel la Champagne est rattachée, et où la diffusion des idées ne peut plus être décrite comme un flux de l'Est vers l'Ouest. Ce domaine culturel apparaît au contraire vecteur d'idées et participe activement au réseau multipolaire de la mise en place des caractères qui définiront les cultures laténiennes à partir du Ve siècle avant notre ère.

Bibliographie

Adam, A.-M. (1996) *Le fibule di tipo celtico nel Trentino*, Patrimonio storico artistico del Trentino 19. Trento, Provincia autonoma di Trento, Ufficio Beni Archeologici.

Baray, L. (2003) *Pratiques funéraires et sociétés de l'âge du Fer dans le Bassin Parisien (fin VIIe-troisième quart du IIe avant J.-C.)*, Supplément *Gallia* 56. Paris, C. N. R. S. Éditions.

Besnard-Vauterin, C.-C. (2009) Ifs, Object'Ifs Sud. Dans *Bilan Scientifique de la région Basse-Normandie 2009*, 59–60. Caen, Direction Régionale des Affaires Culturelles.

Besnard-Vauterin, C.-C. et Guillon, M. (2010) L'ensemble funéraire de la fin du premier au début du second âge du Fer de Mondeville « L'Étoile » (Calvados). In P. Barral, B. Dedet, F. Delrieu, P. Giraud, I. Le Goff, S. Marion et A. Villard-le-Tiec (dir.) *Gestes funéraires en Gaule au second âge du Fer.*

Actes du XXXIIIe colloque international de l'AFEAF, Caen, 20–24 mai 2009, Besançon, 1, 301–313. Presses Universitaires de Franche-Comté, Presses Universitaires de Franche-Comté.

Birkner, R. (1980) *L'image radiologique typique du squelette.* Paris, Maloine.

Brothwell, D. R. (1965) *Digging up Bones. The Excavation, Treatment and Study of Human Skeletal Remains.* London, British Museum Natural History.

Bruzek, J. (2002) A method for visual determination of sex using the human hip bone. *American Journal of Physical Anthropology* 117, 157–168.

Charpy, J.-J. et Roualet, P. (1991) *Les celtes en Champagne. Cinq siècles d'Histoire.* Epernay, Musée d'Epernay.

Chaume, B. (2001) *Vix et son territoire à l'Âge du Fer. Fouilles du mont Lassois et environnement du site princier.* Montagnac, éditions Monique Mergoil.

Collis, J. (2003) *The Celts. Origins, Myths & Inventions.* Stroud, Tempus.

Demoule, J.-P. (1999) Pratiques funéraires et sociétés. Amiens, *Revue Archéologique de Picardie* 15.

Desenne, S., Pommepuy, C. et Demoule, J.-P. (2009) Bucy-le-Long (Aisne) : une nécropole de La Tène ancienne (Ve–IVe siècles avant notre ère). Senlis, *Revue Archéologique de Picardie* Supplément 26.

Fichet de Clairfontaine, F. et Marcigny, C. (2014) 2 000 hectares aux portes de Caen, Comment se renouvelle l'histoire d'un territoire des premiers hommes à l'époque antique. In *L'archéologie préventive : une démarche responsable, actes des rencontres autour de l'archéologie préventive (21–22 novembre 2012)*, 63–76. Paris, éd. Ministère de la Culture et de la Communication, Direction générale des patrimoines – sous-direction de l'archéologie.

Flotté, D. (2010) Soliers, Calvados, Parc d'activités EOLE, tranche B. Parcelles Z8 et 9. Rapport final d'opération, diagnostic archéologique. Caen, Inrap Grand-Ouest, SRA Basse-Normandie.

Grisard, J., Millet, E. et Paresys, C. (2012) Rosières-près-Troyes « Zone Industrielle » (Aube) : une nécropole du premier âge du Fer en haute vallée de la Seine et son contexte sud-champenois. *Bulletin de la Société Archéologique Champenoise* 105 (4), 5–55.

Giraud, P. (2008) Cagny, Décathlon. Dans *Bilan Scientifique de la région Basse-Normandie 2008*, 33–35. Caen, Direction Régionale des Affaires Culturelles.

Hatt, J.-J. et Roualet, P. (1976) Le cimetière des Jogasses en Champagne et les origines de la civilisation de La Tène. *Revue Archéologique de l'Est et du Centre-est* 27, 421–428.

Issenmann, R., Tranchant, C. (dir.), Corrochano, A., Dubreucq, E. et Talluault, O. (2011) Parc d'activités EOLE, SOLIERS (14). Rapport Final d'Opération de fouille. Eveha Caen, Service régional de l'Archéologie de Basse-Normandie.

Jahier, I. (2009) Nécropole d'Éterville « Le Clos des Lilas » (Calvados). Dans F. Delrieu (dir.) *Les gaulois et la mort en Normandie. Les pratiques funéraires à l'âge du Fer (VIIe–Ie siècles avant J.-C.)* 17. OREP éditions, OREP éditions.

Kruta, V. (2000) *Les Celtes. Histoire et dictionnaire, des origines à la romanisation et au christianisme.* Paris, Laffont, collection « Bouquins ».

Lambot, B. et Verger, S. (1995) Une tombe à char de La Tène ancienne à Semide (Ardennes). Reims, *Mémoires de la Société Archéologique Champenoise*, supplément au bulletin 1.

Lepaumier, H. (2007) Cormelles-le-Royal, L'Aire des Gens du Voyage. *Bilan Scientifique de la région Basse-Normandie 2007.* Caen, Direction Régionale des Affaires Culturelles.

Lepaumier, H. (2009) Fleury-sur-Orne, Les Mézerettes. *Bilan Scientifique de la région Basse-Normandie 2009*, Caen, Direction Régionale des Affaires Culturelles.

Lepaumier, H. (2011) « Terre d'Avenir » à Blainville-sur-Orne (Calvados). Etablissement enclos et nécropole de premier âge du Fer en Basse-Normandie. *Bulletin de l'Association Française pour l'Étude de l'Âge du Fer* 29, 39–41.

Lepaumier, H. et Delrieu, F. (2004) *L'âge du Fer en Basse-Normandie (-800 à -52 av.J.-C.).* Bilan de la recherche 1984–2004, In Bilan de la recherche archéologique en Basse-Normandie, 1984–2010 - Vol.1: du Paléolithique à la fin de l'âge du Fer, Editions du Ministère de la Culture et de la Communication, pp. 143–168

Merlange, A. (1979) Sépultures de La Tène dans la vallée de l'Yonne (sauvetages en sablières entre Joigny et Appoigny). In *Les Sénons avant la conquête, à la lumière des dernières découvertes, 6–13.* Sens, Société Archéologique de Sens.

Milcent, P.-Y. (2006) Premier âge du Fer médio-atlantique et genèse multipolaire des cultures matérielles laténiennes. In D. Vitali (dir.) *Celtes et Gaulois, l'archéologie face à l'Histoire, 2 : la préhistoire des Celtes, Actes de la table ronde de Bologne-Monterenzio (28–29 mai 2005)*, 81–105, Bibracte, 12(2). Glux-en-Glenne, Bibracte, Centre archéologique européen.

Milcent, P.-Y. (2004) *Le premier âge du Fer en France centrale.* Paris, Société Préhistorique Française Supplément 34.

Murail, P., Bruzek, J., Houët, F. et Cunha, E. (2005) DSP: a tool for probabilistic sex diagnosis using worldwide variability in hipbone measurements. *Bulletins et Mémoires de la Société d'Anthropologie de Paris* n.s. 3–4 (17), 167–176.

Peake, R. et Delattre, V. (2010) Monumentalité de la Mort : la nécropole diachronique de Jaulnes « Le Bas des Hauts Champs » (Seine-et-Marne). *Bulletin de l'APRAB* 7, 19–22.

San Juan, G. et Le Goff, I. (2003) La nécropole du VIe siècle avant J.-C. de la « Campagne » à Basly (Calvados). In B. Mandy et A. de Saulce (dir.) *Les marges de l'Armorique à l'Age du Fer. Archéologie et Histoire : culture matérielle et sources écrites 59, actes du XXIIIe colloque de l'AFEAF.* Rennes, *Revue Archéologique de l'Ouest* Supplément 10.

Schmitt, A. (2005) Une nouvelle méthode pour estimer l'âge au décès des adultes à partir de la surface sacro-pelvienne iliaque, *Bulletins et Mémoires de la Société d'Anthropologie de Paris* 17 [En ligne] Fascicule 1–2, disponible sur : http://bmsap.revues.org/document943.html (consulté le 5 juillet 2011).

Schaeffer, F. A. (1930) *Les tertres funéraires préhistoriques dans la forêt de Haguenau. Les tumulus de l'Age du Fer.* Bruxelles, Editions Culture et Civilisation.

Stloukal, M. et Hanakova, H. (1978) Die länge der Langsknochen altslawischer Bevölkerungen unter besonderer Berücksichtigung von Wachstumsfragen. *Homo* 29, 53–69.

Ubelaker, D. H. (1978) *Human Skeletal Remains. Excavation, Analysis, Interpretation.* Washington DC, Taraxacum.

Vernay, A. (1993) Les nécropoles de l'âge du Fer en Basse-Normandie. Bilan de trois siècles de découvertes. Dans D. Cliquet et M. Remy-Watte (dir.) *Les celtes en Normandie. Les rites funéraires en Gaule (IIIe–Ier siècle avant J.-C.), 95, Actes du 14e colloque de l'AFEAF. Evreux-mai 1990.* Rennes, *Revue Archéologique de l'Ouest Supplément 6.*

Annexe 11.1 : Résultat des analyses au radiocarbone

Tomasz Goslar (Poznan Radiocarbon Laboratory)

Nom de l'échantillon	N° Lab.	Âge ^{14}C (BP)	Remarques	Date calibrée BC à 68.2 % de probabilité	Date calibrée BC à 95.4 % de probabilité
Soliers ST 140 (diag.: Tr.4–st. 32)	Poz-40956	2420±30	0.7%N 2.7%C	537 (68.2%) 408	748 (15.6%) 687 666 (4.0%) 644 590 (1.0%) 579 556 (74.9%) 401
Soliers ST 120	Poz-40958	2510±35	0.5%N 1.4%C	770 (12.0%) 744 689 (11.6%) 664 647 (44.6%) 551	791 (95.4%) 519
Soliers ST 130	Poz-40959	2490±35	3.4%N 9.3%C	763 (13.4%) 727 693 (4.3%) 681 673 (50.5%) 542	780 (91.3%) 503 493 (0.4%) 488 462 (1.2%) 449 441 (2.5%) 417
Soliers ST 270	Poz-40960	2445±35	0.9%N 3.1%C	736 (17.7%) 690 663 (5.0%) 649 547 (25.6%) 479 471 (19.9%) 414	753 (22.9%) 685 668 (12.4%) 611 597 (60.1%) 408
Soliers Tr. 5 - st. 34	Poz-0	>0	<0.1%N 0.1%C not suitable		

Les données sont des intervalles en âge calendaire, où l'âge réel des échantillons est compris dans des probabilités de 68 % et de 95 %. La calibration a été effectuée avec le logiciel OxCal v4.1.5 Bronk Ramsey (2010) ; r:5 Données atmospheric de Reimer et al. (2009).

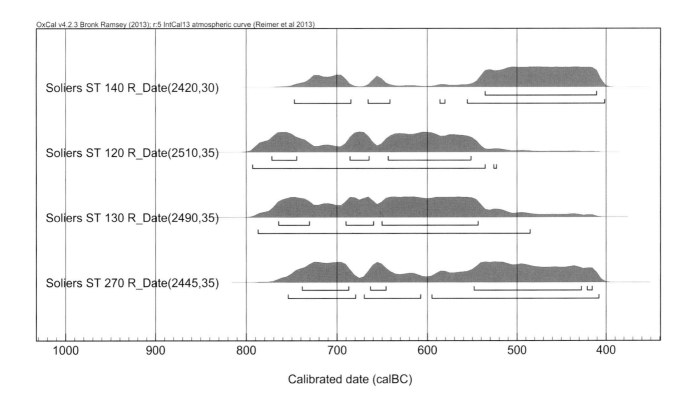

12

Open Bronze Age settlement forms in the north of France: state of knowledge and study strategies

Emmanuelle Leroy-Langelin, Yann Lorin, Armelle Masse,
Angélique Sergent and Marc Talon

Abstract

Owing to the accumulation of data relating to domestic Bronze Age implantations in the Nord/Pas-de-Calais region over the past 30 years, it is now possible to attempt to draw up an overview. The very heterogeneous corpus of open-air settlement sites includes occupations dating mainly from the Middle and Late Bronze Age, identified on the basis of several, or at times more than a hundred, structures. It is not easy to understand these sites due to the difficult identification of habitat buildings. Several circular houses have been identified, marking affiliation to the Channel–North Sea group, but these discoveries are less frequent than in Normandy and across the Channel. Most of the sites in our region are characterised by the absence of traces of structures, probably due to an alternative architectural choice to posts. This lacuna is offset by a large number of pits with varied dimensions and functions. The study of their form, infilling and spatial organisation provides a picture of settlement organisation between the middle of the 2nd and the beginning of the 1st millennia BC in the northwest of France.

Keywords: settlement, buildings, architecture, pits

Résumé

L'accumulation des données depuis une trentaine d'années sur les installations domestiques de l'Âge du bronze dans la région Nord/Pas-de-Calais permet de tenter une synthèse. Le corpus des sites d'habitat ouvert, très hétérogène, réunit des occupations datant essentiellement du Bronze moyen et final, identifiés à partir de quelques structures jusqu'à parfois plus d'une centaine. La compréhension de ces sites n'est pas aisée, en cause la difficile reconnaissance de bâtiments d'habitation. Si quelques maisons circulaires sont attestées, marqueurs d'appartenance au groupe Manche-Mer du Nord, ces découvertes sont moins nombreuses qu'en Normandie et outre-Manche. La plupart des sites de notre région se caractérisent par l'absence de traces de constructions, un choix architectural autre que les poteaux porteurs en est probablement la raison. Cette lacune est compensée par un nombre important de fosses aux dimensions et fonctions variées. Les études de leur forme, de leur remplissage, de leur organisation spatiale permettent actuellement de proposer une vision de l'organisation d'un habitat entre le milieu du IIe et le début du Ier millénaire avant J. C. dans le nord-ouest de la France.

Mots-clés : habitat, bâtiments, architecture, fosses

Introduction

Rescue archaeology has developed extensively over the past 30 years due to territorial developments in the Nord/Pas-de-Calais and Picardy regions. As far as the Bronze Age is concerned, discoveries made during sandpit monitoring in the 1980s primarily provide evidence from the funerary domain. Since 1988, the main regional linear lines, in particular diverse motorway (A16, A26), railway (TGV Nord) or energy network developments (gas pipelines), have contributed to a profound renewal of our knowledge of this period (Buchez 2011).

An overview of the situation for this flourishing decade was drawn up by Y. Desfossés (1995; 2000). This period marks a decisive step in regional research, by documenting the first recorded habitats and establishing 'trans-Channel' connections.

A growth period of the sectors affected by territorial development (industrial or activity zones, housing developments …) followed. This phase of more systematic requirements relating to vast surfaces led to discoveries enabling us to better assess open settlements.

In Picardy, this progression led to considerations of the coastal Channel and North Sea regions, territories considered to be a 'privileged zone of exchange' (Clark 2004; Needham 2009; Marcigny and Talon 2009; Bourgeois and Talon 2009).

New discoveries and the renewal of the first syntheses enabled us to establish an inventory of the record in 2012, in order to characterise site characteristics in a chronological way. It turned out to be necessary to focus on the structures within the habitat, as they often yield the most informative information. The morphology and organisation (hollows, building plans) of these structures contribute to the interpretation of the site, in the same way as the objects issued from infillings which sometimes act as chronological markers or provide information on the function of the pit.

Chronological description

State of knowledge in 2012 (Fig. 12.1)

During the Early Bronze Age (2100–1600 BC) (Table 12.1), evidence of occupation in the north of France is extremely rare. Only four sites consisting of a single pit have been identified. The latter appear to be related to tree-throws acting as traps for objects.

During the Middle Bronze Age and the early stages of the Late Bronze Age (1600–1150 BC) (Table 12.2), the number of remains increases. In this way 15 sites can be listed. These are mostly pits accidentally discovered during the excavations of other, often more recent periods. Nonetheless, over the past ten years, wider occupations have begun to be identified during surveys and subsequently excavated.

During the middle stage of the Late Bronze Age and the initial phase of the final stage (1150-800 before our era), discoveries remain limited with just 12 represented sites (Table 12.3).

During the Late Bronze Age IIIb, the proportion increases and 23 sites are referenced. This figure expands to 50 if we add sites dating from the transition between the Bronze Age and the first Iron Age (Table 12.4).

The better identification of the more recent occupations is undoubtedly linked to a more intensive recording of hollow structures and more firmly implanted remains in the soil.

Main chronological characteristics of the sites in the regional setting

The rare evidence of Early and Middle Bronze Age settlement sites in the region probably stems from a bias in the identification of remains. Although the world of the dead is well represented during this period by monuments in the Channel-North Sea entity (N. Buchez *et al.* this volume), the world of the living is more difficult to characterise (limited extension, nomadic or ephemeral settlement, few excavation requirements on valley sides and floors …) and necessitates diversified reflection. In addition, the almost inexistent bronze objects and poorly defined pottery render dating difficult. The Early Bronze Age typo-chronology is still very incomplete, and in some cases, only radiocarbon dating can provide information.

The Late Bronze Age is better documented although there are disparities between the different phases, and in particular a very clear over-representation of the Late Bronze Age IIIb. This observation, established for the northern half of France, is sometimes explained by a phase of increase in human demography. The increase in the discovery of sites in the region also seems to be linked to the readability of occupations and can probably be explained by taphonomic factors.

The structures

Houses

The first traces of a Bronze Age building appear during the Middle Bronze Age II and represent a circular structure. In 2012, about ten constructions were recorded (Fig. 12.2). Chronological attribution is generally based on the presence of Deverel-Rimbury tradition material discovered in nearby pits. The pit at Rebecques (Pas-de-Calais: Lorin 2007) is currently linked to this period but it was discovered in a survey context, with no associated objects, and its age is thus uncertain. It is associated with a partial ditch, like some examples from Normandy, such as Malleville-sur-le-Bec (Eure: Mare 2005) and Cahagnes (Calvados: Jahier 2005), or structures without entrance porches at Tatihou (Manche: Marcigny and Ghesquière 2003). However, we

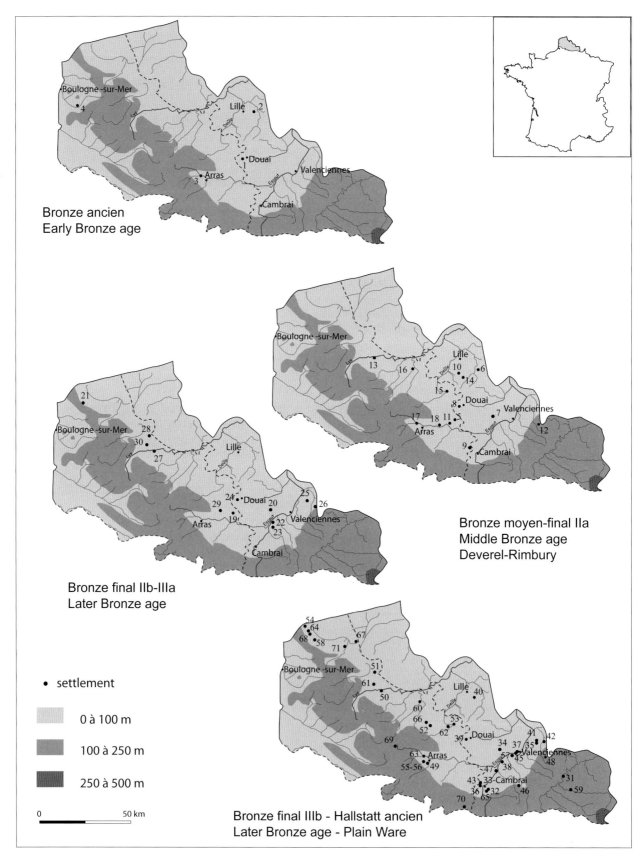

Fig. 12.1. Geographic location of the sites in Nord/Pas-de-Calais by chronological phase.

Table 12.1. Early Bronze Age regional sites.

No.	Dept	Commune	Locality	Discovery	Project director	Organisation	Period	No. of structures
1	59	Lauwin-Planque	ZAC	excavation	E. Leroy-Langelin	Cad-dap	BA	1
2	59	Villeneuve d'Ascq	La Haute Borne	excavation	C. Quérel	Inrap	BA	1
3	62	Maroeuil	rue Curie	excavation	Y. Lorin	Inrap	BA	1
4	62	Samer	route de Desvres	survey	B. Leriche	Inrap	BA	1

Table 12.2. Regional sites from the Middle Bronze Age and the early stage of the Late Bronze Age (BF I–IIa).

No.	Dept	Commune	Locality	Discovery	Project director	Organisation	Period	No. of structures
5	59	Brebières	Zac des Béliers	excavation	Gr. Huvelle	Cad-dap	BM I, BF I–IIa	12
6	59	Cysoing	Le Clos de l'Abbaye	excavation	D. Censier	Cad-dap	BM II–BF I	2
7	59	Erre-Escaudain	RN 455	excavation	E. Leroy Langelin	Cad-dap	BM II–BF I	20
8	59	Lauwin-Planque	ZAC	excavation	E. Leroy Langelin	Cad-dap	BM II–BF I	328 inc. 119 dated
9	59	Marquion	X8	excavation	G. Prilaux	Inrap	BM II–BF I	1
10	59	Seclin	Hauts de Clauwiers	excavation	St. Révillion	CAS	BM ?	11
11	59	Vity-en-Artois	chemin brûlé	diagnostic	N. Cayol	Inrap	BM II–BF I	9
	59	Vity-en-Artois	aérodrome	diagnostic	S. Lacroix	Cad-dap	BM II–BF I	17
12	59	Wargnies-le-Petit	*La Boiscrête* WLP Zone VI	excavation	G. Blanquaert	Afan	BM II–BF I	6
13	62	Aire-sur-la-Lys	La Banlieu	diagnostic	R. Rougier	Afan	BM II–BF I ?	13
14	62	Avelin	RD 549	excavation	M. Germain	Cad-dap	BM II–BF I	1
15	62	Courrières	rue C. Beugnet	excavation	Cl. Barbet	Cad-dap	BM II–BF I	13
16	62	Hinges	zone du Vertannoy	diagnostic	V. Thoquenne	Inrap	BF I ?	13
17	62	Maroeuil	rue Curie	excavation	Y.Lorin	Inrap	BM–BF I	1
18	62	Roeux	château d'eau	excavation	L. Vallin	SRA	BM II	57

must wait for the excavation to confirm this hypothesis. The architecture of these constructions is quite similar, with a diameter between 4.5 m and 7 m, giving a surface of 16–40 m². The outline is not necessarily perfectly circular and posthole spacing is not regular. A porch is sometimes clearly visible, as at Étaples-Tubersent (Pas-de-Calais) or Seclin (Nord). The observed entrances are generally to the east: northeast for Étaples, southeast for Lauwin-Planque

(Nord) and Seclin. The number of postholes varies with the diameter. A central posthole is sometimes identified, as at the sites of Roeux (Pas-de-Calais), Lauwin-Planque and Rebecques. Although certain constructions present an irregular outline, this irregularity can finds a parallel in the Irish site of Corrstown, where circular ditches complete the internal posts, which are not necessarily strictly regular (Ginn and Rathbone 2011).

Table 12.3. Regional sites from the middle stage of the Late Bronze (BF IIb-IIIa).

No.	Dept	Commune	Locality	Discovery	Project director	Organisation	Period	No. of structures
19	59	Brebières	Zac des Béliers	excavation	Gr. Huvelle	Cad-dap	BF IIIa	206
20	59	Erre-Escaudain	RN 455	excavation	E. Leroy Langelin	Cad-dap	BF IIb–IIIa	1
21	59	Guînes	Le couvent	excavation	A. Henton	Inrap	BF IIb–IIIa	1
22	59	Hordain	ZAC Hordain-Hainaut zone 1	excavation	D. Gaillard	Inrap/Cad-dap	BF IIIa	1
23	59	Iwuy	Val de Calvigny II	diagnostic	D. Gaillard	Inrap	BF IIb–IIIa	1
24	59	Lauwin-Planque	ZAC	excavation	E. Leroy Langelin	Cad-dap	BF IIb–IIIa	10
25	59	Onnaing	*Mont de Rétiau* Toyota Sites 10 et 11	excavation	R. Clotuche	Afan	BF IIb–IIIa	21
26	59	Rombies-et-Marchipont	'Le Grand Val, rue de l'Eglise'	excavation	A. Henton	Inrap	BF IIb–IIIa	29
27	62	Aire-sur-la-Lys	phase 3	excavation	Y. lorin	Inrap	BF IIIa	100
28	62	Arques	'ZAC de la Porte de l'Aa, phase 2'	excavation	E. Elleboode	Inrap	BF IIIa	2
29	62	Fresnes-lez-Montauban	*Chemin des Vaches* Transmanche	excavation	G. Blanquaert	Afan	BF IIIa	7
30	62	Inghem	La Fosse	excavation	J.- Fr. Piningre	SRA	BF IIb	36

The function of these constructions has not yet been clearly established in our region. In the absence of large buildings and, in so far as these are the only observed edifices on posts set in the ground, these structures are interpreted as habitats. Nonetheless, the small internal surface contrasts with the large buildings identified in the rest of north-western Europe (Bourgeois 2012, 119). Moreover, these discoveries of circular buildings are exclusively linked to this chronological period and to the Deverel-Rimbury culture, whereas this is not the case in Picardy, where discoveries belong to this phase (Eterpigny-Barleux 'Les Croix Noires'), but also to later phases, such as Nesles *Route de Chaulnes* (Somme) to the Late Bronze Age IIIb (Kieffer 2010), or Méaulte (Somme), to the Middle Hallstatt (Buchez 2012). In Normandy, they occur from the Middle Bronze Age at Tatihou (Marcigny: Ghesquière 2003), but also during the Late Bronze Age and Bronze Age/ Iron Age transition at Malleville-sur-le-Bec and Cahagnes (Marcigny: Talon 2009).

Although there is a clear architectural tradition of the circular form over an, as of yet, unspecified duration of time, larger buildings are practically absent (Fig. 12.3). This absence is even more striking in that during the Late Neolithic (Joseph *et al.* 2011) and the first Iron Age (Leroy-Langelin *et al.* 2012), vast rectangular establishments are known. These are marked by an a pits ridge tile and sometimes by an apse at one end during the Late Neolithic. During the First Iron Age, these differences are more frequent; the architectural model can include an a ridge

tile of an internal supporting structure, a system of posts set into the ground or lying on a low sandpit. This absence could result from an architectural variant leaving very few or no traces in the soil. The site of Choisy-au-Bac (Oise) with constructions on raft foundations (Talon 2013) points to the presence of edifices leaving no traces in the ground. Recent data could shed new light on our knowledge of this theme. The buildings identified on the ZAC of Béliers at Brebières (Pas-de-Calais) can be assimilated to long constructions discovered in Belgium or Normandy. Other cases of constructions are also recorded. At Aire-sur-la-Lys (Pas-de-Calais), a set of constructions on assembled posts is attributed to the earliest phase of the Late Bronze Age. These are square or rectangular buildings, on 4–8 posts, with a ground surface of no more than 16 m². These markers and their concentration in a well-defined space argue for an interpretation of a domestic unit. Further south from this complex, another series of six, systematically paired posts forms a rectangular building of 11 × 5 m. It may delimit an extension with the addition of two extra posts 5 m from the western end that form a cut-off corner. The case of Hordain (Nord) provides a new building module with a cut-off corner attributed to the Late Bronze Age IIIb.

The recent identification of these sites does not account for the absence of local architecture at some sites. These examples remain isolated and do not disprove the hypothesis of buildings without anchors in the substratum, which seem to be predominant in much of northern France during the Late Bronze Age. As there are few analysable elements

Table 12.4. Regional sites from the first phase of the final Late Bronze Age stage (BF IIIb – Early Hall).

No.	Dept	Commune	Locality	Discovery	Project director	Organisation	Period	No. of structures
31	59	Aulnoye-Aymeries	/	diagnostic	J. P. Fagnart	Afan	BF	1
32	59	Awoingt	Rue Pasteur	diagnostic	D. Gaillard	Inrap	BF	5
33	59	Cambrai, Niergnies	contournement de Cambrai	excavation	P. Herbin	CG 59	BF	8, diag
34	59	Erre	rues condorcet et Hubert Parent	diagnostic	P. Neaud	Inrap	BF–Ha ancien	1
35	59	Estreux	*Le Cavin Boissart* (Onnaing, zone 21)	excavation	R. Clotuche	Afan	BF	1
36	59	Fontaine-Notre-Dame	Contournement sud de Cambrai	excavation	D. Gaillard	Inrap	BF IIIb	1
37	59	Hérin	Zac de l'aérodrome Ouest	diagnostic	R. Clothuche	Inrap	BF	2
38	59	Hordain	La queue du cat	excavation or diag nostic	D. Gaillard	Inrap	BF IIIb	20
	59	Hordain	ZAC Hordain-Hainaut secteur 6	excavation	Th. Marcy	Inrap	BF IIIb	1
	59	Hordain	ZAC Hordain-Hainaut secteur 7	excavation	Ch. Séverin	Cad-dap	BF IIIb–Ha ancien	100
39	59	Lauwin-Planque	ZAC	excavation	E. Leroy-Langelin	Cad-dap	BF–Ha ancien	?
40	59	Lesquin	La Haute Borne	excavation	C. Quérel	Inrap	BF	3
41	59	Onnaing	*Abembus* Toyota Simodes	excavation	R. Clotuche	Inrap	BF–Ha ancien	nc
	59	Onnaing	*Mont de Rétiau* Toyota Site 13	excavation	R. Clotuche	Afan	BF	nc
	59	Onnaing	extension du parc d'act. Tranche 2	diagnostic	P. Neaud	Inrap	BF	nc
	59	Onnaing	ZAC vallée de l'Escaut	excavation	R. Clotuche	Inrap	BF	nc
42	59	Quiévrechain	rue Jean Jaurès - Les Vanneaux	excavation	A. Henton	Inrap	BF–Ha ancien	90
43	59	Raillencourt-Sainte-Olle	*Actipôle de l'A2*, le grand camp	excavation	D. Gaillard	Inrap	BF–Ha ancien	5
44	59	Rombies-et-Marchipont	'Le Grand Val, rue de l'Eglise'	excavation	A. Henton	Inrap	BF IIIb	10
45	59	Rouvignies	ZAC du plateau d'Hérin	diagnostic	R. Clotuche	Inrap	BF–Ha ancien	6
46	59	Solesmes	Rd 942, voyette de Vertain	diagnostic	Th. Marcy	Inrap	BF IIIb	4
47	59	Thun L'Évêque	Chemin de Paillencourt	diagnostic	Th. Marcy	Inrap	BF IIIb	nc
48	59	Wargnies-le-Petit	*La Chaudière* WLP Zone V	excavation	G. Blanquaert	Inrap	BF IIIb	1
49	62	Achicourt	'Le Fort'	excavation	Y. Lorin	Inrap	BF IIIb	29
	62	Achicourt	'Le Fort'	excavation	Y. Lorin	Inrap	BF–Ha ancien	4

(Continued)

Table 12.4. Regional sites from the first phase of the final Late Bronze Age stage (BF IIIb – Early Hall). (Continued)

No.	Dept	Commune	Locality	Discovery	Project director	Organisation	Period	No. of structures
50	62	Aire-sur-la-Lys	Hameau Saint Martin	excavation	Y. Lorin	Inrap / CG62	BF–Ha ancien	70
51	62	Arques	ZAC de la Porte de l'Aa, phase 5	diagnostic	E. Elleboode	Inrap	BF–Ha ancien	1
52	62	Bully-Les-Mines	Rue du Docteur Schweitzer	diagnostic	L. Blondiau	Inrap	BF–Ha ancien	1
53	62	Courrières	Rue Beugnet	excavation	Cl. Barbet	Cad-dap	BF–Ha ancien	16
54	62	Coquelles	Rue des Fours	excavation	A 16	Inrap	BF IIIb	nc
55	62	Dainville	Champ Bel air	excavation	A. Masse	CG 62	BF–Ha ancien	195
	62	Dainville	Le Moulin	excavation	D. Favier	Inrap	BF–Ha ancien	41
56	62	Dainville, Achicourt	Le Picotin, Gericho	diagnostic	J. Durier	Inrap	BF–Ha ancien	13
57	59	Douchy-Les-Mines	ZAC du Bois de Douchy Tranche 2	diagnostic	J. Lantoine	Inrap	BF–Ha ancien	8
58	62	Guines	Jardins du Couvent II	excavation	A. Henton	Inrap	BF–Ha ancien	7
59	59	Haut-Lieu	'Carrière de Godin'	diagnostic	J. Lantoine	Inrap	BF–Ha ancien	1
60	62	Hinges	zone du vertannoy	diagnostic	V. Thoquenne	Inrap	BF	3
61	62	Inghem	La fosse	excavation	J.-Fr. Piningre	SRA	BF–Ha ancien	50
62	62	Loison-Sous-Lens	Parc d'activités des Oiseaux	excavation	I. Praud	Inrap	BF IIIb	6
63	62	Maroeuil	rue curie - les capucines	diagnostic	D. Gaillard	Inrap	BF–Ha ancien	3
	62	Maroeuil	rue curie - les capucines	excavation	Y. Lorin	Inrap	BF–Ha ancien	200
64	62	Nielles-les-calais	'RD 304, tronçon B'	diagnostic	P. Neaud	Inrap	BF	nc
65	59	Niergnies	Grand Rue - Le Village	diagnostic	L. Blondiau	Inrap	BF–Ha ancien	12
66	62	Noeux-les-mines	Loisinord II	diagnostic	J.-Fr. Geoffroy	Inrap	BF–Ha ancien	2
67	62	Ruminghem	*Le Quilleval* Transmanche	excavation	G. Blanquaert	Afan	BF–Ha ancien	20
68	62	Saint-Tricat	RD 304	excavation	S. François	CG 62	BF–Ha ancien	12
69	62	Tincques	Béthencourt	diagnostic	B. Behague	Inrap	BF	6
70	62	Ytres	Canal Seine-Nord Europe - ZD 6	diagnostic	Th. Marcy	Inrap	BF	nc
71	62	Zouafsques	'Hameau de Wolphus'	diagnostic	E. Elleboode	Inrap	BF–Ha ancien	1

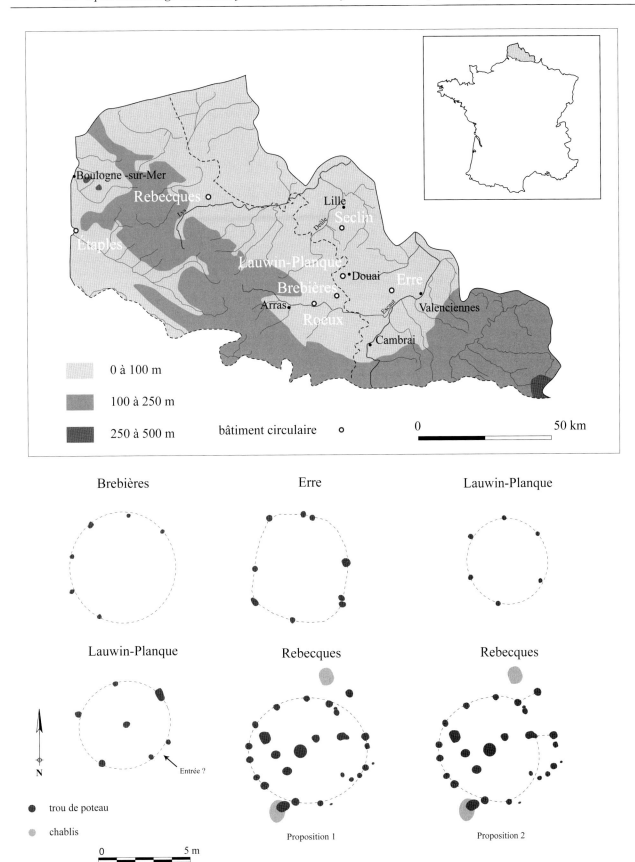

Fig. 12.2. Examples of circular buildings discovered in Nord/Pas-de-Calais, geographic location and plan drawings.

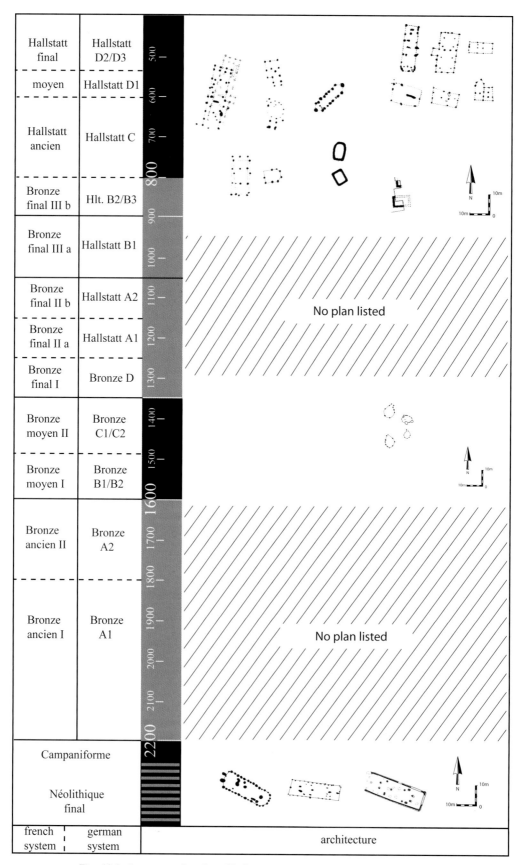

Hallstatt final	Hallstatt D2/D3		
moyen	Hallstatt D1		
Hallstatt ancien	Hallstatt C		
Bronze final III b	Hlt. B2/B3		
Bronze final III a	Hallstatt B1		
Bronze final II b	Hallstatt A2	No plan listed	
Bronze final II a	Hallstatt A1		
Bronze final I	Bronze D		
Bronze moyen II	Bronze C1/C2		
Bronze moyen I	Bronze B1/B2		
Bronze ancien II	Bronze A2		
Bronze ancien I	Bronze A1	No plan listed	
Campaniforme			
Néolithique final			
french system	german system	architecture	

Fig. 12.3. Summary of modes of habitat construction by chronological phase.

linked to 'houses', we must pay greater attention to the other remains of habitat sites.

The other structures

In most descriptions, hollows are related to simple pits, often interpreted in relation to the extraction of silt or chalk, with secondary use as a dump. They are considered to be of the same form. The differential typological analysis of these features has begun and already provides some information. The structures are divided as follows:

Most of the small or medium-sized pits (diameter of less than 2 m) present a vaguely circular or oval shape and a simple bowl-shaped profile.

The larger pits, with a circular or irregular oval outline (length or diameter 2–3 m), have a flat-based profile with more or less oblique walls. Infillings vary depending on the pits. Some hollows contain a first anthropogenic level, with the presence of charcoal and/or archaeological objects. Others display a natural infill in the lower part of the profile. This is characterised by a layer or a lens of whitish, homogeneous leached silt, characterising a phase of water stagnation. Several pockets of the collapse of the silty or limestone walls have also been observed. These markers denote a prolonged open period providing the opportunity to receive direct or indirect evidence of the activities carried out in the vicinity. layers can be strips of earth, detrital rejects in secondary position. A minority of these remains appear to be characteristic. They can be interpreted as sumps, silo type storage structures or combustion structures.

Sumps: these pits can most likely be interpreted as being linked to water provisioning in the habitat (Fig. 12.4). They have an elongated outline, sometimes with a bi-lobed (Quiévrechain, Nord) or regular (Maroeuil, Pas-de-Calais) plot surface. The walls are lined with indurated, rust-coloured silt, and marked by the presence of fine lenses alternating with sand, leached silt and orangy-grey organic clay. The base of the pit corresponds to the low level of the water table. The lower infill level displays alternating layers linked to the regular presence of water. After being abandoned, the hole filled in naturally.

Buried storage: the storage of perishable goods at archaeological sites is identified in several ways: buried storage pots (pots-silos), silos in the ground and granaries (on 4, 6 posts …). A pit can be made to be used as a receptacle for a pot. In this way, almost whole jars are discovered *in situ*. This practice is not frequent and is generally dated to the Middle-Late Bronze Age transition and seems to be abandoned during the course of this latter period (Fig. 12.5a).

During the Middle Bronze Age, simple pits (Fig. 12.5b) are frequently used and can be interpreted as silo-pits. These structures mainly present an oval or circular shape, vertical walls and a flat base. Bottle-neck profiles are rare. The

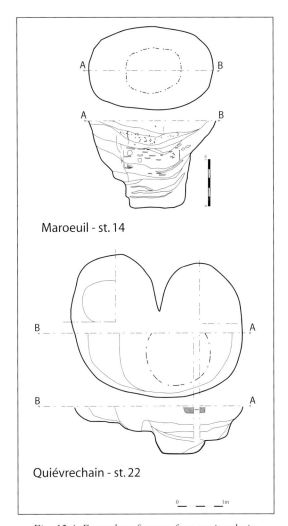

Maroeuil - st. 14

Quiévrechain - st. 22

Fig. 12.4. Examples of sumps from regional pits.

diameter at the opening varies from 0.70 m to 1 m. The upper infill is often made up of dark grey silt containing charcoal and sometimes a considerable quantity of baked clay. The depth of these pits is variable and undoubtedly depends on the levelling of sites, but storage capacity appears to be reduced and may be comparable to that of silo-vases (less than 1 m³). Carpology could lead to the validation of this hypothesis during future excavations.

For the Late Bronze Age, pit profiles are more varied (Fig. 12.5c). In the Arrageois region (Dainville/Bel-Air, Maroeuil, Achicourt), pyriform silos are rare. We observe their appearance from the Late Bronze Age IIIa onwards. The generally stratified infilling contains alternating whitish leached silt levels with charcoal inclusions and sandy silts. The function of these pits was identified through the presence of seeds in the first infill level. The more or less circular opening is between 1.80 m and 2 m, with an original diameter varying between 1.10 m and 1.40 m. Average preserved depth is 1 m.

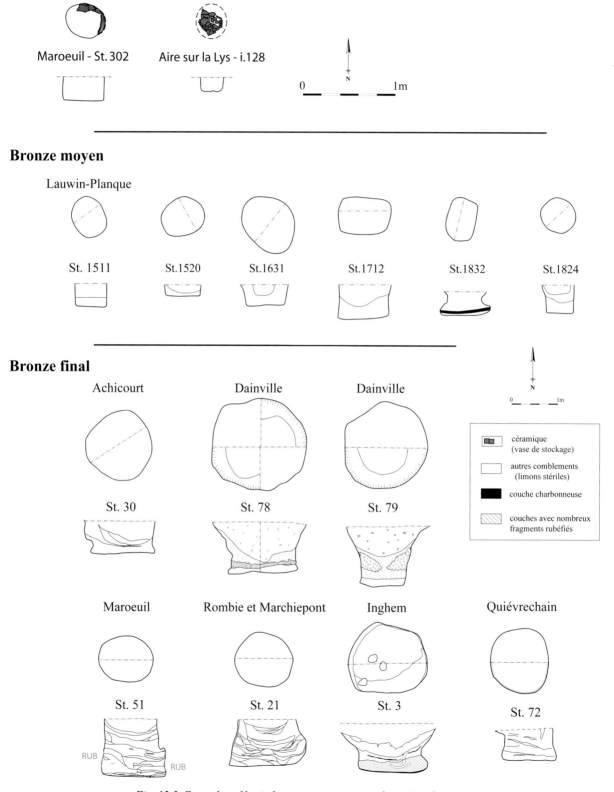

Fig. 12.5. Examples of buried storage structures in the regional corpus.

Large pits (2 to 3.17 m long and 1.36 to 2.80 m wide) could have been used to shelter foodstuffs. This initial pit function (storage, cellar), may have been concealed by subsequent reuse, as the analysis of pit infillings and objects only relates to the final use of these structures (dumps, combustion …) (Fig. 12.6).

Among these large-sized structures attributed to a late phase (from the Bronze Age IIIb?), it is possible to identify a specific category of pits with longitudinal profiles sometimes with evidence of partial re-digging. A characteristic stratigraphy is often brought to light with regular and horizontal levels (silt with charcoal, silt with charcoal and fire-reddened elements), alternating with silt from the surrounding sediments (collapse or intentional recharge?). These stratigraphic units are interpreted as possible recharge levels between evidence of artisanal activities, in different positions in the different structures:

- at the base, as undermining digging (Maroeuil, Aire-sur-la-Lys, Inghem in Pas-de-Calais, …)
- at different intermediary stages of the pit infilling, as 'sheets' (Achicourt) or deepening (Maroeuil, Dainville-Bel-Air)
- on the edge of the structure, as a small portion scorched soil (Quiévrechain, Maroeuil, …).

This is frequently associated with a combustion activity, although the latter is not always well understood. It is thus legitimate to raise the question of a pit linked to a production function (Lorin forthcoming) in order to differentiate storage pits from their first use (conception), or does possible reuse conceal their initial function? (Fig. 12.8).

Above-ground storage: modest constructions are recorded from the Middle Bronze Age, as at Roeux, Aire-sur-La-Lys *la Banlieu* or Lauwin-Planque. Most of them are quadrangular edifices with a floor raised by four posts destined to protect foodstuffs from animals and humidity. The usable area can reach nearly 8 m². This could represent another storage mode where airtightness was not required, unlike for silos. In the absence of datable elements directly associated with these hollows, they are most often supposed to be contemporaneous with the hollows containing objects. During the Late Bronze Age, their number varied according to the general conservation and density of the site. Through their spatial distribution, they are associated, either alone or in pairs, with a group of pits. On denser occupations, they can be assembled in a same sector to define silage zones.

Combustion pits: structures filled with blocks of flint or sandstone have been identified as possible hot stone ovens (Polynesian hearths?). The function of these structures is approached by analysing their shape, the type of infill and the disposition of these blocks. The shapes of these pits are sometimes very elongated (Rouvignies, Nord), rectangular (Maroeuil) or circular hollows (Aire-sur-la-Lys). The walls

are scorched in two cases out of three (Fig. 12.7). Evidence of heating can be more limited, like at Aire-sur-la-Lys where the layout of the stone blocks seems to cover the base to make up the heart of a heating zone or heating area. At Rouvignies, the base is lined with a charcoal level mixed with small fragments of scorched earth. Sandstone blocks are contained in the charcoal infill. At Maroeuil, there is little evidence of heating but the blocks are laid out in a similar way. Although structures with heated stones are more often present in southern France, they are also known in the north since the Neolithic, and present varied morphologies.

Evidence of hearths is provided by scorched areas, most often circular, ranging in diameter from 1 m to 1.2 m. In the absence of constructions, it is not possible to specify whether they are part of the habitat area. This scorching points to the existence of zones hollowed out in the silt or very slightly covered with sediments. These structures can present evidence of more elaborate installations. *In situ* traces are sometimes limited and only elements scorched by fire are described as a layer. These markers correspond to an encased combustion structure, partly covered by a dome or simply a collapsed clay screed. The latter is at least partial, but the conserved data do not provide any more details (important quantity of building earth, refits with no results). Ultimately, these structures with slightly scorched bases and walls are small pits, filled with a charcoal layer, then with building earth. They must be differentiated from other cases, such as infill related to the destruction of a building or intentional backfill after destruction.

Dumps, re-used pits: these are pits with at times more irregular outlines and are not always easy to identify. Sometimes, several days in the open air are necessary to identify the limits of hollowing in the silts by infill oxidation. In some cases, the presence of (sparse or more concentrated) objects leads to defining the remains. These superficial hollows undoubtedly had a special relationship with the domestic area, as shown by deposits of objects. It remains difficult to advance a functional interpretation based on the first use of these pits.

Polylobed pits: pits referred to as 'polylobed' occur in zones with loessial cover. These are hollows made by undermining the walls of an initial hollow. These undercuts develop horizontally in different directions. They are small zones of opportunistic extraction, for architectural functions or production depending on the mechanical properties of the exploited sediments. Regional examples are rare (Aire-sur-la-Lys).

Variable concentrations and new questions

During the Early Bronze Age, remains are often represented by several rare isolated pits and are too scant to extrapolate modes of habitat organisation. It is apparently only from the Middle Bronze Age onwards that structures with

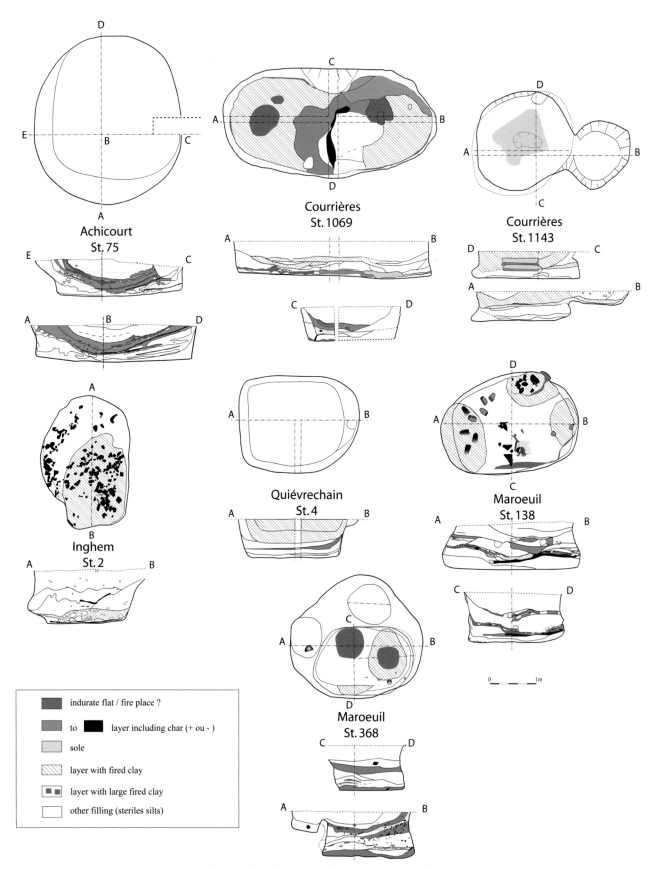

Fig. 12.6. Examples of large-sized pits among regional structures.

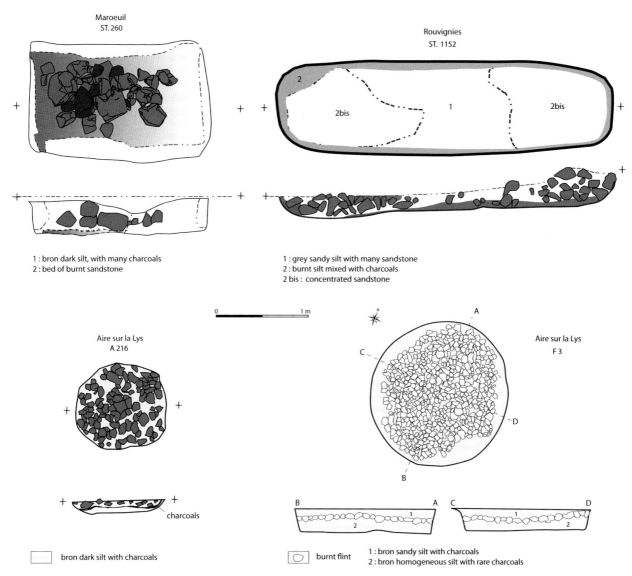

Fig. 12.7. Examples of combustion structures in the regional corpus.

specific functions, such as silos and extraction pits, have been identified. Erosion can explain documentation problems. There are few sites and these are limited to several difficult to interpret remains. The Lauwin-Planque ZAC differs from this schema in that it contains a large expanse of remains from the same period, but it is still an isolated example (Leroy-Langelin and Sergent 2015). Most of the remains identified in the Douai region are materialized by small concentrations of remains cut into be subsequent occupations (Vitry-en-Artois: rue Nobled and Aérodrome, Erre) and the situation is hardly any different for the rest of the region (cf. Table 12.2). It is difficult to identify a denser human presence on the basis of domestic evidence. This lacuna in the settlement record during the early phases of the Bronze Age until the middle of the final phase contrasts with the proliferation of funerary data

from the transition period between the Early and Middle Bronze Age.

In the Middle Bronze Age and at the beginning of the Late Bronze Age, and in parallel with the large funerary monuments, the circular habitat at Roeux provides an image of a small domestic unit extending over a limited surface. It is during this period that the first familial cemeteries appear as pits containing burnt bone remains (Gaudefroy and Le Goff 2004; Blanchet and Talon 2005; Billand *et al.* this volume).

During the following period, corresponding to the middle stage of the Late Bronze Age, at Aire sur la Lys (Pas de Calais: David and Lorin forthcoming), the multiplication of interlinked funerary and domestic sectors confirms settlement densification.

This tendency is reinforced for the last stage of the Late Bronze Age, with the multiplication of recent data (cf. Table 12.3). These results can be compared to the isolated farm model, applied to the Bronze Age in the east of France (Blouet *et al.* 1992) and commonly accepted in our regions. Recent work points to an organisation based on a model of small implantations, grouping a modest community (extended family?) and moving during each generation. However, following a similar observation to that made in Normandy, at the sites of Malleville-sur-le-Bec (Eure) and Cahagnes (Calvados), where important concentrations of remains were discovered in the habitat (Marcigny and Talon 2009), it is reasonable to question the possible contemporaneity of the discovered remains. Does the evidence discovered in these concentrations reflect regular movements or are they related to intermediary (10–40 remains) or concentrated site groupings (above 40), according to the classification advanced by Patrice Brun (Brun *et al.* 2005)? The identification of the number of remains depends on the extent of the cleared surface whereas the size and type of sites depend on other criteria. The effective exploration of large surfaces in our region (as a result of the number of discoveries) raises the question of the coexistence of several synchronous occupations and possible specialisations. The typo-chronological approach to objects does not enable us to assess this interpretative issue in a satisfactory way. The variable number and nature of structures for a given observation point remain characteristic of categories of sites. Occupations are generally not very dense and can be spread out (1.5 ha) as at Dainville, Maroeuil, or Quiévrechain, or even very vast (7.5 ha), as at Aire-sur-la-Lys. At the latter site, the long occupation duration could account for the extensive occupation surface, either by successive movements or the simultaneity of several constructions within the same settlement. These open-air sites do not generally present any overlap between them (cf. Fig. 12.8). In the absence of stratigraphic links, the contemporaneity of these hollows is often solely based on objects. It is envisioned to check whether the spatial distribution of remains and structures could represent organisation within the occupation.

Settlement plans are marked by hollows of varied shapes and it is difficult to observe organisational markers. The thankless nature of sites characterised by simple pit complexes of varying density and by the absence of buildings must not inhibit our analytical efforts. Work on the spatial organisation of sites has begun. It aims to establish pertinent criteria for interpreting plans, structures or object distribution maps. Different work methods have been elaborated to evaluate site organisation, mainly for the Late Bronze Age, which is the only period with enough representative excavations to compare approaches. Simple but recurring observations have been observed:

- these open-air sites do not generally present any link between them. In the absence of stratigraphic

associations, the contemporaneity of the different hollows is often based on objects. However, most of these structures do not contain such evidence. A constant feature is the presence of a 'main' pit with standard dimensions, used as a receptacle for most of the discovered objects. This pit could play an attractive and central role (Achicourt, Maroeuil) and could contribute to defining habitation units, the possible moving of units, or re-use;
- the analysis of the spatial distribution of objects and structures is essential;
- a castrametration project has been undertaken to examine the constants in the orientation or spacing of the main categories of remains. Granaries are oriented, regularly distributed and associated with groups of pits.

The first results of different regional works bring to light characteristics: pits are either regrouped and regularly separated by spaces without remains (Aire-sur-la-Lys, state 3), or classified by type and aligned (Achicourt, state 1). Possible sectorisation between the habitat zone and storage zone has been defined at the sites of Dainville *Bel Air* or Maroeuil *rue Curie*, for example. At Quiévrechain or Rombies and Marchiepont, a cross-analysis of structures and waste distribution was undertaken. The resulting data enable us to propose an analysis of the concentrations and empty zones, in order to spatially interpret the site: definition of domestic units and location of the main building for several occupation phases.

These approaches could be generalised and carried out with targeted questions in order to better understand the ways in which excavated sites are similar or different. The number and type of structures should be assessed using shared analytic criteria. Here, this approach has been used for a first analysis and now needs to be applied systematically.

Conclusion

The identification of habitat zones during this long Bronze Age period (13 centuries) reveals the disparity between data and sometimes the absence of information. Due to the low representativeness of site markers for the early part of this period, we can only propose observations, rather than certitudes.

One of the main elements of this comprehensive approach is the need to define common analytical methods in order to attempt to attenuate the gaps in the record, hastily judged to be thankless, and to continue with a policy of broad requirements for at times tenuous markers.

The characterisation of roundhouses in the north of France represents one of the most striking advances in this domain over these past years (Talon 2013). The identification of morpho-types for hollow structures could mark a new stage in our knowledge. Lastly, the analysis of their distribution could complete this descriptive analysis.

Bibliography

Billand, G., Le Goff, I. and Talon, M. (2017) Évolution des rites et systèmes funéraires à l'Âge du bronze dans le Nord-Ouest de la France. In A. Lehoërff and M. Talon (eds) *Au-delà des frontières, voyager, échanger, communiquer en Europe du IVème au début du Ier millénaire avant notre ère*, actes du colloque international du projet européen BOAT 1550 BC et de l'APRAB, Boulogne-sur-Mer, octobre 2012. Oxford, Oxbow Books.

Blanchet, J.-C. and Talon, M. (2005) L'âge du Bronze dans la moyenne vallée de l'Oise: apports récents. In J. Bourgeois and M. Talon (eds) *L'âge du Bronze du Nord-Ouest de la France dans le contexte européen occidental : nouvelles découvertes et propositions de périodisation*, 232–73, Actes de la table ronde tenue dans le cadre du 125ème Congrès national des sociétés historiques et scientifiques, Lille, Pré-et Protohistoire. Paris, CTHS-APRAB.

Blouet, V., Buzi, P. and Dreidemy, C. (1992) Données récentes sur l'habitat de l'âge du Bronze en Lorraine. In *L'habitat et l'occupation du sol à l'âge du Bronze en Europe*, 177–93, actes du colloque international de Lons-le-Saunier, 1990. Paris, CTHS.

Bourgeois, J. and Talon, M. (2009) From Picardy to Flanders: Transmanche connections in the Bronze Age. In P. Clark (ed.) *Bronze Age Connections: Cultural Contact in Prehistoric Europe*, 38–60. Oxford, Oxbow Books.

Bourgeois, J. (2012) Sint-Gillis-Waas, Kluizenmolen (Flandre Orientale, Belgique). In A. Lehoërff with the collaboration of J. Bourgeois, P. Clark, and M. Talon (eds) *Beyond the Horizon, Societies of the Channel and North Sea 3.500 years ago*, 119, catalogue of the exhibition (Château-Musée de Boulogne-sur-Mer, 30 juin 2012–5 novembre 2012 – Erfgoedcentrum de Ename, 16 décembre 2012–30 mai 2013 – Musée de Douvres, 1er juillet–30 décembre 2013). Paris, coédition BOAT 1550 BC/Somogy éditions d'art.

Brun, P., Cathelinais, C., Chatillon, S., Guichard, Y., Le Guen, P. and Néré, E. (2005) L'âge du Bronze dans la vallée de l'Aisne. In J. Bourgeois and M. Talon (dir.) *L'âge du Bronze du Nord-Ouest de la France dans le contexte européen occidental : nouvelles découvertes et propositions de périodisation*, 189–208, actes de la table ronde tenue dans le cadre du 125ème Congrès national des sociétés historiques et scientifiques, Lille, 2000, Pré- et Protohistoire. Paris, CTHS-APRAB.

Buchez, N. (2011). La protohistoire ancienne. Recherche et fouille des sites de l'âge du Bronze à La Tène ancienne sur les grands tracés linéaires en Picardie occidentale: questions méthodologiques et résultats scientifiques. In N. Buchez, D. Bayard and P. Depaepe (eds) *Quinze ans d'archéologie préventive sur les grands tracés linéaires en Picardie, première partie*, 121–199. Amiens, *Revue Archéologique de Picardie* 3/4.

Buchez, N. (2012) The farm at Méaulte, Somme. In A. Lehoërff with the collaboration of J. Bourgeois, P. Clark and M. Talon (ed.) *Beyond the Horizon, Societies of the Channel and North Sea 3.500 years ago*, 121–2, catalogue of the exhibition (Château-Musée de Boulogne-sur-Mer, 30 juin 2012–5 novembre 2012 – Erfgoedcentrum de Ename, 16 décembre 2012–30 mai 2013 – Musée de Douvres, 1er juillet –30 décembre 2013). Paris, coédition BOAT 1550 BC/Somogy éditions d'art.

Clark, P. (ed.) (2004) *The Dover Boat in Context: Society and Water Transport In Prehistoric Europe*. Oxford, Oxford Books.

Compagnon, E. and Queyrat, I. (2006) *Vitry-en-Artois (Pas-de-Calais), Rue Nobled, site 406-05*, rapport de fouilles. Douai: Direction de l'archéologie préventive de la Communauté d'agglomération du Douaisis. SRA Nord-Pas-de-Calais.

David, A. and Lorin, Y. (forthcoming) *Aire-sur-la-Lys « ZAC Saint-Martin », phase 2*, Rapport Final d'Opération. Inrap Nord-Picardie.

Debiak, R. (1997) *Gazoduc Gournay-sur-Aronde-Arleux-en-Gohelle (Pas-de-Calais) DFS d'évaluation et de surveillance de travaux: Monchy-le-Preux « les Diefs »*, 70–74. Amiens, Afan.

Desfossés, Y. (1995) *Les sites de l'Âge du Bronze de la section Artois du T. G. V. Nord dans le contexte de l'Europe septentrionale*. Mémoire de diplôme de l'E. H. E. S. S.

Desfossés, Y. (2000) *Archéologie préventive en vallée de Canche – les sites protohistoriques fouillés dans le cadre de la réalisation de l'autoroute A 16. Nord-Ouest Archéologie* 11. Berck-sur-mer, C. R. A. D. C.

Gaudefroy, S. and Le Goff, I. (2004) La nécropole du début du Bronze final de Verneuil-en-Halatte (Oise). *Revue archéologique de Picardie* 1–2, 19–32.

Ginn, V. and Rathbone, S. (2011) *Corrstown, a Coastal Community. Excavations of a Bronze Age Village in Northern Ireland*. Oxford, Oxbow Books.

Jahier, I. (2005) Le village de Cahagnes (Calvados), In C. Marcigny, C. Colonna, E. Ghesquière and G. Verron (eds) *La Normandie à l'aube de l'histoire, les découvertes archéologiques de l'âge du Bronze 2300-800 av. J.-C*, 50–1. Paris, Somogy Editions d'art.

Joseph, Fr., Julien, M., Leroy-Langelin, E., Lorin, Y. and Praud, I. (2011) L'architecture domestique des sites du IIIe millénaire before our eradans le Nord de la France. In F. Bostyn, E. Martial and I. Praud (eds) *Le Néolithique du Nord de la France dans son contexte européen: habitat et économie aux 4è et 3è millénaires avant notre ère*, 249–72, 29ème colloque interrégional sur le Néolithique, Villeneuve d'Ascq (Nord, France) –2 et 3 octobre 2009. Buire-le-Sec, Revue Archéologique de Picardie, n° spécial 28.

Kiefer, D. (2010) *Nesles « Route de Chaulnes », Rapport de diagnostic archéologique*. Amiens, Inrap Nord-Picardie, inédit.

Lacroix, S. and Carpentier, F. (2012) *Vitry-en-Artois, « Aerodrome », site 393-09*, rapport final d'opération, Douai: Communauté d'agglomération du Douaisis, Direction de l'archéologie préventive. SRA Nord-Pas-de-Calais.

Leroy-Langelin, E. and Sys, D. (2004) *Escaudain-Erre (Nord), site 376/2004*, fouilles préventives, Douai : Direction de l'archéologie préventive de la Communauté d'agglomération du douaisis. SRA Nord-Pas-de-Calais.

Leroy-Langelin, E., Sergent, A., Séverin, Ch. and Leman-Delerive, G. (2012), Les âges des métaux dans la région de Douai: quoi de neuf? *Revue du Nord* 17, 67–80.

Leroy-Langelin, E. and Sergent, A. (2015), *ZAC Lauwin-Planque, L'âge du Bronze, section 2 (vol. 3a)*, rapport final d'opération, Douai: Communauté d'agglomération du

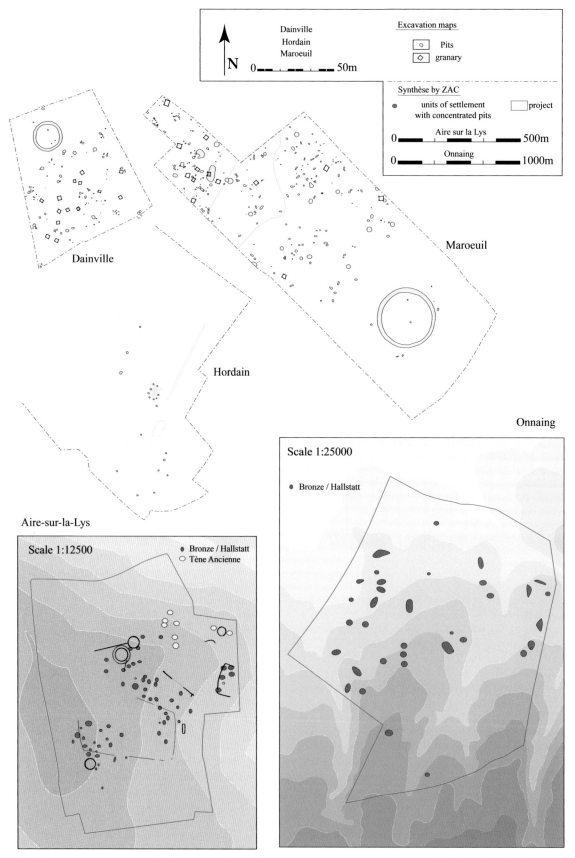

Fig. 12.8. General organization of habitat sites: plans of several occupations representative of the Nord/Pasde-Calais region.

Douaisis, Direction de l'archéologie préventive. SRA Nord-Pas-de-Calais.

Lorin, Y., Pinard, E. and Trawka, H. (2005) Aire-sur-la-Lys, le Hameau St Martin. *Bilan scientifique de la région Nord-Pas-de-Calais*, 128–131.

Lorin, Y. (2007), *Rebecques (Pas-de-Calais) « RD 838 »*. Rapport final d'opération de diagnostic. Douai, Inrap Nord-Picardie.

Marcigny, C. and Ghesquière, E. (dir.) (2003) *L'île de Tatihou (Manche) à l'âge du Bronze: habitats et occupation du sol*, 96. Paris, Éditions de la Maison des sciences de l'Homme,Documents d'archéologie française.

Marcigny, C. and Talon, M. (2009) Sur les rives de la manche. Qu'en est-il du passage de l'âge du bronze à l'âge du fer à partir des découvertes récentes ? In A. Daubigney, P.-Y. Milcent and M.-J. Roulière-Lambert (eds) *De l'âge du Bronze à l'âge du Fer en France et en Europe occidentale (Xe–VIIe siècle av. J.-C.): la moyenne vallée du Rhône aux âges du Fer*, 385–403, actes du XXXe colloque international de l'AFEAF., co-organisé avec l'APRAB, Saint-Romain-en-Gal, 26–28 mai 2006. Dijon, Société archéologique de l'Est, *Revue Archéologique de l'Est*, supplement 27.

Mare, É. (2005) Le village de Malleville-sur-le-Bec (Eure). In C. Marcigny, C. Colonna, E. Ghesquière and G. Verron (dir.) *La Normandie à l'aube de l'histoire, les découvertes archéologiques de l'âge du Bronze 2300-800 av. J.-C*, 52–3. Paris, Somogy Editions d'art.

Needham, S. (2009) Encompassing the sea: 'Maritories' and Bronze Age maritime interactions. In P. Clark (ed.) *Bronze Age Connections: Cultural Contact in Prehistoric Europe*, 12–37. Oxford, Oxbow Books.

Talon, M. (2013) Caractéristiques et évolution de l'architecture à l'âge du Bronze dans le Nord-Ouest de la France. In L. Iakovleva, O. Korvin-Piotrovski and F. Djindjian (dir.) *L'archéologie du bâti, de la Préhistoire au Moyen-Age, à l'Est et à l'Ouest de l'Europe*, 157–82, actes du 3ème Congrès Franco-Ukrainien d'Archéologie. Kiev. EHESS.

13

Les découvertes récentes de mobilier céramique Bronze ancien-début Bronze final dans le nord-ouest de la France

Nathalie Buchez, Marianne Deckers, Caroline Gutierrez,
Alain Henton et Marc Talon

Abstract

The aim of this contribution is to take stock of some unpublished and scattered data in order to put forward a synthetic view and a classification based on typological comparisons and in regard to all the isotopic dates available.

If the body of ceramic finds from the early phases of the Bronze Age is gradually allowing, little by little, the clarification of the periodisation first established by J.-C. Blanchet in 1984, it is proving that some stages remain less well documented (the start of the Early Bronze Age and the start of the Late Bronze Age). On the other hand, the shape of a coherent body apparent in the Deverel-Rimbury horizon, and clearly showing the attachment of northwest France to the Manche-mer-du-Nord (MMN) cultural complex is now emerging for the end of the Middle Bronze Age/beginning of the Late Bronze Age (Bronze C–D).

Keywords: pottery, typo-chronology, isotopic dating, early-middle Bronze Age, Manche-Mer-du-Nord cultural complex

Résumé

L'objectif de cette contribution est de recenser une documentation inédite et éparse afin d'en proposer une vue synthétique et un classement sur la base des comparaisons typologiques et au regard de l'ensemble des datations isotopiques disponibles.

Si le corpus des mobiliers céramiques des phases anciennes de l'Âge du bronze s'étoffe petit à petit permettant de préciser la périodisation initialement établie par J.-C. Blanchet en 1984, il s'avère que certaines étapes restent moins bien documentées (début du Bronze ancien et début du Bronze final). En revanche les contours d'un faciès cohérent apparenté à l'horizon Deverel-Rimbury, et signant clairement le rattachement du nord-ouest de la France au complexe culturel Manche-mer du Nord (MMN), se dégagent désormais pour la fin du Bronze moyen-début du Bronze final (Bronze C-D).

Mots-clés: Céramique, typo-chronologie, datations isotopiques, Bronze ancien-moyen, complexe culturel Manche-mer du Nord

Introduction

Malgré le développement de l'archéologie préventive, notre connaissance des faciès céramiques régionaux des phases anciennes de l'Âge du bronze est encore limitée. Elle s'appuie sur un petit nombre de vases issu d'ensembles funéraires et quelques lots restreints ou tessons isolés représentant les ensembles domestiques. Certains vestiges restent ainsi difficiles à situer dans le temps.

On dispose de fort peu de datations absolues du fait des contextes de découverte (diagnostics ou fouilles relevant de périodes plus récentes). Systématiser les datations pour ces mobiliers, quels que soient ces contextes, est donc une priorité.

Toutefois un tour d'horizon des découvertes récentes (ou plus anciennes mais non publiées) s'appuyant sur ces quelques datations permet de remettre en perspective les éléments de la fin du IIIème millénaire et du début du second et de préciser les contours du faciès *Deverel-Rimbury* de la seconde partie du Bronze moyen-début du Bronze final (Fig 13.1).

Les éléments du Néolithique final-Campaniforme/début du Bronze ancien (début Bronze A1)

Certaines des caractéristiques du mobilier de la structure 447 de Maroeuil (Pas-de-Calais), telle la languette ovalaire (Fig. 13.20), trouvent des prototypes dans la typologie du Néolithique final régional (par exemple Blanchet et Lambot 1985). Toutefois la céramique de cette structure se distingue assez clairement de la typologie du groupe Gord-Deûle-Escaut, tout comme l'abondant mobilier lithique s'en démarque par l'absence de micro-denticulés.

Le mode décoratif de la céramique de la fosse 3643 d'Eterpigny « Les Croix Noires » (Somme) et son organisation (Fig. 13.35) trouvent des parallèles avec certains vases campaniformes (Crombé *et al.* 2011, fig. 8 ; Salanova *et al.* 2011, fig. 7). Une datation le place vers le milieu du IVe millénaire (Table 13.1), dans l'étape 2 du Néolithique final qui correspond au premier impact du Campaniforme dans la région (Salanova *et al.* 2011, 88).

La forme carénée et le décor du vase 1887 d'Eterpigny-Barleux « Les Croix Noires » (Fig. 13.35) ne sont pas sans rappeler le vase de sépulture individuelle de Juvincourt et Damary « Gué de Mauchamps » (Aisne, Salanova 2000, 329) située par une datation radiocarbone dans la fourchette 2400–2150 avant J.-C. correspondant à l'étape 3 du Néolithique final ou Campaniforme récent (Salanova *et al.* 2011).

Dans le cas de la céramique (vase 1, Fig. 13.25) de Saint-Laurent-Blangy « Le Trapèze » (Pas-de-Calais), motifs et organisation du décor sont très proches de ceux des vases de la sépulture d'Arenberg à Wallers dans le Nord (Felix et Hantutte 1969) qui trouvent leurs meilleurs parallèles dans le sud de l'Angleterre et plus particulièrement dans le Wessex (Salanova *et al.* 2011). La forme qui se distingue de celle des vases de Wallers par la présence d'un col court bien différencié (par une concavité dans le haut du profil) est à classer dans un groupe plus caractéristique du nord de l'Angleterre (Needham 2005). Si les vases de la tombe de Wallers paraissent devoir être situés vers 2300-2200 avant J.-C. d'après les chronologies les plus récentes proposées pour l'Angleterre, les morphologies à col sont considérées comme plus récentes.

Les impressions au doigt, souvent réalisées à l'aide de deux doigts opposés (paires d'impressions organisées ou non) sont connues dans le groupe des céramiques communes campaniformes, sur le vase 2 de Saint-Laurent-Blangy « Le Trapèze » et sur le vase de la fosse 152 (Fig. 13.30) d'Argoeuves « Le Moulin d'Argoeuves ». L'association céramique fine de type campaniforme et céramique grossière à décor digité a déjà été signalée régionalement sur le site anciennement fouillé d'Etaples « Bel air II » (Blanchet 1984, 82). Dans le cas du vase d'Argoeuves, la forme et l'association du cordon horizontal placé immédiatement sous le bord sont caractéristiques des céramiques communes campaniformes d'Europe continentale (Besse 2003). Des formes proches, à cordon sous le bord et décor digité couvrant, sont connues en Ile-de-France (Brunet *et al.* 2011) et dans le nord-ouest de la Belgique, avec impressions par paires dans ce cas (Warmenbol 1996). Dans les deux régions, ces découvertes sont situées dans la seconde moitié du IIIème millénaire (Brunet *et al.* 2011 ; Crombé *et al.* 2011).

On retrouve le cordon horizontal placé sous le bord d'une forme à ouverture évasée qui évoque la céramique commune campaniforme du Nord-Ouest de la France (Brunet *et al.* 2008 ; Billard *et al.* 1996) à Pecquencourt « ZAC Barrois » (Nord), en association avec un décor d'incisions couvrantes, larges et profondes, formant un motif en arête de poisson inédit pour la région (Fig. 13.10). Le décor en arête de poisson est connu dans le Bronze ancien du Nord de la France, comme à Hardelot ou à Fréthun « Les Rietz » (Pas-de-Calais, Blanchet 1984 ; Bostyn *et al.* 1992), ainsi que dans la culture Hilversum (Fokkens 2005). Néanmoins, la technique décorative (impression de cordelette) tout comme le profil des vases (biconiques) est alors nettement divergent. C'est finalement sur un vase du site de Mondeville « l'Etoile » (Calvados) attribué au Bronze moyen II ainsi que dans le groupe de *Trevisker*, avec lequel le site de Mondeville présenterait des affinités, que ces incisions trouvent le plus de correspondances (Chancerel *et al.* 2006 ; Gibson *et al.* 1997, 267).

Le profil du vase de Saint-Venant « rue de Garbecque » (Pas-de-Calais), à encolure courte bien démarquée (Fig. 13.27) ne l'inscrit pas parmi ceux du classique « gobelet campaniforme » rencontrés dans les quelques assemblages régionaux mais semble correspondre à une forme tardive de vases à décor à la cordelette (Bardel, en Lançon 2012) que l'on retrouve en association avec des vases à décor plastique et cordons arciformes comme c'est le cas à Compiègne « Le Fond Pernant » (Oise, Blanchet 1984, fig. 44, vases 5 et 3).

Le vase de Monchy-Lagache « La Mare du Flez » (Somme, Buchez et Talon 2005, fig. 2.1), unique à ce jour pour la région, avec son décor digité par pincements qui renvoie au mode décoratif campaniforme et ses cannelures (Fig. 13.39) qui trouvent des parallèles sur la vallée de la Meuse, dans les Ardennes, à Remilly-Aillicourt

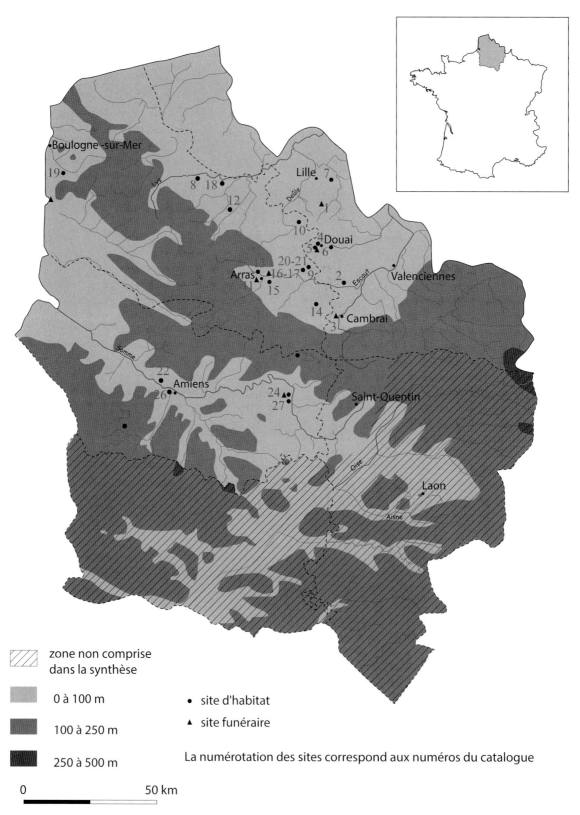

zone non comprise
dans la synthèse

0 à 100 m

100 à 250 m

250 à 500 m

• site d'habitat

▲ site funéraire

La numérotation des sites correspond aux numéros du catalogue

0   50 km

Fig. 13.1. Localisation des découvertes.

Table 13.1. Tableau de l'ensemble des datations isotopiques disponibles se rapportant aux mobiliers céramiques pour la région étudiée.

Dept	Site	Lieu-dit	nature du site		Lab no.	BP	BC cal [1]	Élement daté	Rapport avec le mobilier céramique pris en compte dans l'étude
80	Eterpigny-Barleux	Les Croix Noires	funéraire	tombe du secteur 1	3990±30	2575–2466	2620–2471	bois	boisage de la fosse sépulcrale
60	Compiègne	Le Fond Pernant	habitat	fosse 28	Ly-2964	3890±180	2881/1917	faune	ossement associé à la céramique
59	Avelin	RD 549	funéraire	enclos simple	Beta 281889	3560±40	2023–1772	charbon	niveau sus–jacent à celui contenant la céramique
62	Etaples	Mont Bagarre	habitat	Fossé 100	Ly 308(OXA)	3525±50	2012–1698	charbon	même phase de comblement du fossé que la céramique
59	Avelin	RD 549	funéraire	Enclos à 2 fossés (enclos interne)	Beta 281890	3520±40	1951–1703	charbon	même phase de comblement du fossé que la céramique
62	Etaples	Mont Bagarre	habitat	Fossé 100	Ly 307(OXA)	3515±50	1972–1694	charbon	même phase de comblement du fossé que la céramique
59	Avelin	RD 549	funéraire	Enclos à 2 fossés (enclos externe)	Beta 281891	3470±40	1894–1687	charbon	même phase de comblement du fossé que la céramique
62	Etaples	Mont Bagarre	habitat ?	Fossé 300	Ly 7445	3390±70	1882–1527	charbon	même phase de comblement du fossé que la céramique
62	Fresnes-les-Montauban	Le Motel	funéraire	Enclos 1	Ly 5336	3380±50	1871–1530	inhumation	même monument mais urne funéraire et mobilier des fossés = phase éventuellement différente de l'inhumation
80	Argoeuves	Le Moulin d'Argoeuves	funéraire	Monument A	GrA-44270	3360±35	1744–1534	faune	même phase de comblement que la céramique
62	Fresnes-les-Montauban	Le Motel	funéraire	Enclos 3	Ly 5335	3355±60	1870–1500	inhumation	même monument mais urne funéraire et mobilier des fossés = phase éventuellement différente de l'inhumation

(Continued)

Table 13.1. Tableau de l'ensemble des datations isotopiques disponibles se rapportant aux mobiliers céramiques pour la région étudiée. (Continued)

Dept	Site	Lieu-dit	nature du site		Lab no.	BP	BC cal [1]	Élement daté	Rapport avec le mobilier céramique pris en compte dans l'étude
59	Marquion	Plate-forme canal SNE	funéraire	Incinération en périphérie d'enclos	RICH-20388	3349±35	1739–1531	Incinération	ossement de l'incinération en urne
62	Fréthun	Les Rietz	funéraire	Enclos central	Gif 8928	3310±60	1741–1451	inhumation	même monument mais urne funéraire = phase éventuellement différente de l'inhumation
62	Saint-Laurent-Blangy	Les Soixantes	funéraire	st. 1482	GrA 59617	3325±35	1690–1513	Incinération	même monument mais phase éventuellement différente
59	Lauwin-Planque	Les Dix-neuf	funéraire	Enclos 7, st. 6096	Beta 260098	3290±40	1664–1459	charbon	charbon associé à l'amas osseux en urne
80	Crouy	Les Quatre	funéraire	Enclos ovoïde	GrA-41825	3290±30	1633–1501	Incinération	ossement de l'incinération en urne
62	Etaples	Mont Bagarre	habitat ?	Fossé 400	Ly 309(OXA)	3255±55	1658–1423	charbon	même phase de comblement du fossé que la céramique
62	Vitry-en-Artois	Les Colombiers	funéraire	Incinération principale	Gif-7258	3220±60	1637–1322	charbon	charbon associé à l'amas osseux en urne
80	Argoeuves	Le Moulin d'Argoeuves	funéraire	Monument A	GrA-43447	3170±35	1511–1321	Incinération	ossement de l'incinération en urne
80	Eterpigny-Barleux	Les Croix Noires	habitat	Secteur 3, st. 2111	Beta 349852	3160±30	1501–1323	charbon	même phase d'occupation : vase issue d'une fosse (associée au trou de poteau daté ?)
59	Escaudain-Erre	RN 455	habitat	Fosse 1005	Ly 12974	3150±65	1607–1235	charbon	même phase de comblement que la céramique
80	Eterpigny-Barleux	Les Croix Noires	habitat	Secteur 3, st. 2112	Beta-356164	3130±30	1495–1300	charbon	même phase d'occupation : vase issue d'une fosse (associée au trou de poteau daté ?)
62	Roeux	Le Château d'Eau	habitat	Fosse 10	Ly 5317	3115±50	1498–1261	faune	même phase de comblement que la céramique

(Continued)

Table 13.1. Tableau de l'ensemble des datations isotopiques disponibles se rapportant aux mobiliers céramiques pour la région étudiée. (Continued)

Dept	Site	Lieu-dit	nature du site		Lab no.	BP	BC cal [1]	Élément daté	Rapport avec le mobilier céramique pris en compte dans l'étude
80	Argoeuves	Le Moulin d'Argoeuves	funéraire	Monument B	GrA-44229	3100±35	1436–1266	Bois de cerf	phase finale du comblment du fossé du monument
59	Lauwin-Planque	Les Dix-neuf	funéraire	Fosse 6357	GrA-39120	3080±30	1418–1264	charbon	charbon associé à l'amas osseux en urne
62	Dainville	Les Biefs	funéraire	enclos	GrA-14976	3065±40	1420–1222	Incinération	même monument mais phase éventuellement différente
59	Lauwin-Planque	Milterlotte, B	habitat	Fosse 1832	Beta 339524	3040±30	1397–1216	charbon	même phase de comblement que la céramique
60	La Croix-Saint-Ouen	Le Parc Scientifique	funéraire	enclos	GrA-14511	3035±45	1412–1131	Incinération	rejetée dans le fossé/ postérieur au fossé
62	Aire-sur-la-Lys	ZAC Hameau Saint-Martin	habitat	fosse A70	GrA-51089	3025±30	1395–1132	charbon	même phase de comblement que la céramique
62	Courrières	Carrière Beugnet	habitat	Fosse 1024	Beta 256921	3020±40	1397–1128	charbon	même phase de comblement que la céramique
80	Breuil-Languevoisin	La Sablière	habitat	st. 53	Beta 44804	2980±25	1277–1121	charbon	charbon associé au mobilier céramique

[1]Calibration d'après le programme OxCal, IntCal 13

« La Bonne Fache 1 » (3865 ± 55 BP, 2474–2148 BC cal [1]) en association avec un décor à la cordelette (Blanchet 1984, 105) pourrait aussi être placé dans la fin du IIIème millénaire. Mais si l'on regarde vers la Normandie, les céramiques à motif de cannelures sont attestées dans la phase 1 du site de Tatihou (Manche), placé dans la première moitié du second millénaire (Marcigny et *al.* 2003).

Les décors des quelques tessons résiduels (Fig. 13.31B) issus du remplissage du fossé d'Argoeuves « Le Moulin d'Argoeuves » (monument A) évoquent ceux des vases de Compiègne « le Fond Pernant » (Blanchet 1984, 103) placés dans une fourchette haute, 3890±180 BP (2881–1917 cal BC[2]) qui recouvre l'étape 3 du Néolithique final du nord de la France et le début du Bronze ancien (Salanova et al. 2011), de même que les décors à la cordelette d'Etaples « Mont Bagarre » (enclos 100) (Pas-de-Calais, Desfossés 2000) dont la datation est large (fin Bronze A1-début Bronze A2, Table 13.1) et ceux du vase de Fréthun « Les Rietz » (Bostyn *et al.* 1992). La date dont on dispose pour le site de Fréthun est décalée sur la fin du Bronze ancien et le début du Bronze moyen ou Bronze A2-B (Table 13.1). Cette datation ne concerne cependant pas le vase, trouvé dans le fossé circulaire du monument funéraire, mais une inhumation associée au même monument. Le vase peut donc être antérieur à cette sépulture, bien que sa forme, à carène haute et lèvre oblique est comparable à celle des vases de Crouy « Les Quatre » (Somme, Blanchet 1984, 103) et de Vitry-en-Artois « Les Colombiers » (Pas-de-Calais, Azagury et Demolon, 1990) situés au début du Bronze moyen (Bronze B/Bronze moyen I, Table 13.1). Le fond du fossé du monument A d'Argoeuves a livré un fragment de faune dont la datation est proche de celle de Fréthun (Table 13.1) et, également, de la phase de construction du monument B (Table 13.1) du même site localisé à une cinquantaine de mètres du monument A. Le fait que cet os et les tessons décorés relèvent d'une même phase d'occupation reste cependant de l'ordre de l'hypothèse.

En l'état de nos connaissances, la datation de la forme à col développé et double cordon courbe oblique digité de Villers-Carbonnel, « La Sole d'Applincourt » (Somme, Fig. 13.38) est délicate, même si la forme rentrante à épaulement convexe évoque plutôt des formes anciennes comme celle de Compiègne « Le Fond Pernant » (Blanchet 1984 ; Billard *et al.* 1996).

Fin du Bronze ancien-début du Bronze moyen (fin Bonze A1-Bronze A2–Bronze B)

Plusieurs découvertes récentes sont indubitablement à situer dans cette phase mais, dans certains cas, la datation est plus délicate.

Il en va ainsi du vase de la fosse d'habitat 364 de Maroeuil « Rue Curie » (Pas-de-Calais) dont l'état fragmentaire ne

nous offre aucun renseignement sur la présence éventuelle de décors rapportés (anses arciformes ?) au niveau de la panse. Le décor (restitué, Fig. 13.19) de lignes obliques et espacées d'impressions au peigne ou à la cordelette supporte une datation haute.

Dans le cas des découvertes de Samer « Route de Desvres » (structure 18.1) (Pas-de-Calais), le décor couvrant à l'ongle (Fig. 13.28) rappelle le mode décoratif campaniforme, mais l'une des forme de cet ensemble, ovoïde à lèvre dégagée se retrouve dans l'incinération 600bis d'Etaples « Mont Bagarre », subcontemporaine ou postérieure du fossé 300 pour lequel on dispose d'une datation (Ly 7445: 3390±70 BP, Table 13.1) (Desfossés 2000, fig. 37).

La forme quasi complète à lèvre oblique issue du remplissage supérieur du fossé du monument A d'Argoeuves (Fig. 13.31A) pourrait être rapprochée de certains exemples de la phase 1 du site de Tatihou située à la fin Bronze ancien/début du Bronze moyen (Marcigny et al. 2005, fig. 4), si on lui restitue un profil curviligne peu renflé. Dans l'hypothèse d'un profil segmenté, elle peut s'apparenter aux formes du Translay « Chemin de Morival » (Somme) pour lesquelles une même fourchette chronologique a été proposée (Buchez et Talon 2005, fig. 3). Quoi qu'il en soit, cette forme serait alors antérieure à l'inhumation centrale du monument (Table 13.1) ce qui n'apparaît guère cohérent. La série de datations obtenue pour les fossés d'enclos funéraires du site d'Avelin « Route Départementale 549 » (Nord) qui livrent le même type de céramique que la fosse centrale de ce monument convergent sur la fin du Bronze A1 et le début du Bronze A2 (Table 13.1). Le profil du vase de petite dimension est discontinu, marqué par un épaulement (Fig. 13.2). La lèvre est éversée et amincie. Le décor est représenté par des mamelons tantôt horizontaux tantôt verticaux, probablement au nombre de quatre. Bien que ses contours soient plus mous, le petit vase non décoré associé au monument funéraire de Fontaine-Notre-Dame « Les Dix-Huit » (Nord, Fig. 13.5) est morphologiquement proche de celui d'Avelin. Il rappelle également, en petit module, celle de la céramique 50083-84 de Villeneuve-d'Ascq « La Haute Borne » (Nord, *cf. infra*).

L'ensemble des caractéristiques du vase X8-10 (contexte domestique ?) de Marquion « Plateforme du canal SNE » (Pas-de-Calais) – morphologie générale, bord en biseau, cordon complété de deux oreilles horizontales étirées, marquées sur leur tranche par des impressions digitées (Fig. 13.22) – se retrouvent dans l'urne funéraire de l'enclos 1 de Fresnes-les-Montauban « Le Motel » (Pas-de-Calais) (datation obtenue sur l'inhumation du même monument, 3380±50 BP, Bronze ancien II-début Bronze moyen/Bronze A2-début Bronze B, Table 13.1). La morphologie du vase de 50083-84 de Villeneuve-d'Ascq « La Haute Borne » (Fig. 13.12), muni d'un cordon et de deux éléments arciformes digités est également similaire.

Le profil moins renflé du vase funéraire de Flers-en-Escrebieux « Les Prés Loribes » (Nord) portant des cordons arciformes (Fig. 13.6) est proche de ceux issus de la fosse d'habitat 64 de Cuiry-les-Chaudardes « Le Champ Tortu » (Letterlé 1982).

Le décor d'un cordon digité, horizontal et arciforme, de l'urne de Lauwin-Planque *« Les Dix-neuf »* (Nord, enclos 7, st. 6096, Fig. 13.7) trouve comparaison étroite avec le motif en cordon digité horizontal et arciforme fermé d'un tesson de la même structure de Cuiry-les-Chaudardes. La présence sur ce site d'un moule en calcaire du type Porcieu-Amblagnieu conduit à le situer au Bronze C ou plutôt du début de cette étape (Brun *et al.* 2005). La date de Lauwin-Planque (3290±40 BP, Table 13.1) est effectivement dans une fourchette relativement basse.

Le vase de Saint-Laurent-Blangy « Les Soixantes » (Pas-de-Calais, Fig. 13.26), à carène haute et munie de deux mamelons placés au-dessus de la carène, semble devoir être située dans le même horizon que les céramiques de Vitry-en-Artois « Les Colombiers » (Azagury et Demolon 1990) et du Translay « Le Chemin de Morival », ces dernières ayant été comparées aux mobiliers de Neer dans le Limbourg néerlandais (Buchez et Talon 2005) pour lesquels on dispose d'une date (GrA-14529) qui donne 3340±40 BP (1739–1521 BC cal)[3]. La datation obtenue sur une inhumation d'enfant situé dans le remplissage supérieur du fossé où a été découvert ce vase (Table 13.1) est cohérente avec cette proposition.

L'un des vases du silo 1555 de Brébières « Les Béliers » (Nord) est muni d'un cordon arciforme qui semble se répéter au moins trois fois (Fig. 13.14). La forme, à épaulement rentrant, ressaut et bord évasé à lèvre aplatie (1555-1), trouve aussi des analogies avec l'urne de Vitry-en-Artois et le vase du Translay. Ce type de lèvre est par ailleurs affilié à l'horizon *Hilversum* ancien aux Pays-Bas (type A3) (Fokkens 2005 ; Bourgeois et Talon 2009). Un second individu rencontre sa réplique quasi-exacte à Nonant « La Bergerie » (Calvados) dont les datations [14]C s'étalent autour de 1500–1400 (Marcigny *et al.* 2005). Il s'agit d'un pot tronconique aux parois subverticales (1555-4), présentant un percement dans sa partie supérieure. Les affinités de l'ensemble de Nonant avec le groupe anglais de *Deverel-Rimbury* sont évoquées. Deux bols aux gabarits plus réduits (respectivement 1555-2 et 1555-8) et aux formes plus ubiquistes trouvent des éléments de comparaison avec des vases à profils simples et légèrement rentrants qui semblent caractériser le début de l'Âge du bronze moyen européen comme par exemple dans la phase ancienne du *Hoogkarspel* (Pays-Bas) sur le site éponyme (Fokkens 2005, fig. 13a, 2 et 3). En France, ce sont les sites de Nonant « La Bergerie » (Marcigny *et al.* 2005), Lauwin-Planque « ZAC » (Leroy-Langelin, 2015) et de Roeux « Le Château d'eau » (Pas-de-Calais, Desfossés *et al.* 1992) qui contiennent quelques petits bols similaires. Ces trois sites sont assimilés

au *Deverel-Rimbury*. L'ensemble de Brébières présente donc des composantes se rapportant au Bronze ancien, mais associé à des formes qui paraissent déjà se rattacher à un horizon plus récent, le conduisant à le placer, comme celui de Nonant au début du Bronze moyen (Bronze B).

Fin du Bronze moyen-début du Bronze final (Bronze C–D)

Un faciès cohérent se dégage pour cette période.

La découverte de Renancourt « Le Coup de couteau » (Somme, Fig. 13.37) vient compléter le corpus des formes trapues simples aux parois sub-verticales morphologiquement rattachées à la sphère culturelle *Deverel-Rimbury* déjà connues pour la Somme (Licourt « Carrière Boinet » et Wiencourt-L'Equipée « Fond de Bayonvilliers », Buchez et Talon 2005, fig. 2).

Les récipients de petite taille d'Escaudain-Erre « RN 455 » (Nord), st. 1005 (Fig. 13.4) et Dainville « Les Biefs » (Pas-de-Calais, Fig. 13.17) rappellent la forme à paroi peu oblique et décorée de boutons mise en évidence lors de la fouille de la double enceinte du Bronze moyen de la « ZI sud » de Mondeville en Normandie (Chancerel *et al.* 2006) et renvoient aux découvertes régionales de céramiques légèrement plus hautes telles Croixrault, « Le Fayards » (Somme, st. 323.20), Eterpigny-Barleux « Les Croix Noires » (Somme, st. 62.2) (Figs 13.33 et 13.34). La petite forme pourvue de neuf ergots coniques de Dainville est cependant atypique. Issue du fossé de l'enclos funéraire dont l'aire centrale était occupée par une sépulture à incinération (GrA-14976, 3065±40 BP, 1420–1222 cal BC), elle évoque les vases accessoires mis au jour dans les sépultures du Bronze ancien en Bretagne, dans les îles anglo-normandes et en Grande-Bretagne. Outre-manche, ces petits récipients aux formes variés portent le nom générique de *pigmy cup* et leur fonction reste inconnue.

De façon générale, les formes simples à paroi légèrement obliques (tronconique à légèrement curviligne) ou rentrante portant des éléments plastiques se retrouvent à Etricourt-Manancourt « Le Tarteron » (st. 323.20, Fig. 13.36) dans la Somme, à Vitry-en-Artois « Aérodrome » (Fig. 13.29) et Monchy-le-Preux (Fig. 13.24) dans le Pas-de-Calais et à Villeneuve d'Ascq « La Haute-Borne » (st. 43198, Fig. 13.11), Avelin « Route Départementale 549 » (st. 1501, Fig. 13.3), Lauwin-Planque « Les Dix-neuf » (Fig. 13.8) et « Milterlotte » (zone B, Fig. 13.9) dans le Nord. Les éléments plastiques sont des boutons ou mamelons placés sous le bord, percés verticalement dans le cas du vase d'Avelin où l'arrachement de ceux-ci au niveau des perforations laisse envisager un système de fermeture (couvercle ?). Toujours à Avelin et également à Lauwin-Planque « Milterlotte », ces éléments sont associés à un cordon rapporté lisse ou digité placé sur la partie haute du profil. À Croixrault, le cordon – lisse dans ce cas – apparaît sur un second vase, le premier portant des boutons sous le bord. L'unique vase découvert à Villeneuve-d'Ascq comporte un cordon digité. A Etricourt-Manancourt, il ne s'agit pas de cordons rapportés mais d'un simple épaississement – digité dans un cas – placé au niveau d'une légère inflexion dans le profil. On retrouve cette légère inflexion marquée d'impressions à l'ongle à Vitry-en-Artois « Rue Nobled ».

Ces caractères morphologiques et décoratifs sont apparentés à l'horizon *Deverel-Rimbury*, couvrant la fin du Bronze moyen et le début du Bronze final (Bronze C–D) sur les deux rives de la Manche et de la mer du Nord. Ils remémorent l'assemblage régional de Roeux « Château d'Eau » (Desfossés *et al.* 1992) et ceux de Tatihou (Marcigny et Ghesquière 2003) et de Mondeville « ZI sud » (Chancerel *et al.* 2006) en Normandie. Ils montrent également des affinités culturelles avec les sites britanniques de Puddletown Heath dans le Dorset (Calkin 1964), de Grimes Graves à la frontière entre le Norfolk et le Suffolk (Mercer 1981), de Perry Oaks dans le Middlesex (Every et Mepham), de Merton Rise dans Hampshire (Wright *et al.* 2009).

Une impression à l'ongle sur lèvre aplatie est répertoriée à Vitry-en-Artois « L'aérodrome » (Fig. 13.29). Dans l'état actuel des connaissances, au sein de l'horizon *Deverel-Rimbury* régional, le décor à l'ongle est peu représenté. Il trouve des parentés avec les sites de Roeux « Château d'Eau » (Desfossés *et al.* 1992, 365) et de Lauwin-Planque « Milterlotte, zone B ». De l'autre côté de la Manche, les impressions ongulées sont une composante des assemblages *Deverel-Rimbury* du groupe de la vallée inférieure de la Tamise (*Lower Thames Valley Group*), défini par A. Ellison (Leivers 2008).

On dispose de 4 datations ^{14}C (Lauwin-Planque, Dainville et Escaudain-Erre) se rapportant à la fourchette Bronze C–D (Table 13.1).

Bien que plus renflée, l'urne funéraire d'Argoeuves présentant des mamelons sur la lèvre (Fig. 13.32) se place globalement dans la même fourchette (Table 13.1).

Le site de Courrières « Rue Beuchez-Bouchez » (Pas-de-Calais) également (Table 13.1), mais ses mobiliers (Fig. 13.16), se différencient nettement d'un point de vue morphologique et se caractérisent notamment par de courtes lèvre obliques ou en biseau qui suggèrent d'y voir une phase postérieure à celle des céramiques précédemment évoquées (Buchez et Henton, ce volume).

Les vestiges résiduels du site de Brébières « Les Béliers » (Pas-de-Calais, Fig. 13.15) et ceux de la structure 206 de Maroeuil « Rue Curie » (Pas-de-Calais, Fig. 13.21) qui présentent certaines affinités peuvent être, en première approche et dans l'attente de nouvelles découvertes, associées aux ensembles couvrant globalement le Bronze moyen et une étape ancienne du Bronze final (Bronze B-D-Hallstatt A1, Buchez et Henton ce volume), de même que le site de Hingues « zone de Vertannoy » (Pas-de-Calais, Fig. 13.18). Dans le cas de Brébières, les vases à parois

subverticales ou rentrantes font écho à ceux attribués au *Deverel-Rimbury*. Les formes à profil rentrant ornées d'un décor digité de Brébières et Maroeuil sont aussi connues à Roeux « Château d'Eau » (Pas-de-Calais, Desfossés *et al.* 1992 ; Fig. 13.21). Dans le cas de Maroeuil, si certains éléments, comme les bandeaux appliqués et soulignés d'impressions digitées (03.2 et 03.3), ainsi que les décors d'impressions digitées sur rebord (03.4 et 03.5) sont connus jusqu'à l'aube du premier Âge du fer, certaines formes (03.1 et 04.1) dénotent avec la typologie actuellement reconnue pour la transition Bronze final/ premier Âge du fer dans le Nord-Pas-de-Calais. Le rebord d'écuelle 04.2, à lèvre coupée en marli externe trouve également des parallèles intéressants sur le site de Roeux « Château d'Eau » (Desfossés *et al.* 1992). Le peson associé est par ailleurs plus proche de ceux de Roeux que les exemplaires connus pour le Bronze final, de forme nettement plus sub-trapézoïdale.

Conclusions

Le corpus des mobiliers céramiques des phases anciennes de l'Âge du bronze s'étoffe petit à petit mais certaines étapes restent moins bien documentées (début du Bronze ancien et début du Bronze final).

Ainsi, en l'état des données, nous ne pouvons que reprendre les remarques de nos collègues néolithiciens sur les difficultés à cerner la transition Néolithique-Bronze (Salanova *et al.* 2011) et leur conclusion concernant la fin du IIIème millénaire qui s'appuie sur les datations ^{14}C les plus récentes obtenues pour les sites d'habitat de Bettencourt-St-Ouen (Somme, Martin *et al.* 1996) et Raillencourt-Saint-Olle (Nord, Martial *et al.* 2004). Ces habitats attribués aux groupes Deûle-Escaut livrent de gros assemblages non campaniformes et des éléments campaniformes, apparemment associés, l'articulation entre les deux composantes étant à clarifier.

Sur la base des datations ^{14}C disponibles (Fig. 13.39), le site de Compiègne « Le Fond Pernant » qui livre les attestations les plus anciennes de cordons arciformes reste le seul à pouvoir prendre place dans une étape initiale du Bronze ancien. Le cordon arciforme digité ou lisse, associé ou non à un cordon linéaire est une composante que l'on retrouve ensuite jusqu'au début du Bronze moyen II (Bronze C) d'après les datations proposées pour le site de Cuiry-les-Chaudardes (Brun *et al.* 2005), tout d'abord sur des formes à carène haute et à lèvre/col court oblique qui semblent centrées sur le Bronze moyen I (Fréthun, Crouy) ou sur le vase piriforme de Lauwin-Planque de même datation, puis sur les formes sub-verticales à légèrement rentrantes de type *Deverel Rimbury*. Si les nouvelles datations de Crouy et Lauwin-Planque confirment la distinction de deux faciès, sans décor à la cordelette associé pour le plus récent (« groupe d'Eramecourt » de

Jean-Claude Blanchet (1976) ; Billard *et al.* 1996), les toutes dernières découvertes d'Avelin et Marquion, faisant suite en cela à celle de Monchy-Lagache, mettent surtout l'accent sur la co-existence de différentes composantes et influences au Bronze ancien II–Bronze moyen I (Bronze A2–B), pour certaines issues du Néolithique final et que l'indigence en assemblages domestiques pour ces périodes ne permet pas d'appréhender pleinement. La position haute du vase de Marquion, à profil simple légèrement renflé portant des boutons sous le bord, conduit en outre à poser la question de la genèse de l'ensemble culturel qui s'étend au Bronze moyen II (début du Bronze final I/ Bronze C–début du Bronze D) des deux côtés de la Manche et de la Mer du Nord, induisant celle des processus en jeu dans l'« homogénéisation » de cette entité atlantique dite Manche-Mer-du-Nord (MMN, Bourgeois et Talon 2009 ; Marcigny et Talon 2009).

Pour ce qui est du Bronze final I-Bronze final IIa (Bronze D-Hallstatt A1), la découverte de Courrières, également calée par une datation ^{14}C, vient combler un vide documentaire, et montre un renouvellement des formes par ailleurs observé au sein de cette entité Manche-Mer-du-Nord (Bourgeois et Talon, 2009 ; Marcigny et Talon 2009). Le petit dépôt de parure découvert à peu de distance des deux fosses de Courrières présente des affinités continentales qu'il convient de souligner (Barbet *et al.* 2010). L'étape suivante de l'Âge du bronze – représentée dans notre figure synthétique par les quelques céramiques de datation haute des structures 53–58 de Breuil « La Sablière » (Somme) (Table 13.1) – étant marquée régionalement par la présence significative de composantes continentales (RSFO) (Buchez and Henton, ce volume).

Le corpus n'est pas suffisamment conséquent, quelle que soit la période, pour aborder les questions techniques des façons de faire et de leur évolution, même si à l'échelle micro-régionale (vallée de la Scarpe, Deckers 2010), il semble possible de dégager certaines caractéristiques. De grandes tendances sont néanmoins perceptibles lorsque l'on prend en compte le seul caractère documenté dans toutes les études réalisées (*cf. infra*, catalogue des découvertes) : le dégraissant. On observe à l'échelle de la zone étudiée (Nord, Pas-de-Calais, Somme), la prédominance de l'utilisation de la chamotte pour les phases du Néolithique final 3 (Campaniforme récent)-début Bronze ancien ou début du Bronze A1 (en association ou non, selon les vases, avec des éléments coquillés/calcaire coquillé ou d'os), utilisation qui perdure jusqu'à la fin du Bronze ancien–début du Bronze moyen (Bronze A2–B). L'emploi du silex concassé, souvent dans des proportions importantes, est un caractère récurrent de la période Bronze moyen II–début du Bronze final (Bronze C–D), même si la chamotte est attestée dans certains vases en association ou non avec le silex (questions de chronologie et/ou différences régionales).

Catalogue des découvertes

(La numérotation des sites renvoie à la carte de répartition, Fig. 13.1)

Nord

1. Avelin « Route Départementale 549 » (MD)
En 2010, une opération de fouille a donné lieu à la découverte inattendue de deux monuments funéraires annulaires de l'Âge du bronze ancien (Deckers 2010). Le premier monument correspond à un enclos simple ouvert au diamètre extérieur maximum de 6,46 m. Le second est un enclos à deux fossés interrompus de diamètres de 8,8 m et de 12,30 m. À une distance d'environ 50 m de ces structures fossoyées, une fosse circulaire (st. 1501) a été enregistrée.

AVELIN « ROUTE DEPARTEMENTALE 549 », ENCLOS SIMPLE OUVERT
L'ensemble des tessons collectés dans le remplissage du fossé d'enclos et dans la fosse centrale répondent aux mêmes critères morpho-technologiques, suggérant un seul et même individu (Po 552-079, Fig. 13.2).

– chamotte (module de 1 à 3 mm)/colombins (dépressions au niveau du bas de panse et de la lèvre enregistrées par l'analyse radiographique[4])/surfaces altérées : lissage soigné (pénétration des grains dans la pâte) ?/cuisson en milieu fumigé, avec une phase d'oxydation terminal/mamelons tantôt horizontaux tantôt verticaux probablement au nombre de quatre

AVELIN « ROUTE DEPARTEMENTALE 549 », ENCLOS A DEUX FOSSES INTERROMPUS
Des tessons appartenant à un récipient de profil identique que le vase précédemment cité a été découvert dans le comblement du fossé interne de l'enclos.

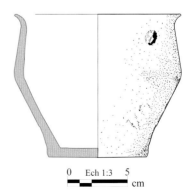

NORD - Avelin
« Route Départementale 549 »,
enclos simple ouvert

0   Ech 1:3   5
                 cm

Fig. 13.2. Nord, Avelin « Route Départementale 549 », enclos simple ouvert.

AVELIN « ROUTE DEPARTEMENTALE 549 », ST. 1501

Une fosse circulaire, aux parois presque verticales et à fond plat, a livré un vase fragmenté (1501-1, Fig. 13.3). L'épaisseur des parois oscillent de 110 à 140 mm. Le fond, épais de 250 à 290 mm.

– chamotte (module de 1 et 6 mm, fréquences de 15 à 20 %, selon la charte d'estimation visuelle de FitzPatrick, 1984) et silex rare (1%, calibre de 1 à 3 mm)/modelage (fond) et colombinage/lissage peu soigné/cuisson en mode réducteur avec une phase d'oxydation terminale/ mamelons à perforation verticale/traces de surchauffe (couleur gris-bleu, déformation de l'ouverture, etc.) et cordon rapporté.

2. Escaudain-Erre « RN 455 », st. 1005 (MD)

En 2004, suite au projet d'agrandissement de la RN 455, une fouille a été effectuée sur une surface de 24 000 m², permettant la mise au jour d'un habitat circulaire sur poteaux (Leroy-Langelin et Sys 2005). À proximité de cette construction, une fosse (st. 1005) a livré du mobilier céramique : 20 tessons se rapportant à 4 individus dont un, reconstitué (1005-4, Fig. 13.4).

– grains de silex (entre 1 mm et 3 mm, fréquence modérée (20%)/ des dépressions circulaires ont été observées sur la paroi externe à la jonction fond-panse/lissage sommaire/ cuisson réductrice à oxydation terminale

3. Fontaine-Notre-Dame « Les Dix-Huit » (NB)

Un double enclos (12 et 37 m de diamètre) a été décapé sur les ¾ de sa surface et étudié lors des diagnostics en vue du contournement de Cambrai en 2004 (Gaillard et Gustiaux 2004). Il était associé à une fosse centrale (oblongue, de 1.50 m de long sur 1 m de large et 0.12 m de profondeur). Intégralement fouillée, la fosse comblée d'un limon sableux brun grisâtre contenant quelques particules charbonneuse a livré un vase (Fig. 13.5), retrouvé couché dans l'angle nord (possible sépulture à inhumation dont les os ne sont pas conservés ?).

– pâte chamottée contenant une petite quantité de grains de silex fins (module ≤ 1 mm, atteignant rarement 2 mm, ajoutés ?)/joint perceptible au niveau du diamètre maximum/ surfaces abîmées (traces horizontales d'un lissage externe de type « main mouillée » ?)/tranche brun foncé à noire et surfaces à tendance brun clair

4. Flers-en-Escrebieu « Les Prés Loribe » (CG)

En 1999, un diagnostic réalisé dans le cadre de l'aménagement d'un échangeur routier sur la commune de Flers-en-Escrebieu a révélé la présence d'une fosse contenant les restes d'une incinération de l'Âge du bronze (Severin 1999). La fosse, oblongue, profonde de 30 cm maximum, contenait dans sa partie orientale les vestiges d'une urne non retournée, qui renfermait un amas osseux.

NORD - Avelin « Route Départementale 549 », structure 1501

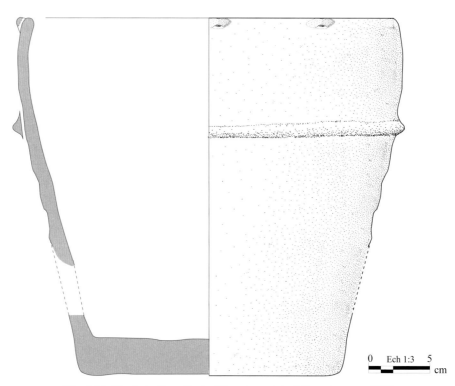

0   Ech 1:3   5
cm

Fig. 13.3. Nord, Avelin « Route Départementale 549 », structure 1501.

Le vase, très érodé, n'a jamais fait l'objet d'une restauration et seule sa partie supérieure a pu être décrite (Fig. 13.6).

– *Chamotte/ pâte noire et surfaces de teinte orangée/trois cordons arciformes, en très mauvais état de conservation, a priori appliqués.*

5. Lauwin-Planque « Les Dix-neuf » / « Milterlotte » (MD)
Le projet d'aménagement d'une « ZAC » à Lauwin-Planque a occasionné la réalisation de diagnostics sur une superficie de 110 hectares (Leroy-Langelin 2015). Au total, 23 hectares ont été fouillés. Onze cercles funéraires, une crémation isolée[5] et un site d'habitat de l'Âge du bronze ont ainsi pu être mis en évidence.

LAUWIN-PLANQUE « LES DIX-NEUF », ENCLOS 7, ST. CENTRALE 6096
Ici, 253 éléments constituent une urne (6096-1, Fig. 13.7) recueillie au sein d'une fosse ovoïde centrée dans l'aire interne de l'enclos annulaire. Déposée en position retournée, elle contenait la crémation. Suite à sa regrettable restauration menant à une mauvaise orientation de la panse, nous nous

limiterons à une proposition de restitution du profil basée sur les extrémités du récipient.

– *silex et chamotte, selon des fréquences de 15% et 20%, de calibrage de 2 mm et de 4 mm/ parois épaisses/cuisson en milieu confiné avec une phase d'oxydation terminale/ finition par lissage simple observable sous le rebord, sur la panse et sur la paroi interne/cordon à impressions digitées alternes, par endroit arciforme (peut-être au nombre de 4)*

LAUWIN-PLANQUE, « LES DIX-NEUF », ST. 6357
À environ 150 m au nord-ouest de la zone B, une fosse ovale a livré un amas osseux accompagné d'un vase (6357-1, Fig. 13.8). Cet amas contient des éléments squelettiques d'au moins quatre individus, dont deux immatures. Le

NORD - Escaudain-Erre « RN 455 »,
structure 1005

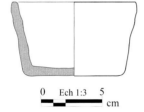

0   Ech 1:3   5
cm

Fig. 13.4. Nord, Escaudin-Erre « RN 455 », structure 1005.

NORD
Fontaine-Notre-Dame
« Les Dix-Huit »

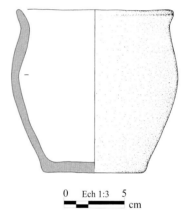

0   Ech 1:3   5
cm

Fig. 13.5. Nord, Fontaine-Notre-Dame « Les Dix-huit ».

NORD - Flers-en-Escrebieu « Les Prés Loribe »

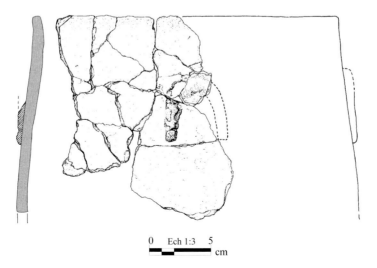

0   Ech 1:3   5
cm

Fig. 13.6. Nord, Flers-en-Escrebieu « Les Prés Loribe ».

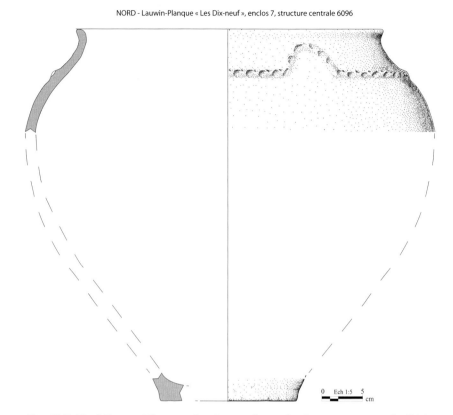

Fig. 13.7. Nord, Lauwin-Planque « Les Dix-neuf », enclos 7, structure centrale 6096.

NORD - Lauwin-Planque « Les Dix-neuf », structure 6357

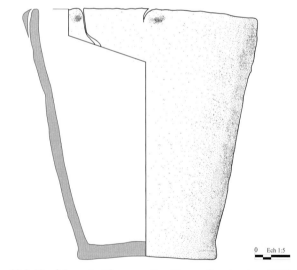

Fig. 13.8. Nord, Lauwin-Planque « Les Dix-neuf », structure 6357.

récipient est complet. Il est déformé, contracté, marqué par une réduction importante de son volume, traduisant un phénomène de re-cuisson ou de surcuisson

– silex et de chamotte en proportion quasi équivalente (fréquences respectives de 15% et 20%), montage aux colombins larges de 1 cm et fond réalisé à partir d'une

galette d'argile/cuisson en atmosphère réductrice avec une phase d'oxydation terminale/ boutons rapportés

LAUWIN-PLANQUE « MILTERLOTTE, ZONE B »
La fouille de la zone B, ouverte au nord de la « ZAC » sur une surface de 14 000 m², a permis de mettre au jour plusieurs structures dont les résultats les plus importants concernent la découverte d'un site d'habitat de l'Âge du bronze moyen II-final I-IIa. Le mobilier céramique (Fig. 13.9) est constitué de 462 tessons se rapportant à 116 individus dont 20 ont été retrouvés en position résiduelle.

– céramique fine (1832-4) dégraissé de chamotte à 5%/pâtes grossières : silex ou associé à de la chamotte/ traitement de surface le plus usité : lissage sommaire/ cuisson de mode réducteur à oxydation terminale externe largement majoritaire/ décors plastiques (cordons digités, mamelons et boutons) et en creux (impressions au doigt et à l'ongle). Ils constituent 3.8% de l'ensemble et témoignent d'une faible représentation des décors mixtes.

6. Pecquencourt « ZAC Barrois », résiduel, (CG)
Un diagnostic réalisé sur une parcelle de 40 ha au printemps 2010 (Rorive 2010) a permis de mettre au jour, dans une tranchée, mais sans structure apparente, un pot composé d'une dizaine de tessons et dont seule la partie supérieure a été conservée (Fig. 13.10).

NORD
Lauwin-Planque « Milterlotte, zone B »

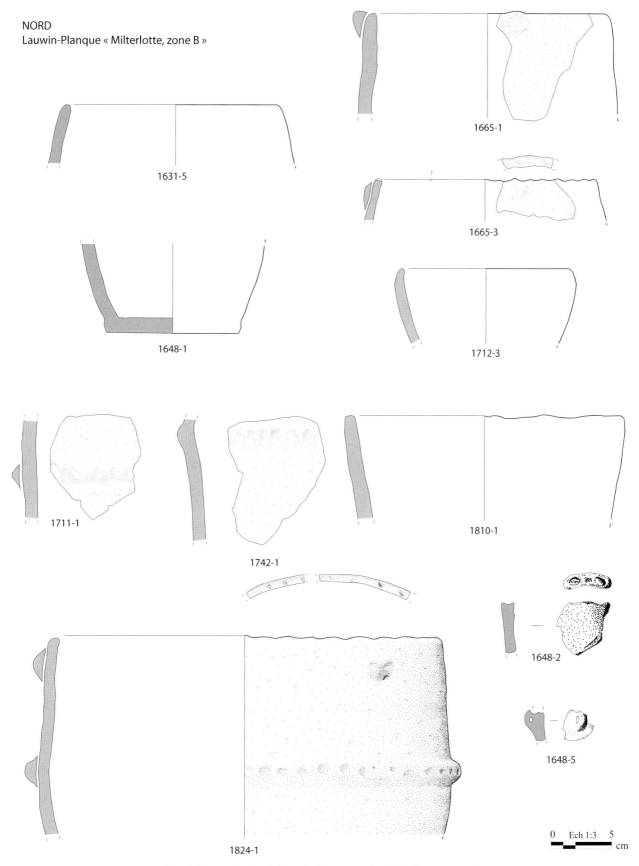

Fig. 13.9. a et b. Nord, Lauwin-Planque « La Milterlotte », zone B.

NORD - Pecquencourt
« ZAC Barrois », mobilier résiduel

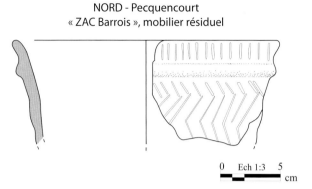

0   Ech 1:3   5

cm

Fig. 13.10. Nord, Pecquencourt « ZAC Barrois », mobilier résiduel.

– *fins grains de chamotte/ intérieur soigneusement lissés (de même que l'extérieur, altéré ?)/ surfaces noires à gris-clair/blanc, en passant par l'orange, avec un cœur noir/cordon horizontal appliqué environ 1,5 cm et larges incisions, a priori couvrantes, formant un motif en arête de poisson.*

7. Villeneuve d'Ascq « La Haute Borne », structure 43198 (AH)
De 2000 à 2005, près de 140 hectares ont été diagnostiqués ou fouillés sur le site du Parc Scientifique de la Haute Borne, à la limite de Villeneuve d'Ascq et de Sainghin-en-Mélantois (Deflorenne 2013). L'Âge du bronze ancien-moyen est représenté par quelques structures diffuses et isolées.

La première structure (fosse ou chablis), St 43198, a livré une quarantaine de tessons d'un même individu (Fig. 13.11).

– *grosse chamotte (8 mm pour les plus gros nodules)/ surfaces faiblement égalisées, irrégulières (dégraissant visible)/gris beige à beige orangé/anses arciformes et cordon appliqué et décor de petites impressions avec traces d'ongles ou simples traces d'ongles verticales (face interne du bord).*

VILLENEUVE D'ASCQ « LA HAUTE BORNE », STRUCTURES 50083 ET 50084 (AH)
Ces fosses proches et de nature indéterminée (Deflorenne 2013) ont été associées suite au remontage de tessons d'un même vase. Près d'une cinquantaine de tessons ont été recueillis dans la structure 50083, représentant un seul individu (Fig. 13.12)

– *silex concassé et chamotte (module de 5 mm max)/ surfaces égalisées et irrégulières (dégraissant visible en surface)/ tranche grise et surfaces grises à beige orangé/ cordon appliqué rehaussé d'impressions digitées profondes avec traces d'ongles.*

Le second ensemble (50084) a livré 5 tessons (*chamotte/ surfaces gris noir (interne) à gris beige (externe)/résidus de combustion visibles sur la surface interne*) associés à un peson de forme cylindrique et de section sub-rectangulaire

(*pâte grise sans dégraissant apparent, surfaces gris à jaune. Perforation centrale. Diam. Peson : 11.5cm, ép. : 5.5 cm, diam. Perforation : 1.2 cm*) et à une douzaine de nodules de torchis cuit, dont des fragments de parois et des possibles fragments d'un second peson.

Pas-de-Calais

8. Aire-sur-La-Lys « ZAC Hameau Saint-Martin » (AH)
Ce site, fouillé en 2004–2005 dans le cadre de l'aménagement d'une ZAC (rapport en cours), a livré une occupation continue du Néolithique final à La Tène moyenne. Les indices d'une occupation datée du Bronze ancien-moyen sont plus rares et sont représentés essentiellement à travers une fosse-silo à vase enterré et écrêté par l'érosion, découverte au diagnostic (A75, NTT : 102, NMI : 1 à 2). Le matériel céramique est accompagné de trois éclats de silex, dont deux chauffés (Fig. 13.13 ; [14]C : Table 13.1).

– *forte concentration de dégraissant minéral (inclusions de silex et de calcaire concassé/pâte grise et surface gris à gris beige, irrégulières (dégraissant apparent)/cordon appliqué rehaussé d'une série d'impressions digitées jointives.*

9. Brébières « Les Béliers » (CG)
Un diagnostic réalisé sur une emprise totale de 60ha entre 2006 et 2007 a permis la mise au jour de vestiges du premier et du second Âge du fer. La fouille de 17 ha, commencée en 2008, a révélé, entre autre, une occupation attribuée au Bronze final III composée d'une palissade cernant des bâtiments quadrangulaires. Aucun mobilier céramique n'y a cependant été recueilli. Toutefois, une centaine de mètres plus au sud, un petit bâtiment circulaire bien caractéristique du Bronze moyen a été découvert. Une fosse implantée à proximité immédiate de cette habitation a livré quelques tessons de céramique, auxquels peuvent s'ajouter quelques éléments issus de structures en partie effacées par les occupations du premier et surtout du second Âge du fer ou en position remaniée dans ces dernières (Huvelle et Lacalmontie, 2012 ; 2015).

BREBIERES « LES BELIERS », ST. 1555
Ce silo a été découvert à environ une centaine de mètres au sud d'un bâtiment circulaire attribué au Bronze moyen. Son comblement, constitué de limon mêlé à du charbon et de l'argile cuite en grande quantité, contenait 86 tessons de céramique, pour un poids d'environ un kg, se rapportant à 11 individus, dont quatre formes identifiables (Fig. 13.14).

1555-1 : grains de silex et de chamotte, de granulométrie moyenne (parfois supérieure à 2 mm), avec une prépondérance d'éléments siliceux/lissage, assez sommaire (grains de dégraissant non intégrés dans la pâte rendant le vase rugueux au toucher)/pâte grise et surfaces zonées

NORD - Villeneuve d'Ascq « La Haute Borne », structure 43198

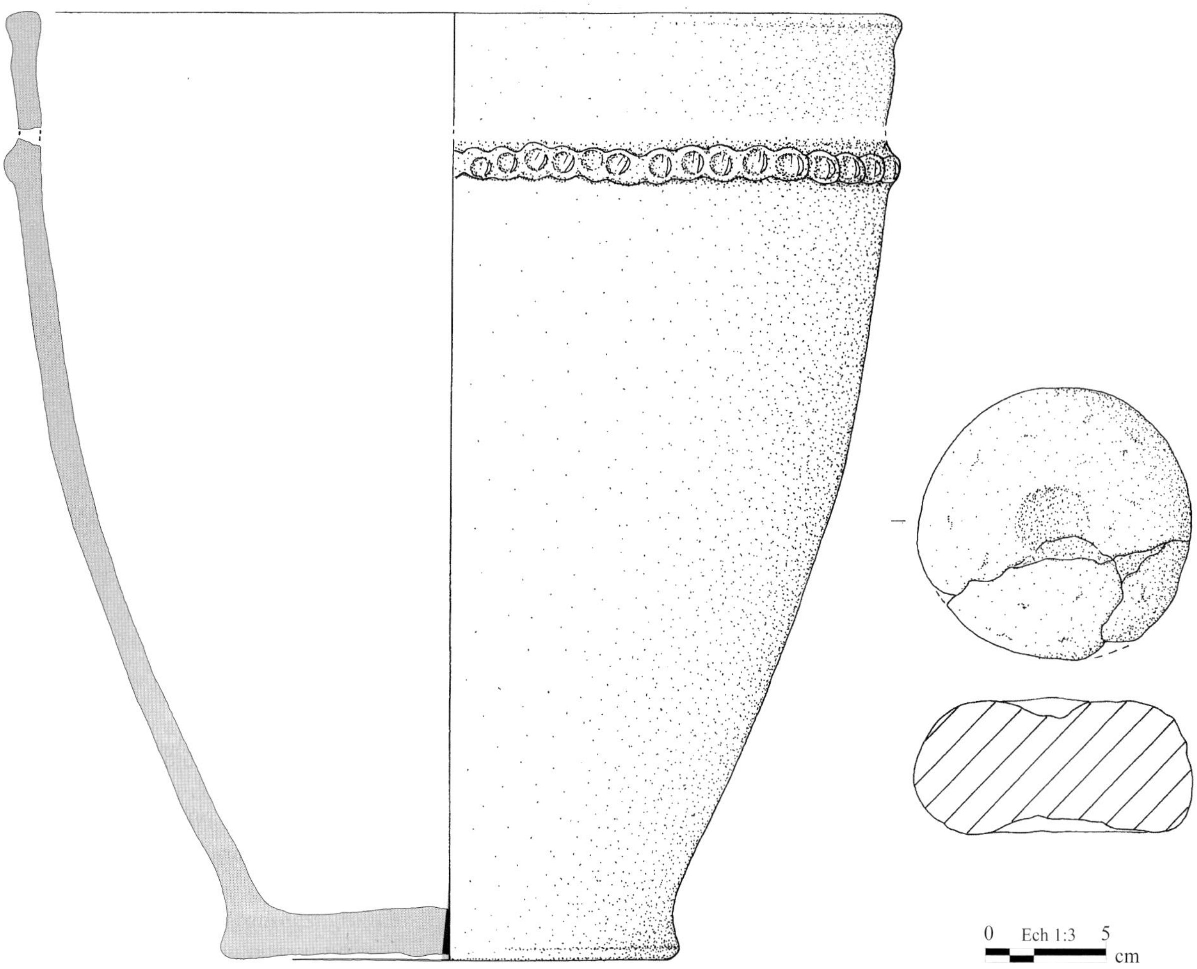

Fig. 13.11. Nord, Villeneuve-d'Asq « La Haute Borne », structure 43198.

allant du gris foncé au niveau de la lèvre et de la surface interne, au brun clair à orangé sur le reste de la panse/ cordon arciforme appliqué au niveau de l'épaule et semblant se répéter au moins trois fois.

1555-4 : dégraissant, peu dense, de chamotte de taille moyenne (jusqu'à 2 mm) et de très rares grains de silex/ parois, bosselées (égalisation sommaire)/teintes sombres, que l'on retrouve dans la tranche/trou de réparation dans sa partie supérieure.

1555-2 : chamotte, de calibre modéré (jusqu'à 2 mm)/ surfaces lissées grossièrement qui restent irrégulières au toucher/pâte de couleur noire et surfaces de tonalité brune

1555-8 : fins grains de chamotte et de silex peu denses/ lissage sommaire (grains saillants/surface externe de couleur blanchâtre (re-cuisson) et paroi interne présentant des tonalités brun-clair

BREBIERES « LES BELIERS » ST. 1010, 1016, 1556, 1557, 1605, 2780, 2795, 1316, 1134 ET MOBILIER RESIDUEL

Une petite série composée d'une centaine de tessons à l'aspect similaire est issue d'une dizaine de fosses réparties inégalement au sein du site. Les quatre premières structures (1010, 1016, 1556, 1557) sont implantées à proximité immédiate du bâtiment circulaire attribué à l'Âge du bronze. Les autres structures sont disséminées dans une large zone au sud des occupations de l'Âge du bronze, au sein des occupations du premier et du second Âge du fer. Dans cette même aire, plusieurs enclos laténiens ont livré du mobilier résiduel que l'on peut rattacher à l'Âge du bronze. Les seuls éléments morphologiques sont issus de la structure 1605 (Fig. 13.16), retrouvée au sein ce cet habitat laténien, à plusieurs centaines de mètres au sud des aires d'occupation de l'Âge du bronze.

Les tessons ont été réunis en raison de la grande homogénéité de leur aspect technique :

– *massivement dégraissés au silex, d'une granulométrie très grossière, certains grains dépassant 4 mm/finition peu poussée (inclusions saillantes, parois rugueuses)/cœur de teinte foncée et surfaces variant du noir au orange, avec une dominante clair/impressions ongulées et cordons digités.*

10. Courrières « Carrière Beugnet », structures 1023 et 1024 (AH)

Ce site a été diagnostiqué par l'Inrap et fouillé en 2008 par la DapCAD dans le cadre d'un projet de lotissement. Au cœur d'une occupation du Bronze final IIIb, deux structures indiquent une occupation antérieure (Barbet 2009). Près de 84 tessons (NMI : 8) ont été dégagés (Fig. 13.16). Notons la proximité d'un dépôt d'objets de parure (4 perles en ambre,

épingle à tête sub-biconique et un rasoir à manche annelé) attribuable au BfI/IIa (Barbet 2010 ; Henton 2013).

– *pâte à forte concentration d'inclusions minérales (silex concassé), quelques tessons à dégraissant mixte (chamotte et silex)/pâte variant du gris au beige orangé et surfaces gris beige à beige orangé, à dégraissant apparent/impressions digitées et cordon appliqué*

11. Dainville « Les Biefs » (MT)

Lors de la fouille réalisée en 1988 par le service archéologique municipal d'Arras à l'emplacement du bassin no. 2 sur la rocade Ouest d'Arras, un enclos funéraire de l'Âge du bronze a été mis au jour. D'un diamètre de 18.60 m, il présente dans son aire centrale les restes d'une sépulture à incinération qui a pu être datée du Bronze moyen (Table 13.1). Dans la partie basse du remplissage du fossé a été découvert un petit

NORD - Villeneuve d'Ascq « La Haute Borne », structures 50083 et 50084

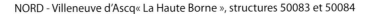

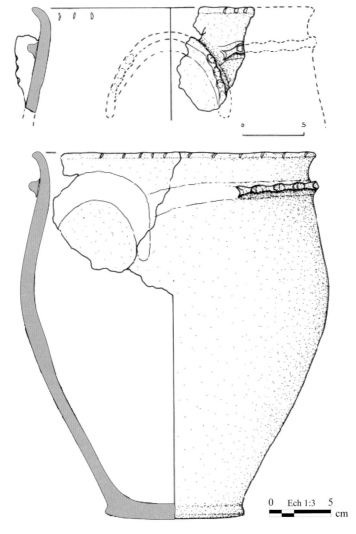

Fig. 13.12. Nord, Villeneuve-d'Asq « La Haute Borne », structures 50083 et 50084.

récipient en céramique de forme presque quadrangulaire (5 × 5.7 cm) de 3.2 cm de hauteur et dont le pourtour est pourvu de neuf petits ergots coniques (Fig. 13.17).

PAS-DE-CALAIS
Aire-sur-la-Lys « ZAC Hameau Saint-Martin »

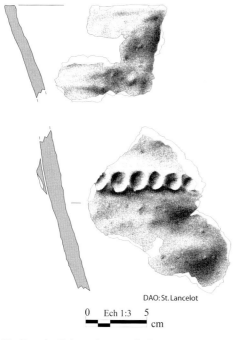

DAO: St. Lancelot

0   Ech 1:3   5
cm

Fig. 13.13. Pas-de-Calais, Aire-sur-la-Lys « ZAC Hameau Saint-Martin ».

– pâte est noire avec un peu de chamotte rouge, dégraissée de petits morceaux de silex en grandes proportions/surface interne grise à rougeâtre et externe de rougeâtre à brun.

12. Hingues « Zone du Vertannoy » », structures 03, 04 et 05 (AH)

Deux fosses et un silo découverts en 2009 lors d'un diagnostic mené sur un projet de lotissement (Thoquenne 2009).

NTT : respectivement 58, 64 et 20, NMI : respectivement : 5, 4 et 3. Mobilier associé à un peu de lithique et à un peson de terre cuite de section sub-ovalaire (Fig. 18)

– silex concassé, particulièrement abondant/pâte grise et surfaces gis beige à beige orangé/impressions digitées sur lèvre et sur cordon appliqué.

13. Maroeuil « Rue Curie » (AH)

Dans le cadre d'un projet de lotissement, ce site a été fouillé sur une surface d'1,8 hectare. L'occupation principale concerne un habitat groupé de l'Âge du bronze final, implanté à peu de distance d'un enclos circulaire de 41 m de diamètre daté du Bronze moyen. A proximité de ce dernier, quelques rares fosses isolées témoignent d'une possible occupation contemporaine de l'enclos, mais aussi d'une plus ancienne (Lorin 2011).

MAROEUIL, STRUCTURE 364, FOSSE D'HABITAT ? (AH)
Cette structure n'a livré que quelques tessons provenant d'un même vase (364.1, Fig. 13.19).

– chamotte associé à un micro tesson à micro-dégraissant coquillier/impressions au peigne ou à la cordelette

PAS-DE-CALAIS - Brebières « Les Béliers », structure 1555

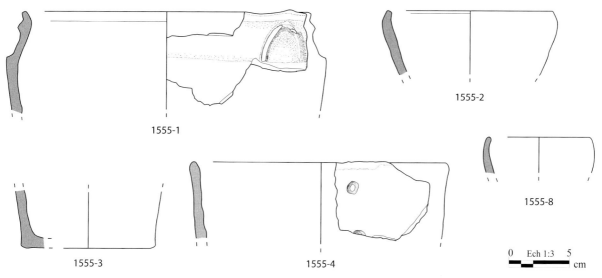

1555-1

1555-2

1555-3

1555-4

1555-8

0   Ech 1:3   5
cm

Fig. 13.14. Pas-de-Calais, Brebières « Les Béliers », structure 1555.

PAS-DE-CALAIS - Brebières « Les Béliers », structure 1605 et mobilier résiduel

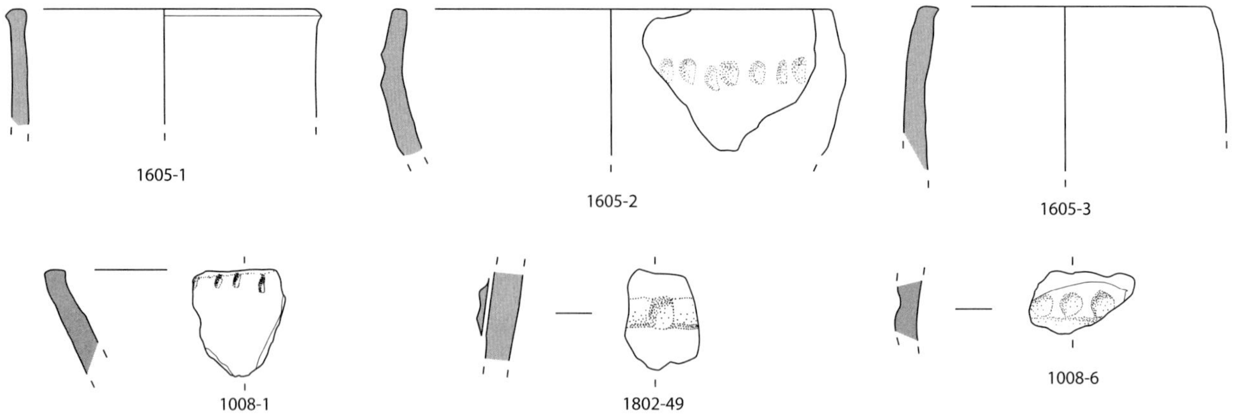

Fig. 13.15. Pas-de-Calais, Brebières « Les Béliers », structure 1605 et mobilier résiduel.

L'état fragmentaire de cette forme ne nous offre aucun renseignement sur la présence éventuelle de décors rapportés (anses arciformes ?) au niveau de la panse.

MAROEUIL,, STRUCTURE 447, FOSSE D'HABITAT ? (AH)
NTT : 172, NMI : 12, isolés : 10 (Fig. 20). Mobilier assez fragmenté et présentant des surfaces relativement altérées (difficulté de restitution graphique).

 – *calcaire coquillé majoritaire, associé suivant les tessons avec de la chamotte ou silex. Quelques tessons à dégraissant unique de chamotte ou associant chamotte et silex/mamelon de préhension (languette ovalaire), bouton appliqué ou l'amorce d'anse (447.8)/traces de doigts en interne sous la lèvre (décor ou traces de montage ?) (447.10).*

MAROEUIL, STRUCTURE 206, FOSSE D'HABITAT ? (AH)
NTT : 28, NMI : 7, isolés : 7 (Fig. 21).
 – *pâte à forte concentration de dégraissant minéral (quartz et calcaire)//impressions digitées (bout de doigt) ou à l'ongle (sur face externe de la lèvre, 206/7).*
 Une forme (206.6), non définissable avec exactitude, pourrait marquer une tasse ou une cuillère.

14. Marquion « Plateforme canal SNE », structures X8-10 et 9 (AH et NB)
La structure X8–10 (fosse ou chablis ?) a livré une cinquantaine de tessons appartenant à un seul individu (Ph. Lefèvre rapport en cours) (Fig. 13.22).
 – *chamotte et rares inclusions de silex concassé/surfaces égalisées/pâte gris foncé et surfaces rouge orangé à gris beige (sur/re-cuisson)/ cordon et oreilles horizontales étirées, impressions digitées (bout de doigt avec traces d'ongle ou non)*

La structure 9 correspond à une incinération retrouvée à l'extérieur d'un fossé d'enclos funéraire, en périphérie de celui-ci (Fig. 13.23).
 – *chamotte abondante et rares inclusions de silex/4 boutons rapportés sous le bord*

15. Monchy-le-Preux « Les Diefs » (NB)
Les opérations menées sur le Gazoduc en 1996 (Debiak 1996) ont abouti à la découverte d'une fosse (structure 20) « isolée » sur la bande de 8 m de large décapée. Subcirculaire (0.70/75 cm de diamètre), à fond plat et de 15 cm de profondeur, elle a livré 3 tessons (NMI : 2–3, Fig. 13.24).
 – *silex pilé visible en surface, bosselée/extérieur brun ou orangé et intérieur plus brun clair, brun gris ou noire/ boutons appliqués sous le bord (et plus bas sur la panse ?), cordon appliqué digité/caramel alimentaire.*

16. Saint-Laurent-Blangy « Le Trapèze » (NB)
À l'occasion de la fouille d'un ensemble funéraire laténien en 2001 (Jacques et Prilaux 2004), six fragments de céramique[6] ont été découverts dans le remplissage d'une dépression allongée (environ 1.80 m pour 0.80 m de large), peu profonde (4 à 20 cm) et aux parois irrégulières, considérée comme un chablis. Les traces de thermo-altération postérieures au bris de l'un des vases et l'association de céramique fine et plus grossière dite commune conduit à faire plutôt l'hypothèse d'un contexte domestique pour cette découverte, plus que funéraire ou correspondant à un dépôt intentionnel.
 Trois vases (Fig. 13. 25) sont représentés par :
 –un minuscule tesson de 6 mm d'épaisseur, en pâte fine *contenant une grande quantité d'inclusions végétales sous la forme de longs éléments tubulaires sub-rectilignes et de feuillets/ surfaces régulières lisses/ intérieur brun foncé/ extérieur orangé*

PAS-DE-CALAIS - Courrières « Carrière Beugnet », structures 1023 et 1024

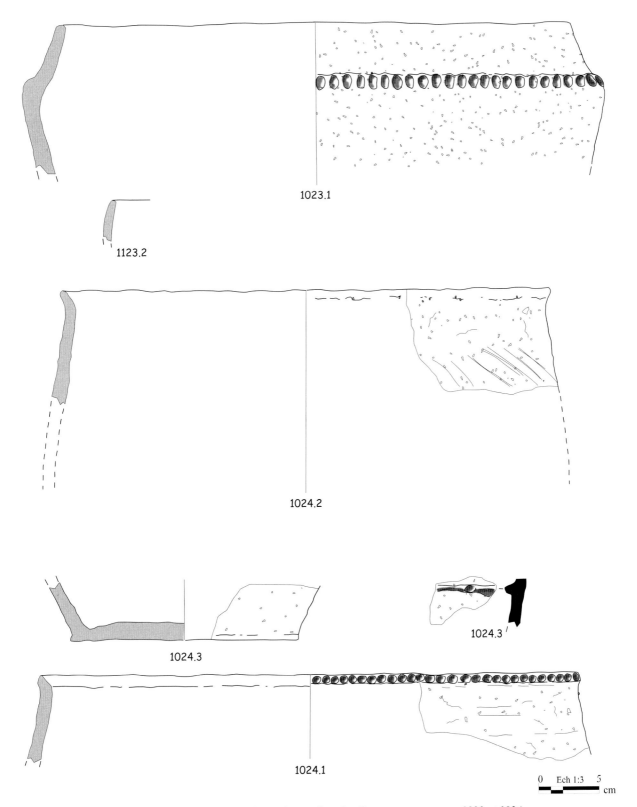

Fig. 13.16. Pas-de-Calais, Courrières « Carrière Beugnet », structures 1023 et 1024.

PAS-DE-CALAIS
Dainville « Les Biefs »

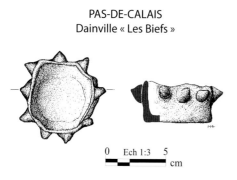

0   Ech 1:3   5
cm

Fig. 13.17. Pas-de-Calais, Dainville « Les Biefs »

– un vase à paroi épaisses (9 mm) en pâte grossière *chamottée/extérieur lisse et légèrement bosselé/léger lustre interne et un aspect finement craquelé (lissage « la main mouillée » par humidification de la surface)/tranche noire et surfaces beiges/décor à l'ongle réalisé à l'aide de deux doigts opposés*

– un demi profil quasi complet en pâte fine et paroi d'épaisseur régulière (5 mm) *chamottée/cassure en biseau et deux fissures filant horizontalement (emploi de colombins et pose interne de ceux-ci ou, tout au moins, d'une partie d'entre eux)/surfaces polies/impressions au peigne incrustées d'un matériau blanc.*

PAS-DE-CALAIS - Hingues « Zone du Vertannoy », structures 03, 04 et 05

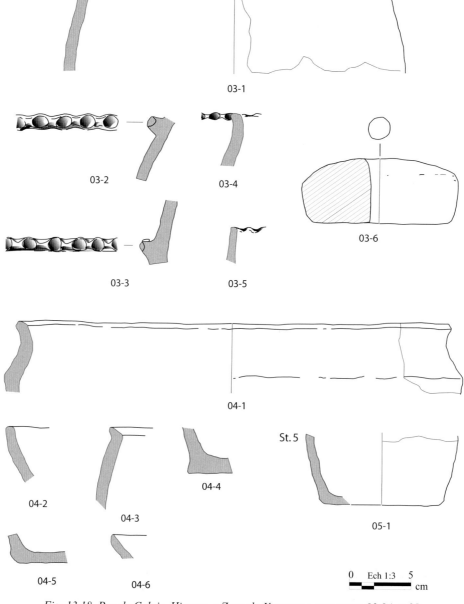

Fig. 13.18. Pas-de-Calais, Hingues « Zone du Vertannoy, structures 03,04 et 05.

PAS-DE-CALAIS - Maroeuil «Rue Curie», structure 364

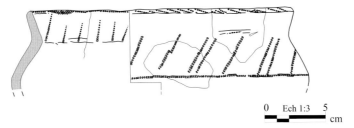

Fig. 13.19. Pas-de-Calais, Marœuil « Rue Curie », structure 364.

PAS-DE-CALAIS - Maroeuil «Rue Curie» structure 447

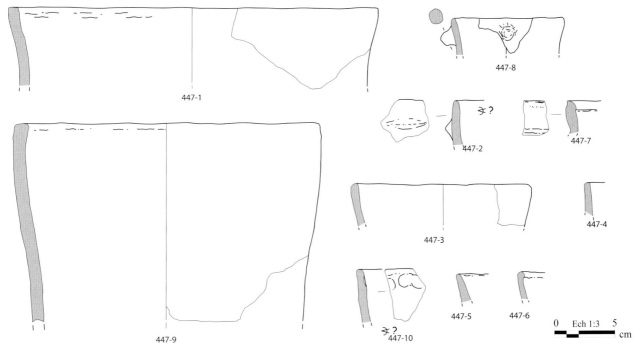

Fig. 13.20. Pas-de-Calais, Marœuil « Rue Curie », structure 447.

PAS-DE-CALAIS - Maroeuil «Rue Curie», structure 206

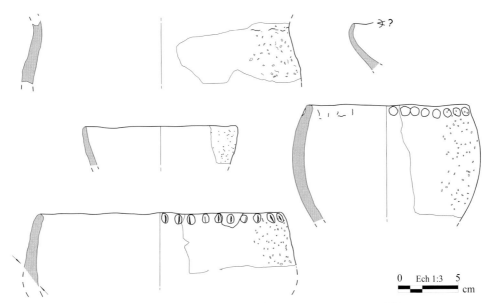

Fig. 13.21. Pas-de-Calais, Marœuil « Rue Curie », structure 206.

PAS-DE-CALAIS - Marquion « Plateforme canal SNE », structure X8-10

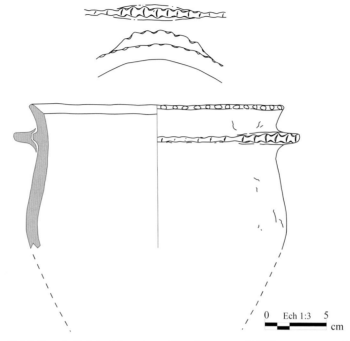

Fig. 13.22. Pas-de-Calais, Marquion « Plateforme canal SNE », structure X8-10.

PAS-DE-CALAIS - Marquion
« Plateforme canal SNE », structure 9

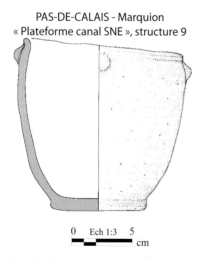

*Fig. 13.23. Pas-de-Calais, Marquion « Plateforme canal SNE »,
structure 9.*

PAS-DE-CALAIS - Monchy-le-Preux «Les Diefs»
structure 20

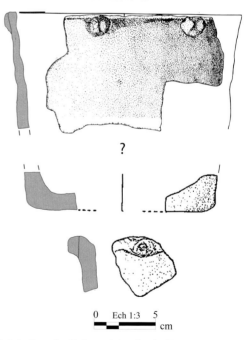

*Fig. 13.24. Pas-de-Calais, Monchy-le-Preux « Les Diefs »,
structure 20.*

La tranche est brun foncé à noire et les surfaces sont orangées, mais la pellicule de même couleur qui s'étend à la surface des cassures témoigne d'une altération thermique postérieure au bris du vase.

Le décor est complexe : il est constitué de trois registres séparés par deux bandeaux lisses, ces registres étant subdivisés en bandes formées de lignes continues superposées, de chevrons simples ou emboîtés, de losanges et de triangles hachurés ou remplis de chevrons. Les lignes continues superposées sont quasiment rectilignes ; les fines

empreintes quadrangulaires les constituants sont de forme régulière. On n'observe de reprise évidente qu'en un point de l'une d'elles et un peigne large (de plus de 13 dents et

PAS-DE-CALAIS - Saint-Laurent-Blangy « Le Trapèze »

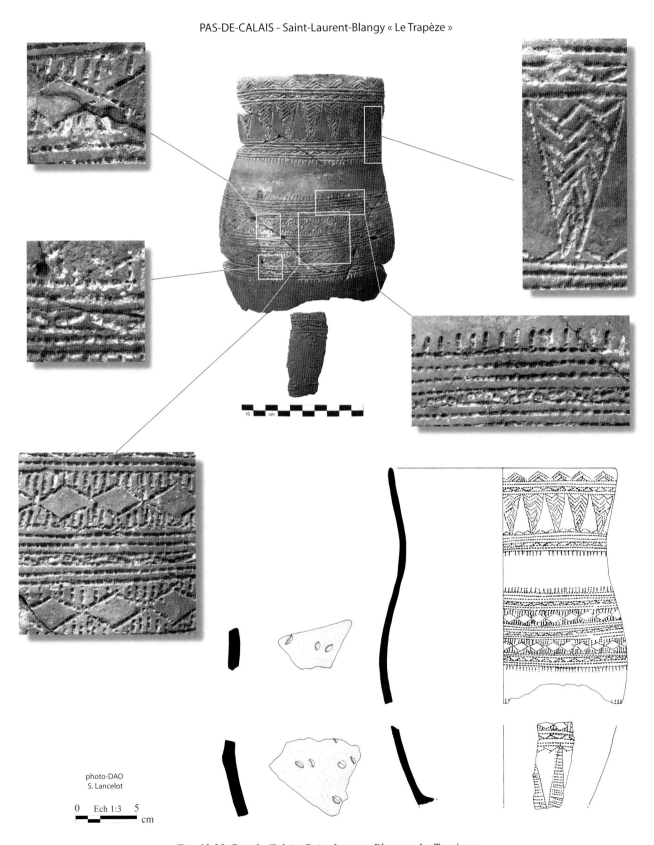

photo-DAO
S. Lancelot

0   Ech 1:3   5
cm

Fig. 13.25. Pas-de-Calais, Saint-Laurent-Blangy « Le Trapèze ».

PAS-DE-CALAIS - Saint-Laurent-Blangy
« Les Soixantes »

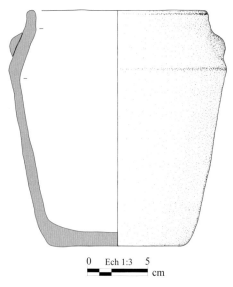

0   Ech 1:3   5
cm

Fig. 13.26. Pas-de-Calais, Saint-Laurent-Blangy « Les Soixantes ».

sans doute à 15 dents, de 2.5 cm) a été utilisé pour leur réalisation.

En revanche, les reprises sont nombreuses sur les lignes formant les bordures des triangles qui sont composées de la juxtaposition de courts tronçons toujours constitués de 5 empreintes également quadrangulaires, quoique moins régulières. Le remplissage de chevrons emboîtés et de hachures horizontales a été réalisé avec le même peigne (de 0.7 cm). Les losanges, chevrons simples, hachures et courts tracés verticaux en bordure des registres sont également composés de courts tronçons dentelés, comprenant de 7 empreintes (losanges et certains chevrons simples à tronçons de 0.8–0.9 cm) à 3 empreintes (dans les autres cas, à tronçons de 0.3 cm). Les différents peignes (à 7, 5 dents plus ou moins régulières et à 3 dents dont deux bien quadrangulaires et l'une moins longue à l'une des extrémités) ont été utilisés pour la bordure terminant le décor sous le bord. Les chevauchements observés montrent que les lignes continues délimitant les bandeaux ont été réalisées préalablement.

PAS-DE-CALAIS - Saint-Venant « rue de Garbecque »

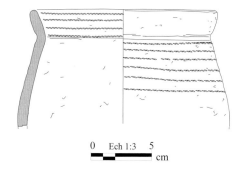

0   Ech 1:3   5
cm

photo-DAO
D. Bardel
0   2,5
cm

Fig. 13.27. Pas-de-Calais, Saint-Venant « Rue Garbecque ».

17. Saint-Laurent-Blangy « Les Soixantes » (NB)

A l'occasion des fouilles d'Actiparc (Favier *et al.* 2004) a été découvert et intégralement fouillé un monument funéraire à fossé sub-circulaire d'environ 8.50 m de diamètre. Son comblement homogène comprend des éléments charbonneux et cendreux ainsi que de nombreux rognons de silex inorganisés mais essentiellement concentrés dans la partie ouest, là où le fossé est le plus large. Un vase presque complet (2 larges fragments disjoints sur la surface interne desquels adhèrent ponctuellement des résidus carbonés) et quelques fragments appartenant à un second vase proviennent de ce secteur (Fig. 13.26). A l'opposé, dans la partie supérieure du comblement, ont été retrouvés les restes d'une inhumation d'enfant mal conservée sur laquelle une datation a pu être effectuée (Table 13.1). L'aire centrale a livré deux épandages charbonneux dont l'une, avec quelques esquilles osseuses pourrait correspondre aux vestiges d'une sépulture à incinération.

– *nombreux grains de silex blancs à gris (module ≤ 3 mm) inégalement répartis dans la pâte/paroi irrégulière mais relativement peu épaisse (6 à 8 mm), sauf au niveau de la carène (10 mm)/un joint oblique interne évident associé à des traces d'étirements externes/surface externe bosselée avec grains de silex pilé visibles, lissage interne avec recouvrement des particules de dégraissant/ tranche et surface internes noires/ étant légèrement plus claire et zoné/ boutons rapportés*

Les quelques tessons représentent un second vase sont issus d'un fond épais (16 mm) associé à une paroi de 6–8 mm.

PAS-DE-CALAIS - Samer « Route de Desvres »

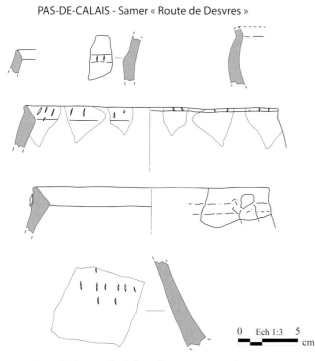

0   Ech 1:3   5
cm

Fig. 13.28. Pas-de-Calais, Samer « Route de Desvres ».

– *petite quantité de grains de silex blanc à gris (module ≤ 3 mm) et forte proportion de chamotte de même module*

18. Saint-Venant « rue de Garbecque »

Lors d'une opération de diagnostic, réalisée en mai 2012, un enclos circulaire a été mis au jour (Lançon *et al.* 2012). À la surface de celui-ci, des tessons à décor à la cordelette ont été découverts. Cette zone fût prescrite et fouillée en mai 2013 sur une emprise de 3040 m². Cette opération a permis de dégager un ensemble de trois cercles dont un double, de cinq incinérations parmi lesquelles deux semblent contemporaines d'un des enclos circulaires, et de deux réseaux de fossés qui traversent l'emprise de part en part (un orienté nord-sud et le second est-ouest) et recoupent les cercles.

La céramique à décor à la cordelette en Z (Fig. 13.27) issue du diagnostic s'avère avoir été retrouvée au niveau du cercle interne du double cercle[7]. Au cours de la fouille seul un tesson a été isolé en surface. Cette céramique semble indiquer la présence d'une occupation antérieure à proximité des cercles mais la surface prescrite n'a pas permis de caractériser celle-ci.

– *pâte fine chamottée/surface lissée plus ou moins régulièrement/couleur sombre et marron en surface/décor externe de 6 lignes d'impressions à la cordelette fine, sur la partie haute de la panse et un décor de 4 lignes identiques sur la partie interne du col.*

19. Samer « Route de Desvres » (AH)

En 2011, lors d'un diagnostic, un puits a été découvert (Leriche 2012). Fouillé partiellement, ce denier a livré du mobilier céramique dans son comblement supérieur (Fig. 13.28).

NTT : 100, NMI : 5. Mobilier céramique associé à une soixantaine d'éclats et d'outils en silex et des fragments de torchis cuit.

– *dégraissant de chamotte majoritaire, avec quelques individus à inclusions de silex/cuisson essentiellement réducto-oxydante, avec surfaces externes beige orangé décor d'impressions au bout d'ongle ou à l'ongle et décor plastique*

20. Vitry-en-Artois « Aérodrome »

Un diagnostic réalisé en 2008 a apporté les indices ténus d'une fréquentation des lieux à l'Âge du bronze moyen. Motivée par la présence d'une *villa* gallo-romaine, la fouille a été effectuée, en 2009 et en 2010, sur une emprise de 24 427 m² (Lacroix 2012). Les installations de l'Âge du bronze se matérialisent au sol par une quinzaine de fosses (*com. pers.* Leroy-Langelin), localisées principalement à l'angle sud-est de la zone prescrite.

L'ensemble de ces structures renferme des tessons (Fig. 13.29) dont l'observation a conduit à l'identification d'un mode de préparation de la pâte analogue :

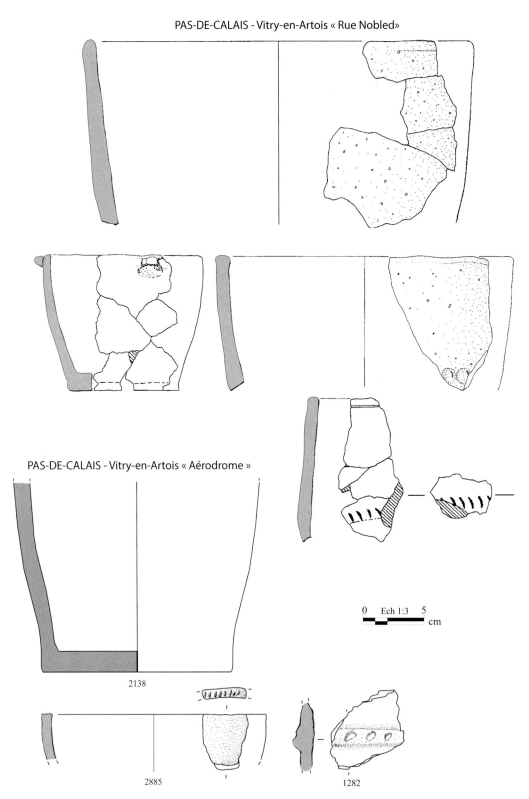

Fig. 13.29. Pas-de-Calais, Vitry-en-Artois « Rue Nobled » et « Aérodrome ».

– dégraissant siliceux (de fréquence modérée définie à partir de l'abaque de FitzPatrick (1984) et de calibre de 1 à 3 mm associée à une finition par lissage sommaire/ cordon appliqué impressions digité (st. 1282) et ongulées (st. 2885).

Argoeuves « Le Moulin d'Argoeuves », fosse 152

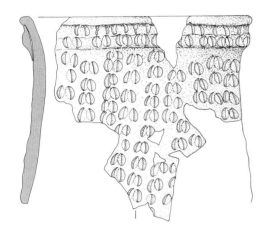

0   Ech 1:3   5
cm

Fig. 13.30. Somme, Argœuves « Moulin d'Argœuves », fosse 152.

Une fosse, aux contours peu perceptibles à la fouille, contenait une forme (Fig. 13.29) dont le profil du bas de panse n'est pas sans rappeler les vases tronconiques de tradition *Deverel-Rimbury* d'Avelin « Route départementale 549 », de Lauwin-Planque « Milterlotte, zone B » et de Roeux « Château d'Eau » (Desfossés *et al.* 1992).

Les mesures d'épaisseur du fond et de la paroi sont respectivement de 150 mm et de 130 mm. – *Ces variations ainsi que la fracture nette au départ du premier colombin indiquent l'emplacement de raccords. L'examen radiographique du fond en plan tangentiel témoigne de son façonnage à partir d'une galette étirée, de diamètre compris entre 150 et 164 mm/silex (fréquence de 15% et de calibre de 1 à 3 mm/lissage sommaire/ cuisson réductrice à oxydation terminale externe.*

21. Vitry-en-Artois « Rue Nobled »

De l'autre côté de la Scarpe par rapport au site de l' « Aérodrome », une fouille réalisée en 2005 a mené à la découverte de neuf structures, 5 fosses et un trou de poteau de l'Âge du bronze (Compagnon *et al.* 2006). La fosse (st. 1126) a livré des rejets d'habitat (fragments de torchis, éclats de grès, 50 silex – cassons, éclats et 1 nucléus – 2 perles en ambre et 61 tessons correspondant à 6 vases différents, Fig. 13.29).

– inclusions de silex (et de chamotte dans 1vase)

Somme

22. Argoeuves « Le Moulin d'Argoeuves » (NB)

Un diagnostic archéologique mené en 2007 a conduit à la découverte de deux monuments funéraires à fossé circulaire

SOMME - Argoeuves « Le Moulin d'Argoeuves »,
monument A, remplissage du fossé

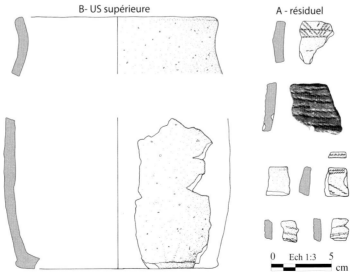

Fig. 13.31. Somme, Argœuves « Moulin d'Argœuves », monument A, remplissage du fossé.

de l'Âge du bronze moyen dont l'un associé avec une incinération sous un vase retourné (st. 18, Soupart 2007). La fouille qui a suivi en 2009 (Buchez 2014) a permis l'étude des fossés et de leur mobilier ainsi que la mise au jour de vestiges céramiques plus anciens (st. 152 et en position résiduelle dans l'un des fossés).

ARGOEUVES « LE MOULIN D'ARGOEUVES », FOSSE 152

La fosse peu profonde, aux contours et parois irrégulières (chablis, creusement intentionnel ?) a livré un vase fragmentaire (Fig. 13.30)

– *nombreuses inclusions blanches, beiges jaunes, grises à noires (tout ou en partie os pilé) et proportion remarquable de grains de chamotte/surfaces zonées (brun foncé à rouge)/ stigmates résiduels d'un polissage sur la surface interne, surface externe soigneusement lissée/décor par pincements*

ARGOEUVES « LE MOULIN D'ARGOEUVES », MONUMENT A, REMPLISSAGE DU FOSSE

Deux groupes de tessons distincts d'un point de vue technologique ne se répartissent pas de la même façon

dans le remplissage du fossé circulaire de ce monument funéraire.

– *Éléments résiduels (Fig. 13.31A)*

Trente-trois tessons à inclusions carbonatées sont dispersés sur 9 m et sur toute la hauteur du comblement du fossé dès la base de la stratigraphie qui commence par des reliquats du sol noir de l'époque issus des bordures du fossé.

– *inclusions blanches à grises à structure feuilletée (coquilles pilées ?) denses à moyennement denses, mais pouvant être occasionnelles (6 tessons représentant au moins 2 vases différents)/surface externe rouge et une surface interne sombre/lissées (léger lustre perceptible dans un cas, à l'extérieur et à l'intérieur/ décor d'impressions réalisées au moyen d'une cordelette (plus ou moins fine) appliquée contre la paroi (décor à la cordelette simple) sur 4 tessons (3 fois à l'extérieur du vase et 1 fois, à l'intérieur)*

L'épaisseur des tessons oscile entre 0.6 et 0.9 cm

– *Remplissage supérieur du fossé*

Les tessons comportant du silex pilé – parfois de larges fragments – proviennent uniquement des niveaux

SOMME - Argoeuves « Le Moulin d'Argoeuves »,
monument A, fosse 18

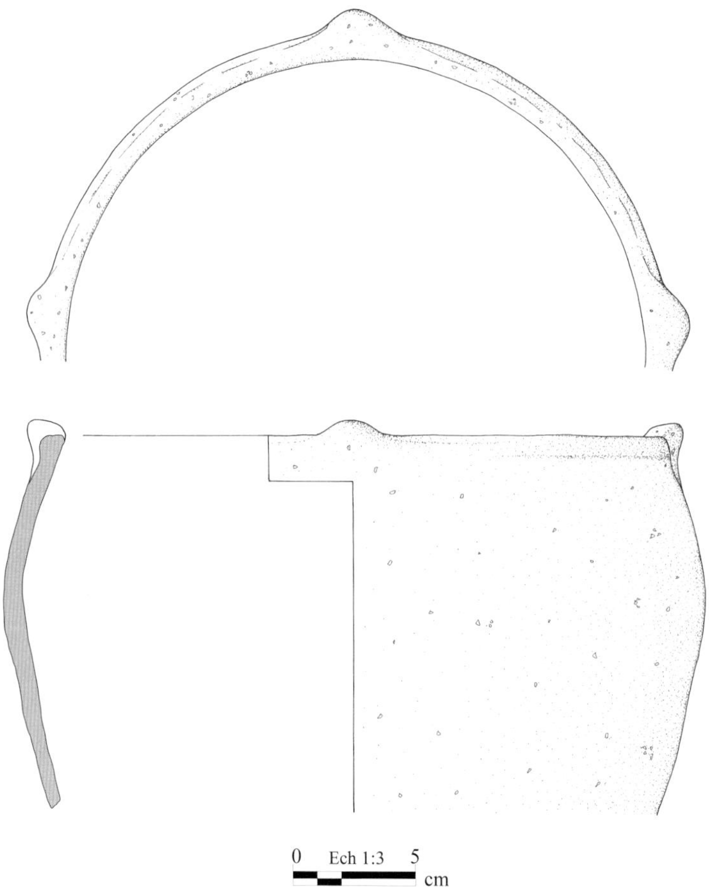

0   Ech 1:3   5
cm

Fig. 13.32. Somme, Argœuves « Moulin d'Argœuves », monument A, fosse centrale (no. 18).

SOMME - Croixrault « Le Fayards », structure 11.51

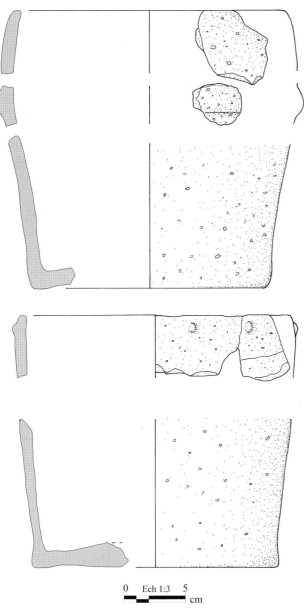

Fig. 13.33. Somme, Croixrault « Le Fayards », structure 11.51.

de comblements supérieurs, postérieurs à l'arrivée dans le fossé des sédiments liés à l'érosion des parties en élévations du monument.

Plusieurs tessons permettant de restituer une forme quasiment archéologiquement complète (Fig. 13.31B) ont été retrouvés à la base du comblement final du fossé d'enclos, en surface d'un lit de blocs de silex relevant d'un possible aménagement (*cf.* Buchez *et al.* dans ce volume).

– forte quantité de grains de silex grossiers (module ≤ 3 mm) blancs/stries sub-horizontales internes de raclage/paroi externe irrégulière dans sa partie basse avec empreintes de façonnage marquant la liaison base/panse (renforcée d'un colombin externe ?) et stries verticales dans sa partie haute/tranche et surfaces à dominante rouge.

ARGOEUVES « LE MOULIN D'ARGOEUVES », MONUMENT A, URNE FUNÉRAIRE (ST. 18)

La fosse aménagée de blocs de silex localisée dans l'aire interne et contenant le dépôt cinéraire mesure 0.40 m sur 0.35 m. Le fond du vase (Fig. 13.32) retourné sur les os a été tronqué par les labours (^{14}C, Table 13.1).

SOMME - Eterpigny-Barleux
« Les Croix Noires », structure 62.2

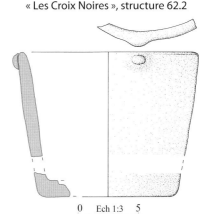

Fig. 13.34. Somme, Eterpigny-Barleux « Les Croix Noires », structure 62.2.

SOMME - Eterpigny-Barleux « Les Croix Noires », structures 1887 et 3643

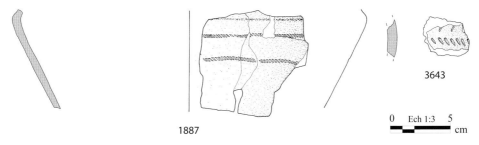

3643

1887

Fig. 13.35. Somme, Eterpigny-Barleux « Les Croix Noires », structures 1887 et 3643.

SOMME - Etricourt-Manancourt « Le Tarteron », structure 323.20

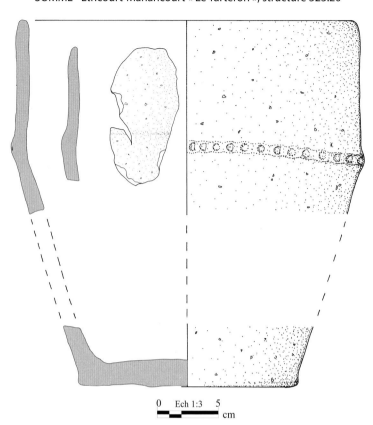

Fig. 13.36. Somme, Etricourt-Manancourt « Le Tarteron », structure 323.20.

– forte quantité de grains de silex grossiers (module ≤ 3 mm) blancs/ lissage de type main mouillée (enrobage des particules de dégraissants)/empreintes liées au montage visibles à l'intérieur/tranche à cœur brun foncé bordé de deux liserés rouges et surfaces brun foncé (à l'intérieur) à brun rouge (à l'extérieur)/ bord muni de mamelons

23. Croixrault « Le Fayards », structure 11.51 (NB)
Un diagnostic réalisé en 2008, sur un secteur qui n'a pas fait l'objet d'investigation plus poussée par la suite, a entraîné la mise au jour d'une vaste fosse (Cayol 2008).

Elle a livré les restes de deux vases archéologiquement complets (Fig. 13.33), un fragment de bord supplémentaire, un peson fragmenté de forme indéterminée ainsi que deux masses argileuses modelées informes comportant des empreintes. Cette association conduit à faire l'hypothèse d'un contexte domestique.

– grains de silex grossiers abondants (≤ 3 mm à 5mm selon les vases avec rares éléments jusqu'à 5 et 8 mm)/cassures longues dans le plan horizontal/traces internes et/ou externes de régularisation de type « main mouillée » (aspect « enrobé » résiduel)/surfaces zonées à dominante clair/ boutons (modelés ou rapportés ?) ou cordon rapporté

24. Eterpigny-Barleux « Les Croix Noires », site 3, structure 62.2 (NB)
Une forme archéologiquement complète a été découverte lors d'un diagnostic en rapport avec les opérations du Canal-Seine-Nord-Europe dans une fosse peu profonde en cuvette de 65 à 90 cm de diamètre (Lamotte 2010). Lors de la fouille de ce secteur[8], du mobilier présentant les mêmes caractéristiques technologiques a été récolté dans plusieurs autres structures et notamment dans l'un des trous de poteau relevant d'un bâtiment de plan circulaire (^{14}C, Table 13.1).

De la structure 62.2 proviennent 22 tessons représentant un même vase (Fig. 13.34). Un dépôt carboné est présent à l'intérieur du vase.

– grains de silex grossiers (≤ 4 mm) blancs à gris bleuté, abondants à moyennement abondants et importante quantité de chamotte grossière/tranche noire et surfaces orangées

ETERPIGNY-BARLEUX « LES CROIX NOIRES », SITE 1-19, STRUCTURES 1887 ET 3643 (NB)
Lors de cette même opération deux attestations d'occupations plus anciennes (Néolithique final/campaniforme) ont été relevées[9].

SOMME - Renancourt « Le Coup de couteau »
structure 96.11

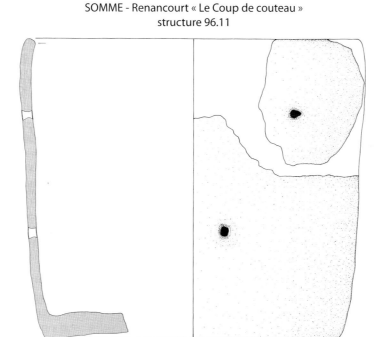

0   Ech 1:3   5
cm

Fig. 13.37. Somme, Renancourt « Le Coup de Couteau », structure 96.11.

SOMME - Villers-Carbonnel
« La Sole d'Applincourt »

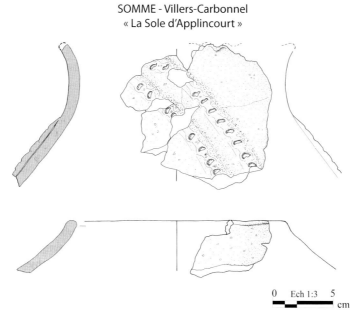

0   Ech 1:3   5
cm

Fig. 13.38. Somme, Villers-Carbonnel « La Sole d'Applincourt ».

La structure 1887 localisée à environ 150 m de l'ensemble de l'Âge du bronze, livre outre du mobilier Bronze final, un tesson plus ancien (Fig. 13.35), peut-être associé à un premier état de la structure.

-pâte fine avec rares grains de chamotte/ lustre externe et aspect finement craquelé/sillons de lissage internes/ tranche brun foncé et surfaces, orangées / impressions à la cordelette simple.

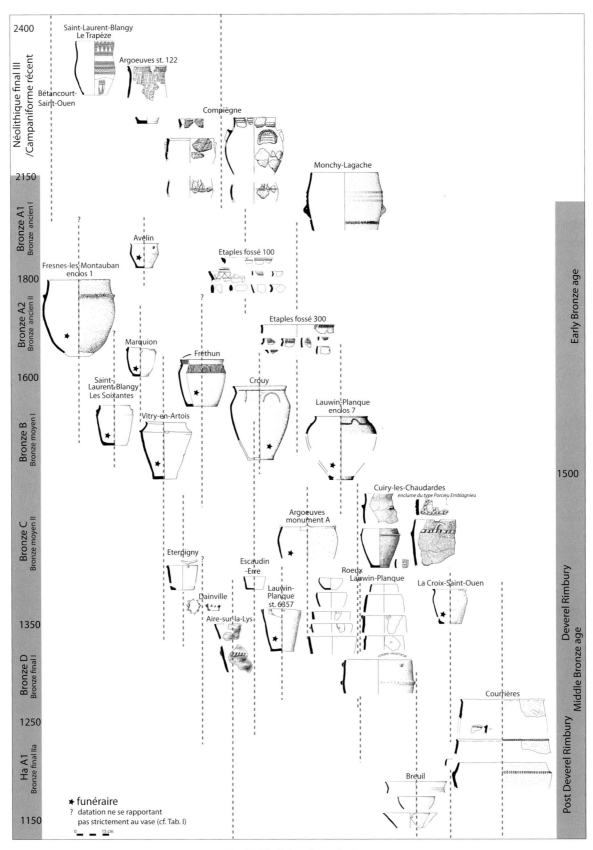

Fig. 13.39. Frise chronologique.

La paroi est fine (4-5 mm). On relève des stigmates en rapport avec une cuisson postérieure à la fabrication du vase (nécrose grise).

Une seconde structure (3643), localisée à 150 m de 1887, semble correspondre à une inhumation en fosse quadrangulaire boisée dont le squelette n'a pas résisté à l'acidité du sol (^{14}C, Table 13.1). Quelques petits tessons (résiduels ?) appartenant à un même vase sont issus de cette tombe (Fig. 13.35). Le décor externe semble couvrir la panse puisqu'on le retrouve sur un minuscule tesson provenant de la base (non dessiné).

– *grains de silex grossiers (module ≤ 4 mm) blancs à gris bleuté, abondants à moyennement abondants et importante quantité de chamotte grossière/tranche noire et surfaces orangées/ impressions ont été réalisées (outil à extrémité plate, courte)*

25. Etricourt-Manancourt « Le Tarteron », structure 323.20 (NB)

Une fosse (d'habitat ?, circulaire, en cuvette, de 0.70 m de diamètre et 0.20 m de profondeur, Lefèvre 2010) découverte en bordure d'une zone de fouille liée aux travaux du Canal Seine-Nord-Europe a livré un lot de 70 tessons issus de 3 ou 4 vases différents (Fig. 13.36).

– *forte proportion de grains de silex blanc (à gris bleuté) grossiers (module ≤ 4 mm)/indices de montage aux colombins (légèrement dépressions linéaires perceptibles sur la paroi interne)/traces de lissage de type « main mouillée » sur les surfaces/tranche et surfaces zonées : rouges à brun-rouge, brun foncé et noires/épaississement plus ou marqué selon les endroits avec impressions digitées ou non*

Le fond conserve des stigmates de recuisson en rapport avec une utilisation comme pot à cuire : une partie de la surface est noircie, une autre est nécrosée rouge clair et grise.

26. Renancourt « Le Coup de couteau », structure 96.11 (NB)

Lors d'un tout récent diagnostic, un vase (Fig. 13.37) a été découvert, dans une zone de limon brun foncé peu lisible (Duvette et Groch 2013). Le vase était posé verticalement, tronqué dans sa partie supérieure. L'intérieur a été comblé par un sédiment qui ne se laisse pas distinguer de l'encaissant. Cette structure qui semble avoir fonctionné « en espace vide » pourrait être rapprochée de celle anciennement découverte au Translay « Le Chemin de Morival » (Buchez et Talon 2005) et d'une série de fosses subcylindriques s'apparentant à des structures de conservation (Leroy-Langelin *et al.* ce volume). Le vase de Renancourt, de relativement grande capacité, peut effectivement avoir servi (au moins dans un deuxième temps de son utilisation ?), à contenir et à conserver des denrées alimentaires à court terme. On observe deux percements réalisés postérieurement à la cuisson du vase, l'un sur le seul fragment de bord préservé, l'autre vers le bas de la panse. Ce qui semble être un dépôt organique adhère à la paroi.

– *forte quantité de silex pilé (grains grossiers gris bleuté à blancs, module ≤ 3 mm)/plaque pour le fond (?) et colombins avec joints obliques internes pour la paroi, visibles à la jonction avec la base et en un point de la hauteur sur la panse associés à quelques empreintes de doigts/traces d'étirements de la pâte à l'extérieur/surfaces lissées (aspect enrobé de la surface)/tranche et surface externe rouge, et surface interne zonée (brun claire à brun foncé et noire)*

27. Villers-Carbonnel, « La Sole d'Applincourt » (NB)

Sept tessons provenant de 2 vases différents (Fig. 13.38) composent un ensemble découvert à l'occasion de la fouille d'un site néolithique fouillé sur une surface de 4.37 ha. sur le tracé du Canal seine Nord Europe. Le mobilier provient d'une cavité de nature indéterminée qui s'inscrit dans l'un des fossés palissadés qui caractérisent l'occupation néolithique (Bostyn 2014).

– *proportion significative de gros grains de silex pouvant atteindre 4 à 5 mm et petit nombre d'impressions allongées et plus ou moins courbes visibles en surface, peut-être en rapport avec la présence de très fines particules organiques/lissage de type main mouillée, conduisant à un enrobage des dégraissants (vase 1)/couleur brun orangé à grise (vase 1) peut-être en rapport avec une cuisson postérieure à sa fabrication/couleur brun foncé (vase 2)/cordons rapportés digités.*

this figure is referenced in the texte (see conclusion)

Notes

1   Calibration d'après le programme OxCal version 4, IntCal.
2   Calibration d'après le programme OxCal version 4, IntCal.
3   Calibration d'après le programme OxCal version 4, IntCal 13.
4   Les examens radiographiques sont réalisés au Laboratoire d'Analyses Physiques et de Caractérisation des Matériaux (LAPCM, CAD-DAP : labo-analyse@douaisis-agglo.com), avec la collaboration de M.-L. Bonte.
5   Deux autres crémations isolées ont été enregistrées. Cependant, leur attribution à l'âge du Bronze reste délicate en raison de l'aspect peu caractéristique de la céramique.
6   Uniquement connue par le dessin de l'un des vases, partiellement inexact (Desfossés *et al.* 2003), cette découverte méritait une publication plus complète.
7   Information A.-L. Sadou, responsable de la fouille.
8   Fouille D. Lamotte, rapport en cours.
9   Fouille D. Lamotte, rapport en cours.

Bibliographie

Azagury, I. et Demolon, P. (1990) Vitry-en-Artois, Les Colombiers. *Cahiers de Préhistoire du Nord* 8, 54–58.

Barbet, C. (2009) Courrières « Rue C. Beugnet et rue P. Bouchez ». Rapport final d'opération de fouille. Douai, Communauté d'Agglomération du Douaisis-Direction de l'Archéologie Préventive, S. R. A. Douai, Nord-Pas-de-Calais.

Barbet, C. (2010) avec la collaboration de Clavel, V. et Henton, A. Le site de Courrières (Pas-de-Calais), les occupations de l'âge du Bronze. *Bulletin de l'APRAB* 7, 71–76.

Besse, M. (2003) *L'Europe du 3ème millénaire avant notre ère : les céramiques communes au Campaniforme*, Cahiers d'Archéologie Romande 94 Lausanne.

Billard, C., Blanchet, J.-C. et Talon, M. (1996) Origine et composante de l'Âge du Bronze ancien dans le Nord-Ouest de la France. In C. Mordant et O. Gaife (dir.) *Cultures et sociétés du Bronze ancien en Europe*, 579–601, actes du 117e congrès national des Sociétés Savantes, Clermont-Ferrand 1992. Paris, CTHS.

Blanchet, J.-C. (1984) *Les premiers métallurgistes en Picardie et dans le Nord de la France.* Paris, Mémoires de la Société Préhistorique 17.

Blanchet, J.-C. et Lambot, B. (1985) Quelques aspects du chalcolithique et du Bronze ancien en Picardie. *Actes du 9ème colloque sur le néolithique, Compiègne, 1982*, 79–118. Amiens, Revue Archéologique de Picardie 3–4.

Bostyn, F., Blancquaert, G., Lanchon, Y. et Auboire, G. (1992) Un enclos triple du Bronze ancien à Fréthun (Pas-de-Calais), *Bulletin de la Société Préhistorique Française* 89, 393–412.

Bostyn, F. (dir.) (2014) Canal Seine-Nord Europe, Fouille 12, Picardie, Somme, Saint-Christ-Briost et Villers-Carbonnel. Des systèmes d'enceintes au Néolithique moyen II. Rapport de fouille. Amiens, Inrap Canal Seine-Nord Europe. Inédit.

Bourgeois, J. et Talon, M. (2009) From Picardy to Flanders: Transmanche connections in the Bronze Age. Dans P. Clark (dir.) *Bronze Age Connections: Cultural Contact in Prehistoric Europe*, 38–60. Oxford, Oxbow Books.

Brun, P., Cathelinais, C., Chatillon, S., Guichard, Y., Le Guen, P. et Nere, E. (2005) L'âge du Bronze dans la vallée de l'Aisne. Dans J. Bourgeois et M. Talon (eds) *L'Age du Bronze du nord de la France dans son contexte européen*. Actes du colloque APRAB de Lille 2000, 189–208. Paris, CTHS.

Brunet, P., Cottiaux, R., Hamon, T., Magne, P., Richard, G., Salanova, L. et Samzun, A. (2008) Les ensembles céramiques de la fin du IIIe millénaire (2300–1900 avant notre ère) dans le Centre-Nord de la France. *Bulletin de la Société préhistorique française* 105, 595–615.

Brunet, P., Hamon, T. et Irribarria, R. (2011) Nouvelle approche de la céramique post-campaniforme et Bronze ancien en Ile-de-France, *Revue Archéologique d'Ile-de-France* 4, 109–136.

Buchez, N. (dir.) (2014) Argoeuves-Saint-Sauveur, Somme, Le Moulin d'Argoeuves. Evolution de l'occupation sur le rebord de plateau du Néolithique final à La Tène *D*. Rapport Final d'Opération. Amiens, Inrap Nord-Picardie.

Buchez, N. et Talon, M. (2005) L'âge du Bronze dans le bassin de la Somme. Bilan et périodisation du mobilier céramique. Dans J. Bourgeois et M. Talon (eds) *L'Age du Bronze du nord de la France dans son contexte européen*. Actes du colloque APRAB de Lille 2000, 159–188. Paris, CTHS.

Calkin, J.-B. (1964) *The Bournemouth Area in the Middle and Late Bronze Age, with the « DeverelRimbury » Problem Reconsidered*. London, Royal Archaeological Institute.

Cayol, N. (2008) Commune de Croixrault et de Theuilloy-L'Abbaye (80), ZAC du Sud-Ouest Amiénois, tranche 1. Rapport de diagnostic. Amiens, Inrap Nord-Picardie.

Chancerel, A., Marcigny, C. et Ghesquière, E. (2006), *Le plateau de Mondeville (Calvados) du Néolithique à l'âge du Bronze*, Document d'Archéologie française 99. Paris, Éditions de la Maison des Sciences de l'Homme.

Compagnon, E. et Queyrat, I. (2006) Vitry-en-Artois. Rue Nobled. Rapport de fouille. Douai, Communauté d'Agglomération du Douaisis-Direction de l'Archéologie Préventive. Douai, S. R. A. Nord-Pas-de-Calais.

Crombe, P., Sergant, J. et Lombaert, L. (2011) L'occupation du nord-ouest de la Belgique aux IVe et IIIe millénaires : bilan des recherches récentes en région sablonneuse. In F. Bostyn, E. Martial et I. Praud (dir.) *Le Néolithique du Nord de la France dans son contexte européen : habitat et économie aux 4e et 3e millénaires avant notre ère*, 103–18, actes du 29ème colloque interrégional sur le néolithique, Villeneuve-d'Ascq, 2–3 octobre 2009, RAP spécial 28. Amiens.

Deckers, M. (2010) L'âge du Bronze. Dans M. Germain (dir.) Avelin « Route départementale 549 » (Nord), Rapport final d'opération de fouille, 41–66. Douai, Communauté d'Agglomération du Douaisis-Direction de l'Archéologie Préventive. Douai. S. R. A., Nord-Pas-de-Calais.

Deflorenne, C. (2013) *Un aperçu de l'occupation du sol à Villeneuve d'Ascq : de la protohistoire au haut Moyen Âge* (Hommages à G. Leman-Delerive) *Revue du Nord* 403, 243–275.

Desfossés, Y. (dir.) (2000) Archéologie préventive en vallée de Canche, les sites protohistoriques fouillés dans le cadre de la réalisation de l'autoroute A16, Nord-Ouest Archéologie 11. Berck-sur-Mer, CRADC.

Desfossés, Y., Jacques, A. et Prilaux, G. (2003) Arras, ZAC Actiparc, Archéologie en Nord-Pas-de-Calais 5. Villeneuve d'Ascq, SRA-DRAC Nord-Pas-de-Calais,.

Desfossés, Y., Martial, E. et Vallin, L. (1992) Le site de l'habitat du Bronze moyen du « Château d'eau » à Roeux (Pas-de-Calais). *Bulletin de la Société préhistorique française*, 89, 59–107.

Duvette, L. et Groch, P.-Y. (2013) Eco-Parc industriel Boréalia, Tranche 1. Rapport de diagnostic, 2013. Amiens, Inrap Nord-Picardie. Inédit.

Every, R. et Mepham, L. Prehistoric pottery from Perry Oaks (resource électronique) 1–47. Accès : World Wide Web. URL: scribb.comm/doc/388460/prehistoric-pottery-from-Perry-Oaks. Année de consultation 2012.

Favier, D., Jacques, A. et Prilaux, G. (2004) ZAC Actiparc (62), Saint-Laurent-Blangy. Les occupations humaines au lieu-dit « Les Soixante ». De la ferme aristocratique gauloise au complexe militaire romain. Document Final de Synthèse. Amiens, Inrap Nord-Picardie, SAM d'Arras. Inédit.

Félix, R. et Hantutte, G. (1969) La sépulture campaniforme d'Aremberg (commune de Wallers-Nord), *Bulletin de la Société préhistorique française* 66, 276–282.

FitzPatrick, E. A. (1984) *Micromorphology of Soils*. London, Chapman and Hall.

Fokkens, H. (2005) Le début de l'âge du Bronze aux Pays-Bas et l'horizon Hilversum ancien. In J. Bourgeois et M. Talon (eds) *L'Age du Bronze du nord de la France dans son contexte européen, 11–33, actes du colloque APRAB de Lille 2000*. Paris, CTHS.

Gaillard, D. et Jacques, A. (2000) Rocade Ouest d'Arras (Pas-de-Calais). DFS de sauvetage urgent de 1995 à 1998. Lille,

AFAN, Service Archéologique Municipal d'Arras et SRA du Nord-Pas-de-Calais.

Gaillard, D. et Gustiaux, M. (2004) Contournement sud de Cambrai, section de Fontaine-Notre-Dame (59). Rapport de diagnostic. Amiens, Inrap Nord-Picardie.

Gibson, A. et Woods, A. (1997) *Prehistoric Pottery for the Archaeologist*. London, Leicester University Press.

Henton, A. (2013) La céramique du Bronze final dans le haut Bassin de l'Escaut et ses marges côtières. Première approche typo-chronologique et culturelle. Dans E. Warmenbol et W. Leclercq (dir.), *Echanges de bons procédés. La céramique du Bronze final dans le Nord-ouest de l'Europe, 145–68*, actes du colloque de Bruxelles (octobre 2010). Bruxelles, Etudes archéologiques, CREA-ULB

Huvelle, G. et Lacalmontie, A. (2012) Habitat enclos, habitat ouvert au Bronze final : deux modèles d'occupations sur le site de Brébières « Les Béliers ». *Revue du Nord*, Hors Série Collection Art et Archéologie 17, 81–89.

Huvelle, G. et Lacalmontie, A. (2015) Brébières « Les Béliers ». Rapport final d'opération. Douai : Communauté d'Agglomération du Douaisis – Direction de l'Archéologie Préventive.

Jacques, A. et Prilaux G. (2004) ZAC Actiparc (62). Rapport de diagnostic pour les sondages et les évaluations, Document Final de Synthèse. Amiens, Inrap Nord-Picardie, SAM d'Arras. Inédit.

Lacroix, S. (dir.) (2012) Vitry-en-Artois « Aérodrome » (Pas-de-Calais). Rapport final d'opération de fouille. Communauté d'Agglomération du Douaisis-Direction de l'Archéologie Préventive, S. R. A. Nord-Pas-de-Calais, Douai.

Lamotte, D. (dir.) (2010) Canal Seine-Nord Europe, PF2, Picardie, Somme, Eterpigny, Barleux. *L'évocation d'un terroir du Néolithique à l'Antiquité au travers des sondages archéologiques de la plate-forme 2 (CSNE) à Eterpigny, Barleux (Somme)*. Rapport de diagnostic archéologique. Croix-Moligneaux, Inrap Canal Seine-Nord Europe.

Lançon, M. (dir.), Bardel, D., Créteur, Y., Gaillard, D. et Notte, L. (2012) « Saint-Venant, Pas-de-Calais Rue de Guarbecque ». Rapport de diagnostic. Lille, SRA Nord-Pas-de-Calais, Inrap Nord-Picardie.

Lefèvre, P. (dir.) (2010) Les occupations humaines du Paléolithique moyen au Bas Moyen Age à Etricourt-Manacourt et Equancourt. Rapport de diagnostic archéologique. Inrap Canal Seine-Nord Europe. Inédit.

Leivers, M. (2008) Prehistoric pottery from Stansted Airport. Dans N. Cooke, F. Brown and C. Phillpotts (dir.), *From Hunter-gatherers to Huntsmen: A History of the Stansted Landscape,* 17.1–17.46 in Chapter 17, the number of the pages is noted in this way :17.1, 17.2 and so on, till 17.46. Oxford and Salisbury, Framework Archaeology,

Leriche, B. (2012) Samer (62). Route de Desvres. Parcelles AD, 435–40. Rapport de diagnostic. Amiens, Inrap Nord-Picardie.

Leroy-Langelin, E. et Sergent, A. (dir.) 2015 Lauwin-Planque « ZAC Lauwin-Planque » (Nord) : L'âge du Bronze. Vol. III. *Rapport final d'opération de fouille*. Douai, Communauté d'Agglomération du Douaisis-Direction de l'Archéologie Préventive, S. R. A. Nord-Pas-de-Calais, section 2.

Leroy-Langelin, E. et Sys, D. (2005) Escaudain-Erre « RN 55 » (Nord). Rapport final d'opération de fouille. Douai,

Communauté d'Agglomération du Douaisis-Direction de l'Archéologie Préventive, S. R. A. Nord-Pas-de-Calais, Douai.

Letterlé, F. (1982) Un site de l'âge du Bronze à Cuiry-les-Chaudardes (Aisne). *Revue Archéologique de Picardie, No. spécial sur la vallée de l'Aisne : cinq années de fouilles protohistoriques*, 175–185.

Lorin, Y. (2011), Maroeuil « Rue Curie, Les Capucines ». *Bilan scientifique du NPDC (2009)*, 170–172.

Marcigny, C. et Ghesquière, E. (2003) *L'île de Tatihou (Manche) à l'âge du Bronze. Habitats et occupation du sol, Document d'Archéologie français 96*. Paris, Éditions de la Maison des Sciences de l'Homme.

Marcigny, C. et Talon, M. (2009) Sur les rives de la Manche : Qu'en est-il du passage de l'âge du bronze à l'âge du Fer ? Dans *De l'âge du Bronze à l'âge du Fer en France et en Europe occidentale (Xe-VIIe siècle av. J.-C. La moyenne vallée du Rhône aux âges du Fer, 385–403*, actes du XXXe colloque international de AFEAF co-organisé avec l'APRAB, St. Romain-en-Gall 26–28 mai 2006. Dijon, RAE, 27e supplément,.

Marcigny, C., Ghesquière, E., Clement-Sauleau, S. et Verney, A. (2005) L'âge du Bronze en Basse-Normandie : définition par le mobilier céramique, une première tentative. Dans J. Bourgeois et M. Talon (eds) *L'Age du Bronze du nord de la France dans son contexte européen, 303–32*, actes du colloque APRAB de Lille 2000. Paris, CTHS.

Martial, E., Praud, Y. et Bostyn, F. (2004) Recherches récentes sur le Néolithique final dans le nord de la France. In M. de Vander Linden et L. Salanova (dir.) *Le troisième millénaire dans la Nord de la France, 49–72, Anthropologica et Praehistorica 115*. Paris, Mémoire XXXV de la société préhistorique française.

Martin, J.-M., Martinez, R. et Prost D. (1996) Le site chalcolithique de Bettencourt-Saint-Ouen (Somme), *Internéo* 1, 114–168.

Mercer, R.-J. (1981) Grimes-Graves, Norfolk: Excavations 1971–1972, vol. 1. London, Her Majesty's Stationery Office.

Needham, S. (2005) Transforming Beaker Culture in north-west Europe: Process of fusion and fission, *Proceedings of the Prehistoric Society* 71, 171–217

Rorive (2010) Pecquencourt ZAC Barrois 'Le Bois de la Chaussée' Tranche I et II. Rapport de diagnostic. Douai, Amiens, DAPCAD-Inrap.

Salanova, L. (2000) *La question du campaniforme en France et dans les îles anglo-normandes. Productions, chronologie et rôles d'un standard céramique, Documents Préhistoriques 13.* Paris, SPF-CTHS.

Salanova, L., Renard, C. et Mille, B. (2011) Réexamen de la sépulture d'Arenberg, Wallers (Nord). In L. Salanova et Y. Tchérémissinoff *Les sépultures individuelles campaniformes en France, 79–95. Gallia préhistoire* XLIe supplément.

Salanova, L., Brunet, P., Cottiaux, R., Hamon, T., Langry-François, F., Martineau, R., Polloni, A., Renard, C. et Sohn, M. (2011) Du néolithique récent à l'âge du Bronze dans le centre nord de la France : les étapes de l'évolution chronoculturelle. In F. Bostyn, E. Martial et I. Praud (dir.) *Le Néolithique du Nord de la France dans son contexte européen : habitat et économie aux 4e et 3e millénaires avant notre ère, 77–101*, actes du 29ème colloque interrégional sur le néolithique, Villeneuve-d'Ascq, 2–3 octobre 2009. *Amiens, RAP no. spécial 28.*

Severin (dir.) (1999) Flers-en-Escrebieux « Les Prés Loribes », échangeur RD20. Evaluation archéologique, Douai, Arkéos-Afan.

Thoquenne, V. (2009) Hingues (62). Zone du Vertannoy. Rapport de diagnostic. Amiens, Inrap Nord-Picardie.

Warmenbol, E. (1996) Les débuts de l'Age du Bronze en Belgique. In C. Mordant et O. Gaife (dir.) *Cultures et sociétés du Bronze*

ancien en Europe, 637–57, actes du 117e congrès national des Sociétés Savantes, Clermont-Ferrand 1992. Paris, CTHS.

Wright, J., Powell, A. B. and Barclay, A. (2009) *Excavation of Prehistoric and Romano-British Sites at Marnel Park and Merton Rise (Popley), Basingstoke, 2004–8*. Salisbury, Wessex Archaeology.

Bronze Age ceramic traditions and the impact of the natural barrier: complex links between decoration, technique and social groups around the Channel

Sébastien Manem

Abstract

The 'Channel–North Sea' complex encompasses Bronze Age populations with numerous shared traits and significant interactions. In this way, pottery production is very similar from a morpho-stylistic viewpoint. However, many studies of the notion of diffusion by borrowing show that there is no systematic correlation between style and cultural identity, unlike for technical traditions. The first may be tied to the consumer, whereas technical traditions depend on producers. This article aims to identify the nature of cross-Channel interactions (a single social group for the region or several social groups separated by this natural barrier) through the study of ceramic shaping chaînes opératoires in Normandy, Cornwall and Hampshire.

Keywords: *Chaîne opératoire*; ceramic traditions; transmission; social boundary

Résumé

Le complexe « Manche–Mer du Nord » englobe les populations de l'Âge du bronze présentant de nombreux traits communs et des interactions significatives. Dans ce cadre, la production céramique est très similaire d'un point de vue morpho-stylistique. Toutefois, de nombreuses études sur la diffusion par emprunt montrent qu'il n'y a pas systématiquement de corrélation entre le style et l'identité culturelle. Le premier peut être affecté par la demande et donc lié au consommateur, tandis que les traditions techniques dépendent des producteurs. Cet article s'attache à identifier la nature des interconnexions transmanches (un groupe social pour une région ou plusieurs groupes sociaux séparés par une barrière naturelle ?) au travers de l'étude des chaînes opératoires de façonnage et de finition en Normandie, Cornwall et Hampshire.

Mots clés : Chaîne opératoire, traditions céramiques, transmission, frontière sociale

Introduction

The 'Channel–North Sea' complex, referred to as 'MMN' (*Manche–Mer du Nord*; Marcigny and Ghesquière 2003; Marcigny *et al.* 2007) or 'Channel Bronze Age' (Needham *et al.* 2006) brings together Bronze Age populations living around the Channel. In spite of the presence of this obvious natural obstacle, these men and women exchange readily and have many traits in common, ranging from material culture to spatial occupation modes. Farms, hamlets and villages are organised around plots of land, like for example on Dartmoor, in the southwest of England. They reveal all the facets of the daily life of these agro-pastoral groups (Bradley 2007; Brück 1999, 2001; Burgess 1980; Fleming 1988; Fowler 1981). This is also the case in Lower Normandy at the sites excavated by

Cyril Marcigny at Tatihou (Manche), Nonant and Mondeville in Calvados (Chancerel *et al.* 2006; Marcigny and Ghesquière 2003; Marcigny *et al.* 2005). Farm size and infrastructures vary from one site to another. Nonant farm is characterized by six buildings inside an enclosure intended for one or two families (Carozza and Marcigny 2007; Marcigny 1999), whereas at Tatihou, about ten buildings have been identified, most of which are designed for specialised functions, such as granaries (Marcigny and Ghesquière 2003).

In the domain of pottery production, Mike Parker Pearson (Parker Pearson 1990) reported the maritime transport of Trevisker-style ceramics over long distances, entailing trans-Channel crossings. Cyril Marcigny also observes strong morpho-stylistic similarities. Ceramics from phases 1 (Early/Middle Bronze Age) and 2 (Middle Bronze Age) from Tatihou Island in Normandy – like elsewhere in the northwest of France (Desfossés and Masson 2000) – are very similar to those produced by potters from the Trevisker Group and from the Deverel-Rimbury Complex (Burgess 1980; Parker Pearson 1990; 1995), located in the south and southwest of England (Marcigny and Ghesquière 2003). These ceramics are mainly characterised by high forms decorated by one or two bands made with a smooth cord or fingerprints. Horizontal fluting and chevrons decorated both English and French vessels (Apsimon and Greenfield 1972; Marcigny and Ghesquière 2003). The shape from Normandy recall the 'Barrel Urns' of the Deverel-Rimbury tradition, as at West Ashby in Lincolnshire (Field 1985; Marcigny and Ghesquière 2003). The high forms from phase 2 from Tatihou or those from Nonant or Mondeville in Normandy (Chancerel *et al.* 2006; Marcigny 1999; Marcigny and Ghesquière 2003; Marcigny *et al.* 2007) are similar to Deverel-Rimbury pottery, for example the bucket-urns, which are also decorated with one or two smooth cord or fingerprint bands, as at Thorny Down or at Latch Farm and Kimpton, all in Hampshire (Burgess 1987; Dacre and Ellison 1981; Piggott 1938; Stone 1941).

It is thus clear that interactions exist between these people implanted on either side of the Channel, and well beyond the sphere of pottery production (Clark 2009). This natural barrier does not seem to have any real impact. On the contrary, the region presents a certain homogeneity. These cross-Channel relations have been described on numerous occasions by scholars (this volume; Bourgeois and Talon 2005; Clark 2009; Leclercq and Warmenbol 2013). However, this natural barrier is by no means neutral, or a simple extension of the grounds (Needham 2009). It is a world in itself, which can be crossed with specific means of locomotion, requiring certain navigation skills. As stated by Naum (2010), boundaries are ambiguous landscapes with several dimensions which can directly or indirectly play a complex social as well as economic role.

Up until now, work focusing on cross-Channel connections has concentrated on the visible aspects of material culture, such as decorative style or the morphology of objects, but rarely on the mechanisms underlying notions of culture, social boundaries or interaction. Although it is commonly accepted that decorative style is cultural, related to identity or proof of social interactions, as well as being a strong chronological marker for the European Bronze Age, it nonetheless remains a complex (Wallaert-Pêtre 2012), or even non-pertinent reference (Stark *et al.* 1998), as revealed by numerous works in psychology, anthropology of techniques and ethnoarchaeology (e.g., Bril 2002; David and Kramer 2001; Hegmon 1998; Reed and Bril 1996). Valentine Roux (2010, 5) recalls 'the absence of regularity between "stylistic provinces" and "social groups"'. Decoration can be linked to a consumption context or mode without necessarily being an identity marker (Dietler and Herbich 1994). In this way, in Mali (Gosselain 2008), potters from Zarmaganda copy the prettier and better-selling decorative style of neighbouring pottery by observation and not through direct learning from another potter. For Bafia potters in Cameroon, decorative patterns have no particular significance and can be made to suit clients (Gosselain 1992), like for the Halpulaar'en in Senegal (Gelbert 2003). In south central Africa, the Ngoni adopt Lwangwa pottery by reinterpreting decoration as the latter is not central to their culture (Collett 1987). All in all, as stated by M. Hegmon (1998), decoration can represent a social marker when it is formalised. This is the case not only for the culture itself, but also for the neighbouring cultures. Invisible stages of pottery shaping are, on the other hand, intricately linked to linguistic groups, cultures, clans, castes, tribes or ethnic groups (e.g., Bowser 2000; De Crits 1994; David and Hennig 1972; Degoy 2008; Dietler and Herbich 1998; Gallay 2000; Gosselain 1992; 2000; 2002; Hegmon 1992; Kramer 1997; Latour and Lemonnier 1994; Lemonnier 1986; 1993; Roux 2013; Stark 1998; Stark *et al.* 2000; 2008).

There is effectively, a fundamental difference between decoration and the shaping phases. The first can be copied and diffused rapidly, without necessarily requiring direct contact between two potters or a shared cultural identity. Conversely, ceramic shaping necessitates a more complex transmission between a master and an apprentice (often from different generations), as it involves the acquisition of motor habits using a model (Bril 2002; Gosselain 2002; Roux 2003; Roux and Corbetta 1989), during a relatively long period (ranging from several years to more than ten years depending on the type of motor habits recquired). Learning operates on the level of material production, but also on the integration of the individual within a social group (Lave and Wenger 1991; Wallaert-Pêtre 2012). Another difference opposes decorative style and technical traditions: the conservatism of the latter is widely recognised. Learned motor habits are effectively much more difficult to change throughout time than stylistic modes (Arnold 1985; Dietler and Herbich 1998; Dobres 2000; Foster 1965; Gosselain 2002; Minar and Crown 2001; Nicklin 1971; Roux 2007; 2010; Wallaert-Pêtre 2001). The same result can also be true of style and function (Rogers and Ehrlich 2008).

The anthropology of techniques thus shows that shaping stages are a very pertinent marker for identifying the nature of links between communities. This reference system is all the more pertinent in that it is an invisible identity trait for the individual who does not belong to the social group, as observed in Senegal for certain shaping methods (Gelbert 2003). A last ethnoarchaeological example illustrates perfectly the absence of links between social groups and the morphology of objects. In southern Ecuador, two current social groups – Cañari, the local original social group, and Chordeleg, descendants of the Spaniards – use the same Tortilla plate (*tortero*). This type of pottery is not directly associated with the identity of Cañari and Chordeleg. Firstly, it is an Inca pottery. Secondly, Cañari and Chordeleg have two different technical traditions. The tortero is shaped by hollowing a lump of clay and beating for Cañari potters, and by wheel for Chordeleg potters (Lara 2015).

The aforementioned cases must not circumvent the existence of pertinent links between the morpho-stylistic aspect of pottery production, cultural identity and the technical traditions involved. The morpho-stylistic study of ceramics from the Middle Bronze Age Duffaits culture revealed that the arrival of the latter in west central France generated a certain stylistic mixing with local pottery production from the Early Bronze Age, but still retained a purely Duffaits continental originality (Gomez de Soto 1995). The same observation was made using the identification of technical traditions (Manem 2008).

On the basis of these principles and examples, the understanding of Bronze Age cultures by means of a classificatory approach clearly appears to be a complex task (e.g. Brun and Mordant 1988; Collectif 1989; Mordant and Gaiffe 1996), if the latter is not combined with a technological analysis in keeping with the principles of the anthropology of techniques (Roux 2010).

The present study focuses in particular on the identification of social boundaries (Stark 1998) by examining material production in this archaeological Channel context and investigating the perimeters of transmission networks. This work will simultaneously broach three complementary questions: (1) Are island and continental technical traditions the same? (2) What is the extent of cross-Channel interactions during the Bronze Age and what is the underlying impact of the Channel as a natural barrier on cross-Channel relationships during the Bronze Age? In other words, is this region settled by one or several social groups? (3) Overall, how is the Channel perceived as a natural barrier: as a territorial boundary or part of the territory? This set of questions inexorably conceals the fundamental debate relating to cross-Channel interactions; were they dominated by intermediaries involved in trading goods and materials or by movements of populations? This latter hypothesis is generally minimised in research, as noted by S. Needham (2009).

Material and method

In order to reply to this question, a long-term study is required to explore the whole 'Channel–North Sea' region. This paper presents a first step conducted on material from archaeological sites in Normandy, Cornwall and Hampshire (Fig. 14.1 and Table 14.1). The study focuses on four sites in France (Chancerel *et al.* 2006; Marcigny and Ghesquière 2003; Marcigny *et al.* 2005) and seven in the United Kingdom (Apsimon and Greenfield 1972; Dacre and Ellison 1981; Davis *et al.* 1994; Jones 1999; Jones *et al.* 1994; Nowakowski 1989; 1991). Site choice was governed by different parameters. First of all, the aim was to centre the study on the Middle Bronze Age but also to consider the Early and Late Bronze Age. In addition, we chose to use sites with complementary and representative functions: farms and hamlets, as at Nonant in Normandy (Marcigny *et al.* 2005), Trethellan in Cornwall (Nowakowski 1991) or a cemetery, as at Kimpton, in Hampshire (Dacre and Ellison 1981). From a chronological viewpoint, the aim was to use single occupation sites or repeatedly settled sites over relatively long periods of time in order to obtain a vision based on several generations of potters and learning networks. Some choices were oriented by the stylistic comparisons conducted by Cyril Marcigny (e.g., 2003: 94–103), in the interest to keep the same reference framework. In order to undertake technological analysis and the reconstruction of *chaînes opératoires*, it is essential to work on well-conserved vessels from a qualitative viewpoint. In other words, it was important to have access to sufficiently complete ceramics to identify all the phases of shaping. Lastly, the study was dependent on the conservation quality of collections in order to reduce interpretation difficulties as much as possible and to enhance analysis resolution. Altogether, 386 ceramics were analysed: 119 ceramics from the French contexts and 267 from the English contexts.

The *chaîne opératoire* is reconstructed based on techniques and methods (Roux 1994). Techniques are 'physical modalities according to which the clay is fashioned'. It depends on the source of energy used, the type of pressures exerted and the mass of clay used and on which pressures are exerted (Roux 2010). Methods are an orderly set of functional operations aimed to transform a clay mass into a container. A method involves phases (the shaping of each part: base, body and neck) and stages such as roughing out and preforming. A roughout is a 'hollow volume which does not present the final geometric characteristics of the pot'. The preform is 'a pot with its final geometrical characteristics but whose surface has not been subjected to finishing techniques' (Courty and Roux 1995, 20). The identification of these elements mainly takes place through the analysis of surface features and the radial sections and fractures with the naked eye and the binocular microscope. Their interpretation is directly linked to experimental and ethnoarchaeological work (e.g. Gallay

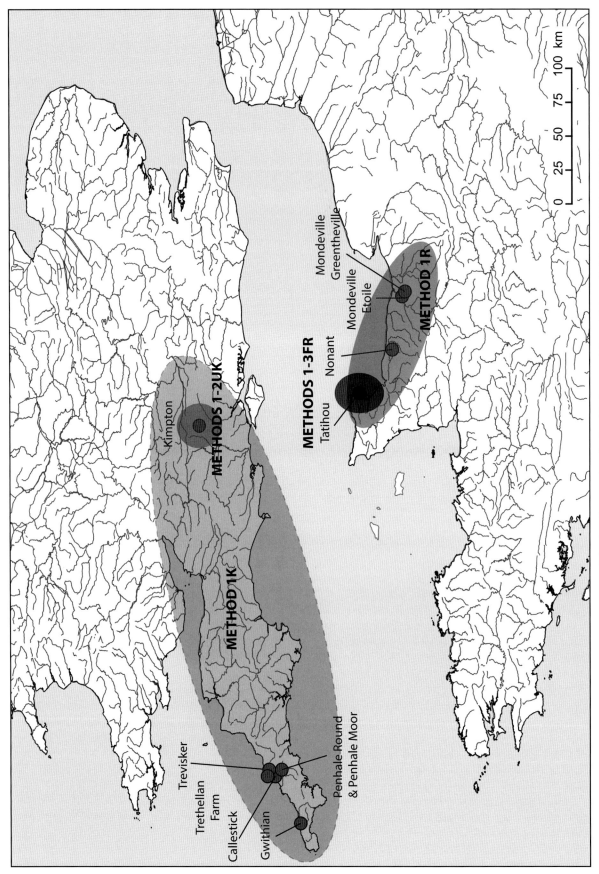

Fig. 14.1. Localisation of Bronze Age site and the distribution of methods of fashioning (Marie Philippe/S. Manem: DIVA-GIS & Natural earth)

Table 14.1. List of archaeological sites and chaînes opératoires associated.

Site	Country/dept/ county	Function	Reference	Initial identification code (chaîne operatoires/site)	Final identification code (chaîne operatoires/site)
Tatihou	France, Normandy	domestic	Marcigny & Ghesquiere 2003	TA1.1–TA1.3, TA2.1, TA3.1	1FR–3FR, 5FR, 6FR
Nonant	France, Normandy	domestic	Marcigny *et al.* 2005	N1.1, N1.2	1FR, 3FR
Mondeville-Etoile	France, Normandy	domestic	Chancerel *et al.* 2006	ME1.1–ME1.3	1FR, 3FR, 4FR
Mondeville-Greentheville	France, Normandy	domestic	Chancerel *et al.* 2006	MG1.1, MG1.2	3FR, 4FR
Trevisker	UK, Cornwall	domestic	Apsimon & Greenfield 1972	Tre1–Tre4	1UK–4UK
Trethellan	UK, Cornwall	domestic	Nowakowski 1991	Treth1.1–Treth1.4	1UK–4UK
Gwithian	UK, Cornwall	domestic	Nowakowski 1989	Gwi1–Gwi3	1UK–3UK
Penhale Moor	UK, Cornwall	domestic	Jones *et al.* 1994	PenhM1.1–PenhM1.2	1UK–3UK
Penhale Round	UK, Cornwall	domestic	Davis *et al.* 1994	PenR1.1–PenhR1.3	1UK–3UK
Callestick	UK, Cornwall	domestic/ ritual	Jones 1999	Call1	1UK
Kimpton	UK, Hampshire	cemetery	Dacre & Ellison 1981	K1.1–K1.3, K2.1–K2.3	1UK–3UK, 5UK–7UK

Reference for *initial identification code of chaînes opératoires:* Manem 2008

2012; Gosselain 2002; Lara 2015; Livingstone Smith 2001; Martineau 2000; May and Tuckson 2000; Rice 1987; Rye 1981). Analysis occurs in two stages: 1) recording data in museums during the observation of macro-traces on the material and taking macro-photographs; 2) validating the recorded data in the laboratory by examining the macro-photos and describing the whole *chaîne opératoire*. For example, observations focused on preferential fractures, junction areas, thickness variations of the section, the presence of flat facets, the oriented inclusions, the type of pressures exerted on the material or the type of clay mass (homogeneous/heterogeneous) worked by the potter, as well as roughing out and preforming techniques.

Results

Normandy pottery

Twelve *chaînes opératoires* were observed for all the sites in Normandy, which are separated by distances of 120 km, at the most. After the comparison of inter-site similarities, a total of six fashioning and finishing *chaînes opératoires* were identified in French contexts (Tables 14.1 and 14.2). However, there are only three fashioning methods (methods 1FR–3FR). All the pots from the studied collections (excepted ceramics associated with the chaîne opératoire no. 6FR) present a base made by modelling (circular slab) (Fig. 14.2: E) from a homogeneous mass of clay and by discontinuous finger pressures (method 1FR: fashioning and finishing *chaîne opératoires* no. 1FR to 4FR). The preforming of some ceramics is realised by beating (method 2FR: *chaîne opératoire* no. 5FR). Lastly, several examples

are entirely made by the technique of hollowing a lump of clay and discontinuous finger pressures (method 3FR: *chaîne opératoire* no. 6FR).

As regards the finishing operations and surface treatments, burnishing and smoothing techniques are observed but the Finishing methods present much more diversity. Some potteries are made totally by surface treatments involving the burnishing technique (*chaîne opératoire* no. 1FR). Other methods combine two techniques. This is the case for the pottery issued from *chaîne opératoire* no. 2FR: the exterior surface is treated by burnishing and the Inner surface is made by smoothing operations. The same methods observed with the burnishing technique are used for the smoothing technique. Smoothing is observed on Inner and exterior surfaces (*chaîne opératoire* no. 3FR), or combined with the burnishing technique: the exterior surface is treated by smoothing and the burnishing technique is used for the Inner surface (*chaîne opératoire* no. 4FR).

Trevisker/Deverel-Rimbury pottery

A total of 23 fashioning and finishing *chaînes opératoires* were identified on the Trevisker and Deverel-Rimbury ceramics from all the studied sites. After comparison of the inter-site similarities of technical traditions, the diversity can be summarised by seven *chaînes opératoires* (Tables 14.1 and 14.3). However, there are only two fashioning methods (methods 1UK and 2UK).

All the bases (Fig. 14.2, C–D) are formed with a coil arranged in a spiral and with discontinuous finger pressures (*chaînes opératoires* 1UK to 7UK). However, in this present case we observe diversity in the techniques

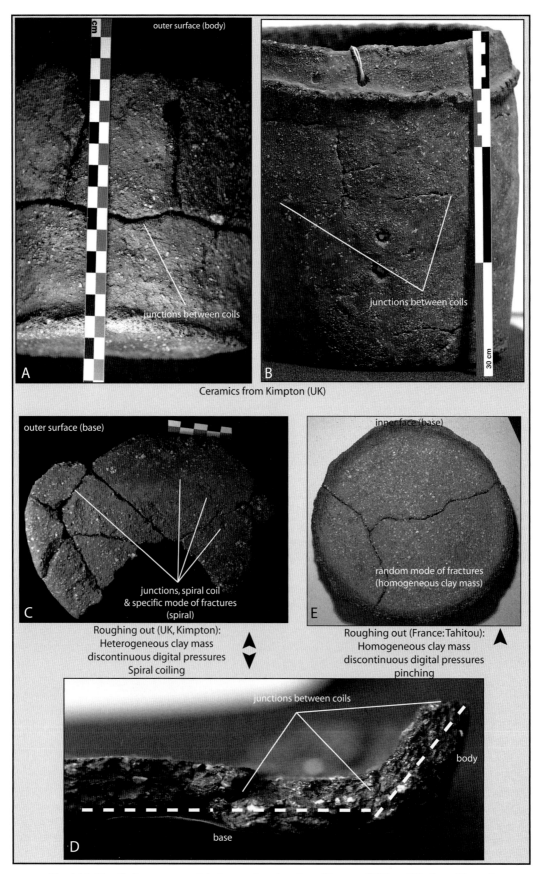

Fig. 14.2. Detailed sequences of chaînes opératoires from Kimpton (UK) and Tatihou (France).

Table 14.2. Short description of Norman chaînes opératoires (Ta: Tatihou; N: Nonant; ME: MondevilleEtoile; MG: Mondeville-Greentheville).

	Chaîne opératoire number	Original name & localisation	Fashioning			Finishing
			Base	body	Neck	
METHOD 1FR	n°1FR	Ta1.1 N1.1 ME1.1	*Roughing out:* Homogeneous clay mass discontinuous digital pressures modelling (circular slab)	*Roughing out:* Heterogeneous clay mass discontinuous digital pressures Coiling	*Roughing out:* Heterogeneous clay mass discontinuous digital pressures Coiling	External/Internal burnishing
	n°2FR	Ta1.2	*Roughing out:* Homogeneous clay mass discontinuous digital pressures modelling (circular slab)	*Roughing out:* Heterogeneous clay mass discontinuous digital pressures Coiling	*Roughing out:* Heterogeneous clay mass discontinuous digital pressures Coiling	External burnishing internal smoothing
	n°3FR	Ta1.3 N1.2 ME1.2 MG1.1	*Roughing out:* Homogeneous clay mass discontinuous digital pressures modelling (circular slab)	*Roughing out:* Heterogeneous clay mass discontinuous digital pressures Coiling	*Roughing out:* Heterogeneous clay mass discontinuous digital pressures Coiling	External/Internal smoothing
	n°4FR	ME1.3 MG1.2	*Roughing out:* Homogeneous clay mass discontinuous digital pressures modelling (circular slab)	*Roughing out:* Heterogeneous clay mass discontinuous digital pressures Coiling	*Roughing out:* Heterogeneous clay mass discontinuous digital pressures Coiling	External smoothing internal burnishing
METHOD 2FR	n°5FR	Ta2.1	*Roughing out:* Homogeneous clay mass discontinuous digital pressures modelling (circular slab)	*Roughing out:* Heterogeneous clay mass discontinuous digital pressures Coiling *Preforming:* Beating	*Roughing out:* Heterogeneous clay mass discontinuous digital pressures Coiling *Preforming:* Beating	External/Internal burnishing
METHOD 3FR	n°6FR	Ta3.1	*Roughing out:* Homogeneous clay mass discontinuous digital pressures hollowing a lump of clay	*Roughing out:* Homogeneous clay mass discontinuous digital pressures hollowing a lump of clay	*Roughing out:* Homogeneous clay mass discontinuous digital pressures hollowing a lump of clay	External/Internal burnishing

Table 14.3. Short description of Trevisker and Deverel-Rimbury chaînes opératoires (Tre: Trevisker; Treth: Trethellan; Gwi: Gwithian; PenhM: Penhale Moor; PenhR: Penhale Round; Call: Callestick; K: Kimpton).

Chaîne opératoire number	Original name & localisation	Fashioning			Finishing
		Base	Body	Neck	
METHOD 1UK					
n°1UK	Tre1; Treth1.1 Gwi1; PenhM1.1 PenhR1.1; Call1 K1.1	*Roughing out:* Heterogeneous clay mass discontinuous digital pressures Spiral coiling	*Roughing out:* Heterogeneous clay mass discontinuous digital pressures Coiling	*Roughing out:* Heterogeneous clay mass discontinuous digital pressures Coiling	External/Internal smoothing
n°2UK	Tre2; Treth1.2; Gwi2; PenhR1.2 K1.2	*Roughing out:* Heterogeneous clay mass discontinuous digital pressures Spiral coiling	*Roughing out:* Heterogeneous clay mass discontinuous digital pressures Coiling	*Roughing out:* Heterogeneous clay mass discontinuous digital pressures Coiling	External/Internal burnishing
n°3UK	Tre3; Treth1.3 Gwi3; PenhM1.2 PenhR1.3; K1.3	*Roughing out:* Heterogeneous clay mass discontinuous digital pressures Spiral coiling	*Roughing out:* Heterogeneous clay mass discontinuous digital pressures Coiling	*Roughing out:* Heterogeneous clay mass discontinuous digital pressures Coiling	External burnishing internal smoothing
n°4UK	Tre4; Treth1.4	*Roughing out:* Heterogeneous clay mass discontinuous digital pressures Spiral coiling	*Roughing out:* Heterogeneous clay mass discontinuous digital pressures Coiling	*Roughing out:* Heterogeneous clay mass discontinuous digital pressures Coiling	External smoothing internal burnishing
METHOD 2UK					
n°5UK	K2.1	*Roughing out:* Heterogeneous clay mass discontinuous digital pressures Spiral coiling	*Roughing out:* Heterogeneous clay mass discontinuous digital pressures Coiling *Preforming:* Beating	*Roughing out:* Heterogeneous clay mass discontinuous digital pressures Coiling *Preforming:* Beating	External/Internal smoothing
n°6UK	K2.2	*Roughing out:* Heterogeneous clay mass discontinuous digital pressures Spiral coiling	*Roughing out:* Heterogeneous clay mass discontinuous digital pressures Coiling *Preforming:* Beating	*Roughing out:* Heterogeneous clay mass discontinuous digital pressures Coiling *Preforming:* Beating	External/Internal burnishing
n°7UK	K2.3	*Roughing out:* Heterogeneous clay mass discontinuous digital pressures Spiral coiling	*Roughing out:* Heterogeneous clay mass discontinuous digital pressures Coiling *Preforming:* Beating	*Roughing out:* Heterogeneous clay mass discontinuous digital pressures Coiling *Preforming:* Beating	External burnishing internal smoothing

and methods for shaping the body and the neck. These latter elements can be shaped with the coil technique (Fig. 14.2, A–B) and by discontinuous finger pressures (method radial: fashioning and finishing *chaînes opératoires* 1UK to 4UK). Ultimately, the distinction between these *chaînes opératoires* is observed for the finishing stages and operates once again according to techniques and methods. Ceramics from *chaîne opératoire* no. 1UK are characterized by a homogeneous surface treatment based on the smoothing technique. We observe the same method for other ceramics but with the burnishing technique (*chaîne opératoire* no. 2UK). This technique is combined with the smoothing technique for ceramics from *chaîne opératoire* no. 3UK: burnishing is used for the exterior surface whereas the Inner surface is treated by smoothing operations. Lastly, this same method is combined with two techniques of homogeneous surface treatment, but applied in reverse: smoothing is observed on the exterior surface and burnishing on the Inner surface (*chaîne opératoire* no. 4UK).

Part of the pottery presents diversity in the technical behaviour used for the shaping operations of the body and neck (method 2UK: shaping and finishing *chaînes opératoires* no. 5UK to 7UK). In other words, the roughing out is similar to the preceding cases, but potteries are preformed by the beating technique. Here again, diversity applies to the finishing operations and surface treatments. We observe whole smoothing (*chaîne opératoire* no. 5UK), comprehensive burnishing (*chaîne opératoire* no. 6UK), or a different method combining both techniques: burnishing is used for the exterior surface and smoothing for the Inner surface (*chaîne opératoire* no. 7UK).

There is a difference between the Trevisker and Deverel-Rimbury productions. Traditions 1UK to 4UK are present in both contexts (method 1UK). However, traditions 5UK to 7UK (method 2UK) only characterise the analysed Deverel-Rimbury potteries.

Discussion

The comparison between the fashioning and finishing *chaînes opératoires* observed on Bronze Age productions in France and the United Kingdom clearly shows that potters do not share the same technical traditions. The main difference derives from the methods, as much for shaping as for finishing *chaînes opératoires*. The main distinction applies to the shaping technique of the base. All the observed English bases are made with the coil technique, unlike the studied Normandy bases, which are made by the modelling (circular slab) from a homogeneous mass of clay. The beating technique for the preforming is known in both island and continental contexts. However, this technique is associated with different methods depending on the insular or continental context. In this way, continental *chaînes opératoires* involving the beating technique are exclusively

characterized by burnishing operations whereas some island potters also used the smoothing technique. The hollowing of a lump of clay is unknown in an island context for the studied collections.

Furthermore, the insular material culture of the Trevisker and Deverel-Rimbury groups is characterised by certain shared technical traditions, although the latter group is differentiated by other aforementioned traditions. This partial similarity could be explained by the older age of the Trevisker group in comparison with the Deverel-Rimbury group (Marcigny and Ghesquière 2003, chronological table, fig. 144). This would probably be the result of a heritage and lineage.

Diffusion by borrowing, in a 'Channel–North Sea' context (France and the United Kingdom) only concerns the shape and the decorative style. In other words, borrowing is only centred on visible elements that can be copied without learning process and without direct contact between potters. In this geographic area, the notion of learning is the keystone to understand this archaeological context. In the domain of technology, Valentine Roux (2010) shows in this way that it is important to distinguish between competence and performance. The first notion is related to motor skills which are acquired by learning from an adult for shaping operations (Bril 2002). On the other hand, operations related to decoration are linked to performances: the individual can easily invent, copy or be inspired by another style during or after learning. There are no motor-type constraints (Roux 2007). Depending on the cultural contexts, decoration may be strictly regulated and linked to identity, whereas in other contexts, the potter may have the freedom to invent or copy a decoration even if he/she rigorously follows the taught shaping stages, like in Mexico for example (Hardin 1977; after Van der Leeuw 1994).

Generally speaking, we now see how Middle Bronze Age traditions are organized in this vast region: the natural boundary of the Channel appears, based on current results, to correspond to boundaries between technical traditions. The Channel limits the extension of learning and transmission networks because the Channel is the boundary between island and continental social groups. We observe a similar impact of natural frontiers among the different communities installed in the islands of the Philippines (Scheans 1977).

The presence of different social groups around the Channel also explains why there is a difference between island and continental Middle Bronze Age domestic architecture (circular in the United Kingdom but rectangular in Normandy), although the structuring of settlements around plots is similar. This difference denotes the habitus characterising each social group (Bourdieu 1977; Hegmon 1998). The different 'technical heritages' (Bonnemaison 2004) show that these are distinctive lineages (Shennan 2013) characterised by these learning networks.

They highlight the social boundaries (Hegmon 1998) defining distinct island and continental communities as regards to identity and culture and only transmit their technical traditions to their descendants. In this 'Channel–North Sea' context, 'each region, whilst aware of and clearly in contact with its neighbours, follows its own particular direction' (Wilkin and Vander Linden 2015, 113).

Although technical traditions are not shared in the 'Channel-North Sea' context, the privileged cross-Channel link brought to light by other scholars is by no means inexact, quite the contrary, provided that the notion of culture for this region is not validated (Marcigny *et al.* 2015). Here again, it depends of the type of transmission between people (direct or indirect) and the actors involved and influencing the production: the style is linked to the consumer thus on demands, whereas technical traditions depend on producers. These opposite results between techniques and styles are understandable when we observe the way of life of Bronze Age groups: families working the land are tied to the earth. However, as pointed out by Cyril Marcigny in his different works, the tempo seems to be identical in the evolution of stylistic modes on both sides of the Channel. This must certainly have induced an indirect link between similar social categories (e.g. farmers) those dealing with trade and exchange networks. From a same generation and the following, they can easily and swiftly follow the same tempo of evolution through rapid and indirect diffusion, where the acquisition of motor skills and technical tradition involves a direct learning between potters or remains strictly confined to the social group where the apprentice learned his/her craft (Herbich 1987). A second hypothesis can be advanced to complete the first; the absence of cultural and identity connotations for decorative style in Normandy. Lastly the limited presence (only observed at Tatihou and Kimpton) of the beating technique for Deverel-Rimbury and Normandy production may – at this stage of analysis – also denote practices without any link between them; nothing more than a possible connection. In the first case, borrowing can be intra-island and intra-continental. For example, beating is known on the continent in the Middle Bronze Age production of the Duffaits culture (Manem 2008). In the second case, only certain isolated traits are involved, inducing in this case, limited and possible borrowing through contact between certain continental and island potters. This borrowing, if it exists, is different from the homogeneous stylistic traits observed in the region, as again, the latter are linked to demand, that is to consumers. Inter-cultural technical borrowing is purely an interaction between producers, and can be linked to technical, economic or social factors. In such cases, the 'sociological composition of the producers' involved is decisive as it conditions borrowing and diffusion modalities (Roux 2016).

The study needs to continue to identify Middle Bronze Age technical traditions throughout the whole Channel–North Sea zone in order to confirm or refine these results. A possible sharing of technical traditions in zones in closer contact, such as the north of France and the south-east of the United Kingdom remains possible (Bourgeois and Talon 2009). If such a case exists, the boundary between social groups could be solely continental, that is, between the north of France and Normandy, for example.

From a diachronic viewpoint, for the moment, the sites studied show that there is no chronological discrepancy in technical practices. In other words, we do not observe the Normandy traditions from the Early Bronze Age/Middle Bronze Age transition (Tatihou phase 1), the Middle Bronze Age (Tatihou phase 2; Nonant) and the Bronze BM2/Late Bronze Age 1 transition (Mondeville) in a Late Bronze Age English context (for instance at Callestick), in the studied sites. There does not seem to be diffusion from the continent towards the United Kingdom in the studied zones: the Channel does not slow down a possible diffusion of technical traditions. The absence of sharing of technical traditions beyond social boundaries during the whole studied period shows stability in social contexts and the preservation of existing balance. It is widely accepted that a significant and sudden change in technical behaviours in a region results from an upheaval or a particular socio-economic context (Roux 2010), such as population movement, for example.

However, the continental Late Bronze Age IIIb analysis remains to be pursued in order to verify, conversely, if there is slow diffusion towards the continent, or even population movement in this direction. In the first case, island Middle Bronze Age traditions could correspond to Late Bronze Age continental traditions.

Conclusion

The 'Channel-North Sea' archaeological context represents a complex case of human interactions. It is characterised by homogeneous morpho-stylistic material production but the analysis of pottery technical traditions clearly shows – for the studied zones and ceramics – a contradiction with current knowledge based on an analytical framework that had not been taken into account up until now. Continental and island technical traditions are different. The Channel seems to be a natural *and* cultural barrier to inter-community connections in terms of transmission by learning and thus in terms of direct links between individuals working the land on either side of the Channel. The combination of these technological results with studies of stylistic similarities and trading carried out by the above cited colleagues thus shows privileged links between these groups living around the Channel, operating above all on the intermediaries and those involved in trade networks. However, the 'Channel–North Sea' context reveals the presence of distinct social and partitioned groups on a cultural and identity level. They only transmit their technical traditions in their respective learning networks. The study must be extended to the rest of the region; however, these results demonstrate that given the stability of technical traditions during the Middle Bronze Age there is no population movement in the zones under consideration.

Acknowledgements

I particularly wish to thank the Fyssen Foundation (Paris) for funding this work. Thanks also to my former supervisor Anthony Harding (University of Exeter and Ludwig-Maximilians-Universität Munich) and to the members of the archaeology department of the University of Exeter for their warm reception during my post doctorate. Thanks to Claude Mordant (Université de Bourgogne), Cyril Marcigny (Inrap) and Valentine Roux (CNRS) for their help and advice. I also wish to thank Ben Roberts (University of Durham) and the British Museum, Jacqueline Nowakowski and Andy Jones (Cornwall Archaeological Unit), Jane Marley (Royal Cornwall Museum), Xavier Savary (service d'archéologie, Conseil Général, Calvados) as well as the Inrap in Lower Normandy for their welcome and access to collections. Thanks to Marie Philippe (Université de Bourgogne), Marc Talon (Inrap) and the referees for observations on the first version of this manuscript. I also wish to thank Anne Lehoerff (Université de Lille) and Marc Talon for the direction of this volume.

Bibliography

Apsimon, A. M. and Greenfield, E. (1972) The excavations of Bronze Age and Iron Age settlements at Trevisker, St Eval, Cornwall. *Proceedings of the Prehistoric Society* 38, 302–381.

Arnold, D. E. (1985) *Ceramic Theory and Cultural Process.* Cambridge, Cambridge University Press.

Bonnemaison, J. (2004) *La géographie culturelle. Cours de l'Université Paris IV – Sorbonne 1994–1997.* Paris, CTHS.

Bourdieu, P. (1977) *Outline of a Theory of Practice.* Cambridge, Cambridge University Press.

Bourgeois, J. and Talon, M. (eds) (2005) *L'âge du Bronze du nord de la France dans son contexte européen. 125e actes des congrès nationaux des sociétés historiques et scientifiques, Lilles, 2000.* Paris, CTHS.

Bourgeois, J. and Talon, M. (2009) From Picardy to Flanders: transmanche connections in the Bronze Age. In P. Clark (ed.) *Bronze Age Connections. Cultural Contact in Prehistoric Europe*, 38–59. Oxford, Oxbow Books.

Bowser, B. J. (2000) From pottery to politics: an ethnoarchaeological study of political factionalism, ethnicity, and domestic pottery style in the Ecuadorian Amazon. *Journal of Archaeological Method and Theory* 7 (3), 219–248.

Bradley, R. (2007) *The Prehistory of Britain and Ireland.* Cambridge, Cambridge University Press.

Bril, B. (2002) L'apprentissage de gestes techniques: ordre de contraintes et variations culturelles. In B. Bril and V. Roux (eds) *Le geste technique: réflexions méthodologiques et anthropologiques*, 113–150. Ramoville Saint-Agne, Éditions Erès (Technologie/Idéologie/Pratiques. Revue d'anthropologie des connaissances).

Brück, J. (1999) Houses, life cycles and deposition on Middle Bronze Age settlements in Southern England. *Proceedings of the Prehistoric Society* 65, 145–166.

Brück, J. (ed.) (2001) *Bronze Age Landscapes: Tradition and Transformation.* Oxford, Oxbow Books.

Brun, P. and Mordant, C. (eds) (1988) *Le Groupe Rhin-Suisse-France orientale et la notion de civilisation des Champs d'Urnes. Actes du colloque international de Nemours*, mémoires du Musée de Préhistoire d'Île-de-France 1. Nemours, A. P. R. A. I. F.

Burgess, C. (1980) *The Age of Stonehenge.* London, Dent.

Burgess, C. (1987) Les rapports entre la France et la Grande-Bretagne pendant l'Âge du Bronze : problèmes de poterie et d'habitats. In J.-C. Blanchet (ed.) *Les relations entre le continent et les Iles Britaniques à l'Âge du Bronze. Actes du colloque de Lille dans le cadre du 22ème congrès préhistorique de France. 2–7 septembre 1984*, 307–318. Paris, Société Préhistorique Française.

Carozza, L. and Marcigny, C. (2007) *L'âge du Bronze en France.* Paris, Éditions La Découverte.

Chancerel, A., Marcigny, C. and Ghesquière, E. (2006) *Le plateau de Mondeville (Calvados) du Néolithique à l'âge du Bronze.* Paris, Éditions de la maison des sciences de l'Homme.

Clark, P. (ed.) (2009) *Bronze Age Connections. Cultural Contact in Prehistoric Europe.* Oxford, Oxbow Books.

Collectif (ed.) (1989) *Dynamique du Bronze moyen en Europe. Actes du 113e Congrès national des Sociétés savantes, Strasbourg, 1988.* Paris, CTHS.

Collett, D. (1987) A contribution to the study of migrations in the archaeological record: the Ngoni and Kololo as a case study. In I. Hodder (ed.) *Archaeology as Long-Term History*, 105–116. Cambridge, Cambridge University Press.

Courty, M.-A. and Roux, V. (1995) Identification of the wheel throwing technique on the basis of ceramic surface features and microfabrics. *Journal of Archaeological Science* 22, 17–50.

Dacre, M. and Ellison, A. (1981) A Bronze Age urn cemetery at Kimpton, Hampshire. *Proceedings of the Prehistoric Society* 47, 147–203.

David, N. and Hennig, H. (1972) The ethnography of pottery: a Fulani case seen in archaeological perspective. *MacCaleb Module in Anthropology* 21, 1–29.

David, N. and Kramer, C. (2001) *Ethnoarchaeology in Action.* Cambridge, Cambridge University Press.

Davis, E., Grove, J., Heathcote, J., Johns, C. and Nowakowski, J. (1994) *A30 project: archive report on the archaeological excavations at Penhale Round, Fraddon, Cornwall 1993.* Truro, Cornwall Archaeological Unit.

De Crits, E. (1994) Style et technique: comparaison interethnique de la poterie subsaharienne. In D. Binder and J. Courtin (eds)

Terre cuite et Société. La céramique, document technique, économique, culturel. Actes des XIVe Rencontres Internationales d'Archéologie et d'Histoire d'Antibes, 327–350. Juan-les-Pins, Editions APDCA.

Degoy, L. (2008) Technical traditions and cultural identity. An ethnoarchaeology study of Andhra Pradesh potters. In M. T. Stark, B. J. Bowser and L. Horne (eds) *Cultural Transmission and Material Culture. Breaking Down Boundaries*, 199–222. Tucson, University of Arizona Press.

Desfossés, Y. and Masson, B. (2000) Les enclos funéraires du 'Motel' à Fresnes-lès-Montauban (Pasde-Calais). In Collectif (ed.) *Habitats et nécropoles à l'Âge du bronze sur le transmanche et le T. G. V. Nord*, 19–58. Paris, Éditions Société Préhistorique Française.

Dietler, M. and Herbich, I. (1994) Ceramics and ethnic identity: ethnoarchaeological observations on the distribution of pottery styles and the relationship between the social contexts of production and consumption. In D. Binder and J. Courtin (eds) *Terre cuite et Société. La céramique, document technique, économique, culturel. Actes des XIVe Rencontres Internationales d'Archéologie et d'Histoire d'Antibes*, 460–472. Juan-les-Pins, Editions APDCA.

Dietler, M. and Herbich, I. (1998) *Habitus*, techniques, style : an integrated approach to the social understanding of material culture and boundaries. In M. T. Stark (ed.) *The Archaeology of Social Boundaries*, 232–263. Washington DC and London, Smithsonian Institution Press.

Dobres, M.-A. (2000) *Technology and Social Agency*. Oxford, Blackwell.

Field, N. (1985) A multi-phased barrow and possible henge monument at West Ashby, Lincolnshire. *Proceedings of the Prehistoric Society* 51, 103–136.

Fleming, A. (1988) *The Dartmoor Reaves. Investigating Prehistoric land divisions*. London, Batsford.

Foster, G.-M. (1965) The sociology of pottery. Questions and hypothesis arising from contemporary Mexican work. In F. Matson (ed.) *Ceramics and Man*, 43–61. Chicago, Aldine.

Fowler, P. J. (1981) *The Farming of Prehistoric Britain*. Cambridge, Cambridge University Press.

Gallay, A. (2000) Peuplement et histoire de la boucle du Niger (Mali) : un exemple de recomposition sociale dans l'artisanat du feu. In P. Pétrequin, P. Fluzin, J. Thiriot and P. Benoit (eds) *Arts du feu et productions artisanales. XXe Rencontres Internationales d'Archéologie et d'Histoire d'Antibes*, 237–260. Antibes, Editions APDCA.

Gallay, A. (2012) *Potières du Sahel. A la découverte des traditions céramiques de la boucle du Niger (Mali)*. Gollion, Infolio.

Gelbert, A. (2003) *Traditions céramiques et emprunts techniques dans la vallée du fleuve Sénégal*. Paris, Editions de la Maison des Sciences de l'Homme, Editions Epistèmes.

Gomez de Soto, J. (1995) *Le Bronze moyen en Occident. La Culture des Duffaits et la Civilisation des Tumulus*. Paris, Picard.

Gosselain, O. (1992) Technology and style: potters and pottery among Bafia of Cameroon. *Man* 27 (3), 559–586.

Gosselain, O. (2000) Materialising identities: an African perspective. *Journal of Archaeological Method and Theory* 7 (3), 187–217.

Gosselain, O. (2002) *Poteries du Cameroun méridional. Styles techniques et rapports à l'identité*. Paris, Editions du CNRS. CRA monographie 26.

Gosselain, O. (2008) Mother Bella was not a Bella. Inherited and transformed traditions in Southwestern Niger. In M. T. Stark, B. J. Bowser and L. Horne (eds) *Cultural Transmission and Material Culture. Breaking Down Boundaries*, 150–177. Tucson, University of Arizona Press.

Hardin, M. A. (1977) Stucture and creativity: family style in Tarascan greenware painting. Unpublished thesis, University of Chicago.

Hegmon, M. (1992) Archaeological research on style. *Annual Review of Anthropology* 21, 517–536.

Hegmon, M. (1998) Technology, style, and social practices: archaeological approaches. In M. T. Stark (ed.) *The Archaeology of Social Boundaries*, 264–279. Washington DC and London, Smithsonian Institute Press.

Herbich, I. (1987) Learning patterns, potter interaction and ceramic style among the Luo of Kenya. *African Archaeological Review* 5, 193–204.

Jones, A. (1999) The excavation of a Later Bronze Age structure at Callestick. *Cornish Archaeology* 38, 1–55.

Jones, A., Jones, A., Nowakowski, J. and Thorpe, C. (1994) *Archive report on the excavation of Penhale Moor Middle Bronze Age site, Fraddon, Cornwall*. Truro, Cornwall Archaeological Unit.

Kramer, C. (1997) *Pottery in Rajasthan. Ethnoarchaeology in Two Indian cities*. Washington DC and London, Smithsonian Institution Press.

Lara, C. (2015) Présence du passé, la poterie contemporaine du sud-est de l'Equateur. *Yachac* 13, 4–46.

Latour, B. and Lemonnier, P. (eds) (1994) *De la préhistoire aux missiles balistiques. L'intelligence sociale des techniques*. Paris, La Découverte (coll. Recherches).

Lave, J. and Wenger, E. (1991) *Situated Learning: Legitimate Peripheral Participation*. Cambridge, Cambridge University Press.

Leclercq, W. and Warmenbol, E. (eds) (2013) *Echanges de bons procédés. La céramique du Bronze final dans le nord-ouest de l'Europe*. Bruxelles, CReA-Patrimoine.

Lemonnier, P. (1986) The study of material culture today: toward an anthropology of technical systems. *Journal of Anthropological Archaeology* 5, 147–186.

Lemonnier, P. (ed.) (1993) *Technological Choices. Transformation in Material Cultures Since the Neolithic*. London and New York, Routledge.

Livingstone Smith, A. (2001) Chaîne opératoire de la poterie: références ethnographiques, analyses et reconstitution. Unpublished thesis, Université Libre de Bruxelles, Faculty of Philosophy and Letters.

Manem, S. (2008) Étude des fondements technologiques de la culture des Duffaits (Âge du Bronze moyen). Unpublished thesis, University of Paris X.

Marcigny, C. (1999) *Une enceinte à vocation domestique de l'Âge du Bronze à Nonant 'La Bergerie' (Calvados). Rapport de fouilles*. Unpublished

Marcigny, C. and Ghesquière, E. (2003) *L'île de Tatihou (Manche) à l'âge du Bronze. Habitats et occupation du sol*. Paris, Éditions de la maison des sciences de l'Homme.

Marcigny, C., Bourgeois, J. and Talon, M. (2015) Cultural geographies, socio-economic complexes and territories along the Channel/Manche–southern sea littoral (Belgium,

England, France). In P. Suchowska-Ducke, S. Scott Reiter and H. Vandkilde (eds) *Forging identities. The modibility of culture in Bronze Age Europe*, 225–233. British Archaeological Report S2772. Oxford, Archaeopress.

Marcigny, C., Ghesquière, E. and Kinnes, I. (2007) Bronze Age cross-channel relations. The Lower-Normandy (France) example: ceramic chronology and first reflections. In C. Burgess, P. Topping and F. Lynch (eds) *Beyond Stonehenge. Essays on the Bronze Age in Honour of Colin Burgess*, 255–267. Oxford, Oxbow Books.

Marcigny, C., Ghesquière, E., Clement-Sauleau, S. and Verney, A. (2005) L'Âge du Bronze en Basse-Normandie: définition par le mobilier céramique, une première tentative. In J. Bourgeois and M. Talon (eds) *L'Âge du Bronze du nord de la France dans son contexte européen*, 303–332. Paris, Editions CTHS.

Martineau, R. (2000) Poterie, techniques et sociétés. Etudes analytiques et expérimentales à Chalain et Clairvaux (Jura), entre 3200 et 2900 av. J.-C. Unpublished thesis, University of Franche-Comté.

May, P. and Tuckson, M. (2000) *The Traditional Pottery of Papua New Guinea*. Sidney, Bay Books.

Minar, C. J. and Crown, P. L. (2001) Learning and craft production: an introduction. *Journal of Anthropological Research* 57 (4), 369–380.

Mordant, C. and Gaiffe, O. (eds) (1996) *Cultures et sociétés du Bronze ancien en Europe. Actes du 117e Congrès national des Sociétés Savantes (Clermont-Ferrand, 1992)*. Paris, CTHS.

Naum, M. (2010) Re-emerging frontiers: postcolonial theory and historical archaeology of the borderlands. *Journal of Archaeological Method and Theory* 17 (2), 101–131. doi: 10.1007/s10816-010-9077-9.

Needham, S. (2009) Encompassing the sea: 'maritories' and Bronze Age maritime interactions. In P. Clark (ed.) *Bronze Age Connections. Cultural Contact in Prehistoric Europe*, 12–37. Oxford, Oxbow Books.

Needham, S., Parfitt, K. and Varndell, G. (eds) (2006) *The Ringlemere Cup: precious cups and the beginning of the Channel Bronze Age*, British Museum Research Publication 163. London, British Museum.

Nicklin, K. (1971) Stability and innovation in pottery manufacture. *World Archaeology* 3 (1), 13–48.

Nowakowski, J. (1989) *Gwithian: an assessment of the Bronze age excavations 1954–1961*. Truro, Cornwall Archaeological Unit.

Nowakowski, J. (1991) Trethellan Farm, newquay: the excavation of a lowland Bronze Age settlement and Iron Age cemetery. *Cornish Archaeology* 30, 5–242.

Parker Pearson, M. (1990) The production and distribution of Bronze Age pottery in south-west Britain. *Cornish Archaeology* 32, 146–152.

Parker Pearson, M. (1995) Southwestern Bronze Age pottery. In I. Kinnes and G. Varndell (eds) *Unbaked Urns of Rudely Shape*, 89–100. Oxford, Oxbow Books.

Piggott, C. M. (1938) A middle Bronze Age barrow and Deverel-Rimbury urnfield at Latch Farm, Christchurch, Hampshire. *Proceedings of the Prehistoric Society* 4, 169–187.

Reed, E. S. and Bril, B. (1996) The primacy of action in development. The primacy of action in development. A commentary of N. Bernstein. In M. Latash and M. Turvey (eds.) *Dexterity and its development*, 431–451. Hillsdale NJ, Erlbaum Associates.

Rice, P. M. (1987) *Pottery Analysis. A Sourcebook*. Chicago and London, University of Chicago Press.

Rogers, D. S. and Ehrlich, P. R. (2008) Natural selection and cultural rates of change. *Proceedings of the National Academy of Sciences of the United States of America* 105 (9), 3416–3420. doi: 10.1073/pnas.0711802105.

Roux, V. (2003) A dynamic systems framework for studying technological change: application to the emergence of the potter's wheel in the southern Levant. *Journal of Archaeological Method and Theory* 10 (1), 1–30.

Roux, V. (2007) Ethnoarchaeology: a non historical science of reference necessary for interpreting the past. *Journal of Archaeological Method and Theory* 14 (2), 153–178. doi: 10.1007/s10816-007-9030-8.

Roux, V. (2010) Lecture anthropologique des assemblages céramiques. Fondements et mise en oeuvre de l'analyse technologique. *Les Nouvelles de l'Archéologie* 119, 4–9.

Roux, V. (2013) Spreading of Innovative technical traits and cumulative technical evolution: continuity or discontinuity? *Journal of Archaeological Method and Theory* 20 (2), 312–330. doi: 10.1007/s10816-012-9153-4

Roux, V. (2016) *Des céramiques et des hommes. Décoder les assemblages archéologiques*. Nanterre, Presses Universitaires de Paris Ouest

Roux, V. and Corbetta, D. (1989) *The Potter's Wheel: Craft Specialization and Technical Competence*. New Delhi, Oxford & IBH Publishing

Rye, O. S. (1981) *Pottery Technology: Principles and Reconstruction 4*. Washington DC, Taraxacum Press.

Scheans, D. J. (1977) *Filipino market potteries*. Manila, National Museum Monograph 3.

Shennan, S. (2013) Lineages of cultural transmission. In R. Ellen, S. J. Lycett and S. E. Johns (eds) *Understanding Cultural Transmission in Anthropology: a Critical Synthesis*, 346–360. New York and Oxford, Berghahn Books.

Stark, M. T. (ed.) (1998) *The Archaeology of Social Boundaries*. Washington DC and London, Smithsonian Institution Press.

Stark, M. T., Bishop, R. L. and Miksa, E. (2000) Ceramic technology and social boundaries: cultural practices in Kalinga clay selection and use. *Journal of Archaeological Method and Theory* 7 (4), 295–331.

Stark, M. T., Bowser, B. J. and Horne, L. (eds) (2008) *Cultural Transmission and Material Culture. Breaking Down Boundaries*. Tucson, University of Arizona Press.

Stark, M. T., Elson, M. D. and Clark, J. J. (1998) Social boundaries and technical choices in Tonto Basin prehistory In M. T. Stark (ed.) *The Archaeology of Social Boundaries*, 208–231. Washington DC and London, Smithsonian Institute Press.

Stone, J. F. S. (1941) The Deverel-Rimbury settlement on Thorny Down, Winterbourne Gunner, S. Wilts. *Proceedings of the Prehistoric Society* 7, 114–133.

Van der Leeuw, S. E. (1994) Innovation et tradition chez les potiers mexicains ou comment les gestes techniques traduisent les dynamiques d'une société. In B. Latour and P. Lemonnier (eds) *De la Préhistoire aux missiles balistiques: l'intelligence sociale des techniques*, 310–328. Paris, La Découverte.

Wallaert-Pêtre, H. (2001) Learning how to make the right pots: apprenticeship strategies and material culture, a case study in handmade pottery from Cameroon. *Journal of Anthropological Research* 57 (4), 471–493.

Wallaert-Pêtre, H. (2012) Apprenticeship and the confirmation of social boundaries. In W. Wendrich (ed.) *Archaeology and Apprenticeship: Body Knowledge, Identity, and Communities of Practice*, 20–42. Tucson, University of Arizona Press.

Wilkin, N. and Vander Linden, M. (2015) What was and what would never be: changing patterns of interaction and archaeological visiblity across north-west Europe from 2,500 to 1,500 cal BC. In H. Anderson-Whymark, D. Garrow and F. Sturt (eds) *Continental Connections: Exploring Cross-Channel Relationships from the Mesolithic to the Iron Age*, 99–121. Oxford, Oxbow Books.

Evolution des faciès céramiques au Bronze final et à l'aube du premier Âge du fer, entre Somme, Escaut et rivages de la Manche (France, région Nord-Picardie)

Alain Henton et Nathalie Buchez

Abstract

The important corpus of pottery recovered over the last two decades in the Nord-Picardie region allows us to propose a new typo-chronological and cultural approach for the period between the 14th and 18th centuries BC. At the early stage of the Late Bronze Age At the early stage of the Late Bronze Age there is a strong technological and typological affinity with English Deverel-Rimbury pottery, at least in its later manifestations. For the middle stage of the Late Bronze Age, this corpus also reinforces a genuine expansion of RSFO traits into the valleys of the Somme and the Scheldt. However, on the coastal margins, if finewares show some RSFO characteristics, the coarsewares show net Deverel-Rimbury/MMN influences. In the final stage of the Late Bronze Age, two distinct styles can be seen on either side of the Scheldt valley. On the left bank, the pottery recalls the Plain Ware style of the Channel coasts, whilst hinting at an underlying RSFO tradition. In the valley of the Somme, the ceramics also relates to Plain Ware, with some attenuated influence of the Ardennes Group. At the dawn of the Iron Age, the Scheldt valley saw the appearance of a new style which finds its parallels in the Belgian and French Ardennes. Regarding the valley of the Somme, the corpus is still too weak to specify its cultural affinities. Hypothetically we can nevertheless assume the presence of a 'Picard' style, more or less associated with the final manifestations of the MMN complex. The cultural homogenisation of the region only begins in the late Halstatt reaching its zenith at the beginning of early La Tène with the expansion of the Marnien style.

Keywords: North Picardy, Somme, Scheldt, pottery, typo-chronology, cultural facies, Deverel-Rimbury, Manche-Mer-du-Nord cultural complex, Rhin-Suisse-France orientale (RSFO), Ardennes group, Late Bronze Age, Early Iron Age

Résumé

L'important corpus céramique dégagé au cours des deux dernières décennies dans la région Nord-Picardie nous autorise à proposer une nouvelle approche typo-chronologique et culturelle pour la période comprise entre les 14e et 8e siècles avant notre ère. A l'étape ancienne du Bronze final, on note de fortes affinités tant technologiques que typologiques avec le Deverel-Rimbury anglais, du moins dans une de ses manifestations tardives. Pour l'étape moyenne du Bronze final, le corpus assez significatif conforte une réelle expansion du faciès RSFO jusque dans les vallées de la Somme et de l'Escaut. Sur les marges littorales toutefois, si la céramique fine montre certains caractères RSFO, la céramique grossière indique quant à elle de nettes influences post-Deverel-Rimbury/MMN. A l'étape finale du Bronze final, deux faciès distincts se font face de part et d'autre de la vallée de l'Escaut. Rive droite, le vaisselier est étroitement associé à celui du Groupe des Ardennes. Rive gauche, le vaisselier se rapporte plus au faciès Plain Ware des rivages de la Manche, tout en laissant deviner un substrat de tradition

RSFO. En vallée de Somme, la céramique se rattacherait elle aussi au faciès Plain Ware, avec certaines influences atténuées du Groupe des Ardennes. A l'aube du premier Âge du fer, la vallée de l'Escaut voit l'apparition d'un nouveau faciès dont les parallèles nous portent vers les Ardennes belges et françaises. En ce qui concerne la vallée de la Somme, le corpus demeure encore trop faible pour préciser les affinités culturelles. De manière hypothétique, nous pouvons toutefois supposer la présence d'un faciès « Picard », plus ou moins apparenté aux dernières manifestations du complexe MMN. L'homogénéisation culturelle de la région ne s'amorcerait qu'au Hallstatt final pour pleinement aboutir à l'aube de la Tène ancienne avec l'expansion du faciès marnien.

Mots-clés : Nord-Picardie, Somme, Escaut, céramique, typo-chronologie, faciès culturels, Deverel-Rimbury, complexe culturel Manche-Mer du Nord (MMN), Rhin-Suisse-France orientale (RSFO), Groupe des Ardennes, Bronze final, premier Âge du fer.

Introduction

Dans le cadre défini par le colloque international de Boulogne, nous avons choisi de présenter ici, sur base d'une approche exclusivement céramologique, les récentes découvertes indiquant un probable basculement culturel progressif d'une partie du territoire de la région française de Nord-Picardie (départements du Nord, du Pas-de-Calais et de la Somme) (Fig. 15.1), au cours de l'Âge du bronze final et du premier Âge du fer. Très clairement affilié à la sphère « atlantique » durant la totalité de l'Âge du bronze ancien et moyen, soit pendant près de 1000 ans, cette zone géographiquement bien définie montre, entre les 13e et 6e siècles, une interpénétration mouvante et complexe de différents faciès, se soldant de manière définitive à l'aube du second Âge du fer par une homogénéisation culturelle, tournée cette fois vers la sphère « continentale ».

A la lecture de certaines études relatives aux connexions culturelles de part et d'autre des rivages de la Manche entre la fin de l'Âge du bronze et le début du premier Âge du fer, il semblait encore voici peu clairement établi que la zone délimitée par les vallées de la Somme, de l'Escaut et les rivages de la Manche soit intégrée aux marges de l'orbite culturelle de l'entité Manche-Mer-du Nord (MMN) (Bourgeois et Talon 2008 ; Marcigny et Talon 2009). Cependant, à la lumière de découvertes récentes de l'archéologie préventive dans les départements de la Somme (80), du Nord (59) et du Pas-de-Calais (62), cette vision dichotomique, confrontant monde continental et monde atlantique, semble devoir être quelque peu tempérée, notamment sur base de l'étude du mobilier céramique.

L'une des difficultés de notre approche se base sur la relative jeunesse de l'archéologie préventive sur une bonne partie de la région Nord-Picardie, ne remontant guère au-delà d'une vingtaine d'année, et surtout sur une prise en compte encore plus récente de la problématique de la protohistoire ancienne.

Une étape ancienne du Bronze final (BF I–IIa/Bz D–Ha A1)?

Si l'existence d'un substrat atlantique couvrant le nord-ouest de la France durant l'Âge du bronze ancien-moyen

ne semble plus devoir être remis en cause (Bourgeois et Talon 2008), les données relatives au tout début du Bronze final demeurent encore trop discrètes pour pouvoir établir avec certitude l'appartenance culturelle de la zone d'étude aux 14e et 13e siècles avant notre ère. Toutefois, quelques ensembles clos, découverts au hasard de diagnostics ou de fouilles préventives permettent d'avancer quelques hypothèses.

En 2008, à Courrières (Pas-de-Calais), deux fosses voisines ont livré un mobilier céramique assez proche du point de vue typologique (pots de stockage de profil haut a priori biconique, à large épaulement rentrant et à pseudo-col court éversé et marqué en interne) et technologique (forte concentration d'inclusions minérales). Une datation absolue (3020±40 BP, 1400–1130 cal BC) couvre l'extrême fin du Bronze moyen II et l'étape ancienne du Bronze final. Cette attribution chronologique semble être confortée par la mise au jour, à quelque distance des deux ensembles clos, d'un petit dépôt associant une épingle à tête sub-biconique, un rasoir à manche annelé et plusieurs perles d'ambre, attribuable au BF I–IIa (Henton 2013). A Maroeuil (Pas-de-Calais), à Hingues « Vertannoy » (Nord) (Buchez *et al.* dans ce volume) et plus récemment à Aire-sur-la-Lys « Hameau de Saint-Martin » (Pas-de-Calais, fouilles Y. Lorin, 2015 d'étude) (Fig. 15.2), des ensembles clos ont livré du mobilier céramique très semblable du point de vue technologique. La typologie restreinte est constituée de bol à panse sphérique et rebord rentrant, de pot à épaulement avec col redressé et lèvre éversée, de tasse, de jatte ou terrine. Le répertoire décoratif se résume à des impressions digitées sur lèvre ou sur bandeau appliqué. A Aire, une série de perforations, à la fonction non reconnue, est visible sous la lèvre d'un grand pot à cordon décoré d'incisions (Fig. 15.2) et renvoie à des contextes du début Bronze final du Norfolk anglais, comme ceux domestiques de Grime's Graves (Mercer 1981), Plumpton Plain (Hawkes 1935) ou funéraire d'Ardleight (Couchman 1975). A noter la présence à Hingues d'un peson de section sub-ovalaire, très différent des pesons sub-cylindriques du Bronze moyen ou sub-trapézoïdaux des étapes moyenne et finale du Bronze final. Si, non étayées par des datations absolues, les études de ces ensembles n'excluent pas une possible attribution au Bronze moyen

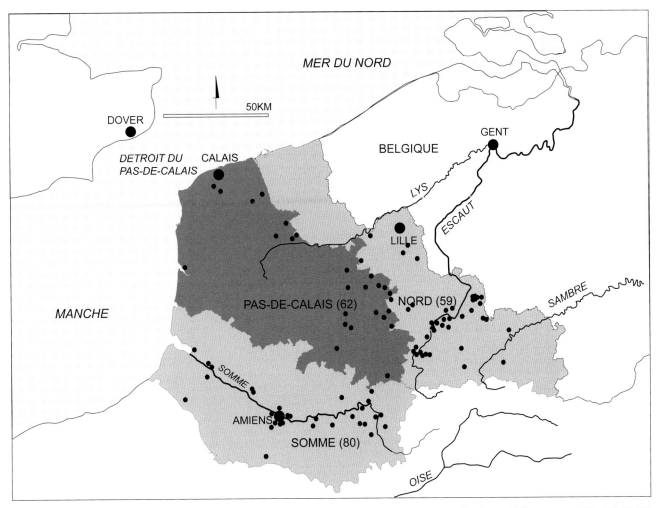

Fig. 15.1. Carte de la zone d'étude, avec implantation des principaux sites d'habitat du BF I/Bz D au Hallstatt moyen/Ha D1 (DAO: A. Henton).

II, certains caractères typologiques plus évolués que sur le site Bronze moyen de Roeux (département du Pas-de-Calais) (Desfossés *et al.* 2000) élargissent cette datation à l'étape ancienne du Bronze final.

Très dissemblant du répertoire typologique de l'étape moyenne du Bronze final, ce mobilier pose donc la question d'un faciès céramique de tradition Manche/Mer du Nord affilié au Deverel-Rimbury dans sa phase finale. Selon toute vraisemblance, et bien que la synchronisation des chronologies allemande et du nord de la France indique une rupture entre le Bronze moyen et le Bronze final vers le milieu du 14e siècle, le répertoire céramique de la zone d'étude à l'aube du Bronze final indiquerait lui une probable continuité culturelle évolutive par rapport à la période directement précédente. Toute la difficulté réside à ce jour sur une distinction claire avec la typologie céramique du Bronze moyen II ; au demeurant elle aussi encore assez mal connue et à laquelle auraient été empruntés certains aspects technologiques (dégraissant), mais aussi sur l'existence d'éventuelles influences extérieures.

Enfin, un autre questionnement concerne le nombre très limité de sites d'habitat reconnus pour cette étape. Cette absence de sites reflète-t-elle une faible occupation du territoire ou plus simplement un problème de reconnaissance archéologique ? Pour le Bronze ancien-moyen, lui aussi caractérisé par une absence remarquée de sites d'habitat, la découverte de très nombreux sites funéraires (enclos fossoyés circulaires) (Henton et Hannois 2014) et d'artefacts métalliques (isolés ou en dépôts) (Blanchet 1984) témoigne d'une occupation relativement plus dense et homogène du territoire et laisse supposer un réel problème de reconnaissance.

L'étape moyenne du Bronze final (BF IIb–IIIa/Ha A2–B1)

Depuis une dizaine d'années, notre perception de la zone d'étude à l'étape moyenne du Bronze final a très fortement évolué, principalement suite à la mise en évidence de nombreux sites d'habitat lors d'opérations d'archéologie

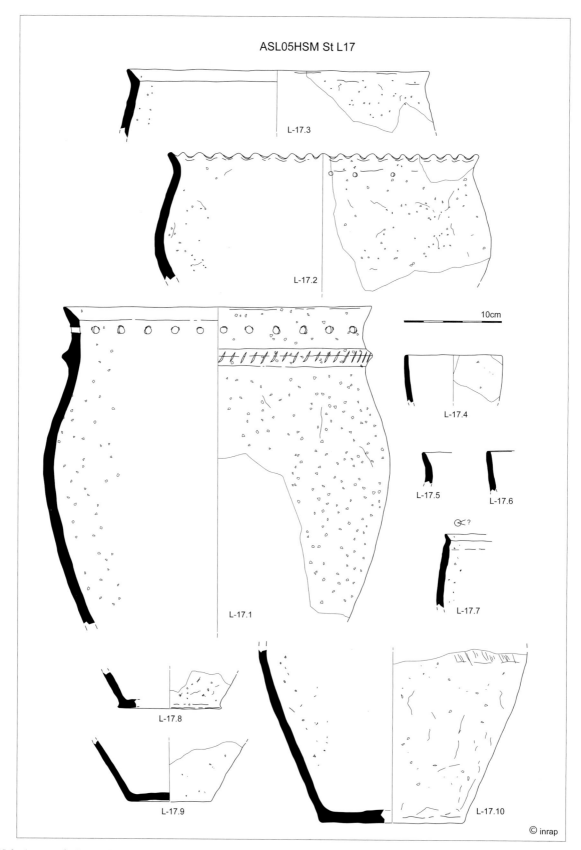

ASL05HSM St L17

L-17.3

L-17.2

10cm

L-17.4

L-17.5   L-17.6

L-17.7

L-17.1

L-17.8

L-17.9

L-17.10

© inrap

Fig. 15.2. Aire-sur-la-Lys « Hameau de Saint-Martin » (Pas-de-Calais), St L17. Ensemble clos du BF I/Bz D (D'après Lorin, en cours).

préventive. Si, voici à peine une quinzaine d'années, moins d'une dizaine de sites pouvaient être mentionnés pour les départements de la Somme, du Nord et du Pas-de-Calais, nous pouvons à ce jour signaler près d'une quarantaine de sites d'habitats, concentrés majoritairement le long des vallées de la Somme et de l'Escaut ou, de manière plus diffuse, entre l'Escaut et les rivages de la Manche. Bien que la grande majorité d'entre eux ne se résume qu'à une ou quelques fosse-dépotoir(s) isolée(s), quelques rares sites se distinguent par un nombre plus important de structures, permettant, comme par exemple à Rombies-et-Marchipont (Nord) (Henton 2007), de définir des plans de petites fermes ouvertes. Outre des données sur l'occupation du territoire, cette profusion récente de sites a notoirement enrichi le corpus céramique. Ce dernier permet actuellement d'argumenter avec plus de précision les changements culturels touchant la zone d'étude entre les 12e et 10e siècles avant notre ère. Notre corpus présente cette particularité d'être exclusivement basé sur du mobilier domestique ; la seule nécropole à incinérations en urnes connue à ce jour, fouillée par l'Inrap en 2013 à Rouvignies (Nord), n'ayant pas encore été étudiée dans son ensemble (informations D. Labarre).

Pour cette étape du Bronze final, notre région, anciennement qualifiée d'atlantique sur base de la typologie d'un mobilier métallique au demeurant peu abondant, semblait jusque récemment être restée dans l'orbite de l'entité MMN, ainsi que le laissait deviner le peu de matériel céramique reconnu. Pour rappel, suivant en cela les données britanniques sur la céramique « *Post Deverel-Rimbury* », le littoral continental de la Manche serait caractérisé du 11e à la fin du 9e siècle par un faciès « *Plain Ware* » (formes simples atypiques avec traces de façonnage et peu décorées) (Marcigny et Talon 2009). Si ce faciès est assez clairement affirmé sur le littoral normand et trouve écho de l'autre côté de la Manche, il convient toutefois de pointer l'absence d'une telle typologie pour le nord de la France et les Flandres belges voisines ; si ce n'est pour quelques formes spécifiques isolées de leurs contextes d'habitat (ex. Inghem et Piningre 2005) ou funéraire (De Mulder 2013). Outre cet ancrage théorique au MMN, la zone d'étude présenterait, toujours pour la même période, l'avantage d'être située au-delà de la zone d'expansion maximale traditionnellement admise pour le complexe nord-alpin, en bordure occidentale de la zone-tampon de mixité culturelle s'étendant le long de la vallée de l'Oise (Brun 2013).

Depuis un peu plus d'une dizaine d'années, ce schéma semble quelque peu perturbé par une « poussée » d'artefacts céramiques de tradition Rhin-Suisse-France orientale (RSFO) hors des limites jusqu'ici définies, atteignant l'Escaut et une partie de la vallée de la Somme et s'étendant même sans vergogne en direction des plages de la Manche. Déjà pressentie auparavant par l'examen du mobilier de quelques sites de la Somme (Feuillères, Vignacourt,

Pont-de-Metz) (Buchez et Talon 2005 ; Buchez 2011) ou du Nord (Onnaing) (Blancquaert *et al.* 2005), l'affiliation d'une partie de la région au complexe (RSFO) semble à ce jour plus clairement défendable. Mesurant bien entendu les implications qu'engendrent cette proposition, nous nous appuyons non seulement sur la présence de marqueurs typologiques ou de thèmes décoratifs caractéristiques du complexe continental, mais aussi sur l'absence assez significative de formes « atlantiques/MMN » au sein des ensembles clos de mobilier céramique étudiés. Cette absence est d'autant plus marquée pour la céramique grossière, *a priori* plus lentement perméables aux fluctuations culturelles que la céramique fine. Fréquemment, les comparaisons renvoient vers des parallèles situés entre la vallée de l'Oise et le Rhin supérieur. C'est entre autre le cas pour les pots à col éversé et marqué en interne, récurrents dans une grande majorité des ensembles clos attribués à l'étape moyenne du Bronze final dans la zone d'étude.

C'est au sein de la catégorie fine la céramique que l'on trouve les marqueurs typo-chronologiques les plus pertinents et les plus nombreux. Pour les plus récurrents parmi ces derniers, nous pouvons citer les gobelets à épaulement, des jattes (ou coupes) à cannelures couvrantes interne ou des pots biconiques ou bi-tronconiques sans bord. Parmi les gobelets, encore peu nombreux et trop fragmentaires, deux gobelets à épaulement court et col rentrant rectilignes, provenant des sites de Vignacourt « Collège-secteur 2 » (Somme) (Fig. 15.3) et de Famars « Technopôle II » (Nord) peuvent être mentionnés pour leur profil et leur décor typiques du RSFO (Buchez 2011 ; Henton 2013). Leurs comparaisons les plus proches renvoient vers la vallée de l'Aisne ou vers la région de Seine-et-Marne. Le site de Rombies-et-Marchipont « Rue de l'Eglise » (Nord) a lui livré un gobelet à épaulement décoré de cannelures et à col rectiligne ouvert (Henton 2013). Son aspect rigide l'éloigne à coup sûr des prototypes rhénans, mais il est associé à un matériel globalement caractéristique du RSFO. Les autres gobelets découverts montrent une certaine variabilité de forme, de biconique simple à lèvre courte éversée (Onnaing « Toyota Z2 ») à profil à épaulement arrondi et col ouvert (Solesmes « Voyette de Vertain », Nord) (Fig. 15.4-04.2). Un gobelet d'Onnaing « Toyota-Simoldes » (Nord) se différentie par un épaulement court et une jonction avec le col soulignée d'une série de fines cannelures horizontales (Fig. 15.4-250.4). Si pour ce dernier un exemplaire assez similaire a récemment été mis au jour en Flandres belges sur le site Bronze final apparenté au RSFO de Sint-Denijs-Westrem (B., *Oost-Vlaanderen*) (information J. Hoorne, DL§H-GATE), une origine jurassienne de cette forme est proposée.

Les jattes sont mieux représentées (une douzaine d'exemplaires) que les gobelets, et ce plus particulièrement pour la vallée de l'Escaut. De forme tronconique ouverte simple, elles présentent fréquemment un décor interne de

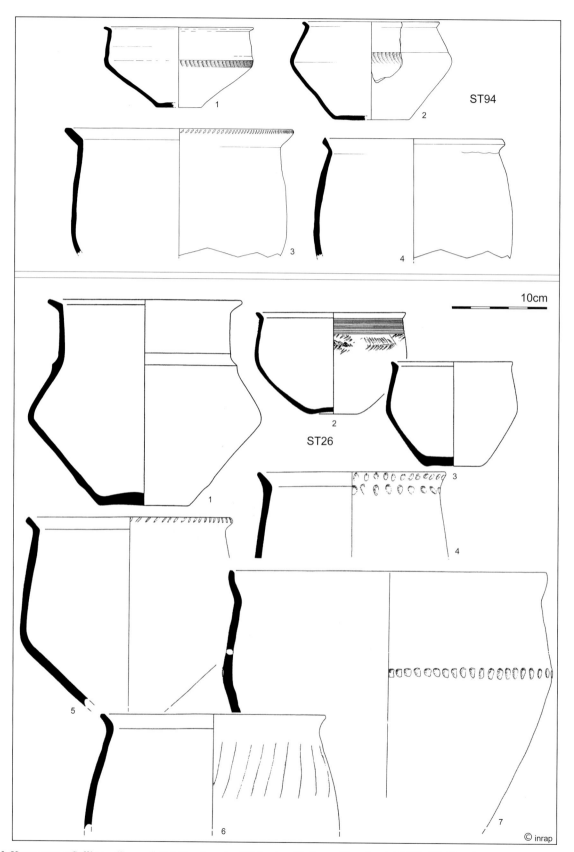

Fig. 15.3. Vignacourt « Collège » (Somme), St 94 (secteur 1) et 26 (secteur 2). Ensembles clos du BF IIb–IIIa/Ha A2–B1 (D'après Buchez 2011).

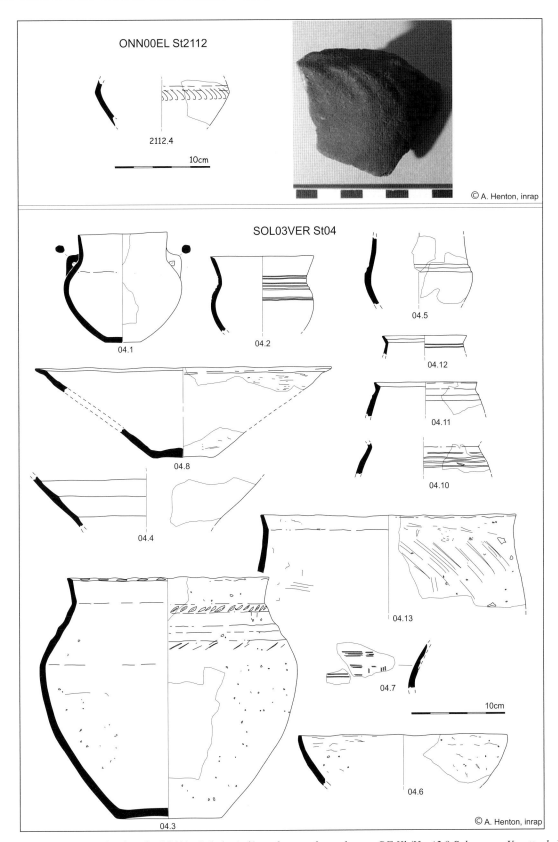

Fig. 15.4. Onnaing « Toyota Z2 » (Nord), St2112. Gobelet à décor de cannelures douces. BF IIb/Ha A2 ? Solesmes « Voyette de Vertain », St04. Ensemble clos du BFIIIa/Ha B1 ? (D'après Henton, en cours).

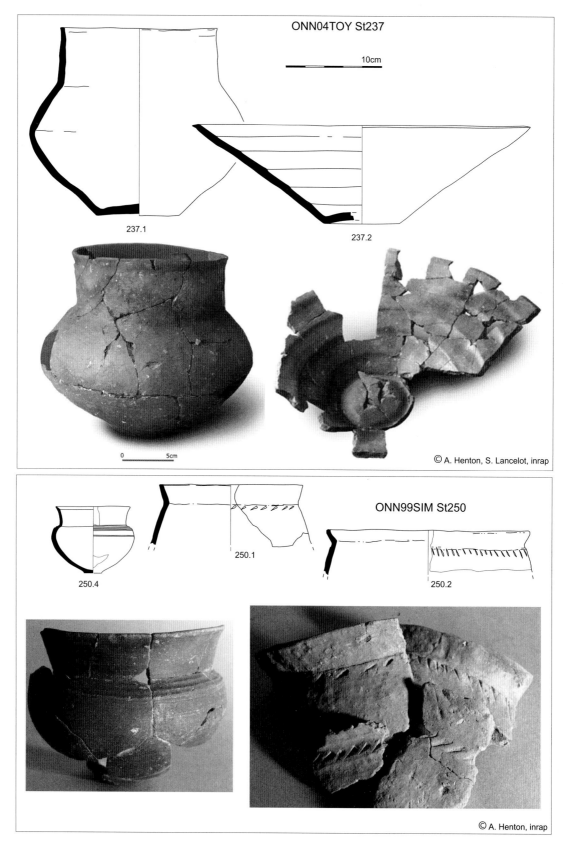

Fig. 15.5. Onnaing « ZAC Vallée de l'Escaut – Toyotomi et Simoldes » (Nord). Ensembles clos du BF IIb–IIIa/Ha A2–B1 (D'après Henton (en cours) et Clotuche 2012).

cannelures larges couvrantes (Fig. 15.5), ou une série de cannelures étroites à la jonction avec le fond. Parmi les autres formes en céramique fine, les profils biconiques sont bien représentés sous une forme haute et fermée ou basse et ouverte, à haut de panse rectiligne et rentrant, terminé par une courte lèvre éversée et marquée. Ces formes ne sont que rarement décorées.

Dans la catégorie de la céramique grossière, une forme se détache très nettement. Il s'agit du pot à tendance biconique et à lèvre éversée et marquée en interne. Cette céramique de préparation ou de stockage montre assez fréquemment un décor d'incisions obliques ou d'impressions digitées situé majoritairement à la jonction panse/col ou sur la face externe de la lèvre (Fig. 15.4-250.1 et 2). Une seconde forme rappelle les vases bitronconiques sans bord (*doppelkonus*) de la cartographie des types RSFO (type 21) (Brun et Mordant 1988). Présente sur le site de Vignacourt « Collège-secteur 2 » (Somme), elle se retrouve le long de la vallée de l'Escaut (Henton 2013), à Onnaing (Fig. 15.5-237.1) ; et ce jusqu'en Belgique dans les nécropoles Champs d'urnes du Groupe de la Flandre (De Mulder 2011).

Outre les formes mentionnées ci-dessus, nous pouvons également mettre en évidence certains thèmes décoratifs propres au RSFO. Bien que la technique de décoration par incisions ait été rencontrée à quelques reprises, la majorité des décors est réalisée à la pointe mousse sous forme de cannelures plus ou moins fines. Les décors au peigne métallique demeurent encore assez exceptionnels (ex. : Onnaing « Simoldes », Fig. 15.4-250.4). Dans la céramique fine, le répertoire des décors est encore assez restreint. Parmi les plus complexes, on peut citer des motifs incisées en zig-zag sur pots à Vignacourt « Le Collège-secteur 2 » et à Plauwin-Planque « ZAC des Hussards » (Buchez 2011, information E. Leroy-Langelin/DapCAD), ou sur rebord d'écuelle à Famars « Technopôle II » ou Etaples-sur-Mer « Bel Air » (Henton 2013). Les décors en triangles ou séries verticales de bâtonnets ont également été observés. Déjà mentionnées pour les jattes, les cannelures couvrantes sont également présentes en externe sur certaines panses de pots, comme par exemple à Aire-sur-la-Lys « Hameau de Saint-Martin » (Pas-de-Calais) ou à Rombies-et-Marchipont « Rue de l'Eglise » (département du Nord). Dans ce dernier cas, le décor concerne un pot à deux anses (« amphore »), proche de formes rhénanes. Récemment mis en évidence, la catégorie des décors en cannelure douce sur carène est représentée par 2 individus à Vignacourt « Collège-secteur 1 » (80) (Buchez 2011) et une à Onnaing « Toyota-Delquignies » (Henton 2013). Dans les trois cas, les cannelures sont du même type que celles mentionnées ailleurs dans l'aire RSFO. L'isolement relatif de ce type de décor aux marges cette aire semble pouvoir être atténué au regard de certaines découvertes similaires mentionnées un peu plus au nord, dans la zone des Flandres belges et intégrées au *Vlaamse groep* (De Mulder 2011). L'existence

de ce type de décor pourrait aussi, indirectement, être confirmée par d'éventuelles imitations. Ainsi, un gobelet (?) biconique, trouvé à Noyelles-sur-Mer (Somme, inédit), montre au dessus de la carène un décor d'incisions obliques encadré de cannelures horizontales. A Etaples-sur-Mer « Bel Air » (département du Pas-de-Calais) (Henton en cours), un grand pot à tendance biconique présente, au niveau de son épaulement une série de hautes cannelures courbes et verticales, qui bien que maladroitement tracées, semblent faire écho aux cannelures douces du répertoire précoce du RSFO (*cf. infra*). Enfin, pour la céramique grossière, le répertoire des décors, assez fréquents, regroupe des séries horizontales, doubles ou simples, d'impressions digitées, des incisions obliques, parfois conjointes sur un même vase (Fig. 15.5).

En marge de ce mobilier étroitement associé au RSFO, il convient de mentionner certains ensembles clos associés à l'étape moyenne, dont la parenté culturelle nous apparaît comme plus problématique. C'est le cas notamment dans la Somme des sites d'Amiens « Champ Pillard », de Pont-de-Metz « Champ Pillard » (Buchez et Talon 2005 ; Buchez 2011) et, dans la zone littorale du Pas-de-Calais, des sites d'Aire-sur-la-Lys « Hameau de Saint Martin », de Guînes « Jardin du Couvent II », d'Etaples « Bel Air » (Lorin, en cours : Henton 2013) ou d'Inghem « La Fosse » (Piningre 2005). Pour la Somme, il avait déjà été mis en évidence la présence simultanée dans certains ensembles de formes apparentées au RSFO et d'autres d'affinité *Plain Ware*, ce qui semble également être le cas en Pas-de-Calais. Il demeure encore trop délicat d'essayer de trancher entre un simple apport d'éléments exogènes « orientaux », un phénomène d'« acculturation » de populations tournées vers la sphère atlantique, le reflet d'une simple évolution typologique ou un problème d'ordre chronologique. Le cas du site d'Etaples « Bel Air », déjà mentionné plus haut, est à ce titre assez symptomatique. Ce site stratifié installé à l'embouchure de la Canche a livré un très abondant mobilier céramique (Fig. 15.6), partiellement étudié et inédit. Une première approche, rendue complexe par la difficulté à définir exactement sa position stratigraphique (et ce malgré un enregistrement exemplaire lors de la fouille menée par H. Mariette en 1963), a très clairement mis en évidence une typologie assez originale. Une grande majorité de la céramique fine présente de nettes influences du RSFO, tant du point de vue typologique (pots biconiques, lèvres éversées …) que des décors (incisions en zigzags, cannelures fines sur lèvre ou épaulement …). La céramique grossière se distingue par des formes à épaulement et col ouvert, mais surtout par ses nombreuses impressions digitées décorant les lèvres, les cols ou des cordons. Outre une absence d'ensembles clos clairement définis et un possible étalement de l'occupation sur plusieurs phases (associées à un artisanat du sel ?), cette typologie mixte rend délicate l'interprétation culturelle du site. Une première hypothèse y voit l'ultime avancée du faciès RSFO vers l'ouest, touchant ainsi les rivages de la Manche dans le courant du BFIIb–IIIa et une seconde hypothèse se base quant à elle sur une évolution typologique locale (BFIIIa–IIIb), sur substrat RSFO et avec influences de faciès régionaux post-Deverel-Rimbury (zone côtière, Angleterre ?).

Du point de vue chronologique, nous ne sommes guère plus avancé, pour les ensembles décris plus haut, qu'à une attribution large couvrant la totalité de la phase moyenne du Bronze final, soit le BFIIb–IIIa/Ha A2–B1. Les dates ^{14}C demeurent rarissimes et ne concernent, comme par exemple à Nesles « Route de Chaulnes » (Somme) (2770±35 BC, soit 1002–830 cal BC), que du matériel de transition BFIIIa–IIIb. Nous regrettons également l'absence totale d'association assurée entre mobilier métallique et mobilier céramique.

Il nous est impossible pour l'heure de dater avec précision les premières manifestations du RSFO au niveau régional. Toutefois, certains indices de la typologie céramique tendent à supposer une apparition relativement précoce de ce faciès, dès le BFIIb/Ha A2 (cannelures douces). En Hainaut-Cambrésis et dans la Somme, certaines dates obtenues pour les phases précoces du BFIIIb indiquent clairement une disparition d'une bonne partie de la typologie RSFO avant le milieu du 10ᵉ siècle.

L'étape finale du Bronze final (BF IIIb/Ha B2–3)

En comparaison avec les périodes précédentes, la fin du Bronze final a été particulièrement favorisée au cours des dernières années. Au niveau régional, plus d'une cinquantaine de sites d'habitat peut assurément être attribuée à cette période. Cette augmentation soudaine de données résulte de plusieurs facteurs, dont le principal semble être l'accroissement notoire des opérations d'archéologie préventive dans des secteurs géographiques spécifiques, telles que la haute vallée de la Somme ou la vallée de l'Escaut. C'est d'ailleurs le long de cette dernière, en Hainaut-Cambrésis, que sont concentrés plus de 50% des sites de cette étape. Pour cette zone bien documentée, élargie au Hainaut belge, nous pouvons prudemment parler d'une réelle augmentation de l'occupation du territoire au cours des 10e et 9e siècles avant notre ère. Tout en prenant en compte une dispersion inégale des interventions archéologiques sur les autres secteurs régionaux, ceci semble néanmoins contraster avec une répartition *a priori* plus faible des sites dans la zone comprise entre les vallées de la Somme, de l'Escaut et les rivages de la Manche. Il demeure bien entendu impossible, à la lumière des connaissances actuelles, d'expliquer ce phénomène ; si ce n'est par une simple énumération de différents facteurs, tels que typologie de l'habitat (fermes isolées ou habitat groupé) ou position des occupations dans le paysage et/ou sur les différents types de substrat …

Si, pour l'étape précédente, une certaine homogénéisation culturelle semble caractériser notre zone d'étude, de profondes modifications transparaissent pour l'étape finale. Globalement, nous pouvons opposer une zone de nature continentale très clairement affiliée, par la céramique, au faciès du Groupe des Ardennes à une zone nettement plus tournée vers la façade maritime et apparentée, toujours pour la céramique, au faciès MMN/*Decorated ware*. Ceci semble très clairement aller dans le sens d'un morcellement culturel tel que défini par P. Brun (1986) pour l'étape 3 des « Champs d'urnes » du Bassin parisien. Pour la moitié septentrionale de notre zone, nous présentions déjà, voici quelques années, le rôle majeur de la vallée de l'Escaut dans la mise en place des groupes culturels régionaux (Henton 2013). Les récentes données mises à disposition confirment un rôle de « frontière » ou de limite d'expansion de ces groupes, répartis de part et d'autre de ce fleuve sinueux à la vallée plus ou moins large et bien marquée dans le paysage.

Rive droite de l'Escaut, l'ensemble des sites attribués à l'étape finale du Bronze final ne concerne que de l'habitat. Inscrites dans de petites fermes ouvertes, *a priori* isolées dans un terroir (cf. Leroy-Langelin *et al.* dans ce volume) des fosses ont livré un abondant mobilier céramique caractérisé par une très forte homogénéité typologique et assurément affilié au Groupe des Ardennes. Déjà décris à plusieurs reprises (Henton et Demarez 2005 ; Henton 2013), une série de marqueurs typo-chronologiques fiables permettent maintenant d'isoler et d'associer avec une certaine précision les ensembles clos attribués à ce faciès. Rappelons ici rapidement la présence, quasi systématique dans les assemblages, de jattes tronconiques ouvertes, de gobelets en « bulbe d'oignon » ou de gobelets cylindriques. Les dernières études, facilitées par un approvisionnement régulier de nouvelles découvertes, permettent maintenant d'affiner quelque peu notre approche de ce mobilier, tant du point de vue chronologique que de son expansion géographique, mais aussi de ses liens avec le RSFO. Du point de vue chronologique, il nous est maintenant possible d'isoler des ensembles précoces au sein même de ce faciès (Henton 2013). Ceux-ci sont définis, entre autre, par la présence de certaines formes ou thèmes décoratifs proches du répertoire RSFO antérieur (jatte à cannelures internes ou à décor géométrique couvrant …) (Fig. 15.7). L'un des indices de précocité concerne également les gobelets cylindriques. Cette forme, non encore décelée dans les ensembles régionaux de l'étape moyenne, semble apparaître soudainement au cours de la seconde moitié du 10ᵉ siècle. Si son origine demeure obscure (prototypes jurassiens ?), il apparaît que les plus anciens individus sont très fréquemment décorés et offrent un répertoire décoratif assez riche. Découvert sur le contournement routier de Cambrai (fouilles CG59 inédites), un individu peut être mis en évidence pour son décor géométrique réalisé au peigne métallique (Fig. 15.7-200.2) ; seul cas actuellement connu

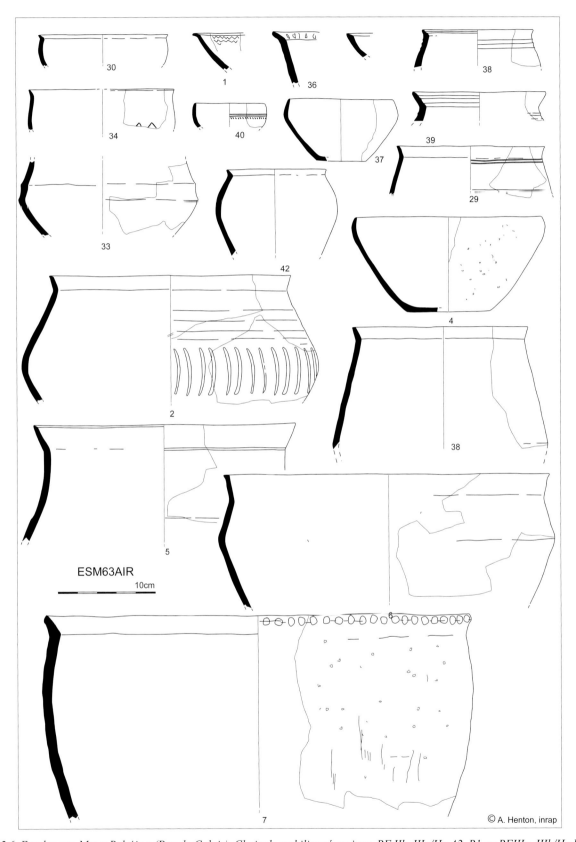

ESM63AIR

10cm

© A. Henton, inrap

Fig. 15.6. Etaples-sur-Mer « Bel Air » (Pas-de-Calais). Choix de mobilier céramique. BF IIb–IIIa/Ha A2–B1 ou BFIIIa–IIIb/Ha B1–B2 ?

au niveau régional. Ce gobelet était en outre associé à des jattes à cannelure internes et d'autre à décors couvrant imitant les guirlandes du répertoire RSFO.

Pour les ensembles plus récents (fin du 9e siècle) (Fig. 15.8), on note une diminution de la fréquence des décors sur la céramique fine (gobelets cylindriques), l'évolution sensible de certaines formes (jattes tronconiques tendant vers un profil plus arrondi) ou encore l'augmentation du décor d'impressions digitées sur la céramique grossière. Dans certains ensembles, l'apparition de nouvelles formes (terrines ouvertes à panse basse hémisphérique et lèvres à impressions digitées) pourrait laisser supposer une porosité grandissante de la zone de contact avec le faciès voisin apparenté au MMN.

Ces données nous laissent entrapercevoir une probable périodisation régionale du faciès Bronze final du Groupe des Ardennes en Hainaut-Cambrésis et permettent l'utilisation d'une chronologie plus affinée basée sur un BFIIIb ancien/Ha B2, couvrant la seconde moitié du 10e siècle et un BFIIIb récent/Ha B3 couvrant le 9e siècle. La répartition géographique de ce faciès montre donc une forte concentration en Hainaut-Cambrésis (à cheval sur le département du Nord et la province belge du Hainaut). Ce territoire bien défini du point de vue géographique est bordé à l'ouest par la vallée de l'Escaut, à l'Est par la vallée de la Sambre, au nord par les collines des Ardennes flamandes et au sud par la limite entre la vallée de l'Escaut et celle de la Somme. Si pour ce territoire, et comme indiqué plus haut, on note une forte homogénéité du mobilier, il convient de mentionner une zone située à ses marges sud-ouest, dans la vallée de la Somme entre Saint-Quentin et Amiens, où les marqueurs typo-chronologiques apparaissent comme moins pertinents, mais présente néanmoins une certaine parenté avec le Hainaut-Cambrésis. Les recherches menées à Nesles « Rue de Chaulnes », Amiens « Intercampus » (fouilles inédites) ou encore Framerville-Rainecourt « Le Fond d'Herleville » (Buchez et Talon 2005) ont révélé un mobilier contenant des formes proches du Groupe des Ardennes (gobelets, jattes, bols/tasses) mais associées à quelques formes s'en différentiant et pouvant être inspirées du répertoire MMN. La place que tient notre faciès dans le Groupe des Ardennes commence à s'éclaircir. Un lien assez étroit semble unir, uniquement au BFIIIb/Ha B2-3, celui-ci à une partie de la vallée de l'Aisne, ainsi que le laisse deviner le matériel céramique des sites de Bucy-le-Long « la Heronnière », Limé « les Fusils », Berry-au-Bac « Le vieux Tordoir » et surtout Nanteuil-sur-Aisne « l'Entrée des Ecouaires » (Brun *et al.* 2005 ; Lambot 1977). Hors de cette aire de répartition, localisée aux marges ouest et sud-ouest du massif ardennais, les données archéologiques disponibles pour le sud de la Belgique ou le nord du département des Ardennes ne permettent actuellement pas d'étendre ce faciès du Bronze final vers l'est. Seul un hypothétique rapprochement avec le faciès présent en Hesbaye belge,

bordant la vallée mosane à environ 120 kilomètres au nord-est du Hainaut-Cambrésis, pourrait être envisagé sur base du mobilier d'habitat (Destexhe 1986).

La seconde composante culturelle présente au niveau régional à la fin du Bronze final, apparentée à l'entité MMN, s'étend à l'ouest de l'Escaut, entre ce fleuve et les rivages de la Manche et, vers le sud, couvre une partie de la vallée de la Somme. Contrairement au faciès affilié au Groupe des Ardennes, cette composante demeure encore largement méconnue et n'est basée qu'au maximum sur une vingtaine de sites d'habitat. Ces derniers se répartissent de manière assez irrégulière et se concentrent autour de quelques zones à forte activité archéologique. La première, en Pas-de-Calais, concerne l'Arrageois et la région de Lens. Autour d'Arras (Pas-de-Calais), des fouilles préventives ont ainsi permis de dégager des sites d'habitat contenant une grande quantité de mobilier céramique, à Achicourt « Aire des Gens du Voyage » (Fig. 15.9), Maroeuil « Rue Curie » ou Dainville « Bel Air » (Lorin 2008 ; Masse 2013 ; Henton 2013). Ces sites se caractérisent par une forte concentration de fosses et de silos, mais aussi de bâtiments de stockage (greniers). Ces structures semblent définir un habitat de type groupé (cf. Leroy-Langelin *et al.* dans ce volume). Une seconde zone se situe en bordure de la vallée de Lys et de la Plaine maritime. Le site le plus emblématique est celui d'Aire-sur-la-Lys « Hameau de Saint-Martin », où un habitat de type groupé, de même type que ceux de la région d'Arras, côtoie une aire funéraire associant un *landgräbben* et des incinérations en fosse (Lorin, en cours). Une troisième zone concerne la vallée de la Somme et plus spécifiquement l'Amiénois, avec entre autres le site de Glisy « Terre de Ville » (Buchez 2011).

En Pas-de-Calais, le corpus céramique est très important du point de vue quantitatif (plusieurs milliers de tessons) et permet de dresser une première typologie et de mettre en évidence les marqueurs les plus caractéristiques (Henton 2013). Parmi ces derniers, signalons rapidement pour la vaisselle de table des pots à carène marquée et col concave, des gobelets, des tasses à anse, des bols, des terrines ou encore des jattes à bord lobés ou festonné. Pour la vaisselle de stockage, des hauts pots à large épaule arrondie et col ouvert et des pots biconiques et à col éversé sont les plus fréquents. Les gobelets, relativement nombreux, se déclinent en plusieurs types (à épaule arrondie, à carène et col court concave, à tendance biconique …). Interprétés encore voici peu (Henton 2013) comme n'étant que de simples copies ou variantes des gobelets du faciès du Groupe des Ardennes (dont ceux en bulbe d'oignon), ces gobelets apparaissent maintenant comme une composante à part entière de la typologie. Leur dissemblance avec les gobelets RSFO de l'étape moyenne ne permet pas pour l'heure d'en connaître l'origine. A ce stade des connaissances, certaines formes typiques du vaisselier du Groupe des Ardennes semblent absentes ou très faiblement représentées dans ce faciès.

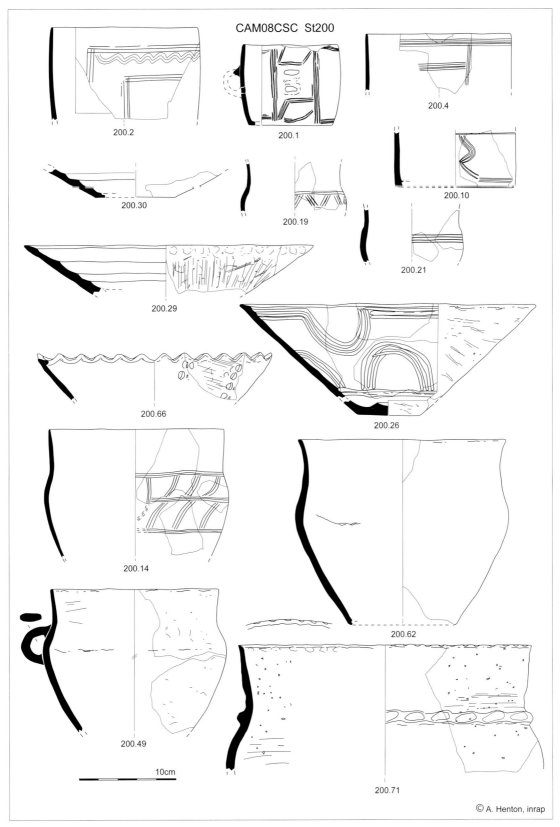

Fig. 15.7. Cambrai « Contournement Sud » (Nord), St 200. Choix de mobilier céramique de l'ensemble clos. BF IIIb–ancien/Ha B2. Faciès Groupe des Ardennes du Hainaut-Cambrésis (D'après Henton (en cours) et données inédites du Service archéologique du CG59).

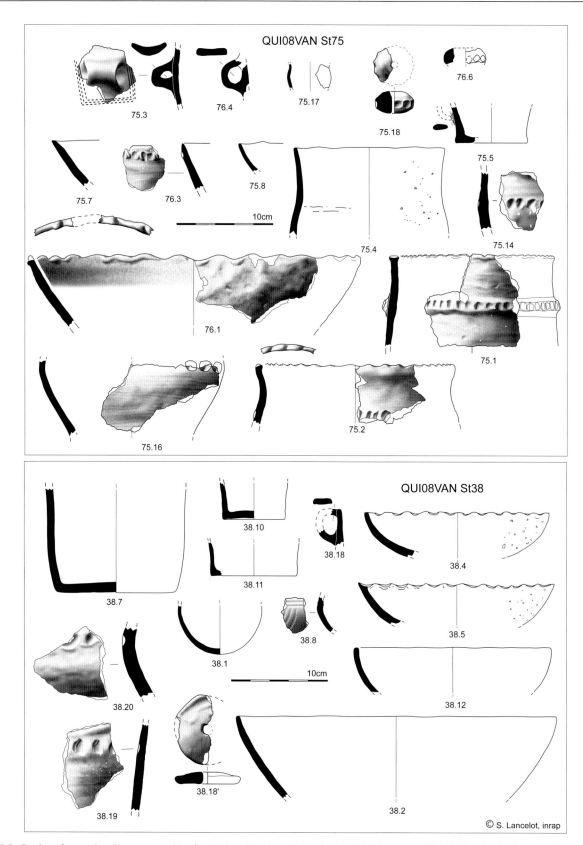

Fig. 15.8. Quiévrechain « Les Vanneaux » (Nord), St 38 et 75. Ensembles clos du BF IIIb–récent/Ha B3. Faciès du Groupe des Ardennes du Hainaut-Cambrésis (D'après Henton en cours).

C'est le cas des jattes tronconiques ou encore des gobelets cylindriques. Cette céramique présente certaines spécificités technologiques la différenciant de celle du faciès voisin scaldien. Si le colombin semble être utilisé pour une partie de la vaisselle de table, une seconde technique de montage se distingue pour la grande majorité des vases, principalement pour la céramique plus grossière. Dans l'attente d'études spécialisées, nous optons pour un montage en plaque ou par battage, voire dans certains cas mixte (plaque/battage/ colombin large). L'utilisation préférentielle d'un dégraissant minéral est également à noter. Rien ne permet toutefois de voir dans cette dernière une différentiation culturelle par rapport au faciès du Groupe des Ardennes, où prédomine le dégraissant de chamotte, ou, plus simplement le reflet d'un faciès implanté essentiellement dans une zone géographique caractérisée par un substrat de craie à niveaux de silex.

En vallée de Somme, le corpus demeure encore trop peu étoffé pour clairement mettre en évidence certains marqueurs typo-chronologiques fiables. L'un des sites ayant livré le mobilier le plus significatif, à Glisy « Terre de Ville » (Buchez 2011) (Fig. 15.10), semble toutefois indiquer une relative parenté avec les ensembles du Pas-de-Calais, pour ce qui est notamment des gobelets ou des vases de stockage. Certaines formes apparaissent toutefois comme originales, comme par exemple un vase à haute panse tronconique, épaule courte arrondie et col haut fortement ouvert, préfigurant certains vases du premier Âge du fer de la vallée de Somme.

Apparenté par certaines de ses caractéristiques à la céramique de type *Plain Ware* anglaise des périodes 6 et 7 de Needham (1996), le faciès présent à la dernière période du Bronze final dans la moitié occidentale du Pas-de-Calais et dans une partie de la Somme semble donc pouvoir être rattaché à la culture Manche-Mer du Nord ; du moins dans l'une de ses expressions tardives. Cependant, il convient de rappeler ici, ainsi que cela avait déjà été observé pour d'autres sites plus méridionaux (Marcigny et Talon 2009), une certaine proportion de formes présentant des influences orientales. Pour quelques unes d'entre elles, issues de la céramique fine de table, se pose même la question d'un lien direct ou indirect avec la céramique RSFO régionale de l'étape moyenne. C'est le cas pour une série de pots biconiques à col éversé ou de pots à deux anses (amphores). Un tel lien serait aussi discernable dans certains motifs de décoration de la céramique fine.

Cette question inhérente à ces influences ouvre bien entendu sur celle de l'origine même de ce faciès MMN tardif/*Plain ware* au niveau régional. Deux hypothèses sont envisagées, sans prévalence de l'une ou l'autre à ce stade des connaissances. La première privilégie une évolution locale d'un substrat culturel de nature continentale ou mixte, avec influences marquées des faciès *Plain Ware* des rivages de la Manche. La seconde se base sur une expansion directe d'un faciès *Plain Ware* originaire de la zone littorale située au sud

de la vallée de la Somme (Normandie ?). Enfin, mentionnons ici de très possibles contacts avec l'Angleterre, au point de passage le plus étroit entre celle-ci et le continent (détroit du Pas-de-Calais/*Dover strait*). Outre Manche, quelques parallèles peuvent être tentés avec le mobilier céramique (*Late Bronze Age*) de Runnymede Bridge (GB, Berkshire) (Needham 1978), Mucking « South rings » (GB, Essex) (Jones and Bond 1980) ou encore Mill Hill (GB, Kent) (Champion 1980).

Du point de vue chronologique, les dates ^{14}C disponibles pour la Somme (Glisy) ou le Pas-de-Calais (Aire-sur-la-Lys, Achicourt et Dainville) se cantonnent entre la fin du 9e siècle et la fin du 8e siècle, soit la fourchette admise pour le BFIIIb/Ha B2–3. A l'inverse du faciès contemporain du Groupe des Ardennes scaldien, il n'est pas possible pour l'heure de distinguer un sous-phasage chronologique de la typologie céramique.

La répartition actuelle des sites représentatifs de ce faciès n'autorise que quelques hypothèses quant à son expansion géographique. La plus assurée concerne sa limite orientale. La vallée de l'Escaut fait ainsi très clairement office de zone « frontière » avec le faciès contemporain du Groupe des Ardennes du Hainaut-Cambrésis. Dans le détail bien entendu, cette zone de jonction n'est pas hermétique au brassage de certaines influences entre les deux faciès et l'implantation d'habitats de l'un ou l'autre faciès sur la rive « opposée » n'est pas exclue. Vers le nord, le manque de données de part et d'autre de la zone frontière avec la Belgique ne permet pas d'étendre les limites du faciès au-delà de la région d'Aire-sur-la-Lys et des abords de la Plaine maritime française. Notons que le corpus céramique connu pour le nord des Flandres belges ne présente que très peu de parallèles typologiques ; même si des formes de céramiques atlantiques y sont mentionnées (De Mulder 2013).

Au sud de la vallée de la Somme, les découvertes réalisées en Calvados (Cussy et Ifs) et en Eure (Maleville-le-Bec) (Manen *et al.* 2013) indiquent une filiation culturelle évidente, mais laissent également transparaître certaines différences quant aux assemblages typologiques, accréditant peut-être une multiplication de faciès régionaux ou micro-régionaux au sein même du MMN tardif.

L'aube du premier Âge du fer (Ha C/Hallstatt ancien)

Jusqu'il y peu encore, les plus anciennes manifestations du premier Âge du fer au niveau régional étaient, par la force des choses, noyées dans une phase chronologique à la terminologie volontairement floue de « transition Bronze final/Hallstatt » ou « Ha B/C ». Au cours des dernières années, le premier Âge du fer a cependant bénéficié, au même titre que l'Âge du bronze final, des apports de l'archéologie préventive, rendant dès lors possible l'établissement d'une typologie céramique propre

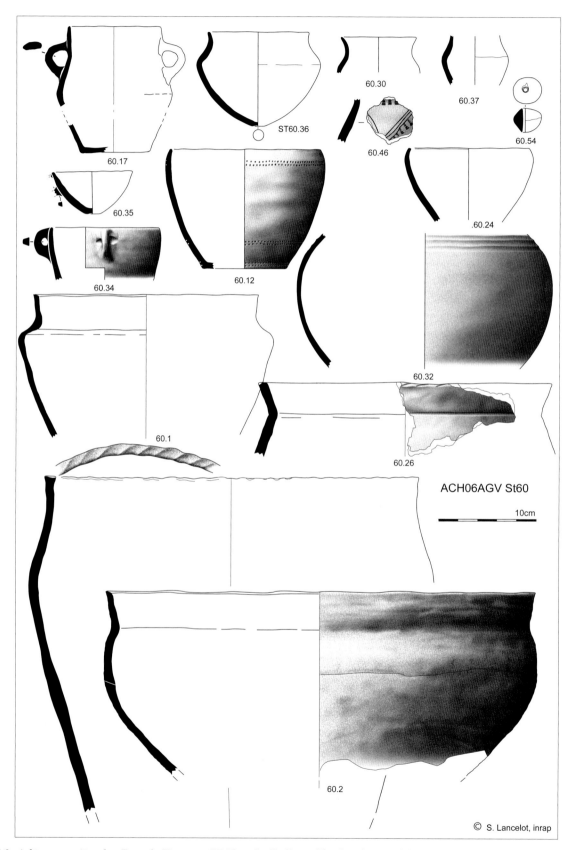

Fig. 15.9. Achicourt « Aire des Gens du Voyage – RD60 », St 60. Ensemble clos du BFIIIb/Ha B2–3. Faciès MMN tardif/Plain-Ware (D'après Lorin 2008).

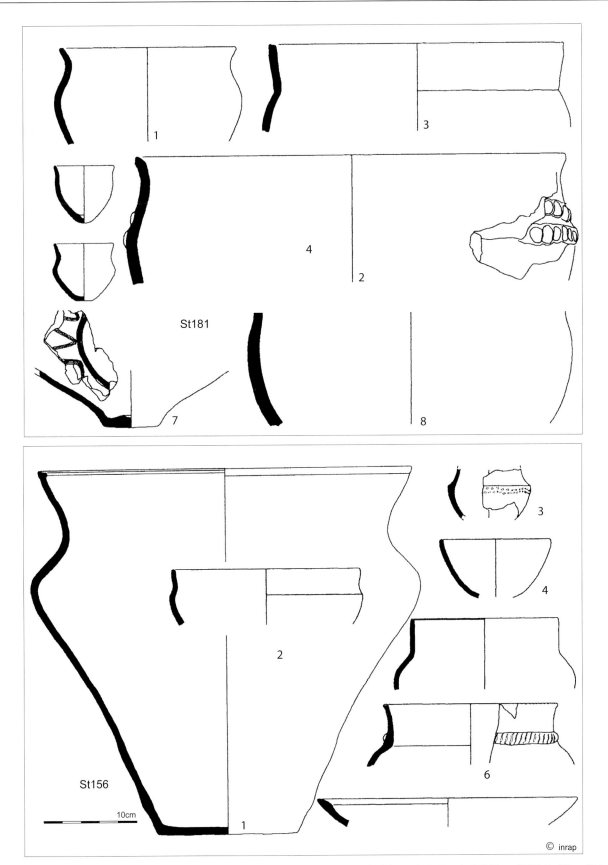

Fig. 15.10. Glisy « Terre de Ville » (Somme), St 181 et 156. Ensembles clos du BfIIIb/Ha B2–3. Faciès MMN tardif/Plain-Ware (D'après Buchez 2011).

et clairement dissociable de celle de l'époque précédente. Cette typologie indique clairement l'existence de faciès distincts et *a priori* contemporains : un faciès hallstattien du Hainaut-Cambrésis, un hypothétique faciès de tradition Bronze final MMN tardif et un faciès « picard ».

Le premier, déjà mis en évidence en Hainaut occidental belge voici une vingtaine d'années (Henton 1994), s'installe directement sur l'aire géographique couverte par le faciès céramique Bronze final du Groupe des Ardennes. Une quarantaine de sites d'habitats se répartissent en rive droite de l'Escaut sur environ 80 km du nord au sud, majoritairement dans le département du Nord et en Hainaut belge. Si la ferme ouverte semble toujours être le modèle de base de l'habitat, on note toutefois, pour certains sites fouillés en décapage extensif, l'apparition de grands bâtiments sur poteaux, de type maison-étable, accompagnés de constructions secondaires. Bien que les données demeurent encore trop lacunaires, il est tentant d'imaginer une possible hiérarchisation entre sites, peut-être regroupés en « domaines » sur un terroir donné (exemple : Onnaing « ZAC de la vallée de l'Escaut/ Toyota » ; Henton en cours).

La céramique se distingue très nettement de celle du Bronze final, tant par la disparition de certains marqueurs typologiques (jattes tronconiques, gobelets cylindriques) que par l'apparition de marqueurs spécifiques (Fig. 15.11). On note une généralisation des formes à épaule arrondie surmontées d'un col ouvert plus ou moins haut et de tendance rectiligne, et déclinées en terrines basses ouvertes ou pots. L'une des formes nouvelles les plus significatives se défini comme un plat tronconique ouvert, systématiquement terminé par un large rebord épaissi formant un marli interne. Si les petits gobelets en bulbe d'oignon du Bronze final ont disparu, ils sont remplacés par des gobelets de plus grande taille, à panse basse, épaule arrondie et col haut. Des jattes à bord lobés et à décor couvrant externe font leur apparition, préfigurant les jattes à bord festonné du Ha D2–3 et de la Tène ancienne. Le répertoire décoratif est plus restreint qu'à la période précédente, totalement absent de la céramique fine et cantonné, sous forme d'impressions digitées, aux récipients de préparation ou de stockage. Vraisemblablement plus décoratives (voire symboliques ?) que réellement fonctionnelles, des petites languettes horizontales, avec ou sans dépression centrale et non perforées, garnissent assez fréquemment les formes à épaule arrondie.

L'origine de cette cassure de la typologie céramique très nette entre ce faciès hallstattien et le faciès Bronze final du Groupe des Ardennes du Hainaut-Cambrésis demeure encore problématique, tant pour sa position chronologique que pour son origine. Une apparition relativement précoce, probablement dès l'aube du 8e siècle, est à ce jour privilégiée, bien que n'étant confortée que par de trop rares datations [14]C. Le changement entre le vaisselier du BFIIIB et le vaisselier hallstattien apparait comme relativement brutal. Très rares sont les ensembles clos montrant une réelle mixité de forme

et pouvant induire une évolution linéaire de la typologie aux alentours de 800 avant notre ère. Parallèlement à une modification de la structuration de l'habitat et, de manière hypothétique, du rituel funéraire (passage à l'incinération sous tombelle), la typologie céramique pourrait signaler l'implantation d'un nouveau groupe humain (peut-être restreint) et son essaimage rapide sur un territoire micro-régional, côtoyant (voire acculturant ?) pendant quelques décennies une population de tradition culturelle Bronze final. Ecartant bien entendu la vision chère à M.-E. Mariën du déferlement de cavaliers hallstattiens issus des contrées orientales, nous nous heurtons cependant à la question de l'origine géographique de cette hypothétique nouvelle population. Les parallèles les plus significatifs connus à ce jour ne nous renvoient de manière assurée, pour la typologie céramique et les rituels funéraires, que vers la lorraine belge à Saint-Vincent « Le Grand-Bois » (B., Luxembourg) ou en Argonne à Vieille-la-Ville « Haulzy » (Marne), mais aussi plus ponctuellement en provinces belges du Brabant wallon (Court-Saint-Etienne « La Quenique ») et de Namur (Louette-Saint-Pierre « La Fosse-aux-Morts », Gedinnes « Chevaudos ») (Goury 1911 ; Guillaume 2005).

L'expansion de ce faciès céramique hallstattien du Hainaut-Cambrésis à l'ensemble de la zone de comparaison reste cependant délicate. En effet, les sites mentionnés ci-dessus ne concernent que des occupations funéraires et le mobilier céramique des habitats associés à ces dernières demeures quasiment inconnus. Ces mêmes incertitudes nous empêchent pour l'heure d'associer notre faciès à la phase hallstattienne du Groupe des Ardennes qui, il faut le rappeler, a été défini quasi-exclusivement sur base d'assemblages de mobilier funéraire (Brun 1986).

Pour la région située entre la rive droite de l'Escaut, les côtes de la Manche et la vallée de la Somme, nous devons ici concéder une réelle méconnaissance pour ce qui est du début du premier Âge du fer. Ceci résulte essentiellement d'une pauvreté avérée du corpus céramique, mais aussi probablement de notre incapacité à discerner des ensembles récents au cœur d'un mobilier n'évoluant guère à la transition entre l'Âge du bronze final et le premier Âge du fer.

Pour les départements du Nord et du Pas-de-Calais, aucun ensemble ne peut être daté avec certitude du Hallstatt ancien/Ha C. Seuls quelques rares ensembles clos dégagés sur le site d'Aire-sur-la-Lys ont été situés sans plus de certitude entre la phase Bronze final et la phase du Ha D du site, notamment sur base de l'absence d'influences RSFO. Assez récemment toutefois, une fosse fouillée en 2011 à Wittes (Pas-de-Calais), à quelques kilomètres d'Aire, a livré un mobilier se distinguant du faciès Bronze final du MMN tardif (informations V. Thoquenne). On y retrouve notamment des tasses à panse basse sur ombilic, carène et col haut concave et des pots à col haut concave et plus ou moins ouvert. La forme des tasses pose ici la question d'une influence plus ou moins directe du Bronze final

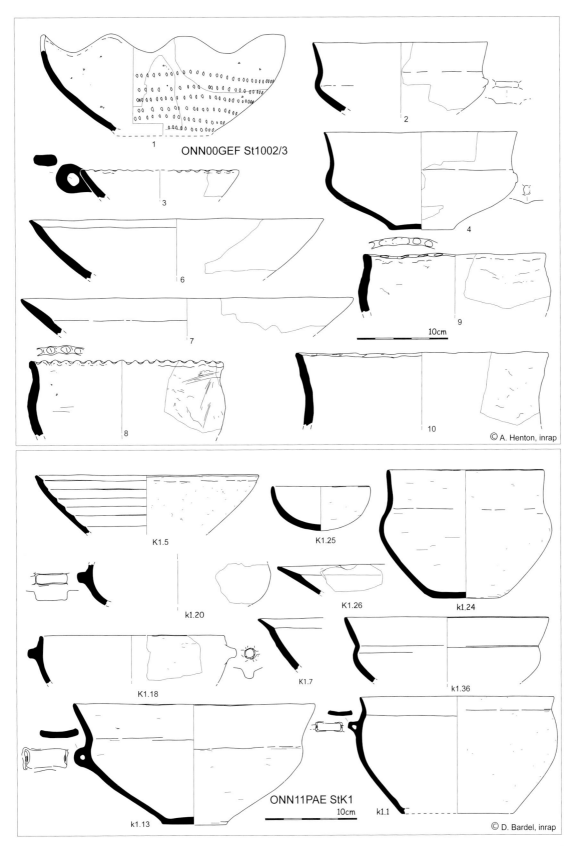

Fig. 15.11. Onnaing « ZAC de la Vallée de l'Escaut-Gefco et PAVE2 ». Ensembles clos du Hallstatt ancien/HaC. Faciès hallstattien du Hainaut-Cambrésis. D'après Henton (en cours) et Neaud et al 2014).

Alain Henton et Nathalie Buchez

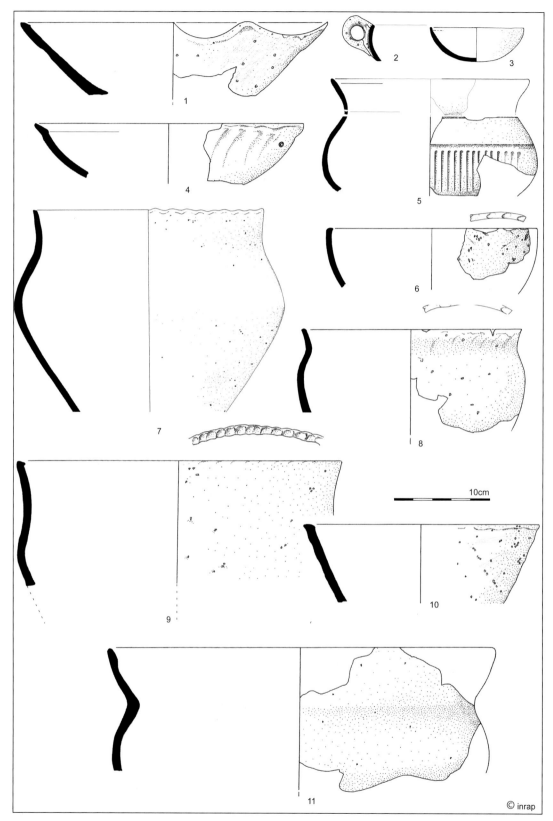

Fig. 15.12. Pont-de-Metz « Le Chant aux Oisons » (Somme). Choix de mobilier céramique. Hallstatt ancien/Ha C. Faciès picard du début du premier Âge du fer (D'après Buchez 2011).

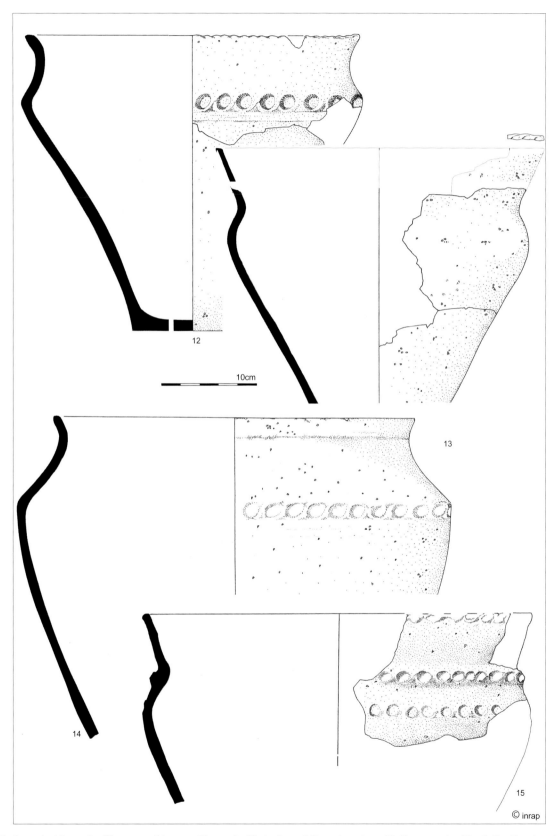

Fig. 15.13. Pont-de-Metz « Le Chant aux Oisons » (Somme). Choix de mobilier céramique. Hallstatt ancien/Ha C. Faciès picard du début du premier Âge du fer (D'après Buchez 2011).

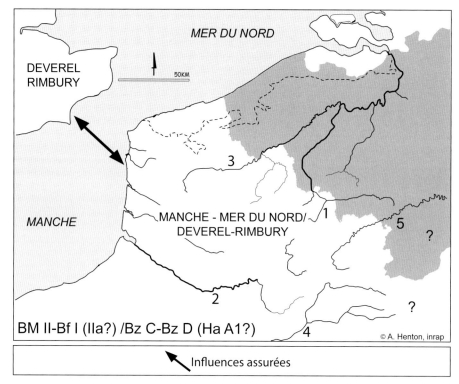

Fig. 15.14. Carte de synthèse du faciès culturel présent dans la zone d'étude au BM II–BF1 (IIa ?)/BZ C–D (Ha A1 ?). 1 : Escaut, 2 : Somme, 3 : Lys, 4 : Oise, 5 : Sambre.

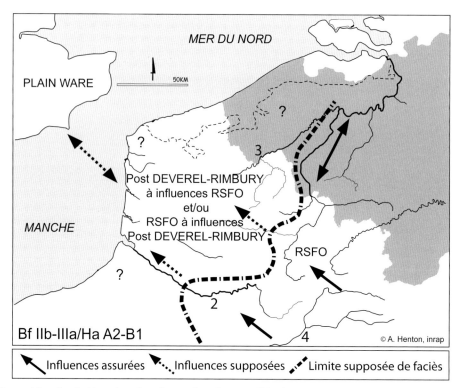

Fig. 15.15. Carte de synthèse des faciès culturels présents dans la zone d'étude au BF IIb–IIIa/Ha A2–B1. 1 : Escaut, 2 : Somme, 3 : Lys, 4 : Oise, 5 : Sambre.

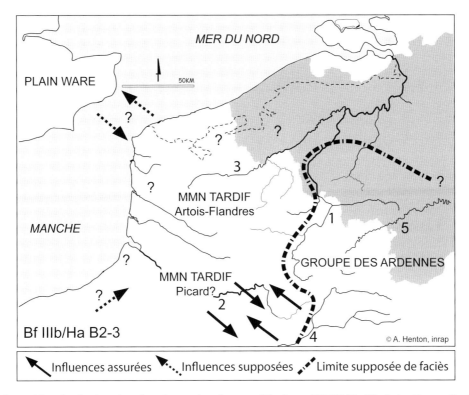

Fig. 15.16. Carte de synthèse des faciès culturels présents dans la zone d'étude au BF IIIb/Ha B2–3. 1 : Escaut, 2 : Somme, 3 : Lys, 4 : Oise, 5 : Sambre.

d'Outre-Manche. Dans l'attente d'une datation absolue, cette fosse a été prudemment datée du Ha C–D1. La définition d'un faciès « hallstattien » évoluant à partir d'un faciès Bronze final MMN tardif demeure donc à ce jour purement hypothétique.

Pour la Somme, quelques rares sites viennent éclairer quelque peu l'aube du premier Âge du fer. Le plus caractéristique a été fouillé à Pont-de-Metz « Le champ aux Oisons » (Buchez 2011) (Figs 15.12 et 15.13). Parmi le mobilier céramique, il faut signaler des profils simples, curvilignes ou rectilignes et des profils complexes, dont des pots à panse carénée ou épaule haute surmontée d'un col rectiligne ou concave. Ces derniers sembleraient être l'évolution de prototypes du Bronze final connus sur le site de Glisy (cf. *supra*). Ce mobilier de Pont-de-Metz présente certaines similitudes avec le mobilier découvert anciennement dans la vallée de la Somme (Amiens « La Madeleine-au-Lait ») (Blanchet et Fournier, 1978) ou dans la vallée de l'Oise (phases 2 et 3 de Choisy-au-Bac « Le Confluent ») (Talon 1984 ; 1987) et daté de la période II du premier Âge du fer de Blanchet (1984).

La répartition des sites de comparaison pose donc la question d'un faciès « picard » du Hallstatt ancien-moyen couvrant une partie de la vallée de la Somme et de celle de l'Oise au début du premier Âge du fer. Cette question des influences culturelles demeure toujours ouverte, même

si un bruit de fond atlantique (MMN) demeure plus que perceptible. Evoluant au Hallstatt final, notamment par l'adoption des formes carénées pour les jattes et les écuelles, ce faciès « picard » de la vallée de la Somme et du nord de l'Aisne présentera alors certains trais culturels de convergence « médio-atlantique » (Milcent 2006). Il s'étendra vers le nord, en longeant la vallée de l'Escaut (rive gauche) pour atteindre le Douaisis, en diluant certaines influences du Hainaut-Cambrésis, et vers le nord-ouest, en direction des côtes de la Manche (Bardel *et al.* 2014).

A l'issue de ce rapide tour d'horizon des faciès céramique présent au Bronze final et au premier Âge du fer entre Escaut, Somme et rivages de la Manche, nous pouvons donc constater une certaine fluctuation des influences culturelles. Affiliée clairement à la sphère atlantique au Bronze ancien-moyen, dans l'orbite du complexe Manche-Mer du Nord (MMN) (Fig. 15.14), notre zone d'étude voit une première percée d'influences continentales au cours du BFIIb–IIIa/Ha A2–B1. Celles-ci repoussent les limites généralement admiscs de la culture RSFO jusqu'à la vallée de l'Escaut et le long d'une partie de la vallée de la Somme. En direction des rivages de la Manche, les données actuellement disponibles montrent une mixité culturelle mélangeant influences RSFO et influences MMN (Fig. 15.15). A l'étape finale (BFIIIb/Ha B2–3), deux faciès céramiques contemporains se font face de part et d'autre de la vallée de l'Escaut.

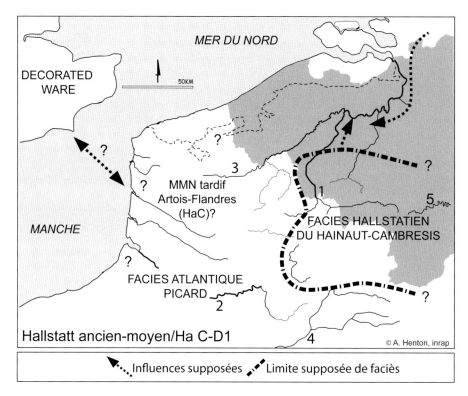

Fig. 15.17. Carte de synthèse des faciès culturels présents dans la zone d'étude au Hallstatt ancien–moyen/Ha C–D1. 1 : Escaut, 2 : Somme, 3 : Lys, 4 : Oise, 5 : Sambre.

Rive droite, le mobilier céramique s'intègre parfaitement à la typologie Bronze final du Groupe des Ardennes et se raccroche aisément à celui présent dans la vallée de l'Aisne. Rive gauche de l'Escaut et dans la moyenne vallée de la Somme, un faciès particulier voit le jour, de parenté MMN assurée (MMN tardif/*Plain ware*), mais encore emprunt de caractères antérieurs RSFO (Fig. 15.16).

Au Ha C/Hallstatt ancien, l'Escaut demeure une zone de contact privilégiée entre monde continental et monde atlantique. Rive droite, un faciès hallstattien du Hainaut-Cambrésis apparaît sur le territoire jusqu'à lors occupé par le faciès Bronze final du Groupe des Ardennes ; et ce probablement dès l'aube du 8e siècle av. notre ère. Un renouvellement complet du vaisselier céramique pose la question de l'éventualité de l'implantation d'un nouveau groupe humain. Entre la rive gauche et la Manche, des incertitudes demeurent, privilégiant un hypothétique faciès MMN tardif. Dans la vallée de la Somme, quelques ensembles laisseraient envisager un faciès « picard » de nature atlantique (Fig. 15.17).

Faciès hallstattien du Hainaut-Cambrésis et faciès « picard » évolueront et se côtoieront de manière plus ou moins active jusqu'au Hallstatt final, avant que l'ensemble de notre zone d'étude ne soit réunie de manière définitive, par l'expansion du complexe Aisne-Marne à l'aube du second Âge du fer.

Bibliographie

Bardel, D., Buchez, N., Henton, A., Leroy-Langelin, E., Sergent, A. et Gutierrez, C. (2014) *Du répertoire hallstattien au répertoire laténien dans le nord de la France. Première analyse typologique, chronologique et culturelle des corpus céramiques du Hallstatt D à la Tène ancienne A1 (7e–5e s. av. J.-C.), 143–92*, Revue du Nord, tome 95 (hommages à Germaine Leman-Delerive) 403. Villeneuve d'Ascq, Université Lille III.

Blanchet, J.-C. (1984) *Les premiers métallurgistes en Picardie et dans le nord de la France*, Mémoires de la Société Préhistorique Française 17. Paris, Société Préhistorique Française.

Blanchet, J.-C. et Talon, M. (2005) L'Âge du Bronze dans la moyenne vallée de l'Oise : apports récents. Dans J. Bourgeois et M. Talon (éd.), *L'Âge du Bronze dans son contexte européen, 227–68*, actes des CTHS 125e (Lille 2000). Paris, Comité des Travaux Historiques et Scientifiques.

Blanchet, J.-C., Fournier, J., et Fournier C. (1978) Une découverte du premier Age du Fer à Amiens (Somme), « La Madeleine-au-Lait ». *Cahiers Archéologiques de Picardie* 5, 279–283.

Blancquaert, G., Feray, Ph. et Robert, B. (2005) L'Age du Bronze dans le nord de la France : découvertes récentes. Dans J. Bourgeois et M. Talon (éd.), *L'Âge du Bronze dans son contexte européen, 83–101*, actes des CTHS, 125e (Lille 2000). Paris, Comité des Travaux Historiques et Scientifiques.

Bourgeois, J. et Cherretté, B. (2005) L'Age du Bronze et le premier Age du Fer dans les Flandres occidentale et orientale (Belgique) : un état de la question. Dans J. Bourgeois et M. Talon (éd.), *L'Âge du Bronze dans son contexte européen,*

43–81, actes des CTHS, 125e (Lille 2000). Paris, Comité des Travaux Historiques et Scientifiques.

Bourgeois, J. et Talon, M. (2008) From Picardy to Flanders: transmanche connections in the Bronze Age. Dans P. Clark (dir.), *Bronze Age Connections: Cultural Contact in Prehistoric Europe*, 38–59. Oxford, Oxbow Books.

Bretagne, P., Catteddu, I., Clavel, V., Clotuche, C., de Saulce, A., Decanter, F., Deschodt, L., Fosse, G., Frenée, E., Gaudefroy, S., Lantoine, J., Lefebvre, A., Martial, E., Mervelet, P., Michel, K., Olszewski, M., Praud, I., Robert, S., Robert, B., Roger, D., Soupard, N., Thévenard, J.-J. et Vialet, P. (2000) Rapport de fouilles archéologiques réalisées sur le site Toyota, sauvetage urgent 8/06/98–14/08/98. Villeneuve d'Ascq : AFAN et S.R.A. Nord-Pas-de-Calais.

Brun, P. (1986) *La civilisation des Champs d'Urnes. Etude critique dans le Bassin Parisien*, Documents d'Archéologie française 4. Paris, Ed. de la Maison des Sciences de l'Homme.

Brun, P. (2013) La culture des Champs d'Urnes : problèmes et définition. Dans E. Warmenbol et W. Leclercq (éd.), *Échanges de bons procédés. La céramique du Bronze final dans le nord-ouest de l'Europe. Actes du colloque de Bruxelles, octobre 2010*, 13–21, Études archéologiques (Centre de Recherches en Archéologie et patrimoine de l'ULB). Bruxelles, CReA-Patrimoine.

Brun, P. et Mordant, C. (1988) Le Groupe Rhin-Suisse-France orientale et la notion de civilisation des Champs d'Urnes. Actes du colloque international de Nemours 1986. *Mémoires du Musée de Préhistoire d'Ile-de-France* 1, 627–659.

Brun, P., Cathelinais, C., Chatillon, S., Guichard, Y., Le Guen, P. et Nere, E. (2005) L'Âge du Bronze dans la vallée de l'Aisne. Dans J. Bourgeois et M. Talon (éd.), *L'Âge du Bronze dans son contexte européen, 189–208*, actes des CTHS, 125e, Lille 2000. Paris, Comité des Travaux Historiques et Scientifiques.

Buchez, N. (2011). La protohistoire ancienne. Recherche et fouille des sites de l'âge du Bronze à La Tène ancienne sur les grands tracés linéaires en Picardie occidentale : questions méthodologiques et résultats scientifiques. Dans N. Buchez, D. Bayard et P. Depaepe (dir.) *Quinze ans d'archéologie préventive sur les grands tracés linéaires en Picardie, première partie, 121–99*, Revue Archéologique de Picardie 3/4. Amiens, Société archéologique de Picardie.

Buchez, N. et Talon, M. (2005) L'âge du Bronze dans le bassin de la Somme. Bilan et périodisation du mobilier céramique. Dans J. Bourgeois et M. Talon (éd.), *L'Âge du Bronze dans son contexte européen, 159–88* Actes des CTHS, 125e (Lille 2000). Paris, Comité des Travaux Historiques et Scientifiques.

Champion, T. (1980) Settlement and environment in later Bronze Age Kent. Dans J. Barrett et R. Bradley (éd.). *Settlement and Society in the British Later Bronze Age, 243–46*, British Archaeological Report 83. Oxford. British Archaeological Reports.

Clotuche, R. (2012) Onnaing, Z. A. C. de la vallée de l'Escaut, Opération Delquignies–BilsDeroo. Occupations Bronze/Hallstatt et artisanat gallo-romain (1er–3e s.), Rapport final d'opération, inédit. Amiens, SRA Nord/Pas-de-Calais.

De Mulder, G. (2011) Funeraire rituelen in het Scheldebekken tijdens de late bronstijd en de vroege ijzertijd: de grafvelden in hun maatschappelijke en sociale context. Proefschrift voorgedagen tot het bekomen van de graad van Doctor in de Archeologie. Universiteit Gent.

De Mulder, G. (2013) La céramique de Bronze final dans l'ouest de la Belgique. Entre le monde atlantique et le groupe Rhin-Suisse-France orientale. Dans E. Warmenbol et W. Leclercq (éd.), *Échanges de bons procédés. La céramique du Bronze final dans le nord-ouest de l'Europe. Actes du colloque de Bruxelles, octobre 2010*, 217–38, études archéologiques (Centre de Recherches en Archéologie et patrimoine de l'ULB). Bruxelles, CReA-Patrimoine.

Desfossés, Y., Martial, E. et Vallin, L. (2000) Le site d'habitat du Bronze moyen du « Château d'Eau » à Roeux (Pas-de-Calais). *Bulletin de la Société Préhistorique Française* 89, 10–12.

Destexhe, G. (1986) La protohistoire en Hesbaye centrale. Du Bronze final à la romanisation. *Archéologie hesbignonne* 5, 77–91.

Guillaume, A. (2005) 150 ans de recherches hallstattiennes en Wallonie. Les rites funéraires », *Bulletin du Cercle archéologique Hesbaye-Condoz, t. XXVII 2003*.

Henton, A. (1994) L'Âge du Bronze final et le premier Âge du Fer en Hainaut occidental. Nouvelles perspectives de recherches. *Lunula. Archaeologia protohistorica* 2, 31–32.

Henton, A. (2007) Rombies et Marchipont « Rue de l'Eglise ». Rapport final d'opération, inédit. Villeneuve d'Ascq, SRA Nord/Pas-de-Calais.

Henton, A. (2013) La céramique du Bronze final dans le haut bassin de l'Escaut et ses marges côtières. Première approche typo-chronologique et culturelle. In E. Warmenbol et W. Leclercq (éd.), *Échanges de bons procédés. La céramique du Bronze final dans le nord-ouest de l'Europe. Actes du colloque de Bruxelles, octobre 2010*, 145–68, études archéologiques (Centre de Recherches en Archéologie et patrimoine de l'ULB). Bruxelles, CReA-Patrimoine.

Henton, A. (en cours) Approche typo-chronologique et culturelle du mobilier céramique de l'âge du Bronze final et du premier âge du Fer dans le Haut Bassin de l'Escaut et ses marges littorales. Mémoire de thèse de doctorat en archéologie. Universiteit Gent.

Henton, A. et Demarez, L. (2005) L'Âge du Bronze en Hainaut belge. Dans J. Bourgeois et M. Talon (éd.), *L'Âge du Bronze dans son contexte européen, 83–101*, actes des CTHS, 125e (Lille 2000). Paris, Comité des Travaux Historiques et Scientifiques.

Henton, A. et Hannois, P. (2014) Prospection archéologique par ortho-photographies aériennes et images satellitaires en Nord-Pas-de-Calais (France). *Lunula. Archaeologia protohistorica* 22, 23–31.

Jones, M. U. et Bond, D. (1980) Later Bronze Age settlement at Mucking, Essex. Dans J. Barrett, et R. Bradley (éd.), *Settlement and Society in the British Later Bronze Age, 471–82*, British Archaeological Report 83. Oxford, British Archaeological Reports.

Lambot, B. (1977) Nanteuil-sur-Aisne. Un site du Bronze final dans le Sud ardennais. *Bulletin de la Société Archéologique Champenoise* 4, 17–58.

Lorin, Y. (2008) Achicourt (Pas-de-Calais) « Aire des gens du voyage – Route départementale 60. Fouille d'une occupation rurale de la transition Bronze/premier Fer. RFO de fouille. Achicourt : Inrap, déposé au SRA Nord-Pas-de-Calais.

Lorin, Y. (2015) Aire-sur-la-Lys « Hameau de Saint-Martin. Rapport final d'opération, inédit. Achicourt : Inrap, déposé au SRA Nord/Pas de Calais.

Manem, S., Marcigny, C. et Talon, M. (2013) Vivre, produire et transmettre autour de la Manche. Regards sur les comportements des hommes entre Deverel-Rimbury et post Deverel-Rimbury en Normandie et dans le sud de l'Angleterre. Dans E. Warmenbol et W. Leclercq (éd.) *Échanges de bons procédés. La céramique du Bronze final dans le nord-ouest de l'Europe. Actes du colloque de Bruxelles, octobre 2010, 245–66*, études archéologiques (Centre de Recherches en Archéologie et patrimoine de l'ULB). Bruxelles, CReA-Patrimoine.

Marcigny, C. et Talon, M. (2009) Sur les rives de la Manche : Qu'en est il du passage de l'Âge du Bronze à l'Âge du Fer. Dans *De l'Âge du Bronze à l'Âge du Fer (X–VIIème siècle av. J-C), 385–403*, actes du colloque international APRAB-AFEAF de Saint-Romain-en-Gall 2005, Revue Archéologique de l'Est, Supplément 27. Dijon, Société archéologique de l'Est.

Masse, A. (2013) Dainville (Pas-de-Calais) « Le Champ Bel Air ». RFO de fouille. Dainville : Service archéologique du Pas-de-Calais, déposé au SRA Nord-Pas-de-Calais.

Milcent, P.-Y. (2006) Premier âge du Fer médio-atlantique et genèse multipolaire des cultures matérielles laténiennes. In D. Vitali (dir.) *Celtes et Gaulois. L'Archéologie face à l'Histoire : La Préhistoire des Celtes, 81–106*, actes de la table ronde de Bologne, 28–29 mai 2005. Glux-en-Glenne, Bibracte.

Neaud, P., Bardel, D. et Henton, A. (2014) Onnaing (NPDC), Extension du Parc d'Activités du Val d'Escaut (PAVE2). Occupations du Bronze final et du Hallstatt ancien. RFO de fouille. Achicourt : Inrap, déposé au SRA Nord-Pas-de-Calais.

Needham, S. P. (1991) *Excavation and Salvage at Runnymede Bridge 1978. The Late Bronze Age Waterfront Site*. London, British Museum Press.

Needham, S. (1996) Chronology and periodisation in the British Bronze Age. Dans K. Randsborg (dir.) *Absolute Chronology, Archaeological Europe 2500–500 BC, 121–40*, Acta Archaeologica 67. Copenhague, Wiley-Blackwell.

Piningre, J.-F. (2005) Un habitat de la fin de l'Age du Bronze : le site d'Inghem (Pas-de-Calais). Dans J. Bourgeois et M. Talon (éd.) *L'Âge du Bronze dans son contexte européen, 137–58*, actes des CTHS, 125e, Lille 2000. Paris, Comité des Travaux Historiques et Scientifiques.

Talon, M. (1984) *Les formes céramiques Bronze final et premier Âge du Fer de l'habitat de Choisy-au-Bac (Oise)*, mémoire de Maîtrise de l'Université de Paris I. Paris, Université Paris I.

Talon, M. (1987) Les formes céramiques Bronze final et premier Âge du Fer de l'habitat de Choisy-au-Bac (Oise). Dans *Les relations entre le continent et les Îles britanniques à l'Âge du Bronze, 255–73*, actes du colloque Bronze de Lille (1984), no. spécial *Revue Archéologique de Picardie* et S. P. F. Amiens, Société archéologique de Picardie.

16

The Channel: border and link during the Bronze Age

Patrice Brun

Abstract

The cultural geography of the Atlantic seaboard remained elusive for a long time due to the scarcity of the pottery record. As a result of recent advances in the development of rescue archaeology it is now possible to assess earlier proposals based almost exclusively on metal materials. These data also call for reflection on the ambivalence of maritime corridors for coastal societies. These long straits are natural borders and favoured crossing points and produced dramatically variable effects depending on the social context of the time. This paradoxical situation is particularly marked during the Bronze Age, characterised by the intensification of trade in raw materials and finished metal goods between Great Britain and the Continent.

Keywords: Atlantic Bronze Age, exchange, identities, Bronze Age cultures

Résumé

La géographie culturelle de la façade atlantique est longtemps restée difficile à saisir en raison d'une documentation céramique peu abondante. Les récents progrès réalisés grâce au développement de l'archéologie préventive permettent de préciser les propositions antérieures fondées presque exclusivement sur la documentation métallique. Ils invitent aussi à réfléchir sur l'ambivalence des couloirs maritimes pour les sociétés riveraines. À la fois frontières naturelles et lieux de traversée privilégiés, ces détroits allongés produisaient des effets susceptibles de varier du tout au tout en fonction du contexte social du moment. Cette situation paradoxale prend un relief particulièrement accusé à l'Âge du bronze, caractérisé par l'intensification des échanges de matières premières et de produits finis métalliques entre la Grande-Bretagne et le continent.

Mots-clés : Âge du bronze Atlantique, échanges, identités, cultures de l'Âge du bronze

Introduction

In order to assess ambitious issues from a historical and sociological viewpoint, protohistoric archaeology has to reconstruct cultural geography as accurately as possible. Metal remains, in the form of non-funerary terrestrial and aquatic deposits, are abundant in coastal Channel regions but pottery remains have only been revealed there recently. With these precious complements, it will be possible to validate and clarify reconstructions proposed earlier. Recent publications provide eloquent evidence of the necessity to carry out quantitative analyses of pottery types in order

to define cultural entities. In view of this, it is appropriate to recall the methodological, theoretical and contextual framework. Such rigour is essential in order to interpret cultural entities as pertinently as possible, as archaeologists do not generally grasp the full significance of these entities. In the absence of texts, these stylistic groups are the best sources at our disposal for gaining access to expressions of identity, which are crucial for interpreting the organisation and political, economic and ideological choices of the people in question. In this paper, this leads us to develop several reflections on the continental side of the Channel during the

Bronze Age and to consider that this maritime strait played a double role of border and link at this time.

The methodological, theoretical and contextual framework

An enhanced understanding of the question of trans-Channel links requires the development of a protocol for evaluating the level of similarity of human productions and their distribution throughout time and space. Since the work of J.-C. Gardin (1979), this protocol has become standard in archaeology and consists of:

- elaborating a typology;
- assessing the frequency of association of the defined types;
- determining the significance (chronological, spatial or functional) of frequently associated types of groups;
- ordering and mapping cultural entities.

This type of classification requires a precise definition of the notion of archaeological culture as this concept is still often used in a rather vague way. It was coined in the 19th century to designate complexes of objects, tombs, buildings or establishments showing relative stylistic consistency and was consequently considered to be the material expression of a common culture. In this way, it was generally assumed that the human communities corresponding to the ethnic groups, tribes and nations evoked by ethnographic and historic sources could be geographically positioned. Work carried out in this domain was obscured by studies using simplistic methodological analysis (the arbitrary selection of *fossiles directeurs)* and especially by interpretations intended to back up the original sovereignty, or even the racial superiority of a population living or having lived on a specific territory (see the theses advanced by G. Kossinna (1912), revisited by the Nazi Party, then by the Nazi regime). As is often the case, this abuse led to throwing the baby out with the bathwater, that is to say, to outlawing this type of ethically incorrect research. Fortunately, non-conventional personalities, in particular the talented V. G. Childe, endeavoured to study this crucial question further by defining archaeological cultures more accurately. He proposed a version of typological correlations, founded on the repetition of associated types classifiable by statistics or polythetics (Childe 1942; Klejn 1982). In this vein, we can successfully define an archaeological culture as 'a polythetic assemblage of elements more frequently associated within a limited geographic area than outside it' (Brun 1991). The polythetic dimension is clearly essential for underlining the fact that these assemblages are made up of several types of objects and each of them can be present elsewhere, but only in a marginal way in combination with the other types. The frequency of association is absolutely decisive here. In more sociological terms, an archaeological culture is the materialisation of a group of human communities with more contacts between them than with others. It goes without saying that the identification of these similarities conditions our likelihood of grasping the economic, political and ideological organisation of these societies, in the absence of sufficiently explicit textual sources.

When the archaeological record is sufficiently abundant, we still differentiate cultural assemblages with different levels of similarity and disproportionate surface areas, which fit together, ranging from the cultural group to the cultural complex, and including the culture or group of cultures, to use the terminology proposed by D. Clarke (1968). If we concentrate on the Bronze Age, several tens of thousands of objects from this period have been recorded throughout Europe. These adornments, weapons, tools, harness implements and tableware are very similar across the continent, but details of more frequently associated forms and decorations reveal the existence of about a dozen distinctive stylistic zones, which we call cultural complexes. In each of these, almost identical, objects prove that preferential links were maintained over hundreds of kilometres. This is the case along the Atlantic coastline, from Scotland to Andalucía (Briggs 1987; Brun 1991; 1998; Coffyn 1985; Quilliec 2003; Savory 1949) (Figs 16.1 and 16.2). There, maritime transport undoubtedly facilitated contacts, which favoured mutual borrowing and a certain degree of cultural homogeneity.

Studies increasingly show that the Channel played a key role in the group of northern Atlantic complex cultures (Blanchet *et al.* 1989; Briard 1965; 1984; De Laet 1974; O'Connor 1980). We can discern the beginnings of an Atlantic community well before the Bronze Age. The same regions used megalithic funerary practices from the 5th millennium BC. However, these practices are shared with certain sectors of the Mediterranean on one hand and the Baltic Sea on the other, outlining the perimeter of the pioneering front of the first sedentary farmers, advancing slowly from the Danube Basin before gaining the Paris Basin at around 5000 BC. These peripheral communities adopted a production economy characterized by the later domestication of plants. A cultural feature, perhaps even the conscience of a distinctive collective identity from that of the farmers from the Danube melting pot, could have paved the way for the emergence of an Atlantic cultural complex. These regions provide evidence of renewed links from about 2600 BC onwards, through Beaker ware (goblets in the shape of an upside-down bell and decorated all the way up -) and a kit of very specific objects (copper dagger, stemmed and barbed arrowheads, archer armlet and sometimes gold or amber jewellery). The distribution of these objects, which indicates active working trade networks driven by social elites, is not limited to the westernmost maritime edge of Europe, as it extends to Poland and Hungary. However, they seem to form a slightly separate sub-complex in this vast network where some individuals, namely those bringing the

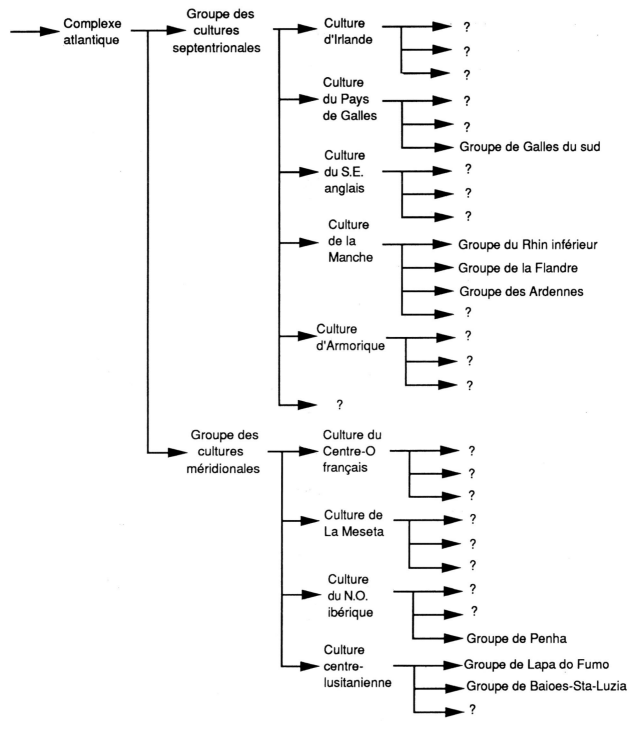

Fig. 16.1. Proposed dendrogram of cultural entities from the north Alpine complex at the end of the Bronze Age (after Brun 1991, Fig. 3).

famous kit to the grave as though to display their links to distant allies, probably played a crucial role (Harrison 1986).

These connections led to the completion of the extension of copper metallurgy in Europe; a long process that began in the southeast of the continent. Then, an unexpected, revealing and exciting phenomenon occurred. As soon as they had mastered this metallurgical technique, communities in the British Isles innovated by alloying tin with copper and began producing true bronze with tin before any other community (Gerloff 1993; Pare 2000). In this way, peripheral and marginal societies, from an economic viewpoint, were suddenly, almost without transition, at the cutting edge of technical innovation, which advanced in exactly the opposite direction to that of copper. True

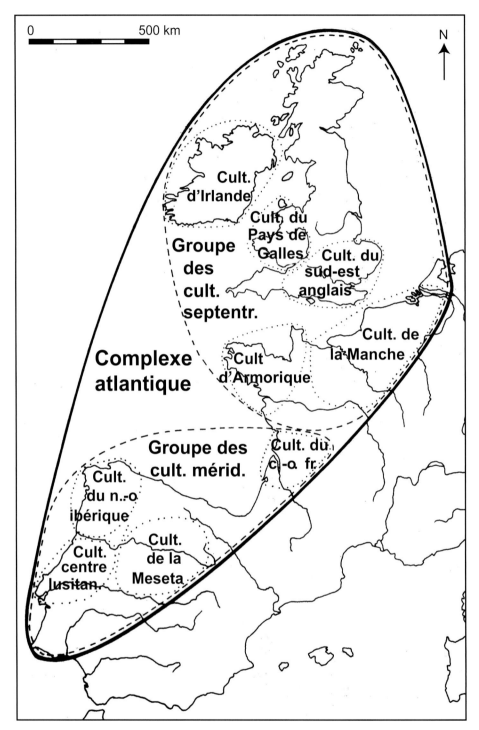

Fig. 16.2. Attempt at mapping the cultural subdivisions of the north Alpine complex at the end of the Bronze Age (after Brun 1991, fig. 4).

bronze, with more than 8% of tin, began to dominate British metal products from as early as 2100 BC. In Germany and Central Europe, this did not occur until 1800 BC and 1700 BC in the Balkans. It is true that the Atlantic regions had considerable advantages for the production of metal goods of superior quality to those in pure copper and even copper deliberately alloyed with arsenic, misleadingly called bronze by some. In Galicia, on the edge of the Massif Central, in

Armorica or in Cornwall, copper and tin ores are located close to each other, whereas they rarely occur alongside each other elsewhere on the continent. The exploration of these exceptional resources appears to partly explain the social changes so clearly displayed in the rich funerary hoards of the Armorican and Wessex tumuli. These ostentatious displays of wealth and power disappeared during the 16th century BC. All the communities in this Atlantic world then chose very simple funerary practices, without necessarily calling into question their hierarchical social organization. It is certain, in any case, that this discretion does not correspond to economic decline, as shown by frequently buried hoards containing large quantities of bronze objects (Pennors 2004; Brun *et al.* 2010).

These non-funerary hoards dissimulated very varied complexes: weapons and adornments that were undoubtedly not accessible to everyone, but also tools, often made up of series of rather heavy axes. Normandy became a production region, as shown by its own variants. Normandy appears to supplant Armorica from the 15th century BC in terms of the number and richness of hoards. There is every indication that the communities standing to gain the most from the bronze 'trade' were no longer those controlling raw material extraction, but those in charge of the main circulation routes. The control of the mouth of the Seine, a major crossing point between the Cornwall or Armorica hoards on one hand, and Burgundy opening onto the Alpine and Danube regions on the other, was a major economic advantage in such a context. A comparable phenomenon occurred at the same time on the other side of the Channel: the region of Wessex declined while the lower Thames Valley, like the Seine, began attracting a considerable proportion of the metal in circulation (Burgess 1980). This influx of goods inevitably entailed a procession of potentially destabilising developments for local social stability; perhaps resulting in more abundant offerings than elsewhere to divinities called upon to end an unfavourable event: internal or external conflict, interruption of provisions, epidemics, climatic perturbation ... or to grant forgiveness. History and ethnology have taught us that social difficulties very often lead to intensified religious practices.

Although the coastal Channel regions lack copper and tin deposits, they became very innovative production centres of bronze objects, particularly swords, which were the most emblematic object of masculine 'aristocratic' equipment in Europe from the 14th to the 9th centuries BC. Consequently, the distribution of these hand weapons not only reveals social elite trade networks, but also the most advanced technical investment of that time and socially prestigious practices. It shows that during the whole of the Final Bronze Age, Normandy and Picardy, on one side, and the basin of London, on the other, were centres of invention for successive types of swords, which then extended, often by imitation, to the rest of the Atlantic cultural complex (Quilliec 2003).

The social value of bronze quickly played a leading role for societies at that time. Bronze objects produced in series were indispensable to the elite for appearances and combats and probably facilitated fundamental transactions for traditional societies (price of the fiancé, dowry or blood money). Bronze was also used for making agricultural tools and probably contributed to the increase in agro-pastoral productivity. Metal axes and sickles definitively replaced their stone counterparts. This point is essential as although long distance trade was important, it was necessarily based

on the potential of the subsistence economy of food and clothing. This also explains the increase in communities in large valleys. Indeed, social dynamics are based on demography and spatial occupation conditions.

For the purposes of the Channel during the Bronze Age, the cultural complex in question is the Atlantic complex and more precisely, the group of northern cultures from this complex, identified as a cultural community by H. N. Savory in 1949, then by J. Briard in 1965. The attempt at classification several years ago (Brun 1988), using only metal objects, as the pottery record only began to develop recently, led to the identification of rather clearly distinct cultures and more evanescent cultural groups for the end of the Late Bronze Age (Fig. 16.1).

It is only over the past few years that archaeologists have begun to question the identity principle, although it is a behavioural human trait founding the very formation of the cultural entities that they endeavour to identify. Psychologists and sociologists explained this principle in the 1980s (Forsé 1989). The identity of an individual emerges through the mimetic adoption of models from the community in which he grew up, but also through differentiation from foreigners and, more imperceptibly, from the preceding generation, or even from others in general. This distinction naturally occurs to different degrees. Generally, it requires a model to imitate (the cultural baggage of the family, residence group), and another, the foreign model, from which to differentiate. This formation process of the individual and collective personality is essential. Naturally, the degree of imitation and distinction is variable, depending on the distance to be marked out. The cultural entities assessed by archaeologists are also differentiated and ordered by the volume, frequency and conditions of trade at the time. Distance is a major restriction for these three criteria.

We thus gain a better understanding of the crucial importance of identity, the fact that its social and spatial manifestations change constantly, but at different scales and rhythms, and that they can conserve the same geographic limits for a very long time. This principle of concomitant standardization and increased heterogeneity explains cultural expansion by the formation of matrimonial and cultural networks, without mechanically using migration hypothesis, leads to an understanding of the hierarchy of the entities within the main complexes and accounts for the existence of the conservation of different cultural entities.

Several considerations on the continental side of the Channel

The documentary disparity between the east and the west of France upheld the notion of northwestern inferiority for a long time. The Atlantic regions were perceived as the extreme periphery of technical, stylistic and social changes. What is true of the Neolithic and then the Iron Age, during which time a vast economic system centred on the Mediterranean developed, does not necessarily apply to the Bronze Age, in particular in relation to the north Alpine zone. The metal record shows, on the contrary, active competition between the respective productis from these cultural complexes, a sort of reciprocal emulation illustrated by rapid borrowing and adaptation to local tastes.

How could it be any other way in a context where bronze raw material trade is indispensable and illustrates the use of different deposits with overlapping circulation channels over long distances (Northover 1982)? The analysis of the frequency of association of types in mixed hoards shows that the Atlantic world displays no delay, no systematic time

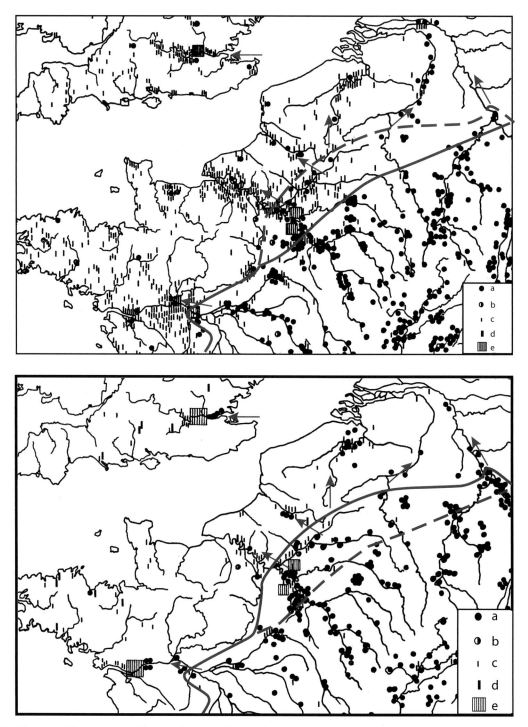

Fig. 16.3. Identification of the opposition between the north Alpine cultural complex and its Atlantic counterpart; top: Br D–Ha A1; bottom: Ha A2–B1; a: north Alpine type object; b: mixed hoard; c: Atlantic type object; e: concentration of aquatic hoards; in red: evolution of the inferred limit between north Alpine and Atlantic complexes (after Brun 1988, figs 3 and 4).

lag in the adoption of technical innovations. Indeed, more than other regions, the Atlantic complex necessarily became highly efficient in the domain of maritime transport. This is implied by the cultural community that not only included Scotland and Portugal, but also persisted for a long time through the successive modification of large sections of the material culture. This represents a privileged sphere of exchanges where participants developed their own styles for expressing their belonging to this community and their difference in relation to others. This principle operated at several different scales: from an individual scale to that of humanity as a whole. At the beginning of the Bronze Age, very dense inter-Atlantic cultural links united the north of the Atlantic coastline, from the Loire to the Rhine delta and the Ardennes to Ireland. This complex only incontestably appears to have fused with the southwest of France and the west of Iberia during the second stage of the final Bronze Age. The most extensive networks, which were probably more fragile, visibly experienced temporary eclipses.

For a long time, the archaeological record was made up bronze objects, mostly from non-funerary hoards. Through the development of rescue archaeology, the pottery corpus now provides bases for reflection that were sorely lacking up until now. Our knowledge of the distribution of pottery forms and decoration is still clearly lagging a long way behind the north Alpine sphere, but it is now challenging to attempt to outline the cultural geography of the zones around the Channel. The following section is based on data kindly supplied before publication by W. Leclercq (2013), G. de Mulder (2013) and A. Henton (2013). Pottery types with light fluting from Br D–Ha A1, then RSFO from Ha

A2–B1, exist to the northwest of the limits suggested by the distribution of metal types, but they remain sporadic and marginal, and more so if we exclude ubiquitous types such as the *doppelkonus*, which are particularly frequent in a culturally different sector from the north Alpine area; that of the Ruhr. The Ha B2–3 types can also generate confusion, as an evolution of Plain Ware to Decorated Ware occurred during this chronological stage, characterized by forms and decorations that are at times still similar to north Alpine RSFO types. It is important, in this respect, to underline frequent confusion consisting in calling Ha B2–3 pottery types RSFO for the north Alpine zone as well. Although there is a clear link with types from the RSFO culture, there are evident changes that give rise to cultural groups with much more marked stylistic characteristics than beforehand. This very marginal presence, during Ha A2–B1 in the coastal Channel zone is not surprising. It merely confirms the cultural geography suggested by bronze according to a polythetic conception of cultural entities (Fig. 16.3).

These marginal foreign elements are located at a moderate distance from their zone of origin and the main north Alpine bronze export channels. They are probably presents from north Alpine travellers, or elements from the trousseaus of north Alpine women living there after matrimonial exchanges. North Alpine bronze exportation channels towards Great Britain were identified very early on by N. Roymans (1991), in a very relevant way, with details of his use of the term 'Urnfield group', which created ambiguity and generated confusion as the north Alpine complex was still commonly called the Urnfield culture in Germany (Fig. 16.4). In that article, N. Roymans showed

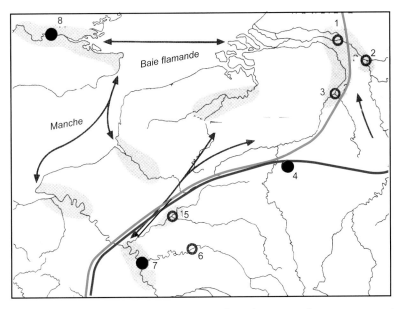

Fig. 16.4. Zones with concentrations of Ha B2/3 swords. Arrows: major long distance trade routes; empty circles: concentrations (more than 30 objects in aquatic hoards); filled circles: concentrations (more than 100 objects in aquatic hoards); 1: Nijmegen/Millingen; 2: Wesel-'Aue'; 3: Roermond; 4: Hansur-Lesse; 5: Compiègne/Choisy-au-Bac; 6: Brasles; 7: Paris; 8: London (after Roymans 1991, Fig. 9, modified and completed by the cultural complex limits: Atlantic in blue, north Alpine in red).

the intensity of bronze trade, particularly of weapons and adornments, between the different cultural complexes in contact with each other in the middle of the Paris Basin, i.e., not far from the Channel and the Flemish coastline at the southern end of the North Sea, especially between the Seine estuary and the Rhine delta. The importance of the Seine and Rhine axes emerged a long time ago after fluvial dredging, but the Brasles-Compiègne-Somme Bay axis is gradually becoming better known, as is that of Escaut. These four axes visibly converge towards England, with intensified traffic in both directions, well-marked by trade, technological transfers and reciprocal imitations between the north Alpine and Atlantic worlds. The fact that the famous large Hallstattian iron sword came from a bronze Atlantic culture prototype, the Ewart-Park type, is a good example of this, but only reflects the continuation of a long history of mutual inspiration (Brun *et al.* 2009).

Conclusion

Maritime zones are often perceived as barriers. It is true that they impede human mobility, which is why political borders comply with their morphology. Major rivers or mountain chains played a similar role. With the development of technical and organisational skills, it became possible for human societies to cross these hydrographical or topographical barriers. This resulted in a gradual increase in capacities to channel, harness and control the movement of people, goods and ideas. In sum, these natural obstacles played the role of a filter, paradoxically favourable to exchanges, depending on the progress made in the technical domain (metal tools, naval architecture, etc.) and in the sphere of collective organisation (development, mobilisation, crew maintenance, etc.).

During the Bronze Age in particular the Channel was both a barrier and a link. This situation began with the development of the 'Beaker complex' networks, through which north-western European societies acquired copper metallurgy. The whole tip of Western Europe (the west of the Iberian Peninsula, the French Massif Central, the Armorican Massif and British Cornwall) produced bronze weapons and adornments, then tools, as these zones contained exceptionally rich tin deposits. The rather rapid replacement of stone by bronze as a raw material occurred everywhere over several centuries, not only in metal-bearing massifs, but also in large sedimentary basins lacking such deposits, such as the Paris and London basins. For these societies, this dependence on bronze logically required constant efforts to ensure indispensable supplies for their survival. In a context where trade was probably prone to various possible causes of interruption (decreases in producers' output, convoy attacks, shipwrecks, hijacking by other persons, breached alliances, wars, etc.), one of the ways of making these crucial supplies less uncertain was to diversify the sources. The Channel

thus became an extremely important link, for crossing and for coastal trade convoys of copper and tin loads towards the mouth of the rivers opening onto large expanses of rich inland farming land. Crossing in both directions was of course indispensable, in order to compensate for the inevitable defections of the nearest suppliers. The supply and demand of copper and tin were probably the backbone of this spectacular economic dynamism. This appears to be largely confirmed by the correlation of its decline with the increased competition from iron.

Bibliography

Blanchet, J.-C., Brun, P. et Talon, M. (1989) Le Bronze moyen en Picardie et dans le Nord-Pas-de-Calais. In *Dynamique du Bronze moyen en Europe occidentale, 491–500*, actes du 113e Congrès national des Sociétés savantes, Strasbourg-Haguenau, 1988. Paris, CTHS.

Briard, J. (1965) *Les dépôts bretons et l'âge du Bronze atlantique*. Rennes, Laboratoire d'anthropologie préhistorique de la Faculté des Sciences de Rennes.

Briard, J. (1984) *Les tumulus d'Armorique*. L'âge du Bronze en France 3, Paris, Picard.

Briggs, C. S. (1987) Buckets and cauldrons in the Late Bronze Age of north-west Europe: a review. In *Les relations entre le continent et les îles britanniques à l'Age du Bronze, 161–87*, actes du Colloque de Lille dans le cadre du 22e Congrès préhistorique de France, 1984. Paris, Revue archéologique de Picardie et Société préhistorique française.

Brun, P. (1988) L'entité 'Rhin-Suisse-France orientale': nature et évolution. In P Brun and C. Mordant (eds) *Le groupe Rhin-Suisse-France orientale et la notion de civilisation des Champs d'Urnes, 599–618*, actes du Colloque international de Nemours, 1986. Nemours, Mémoires du Musée de Préhistoire d'Ile-de-France 1.

Brun, P. (1991) Le Bronze atlantique et ses subdivisions culturelles : essai de définition. In C. Chevillot and A. Coffyn (eds) *L'âge du Bronze atlantique: ses faciès, de l'Ecosse à l'Andalousie et leurs relations avec le bronze continental et la Méditerranée, 11–24*, actes du 1er Colloque du Parc archéologique de Beynac, 10–14 Sept. 1990. Beynac-et-Cazenac, publication de l'association des musées du Sarladais.

Brun, P. (1998) Le complexe culturel atlantique: entre le cristal et la fumée. In S. Oliveira Jorge (ed.) *Existe una Idade do Bronze atlântico? 40–51*. Lisbonne, Instituto Português de Arqueologia.

Brun, P., Chaume, B., Dhennequin, L. and Quilliec, B. (2009) Le passage de l'âge du Bronze à l'âge du Fer … au fil de l'épée. In M.-J. Roulière-Lambert, A. Daubigney, P.-Y. Milcent, M. Talon and J. Vital (eds) *De l'âge du Bronze à l'âge du Fer en France et en Europe occidentale (Xe–VIIe siècle av. J.-C.), 477–86*, actes du XXXe Colloque International de l'AFEAF, mai 2006. St-Romain-en-Gal/Vienne, Revue archéologique de l'Est.

Brun, P., Aubry, L., Galinand, C., Pennors, F., Quenol, V. and Ruby, P. (2010) Elite and prestige goods during the early and middle Bronze Age in France. In H. Meller and F. Bertemes (eds) *Der Griff nach den Sternen. Wie Europas Eliten zu Macht und Reichtum Kamen, 199–206*, international symposium (16–21 02–2005). Halle, Landesamt für Denkmalpflege und Archäologie Sachsen-Anhalt – Landesmuseum für Vorgeschichte Halle.

Burgess, C. (1980) *The Age of Stonehenge*. Londres, Dent.

Childe, G. (1942) *What Happened in History*. Harmondsworth, Penguin (Trad. fr. 1961. *De la préhistoire à l'histoire*. Paris, B. Arthaud).

Clarke, D. L. (1968) *Analytical Archaeology*. London, Methuen.

Coffyn, A. (1985) *Le Bronze final atlantique dans la Péninsule Ibérique*. Paris, De Boccard.

De Laet, S. J. (1974) *Prehistorische Kulturen in bet zuiden der Lagelanden*. Wetteren, Universa bvba.

De Mulder, G. (2013) La céramique du Bronze final dans l'Ouest de la Belgique. Entre le monde atlantique et le groupe Rhin-Suisse-France orientale. In W. Leclercq and E. Warmembol (eds) *Echanges de bons procédés. La céramique du Bronze final dans le nord-ouest de l'Europe*, 223–244. Bruxelles, CReA-Patrimoine.

Forsé, M. (1989) *L'Ordre improbable. Entropie et processus sociaux*. Paris, Presses universitaires de France.

Gardin, J.-C. (1979) *Une archéologie théorique*. Paris, Hachette.

Gerloff, S. (1993) Zu Fragen mittelmeerländischer Kontakte und absoluter Chronologie der Frühbronzezeit in Mittel- und Westeuropa. *Prähistorische Zeitschrift* 68, 58–102

Harrison, R. J. (1986) *L'âge du Cuivre: la civilisation du vase campaniforme*. Paris, Errance.

Henton, A. (2013) La céramique du Bronze final dans le haut Bassin de l'Escaut et ses marges côtières. Première approche typo-chronologique et culturelle. In W Leclercq and E. Warmembol (eds) *Echanges de bons procédés. La céramique du Bronze final dans le nord-ouest de l'Europe*, 145–168. Bruxelles, CReA-Patrimoine.

Klejn, L. S. (1982) *Archaeological Typology*. British Archaeological Report S53. Oxford, British Archaeological Reports.

Kossina, G. (1912) *Die deutsche Vorgeschichte, eine hervorragend nationale Wissenschaft*. Leipzig, Curt Kabitzsch.

Leclercq, W. (2013) Regards sur l'Orient : analyse des rapports entre les bassins rhénan, mosan et scaldien à travers une approche typologique du matériel céramique du Bronze final. In W. Leclercq and E. Warmembol (eds) *Echanges de bons procédés. La céramique du Bronze final dans le nord-ouest de l'Europe*, 199–222. Bruxelles, CReA-Patrimoine.

Northover, J.-P. (1982) The exploration of long-distance movement of bronze in Bronze and Early Iron Age Europe. *Institute of Archaeology Bulletin* 19, 45–72.

O'Connor, B. (1980) *Cross-Chanel Relations in the Later Bronze Age*. British Archaeological Report S91. Oxford, British Archaeological Reports.

Pare, C. (2000) (ed.) *Metals Make the World go Round. The Supply and Circulation of Metals in Bronze Age Europe*. Oxford, Oxbow Books.

Pennors, F. (2004) Analyse fonctionnelle et pondérale des dépôts et trouvailles isolées de l'âge du Bronze en France. Thèse de Doctorat, (dactylographié). Paris, University of Paris I.

Quilliec, B. (2003) L'épée atlantique : échanges et prestige au Bronze final. Thèse de Doctorat, (dactylographié). Paris, University of Paris I.

Roymans, N. (1991) Late urnfield societies in the Northwest European Plain and the expanding networks of Central European Hallstatt groups. In N. Roymans and F. Theuws (eds) *Images of the Past. Studies on Ancient Societies in Northwestern Europe. Studies in Pre- en Protohistorie 7*, 9–89. Amsterdam, Instituut voor Pre- en Protohistorische Archeologie.

Savory, H. N. (1949) The Atlantic Bronze Age in south-west Europe. *Proceedings of the Prehistoric Society* 15, 128–155.

Water between two worlds – reflections on the explanatory value of archaeological finds in a Bronze Age river landscape

Christoph Huth

Abstract

This article explores the explicative value of Bronze Age archaeological finds from the Upper Rhine valley. It discusses various aspects of the metal finds dredged from the river – their quality and quantity, the circumstances of their discovery and their distribution in space and time – and proposes the notion of the river as a border zone between different spheres of the Bronze Age world. The liminal character of the Rhine as a frontier between the world of the living and the other-world is particularly evident in the deposition of metal objects in the river. This practice is placed in a long-term perspective by comparing the river finds of the Bronze Age with religious sites of the Iron Age. Brief mention is made of the potential of contextualising archaeological finds of all kinds (depositions, settlements, burials) in the geographical, geological and environmental data.

Keywords: Upper Rhine, river landscape, Bronze Age, settlement archaeology, archaeological formation processes, explicative value of archaeological finds, archaeology of religion.

Résumé

Cet article traite de l'interprétation des découvertes archéologiques de la vallée du Haut Rhin. Il discute des différents aspects des trouvailles draguées dans la rivière : leur qualité et quantité, les circonstances de leur découverte et leur distribution entre d'espace et de date ; il propose d'appréhender la notion de rivière comme une zone frontière entre différentes sphères du monde de l'Âge du bronze. Le caractère de limite du Rhin comme frontière entre le monde des vivants et les autres mondes est particulièrement évident dans la pratique du dépôt d'objets métalliques dans le fleuve. Cette pratique est mise en perspective sur la longue durée grâce à des comparaisons entre les trouvailles en rivière de l'Âge du bronze et les sites religieux de l'Âge du fer. Une brève mention est faite sur le potentiel d'une contextualisation des trouvailles archéologiques de différents types (dépôts, habitats, tombes) dans un cadre géographique, géologique et environnemental.

Mots-clés: Rhin supérieur, fond de vallée alluviale, Âge du Bronze, archéologie de l'habitat, processus de formation des gisements archéologiques, valeur informative des faits archéologiques, archéologie de la religion.

Introduction

'The Rhine is the river of which all world speaks yet no one explores, which everyone visits yet no one knows, which you perceive in passing and then quickly forget, which gets swept by every glance yet no one intellectually examines.' Victor Hugo, *Le Rhin* (1842)

The Rhine has always been a means of communication and trade between landscapes and settlements. It is a connective route as well as a natural barrier, and with its floodplains it is an important economic resource. The Rhine is the only river that connects the Alps to the North Sea.

Yet there are not only links between landscapes and people, but also between different spheres of the world, i.e. the world of the living and the other-world. For the Bronze Age one can assume that this dimension of the Rhine, and of water in general, held special importance. In the following the Rhine of the Bronze Age will be regarded mainly from an archaeo-religious angle. Furthermore, its role as an economic and settlement area as well as its historical importance will be examined. The focus will be on the Upper Rhine, which refers to the 350 km between Basel and Bingen. Of course, most of the discussed issues are applicable to the Rhine in general.

The Rhine is Germany's longest and biggest river. The symbolic significance of the Rhine is well known among romanticists, especially in Germany. Yet the most beautiful exaggeration was written by a French poet, Alphonse de Lamartine, who in his Marseillaise of 1841 described the Rhine as 'the Nile of the Occident'. Whether the Rhine of the Bronze Age can live up to this comparison remains to be verified.

Geographical conditions

We must however begin with a critical evaluation of the archaeological sources, particularly when examining landscapes which undergo extreme changes, as is the case with river landscapes. The appearance of the Rhine has drastically changed, primarily over the last two centuries (Musall 1969). What remains is a watercourse which has been completely domesticated by construction projects. Furthermore, the landscape of the Rhine Valley has been severely marked by its intensive industrial use, and agriculture has lastingly altered its original appearance.

The transformation of the landscape is not solely due to humans. Before the Rhine was artificially regulated it continually changed its appearance and found new paths for itself (Galluser and Schenker 1992). The original, non-regulated river, flowed between Basel and Mainz in steadily changing paths (Fig. 17.1). In the south, between Basel and Strasbourg, is the so called braided river zone, in which the Rhine has a 2–3 km wide drainage area with numerous smaller branches and islands. The area between Strasbourg and Karlsruhe is a transitional zone in which the meanders, which are typical for the northern section of the Rhine, gradually start to emerge. In this meander zone the Rhine flows in a single riverbed which cuts through the landscape in large winding loops which incorporate all of the Rhine valley. The southern part of the upper Rhine plain is also crossed by a further river: the Ill, which flows in parallel to the Rhine and gave the whole landscape its name, the Alsace (German *Elsass*).

One can easily imagine that conditions for the preservation of archaeological material in the described circumstances are conceivably poor. In the braided river zone the water changes its course with every flood. In the meander zone the changes take place over a longer period but affect the whole floodplain up to the edge of the alluvial terrace. Without question the river has washed away a lot of archaeological material.

It is not simply about the circumstances in which the archaeological material is preserved. It is just as important to gain an idea of what the landscape originally looked like. The meander zone describes a winding river including stagnant ponds of water and swamps. The braided river zone is made up of countless smaller rivers and gravel islands surrounded by softwood. The hardwood plains are almost devoid of streams; on the outer edge of the floodplain there are many pools and crystal clear springs. We are certainly dealing with an extremely variable water landscape which is very different to the one we see today. Naturally the vegetation was also altered by human interference. Originally the floodplain was covered by woods. Therefore, the upper Rhine valley was an area that was several kilometres across, not easily accessible, and if crossed most certainly required exact geographical knowledge of the area.

Thus the Rhine did not only connect people, it also separated them. One can assume that this double meaning of the river played an important role in the perception of life and religion for Bronze Age society, particularly so when viewing its role as a border between two worlds, the world of the living and the other-world.

River finds

All the previously discussed topics are important when analysing the archaeological data of such a landscape. Metal artefacts from the river are the most prominent group. River finds are typical of, yet not exclusive to, the Bronze Age (Torbrügge 1996). They are first found in the Neolithic and appear throughout prehistory in various forms. Bronze Age metalwork is also found in the Rhine, yet not in the Nile (Wegner 1976; Logel 2007; Huth *et al.* 2008; Behrends 1999; Görner 2003; Zimmermann 1970). Throughout this period metal objects were deposited in many different bodies of water: rivers, lakes and bogs, in springs and even in the ocean. Rivers that are especially known for the sheer number of metal artefacts are the Thames (Needham and Burgess 1980; York 2002), the Loire (Briard 1971; Cordier 1985), the Seine (Mohen 1977), the Saône (Bonnamour 2000a) as well as the Rhine, the Main, the Inn and the Danube (Torbrügge 1972). The finds are not spread evenly along the rivers, but gather in certain places and are completely absent in others. A recent map which shows metalwork from rivers in southern Germany during the periods Bz C to Ha A demonstrates this in a striking way (Falkenstein 2005).

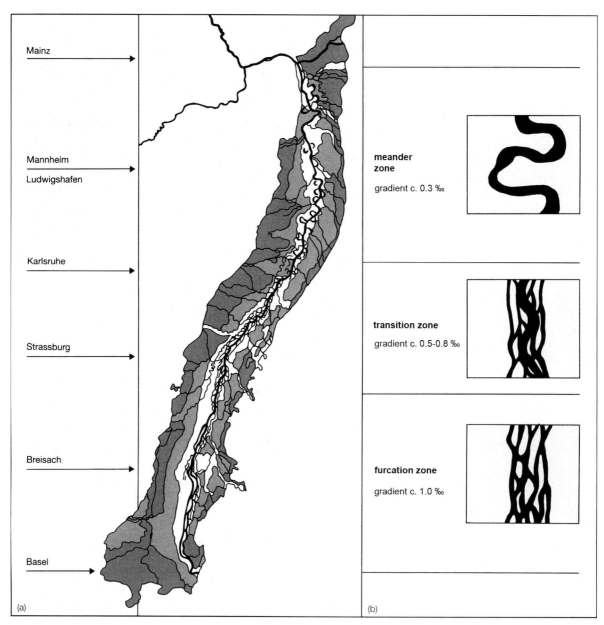

Fig. 17.1. Flowing regime of the upper Rhine between Basel and Mainz (after Galluser and Schenker 1992, 5 Fig. 3).

The complete absence of finds on the southern part of the upper Rhine is particularly eye-catching.

The distribution of river finds strongly depends on the conditions of discovery. The finds accumulate anywhere the riverbed is being dredged or gravel is being extracted. Heritage institutions and museums with curators willing to purchase new objects also add to the total of objects known. There are certain places that are well known for their accumulation of artefacts like the Rhine near Mainz (Wegner 1976), the Thames near London (Needham and Burgess 1980) or the Seine near Paris (Mohen 1977). However, one has to be very careful with regard to the provenance of these finds, which are extremely inaccurate

considering the size of Paris or London. Nevertheless, it has been demonstrated that in all three cases – Paris, London and Mainz – the tremendous number of retrieved objects actually reflects prehistoric realities to a great extent (Wegner 1976, Needham and burgess 1980; Mohen 1977). So, it is always of utmost importance to understand exactly why and how the objects were discovered and which archaeological formation processes played a role.

Under closer scrutiny however the complete lack of archaeological material in the southern region of the upper Rhine turns out to be an artefact (Fig. 17.2). Recent investigations in local heritage institutions on the upper Rhine, in museums and private collections have produced an impressive amount of objects stemming from virtually all periods (Logel 2007; Huth *et al.* 2008). These not only included artefacts from the Rhine, the Ill, and other watercourses but all objects discovered on the floodplains between the glacial terraces. Remembering the change the river flow has undergone over time, it makes sense to consider any object that is not directly associated with a grave, settlement or hoard to be a potential river find. In this way the empty area starts filling up, yet spaces void of metalwork still remain. Also, the overall amount of objects still does not compare to that of other sections of the river.

As in most other places the finds are mainly comprised of weapons, axes and ornaments, *i.e.* objects which are worn directly upon the body. The artefacts are in useable condition, certainly not new but not damaged beyond repair. Many objects are very precious due to their rarity, such as the helmet that was found in the Rhine near Basel (Logel 2007, 50 fig. 7; *cf.* Wirth 2007) or the pendant and the wild boar tusk which were found in the Karlsruhe area (Figs 17.3–4). It is well known that intact defensive arms are mainly found in waters, while fragments are also known from scrap hoards.

Tools are relatively rare among river finds. Sickles are probably the most common tools documented. Awls may occasionally have been tools but can also be seen as part of the toiletry. They may have been used as tattoo needles and thus belong to the artefacts that have a close physical connection to their owner. Fishing hooks are generally categorised as accidental losses. This however may have been a rash interpretation as fishing hooks are also known from Bronze and Iron Age graves where they seem to have specific meaning (Huth 2003, 256 with footnote 598).

The selection and condition of metalwork makes it plausible that the finds are not merely accidental losses or objects that were washed away from settlement sites or graves. Many years ago Walter Torbrügge pointed out that these finds must primarily be religious offerings and ever since then his conclusion has been repeated many times, often without giving it further thought (Torbrügge 1972).

Torbrügge's assertion may readily apply to most objects from rivers. But the picture we get of the original circumstances is often distorted by various filters active in the archaeological record. This refers to the very conspicuous fact that most artefacts are intact. Generally, it is assumed that smaller objects are missing because they are simply overlooked during the dredging of the riverbed or gravel pit. But this is not the case as can be seen by the fishing hooks and awls that have been found. The line of separation can be seen between the intact and recognizable objects on the one hand and the damaged and less identifiable ones on the other. Objects that are intact and recognizable in form and function are more likely to be picked up and recognized for what they are. This is a well-known and well documented

phenomenon with hoards and it is no different when it comes to finds from waters (Huth 2008, 132).

This is demonstrated by a collection of finds that were recovered in exceptionally good condition from the Silbersee near Roxheim (Sperber 2006). The complex is comprised of 412 objects, most stemming from the 11th–9th century BC (Figs 17.5–7). The selection is essentially made up of ornaments and weapons, among them 100 pins, 49 smaller rings and 25 bracelets, also 33 spearheads, 27 swords, 18 axes and 1 fragment of a helmet. The sheer number of very small, intricate objects such as awls, burins, sewing needles and all kinds of dress fittings is astounding. Sickles are dominant among the tools numbering ten in total. The seven fishing hooks also correspond to the range of objects found in rivers elsewhere. In contrast, fragments from wagons or horse-gear are rarely found. Metalwork debris, rough copper and ingot fragments are rare but occasionally also known from other rivers.

Many of the objects seem to have been willfully destroyed or damaged before being deposited, some of them also showing visible fire damage. The weapons are especially damaged, ornaments and other artefacts to a much lesser extent. Most of the smaller objects seem completely undamaged. At first glance the corpus of finds resembles the scrap hoards known from the late Bronze Age, especially those from France, and indeed many types originating in Western Europe can be found among the artefacts. But under closer examination fundamental differences quickly become apparent, such as the fact that many fragments fit together perfectly which is rarely the case in hoards. Furthermore, it is highly unlikely that we are dealing with a closed find considering that the objects originate from a period spanning two to three centuries.

It is also very uncommon to find fire damaged bronzes in hoards. In contrast to this bigger lumps of molten and fused bronzes are well known from rivers (Fig. 17.8) such as the Thames (Burgess *et al.* 1972, 266 fig. 24) and the Seine (Mohen 1977, 181 figs 361–71) and also from Lake Neuchâtel (Müller 1993, 81 fig. 7). It has been proven that these are not the relics of a cancelled production process. If the goal was to melt down older bronzes and reuse the metal for new items the bronzes would have had to have been broken down into much smaller pieces. Rather these partly fused lumps of bronze show that specific actions preceded the deposition, meaning that at least some objects were not just simply thrown into the water.

The example of Roxheim illustrates that we also need to reckon with completely different things than before if the observational circumstances are good. This is also supported by the detailed investigations into the files of the heritage institutions. In any case this opens up entirely new approaches to the interpretation of finds from water. However, in the face of all this, it is important not to forget all the intact weapons and ornaments found in

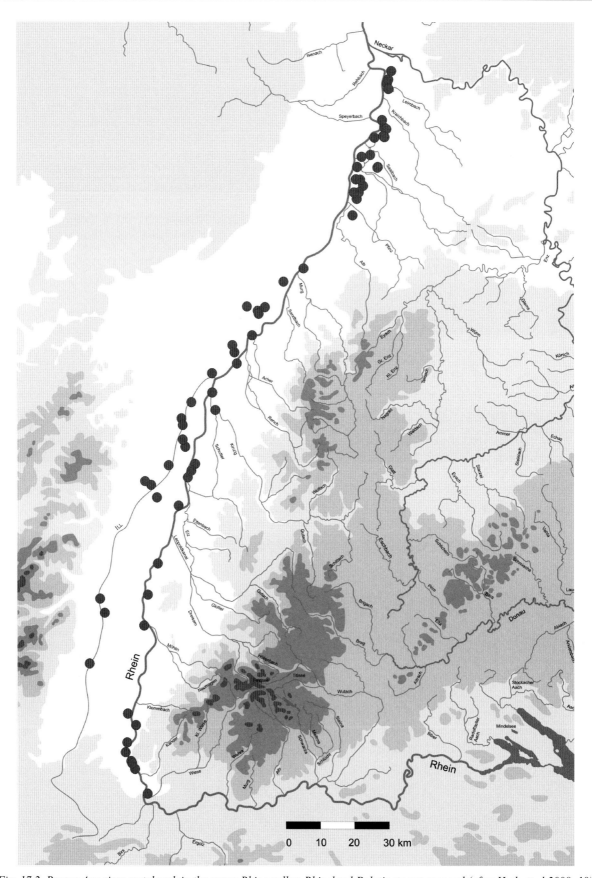

Fig. 17.2. Bronze Age river metalwork in the upper Rhine valley. Rhineland-Palatinate not mapped (after Huth et al 2008, 19).

Fig. 17.3. Karlsruhe-Neureut. Bronze pectoral. Length as illustrated c 64 cm (after Behrends 1999, 88 Fig. 3).

watercourses that do not appear in graves, settlements or hoards in this form.

Encounters with the numinous

There are many theories as to why bronzes were deposited in water. Walter Torbrügge has presented many of these, especially the idea that water is a boundary between the worlds of the living and the dead which is well-known from ancient times (Torbrügge 1972; 1996). In more recent times the assumption has been put forward that it may be a case of ostentatiously destroyed prestige goods (Bradley 1990). German researchers however favor the theory that these bronzes are gifts to the gods (Hänsel and Hänsel 1997).

Each of these theories has convincing arguments on its side, but these will not be further discussed. Instead the archaeological record shall be regarded from a long term perspective. First of all it stands out that throughout time there are only very few river finds. They occur sporadically, although they do seem to cumulate in certain places. Large accumulations of metalwork, such as the one in Roxheim or from the Rhine near Mainz are the exception. Even if one accounts for the disparate chances of discovery combined with the high loss rate in the archaeological record one has to reach the conclusion that bronzes being deposited in waters are an entirely ephemeral occurrence. That special locations are sought out over a longer period of time for the purpose of performing religious acts is probably only true for particular cases. Thus we are not dealing with a long lasting tradition, especially not the formation of downright cults, meaning a larger community of people who congregate to fulfill their collective religious duties.

The contrast becomes more apparent when comparing the corpus of finds to that of other locations with religious relevance. Think of the numerous rock carvings at Mont Bégo (de Lumley 1995) and in Valcamonica (Huth 2006),

where evidence of religious activities can be found in their thousands. The conditions for preservation of the rock carvings are of course conceivably better than those for the water finds. But the Bronze Age river finds cannot even compare to places such as La Tène (Betschart 2007) or the Duchcov spring in Bohemia (Kruta 1971) and especially not to sanctuaries like in Venetia (Pascucci 1990) or by the sources of the river Seine (Deyts 1983).

The sanctuaries of the Iron Age, more than any others, illustrate the change in conditions compared to the Bronze Age. As different as each of these sites may seem, they share a number of characteristics that cannot be found in the Bronze Age. Among these are the sheer number of finds combined with the continual use of these sites over several centuries, the catchment area of these sanctuaries that reaches far beyond the local settlement and finally the change over from votive objects to figural, particularly anthropomorphic offerings. Regardless of whether these anthropomorphic figures symbolize the deity, the donor or both, it is a type of personification and concretion of something that previously only appeared in very vague forms. Not least the first theonyms are also known from this time (Huth 2003, 220–2).

The appearance of anthropomorphic artwork and the encounter with the deity in a specific place expresses increased self-awareness, a greater capability of taking action in face of the numinous that is now being faced head on. This self-awareness is part of a decentralization process in which man distances himself from the natural order of things and increasingly begins to organize himself (Dux 1994, 207–9; Huth 2003, 271–94).

None of this can be found in the Bronze Age. Meanwhile the ephemeral nature of Bronze Age finds correlates well with the nature of the offerings. Predominantly these objects are carried directly upon the body, notably weapons or ornaments, *i.e.* personal possessions. It is fair to assume

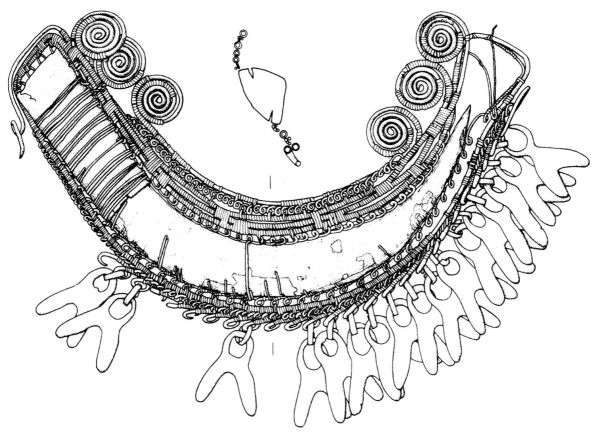

Fig. 17.4. Karlsruhe-Neureut. Tusk of a wild boar ornamented with bronze fittings. Length approximately 20 cm (after Behrends 1999, 92 Fig. 8).

that these artefacts are supposed to symbolize the donor himself.

Making contact with the numinous by offering up personal belongings is characteristic of any religious act throughout prehistoric times. It is not relevant to what shape this numinous entity takes – be it deities, ancestral spirits or any kind of supernatural power. Much more important is that this numinous power is not faced in person, as is the case with later anthropomorphic figures. Instead a personal object is offered up, taking the place of its owner (Kossack 1999). Surely these were not purely material goods, but objects that were of great personal value to their owner. Georg Kossack meaningfully described this as the secret life-force of an item. It is no accident that many artefacts are decorated with religious symbols, such as the stylized water bird on the hilts of Late Bronze Age swords (Lenerz-de Wilde 2009). The lancet shaped pendants on the pectoral found in Karlsruhe-Neureut may also have a symbolic meaning (Kossack 1998).

Communities that do not have a permanent sanctuary will not have any temples either. They simply do not exist in the Bronze Age apart from the alleged temple from Barger-Oosterveld in the province of Drenthe cf. van den Broeke 2005). The numinous is not domesticated; it does not reside in one specific place, but it is present anywhere it appears in whatever shape this may be. In the Bronze Age, and especially during the urnfield period this most certainly means water in any of its forms, a river, stream, spring, well, lake, bog, or ocean. Acts of devotion are restricted to individuals, to a group of families or smaller settlement communities. It never transgresses to a higher level, to supra-local cults which are independent of single families and settlements. Temples and anthropomorphic figures as offerings only start appearing in the Iron Age (Kossack 1999). Liminal places at the very edge of the settled area are sought out instead.

Settlements, graves and routes

The following lines will give a short overview of the settlement areas. Analyzing the settlement history along the Rhine is difficult because the impression we get at any given place strongly depends on the current state of research. In many regions there is a lot of work that has yet to be done. The area around Freiburg is the only region that has an up-to-date study available (Mischka 2007; for the regions on the left bank of the Rhine see Treffort 2009).

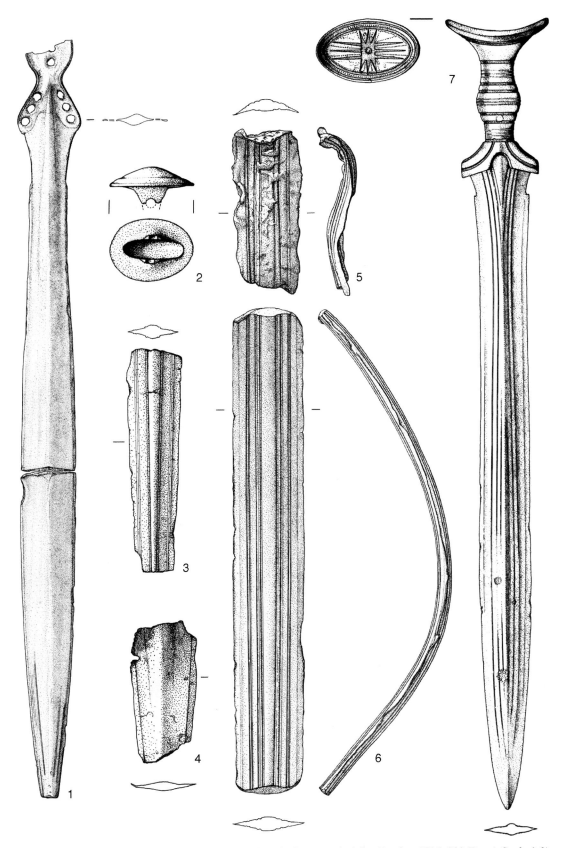

Fig. 17.5. Silbersee near Bobenheim-Roxheim, Lkr. Ludwigshafen: swords (after Sperber 2006, 202 Fig. 4. Scale 1:2).

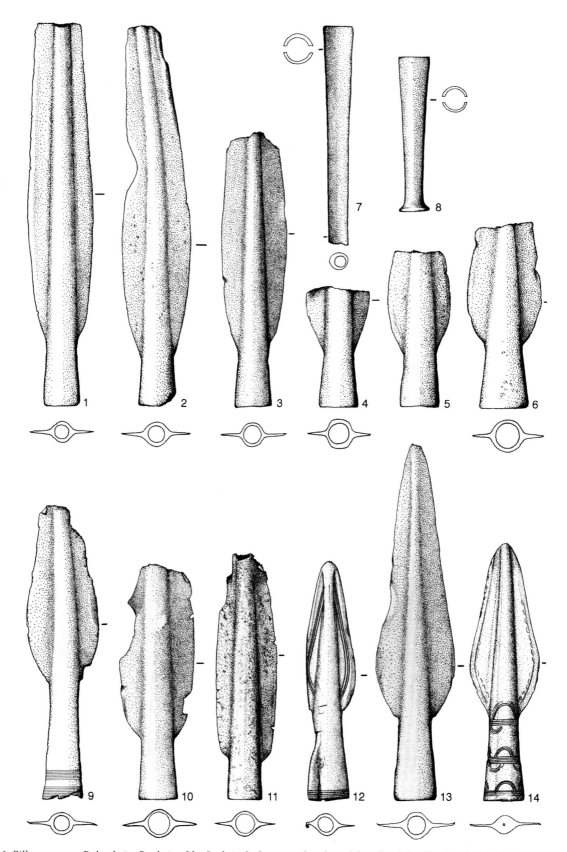

Fig. 17.6. Silbersee near Bobenheim-Roxheim, Lkr. Ludwigshafen: spearheads and ferrules (after Sperber 2006, 204 Fig. 6. Scale 1:2).

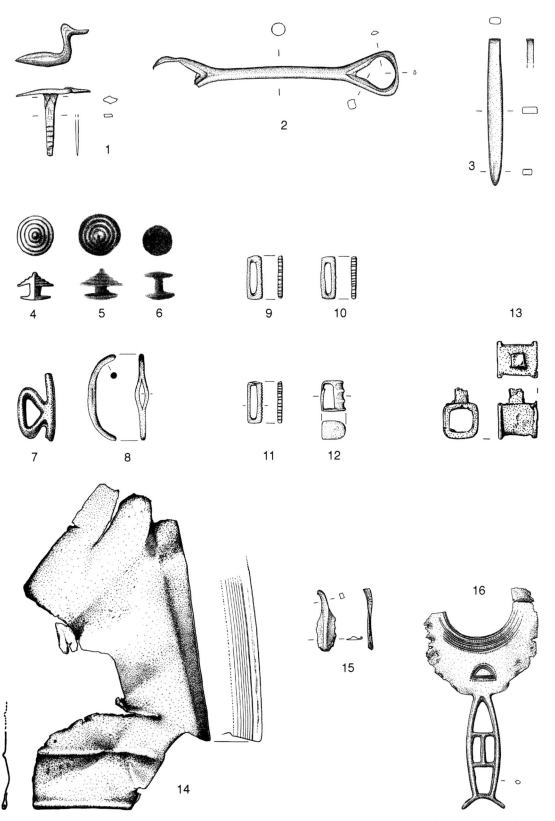

Fig. 17.7. Silbersee near Bobenheim-Roxheim, Lkr. Ludwigshafen: small objects (after Sperber 2006, 205 Fig. 7. Scale 1:2).

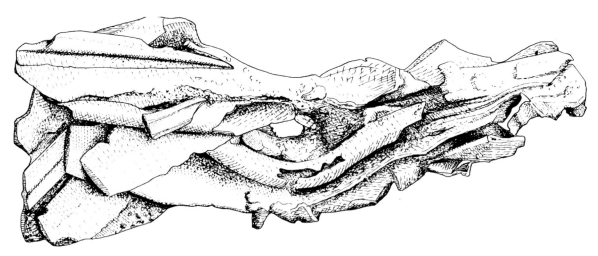

Fig. 17.8. Molten lumps of bronzes (socketed axe, sword fragments, chapes, spearhead, ferrules) from the river Seine near Paris (after Mohen 1977, 131 Fig. 361–71. Not to scale).

When studying a settlement area it is again important to consider the archaeological formation processes. The emerging picture we get of the southern upper Rhine is revealing (Fig. 17.9). Settlement areas are safe from floods and have good soils which are easy to farm. Besides open settlements there are also hilltop settlements, namely the Isteiner Klotz, the Burgberg near Burkheim, and perhaps also the Schönberg near Freiburg. The hilltop settlements situated directly on the Rhine were most likely distribution places for goods, a role which did not change much throughout historic times. The publication of finds from the excavations in Breisach and Burkheim should be awaited before drawing further conclusions.

There is little proof of boats being used for transportation on the Rhine. However, this is not significant considering there is only one known boat find on the upper Rhine from the Middle Ages. As expected, the floodplains did not yield any settlement sites, even though some subsistence activities are to be expected there. A seasonal occupation of gravel islands by hunters, trappers and fishers is conceivable.

One of the indicators for settlements are graves. They are normally found within the settlement area (Mischka 2007). This rule however does not apply to burial mounds. The Ried near Strasbourg, a swampy area with many rivers, is a good example of this. No settlement in the Ried can be proven since the Bronze Age, yet there are many tumuli, some of which also date to the Iron Age (Flotté and Fuchs 2000, 438–43), indicating both Bronze and Iron Age settlement. Beyond the alluvial plains there are burial mounds constructed along the glacial terraces, thus right on the border between the settlement area on the high ground and the water meadows (Logel 2007). And with this we suddenly find ourselves back on the topic of frontiers and connecting paths. The double symbolism of the topographic

and the religious liminality is obvious. Where should the burial mounds be built, if not there?

When contemplating the borders and connecting paths of the Rhine valley on a large scale one quickly reaches the conclusion that these are often not recognizable, especially not on distribution maps. As usual we are dealing with distribution patterns that overlap each other and follow a polythetic order. This means that depending on which map we chose we may be in the center or more towards the periphery of things. Another complicating factor is that existing maps, most of them from the *Prähistorische Bronzefunde* project (PBF), always use the Rhine as their border. Maps transgressing the Rhine are nowhere to be found, and are arduous to produce.

On a small scale it is a completely different matter, especially when including all archaeological parameters, not just the finds themselves but also settlements, graves and geographical factors. Thierry Logel applied this to the southern region of the upper Rhine. In fact we mainly find connections across the Rhine, particularly when keeping in mind the locations of hilltop settlements and possible points of crossing the Rhine (Logel 2007). By the way this is also the case during the Iron Age.

So, there are many questions that remain to be answered, both on a large scale and in detail. Studies including all available archaeological data and geographical parameters are especially important. Of course, this is only possible for smaller areas and calls for a lot of dedication and diligence. But the potential for new insights is all the greater. Elsewhere, particularly in France, research into Bronze Age river landscapes is much further advanced – so much so that handbooks on the subject matter have been published (Bonnamour 2000b; Dumont 2006)

What remains to be discussed is the Rhine as a historical area. Comparing the historical importance of the Rhine and

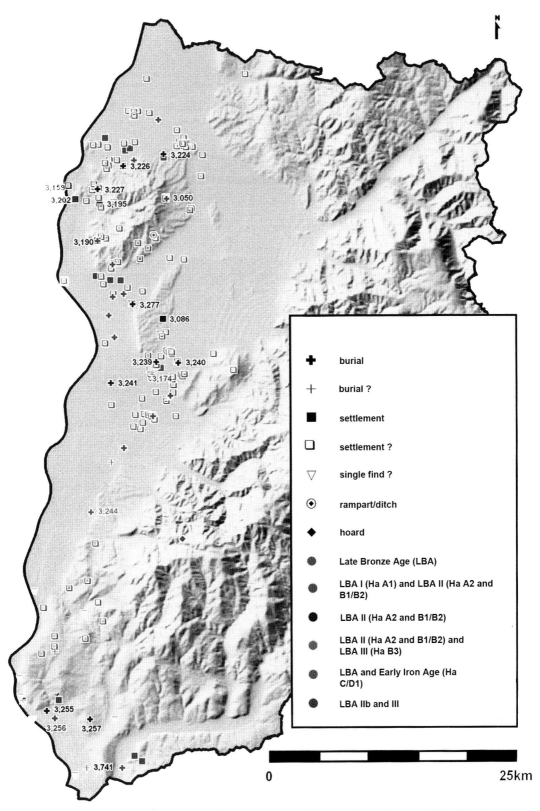

Legend:

+ burial

+ burial ?

■ settlement

□ settlement ?

▽ single find ?

◉ rampart/ditch

◆ hoard

● Late Bronze Age (LBA)

● LBA I (Ha A1) and LBA II (Ha A2 and B1/B2)

● LBA II (Ha A2 and B1/B2)

● LBA II (Ha A2 and B1/B2) and LBA III (Ha B3)

● LBA and Early Iron Age (Ha C/D1)

● LBA IIb and III

0   25km

Fig. 17.9. Late Bronze Age settlement indicators between Basel and Freiburg (after Mischka 2007, 183 Fig. 6.25).

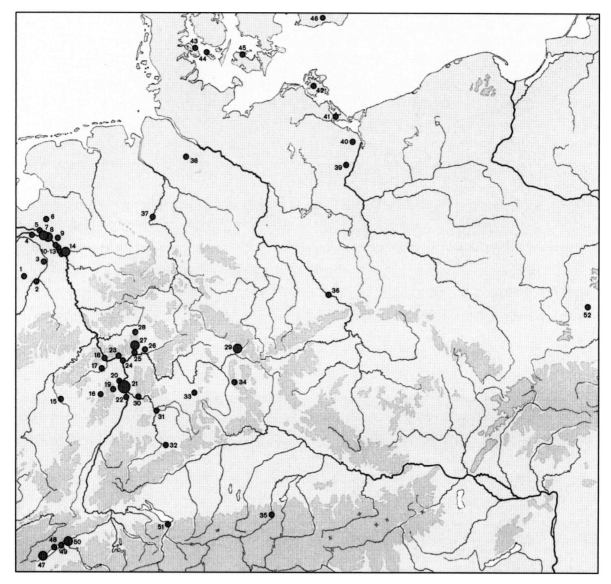

Fig. 17.10. Atlantic metalwork in central Europe at the end of the Bronze Age (Hallstatt B3) (after Sperber 2006, 363 Fig. 3).

the Nile during the Bronze Age, the Nile wins hands down. One does not have to be stuck on the idea of *ex oriente lux* to realize that other European rivers, such as the Rhône or the Danube hold greater importance than the Rhine, at least from a cultural geographic point of view. An exaggeration would be that the Rhine simply flows in the wrong direction. Yet even in the Bronze Age not everything was imported from the South or Southwest. Just think of the major influx of atlantic bronzes in central Europe towards the end of the Bronze Age (Fig. 17.10), which can be seen at Roxheim as well as in the scrap hoards from the Rhine-Main area (Sperber 2006b, 363 fig. 3). Influx is probably the most fitting word, considering that the Rhine most likely played an essential role.

Bibliography

Behrends, R.-H. (1999) Zwei außergewöhnliche Fundstücke aus Karlsruhe-Neureut. *Fundberichte aus Baden-Württemberg* 23, 87–94.

Betschart, M. (ed.) (2007) *La Tène. Die Untersuchung – Die Fragen – Die Antworten*. Biel, Museum Schwab Biel.

Bonnamour, L. (ed.) (2000a) *Archéologie de la Saône*. Paris, Errance.

Bonnamour, L. (ed.) (2000b) *Archéologie des fleuves et des rivières*. Paris, Errance.

Bradley, R. (1990) *The Passage of Arms*. Cambridge, Cambridge University Press.

Briard, J. (1971) Epées de Bretagne et d'ailleurs jetées dans les rivières à l'âge du Bronze. *Annales de Bretagne* 78 (1), 47–58.

van den Broeke, P. (2005) Gifts to the Gods. Rites and cult sites in the Bronze Age and the Iron Age. In L. P. Louwe Kooijmans, P. W. van den Broeke, H. Fokkens and A. L. van Gijn (eds) *The Prehistory of the Netherlands*, 659–677. Amsterdam, Amsterdam University Press.

Burgess, C., Coombs, D. and Davies, G. (1972) The Broadward Complex and barbed spearheads. In F. Lynch and C. Burgess (eds) *Prehistoric Man in Wales and the West. Essays in Honour of Lily F. Chitty*, 211–283. Bath, Adams & Dart.

Cordier, G. (1985) 'Nouveaux' objets de l'Age du Bronze tirés de la Loire. *Revue archéologique du Centre de la France* 24 (1), 63–68.

Deyts, S. (1983) *Les bois sculptés des sources de la Seine*. Paris, CNRS.

Dumont, A. (ed.) (2006) *Archéologie des lacs et des cours d'eau*. Paris, Errance.

Dux, G. (1994) Die ontogenetische und historische Entwicklung des Geistes. In G. Dux and U. Wenzel (eds) *Der Prozeß der Geistesgeschichte. Studien zur ontogenetischen und historischen Entwicklung des Geistes*, 173–224. Frankfurt, Suhrkamp.

Falkenstein, F. (2005) Zu den Gewässerfunden der älteren Urnenfelderzeit in Süddeutschland. In B. Horejs, R. Jung, E. Kaiser and B. Teržan (eds) *Interpretationsraum Bronzezeit. Bernhard Hänsel von seinen Schülern gewidmet*, 491–504. Bonn, Habelt.

Flotté, P. and Fuchs, M. (2000) Le Bas-Rhin. *Carte archéologique de la Gaule* 67-1. Paris, Académie des Inscriptions et Belles-Lettres.

Galluser, W. A. and Schenker, A. (1992) *Die Auen am Oberrhein – Les zones alluviales du Rhin supérieur*. Basel, Birkhäuser.

Görner, I. (2003) Die Mittel- und Spätbronzezeit zwischen Mannheim und Karlsruhe. *Fundberichte aus Baden-Württemberg* 27, 79–279.

Hänsel, A. and Hänsel, B. (eds) (1997) *Gaben an die Götter. Schätze der Bronzezeit Europas*. Berlin, Staatliche Museen zu Berlin – Preußischer Kulturbesitz.

Huth, C. (2003) *Menschenbilder und Menschenbild. Anthropomorphe Bildwerke der frühen Eisenzeit*. Berlin, Reimer.

Huth, C. (2006) s.v. Valcamonica. In H. Beck, D. Geuenich and H. Steuer (eds) *Reallexikon der Germanischen Altertumskunde 32*, 34–40. Berlin, de Gruyter.

Huth, C. (2008) Horte als Geschichtsquelle. In K. Schmotz (ed.), *Vorträge des 26. Niederbayerischen Archäologentages*, 131–162. Rahden/Westfalen, Leidorf.

Huth, C., Logel, T. and Schmid, C. (2008) Versenkt, verloren, vergessen – bronzezeitliche Gewässerfunde vom Oberrhein. *Archäologische Nachrichten aus Baden* 76–7, 18–19.

Kossack, G. (1998) Von der verborgenen Lebenskraft der Dinge. Nordtiroler Gehängefibeln aus der frühen Eisenzeit als sakrale Zeichen. *Veröffentlichungen des Tiroler Landesmuseums Ferdinandeum* 78, 71–87.

Kossack, G. (1999) *Religiöses Denken in dinglicher und bildlicher Überlieferung Alteuropas aus der Spätbronze- und frühen Eisenzeit (9.–6. Jahrhundert v. Chr. Geb.)*. München, Bayerische Akademie der Wissenschaften.

Kruta, V. (1971) *Le trésor de Duchcov dans les collections tschéchoslovaques*. Duchcov, Severočeské Naklad.

Lenerz-de Wilde, M. (2009) Wasservögel – Sonnenbarken – eine Schiffsreise. In S. Grunwald, J. K. Koch, D. Mölders, U. Sommer and S. Wolfram (eds) *Artefact. Festschrift für Sabine Rieckhoff zum 65. Geburtstag*, 723–736. Bonn, Habelt.

Logel, T. (2007) Les dépôts de métal en milieu humide et les gués sur le Rhin et l'Ill à l'Âge du Bronze: présentation préliminaire. *Cahiers alsaciens d'archéologie, d'art et d'histoire* 50, 27–50.

de Lumley, H. (ed.) (1995) *Le grandiose et le sacré*. Aix-en-Provence, Edisud.

Mischka, D. (2007) *Methodische Aspekte zur Rekonstruktion prähistorischer Siedlungsmuster. Landschaftsgenese vom Ende des Neolithikums bis zur Eisenzeit im Gebiet des südlichen Oberrheins*. Rahden/Westfalen, Leidorf.

Mohen, J.-P. (1977) *L'Age du Bronze dans la région de Paris*. Paris, Éditions des Musées Nationaux.

Müller, F. (1993) Argumente zur Deutung von 'Pfahlbaubronzen'. *Jahrbuch der Schweizerischen Gesellschaft für Ur- und Frühgeschichte* 76, 71–92.

Musall, H. (1969) *Die Entwicklung der Kulturlandschaft der Rheinniederung zwischen Karlsruhe und Speyer vom Ende des 16. bis zum Ende des 19. Jahrhunderts*. Heidelberg, Geographisches Institut der Universität Heidelberg.

Needham, S. and Burgess, C. B. (1980) The later Bronze Age in the lower Thames valley: the metalwork evidence. In J. C. Barrett and R. J. Bradley (eds) *Settlement and Society in the British Later Bronze Age, 437–70*, British Archaeological Report 83. Oxford, British Archaeological Reports.

Pascucci, P. (1990) *I depositi votivi Paleoveneti. Per un'archeologia del culto*. Padova, Archaeologia Veneta.

Sperber, L. (2006) Bronzezeitliche Flussdeponierungen aus dem Altrhein bei Roxheim, Gde. Bobenheim-Roxheim, Lkr. Ludwigshafen – Ein Vorbericht. *Archäologisches Korrespondenzblatt* 36 (2), 195–214; 36 (3), 359–368.

Torbrügge, W. (1972) Vor- und frühgeschichtliche Flußfunde. Zur Ordnung und Bestimmung einer Denkmälergruppe. *Bericht der Römisch-Germanischen Kommission* 51–2, 1–146.

Torbrügge, W. (1996) Spuren in eine andere Welt. Archäologie der vorzeitlichen Wasserkulte. In M. Almagro-Gorbea *et al. Archäologische Forschungen zum Kultgeschehen in der jüngeren Bronzezeit und frühen Eisenzeit Alteuropas*, 567–581. Regensburg, Universitätsverlag Regensburg.

Treffort, J.-M. (2009) L'âge du Bronze. In M. Châtelet (ed.), *Fouilles et découvertes en Alsace*, 42–57. Rennes, Éditions Ouest-France.

Wegner, G. (1976) *Die vorgeschichtlichen Flußfunde aus dem Main und aus dem Rhein bei Mainz*. Kallmünz, Lassleben.

Wirth, St. (2007) Tombé dans l'eau? Les découvertes de casques en milieu humide. In Ph. Barral, A. Daubigney, C. Dunning, G. Kaenel and M.-J. Roulière-Lambert (eds) *L'âge du fer dans l'arc jurassien et ses marges*, 449–461. Besançon, Presses Uni Franche Comté.

York, J. (2002) The life cycle of bronze age metalwork from the Thames. *Oxford Journal of Archaeology* 21 (1), 77–92.

Zimmermann, W. H. (1970) Urgeschichtliche Opferfunde aus Flüssen, Mooren, Quellen und Brunnen Südwestdeutschlands. *Neue Ausgrabungen und Forschungen in Niedersachsen* 6, 53–92.

18

Le passage des Alpes : voyages et échanges entre l'Italie et la Suisse (2200–700 av. J.-C.)

Mireille David-Elbiali

Abstract

Very old privileged relationships exist between Piedmont, Western Lombardy, Western Alpine regions and those located northwest of the Alps. In the alpine area of western Switzerland, they can be highlighted for the Bronze Age thanks to the archaeological material, particularly bronze objects: some have a distribution limited to the alpine zone, others were on both sides of the Alps or reached remote areas, and there are also copies of foreign objects and very few real imports. Most of these objects are related to exchanges associated with normal activities of the alpine populations, which include limited movements north and south of the Alps, especially from craftsmen or colporteurs. Some evoke exceptional long-distance travels and a third group, also including ceramics, suggests the possibility of population movements, in connection with the RSFO's extension from the 12th century BC. Outside this last period, the influence of the area south of the Alps seems dominant and demonstrates a more rapid cultural change and of a higher level in Northern Italy, due to the proximity of urban civilisations.

Keywords: Alpine region, Bronze Age, exchange, bronze artefacts, ceramics

Résumé

Des liens privilégiés très anciens existent entre le Piémont, la Lombardie occidentale, les régions alpines occidentales et celles situées au nord-ouest des Alpes. Dans la zone alpine de Suisse occidentale, ils peuvent être mis en évidence pour l'Âge du bronze grâce au matériel archéologique, en particulier les objets en bronze : certains ont une diffusion limitée à la zone alpine, d'autres se retrouvent de part et d'autre des Alpes ou ont atteint des régions éloignées, il existe aussi des copies d'objets étrangers et de très rares vraies importations. La plupart de ces objets se rapportent à des échanges liés aux activités normales des populations alpines, qui comprennent des déplacements limités au nord et au sud des Alpes, probablement d'artisans ou de colporteurs ; quelques-uns évoquent des déplacements exceptionnels à longue distance et un troisième groupe, comprenant aussi de la céramique, laisse présumer des déplacements de population de plus grande ampleur, en relation avec l'extension du RSFO à partir du 12e siècle av. J.-C. En dehors de cette dernière période, les influences du sud des Alpes semblent dominantes et témoigner d'une évolution culturelle plus rapide et d'un niveau plus élevé en Italie du Nord, en raison de la proximité des civilisations urbaines.

Mots-clés : région alpine, l'Âge du bronze, échange, objets en bronze, céramique

Introduction

Cette contribution traite des voyages et des échanges dans la partie centre-occidentale des Alpes, entre la Suisse et l'Italie, durant le deuxième millénaire et le début du premier av. J.-C., soit du Bronze ancien au début de l'Âge du fer. L'examen des données archéologiques montre l'existence de liens privilégiés très anciens entre le Piémont, la Lombardie occidentale, les régions alpines occidentales et celles situées au nord-ouest des Alpes. Ces territoires se distinguent culturellement de ceux situés plus à l'est et ceci va perdurer tout au long de la période historique. Cette convergence culturelle semble liée à des réseaux privilégiés de contact et d'échange qui se mettent en place dès le Néolithique.

Quelles analogies entre mer et montagne ?

Bien que cela puisse sembler surprenant de prime abord, la mer et la montagne présentent des caractéristiques similaires sur le plan des voyages et des échanges (Fig. 18.1). Les conditions dans lesquelles ils s'effectuent sont en effet influencées par la topographie ; il est *a priori* plus facile de traverser un paysage terrestre ouvert que de franchir un bras de mer ou une chaîne de montagne. La Manche, pierre angulaire de ce colloque, sert pourtant de trait d'union entre deux rives qui abritent des populations possédant de nombreux traits culturels communs. Les Alpes non plus n'ont jamais représenté une barrière, mais un monde en soi au même titre que la mer. Le monde intra-alpin est formé de vallées et de zones de haute altitude. Ces dernières, tout comme la mer, ne sont pas des lieux d'établissement, mais constituent des territoires exploités pour leurs ressources en matières premières, faune et végétation et parcourus pour se rendre d'un point à un autre. Ce monde intra-alpin est fréquenté par des communautés locales, qui y vivent et entretiennent des rapports réguliers avec les régions de plaine situées au nord comme au sud. Ce sont des membres de ces communautés qui empruntent les chemins qui permettent de franchir les montagnes. Comme la mer, la haute montagne est un territoire dangereux où il est peu recommandé de s'aventurer sans connaissance précise des itinéraires, des temps de parcours et des conditions climatiques. Un équipement adéquat, des provisions, savoir où sont situées les haltes, notamment en cas de mauvais temps, sont nécessaires pour les traverser en minimisant les risques. Ce sont donc les communautés alpines qui assurent le contrôle de ces territoires et la transmission des biens et des idées de part et d'autre de la chaîne, car par leur mode de vie, elles connaissent les différents étages alpins et leurs ressources spécifiques (Fig. 18.2). Elles tireront probablement assez tôt des revenus de leur situation particulière.

Les similitudes entre mer et montagne peuvent se résumer en trois points :

(a) une zone parcourue mais non habitée – pleine mer ou territoires de haute altitude – qui sert plus de trait d'union que de frontière entre des groupes humains installés sur ses marges – rivages ou vallées alpines – ;

(b) des groupes humains qui partagent le même mode de vie de part et d'autre de ces écosystèmes, qui peuvent être qualifiés d'extrêmes, car non habitables ; ils sont souvent plus proches entre eux qu'ils ne le sont des groupes humains qui vivent dans les plaines du même côté de la mer ou des Alpes ;

(c) des écosystèmes qui exigent de leurs riverains le développement de connaissances spécifiques, car les deux peuvent être fatals si on les affronte sans préparation adéquate, ce qui a aussi pour corollaire que des membres de ces populations sont sollicités par les voyageurs qui souhaitent franchir ce qui leur apparaît, à eux, comme des « obstacles » et qu'il est ainsi aisé de contrôler les passages et d'en tirer des revenus.

Caractéristiques géographiques du territoire examiné

Les 750 km de frontière qui séparent l'Italie et la Suisse courent le long des lignes de crête de la chaîne alpine, à l'exception de la plaine tessinoise qui appartient du point de vue géographique et aussi culturel à l'Italie du Nord (Fig. 18.3). C'est dans la partie centre-occidentale que la chaîne alpine est la plus élevée avec des massifs qui atteignent plus de 4000 m d'altitude ; ainsi seuls des cols d'altitude assurent un accès direct entre les deux régions. Ces passages sont limités et ils peuvent devenir infranchissables à certaines saisons ou lors de phases climatiques défavorables. Cet obstacle topographique et climatique n'a toutefois jamais empêché les relations entre les deux versants.

La zone alpine occupe plus de la moitié du territoire suisse et pour passer de l'Italie au Plateau, qui est la région la plus peuplée, il faut encore franchir une vallée intra-alpine et un second col, que ce soit en Valais à l'ouest ou dans les Grisons à l'est, sauf si on emprunte le massif du Gothard à partir du Tessin.

Bref historique du peuplement

Le peuplement alpin, aussi bien sur le versant nord que sur le versant sud, est constitué de groupes culturellement très proches entre lesquels les échanges sont nombreux. Une frontière plus nette semble se marquer avec les populations des plaines. Du point de vue culturel, le monde alpin reçoit des influences qui fluctuent au cours du temps.

Les Alpes de Suisse occidentale, dont il sera question ci-dessous, ont été colonisées progressivement à partir de la fin de la dernière glaciation. Elles ont d'abord été parcourues par des chasseurs mésolithiques venant du sud des Alpes et dont les traces ont été identifiées en haute montagne, notamment dans la région du Cervin et celle du Simplon sur les versants italiens et suisses (Curdy et Praz 2002 ; Curdy 2010, 152). Les installations néolithiques les plus anciennes de la haute vallée du Rhône ont livré une céramique qui montre des liens étroits avec la région de Varese au sud des Alpes (Banchieri 2009, 7–9 ; Gallay 2008, 178). La vallée

intra-alpine du Rhône (Valais) est en étroit contact avec celle de la Dora Baltea (Vallée d'Aoste) pendant tout le Néolithique (Gallay 2008). A l'Âge du bronze, les influences dominantes proviennent le plus souvent du sud des Alpes, mais parfois aussi du nord, comme c'est le cas entre le 11e et le 9e siècle av. J.-C. ; elles côtoient évidemment aussi des traits culturels proprement alpins.

Nature et identification des échanges

Les échanges à distance constituent une part importante de la vie sociale des communautés humaines, ainsi que l'illustre la littérature ethnographique. Ils sont polymorphes : échanges de matières premières et d'objets, d'idées et de personnes (notamment échanges matrimoniaux). Ils impliquent obligatoirement des déplacements de personnes et de biens. Pour les reconstruire, il faut être en mesure d'identifier « l'objet » échangé et, souvent, plus il provient de loin, plus il est facile à reconnaître. En l'absence de récits et de textes pour les temps pré-et protohistoriques, cela concerne exclusivement des vestiges matériels. Pour les matières premières, il est possible de savoir ce qui est disponible et indisponible dans une région donnée. Pour les objets manufacturés, ils doivent être suffisamment différents par leur forme et leur décor de ceux du groupe receveur pour qu'ils soient perçus comment venant d'ailleurs. Pour certains matériaux comme les objets en métal, la céramique et les squelettes humains, des analyses permettent de démontrer qu'ils ne sont pas « locaux » ; il est par contre beaucoup plus difficile et aléatoire de repérer d'où ils viennent. Ces

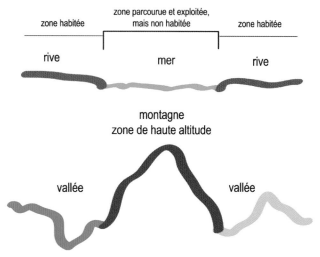

Fig. 18.1. Schéma montrant les analogies entre mer et montagne dans le cadre des échanges.

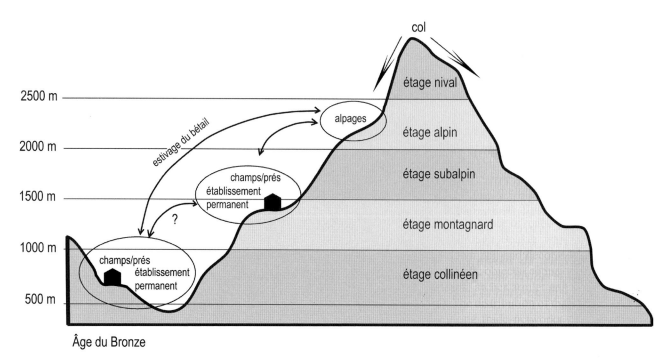

Fig. 18.2. Schéma des zones altitudinales investies par l'économie alpine (Curdy 1995, modifié).

analyses sont en général effectuées sur des objets pour lesquels existe déjà un soupçon, elles sont encore peu répandues et leur interprétation n'est pas toujours univoque, soit en raison du manque de données de référence soit de la faiblesse de la méthode, comme ce peut être le cas pour les analyses du strontium (Sr) sur les ossements humains.

Echanges et voyages à l'Âge du bronze

C'est l'examen des objets archéologiques – bronzes, céramiques, etc. – qui permet de mettre en évidence les échanges, notamment ceux résultant des relations transalpines. A l'Âge du bronze, la présence d'objets d'origine extérieure n'est pas liée à des pratiques étroitement commerciales, comme elle commencera à l'être à partir de l'Âge du fer, et elle peut s'expliquer par trois principaux cas de figure :

(a) des objets liés à l'activité normale des populations alpines, qui ont des contacts réguliers avec les populations des plaines au nord comme au sud des Alpes et qui servent ainsi de vecteurs pour la transmission des éléments culturels : artisans, colporteurs, échanges de biens, échanges matrimoniaux … ;

(b) des objets isolés liés aux déplacements occasionnels d'individus, notamment dans le cadre des contacts qui existent alors entre les élites européennes, qui partagent les mêmes symboles de statut : prospecteurs à la recherche de matières premières, ambassadeurs ou messagers, membres des élites elles-mêmes qui dirigent des expéditions, comme ça a été le cas avec les Argonautes ;

(c) des objets amenés par des groupes humains qui se déplacent : migration ou conquête.

Objets en métal

Parmi les objets archéologiques, ceux en métal occupent une place prépondérante, car ils voyagent plus facilement que la céramique et leur classification typologique est plus précise. Ils peuvent être répartis en quatre catégories : ceux d'origine locale à diffusion restreinte, ceux d'origine locale à diffusion élargie, les copies locales d'objets extérieurs et les vraies importations.

Objets en métal d'origine locale à diffusion restreinte

Plusieurs formes locales ont une diffusion limitée à leur région d'origine. C'est notamment le cas des brassards de type valaisan en tôle de cuivre martelée et ciselés de motifs géométriques fabriqués vers 2000-1900 av. J.-C., ou encore des gorgerins et des épingles à tête en disque cantonnée de type Drône, qui remontent aux environs de 1550 av. J.-C. et sont encore réalisés selon l'ancienne technique en tôle de bronze martelée puis décorée au ciselet (Fig. 18.4) (David-Elbiali 2000, 147–8, 229–31, 250). Ces exemples appartiennent à la région intra-alpine de la culture du Rhône, qui s'étend sur une grande partie de la Suisse occidentale durant le Bronze ancien. Il est plus difficile d'en mettre en évidence pour les phases ultérieures de l'Âge du bronze.

Objets en métal d'origine locale à diffusion élargie

Il existe aussi des formes d'origine locale dont la diffusion s'étend de part et d'autre des Alpes et on peut retrouver au nord et au sud des pièces pratiquement identiques, comme cette association d'une épingle proche des types tréflés avec extrémité enroulée et d'une hache de type

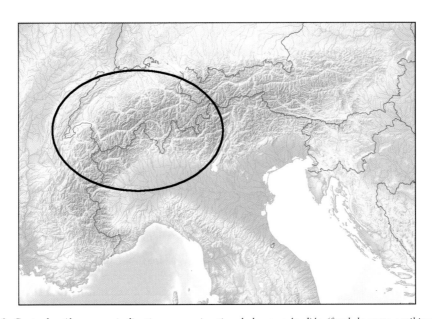

Fig. 18.3. Carte des Alpes avec indication approximative de la zone étudiée (fond de carte : wikipedia.org).

Langquaid II : un lot provient du village palafittique Ponti et l'autre du niveau A de Meilen-Schellen sur le lac de Zurich, daté par la dendrochronologie entre 1647 et 1641 av. J.-C. (Conscience *et al.* 2005) (Fig. 18.5). Autre exemple, la sépulture de Casale Monferrato au Piémont, datée des environs de 1600 av. J.-C., qui a aussi livré des objets de types nord-alpins, soit une hache proche du type Mägerkingen et un poignard de type Broc (Venturino et Villa 1993) qui peuvent être comparés respectivement à une hache découverte à Genève (Abels 1972, pl. 28, 404) et à un poignard d'Ollon – Saint-Triphon dans le canton de Vaud (David-Elbiali 2000, ill. 4).

Cette présence de bronzes de types nord-alpins dans la partie nord-occidentale de l'Italie s'observe encore au Bronze moyen, par exemple dans le dépôt de la Cascina Ranza à Milan (de Marinis 2012) ou à Viverone au Piémont dans un village palafittique (de Marinis 1998 ; Rubat Borel 2010a). Parmi les objets répertoriés, ce sont les haches qui présentent le plus de parenté avec les exemplaires nord-alpins (Fig. 18.6), or la Culture du Rhône du Bronze ancien se distingue précisément par une grande production de types originaux de haches (Abels 1972, 94–5).

Seuls les bronzes présentent des analogies marquées. Dans le cas de la céramique, il n'y a pas de parenté étroite entre le matériel nord-et sud-alpin. Si durant la première moitié du Bronze ancien, certaines formes peuvent se ressembler, l'écart se creuse dès la fin du Bronze ancien. Aux environs de 1550 av. J.-C. se développe au Piémont le faciès de Mercurago, qui est caractérisé par des tasses munies d'une anse surélevée en forme de hache, dite anse *ad ascia* ; elles sont répandues dans toute l'Italie nord-occidentale, Piémont, Lombardie occidentale, Ligurie et Emilie occidentale incluses, mais restent inconnues au nord des Alpes, à l'exception d'un exemplaire isolé et fragmenté, découvert durant la seconde moitié du 19e s. à Thônex-Vallard dans le canton de Genève (Fig. 18.7).

Pour expliquer la présence de ces bronzes qui montrent des liens étroits avec les productions nord-alpines, alors que cette parenté ne semble pas aussi marquée avec la province palafittique nord-orientale et la zone des terramares, il faut envisager des échanges réguliers entre ces deux territoires. Il pourrait s'agir d'artisans bronziers, qui se déplacent de façon saisonnière et qui fabriquent à la demande des objets, ce qui pourrait expliquer les quelques nuances qui existent entre productions nord-et sud-alpines (David-Elbiali et Venturino Gambari 2016). Il pourrait aussi s'agir de colporteurs, qui échangent des pièces ramenées du nord des Alpes.

Les objets diffusés à grande distance sont nettement plus rares. Les plus remarquables sont les haches de type Bevaix, une forme très caractéristique de la fin du Bronze ancien répandue surtout dans la zone alpine, mais dont quelques exemplaires ont atteint des régions éloignées. Parmi eux, deux pièces ne sont pas de simples trouvailles isolées, mais appartiennent à des dépôts, dont celui de la Baragalla est situé au sud de la plaine padane et celui de Kläden en Allemagne du Nord (de Marinis 1976 ; von Brunn 1959, 61, pl. 54 ; David-Elbiali et Hafner 2010, fig. 22). Dans ce cas, les mécanismes de diffusion sont probablement différents : il pourrait s'agir de déplacements exceptionnels, tels qu'ils ont été définis ci-dessus, ou d'objets qui connaissent différents propriétaires.

Copies d'objets en métal d'origine extérieure

Il existe aussi des formes étrangères qui sont imitées dans la zone alpine, par exemple les épingles à tête en disque décorée de cercles concentriques hachurés et d'une croix centrale, qui sont déposées souvent par paire dans les sépultures féminines en Autriche orientale et en Slovaquie au début du Bronze ancien. Des pièces apparentées, mais pas identiques, sont utilisées dans la zone alpine de la Culture du Rhône (David-Elbiali 2000, ill. 58, fig. 13, cartes 24–5 ; David-Elbiali et David 2009, 318). Il s'agit d'objets qui reproduisent un modèle, mais sans le copier de façon fidèle. A-t-on voulu l'adapter au goût local ou était-on incapable de le reproduire mieux, parce que la connaissance du modèle original était insuffisante ? Ce dernier cas de figure se rencontre dans la peinture ancienne. Ainsi Giotto dans son adoration des mages peinte dans la chapelle *degli Scrovegni* à Padoue a reproduit des dromadaires en s'inspirant d'un autre peintre avec un résultat particulier : ils ont des oreilles et un regard de biche, ce qui explique leur étrangeté et c'est cette même étrangeté que l'on ressent en comparant certains bronzes de même type, mais qui sont originaires de régions éloignées.

Objets importés

Les objets qui proviennent vraiment d'autres régions et qui n'ont pas été simplement copiés sont très peu nombreux et, sans analyse, le doute demeure quant à leur origine. Quelques exemples sont présentés ci-dessous.

Un minuscule annelet temporal en or mélangé, qui appartient à la famille des *Noppenringe*, a été retrouvé dans le dolmen V de Sion-Petit-Chasseur (canton du Valais), sans position stratigraphique précise. Longtemps attribué au Néolithique (Gallay 2008, fig. 109), il trouve en fait d'excellents parallèles au Bronze ancien, notamment dans le complexe d'Ùnetice, où plusieurs sépultures ont livré des objets analogues, par exemple la tombe 1 de Goseck (Ldkr. Weißenfels) dans l'est de l'Allemagne (Genz et Schwarz 2004). De la même nécropole du Petit-Chasseur, mais dans le dolmen VI a été exhumé un anneau de chevelure en argent attribué à la période campaniforme. L'analyse du métal montre que cette pièce n'est pas indigène, mais qu'elle a été importée soit d'Europe de l'Est, soit de la Méditerranée orientale, soit du Proche-Orient (Primas *et al.* 1998).

Au dépôt de Sigriswil situé dans les Alpes bernoises, appartenait aussi une pointe de lance, dont il ne subsiste malheureusement qu'un dessin (Strahm 1968, fig. 6,24 ; David-Elbiali 2000, pl. 23,4). Le décor de cet objet était identique à celui observé sur des pièces retrouvées surtout en Slovaquie et datées de la seconde moitié du Bronze ancien, vers 1650 av. J.-C. (David 2006, pl. 5, 1–6).

Une fosse du site d'Onnens-Les Côtes dans le canton de Vaud, près de la rive occidentale du lac de Neuchâtel, a livré une tasse à proto-anse, qui semble provenir d'Italie nord-orientale ; elle trouve son meilleur parallèle dans une tasse issue de la terramare de Bellaguarda (province de Mantova) (de Marinis 2002, fig. 47, US64) (Fig. 18.8). Une étude de la pâte devrait encore confirmer l'origine de cette pièce. Le reste du mobilier est de typologie locale et remonte au BzD1. Cette structure appartient à un ensemble de six fosses à vocation rituelle (David-Elbiali, Falquet, Niţu *et al. 2014*).

La tombe 1/95 de la nécropole de Morano sul Po (province d'Alessandria) a livré une tête d'épingle céphalaire (Venturino Gambari 2006, 99–101, fig. 93,6), une forme dont l'extension est quasiment limitée au Plateau suisse et à ses marges ; V. Rychner la qualifia du reste « d'emblème des palafittes suisses » (Hochuli, Niffeler, Rychner 1998, 129). Ce type date de la première moitié du 10ᵉ siècle av. J.-C. Cette incinération était celle d'un adulte de sexe indéterminé, plutôt masculin. A part l'épingle céphalaire, il était associé à trois autres épingles à tête conique et à une urne munie d'une écuelle-couvercle, toutes caractéristiques du Protogolasecca. Il ne semble donc pas s'agir d'un individu d'origine étrangère, mais d'un autochtone en possession de ce fragment d'épingle.

Durant le 9ᵉ siècle av. J.-C., un certain nombre d'objets témoignent d'échanges entre le Plateau suisse et l'Italie du Nord. Les perles en verre, qu'on retrouve régulièrement dans les sépultures et dans les palafittes sont fabriquées dans la basse plaine du Pô en Vénétie (Rychner-Faraggi 1993, 64). Il y a aussi les objets qui proviennent de la zone des lacs de la culture de Golasecca, comme les fibules à arc simple ou à côtes de type Mörigen (Fig. 18.9). Toutes ces pièces ont transité par la région alpine.

Evolution des échanges au cours de l'Âge du bronze et à l'Âge du fer

Les liens qui unissent le nord et le sud des Alpes centre-occidentales sont déjà bien établis à l'époque néolithique. Cet état de fait se poursuit au Bronze ancien avec des formes d'objets en bronze identiques ou étroitement apparentées présentes sur les deux versants et quelques cas possibles d'objets importés, alors que certaines productions alpines circulent dans des régions éloignées.

Le Bronze moyen est une période qui reste mal connue. On se retrouve ainsi avec le paradoxe suivant. Dans le lac Viverone, un petit plan d'eau situé au nord du Piémont, de nombreux bronzes d'origine nord-alpine ont été retrouvés lors de fouilles subaquatiques. Ils étaient accompagnés par de la céramique abondante, dont l'étude a permis de définir précisément la culture de Viverone, qui est un faciès caractéristique du milieu du Bronze moyen au Piémont, au sud du Tessin et en Lombardie occidentale (de Marinis 1998 ; Rubat Borel 2009 ; 2010b ; 2011). Les bronzes présentent des affinités évidentes avec ceux du Jura souabe dans le sud de l'Allemagne, mais aucun parallèle n'est connu sur le territoire suisse et pourtant ils ont à coup sûr passé par les Alpes. C'est surtout à partir de la fin du Bronze moyen et au Bronze récent qu'apparaissent de nombreux habitats en position dominante, situés sur les routes de transit à travers les Alpes (Benkert *et al.* 2010). A cette période, les vallées les plus méridionales ont livré de la céramique proche de celle du sud des Alpes.

Au cours du Bronze final, les échanges se poursuivent. En ce qui concerne la céramique, il semble aussi qu'il y ait une certaine convergence du goût esthétique – par exemple l'évolution de la forme des pots biconiques, la décoration de cannelures incurvées sous l'anse, la morphologie des gobelets à corps globuleux ornés d'un registre de cannelures – qui atteste de rapports réguliers entre les communautés du nord et du sud des Alpes centre-occidentales (David-Elbiali, *2014*, fig. 8–9 ; 2013, fig. 6–7).

Après l'Âge du bronze, à partir du 7ᵉ siècle av. J.-C., avec l'extension des comptoirs étrusques et la formation des cultures proto-urbaines en Italie du Nord, le commerce se développe. Au centre-ouest des Alpes, les produits étrusques et méditerranéens transitent par le territoire de la culture de Golasecca, qui exporte aussi ses propres productions (de Marinis 1997). Au second Âge du fer, vers le 4ᵉ siècle av. J.-C., la présence de mercenaires reste une question ouverte. La conquête des Alpes par les Romains entre 25 et 13 av. J.-C. et l'intégration de ce territoire à l'Empire vont encore intensifier le transit à travers les Alpes.

Conclusion

Si on se réfère aux trois cas de figure qui peuvent expliquer la présence d'objets étrangers, la plupart des exemples évoqués ci-dessus se rapportent à des échanges liés aux activités normales des populations alpines, qui comprennent des déplacements limités au nord et au sud des Alpes, notamment d'artisans ou de colporteurs. Quelques objets sont clairement liés à des déplacements exceptionnels, reste à identifier ce qui pourrait concerner une migration ou une colonisation. En fait, durant le passage du Bronze récent au Bronze final, des indices évoquent des changements

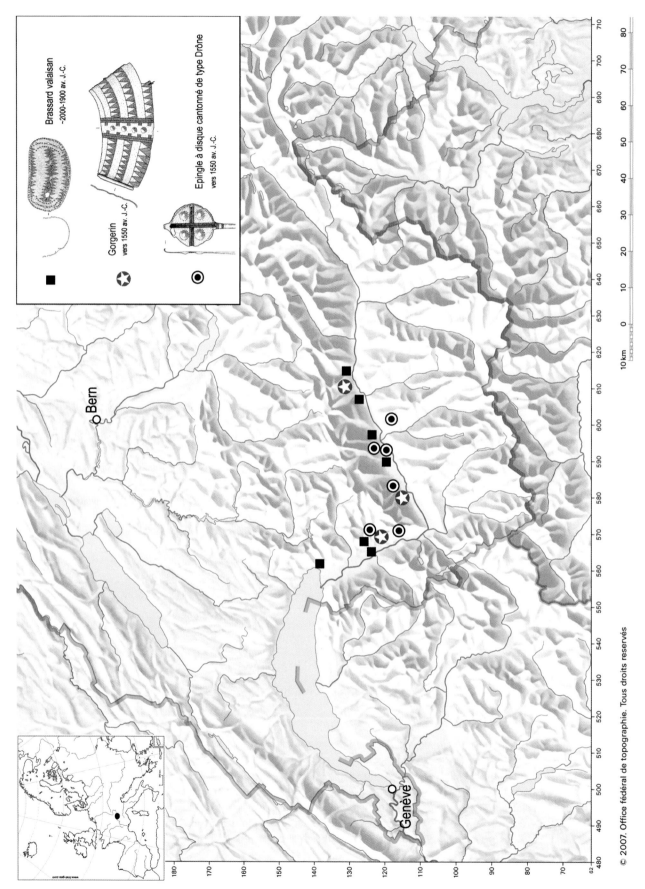

Brassard valaisan
~2000-1900 av. J.-C.

Gorgerin
vers 1550 av. J.-C.

Epingle à disque cantonné de type Drône
vers 1550 av. J.-C.

Bern

Genève

10 km

Fig. 18.4. Carte de répartition de trois types d'objets en bronze de la culture du Rhône à diffusion restreinte.

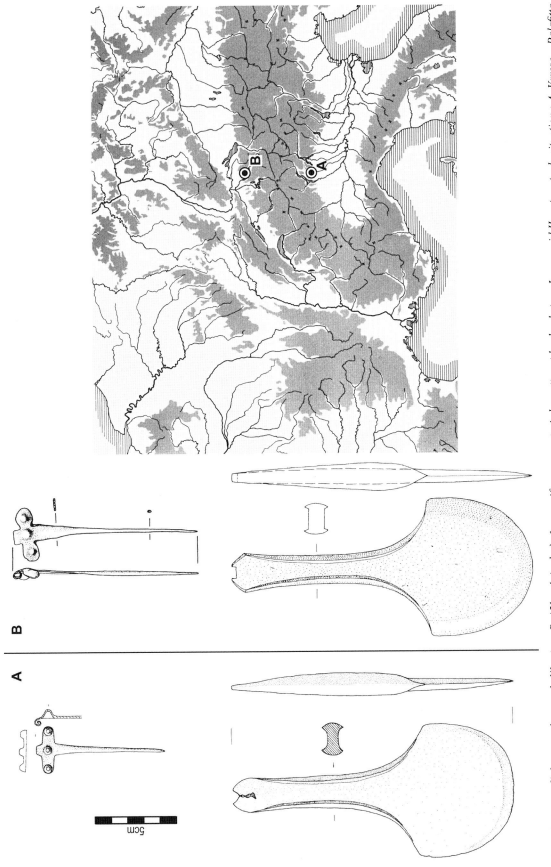

Fig. 18.5. Lots d'objets analogues de l'horizon BzA2b – épingle à tête cruciforme avec trois bossettes et hache de type Langquaid II – et carte de situation : A. Varese – Palafitta Ponti, Italie (de Marinis, Massa, Pizzo 2009) ; B. Meilen – Schellen, Suisse (Conscience 2005).

Mireille David-Elbiali

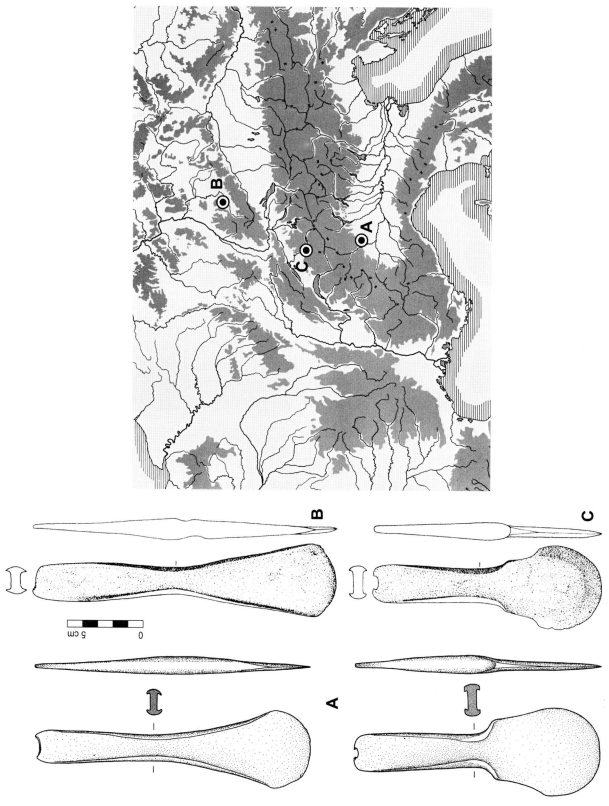

Fig. 18.6. Exemples de haches du Bronze moyen et carte de situation : A. Viverone, Italie (de Marinis 1995) ; B. Pfullingen, Allemagne (Abels 1972) ; C. Thun, Suisse (Abels 1972).

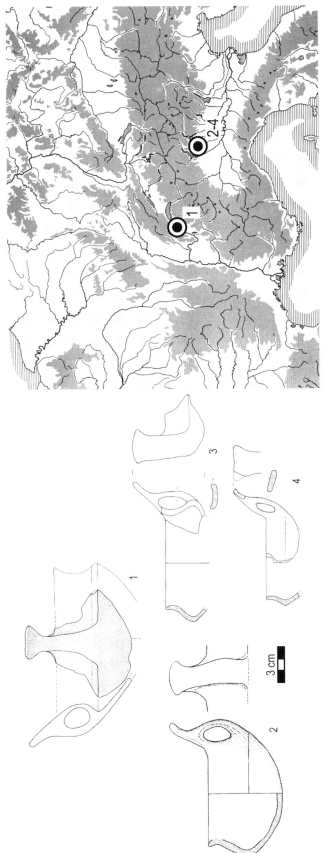

Fig. 18.7. Tasses avec anse ad ascia et carte de situation : 1. Thônex-Vallard, Genève, Suisse (dessin de l'auteur) ; 2–4. Varese-Sabbione, Italie (de Marinis, Massa, Pizzo 2009).

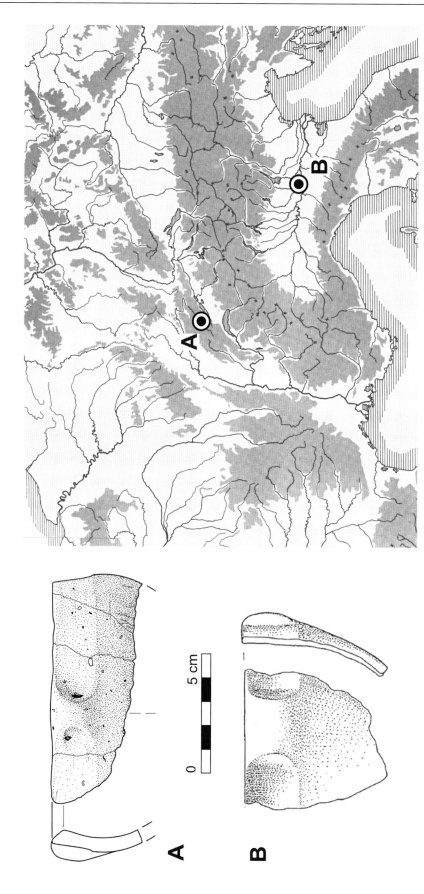

Fig. 18.8. Tasses à proto-anse du Bronze récent et carte de situation : A. Onnens – Les Côtes, Suisse (David-Elbiali, Falquet, Niţu et al. 2014) ; B. Bellaguarda, Italie (de Marinis 2002).

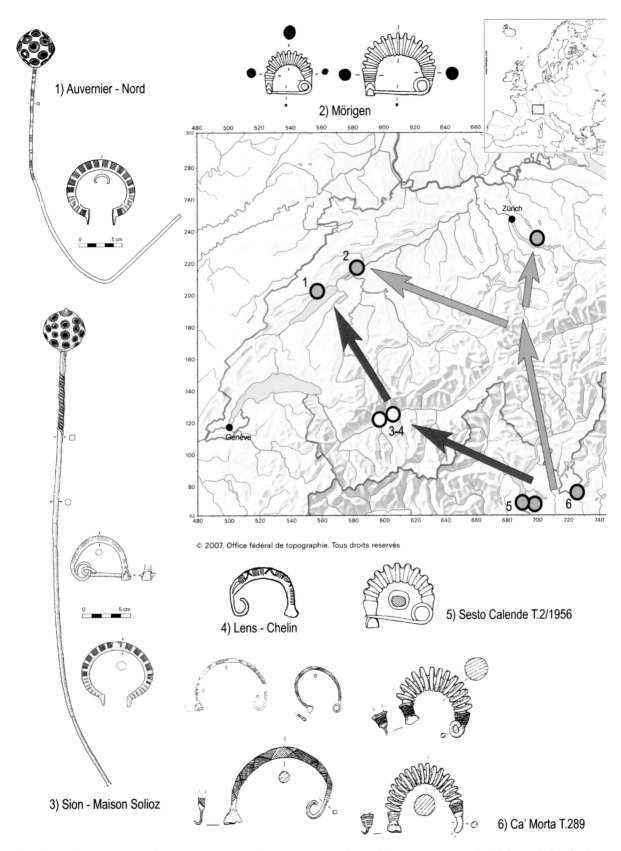

© 2007. Office fédéral de topographie. Tous droits réservés

1) Auvernier - Nord

2) Mörigen

3) Sion - Maison Solioz

4) Lens - Chelin

5) Sesto Calende T.2/1956

6) Ca' Morta T.289

Fig. 18.9. Exemples d'objets circulant entre le nord de l'Italie, la zone alpine et le Plateau suisse au 9e siècle av. J.-C. : 1) Auvernier-Nord (Rychner 1987) ; 2) Mörigen (Bernatzky-Goetze 1987) ; 3) Sion - Maison Solioz (dessin de l'auteur) ; 4) Lens-Chelin (Bocksberger 1964) ; 5) Sesto Calende (de Marinis, Gambari 2005) ; 6) Ca' Morta (de Marinis 1995).

de culture dominante, qui cachent peut-être de vrais déplacements de population.

Il faut tout d'abord constater, surtout à partir du Bronze moyen et récent (15e–13e s. av. J.-C.), l'apparition d'habitats en position dominante, situés sur les routes de transit à travers les Alpes. A la même période, les sites des vallées de l'ubac valaisan, qui sont celles qui conduisent aux cols menant au sud des Alpes, livrent de la céramique de type sud-alpin, soit de la céramique de type Viverone à Zeneggen-Kastelschuggen, dans la vallée de la Vispa sur le chemin du col du Théodule, et de la céramique de type Canegrate à Sembrancher, sur la route du col du Grand Saint-Bernard, et à Viège – In Albon, cette fois dans la vallée du Rhône au débouché de la vallée de la Vispa (David-Elbiali et Chaix 1987 ; David-Elbiali 1994). Cet ensemble d'éléments montre que les vallées méridionales du Valais sont dans le giron des cultures du sud des Alpes à cette période.

On assiste à un renversement de situation au Bronze final avec l'arrivée du Rhin-Suisse-France orientale à partir du 12e s. av. J.-C., qui s'arrête dans la même grotte In Albon que les représentants de la culture de Canegrate (David-Elbiali et Chaix 1987) et qui étend son influence au sud des Alpes avec la formation du groupe de Pont-Valperga dans le nord-ouest du Piémont, qui présente un mélange de caractères culturels de Rhin-Suisse-France orientale et de Protogolasecca (Rubat Borel 2006).

D'autre part, à partir de la seconde moitié du Bronze moyen et durant le Bronze récent, la distance culturelle semble s'approfondir entre les groupes du versant méridional des Alpes et ceux du versant septentrional. Ceci se voit particulièrement dans les rites funéraires, même s'il ne faut pas oublier que les témoignages du Bronze ancien et du début du Bronze moyen sont très rares. La démographie a pu jouer un rôle important sur le versant méridional plus peuplé. Inévitablement en contact avec la société terramaricole qui est sa voisine de l'Est, dont l'avancement culturel est indéniable et qui entretient des rapports directs ou indirects avec les Mycéniens, la province occidentale, même si elle préserve jalousement sa spécificité, probablement à cause de ses origines ethniques différentes et de l'usage probable d'un autre idiome, cette province occidentale est emmenée sur la voie de la civilisation à un rythme très différent de celui des cousins qui occupent les territoires nord-alpins. La poussée assez forte des groupes dits « des Champs d'urnes », qui étendent leur influence et pénètrent physiquement par petits groupes jusqu'au sud des Alpes, notamment au nord-ouest du Piémont, ne modifie pas cet état de fait.

En conclusion, il semble concevable que les deux versants des Alpes centre-occidentales aient été occupés par des populations d'origine commune et possiblement de langue apparentée, ce qui sera le cas à l'époque historique, qui vont continuer à entretenir des rapports étroits durant tout l'Âge du bronze. Peu à peu, la proximité de cultures de niveau plus élevé, puis de civilisations urbaines, conduit à une accélération de l'évolution sur le versant méridional, alors que le versant septentrional accuse, sur ce plan, un retard qui va durer longtemps.

Bibliographie

Abels, B.-U. (1972) *Die Randleistenbeile in Baden-Württemberg, dem Elsass, der Franche-Comté und der Schweiz*, Prähistorische Bronzefunde 9/4. München, C. H. Beck.

Banchieri, D. G. (2009) La Preistoria del territorio di Varese. Dans R. C. de Marinis, S. Massa et M. Pizzo, (ed.) *Alle origini di Varese e del suo territorio: le collezioni del sistema archeologico provinciale*, 3–10, Biblioteca archeologica 44. Roma, 'L'Erma' di Bretschneider.

Benkert, A., Curdy, P. et David-Elbiali, M. (2010) Sites de hauteur et contrôle du territoire aux âges des métaux dans la vallée du Rhône (Suisse/cantons du Valais et de Vaud). *Bulletin d'Etudes Préhistoriques et Archéologiques Alpines* (Aoste) 21, 171–191.

Bernatzky-Goetze, M. (1987) *Mörigen : die spätbronzezeitlichen Funde*, Antiqua 16. Basel, Schweizerische Gesellschaft für Ur- und Frühgeschichte.

Bocksberger, O.-J. (1964) *Age du Bronze en Valais et dans le Chablais vaudois*. Lausanne, Imprimerie centrale (Thèse).

Conscience, A.-C., Brombacher, C., Ghiggi, D., Jacomet, S. et Rehazek, A. (2005) *Seeufersiedlungen, Wädenswil-Vorder Au : eine Seeufersiedlung am Übergang vom 17. zum 16. Jh. v. Chr. im Rahmen der Frühbronzezeit am Zürichsee. Unter besonderer Berücksichtigung der frühbronzezeitlichen Funde und Befunde von Meilen-Schellen*, Zürcher Archäologie 19. Zürich und Egg, Baudirektion Kanton Zürich, Hochbauamt, Kantonsarchäologie.

Curdy, P. (1995) Ecologie du territoire. Dans A. Gallay (ed.) *Dans les Alpes à l'aube du métal, archéologie et bande dessinée*, 143–7. Sion, Musées cantonaux du Valais (catalogue d'exposition).

Curdy, P. (2010) Les passages des Alpes centrales à l'Âge du Fer, quelques réflexions. Dans J.-C. Le Bihan et J.-P. Guillaumet (ed.) *Routes du monde et passages obligés de la Protohistoire au haut Moyen Âge,* 143–60, actes du colloque international d'Ouessant (27–28 septembre 2007). Quimper, Centre de recherche archéologique du Finistère.

Curdy, P. et Praz, J.-C. (ed.) (2002) *Premiers hommes dans les Alpes de 50'000 à 5'000 avant Jésus-Christ*. Lausanne, Payot, Sion : Musées cantonaux du Valais (catalogue d'exposition).

David, W. (2006) Aus der großen ungarischen Tiefebene bis zum Fuß der italienischen See-Alpen: reichverzierte Lanzenspitzen aus Zeugen überregionaler Beziehungen altbronzezeitlicher Eliten. Dans *Studi di protostoria in onore di Renato Peroni*, 101–119. Borgo San Lorenzo (Firenze), All'Insegna del Giglio.

David-Elbiali, M. (1994) Les influences culturelles en Valais au début du Bronze final au travers des découvertes de Zeneggen VS-Kasteltschuggen. *Annuaire de la Société suisse de préhistoire et d'archéologie* 77, 35–52.

David-Elbiali, M. (2000) *La Suisse occidentale au IIème millénaire av. J.-C. : chronologie, culture et intégration européenne*, Cahier d'archéologie romande 80. Lausanne, Cahiers d'archéologie romande.

David-Elbiali, M. (2014) Il cammino tra le Alpi. Elementi di riflessione per una storia dei rapporti transalpini nella zona alpina centro-occidentale all'età del Bronzo.Dans B. Grassi, M. Pizzo (ed.) *Gallorum Insubrum fines. Ricerche e progetti archeologici nel territorio di Varese.* Atti della giornata di studio (Varese, Villa Recalcati, 29 gennaio 2010). Roma, L'Erma di Bretschneider, Studia Archaeologica 200, 43-64.

David-Elbiali, M. (2013) La chronologie nord-alpine du Bronze final (1200–800 av. J.-C.): entre métal, céramique et dendrochronologie. Dans W. Leclercq et E. Warmenbol (ed.) *Echanges de bons procédés: la céramique du Bronze Final dans le Nord-Ouest de l'Europe* (Université libre de Bruxelles, 1–2 octobre 2010). Bruxelles, Université libre / Centre de Recherches en Archéologie et Patrimoine (CReA-Patrimoine), Études d'archéologie 6, 181-197.

David-Elbiali, M. et Chaix, L. (1987) Occupation en grotte à l'âge du Bronze récent/final en Haut-Valais (Grotte In Albon). *Annuaire de la Société suisse de préhistoire et d'archéologie* 70, 65–76.

David-Elbiali, M. et David, W. (2009) A la suite de Jacques-Pierre Millotte, l'actualité des recherches en typologie. Le Bronze ancien et le début du Bronze moyen : cadre chronologique et liens culturels entre l'Europe nord-alpine occidentale, le monde danubien et l'Italie du Nord. Dans A. Richard, P. Barral, A. Daubigney, G. Kaenel, C. Mordant et J.-F. Piningre (ed.) *L'isthme européen Rhin-Saône-Rhône dans la Protohistoire. Approches nouvelles en hommage à Jacques-Pierre Millotte* (Besançon, 16–18 octobre 2006), 295–324. Besançon, Presses universitaires de Franche-Comté (Annales Littéraires; Série « Environnement, sociétés et archéologie »).

David-Elbiali, M. and Hafner, A. (2010) Gräber, Horte und Pfahlbauten zwischen Jura und Alpen. Die Entwicklung elitärer sozialer Strukturen in der frühen Bronzezeit der Westschweiz. Dans H. Meller et F. Bertemes (ed.) *Der Griff nach den Sternen: wie Europas Eliten zu Macht und Reichtum kamen,* 217–38. Internationales Symposium in Halle (Saale) 16–21 Februar 2005, Tagungen des Landesmuseums für Vorgeschichte Halle 5 (1). Halle (Saale), Landesmuseum für Vorgeschichte.

David-Elbiali, M., Falquet, C., Nițu, C., Studer, J. avec des contributions de Glauser, D., Jacquat, C., Katona Serneels, I., Serneels, V. (2014). *Ensemble de fosses à fonction rituelle à Onnens / Corcelles-Près-Concise – Les Côtes (canton de Vaud, Suisse) sur le tracé de l'autoroute A5: pratiques sacrificielles au pied du Jura au 13e siècle av. J.- C.? Contribution à la définition de la phase DzD1 en Suisse occidentale.* Cahier d'archéologie romande 147, Lausanne, Cahiers d'archéologie romande.

David-Elbiali, M., Venturino Gambari, M., (2016) Artisans métallurgistes de l'âge du Bronze à travers les Alpes?. *Bulletin d'études préhistoriques et archéologiques alpines* (Aoste) 27, 171–184.

De Marinis, R. C. (1976) Il ripostiglio dell'antica età del Bronzo della Baragalla presso Reggio Emilia. *Atti della riunione scientifica dell'Istituto Italiano di Preistoria e Protostoria* 19 (Firenze, 11–14 ott. 1975), 213–242. Firenze, Istituto Italiano di Preistoria e Protostoria.

De Marinis, R. C. (1995) La tomba 289 della Ca' Morta e l'inizio dell'Età del Ferro nelle necropoli dei dintorni di Como. Dans B. Schmid-Sikimić et P. Della Casa (ed.) *Trans Europam : Beiträge zur Bronze- und Eisenzeit zwischen Atlantik und Altai. Festschrift für Margarita Primas,* Antiquas, Reihe 3, Bd. 34, 93–102. Bonn, Rudolf Habelt,

De Marinis, R. C. (1997) Golasecca : I più antichi Celti d'Italia. In Antico Gallina, M. (ed.) *Popoli italici e culture regionali. Popoli dell'Italia antica,* 10–41. Milano, Amilcare Pizzi S.p.A., Laboratori Guidotti.

De Marinis, R. C. (1998) La metallurgia dell'antica e media età del Bronzo in Piemonte. Dans L. Mercando et M. Venturino Gambari (ed.) *Archeologia in Piemonte: la Preistoria,* 157–86. Torino. Soprintendenza archeologica del Piemonte

De Marinis, R. C. (2002) Towards a relative and absolute chronology of the Bronze Age in Northern Italy. *Notizie archeologiche bergomensi 7/1999,* 23–100.

De Marinis, R.C. (2012) Das Depot der Cascina Ranza bei Mailand. Dans *Waffen für die Götter. Krieger, Trophäen, Heiligtümer,* Innsbruck, Tiroler Landesmuseum Ferdinandeum, 54–62.

De Marinis, R. C., Gambari F. M. (2005) La cultura di Golasecca dal X agli inizi del VII secolo a.C. : cronologia relativa e correlazioni con altre aree culturali. Dans G. Bartoloni et F. Delpino (ed.) *Oriente e Occidente : metodi e discipline a confronto. Riflessioni sulla cronologia dell'età del ferro italiana,* 197–225. Atti dell'Incontro di studi (Roma, 30–31 ottobre 2003), Mediterranea I-200. Mediterranea (Roma) I-2004, 197-225.

De Marinis, R. C., Massa, S. and Pizzo, M. (ed.) (2009) *Alle origini di Varese e del suo territorio : le collezioni del sistema archeologico provinciale,* Biblioteca archeologica 44. Roma, 'L'Erma' di Bretschneider.

Gallay, A. (ed.) (2008) *Des Alpes au Léman : images de la préhistoire.* Gollion, In Folio.

Genz, H. et Schwarz, R. (2004) Von Häuptlingen und anderen Oberhäuptern: reich ausgestattete Gräber in der Frühbronzezeit. Dans H. Meller (ed.) *Der geschmiedete Himmel: die weite Welt im Herzen Europas vor 3600 Jahren,* 162–5. Stuttgart, K. Theiss (catalogue d'exposition).

Hochuli, S., Niffeler, U. et Rychner, V. (ed.) (1998) *Âge du Bronze,* La Suisse du Paléolithique à l'aube du Moyen-Age 3. Bâle, Société suisse de Préhistoire et d'Archéologie.

Primas, M., Wanner, B. et Boll, P. O. (1998) The interpretation of metal analyses : a case study based on the silver spiral from Sion (Valais, Switzerland). Dans C. Mordant, M. Pernot et V. Rychner (ed.) *Les analyses de composition du métal : leur apport à l'archéologie de l'Age du Bronze. Actes du colloque international 'Bronze 96' (Neuchâtel et Dijon, 1996),* 53–62. L'Atelier du bronzier en Europe du XXe au VIIIe siècle avant notre ère, tome 1, session de Neuchâtel. Paris, CTHS.

Rubat Borel, F. (2006) Il Bronzo Finale nell'estremo Nord-Ovest italiano: il gruppo Pont-Valperga, *Rivista di Scienze Preistoriche* 56, 429–482.

Rubat Borel, F. (2009) La Media età del Bronzo nel Nord-Ovest italiano: la facies di Viverone e il sito eponimo. Padova : Dipartimento di Archeologia dell'Università degli Studi di Padova (thèse de doctorat).

Rubat Borel, F. (2010a) Testimonianze del potere nella Media età del Bronzo a Viverone : le armi del guerriero e gli ornamenti femminili. *Bulletin d'Etudes préhistoriques alpines* 21, 377–403.

Rubat Borel, F. (2010b) La ceramica della media età del Bronzo dall'abitato perilacustre di Viverone. *Quaderni della Soprintendenza archeologica del Piemonte* 25, 31–70.

Rubat Borel, F. (2011) Gli ornamenti del Bronzo Medio dall'abitato nel lago di Viverone: il costume femminile tra Italia nordoccidentale e cerchia nordalpina. Dans *Il filo del tempo. Studi in onore di Raffaele C. de Marinis. Notizie Archeologiche Bergomensi* 19, 205–219.

Rychner, V. (1987) *Auvernier 1968–1975 : le mobilier métallique du Bronze final : formes et techniques*, Auvernier 6, Cahiers d'archéologie romande 37. Lausanne, Bibliothèque historique vaudoise.

Rychner-Faraggi, A.-M. (1993) *Hauterive Champréveyres, 9 : métal et parure au Bronze final*, Archéologie neuchâteloise 17. Neuchâtel, Musée cantonal d'archéologie.

Strahm, C. (1965–6). Renzenbühl und Ringoldswil : die Fundgeschichte zweier frühbronzezeitlicher Komplexe. *Jahrbuch des Bernischen Historischen Museums* 45–6, 321–371.

Venturino Gambari, M. (ed.) (2006) *Navigando lungo l'Eridano. La necropoli protogolasecchiana di Morano sul Po*. Casale Monferrato : Museo Civico. Torino, Soprintendenza per i beni archeologici del Piemonte e del museo antichità egizie.

Venturino, M. and Villa, G. (1993) Casale Monferrato, fraz. S. Germano, loc. Vallare. *Quaderni della Soprintendenza archeologica del Piemonte* 11, 199–202.

Von Brunn, W. A. (1959) *Die Hortfunde der frühen Bronzezeit aus Sachsen-Anhalt, Sachsen und Thüringen*, Schriften der Sektion Vor-und Frühgeschichte 7. Berlin, Deutsche Akademie der Wissenschaften.